D1633728

THE STATE OF THE EUROI

VOLUME 5

A project of the European Community Studies Association

The State of the European Union

Risks, Reform, Resistance, and Revival

VOLUME 5

edited by

MARIA GREEN COWLES and MICHAEL SMITH

OXFORD
UNIVERSITY PRESS

OXFORD

UNIVERSITY PRESS

Great Clarendon Street, Oxford OX2 6DP

Oxford University Press is a department of the University of Oxford.
It furthers the University's objective of excellence in research, scholarship,
and education by publishing worldwide in

Oxford New York

Athens Auckland Bangkok Bogotá Buenos Aires Calcutta
Cape Town Chennai Dar es Salaam Delhi Florence Hong Kong Istanbul
Karachi Kuala Lumpur Madrid Melbourne Mexico City Mumbai
Nairobi Paris São Paulo Shanghai Singapore Taipei Tokyo Toronto Warsaw

and associated companies in Berlin Ibadan

Oxford is a registered trade mark of Oxford University Press
in the UK and in certain other countries

Published in the United States
by Oxford University Press Inc., New York

British Library Cataloguing in Publication Data

Data available

Library of Congress Cataloging in Publication Data
The State of the European Union: risks, reform, resistance, and revival /
edited by Maria Green Cowles and Michael Smith.
p. cm.
Includes bibliographical references and index.
1. European Union. 2. Monetary unions—European Union countries.
3. Europe—Economic integration. 4. European Union countries—Politics and government.
I. Green Cowles, Maria. II. Smith, Michael.
JN30.S725 2000 341.242′2—dc21 00–044603

ISBN 0–19–829752–1
ISBN 0–19–829757–2 (pbk.)

1 3 5 7 9 10 8 6 4 2

Typeset by Hope Services (Abingdon) Ltd.
Printed in Great Britain on acid-free paper by
Biddles Ltd., Guildford and King's Lynn

To
Adam and Annika
To
Dorothy, Kate, and Caroline

PREFACE

This book represents the relaunching of the *State of the European Union* series sponsored by the European Community Studies Association (ECSA). When the first volume in the series was published in 1991, there was a relative dearth of information on the then-European Community. That volume, *The State of the European Community: Politics, Institutions, and Debates in the Transition Years*, came on the heels of the creation of ECSA itself in 1988. It represented one of the first efforts to catalogue the state of affairs in the burgeoning European integration project.

Nine years later, of course, the study of the European Union has changed dramatically—as has the European Union itself. Today, there are no fewer than seven journals dedicated to coverage of EU issues and books on the subject abound. With this in mind, the ECSA Executive Committee questioned whether or not the series should be continued. In discussions with ECSA members, however, it became clear that the need for such a volume still exists for both scholarly and classroom purposes. We are particularly grateful to a number of people whose insights and expertise were immensely helpful in relaunching this volume, in particular, Erik Jones, Gary Marks, John Peterson, Mark Pollack, Vivien Schmidt, and Valerie Staats.

We also thank Dominic Byatt of Oxford University Press for sharing and promoting our desire to relaunch this series with a timely publication in both hardcover and paperback. In terms of the book's production, we thank Amanda Watkins for her patience and professionalism in overseeing the manuscript. Our appreciation also goes to Emily Schuster and Susanna Suo-Heikki of American University for their painstaking work on the bibliography, to Felix Klimpacher for serving as computer-guru extraordinaire, and to Margo Thoreson and Sheryl Novick for their overall production support.

Of course, our appreciation also extends to the contributors in this volume. The ECSA series has always brought two scholars from the United States and Europe to serve as editors. With this fifth volume, however, we have sought to make this a truly transatlantic – if not global – production. The book features leading junior and senior scholars representing Canada, Greece, Hungary, Ireland, Italy, Luxembourg, the Netherlands, the United Kingdom, the United States – and even New Zealand. While coordinating such a diverse group might be an editor's nightmare, we were continually delighted with the high level of scholarship, professionalism, and dedication of everyone involved in the book.

Our final thanks go to our families – our spouses and children – for their patience and support throughout this project. It is to them that this volume is dedicated.

Maria Green Cowles
Michael Smith
April 2000

CONTENTS

LIST OF FIGURES

LIST OF TABLES

THE EDITORS

MARIA GREEN COWLES is an Assistant Professor at American University, Washington, DC, and Vice-Chair of the European Community Studies Association (ECSA), USA. She is co-editor with James Caporaso and Thomas Risse of *Transforming Europe: Europeanization and Domestic Change* (2000), and author of numerous articles and book chapters on the role of multinational firms in the European Union. Her current work focuses on the impact of the European Union on domestic institutions, the Transatlantic Business Dialogue, and the political activities of large companies in global regulatory policy-making.

MICHAEL SMITH is Jean Monnet Professor of European Politics at Loughborough University, UK, and past chair of the University Association for Contemporary European Studies (UACES), UK. He is author, co-author, and editor of numerous books, including *Beyond Foreign Economic Policy: The United States, the Single European Market and the Changing World Economy*, with Brian Hocking (1997), and *Europe's Experimental Union: Rethinking Integration*, with Brigin Laffan and Rory O'Donnell (2000). He is currently writing on the interaction of public and private in EU–US relations, on EU commercial policy-making, and on negotiations in and by the EU.

LIST OF CONTRIBUTORS

STEFANI BÄR is Senior Fellow at Ecologic, Centre for International and European Environmental Research, Berlin, Germany.

ELIZABETH BOMBERG is Lecturer in Politics at the University of Edinburgh, Scotland, UK.

MIRIAM L. CAMPANELLA is Associate Professor in International Political Economy at the University of Turin, Italy.

ALEXANDER CARIUS is Director of Ecologic, Centre for International and European Environmental Research, Berlin, Germany.

J. BRYAN COLLESTER is Professor of Political Science and Director, School of Government, Principia College, Elsah, Ill., USA.

LYKKE FRIIS is Senior Research Fellow at the Danish Institute of International Affairs, Copenhagen, Denmark.

DAVID MICHAEL GREEN is Assistant Professor of Political Science at Hofstra University, Hempstead, NY, USA.

SIEGLINDE GSTÖHL is Assistant Professor of International Politics at Humboldt University Berlin, Germany.

MARTIN HOLLAND is Director of the Centre for Research on Europe, University of Canterbury, Christchurch, New Zealand.

ERIK JONES is Senior Lecturer in Politics at the University of Nottingham, UK.

SOPHIE MEUNIER is Visiting Research Fellow and Lecturer in Public and International Affairs, Princeton University, USA.

PAUL FABIAN MULLEN is a Ph.D. Candidate in Political Science, University of Pittsburgh, USA.

ANNA MURPHY is Jean Monnet Fellow, Robert Schuman Center, European University Institute, Florence, Italy.

KALYPSO NICOLAÏDIS is University Lecturer at St Antony's College, Oxford, UK.

JOHN PETERSON is Jean Monnet Professor of European Politics, University of Glasgow, Scotland, UK, and Visiting Professor at the College of Europe, Bruges, Belgium.

MARK A. POLLACK is Assistant Professor of Political Science at the University of Wisconsin, Madison, USA.

ROGER M. SCULLY is Lecturer in European Politics, University of Wales, Aberystwyth, UK.

ULRICH SEDELMEIER is Assistant Professor of International Relations and European Studies at the Central European University, Budapest, Hungary.

JO SHAW is Professor of European Law at the University of Leeds, UK.

MITCHELL SMITH is Assistant Professor of Political Science, University of Oklahoma, USA.

AMY VERDUN is Assistant Professor of Political Science at the University of Victoria, British Columbia, Canada.

INGMAR VON HOMEYER is Research Fellow at Ecologic, Centre for International & European Environmental Research, Berlin, Germany.

HELEN WALLACE is Co-Director of the Sussex European Institute, University of Sussex, UK.

ANTJE WIENER is Reader in European Studies at the Queen's University of Belfast, Northern Ireland, UK.

I

Introduction

1

Risks, Reform, Resistance, and Revival

MARIA GREEN COWLES AND MICHAEL SMITH

The last two years in the history of the European Union have been times of trial, error, and uncertainty. Of course, it might be claimed that this has always been the case with the 'great experiment' which has been going on in Europe since the 1950s. A rapid review of some key areas in European integration, however, shows some of the ways in which the late 1990s were distinctive if not unique.

First, there has been a more explicit emphasis than at any time since the late 1960s on the institutional assets and liabilities of the European integration project. The Treaty of Amsterdam (1997) was designed on the face of it to adapt the institutions to the demands both of the changing world political economy and of the changing essence of the Union itself (for instance in the area of membership and its enlargement). But the Treaty was widely criticized—rightly or wrongly—for shirking the challenges faced in the field of institutional reform. More dramatically, during 1999 the credentials and legitimacy of institutions themselves, and particularly of the European Commission, were at the center of a kind of 'constitutional crisis'. The resignation of the Santer Commission, and its replacement by the Prodi Commission, will feature in the histories of the EU as a watershed in the design and functioning of the 'Brussels machine'.

We have already mentioned the ways in which prospective enlargement of the Union fed into the institutional debates of the late 1990s, but it is also important to underline the importance and complexity of the enlargement negotiations themselves. While the accession of Finland, Sweden, and Austria in 1995 had been carried out according to long-standing assumptions and expectations, the handling of a long and lengthening line of prospective members from Central and Eastern Europe and the Mediterranean posed new challenges. Some of these challenges were institutional: did the Union have the capacity to carry forward negotiations with up to a dozen potential members, at the same time as it dealt with its own internal needs and with the challenges of European and world order? Others were political: could the Union arrive at and sustain a coherent negotiating position in the light of an expanded range of demands and expectations? Yet others were challenges of identity and legitimacy: could the Union retain its solidarity and its painfully acquired international credentials in the face of large-scale expansion?

Enlargement was not the only area in which such questions were raised. Most obviously, the implementation of Economic and Monetary Union (EMU) created major issues of both an administrative and a political/economic nature. Internally, the Union had to face the fact that 'Euroland' included only eleven of the EU's fifteen members, and that the advantages of uniform monetary management were thus to some degree diluted. Externally, the Euro had to make its way in a turbulent global economy and to match up to the challenge of the dollar as well as of the financial crisis in the Asia-Pacific. The steady decline of the Euro in the first year of its existence did not prove it a failure; in many ways, it actually demonstrated that it was behaving as a 'normal' internationally traded currency. But the challenges of internal coordination and external legitimacy would persist.

Alongside the challenges of institutional adaptation, of enlargement, and of the Euro, the Union in the late 1990s had to face the consequences of its engagement with the European security order. Indeed, many of the issues mentioned already can be viewed as part of this existential dilemma. The mid-1990s were to say the least a period of uncertainty in this field, with the harsh lessons of the conflicts in former Yugoslavia to be absorbed and the infrastructure of the Common Foreign and Security Policy still underdeveloped. The years 1998 and 1999 may yet come to be seen as the turning-point in European security developments, for a number of reasons. On the one hand, the conflict in Kosovo underlined once more the limits of an EU security policy and the primacy of NATO as a vehicle for intervention. At the same time, the role of the EU in orchestrating the post-conflict peace-building process was also reaffirmed. While the sound and fury of Kosovo dominated the headlines, other moves enhanced the possibility of an eventual EU defense and security dimension. The St Malô meeting of the British and French leaders in the autumn of 1998, and subsequent developments in the implementation of the Amsterdam provisions for CFSP, gave grounds for thinking that a significant impetus had been gained.

If nothing else, these examples demonstrate the complex and mixed character of the 'EU experience' in the late 1990s. We could extend the list almost indefinitely: EU–US relations continued to be a frustrating mixture of institutionalization, cooperation, and outright conflict over trade; the Common Agricultural Policy (CAP) and the Community budget continued to demand reform but also to resist political accommodation; the tension between the forces of transnational production and exchange in a single market and the persistence of national or regional difference continued to echo throughout the Union.

How are we to explore these complex and coexisting trends and tensions? This volume takes as its central theme the 'four Rs' contained in its title. We argue that in the final years of the twentieth century, and the first years of the twenty-first, as before, the progress of the European project can be judged in terms of a fluctuating balance between four forces: risk, reform, resistance, and revival. The purpose of this Introduction is to outline what we understand by the four elements and by the balance between them, and to suggest some of the ways in which they can be used to explore the current development of the European project.

Risk, Reform, Resistance and Revival in the European Project

What do we mean by the 'four Rs', and how do they relate to the development both of the European project and of scholarship in European integration?[1] This section presents first a set of initial definitions and conceptualizations, next an outline of how they might be applied to the 'history' of the European project, and finally a set of connections to scholarship about the EU.

First, the definitions. We conceive of *risk* in terms of the stakes attaching to the European project, and in terms of the challenges it faces both from within and from external sources. It is important to note that perceptions both of the risks and of the challenges will differ between different groups involved in the process of European integration: for example, large and small member states, the different European institutions, those countries aspiring to membership, large and small companies, and so on. Perceptions of risk will also change over time and between different issue areas in which European integration is at stake, and these fluctuations will be important in shaping what member states and other groupings will accept or commit themselves to. For an example, we need look no further than the introduction of EMU, which revolved for many governments and non-governmental groupings precisely around the allocation of costs and benefits in an uncertain world economy.

Our conception of *reform* is also a variable one. In broad terms, we see reform as the attempt to shape and reshape the European project in pursuit of a number of aims: efficiency, effectiveness, and avoidance of the risks of non-reform. As with risk, the perception of the need for reform

[1] We thank John Peterson for originally suggesting 'Risks, Reform, Resistance' as a theme for this book.

and of its practicality will vary between groupings involved in the process of integration and across issue areas. There is also an important question to be asked about how reform should be tackled; can it be imposed from above, by grand bargains between member states and institutions, or is it more likely to emerge from the bottom up, through the evolution of activities and the tackling of practical problems? The example cited earlier, of the projected reforms which were at the center of the Amsterdam process and of the crisis over the role of the Commission during 1999, illustrates at least some of the questions which are prompted by this concept.

The third force is that of *resistance*. We see resistance in some ways as the other side of the impetus to reform, since it is clear that in European integration as in other social processes, each movement forward can be countered by forces operating in favor of the established way of doing thing. Each additional area of policy added to the European portfolio has both its supporters and its opponents. There is also a link here to risk, since what drives resistance is often the feeling that the risks of reform outweigh the potential benefits. Very often, the resistors are to be found among member states, but there is no inevitability about who will resist what, and when or how they will do it. Resistance can also arise from social forces or groupings at the non-governmental level, or from outside the EU altogether. Thus, the process of enlargement has engendered a complex set of coalitions and tactics both within the EU and between the EU and potential new members, many of them prompted by resistance to anticipated institutional or policy changes, for example in the distribution of regional aid or finance under the CAP.

Finally, we focus on *revival*. The combination of risk, reform, and resistance can at times lead to stalemate, and to the phenomenon sometimes described as 'Eurosclerosis', in which the project almost literally seizes up because of the balance between the forces of movement and the forces of conservatism. It can, though, also lead to breakthroughs, 'relaunchings', or other forms of revival, precipitated by shifts in the balance between risk, reform, and resistance. Perceptions of risk can change, sometimes dramatically; processes of reform previously stalled can be revitalized; the forces of resistance can be reduced by political change or by shifts within or between institutions. In these circumstances, the catalyst for change can come from within the European Union or from the wider world, and sometimes it can be largely unrecognized as the decisive element in the process of revival. The earlier discussion of foreign and security policy suggests that important steps forward can often be masked by the 'noise' of dramatic events, and also that out of adversity can come a new impetus for reform.

It is clear from what we have said that no one of these four elements can be taken in isolation. It is their coexistence, and the fluctuating balance between them, that influences the direction and the momentum of the European project. If we examine the broad 'history' of the European integration process, it becomes clearer that certain key phases and periods of development can be viewed in the light of the 'four Rs'. The formative period of the early 1950s, in which the European Coal and Steel Community was established but the European Defense Community was not, can be seen as a phase in which key countries (especially France and Germany) were ready to take certain risks, but either unwilling or unable to take other risks—specifically, the risk of moving into the area of 'hard security' and military integration. Some countries, the United Kingdom in particular, were unwilling to take the risks at all, and placed a higher premium on resistance to supranational projects. The relaunching of European integration at Messina and its expression in the Treaty of Rome (1957) can be seen as a process in which the momentum created by the ECSC and other economic developments, combined with the pressure for reform, overcame elements of resistance to produce a major revival. But this did not mean that the elements of resistance and the perception of unacceptable risk had gone away.

Seen in this light, the 'integration crisis' of the late 1960s represents a phase in which the forces of resistance, particularly from Gaullist France, were effective in shaping the development of European integration. In this, they were assisted by the sharpened perceptions of risk and potential cost in going beyond the core activities of the Common Market and the Treaty of Rome. This in turn was not unconnected to the turbulence of the world economy and the heightened tensions of the cold war. But these conditions also helped to create pressures for moves further into the integration project, because of the perceived need to engage with challenging political and economic problems in the 1970s. Although that decade is often seen as the prime example of 'Eurosclerosis', with the first enlargement and the crisis of the world economy showing up the limitations of the integration process, it can also be seen as the time at which, gradually, the forces of reform and revival began to gather.

The renewed impetus for reform and revival, in terms of our analysis, came to a head in the early 1980s. The eventual 'digestion' of the United Kingdom and the settlement of the EEC's budgetary problems were combined with increasing perceptions of the risk arising from US and Japanese competition in the world political economy, to create a context in which institutional reform (the Single European Act of 1986) and policy expansion (the Single Market Program) were possible. Not only this, but the perceptions of the risk of inaction in the political and security spheres, in the face of militant Reaganism in the USA, created conditions in which it was possible to revive the notion of a European security identity. For a while, it appeared that the forces of resistance had been effectively muted, and that in place of 'Eurosclerosis' the predominant feeling was one of 'Europhoria', in which new expansions of policy and further institutional innovation could be contemplated.

This feeling of confidence and expansiveness persisted into the early 1990s, fuelled by the events in Central and Eastern Europe and the former Soviet Union which seemed to imply a new role for the European Community as a European 'pacifier'. Not only this, but the project of Economic and Monetary Union (EMU) seemed to presage a period in which the European Community and then the Union could move further towards the acquisition of 'state powers'. This mood, which generated the impetus toward the Maastricht Treaty, did not persist. Instead, it was first joined and then almost replaced by a mood of resistance and by a perception of enhanced risk. The resistance was most obviously expressed in the difficulties first in negotiating the Treaty on European Union and then in achieving its ratification after initial rejection by the Danish electorate. Perception of enhanced risk was apparent both in the EU's uncertainty in the light of post-cold war crises (most obviously in former Yugoslavia) and in respect of the halting progress towards EMU. It appeared by the mid-1990s that the balance between the 'four Rs' had shifted decisively away from the reform/revival end of the spectrum and towards the risk/resistance end.

It is important to emphasize, however, that the history of the integration project is not one of absolutes. When the forces of reform and revival seem predominant, there is still a role for risk and resistance. Likewise, when risk and resistance seem to have won the day, when fragmentation rather than integration seems to be the prime political and economic motif, there is still a role for reform and revival. So it proved in the late 1990s. Progress towards EMU was hard, but it was achieved. Maastricht was followed by Amsterdam; not a resounding triumph for the forces of reform and revival, but a treaty that could be and was ratified and which was also more substantial than its critics might imply. The Common Foreign and Security Policy was battered by Bosnia and then by Kosovo, but in 1998 and 1999 there were important developments in the moves towards security co-operation and 'convergence criteria' for defense policies. Enlargement negotiations were complex, often frustrating, and certain to be long drawn out, but they were initiated and sustained. The institutions, especially the Commission, were assailed by critics and by other institutions, to such effect that in 1999 the incumbent Commission was forced to resign; but it could be argued that this in itself was the catalyst for a more realistic and effective perspective on the Commission, both on the part of its members and on the part of outsiders.

To argue thus is not to adopt a naïve optimism that all will be well in the end for the European project. Rather, it is to follow the logic of our 'four Rs' and to underline the fact that we are not dealing in absolutes so much as in balances and nuances. Such a view also alerts us to two other vital factors. First, if we take the long view on such issues as the accumulation of legitimacy by the European institutions, we become aware that dramatic or sudden shifts in the balance of forces are often less important than the long-term trend line which runs through the middle of the contending forces. Second, we also become aware that the quiet, everyday activity of European integration may well be as significant as the grand bargains and the grand conflicts epitomized by Maastricht or the initiation of EMU. Although the 'four Rs' are present today, as they have been present throughout the history of the European project, the project itself has created a new context for their interplay. As a result, although it might be argued that the load on the EU system today is both more extensive and more challenging than it has been in other periods, it is also clear that there is not the gloom and 'Europessimism' of earlier periods such as the 1970s. Could it be that this is because the European project has moved from being a project to being a polity, with accompanying implications for both the political economy of the process and the political identity and aspirations of its participants (Laffan, O'Donnell, and Smith 2000)?

If indeed it is becoming possible to explore the EU as a polity rather than a project, how can we see this reflected in the development of scholarship? A recent review of the field (Begg and Peterson 1999) argued that theory-building predominated over theory-testing in the study of European integration, and that the empirical application and exploration of theoretical frameworks were still underdeveloped. The authors went on to identify a series of gaps in the analysis of European integration which demanded attention, and in particular to argue that new forms of policy process or new forms of linkages between the EU and its environment should be accommodated by theory. Such arguments can not only be accommodated within our framework; they are good examples of the ways in which the 'four Rs' help us to think about the shifting balances of European integration. For instance, in examining the links between the EU and its global or regional environment, the 'four Rs' indicate that we should explore the perceived risks and challenges of those linkages; the ways in which policy reform can accommodate to changes in the linkages; the potential areas of resistance to particular linkages; and the ways in which the stimulus of global or regional change can lead to revival of the European project.

Thus, there is a sense in which our notion of the 'four Rs' helps us to engage with the theoretical debate about European integration as well.

During the late 1990s, there has been a self-conscious effort by many scholars to locate the European project in terms of frameworks of theory going beyond the established range: for example, comparative politics, governance and regulation, institutionalism, social constructivism, post-modernism, and the politics of identity. The growing pluralism of theory applied to the European project appears to reflect, on the one hand, the continuing fluidity of the balance between the 'four Rs' in the practical evolution of the EU. Because there are a number of coexisting and often competing forces operating on the EU, it is increasingly difficult to develop any 'grand theory' unifying the whole field of analysis. On the other hand, there is also the theoretical movement which points to the growing institutionalization of the EU policy process at the same time as it indicates the 'Europeification' or 'Europeanization' of national politics and policy-making (Cowles, Caporaso, and Risse 2000). This means that there is a substantial basis for investing effort in theorizing, because the EU is not going to go away; it is now a permanent feature of the political, economic, and social landscape, and thus susceptible to cumulative the-ory-building and testing in a variety of areas. It would be quite possible in principle to evaluate every one of the approaches mentioned above in terms of its 'fit' with the 'four Rs' identified in this Introduction, and in terms of its contribution to a cumulative set of theories of European integr-ation. It is more appropriate, however, to leave this as one of the starting-points for our contributors and to turn now to the structure and scope of the volume.

The Structure and Scope of the Volume

The book is structured around five substantive parts, each dealing with major issues arising from the exploration of the 'four Rs'. Part II is con-cerned with the characteristics of the EU as an 'evolving' polity, and with the ways in which this might be theorized. Parts III and IV deal with the two most salient areas in which the 'contours' of the EU are changing in the early years of the new millennium: first, the establishment and opera-tion of EMU, and second, the process of enlargement. Part V focuses on the ways in which the EU's institutions are shaped, on questions of insti-tutional capacity, and on the issues of legitimacy and identity. Finally, Part VI deals with the scope of policy and movements for policy reform in four major sectors, exploring the challenges faced and the resources available to meet changing demands.

In dealing with the nature of the EU as a 'political animal', the authors in Part II uncover a number of important themes. John Peterson and

Elizabeth Bomberg take as their starting-point the balance between continuity and change in the EU, and more particularly the ways in which the
EU can confront and overcome successive challenges and apparent set-
backs. This capacity of the EU to 'reinvent' itself emanates not simply
from the resilience of institutional and organizational structures, but also
from the evolution of norms and patterns of behavior: the practices as well
as the institutions of the Union. One implication of this process is that it
may be more appropriate to conceptualize the EU as a 'polycentric polity',
with differentiated systems and practices of decision-making reflecting not
only pressures from within but also the broader environmental challenges
of globalization. Sieglinde Gstöhl, in turn, develops the theme of differentiation and flexibility within the European project. Her concern is specifically with the concept of 'differentiated integration' and with the ways in
which this has become formalized with the Treaty of Amsterdam. Does
this formalization reflect the 'grand bargains' which are the subject of
liberal intergovernmentalist theory, or the evolution of practices which are
more the stuff of 'everyday integration'? Gstöhl proposes a linkage
between 'grand bargains' and 'everyday integration'—a linkage that
emerges from the development of 'institutionalized international governance' and which places the 'high politics' of Intergovernmental
Conferences within the context of broader processes of implementation
and compliance. The third chapter in Part II, by Jo Shaw and Antje
Wiener, also deals with issues of differentiation and institutionalization.
However, Shaw and Wiener take the argument significantly further by
situating the EU's legal order not only in terms of formal institutions and
rules but also in terms of developing understandings and identities. In
contrast to the broadly positivist arguments of Gstöhl (and, to a lesser
extent, Peterson and Bomberg), Shaw and Wiener take a position based
on social constructivism, thereby reflecting a significant new element in
debates about the EU as it enters the new millennium. By doing so, they
can uncover the ways in which earlier analyses of the EU have been governed by statist assumptions, and can deal with a range of issues merging
from social interaction, social learning, and the generation of norms
within the EU legal order.

Part III focuses on the major institutional innovation and expansion of
policy scope generated during the 1990s: Economic and Monetary Union.
Chapter 5, by Amy Verdun, explores the ways in which EMU developed;
in other words, it asks about the process through which EMU came to be
embedded in the EU structure, and through which it expressed the interplay of member-state preferences, negotiating positions, and a developing
consensus. According to Verdun, ideas constitute a vital factor in overcoming perceptions of risk and points of resistance among the major

participants. These ideas help us to account for the ways in which EMU has come to acquire credibility and legitimacy both within the Union and outside. Miriam Campanella is also concerned with the interplay of conflicting forces within the EMU, but her analysis is based on different conceptual foundations. Analyzing the establishment of EMU initially as a strategic game played out between the member states and the European Central Bank (ECB), she is able to show how the debates about political accountability and control go beyond simple rational calculation, and how the contest over the independence of the European Central Bank has been fought so far. In Chapter 7, Erik Jones takes the analysis of EMU and its impact much further by focusing on the ways in which adjustment has been demanded and achieved within the system. This is a crucial issue for the longer term sustainability of EMU, and it engages with a host of major questions about state motivations, strategies, and autonomy. Jones argues that analysis of EMU is best conducted by seeing it as a mechanism for adjustment, and as part of an increasingly embedded status quo to which national and regional adjustment strategies are a response. In doing so, he engages both with the ideational approach put forward by Verdun and with the strategic approach espoused by Campanella.

In Part IV, the changing shape of the EU is viewed from another perspective, that of enlargement. Helen Wallace begins this section by arguing that enlargement is undertheorized in the EU literature, and that it is vital to conceptualize it as part of the project itself. In other words, enlargement is one of the essential characteristics of the 'evolving polity', and from this flows a series of questions about the stability of the system, its mechanisms for distributing costs and benefits, and its institutional capacity. Wallace also points out that in discussion of enlargement (as in other areas of EU studies) there is an important interaction between theorists and practitioners, which can skew the terms of debate and of analysis. As in some of the earlier chapters, Wallace's argument alerts us to important normative issues, by pointing to the growth of 'common sense' assumptions about the risks, potential costs and benefits, and the broader impact of enlargement. This broader impact, on European order, on the domestic politics and economics of member states and candidates, and on the global arena, is not a one-way process; the EU is affected by variations in these areas as much as it affects them. Wallace's analysis of the linkages between enlargement and integration is then given further expression. In Chapter 9 Ulrich Sedelmeier draws attention to the ways in which enlargement is not simply a problem in EU external policy-making. He argues that, rather than viewing enlargement as a collective action problem pure and simple, we should build into our analysis the ways in which enlargement for member states constitutes an 'enactment of their collective identity'. This helps us to explain why, despite the many conflicting interests and national positions evoked by enlargement, there is none the less little scope to veto the process which possesses an expansive logic of its own. This takes us further down the track of building enlargement into the integration process, by calling into action some of the elements of social learning and social construction proposed in earlier chapters by Shaw and Wiener and Verdun. In Chapter 10, Lykke Friis and Anna Murphy undertake a detailed analysis of the ways in which notions of governance and boundaries can be factored into the enlargement process. They are concerned with the specific impacts of many of the general conditions clarified by Helen Wallace, and they provide an important insight into the dynamics of the negotiating processes which have been generated by the prospective enlargement into Central and Eastern Europe. They take a more 'externally oriented' view than Sedelmeier, and by doing so can point out the ways in which enlargement creates external challenges and demands as well as the ways in which candidate countries can become internalized into the EU process.

Part V takes us into rather different areas of the European integration project, by focusing on the interaction between institutions, political change, and changing identities. Not surprisingly, the 'evolving polity'—notably the development both of EMU and of the enlargement process—has instigated many of the institutional questions raised here. Chapter 11, by Mitchell Smith, explores the challenges faced by the Commission, and particularly the ways in which the Commission has encountered 'diminishing returns to political entrepreneurship'. This approach helps us to understand why the status of the Commission has been put at risk, and why there are pressures for reform generated by perceptions of institutional incapacity. It also helps us to identify the ways in which the technocratic style of Commission action has become subject to politicization and challenge, raising issues of legitimacy and accountability. Roger Scully argues in Chapter 12 that some of the same questions about legitimacy and institutional status can be posed in relation to the European Parliament. While the EP has experienced significant enhancement of its status as the result of successive IGCs, this does not mean that its legitimacy has expanded in step with its activity. Indeed, by deploying the literature of comparative legislative studies, Scully can argue that the EP is a 'vulnerable' legislature whose capacities could be tested to destruction, for example by the consequences of the next enlargement. The implications of enlargement are also central to the study by Paul Mullen of the Court of Justice, and in particular of its translation services. By focusing on this little-studied aspect of 'integration in practice', Mullen is able to pose important questions about institutional capacity and legitimacy, and about the relationship between everyday activities and the integration process (issues raised in earlier chapters dealing with the theorization of the EU). The final two chapters in this section deal with the broader political and attitudinal context for the operation of EU institutions and development of an EU identity. In Chapter 14 Mark Pollack deals with the impact of political change, specifically the rise of center-left governments in Europe, and the potential impact of the 'third way'—or what is sometimes termed 'Blairism' in the UK—on EU policy-making. Pollack explores the competing ideas among the political leaders of the European left, as well as the ways in which their agendas influence the EU political process. He suggests that there is not a single 'third way', but multiple ways in which the European left might pursue a European social model at the EU level in the twenty-first century. In Chapter 15 David Green tackles the issue of 'being a European'. Deploying extensive data on public attitudes across the Union, Green is able to generate substantive questions about the prospects for democratic legitimacy in a changing EU, and about the ways in which diffuse support for the 'idea of Europe' does or does not translate into specific grants of legitimacy to institutions or policy initiatives. He maintains that there is a diffuse European identity in Europe but questions whether or not this 'insurance policy' will provide the EU with the support necessary to cope with major risks or challenges. Green concludes that the answer to this question depends on how one conceptualizes the European polity itself—thus hearkening back to the earlier debates in Part II.

The final section of this book deals with some of the specific policy challenges which might crystallize perceptions of risk, the need for reform, and the interplay of resistance and revival. Sophie Meunier and Kalypso Nicolaïdis take further the arguments in earlier chapters about policy challenges and institutional capacity, by exploring the question 'who should speak for Europe?' in trade policy. Using principal-agent analysis, they are able to identify central issues of competence and control in external trade policy, and to trace the ways in which the shifting parameters of institutional reform are initiated and determined. In particular, they focus on issues of democratic accountability—an important focus in an area of European policy-making that has traditionally been highly technocratic. As the authors of several other chapters do, they identify trends towards differentiation in EU policy-making and implementation, and explore the problems of fragmentation that might result. In Chapter 17 Ingmar von Homeyer, Alexander Carius, and Stefani Bär undertake a detailed analysis of issues arising in environmental policy as the result of prospective enlargement. By doing so, they give a different angle on questions relating to the *acquis*—the set of competences and stipulations contained in

European legislation, as well as less formal expectations. They cast their argument particularly in terms of the tensions between Europeanization and renationalization of environmental policies, and are able to identify problems relating to the allocation of costs and to the implementation of policies. An intergovernmentalist analysis might predict that in these conditions there would be incentives to renationalize policy. However, an institutionalist analysis indicates the ways in which expectations about environmental policies have become embedded and legitimized at the EU level, and also the ways in which institutional adaptation and flexibility can 'rescue' policies at risk. Chapter 18, by J. Bryan Collester, focuses on the policy challenges and responses encountered in the development of a European defense. Specifically, he examines the ways in which, after discouraging experiences in the early 1990s, the development of a European Security and Defense Identity (ESDI) took significant steps forward during 1998 and 1999. His analysis focuses on three interacting forces: the changes in political élites and their interests, the growing public awareness of the EU's shortcomings in defense, and the corporate restructuring of defense industries in the EU. These converged, Collester argues, to provide a context in which the Western European Union (WEU) could act as the vehicle for 'spillover' into new areas of activity, and also to provide safeguards against 'spillback' or the renationalization of particular areas of defense policy. The final chapter, by Martin Holland, takes the discussion of policy further by analyzing the processes of negotiation centering on the Lomé Convention during the late 1990s. Holland is particularly concerned with the ways in which the changing global context for development created incentives to reform the Lomé structures, but also created substantial obstacles to innovative institutional solutions. In taking this line of attack, he brings us back to issues of institutional capacity, but also to ways in which the idea of EU–developing-country partnership has evolved and to the interaction between uncertain consensus and fragile institutions.

The chapters gathered together here thus cover a very wide range of analytical and policy issues. By doing so, they give a broad and variegated impression of the 'state of the European Union' on the threshold of the twenty-first century. They also provide a strong impression of the methodological pluralism that characterizes the area of EU studies in the contemporary era, and thus in a sense of the 'state of EU studies'. There are, though, a number of threads that run through all of the chapters, and that relate back strongly to our themes: risk, reform, resistance, and revival. Among these themes, the following stand out:

• The development of the 'EU order', not just in terms of formal institutions but also as a normative order engaging the social forces at play in the Union.

I

Conceptualizing the European Union

2

The EU after the 1990s: Explaining Continuity and Change

JOHN PETERSON AND ELIZABETH BOMBERG

Predictably, the arrival of the New Millennium brought a glut of Toffleresque predictions of looming, revolutionary change in all arenas of social and political life. Many were far-fetched enough to make sober reflection on the future of modern governance seem like a lost art. Nevertheless, the European Union (EU) genuinely appeared on the brink of dramatic and perhaps wholesale change. Monetary union was established but many of its effects were still unknown. EU enlargement was given an unexpected shot in the arm by the war in Kosovo. The Balkan wars of the 1990s, combined with a dramatic turnaround in the United Kingdom's position on European security cooperation, made an unprecedented pooling of defense capabilities seem inevitable, and perhaps even near at hand. After a newly emboldened European Parliament (EP) forced the resignation of Jacques Santer and the European Commission in 1999, Santer's successor—the former Italian Prime Minister, Romano Prodi—set out to transform the Commission into a 'European government'. Often unnoticed amidst all the ruptures, EU member states agreed to convene yet *another* intergovernmental conference (IGC), the Union's third in 14 years, to consider reform of its Treaties. Symbolically, at least, the emergence of a 'new' EU—what Prodi called a 'political Europe'—was signaled by the start of the IGC in early 2000.

Our purpose here is to identify what about the EU is changing and what is not. We build on recent work into how the EU makes *decisions*: choices or solutions that end some uncertainty or reduce contention (see Peterson and Bomberg 1999). First we offer an overview of recent developments in the EU, then consider how theory can be deployed to explain changing (and unchanging) patterns of EU decision-making. Next, we identify evolving norms in EU decision-making, or changing principles of 'right action' that guide, control, or regulate it. Then we highlight enduring patterns, or ones that are so embedded and institutionalized as to resist much change anytime soon.

Our essential argument is that the EU is set to be transformed in the twenty-first century in important ways. Monetary union and enlargement are the two most obvious catalysts. Yet, more generally, the EU faces new pressures and incentives to become a more unified global actor and to innovate institutionally, including in ways that defy the traditional Community method of decision-making. The EU is becoming more poly-centric, with more and more diverse centers of power, development, and control. Despite our aesthetic need to get a 'handle' on the EU, particu-larly given the curiosity and confusion of non-specialists,[1] it is increasingly difficult to generalize about the European Union and how it makes deci-sions. We do our best here, but also concede (a bit wearily) that the multi-level polity we began to understand in the 1990s seems to be transmuting into what, effectively, are multiple and different polities.

The 'New' European Union

Our contribution to the last *State of the European Union* accented the rel-ative calm of the post-Maastricht EU (Peterson and Bomberg 1998: 59). After the turmoil surrounding the ratification (in 1993) of the Maastricht Treaty, northern enlargement in 1995 was the smoothest, least disruptive enlargement in the Community's history. The incoming Santer Commission pledged to 'do less but do it better'. Decision-making pat-terns were essentially frozen in advance of another IGC (which began in 1996) and so were most policies ahead of negotiations on a new six-year Community budget.

It was always clear that the quiet could not last, particularly given plans to launch the Euro in 1999 and to agree to a new set of Treaty reforms before then. Of course, the resignation of the Santer Commission and war in Kosovo were far more unexpected. But all were defining events in the EU's development. Their combined effect was to spur the rise of a some-thing like a 'new' European Union.

European Monetary Union is the subject of Part III of this volume. For our purposes, it is enough to note three basic effects on EU decision-making. First, the launch of the Euro makes the EU a significantly more polycentric polity (see Snyder 1998). No other EU policy explicitly creates such a division between member states who are 'ins' and those who are 'outs', while still drawing (deeply) on the Union's common resources and institutions. No other gives as much autonomy to non-elected officials—

---

[1] This point was made eloquently by Daniel Elazar in his contribution to a conference on 'Rethinking Federalism in the EU and US', Kennedy School, Harvard University, 19–20 Apr. 1999.

heads of national central banks and the European Central Bank's (ECB) executive committee—to take such weighty decisions (such as on interest rates and national public budget deficits). Despite its profound effects on a wide range of other EU policies (Crouch 2000), monetary union has given birth to a system of decision-making that is unique, cloistered, and mostly 'stands alone'.

Second, as a partial counterpoint, many of the institutional consequences of monetary union are still largely unknown. Even after a declaration was agreed on the division of labor between the EU-15 Council of Economic and Finance Ministers (ECOFIN) and the 'Euro-11' Council at the 1999 Helsinki summit, it was unclear how the relationship between the two might evolve (particularly after eastern enlargement). Rules designed to ensure accountability, openness, and transparency in the management of the Euro were ambiguous and contested (see Buiter 1999; Issing 1999*a*). The ECB President was obliged to report four times a year to the EP, and scrutinizing European monetary policy gave the Parliament a potentially significant opportunity to raise its profile and legitimacy. Yet, MEPs clearly would have to work hard to establish their credibility with a set of actors—central bankers—who were generally unaccustomed to scrutiny by elected politicians.

Third, the external implications of EMU are considerable and often underappreciated (see Commission 1997*d*). The Euro's development into a major international currency will be gradual. Regardless, the EU's position in major international institutions clearly will be enhanced. The power that comes with responsibility for managing a reserve currency will not be easy for the Union to handle. The Euro area is a relatively closed economy (more so than the EU as a whole), with far more trade occurring within it than between Euro-land and the outside world. Most economists expect more fluctuation between the dollar and Euro—because of 'benign neglect' of exchange rates in both the USA and EU—than has traditionally occurred, say, between the dollar and German mark. The bad-tempered squabble with the USA over the EU's representation in Group of Eight meetings of finance ministers may foreshadow similar disputes in other international forums.

In many respects, EMU acted to overshadow the *Amsterdam Treaty*, which did not contain many significant institutional reforms. Arguably, the Treaty's most notable provisions sought to create antidotes to problems engendered by EMU: unemployment and fiscal solvency (Peterson and Jones 2000). Still, the Treaty sanctioned at least four potentially important changes to EU decision-making.

The first concerned 'flexibility': allowing subgroups of member states to deepen cooperation between themselves (see Philippart and Edwards

1999, and Chapter 3, below, by Gstöhl). The EU was not without precedents: the Social Chapter allowed a UK opt-out and the first wave of EMU saw only eleven Member States join the Euro. However, despite numerous 'catches' to limit their application (Peterson and Bomberg 1999: 19), Amsterdam's flexibility provisions marked a step-level change away from a Union where all member states sail at one speed as often as possible. A committee of 'Wise Men', reporting to the Commission in advance of the Millennium IGC, pushed the boat out even further. The so-called Dehaene (*et al.* 1999) Report argued that Amsterdam's flexibility provisions were 'so complex and subject to such conditions and criteria that they are unworkable' and insisted that an enlarged EU required increased institutional flexibility and less restrictive procedures for triggering this flexibility. In short, Amsterdam accelerated the drift towards a more differentiated, à la carte European Union.

Second, the extension of co-decision was, apparently, relatively uncontroversial in the negotiations on the Amsterdam Treaty (Moravcsik and Nicolaïdis 1999: 80–1). It kept the EU on a consistent path of change: every time the Treaties have been revised, the EP has been awarded more powers. As a consequence, the EU has moved much closer to being a parliamentary democracy than it was at the beginning of the 1990s—a point discussed at greater length by Scully in Chapter 12.

Third, the Amsterdam Treaty mandated important, even dramatic changes to the EU's intergovernmental pillars. Pillar III was the surprise star of the Treaty, with significant elements of justice and home affairs (JHA) policies—particularly border controls, asylum, and immigration—elided into pillar I, albeit with yet another complicated series of brakes, catches, and caveats. For example, unanimous voting (not qualified majority voting, or QMV) will apply to all JHA policies moved to Pillar I for at least five years after the Treaty becomes effective. Member states will enjoy the right of initiative and share it with the Commission, in a startling reversal of past Pillar I procedure. The communitarization of Pillar III was a messy one, which gives the EU more—not fewer—different methods of reaching decisions (Barrett 1997).

The Amsterdam reforms of the Common Foreign and Security Policy (CFSP) look modest on paper (see Peterson and Sjursen 1998). The European Council was given enhanced responsibility for decision-making, but there was no clear move to more QMV on Pillar II issues. Here, as in the Treaty's creation of a new 'High Representative' for the CFSP and a Policy Planning and Early Warning Unit, *how* the Treaty is implemented will matter more than what it says.

Fourth, perhaps the most important outcome of the 1997 Amsterdam summit was a series of 'non-decisions' on institutional reform. After long and tortured debate, a deal trading off a reduction in the size of the Commission (with larger member states giving up their right to appoint two Commissioners) in exchange for a reweighting of Council votes under QMV (with larger states gaining more) collapsed. None the less, a protocol attached to the Treaty made it clear that the trade-off would be the centerpiece of the next IGC. The protocol also stated that the EU would undertake a 'comprehensive review' of EU decision-making procedures at least a year before its membership exceeded twenty, thus creating a new potential barrier to enlargement. In effect, the protocol mandated a two-step reform process: a quick set of reforms in 2000 (to seal the deal which was nearly sealed at Amsterdam) and then a more comprehensive round several years later.

Yet, the Dehaene (*et al.* 1999: 1–2) Report urged that 'comprehensive reform should be undertaken right now. There might be no better occasion in future'. Resistance to 'comprehensive reform' was abundant and widely distributed among national capitals, but the possibility of a broad-ranging IGC in 2000, as opposed to a narrow one, was at least placed on the Union's agenda.

The *Santer Commission* kept a low profile during the Amsterdam IGC. Santer learned from the mistakes of his predecessor, Jacques Delors, and focused on a few selected priorities while avoiding 'proposals which were too visionary' as Delors had done to the Commission's cost in the Maastricht IGC.[2] Yet, member states effectively ignored the Commission's preferences on three issues of crucial importance to Santer: 'new' external trade issues (services and intellectual property), the High Representative for the CFSP, and the communitarization of Pillar III (see Moravcsik and Nicolaïdis 1999). In all three cases, member states reserved for themselves an upper hand in decision-making.

However, Santer got what he wanted on two other priority issues. First, Amsterdam extended QMV to all stages of decision-making on research policy, thus eliminating a rogue version of co-decision which required the Council to agree unanimously on budgets and general priorities for the Framework R&D program, inevitably producing long delays (see Peterson 1995*b*). Second, Santer convinced member states to elevate the Commission President from 'first among equals' on the college of Commissioners to its clear political leader. The new Treaty stated that future Commissioners would be nominated 'by common accord with the nominee for President' and then would 'work under the political guidance of the President'.

---

[2] Santer quoted in Peterson 1999*b*: 52.

Of course, Santer will be remembered more for his downfall in spring 1999 than for anything achieved under his Presidency. After a shocking report by the EP-instigated Committee of Independent Experts found evidence of nepotism and mismanagement in the Commission, Santer's stubborn defense of himself and his team was poorly judged, cack-handed, and sealed his doom. Yet, while Santer was by no means a strong or forceful President, he embraced reform of the Commission far more than any of his predecessors had done. Nine months before the Commission resigned, the final declaration of the Cardiff summit con-gratulated Santer and his team for their efforts to improve the efficiency and management of the Commission (Peterson 1999*b*: 57; see also Laffan 1997; Cram 1999). Santer became the EU's Gorbachev: a reformer swept away by the powerful forces he himself unleashed (Peterson 1999*a*).

Santer's resignation created a window of opportunity for a fundamen-tal reinvention of the Commission under Prodi. The decision to choose Prodi was taken extraordinarily quickly. Convened within a week of Santer's resignation, the Berlin summit also agreed a sweeping five-year budget deal, accepting the broad outlines of the Commission's (1997*a*) *Agenda 2000* proposal. The European Council's formidable agency—or ability to wield power and act decisively—was displayed clearly.

The EU's impressive recovery from one of its darkest moments was barely noticed, however, as NATO airstrikes against Serbia began on the first night of the Berlin summit. *Kosovo* goaded the EU into action: the Union immediately agreed to impose an oil embargo on Serbia and dis-patched the Finnish President, Martti Ahtisaari, to negotiate (success-fully, as it turned out) a political settlement to end the war. Within a few days of the Berlin summit, Prodi and the President-in-Office of the Council, German Foreign Minister Joschka Fischer, both began arguing for a new kind of partnership between the EU and the Balkans. Prodi floated plans for a 'New Southeast Europe'. Fischer lobbied hard for a rapid EU offer of association to Albania and Macedonia, as well as a new 'Stability Pact' for the Balkans.

Almost as soon as the war ended, the EU was shackled by familiar problems: low levels of Community funding for post-war reconstruction, slow and small national aid contributions, continued reliance on NATO firepower, and an ugly row about whether the Union would base its aid effort in Kosovo or Greece. Yet Kosovo had three immediate effects on thinking about the EU's future. First, it transformed the debate about the EU's enlargement, which had almost disappeared from political radar screens as the accession negotiations grinded away. After Kosovo, rapid EU enlargement—although fraught with risks and costs—seemed less risky or costly than allowing the process to stagnate. Second, Kosovo gave

stimulus to ongoing discussions, led by the UK and France, about consolidating European military capabilities and discussing them in the next
IGC. Third, the EU clearly faced a litmus test in the Balkans. If it succeeded in bringing peace, stability, and prosperity to the region, its status
as a political superpower would be never again be questioned. If it failed,
the EU would be relegated to the sidelines in some new, undefined political settlement in twenty-first-century Europe.

Explaining Change and Continuity

If one central point of consensus has emerged out of recent scholarship on
the EU, it is that the Union has become a 'multi-level' system of governance. Moravcsik's (1998: 61) masterful study of five transformative decisions in post-war European integration distinguishes between the 'high
politics' of treaty-amending negotiations and the 'low politics' of the EU's
'everyday legislative process'. Elsewhere (Peterson and Bomberg 1999), we
have sought to specify, as analytical categories, three different types of EU
decision: history-making (the kind that preoccupy Moravcsik), policy-
setting (which determine EU policy), and policy-shaping (which determine policy options or technology). Each tends to be taken at distinct,
identifiable levels of governance in most EU policy sectors.

The best-known treatment of multi-level governance remains that of
Gary Marks, Liesbet Hooghe and colleagues (see Marks *et al.* 1996*a*;
1996*b*; Hooghe and Marks 1997*a*). It is based on three core assumptions.
First, 'decision-making is shared by actors at different levels rather than
monopolized by state executives'. Second, 'collective decision-making
among states involves a significant loss of control for individual state executives'. Third, 'political arenas are interconnected rather than nested', and
in particular subnational actors are *not* nested exclusively within states
(Hooghe and Marks 1997a: 23).

In a recent exposition, Hooghe and Marks (1999) explain how and why
the EU emerged as a (multi-level) polity in its own right. They argue that
the Single European Act 'institutionalized a double shift of decision making away from national states—to the market and to the European level'
in the 1980s. One consequence was a 'broadening of participation' in EU
decision-making, which became 'less technocratic and more contentious.
Fewer decisions are resolved by rational-scientific methods, by ascertaining the most efficient means to given ends, while more decisions involve
political contention concerning the fundamental goals of European integration' (Hooghe and Marks 1999: 73–4). Hooghe and Marks offer a per-
ceptive and plausible explanation of what changed and why in the 1980s.

We are not convinced that this framework explains change (or continuity) in the late 1990s very well, for three reasons. First, it is easy to exaggerate the extent to which EU decision-making has become 'participatory-politicized'. In particular, élitist-technocratic decision-making remains firmly entrenched at the deeper recesses of the EU, and usually introduces a bias for policy continuity instead of change. Second, Hooghe and Marks focus mainly on the internal logic of EU polity-building: creating the internal market required changes in formal institutions and decision rules which led to a more open, contestable style of politics. Yet, change in EU decision-making is now, more than ever, driven by forces external to the EU itself: globalization, international monetary politics, and instability in the EU's 'near abroad'. Third, the EU is distinctively multi-level, but recent changes—particularly EMU and the creation and evolution of Pillars II and III—have produced a far more polycentric polity, or one with multiple centers of development and control. Explaining change and continuity in EU decision-making requires analysis of decisions at different levels and across different centers of power.

An EU 'Decision-Making Style'?

Considerable academic effort has been expended on identifying a distinctive EU policy or decision-making 'style' (see Richardson 1996; Hooghe and Marks 1999). Characterizations of national policy styles—anticipatory or reactive, élitist or participatory—were always presented as ideal types, which facilitated the deriving of comparative insights (Richardson 1982). Still, if the EU has become a polity in its own right, has it not developed a style of its own?

Certainly, EU politics have become 'domesticated' in that 'politics in the EU is more like that found *within* nation states than *among* them' (Hooghe and Marks 1999: 75). In some policy areas the EU has become more partisan, politicized, and participatory (see McGowan and Wallace 1996; Peterson 1997; Pollack 1997*b*; Wallace and Young 1997; Greenwood and Aspinwall 1998; Mazey 1998). The expansion of the EU's reach to social, environmental, research, and cultural policies means that more actors have a stake in EU decision-making and focus more of their lobbying on Brussels and Strasbourg. 'Europe' has become a domestic political issue in many member states and Euroscepticism a source of identity for political parties ranging from the British Conservatives to Nordic Social Democrats to French Gaullists.

On balance, these changes made it more—not less—difficult to identify a single EU decision-making style, and more so now than in the 1980s. Manufacturing one does not help us explain how the EU changes (or does not). What *does* help is to focus on how different kinds of decision are taken at distinct levels of governance. These levels are visible and (more or less) distinct in most EU policy sectors and are marked by different norms, rules, and 'styles'. At the highest political levels, history-making decisions result from bargaining which is effectively intergovernmental. Nearly all are taken unanimously by policy generalists (not specialists). Repeated rounds of sweeping, quasi-constitutional changes (in IGCs) since the mid-1980s suggest that the EU's heads of state and government—convening as the European Council—remain the most important source of agency in EU decision-making. The emergence of Europe as a domestic political issue in the 1990s places new constraints on high-level bargaining. Witness, for example, John Major's insistence on British opt-outs from the Maastricht Treaty or Helmut Kohl's resistance to extending QMV in the Amsterdam Treaty (Peterson and Bomberg 1999: 18–19, 212). However, the steady (if slow) expansion of the EU's competence, the unremitting empowerment of the EP, and the successful drive to EMU all suggest that integration continues to beget more integration. If liberal intergovernmentalism (LI) explains how high-level bargaining yields history-making decisions, then neofunctionalism remains a surprisingly plausible theory of how the context for intergovernmental bargaining evolved during the 1990s (see Caporaso 1998; Moravcsik 1999).

Even if the search for an EU policy style seems unprofitable, the traditional focus of most scholarship on grand bargains has left us bereft of a theory of the 'domestic politics' of the EU as a political system (see Hix 1999). At this 'systemic' level, especially given expanded QMV and EP empowerment, policy outcomes are now as much (often more) a product of inter-institutional than intergovernmental bargaining. Each sector of EU policy—the internal market, cohesion policy, the CFSP—has its own dedicated institutions. The institutional frameworks that have grown up around each have tended to become more unique, differentiated, and dominated by policy specialists.

When EU policies are set, it is after bargaining within relatively autonomous and sector-specific clusters of institutions. If few EU policies changed radically in 1990s, an important reason why is surely because institutions offer 'relatively stable or at least "sticky" frameworks for political choice' (Remmer 1997: 59). Path dependency is powerful in EU decision-making: past bargains are treated with great reverence and package deals are rarely unpicked. Thus, institutional theory offers considerable leverage as a theory of the 'domestic politics' of EU decision-making, not least because it 'characteristically provide[s] better answers for stability than change' (Remmer 1997: 59).

Even if decisions taken by the Council, the EP, the college of Commissioners, and the European Court of Justice (ECJ) attract the most academic, media, and popular attention, the vast majority of actual decisions in EU governance are taken within its vast labyrinth of committees. This subterranean, or subsystemic, level of governance is difficult to study since it rarely yields public documents or voting records. It *is* clear that the very nature of the EU means that the subsystemic level implicates a wide variety of different types of actor—political and administrative, public and private, national and supranational (and subnational)—who share a stake in EU policy outcomes. As such, the concept of 'policy networks', whatever its shortcomings as a theoretical construct (see Peters 1998; Thatcher 1998), has become a more common analytical tool of EU policy analysis. Policy networks are clusters of actors, or 'stakeholders', each with an interest in a given EU policy sector and the capacity to help determine policy success or failure. More than in most other polities, EU policies are shaped—options debated and defined—at a level quite far removed from the politicized worlds of ministers, Commissioners, and EP party group leaders. Policy specialists, not generalists, dominate EU policy networks. Members tend to share technical expertise, causal knowledge, and functional loyalties.

Fresh gusts of political wind often lose force by the time they reach the subsystemic level. After the Kosovo war ended, a new impetus for rapid EU enlargement became palpable, with Prodi proclaiming 'the first opportunity of reuniting Europe since the fall of the Roman Empire'.[3] However, the Commission's chief negotiator on enlargement, Niklaus van der Pas, bluntly asserted: 'There is no possibility of speeding up the process. That would mean opening up more chapters per presidency, i.e. producing more draft common positions, but there is a limit on our ability to absorb the positions that the applicant countries present to us and on their ability to produce new positions.'[4] The EU's decision-making style at the subsystemic level is often cloistered, technocratic, and conservative.

In short, testable theoretical models of how the EU changes, and how and why change is resisted, do exist. But there is no single EU decision-making or 'policy style'. Moreover, the Union is evolving in ways that make the search for one increasingly fruitless.

External Impulses, Internal Change

However else the EU changed during the 1990s, it clearly emerged as a global power (see Peterson and Sjursen 1998; Bretherton and Vogler 1999). After widespread fears of a new 'Fortress Europe' in the 1980s, the

---

[3] Quoted in *European Voice* (10–17 Nov. 1999).
[4] Quoted in *European Voice* (22–8 July 1999).

EU played a surprisingly constructive role in the Uruguay Round and construction of the new World Trade Organization (see Pelkmans 1995). The geopolitical earthquakes of 1989–91 left the EU leading the Western effort to aid political and economic reform in the former Soviet bloc. The CFSP (created via the Maastricht Treaty) marked an attempt to ratchet up the EU's capabilities to keep pace with the outside world's expectations (Hill 1993).

The Union is a young superpower. The balance sheet of the 1990s probably contains more external policy failures—Bosnia, bananas, Russia—than successes. The Maastricht Treaty's commitment to 'the eventual framing of a common defense policy, which might in time lead to a common defense' has often seemed an empty one. In external trade policy, history-making decisions to open up the EU's huge market to foreign competition have frequently been stifled by subsystemic decisions to deploy anti-dumping or other protective measures. Europe's inability to respond quickly to crises in Rwanda, Algeria, or (especially) the Balkans was not enough to inspire a fundamental overhaul of the CFSP in the Amsterdam Treaty.

Explaining how the EU changes has always meant investigating how the Union responds to pressures emanating from beyond Europe itself (see Sandholtz and Zysman 1989; Cowles 1995; Caporaso 1998). Yet the Union's new global responsibilities make the EU far more responsive to external impulses than was the case in the 1980s. Its two most important recent projects—eastern enlargement and EMU—both expose the EU to intense new pressures from beyond its own borders. Meanwhile, globalization implies a steady and profound shift in the international backdrop against which the EU operates (see Anderson 1999). Increasingly, explaining change in EU decision-making means examining how the Union decides to respond to globalization: embracing it, accelerating it, or seeking to limit its effects—and why it chooses one of these goals over the others. The internal logic of the European project continues to matter, but external impulses increasingly determine choices about how it evolves.

Polycentricity: The New Paradigm?

The EU ended the 1990s as a far more 'differentiated polity', or one fragmented into more and more diverse centers of decision-making (see Rhodes 1997). The Union's expanding remit and ragged institutional reform combined to make its multiple, multi-layered centers of decision-making more distinctive, nuanced, and different from one another. In some cases, new cooperation was organized in ways designed to take politics out of policy-making. Take, for example, EMU and food safety. The

European Central Bank was given one of the most powerful forms of independence enjoyed by any central bank in the world. A new hierarchy of technocratic food safety committees effectively removed much decision-making from ministers.

Elsewhere, member states decided to retain stricter control over decision-making than they enjoy as the Council of Ministers under the traditional Community method (Devuyst 1999). The Maastricht Treaty's pillars for justice and home affairs policies and the CFSP are the most obvious examples. In particular, the CFSP became a law unto itself, with member states 'Brusselizing' their national foreign policies but giving the EU's institutions only marginal roles in decision-making (see Allen 1998). How the Amsterdam Treaty's provisions for flexibility will play out in practice is an open question. But it is clear that, to the extent they are used, they will produce more differentiation and fragmentation.

The wider point is that the EU became far more polycentric in the 1990s, with more diverse and anomalous arrangements for decision-making. Given the profusion of new and different structures, EU scholars have begun borrowing from the emerging 'constructivist' literature on international relations, which 'emphasizes the role of social structures and norms at the expense of the agents who help create them and change them in the first place' (Checkel 1998: 325; see also Chapter 4 below). The results (see Jachtenfuchs 1995; Christiansen *et al.* 1999) are often stimulating, but somewhat vague and prone to claims that cannot 'even in principle, be declared empirically invalid' (Moravcsik 1999: 670).

Still, much EU scholarship starts with the increasingly tenuous assumption that the Union and its institutions are only as powerful as member states want them to be. It must be accepted that actors in EU decision-making, particularly at the systemic and subsystemic levels, do not form their preferences in a purely exogenous fashion that takes no account of the context of the EU itself. To explain outcomes, we may often need to open up the black box of interest and identity formation in a way that is sensitive to the increasingly varied structural contexts within which iterated EU bargaining takes place.

To be sure, given the EU's abundance of veto points, the frequency with which agency seems to trump structure in EU decision-making often seems miraculous (see Peterson and Bomberg 1999: 254–6). But we cannot neglect the profusion of different EU structures, and how agency is shaped and constrained by them. In effect, the EU has become many different systems of governance, which may have different historical trajectories, and no longer just one.

Evolving Norms in EU Decision-Making

The precise contours of the 'new' EU will not become visible until the next edition of the *State of the European Union*. Yet, recent events have accelerated the evolution of norms that govern exchanges between EU institutions and member states, and provide a structural context for agency in EU decision-making. We highlight four such changing norms here.

The first and most significant arises primarily from the launch of EMU, in the teeth of daunting political opposition and risks. One upshot may be categorized as an evolving norm: in terms of new initiatives, *the parameters of what has become thinkable have broadened*. The point cannot go unqualified: in important respects, expectations about what powers the EU should take on have diminished. The end of Kohl's long reign as German Chancellor, and replacement by Gerhard Schröder, a pragmatist and occasional Eurosceptic, signaled new limits. It also united German, British, and French attitudes towards subsidiarity as never before (Peterson and Bomberg 1999: 57). Still, if the European Union can succeed in delivering on its most audacious project, with origins in the late 1960s, then other new projects with high ambitions cannot be dismissed out of hand.

The point was illustrated by Prodi's calls for a new 'European army' during the Kosovo crisis. An EU defense capability will not be constructed quickly and Eurosceptic parties can be expected to rally around the issue. However, a stunning U-turn by the UK, after Blair's passionate insistence on the primacy of NATO at the Amsterdam summit, meant that the EU's three most powerful member states shared a broad agenda on defense (see Chapter 18 below). Germany's modest, but symbolically potent military contribution to the Kosovo campaign also shifted the debate. Attempts by the 1999 Finnish Council Presidency to keep the 2000 IGC focused on a short agenda of institutional reform issues left over from Amsterdam were challenged by demands for a debate about an EU defense policy, and specifically by a Anglo-Franco proposal for a 60,000 strong EU peacekeeping force.

The logic of defense integration is functional, as much as political, as Europe's military weakness was exposed as never before by the Balkan wars. The Growth and Stability Pact agreed alongside the Amsterdam Treaty placed strict limits on attempts—barely imaginable anyway—by member states to try to fix the problem by markedly increasing national defense budgets. EMU and the politics of European defense cooperation were linked in more ways than one.

Evidence that EMU made thinkable what was previously unthinkable was visible in other areas. One was taxation: the row which ensued after the ill-fated German Finance Minister, Oskar Lafontaine, was joined by his (also ill-fated) French counterpart, Dominique Strauss-Kahn, in calling for serious tax harmonization in 1998 was a storm in a teacup. Still, pressures for the harmonization of savings and business taxes were measurably stronger post-EMU. In an illustration of both the EU's increased polycentricity and the increasing use of peer pressure in policing the internal market, the pressures were partially defused by a comprehensive survey of national tax breaks and a new (non-binding) code of conduct to regulate them.

Competition policy was another sector where the EU seemed poised to go boldly where it had never gone before. A Commission White Paper on competition policy reform, unveiled in May 1999, shocked many EU watchers (EU 1999). Proposals to decentralize the enforcement of EU competition rules, while giving the Commission the right to snatch cases from national authorities if it deemed necessary, faced numerous political obstacles (particularly from Germany). Still, EMU promised to lead to an increase in mergers, acquisitions, and joint ventures and threatened to swamp the Commission's competition authorities. Since the status quo was unsustainable anyway, the Commission did not shirk from proposing radical change. (For further discussion on this point, see Chapter 11 below.)

These initiatives all revealed a second evolving norm: *a willingness to embrace new and more diverse decision-making arrangements* to suit specific needs and priorities. Again, there were precedents: take social policy, with decision-making based on a 'social dialogue' between employers and trade unions and a bias towards voluntary agreements instead of regulation (Peterson and Bomberg 1999: 82–3). Still, a greater willingness to experiment flowed from eastern enlargement, and the inevitability of new kinds of variable geometry in an EU of twenty-five or more member states (see Dehaene *et al.* 1999). Applicant states themselves reacted by tabling new demands for special treatment. Both Poland and Hungary insisted on the right to restrict the purchase of farmland by non-nationals. Poland demanded that designated Special Economic Zones targeted for redevelopment should be exempt from EU state aid rules until 2017. To an extent previously unseen, EU decision-makers began to concede that the longstanding imperative to preserve one *acquis* for all and the somewhat newer imperative to simplify and standardize EU decision rules were incompatible with anything but long delays to eastern enlargement.

The new determination to push ahead with enlargement, as well to deepen defense cooperation, reflected a third evolving norm: *consensus that the EU must become a more effective global actor*. In facing up to its international responsibilities, the EU had to find new ways to allow interested non-EU states (especially applicant states) a voice in its policy debates. Again, EMU was critical in raising the Union's profile in international economic diplomacy, as was the inescapable fact that the Union's most powerful foreign policy tool was its ability to offer association or membership to states to its east. Perhaps above all, the 'new' EU seemed determined to learn from its perceived failure in Bosnia and success in Kosovo. This norm both underlines and enhances the growing importance of external forces in shaping EU decision-making.

There is little point in debating whether the Amsterdam Treaty would have yielded radical reforms of the CFSP if it had been agreed after, rather than before Kosovo. In any event, the CFSP's formal rules matter far less than how they are used: the appointment of Javier Solana as the first CFSP High Representative, after impressive performances as Spanish Foreign Minister and secretary-general of NATO during Kosovo, probably mattered more than anything agreed on pillar II at Amsterdam. Even outside the confines of the EU, the Blair government's decision to nominate George Robertson, who had also had a 'good war' as British Defense Secretary during Kosovo, to replace Solana at NATO was indicative of new will to upgrade Europe's international presence. Robertson was a keen advocate of closer European defense cooperation. His appointment was enthusiastically supported by France, whose government was motivated by deep concerns—reflected clearly in public opinion—about a 'new American hegemony' (see Peterson 2000). Yet different motivations among leading member states did not preclude a convergence of views about the need to make the EU into an international power that could punch its weight.

This convergence extended to Prodi as he assembled his new team of Commissioners. One of the heavyweights of the Prodi Commission, the former Conservative British minister (and last governor of Hong Kong), Chris Patten, was given the general external relations portfolio. Prodi's determination to channel strong national preferences into effective political agency led to the surprise choices of Germany's Gunter Verheugen as Commissioner for enlargement and France's Pascal Lamy as Commissioner for trade. Prodi brushed aside suggestions that Germany's pro-enlargement agenda made it politically unacceptable to give Verheugen the enlargement dossier. Lamy's appointment raised eyebrows, but his Atlanticist and pro-free trade credentials made his appointment seem a political masterstroke, particularly given the predictable difficulties of selling any new world trade deal to the French.

The dawn of the Prodi era signaled a fourth evolving norm: a new *determination to reform the European Commission*, and make it more effective, efficient, and respected. Arguably, Prodi ended up with a less impressive line-up of Commissioners than Santer did (see Peterson 1999a). Despite his new, stronger appointment prerogatives, Prodi was forced to work within clearly defined political limits, particularly the need to achieve gender and party-political balance. He did not veto any national candidate. However, several of his preferences were heeded in, for example, Blair's appointment of Patten instead of the British Conservative Party's favored candidate, Alistair Goodlad, and Italy's choice of Mario Monti over Emma Bonino (the latter two being holdovers from Santer's Commission).

Meanwhile, Prodi openly acknowledged his ambition to make the Commission a 'European government'. Portfolios were matched to the expertise of national nominees. Prodi designated himself a virtual 'Prime Minister' without portfolio. Despite the lack of any formal rule to sanctify it, Prodi insisted that he would not hesitate to reshuffle portfolios if he thought it necessary.

Even before the new Commission's investiture by the EP, Prodi announced sweeping internal reforms, especially ones designed to separate political from administrative tasks and reduce the influence of national capitals on the college. In particular, Prodi imposed new limits on the power of Commissioners' *cabinets* of personal advisers. He also insisted that all Commissioners appoint either a *chef* (head) or deputy *chef* to their *cabinet* who did not share their own nationality, and drove the point home by choosing an Irishman, David O'Sullivan, as his own *chef* (before Sullivan became the Commission's Secretary General). Above all, Prodi curtailed the power of any single Commissioner to block or delay decisions opposed by their home government, as had repeatedly occurred during the Santer era (see Peterson and Bomberg 1999: 76).

The job of reforming the Commission's services was given to Neil Kinnock, one of two Commission Vice-Presidents. The Directorates began to look far more like national ministries, with Kinnock requiring Commissioners physically to be present in the same buildings as their service. No Commissioner and Director-General (top permanent official) of any service could hail from the same member state.

Prodi had far to go before he could claim credit for creating a 'strong Commission, an autonomous Commission, an independent Commission, an accountable Commission'.[5] A true revolution was required before the analytical distinction, drawn frequently by EU scholars, between 'national governments' and 'EU institutions', had basis in empirical reality. However, most member states clearly wanted a new model Commission, even if there was little consensus about what it might look like.

[5] Quoted in *European Voice* (22–8 July 1999).

Enduring Patterns

In many respects the EU has changed beyond recognition since the mid-1980s. Radical policy shifts have occurred in telecommunications, external trade, and environmental protection. It would be surprising if EMU and enlargement did not further transform EU decision-making in fundamental ways. Still, decision-making is heavily routinized in many sectors, even if it has become less standardized and uniform across the EU as a whole. Much recent EU scholarship has accentuated continuity more than change: prominent themes include 'path dependency', 'lock-in' and simple inertia (see Armstrong and Bulmer 1998; Grant 1997; Michael E. Smith 1998; Peterson and Sharp 1998; Pierson 1998). In this section we identify three broad patterns which have endured and are likely to endure in the 'new' European Union.

The first concerns *the role of the European Parliament*. Given the EP's new self-confidence, symbolized above all by Santer's resignation, the empowerment of the EP may seem to signal change rather than continuity. Yet, the EP has been the institutional winner each time the Treaties have been revised. Empowering the EP is almost a default outcome when institutional change reaches the top of the EU's agenda. The perceived need of member states, above all Germany and the Benelux and Nordic states, to fight domestic Euroscepticism by arguing that the EU is evolving into a parliamentary democracy is powerful. Member states that have traditionally resisted EP empowerment—France, the UK, Denmark, and Greece—have trouble making a principled argument against upgrading the powers of what is, on paper at least, the EU's most democratically legitimate institution.

The gradual empowerment of the EP has *not* been accompanied by radical change in its collective behavior. Where co-decision applies—particularly the internal market—the EP has won significant victories *vis-à-vis* the Council, especially on matters of detail which make EU policy more consumer- or environment-friendly. But the EP maximizes its influence under co-decision only when it collectively judges how far it can push the Council. Since it must speak with one voice, and has such enormous difficulties doing so, the most common outcome of co-decision is a creative 'shifting of goalposts', or a retrospective revision of the stated goals of a measure so that all can claim some kind of victory (Bomberg and Burns 1999).

Even if the most important cleavage in most EU policy debates—particularly under co-decision—is inter-institutional, other cleavages still matter. Party group cohesion remains far lower than in most national

European parliaments, but there is evidence of an increasingly partisan style of politics in the EP (Kreppel 1999). EP party groups mobilized quickly to squeeze concessions out of Prodi after his nomination, with new Amsterdam Treaty rules making a positive EP vote a legal prerequisite of the Commission's investiture. The European Peoples' Party (EPP), which made significant gains in the 1999 EP election (gaining a plurality of seats), indulged in considerable saber-rattling about the perceived under-representation of Christian Democrats (only six of twenty nominees) in the Prodi Commission. These public displays of indignation were, more than anything else, a tactic to force Prodi to appoint EPP sympathizers to senior positions as Commission Directors-General, after Prodi promised to weed out technocrats who were poor managers. The strategy revealed the continuing importance of both party-based advocacy coalitions in EU decision-making (see Sabatier 1998) *and* the salience of political affiliations amongst formally apolitical actors working mostly at the subsystemic level. In fact, Prodi's determination to abolish the informal system of national quotas on senior Commission posts made it likely that party-political loyalties—instead of national origins—would become the primary determinant of who got what Commission job.

As for the EP, its post-1999 cohort was an unusually motley collection of individuals, who were likely to disappoint raised expectations of the Parliament. A large influx of members from fringe parties meant that turnover amongst MEPs was higher in the 1999 EP election than in any previous election. Meanwhile, with voter turnout hitting an all-time low, the election was a collective disaster for the EP. The Parliament looked set to remain a relatively unpredictable and ill-disciplined actor in EU decision-making. The steady institutional advances of the EP, and its continued difficulties in wielding its powers, constitute lines of continuity more than change.

A second enduring pattern is *stagnation in most EU policy outcomes*, with change usually occurring abruptly when it occurs at all. This pattern underscores the importance of identifying the sources of continuity and change at different levels of governance. The post-Maastricht period is rife with examples of policies—the EU's banana regime, subsidies for collaborative R&D, water-quality standards—which survived past their 'sell-by' dates in the absence of intervention from the highest political levels. Two recent examples, both arising from the Commission's *Agenda 2000* package, are also illustrative. First, the Commission's proposals for CAP reform highlighted the need for a 'coherent rural policy', or the integration of the Union's various rural initiatives and budgets. It also suggested renationalization of as much as one-quarter of EU farm spending, and large cuts in agricultural support prices. After virtually every member state trashed the proposals, the Commission made serious headway in negotiations leading up to the Berlin summit of 1999. A week before the summit, the Agriculture Council agreed to quite significant reforms. However, they were watered down considerably by the European Council at Berlin when Schröder both wilted under French pressure and bowed to the perceived need for a deal, any deal, with the Commission's resignation and Kosovo both requiring urgent attention.

A second example—cohesion policy—suggests that stagnation often occurs because the EU avoids decisions until it is forced to make them. Agenda 2000 proposed fundamental changes to the structural funds, such as narrowing the percentage of the EU's population covered by cohesion funding from 51 per cent to between 35 and 40 per cent. The European Council accepted most of the Commission's proposals for rejigging the basic principles of the structural funds (see Peterson and Bomberg 1999: 154), but insisted on very long transition periods for those areas to be 'weaned' off EU aid. With the first elections to the Scottish Parliament a few months away, the British government even came away with as much funding for the Scottish Highlands and Islands as the region would have received under the old rules.

A third pattern has persisted despite the decline of the EU's traditional permissive consensus 'from below': that is, placid publics with little interest or engagement in what the EU does. The pattern sees a broad consensus emerge at the highest political levels, among policy generalists such as Prime or Foreign Ministers, for change in EU governance or policy. Good examples include agreement on the need for a 'social Europe' in the early 1990s or, more recently, Commission reform or a 'new Southeast Europe'. But consensus for change is often vague, extending only to broad principles as opposed to the details of new instruments or reforms. The effect is to create *a permissive consensus 'from above'*, allowing policy specialists to shape, prepare, and table tangible policy proposals.

The EU's affinity for delegating to 'a small and powerful committee able to make far-reaching decisions' is time-honored (Milward 1992: 336). It reflects the simple reality that political actors can usually only agree on basic objectives, and thus must leave tough choices about how to realize them to experts. But the EU relies on this method of policy development far more than do most other systems of government. To illustrate the point, the emergence of consensus (amongst mostly Socialist governments) for an EU social policy to 'flank' the internal market, eventually led to the Social Chapter. A social policy network spanning the Commission, EP, and European labor organizations was crucial in pushing for an expansive reading of Article 100a (on worker health and safety). This interpretation resulted in several measures (such as the Working

Time Directive) which were enacted even before the Social Chapter existed (see Eichener 1993; Leibfried and Pearson 1996). It is not implausible that one of its cornerstones, the social dialogue, was the brainchild of one academic at the European University Institute (see Bercusson 1994: 184).

Another example of a 'permissive consensus reversed' is Prodi's campaign to turn the Commission into a European government. By late 1999, it had vastly overtaken the reform plans tabled (by Germany and the UK amongst others) after the fall of Santer, and made them look very modest. It was also evident that Prodi was courting support for his plans from allies in the EP and transnational lobbies in Brussels. Meanwhile, Prodi's 'new Southeast Europe' initiative embraced almost verbatim proposals developed by the Brussels think tank, the Centre for European Policy Studies, for a new set of association agreements in the region.

Change in EU governance does not usually come from the bottom up, and there are stark limits on the extent to which the EU has become more politicized or participatory. The gradual thickening of interest representation in Brussels has not eliminated the 'advocacy void' which arises from a general lack of strong transnational pressure groups or European political parties (Aspinwall 1998). The point is that consensus for change is often very broad and unspecified when EU governments manage to agree one, and a few well-placed, fast-acting agents can often determine what and how much changes.

Fourth, the most enduring pattern in EU decision-making is one that may be left mostly unadorned: virtually *everything remains negotiable*. The Union does not lack formal rules of decision-making, and the ECJ is a powerful enforcer of them. Yet, whether or not the EU's Treaties are becoming, in effect, a 'constitution' (see Weiler 1997; Snyder 1998), they are much more vague and less detailed than most national constitutions.

One consequence is that formal rules continue to matter far less than informal norms. It was possible, for example, that the EU's determination to raise its international profile might mean that post-Amsterdam reforms to the CFSP would produce a 'significant extension' of QMV in pillar II (Roper 1997: 2). Although the Maastricht Treaty clearly indicated that the President of the ECB would serve an eight-year term, the French President, Jacques Chirac, seized on the norm that top EU jobs are shared out amongst member states. Thus, Chirac secured an informal understanding that Wim Duisenberg, the ECB's first President, would stand down 'voluntarily' to make way for a French successor halfway through his term. (Peterson and Bomberg 1999: 262–3).

Many EU scholars would protest that the Union has emerged from the 1990s more politically mature, less experimental, and more like a rules-based 'political system' (Hix 1999). Logically, they seek to generalize about it: identifying an EU policy style, developing a comprehensive 'meta-theory' of EU decision-making, trying to get a handle on this strange, amorphous polity. Yet, the European Union continues to defy general characterizations, with new structures constantly emerging, old ones continually altered, and polycentricity ceaselessly reinforced. As Bob Dylan's dream polity, the EU remains Forever Young, thus allowing it to capitalize on its greatest strength: its apparently limitless capacity for improvisation.

Conclusion

In a sense, frequent change became routine for the EU of the 1990s, and ironically represents a kind of continuity. But, as we have argued, understanding change and continuity in EU governance means recognizing that the Union operates in fundamentally different ways at different levels of governance and increasingly spawns new and distinct centers of power. More than any other polity in existence, it resists neat, simple generalizations.

Our final task is to consider what insights our analysis offers to students of risk, reform, resistance, and revival in the evolution of the European project. The project has always been a *risky* enterprise, involving unprecedented and experimental acts of cooperation between sovereign nation-states. Risks are inevitably weighed by decision-makers before they select choices. Most decision-makers are risk averse, and try to minimize future costs arising from current choices. Risk-averse behavior is certainly a prime characteristic of EU decision-making and helps explain the EU's tendency towards lowest common denominator outcomes. Yet, the risks of inertia, inaction (especially in external policy), and policy stagnation have perceptibly increased for the EU in the 1990s.

An important reason why is that the freeing of the world's largest single capitalist market—a project far closer to completion at the end of the decade than at the start—unleashed enormously strong market forces. The internal market has the power to overwhelm public power entirely unless it is wielded collectively at the EU level. When the EU is literally forced to act, or face unacceptable consequences, the effect is usually to encourage compromise, empower the EU's supranational institutions (especially the Commission), and create a 'permissive consensus reversed' (see Pollack 1997*a*). Take, for example, (electronic) 'e-commerce': a largely unregulated global market worth $8 billion in 1998, but expected to grow to $325 billion by 2002 (Bar and Murase 1999: 39). Despite consumer-group resistance, member states accepted the Commission's controversial proposal to regulate e-commerce in June 1999, with virtually all conceding that a flawed directive was better than none.

The launch of the Euro further unleashes the market and brings new risks. Transforming 'outs' from the first wave of EMU—Denmark, Greece, Sweden, and the UK—into 'ins' is not without perils, and problems in the transition to the 'hard' Euro in 2002 cannot be excluded. Assertions, many of them American (summarized by Moravcsik and Nicolaïdis 1999: 36), that the collapse of monetary union could lead to the return of armed conflict in Western Europe are difficult to take seriously. But, in broad terms, the European project cannot succeed if monetary union fails.

EMU has given succor to another multiplier of risks: increased expectations of the EU in the eyes of the world. Sometimes, the costs of failing to meet them are made plain. Take, for example, the indignant protests of many African, Caribbean, and Pacific (ACP) states to EU attempts to enshrine 'clean governance' criteria in eligibility rules for aid under a reformed Lomé Convention (see Chapter 19 below). A bit rich, complained many ACP voices, when the Santer Commission had to resign for its own lack of 'cleanliness'. As the rest of world pays more attention to the EU, not only does the Union respond with more alacrity to external impulses. The risks of failure also increase.

The impulse to *reform* the EU has, in crucial respects, never been stronger, as shown by Prodi's reformist zeal. Institutional and policy reforms of a magnitude never before witnessed in the EU's past were clearly needed by the end of the 1990s to avoid the greatest risk of all: an enlarged EU which seizes up and becomes incapable of taking decisions. Attempts to keep Millennium IGC's agenda short and focused were under challenge by late 1999, as enlargement did much to focus minds on big, essential questions.

Resistance blocks or prevents change. The 1999 EP election revealed continued popular reluctance to embrace the European project. The transformation of previously pliant member states—especially Germany and the Netherlands—to far more hardheaded positions on the EU's budget created new sources of resistance. Yet, there was no clear or simple relationship between popular Euroscepticism and national preferences in EU decision-making. Dutch citizens, for example, were more likely to think their state's EU membership is a 'good thing' than were those of most other member states.[6] Fischer's admirable performance during the Kosovo crisis, and the appointment of the first Green Commissioner (Michaele Schreyer) under Prodi, muffled anti-EU sentiment amongst

[6] Commission, Eurobarometer, *Public Opinion in the European Union*, 53 (April 2000), http://europa.eu.int/comm/dg10/epo/eb/eb52/eb52.html, pp. 22, 38.

Green parties, which were growing in strength by the late 1990s. A broad range of factors—lower prices from EMU, aversion to American hegemony, and a strong popular will to avoid future Kosovos—suggest that citizen resistance to a reformed, 'new' EU cannot be assumed.

The EU's *revival* depends, fundamentally, on the success of EMU and enlargement. In particular, the need to revive Europe's economy in the face of the challenges posed by globalization acts to embolden EU decision-makers and encourages risk-taking. In the 1980s, the freeing of the internal market was risky, although arguably leaving Europe's uncommon market unaltered was even riskier. In the 1990s, it became easier, in important respects, to complete EMU than to abandon it.

Crucially, both EMU and the internal market were linked, however tenuously, to desirable outcomes. The potential benefits of the freeing of the internal market—always much hyped and far-fetched (see Cecchini 1988)—never really materialized. But the coincidence of fresh evidence that the 1992 project had created nearly one million jobs and helped ease the continental recession of the early 1990s gave crucial sustenance to EMU (see Commission 1998*f*). Meanwhile, economic growth rates began to pick up in 1999 just as the Euro was created. EMU clearly helped immunize Europe from the undesirable consequences of the Asian financial crisis, thus illustrating how the EU sometimes allows its member states to defend themselves from the vagaries of globalization.

The revival of the European project is difficult to reconcile with enlargement. None the less, the Kosovo conflict altered the equation in important respects, as did agreement on the need for yet another IGC in 2000. There was a palpable, growing sense in European capitals that the EU needed to compensate for the inevitable decline in its political unity which enlargement threatened to bring about. Whether it would be sustainable, and with what effect, remained open questions.

3

The European Union after Amsterdam: Towards a Theoretical Approach to (Differentiated) Integration

SIEGLINDE GSTÖHL

The Triumph of Diversity

Until recently, the European Union traditionally aspired to an invariable and (except for some specific transitional periods) simultaneous integration of its member states. Any deviations from the *acquis communautaire* needed to be objectively justified, temporary, and Community-controlled. Interests which only some of the member states shared had to be organized outside the Community treaties and institutions, such as the European Monetary System, the Schengen Agreements, social policy, the Eurocorps, and various research programs. This orthodox 'Community method' in favor of uniform integration loosened in the 1990s.

The Maastricht Treaty on European Union, besides granting Britain and Denmark certain opt-outs, sanctioned a 'Europe at different speeds' in the form of the Economic and Monetary Union (EMU). Moreover, it set up the intergovernmental second and third pillars outside the Community structures and explicitly allowed for closer cooperation in the Common Foreign and Security Policy (CFSP) and in justice and home affairs. The Amsterdam Treaty institutionalized, if not constitutionalized, differentiated integration.[1] New clauses enable the member states ready to develop deeper integration within the Union's framework to go ahead under certain conditions. Hence, while Maastricht showed that unwilling member states cannot be forced to integrate, Amsterdam made clear that

I would like to thank the editors of this volume for most useful comments.

[1] For the purpose of this article, 'flexibility', 'differentiated integration', and 'closer cooperation' are used interchangeably, as an overall notion of integration that does not comprise all the EU member states. By comparison, 'multi-speed' allows for flexibility in the pace of integration, 'variable geometry' permits different groups of member states to integrate in different policy areas, and 'à la carte' integration entitles individual states to pick and choose (cf. Stubb 1996).

the reluctant countries cannot keep the others from further deepening. After the accession of three neutral countries in 1995 and in view of the long, heterogeneous queue of candidates, the Treaties finally acknowledged Europe's diversity.

Even though the issue has received much attention in the context of the 1996–7 Intergovernmental Conference, the study of differentiated integration has so far been limited to the categorization of flexibility concepts (e.g. Stubb 1996), a few case-studies (e.g. Grabitz 1984; Manin and Louis 1996) and some (legal) discussions of the Amsterdam provisions on closer cooperation (e.g. Ehlermann 1998; Kortenberg 1998). Given the EU's imminent widening and, hence, its increasing heterogeneity, as well as the growing popular skepticism towards further deepening, it becomes more and more salient for the Union's future to understand variable geometry and its implications.

This chapter argues that a different theoretical approach is needed to explain these changes in the Union's constitution and their consequences—specifically, the ways in which the 'grand bargains' over differentiated integration can be related to the actual and potential growth of variable geometry through 'everyday' practices of integration within the EU. No analytical framework is available to account for both treaty amendments and normal Community legislation in a single framework. Yet 'history-making' and 'everyday' politics interact. On the one hand, the possibility of capitalizing on the continuing daily business within the Union during an IGC offers the actors greater leeway in the negotiations. On the other hand, some well-entrenched policies may be easier to change at the IGC level even if they could be taken care of in the normal EU framework. In addition, past decisions influence future ones. Policy feedbacks from a 'constitutional' change may work through everyday politics to influence the next grand bargain. The prenegotiation phase helps shape the agenda, while the post-IGC phase (ratification and implementation) may change the original deal or induce new negotiations.

This chapter provides a first step toward providing a framework that brings together the 'history-making' and 'everyday' politics in an effort to shed light on the changing European Union. Specifically, I argue that the combination of liberal intergovernmentalism (LI) and institutionalized international governance (IIG) opens a research avenue towards a new theoretical approach to differentiated integration and beyond. Alone, neither theory is adequate. While LI offers a powerful explanation for the creation of differentiated integration, it fails to capture some key dynamics of ordinary EU policy-making such as the role of institutions and norms. By bringing in insights from IIG and examining EU decision-making from a perspective that encompasses both 'history-making' and 'everyday' politics in a multi-step approach, a more powerful framework can be offered.

Both in theoretical and substantive terms, these considerations link closely with the themes of this volume: the 'four Rs' of risks, reform, resistance, and revival. Differentiated integration concepts are in many ways a direct response to the risks arising from increasing diversity and the possible onset of 'Eurosclerosis'. At the same time, they carry with them a risk of fragmentation. The development of flexibility norms is also related to the perceived need for reform of institutions and practices as a means of handling the growing Union. It remains, however, unclear whether it is 'grand bargains' that introduce the practices of differentiation or whether the 'grand bargains' are a means of ratifying practices already established at the 'everyday' level. Empirically, it is apparent that the emergence of flexibility concepts has focused forces of resistance and revival, in particular in the Amsterdam process, and hence raised important issues about the origins and the impact of shifts in preferences among member states and other actors. There is thus much to hope for from the development of new frameworks for understanding differentiated integration.

This chapter begins with a review of current approaches to 'grand' EU bargains and 'everyday' EU politics and their shortcomings in explaining differentiated integration. It then proposes a multi-step framework to analyze the integration process. Finally, the framework is applied to the Amsterdam Treaty as a 'plausibility test' and provides some preliminary evidence with regard to the case of flexibility as the latest addition to the EU's constitutional principles.

The Case for New Theorizing

Different approaches explain different phenomena, according to their level of analysis. Hence, we must theorize the distinction between 'constitutional' and 'daily' decisions of EU politics (Scharpf 1999: 167). The brief review in this section will show that the existing approaches are not sufficient to explain closer cooperation in the European Union.

'Grand' EU Bargains

Differentiated integration has not been a topic in the classical integration theories. Nevertheless, (neo) federalism *could* interpret a 'multi-speed Europe' as a temporary situation in which the laggards are to catch up with full integration. Yet, even in such a gradual federalizing process (Pinder 1985/6: 51), permanent exemptions, the lack of political will, or codified variable geometry rules are hard to imagine. Hence, one could argue from a federalist perspective, that the Amsterdam Treaty's provisions on closer cooperation are an anomaly.

Neofunctionalist theory would expect the expansive logic of sector integration to ensure uniform integration (Haas 1958: ch. 8). However, instead of a smooth transition from the internal market to monetary union and 'high' politics, instances of differentiation have proliferated in recent years. Neofunctionalist explanations *could* be stretched to account for those 'avant-garde' cases where all member states are willing but not yet able to join an integration step. However, they fail to explain the motives of able but unwilling governments. Already de Gaulle's policy in the 1960s showed that disregarding nationalist policy motivations and assuming a predictable institutional outcome was a mistake (cf. Haas 1975: ch. 1). The nation-state might have been transformed, but is not withering away.

From a transactionalist perspective, the attainment of a 'we-feeling' in a (pluralistic) security community does not require much institutionalization. Transactionalists *might* anticipate some differentiation where interdependence in terms of transaction flows is very low (Deutsch 1957: ch. 2). In today's amalgamated European Union, transactionalists would argue, no demand for exceptions should arise and the high and increasing transaction flows in the internal market should not produce any differentiation in social or monetary policy.

Stone Sweet and Sandholtz's (1998) recent model of 'supranational governance' relies heavily on transactionalist and neofunctionalist theory. It seeks to explain why some sectors in the EU have over time become more integrated than others. However, supranational governance only accounts for integration which has been triggered by transnational exchange and does not explain variable geometry driven by some reluctant or eager member states. It tends 'to overlook the importance of the interplay of national economic interests in the motoring of European integration, and to devalue the influence of the EU's intergovernmental institutions' (Puchala 1999: 323). Governance in Europe is both supranational and intergovernmental.

These conventional integration theories leave us puzzled when it comes to variable geometry. On the one hand, they do not cater explicitly to political bargains that lead to exemptions or to the possibility of closer cooperation between some member states. On the other hand, they find it difficult to accommodate unevenness in the integration process, arising from the playing out of the economic, political, and institutional forces created by the process itself. Of the existing integration theories, only the intergovernmentalist school offers a clue as to why countries might be unwilling to integrate. Inspired by neorealism, intergovernmentalism views nation-states as the dominant actors pursuing their national interests which may consist in opt-outs from integration. As Hoffmann (1966: 867) argued, integration 'can fail not only when there is a surge of nationalism in one important part, but also when there are differences in assessments of the national interest that rule out agreement on the shape and on the world role of the new, supranational whole'. Neofunctionalism, (neo) federalism, and transactionalism focus on integration, intergovernmentalism on non-integration, yet variable geometry embraces both. The logic of diversity sets limits to the spillover process. However, intergovernmentalism remains too static if it does not take into account the roots of national preferences. This is where liberal intergovernmentalism (LI) comes in.

Liberal Intergovernmentalism Revisited

LI argues that a tripartite explanation of integration—economic interests, relative power, credible commitments—accounts for the form, substance, and timing of major steps toward European integration (Moravcsik 1998: 4). The decision-making process is divided into national preference formation and international negotiations (i.e. interstate bargaining and institutional choice). LI provides a good starting-point as forms of differentiated integration are typically agreed upon in intergovernmental negotiations based on national interests. Yet its view of preference formation does not capture all the 'Eurosceptic' cases.

Assuming that, in pluralist democracies, governments aggregate the demands which interest groups articulate on the basis of their expected gains and losses as well as uncertainty and risk, Moravcsik (1998: 35–50) argues that economic interests dominate, except for issues of 'high' politics. However, geopolitics is not the only potential source for a reluctant or integrationist policy, and the analysis of political factors is not only important where economic interests are weak. In member states like Denmark, Great Britain, or Sweden (not to mention would-be members such as Norway or Switzerland), the anticipated large economic benefits of integration have often been outweighed by deeply rooted political impediments to it (cf. Gstöhl 1998). These constraints of a domestic or geohistorical nature may well go beyond security externalities and touch upon questions of national identity. A liberal approach to preference formation may well take into account ideational factors such as collective ideas about national identity which reflect underlying societal values. Among those potential determinants are domestic institutions (such as direct democracy, welfare models, federalism, and parliamentary sovereignty), societal cleavages (of a religious, ethno-linguistic, or regional nature), the foreign policy tradition (e.g. the lack of an 'integration-compatible' foreign policy or claims to leadership in Europe), and historical experiences of 'integration' in terms either of foreign rule (e.g. colonization, satellization, occupation in the Second World War) or of multi-ethnic empires. In such cases, Moravcsik's version of the preference-formation process with its emphasis on (commercial) interests stemming from economic interdependence may not capture all relevant motivations. Further empirical research is required to investigate how not only geohistorical factors but domestic institutions and cleavages shape preferences (Caporaso 1999: 162; Risse-Kappen 1996: 64–5). A modification of LI to include such potential obstacles or incentives to integration would actually enhance the liberal intergovernmentalist case.

Another way in which LI can be modified is to take account of how EU membership as a long-term 'socialization process' affects the formation of preferences beyond purely domestic determinants (Sandholtz 1996: 427). It is not clear whether and how interest groups or political élites 'endogenize' European issues, yet such an effect is likely to be more important in daily EU business than in treaty amendments.

LI offers a sound explanation of intergovernmental negotiations, even if it has not explicitly considered differentiated integration. The bargaining power of member states is shaped by the relative intensity of preferences, and the outcome is likely to reflect the value of unilateral policy alternatives (credible threats to veto), coalitional alternatives (credible threats to exclude), and the opportunities for issue linkage and side-payments in package deals (Moravcsik 1998: 60–7). These strategies are most significant for member governments in need of derogations. The most reluctant participant tends to define the range of possible agreements. If the threat of exclusion as well as linkages and side-payments fail to convince the unwilling state, the result is either no agreement or differentiated integration (e.g. in the form of opt-outs).

In treaty-amending negotiations, the focus on governments as the main actors seems justified. They may act 'as if' they were unitary and pursue a stable net national position as long as their internal cleavages do not alter the national negotiating stance. The role of non-state actors is marginal. Sub- and transnational actors may affect EU negotiations only indirectly, via the member governments. The Commission may gain some influence on IGC negotiations via its technical expertise in treaty reform, its gate-keeper position *vis-à-vis* non-governmental interests and a close cooperation with the Presidency and the Council Secretariat which draft the treaty blueprints (Christiansen and Jørgensen 1998: 449–50). In the end, however, the heads of state and government may do whatever they like to these draft treaties.

Finally, governments transfer sovereignty to EU institutions where potential joint gains are large and other means to secure compliance by all governments are likely to be ineffective (Moravcsik 1998: 73–7). While the interstate bargain basically decides on the principles, norms, and rules of a regime, institutional choice means agreement on its procedures.

Hence, a modified version of LI offers the best explanation for the creation of flexibility norms of an *ad hoc* or institutionalized nature. Yet it does not specify the capacity of policy feedbacks to affect future negotiations, for example through the repercussions of earlier 'grand bargains' on the powers of the supranational actors or the incorporation of the day-to-day practice of Community institutions into the treaties (Wincott 1995: 603–6). At most, it concedes that the integration process is path-dependent by accepting previous agreements and the societal adaptations to them as a new status quo (Moravcsik 1995: 612).

With its focus on 'grand bargains', liberal intergovernmentalism confines itself to the constitutional norm-molding process and does not tell us anything about the application of norms and the factors relevant in the EU's daily decision-making. Therefore, we need to search for appropriate extensions of LI.

'Everyday' EU Politics

Comparative politics has generated many studies of 'everyday' EU policy-making in terms of governance, policy networks, or other institutional approaches which focus on decision-making processes (and less on preference formation or negotiation analysis).

Marks (1993: 392) describes multi-level governance as a system of continuous negotiation among nested governments at several territorial tiers. Thus, decision-making competencies are shared by actors at different levels rather than monopolized by state executives, and political arenas are interconnected in the sense that subnational actors are not confined to the national level. The concept of governance thus seems relevant for everyday EU politics. Policy networks as one form of governance structure, which Peterson (1995*a*: 76) defines as arenas for the mediation of the interests of government and interest groups, are less useful since they deal mainly with the (technocratic) meso-level of transnational policy formulation and neglect the role of EU institutions. From this comes the need of Peterson (1995*a*: 84–5) to supplant policy networks with an institutionalist approach.

Institutionalist approaches claim that institutional structures and rules constrain the governments' scope of action and that EU institutions may develop their own interests (Bulmer 1998: 370; Pollack 1997*a*: 101). Sandholtz (1996), for example, argues that EU institutions can affect member states' behavior by becoming autonomous actors, by creating options for domestic actors in their choice of allies and arenas, and by inducing changes in domestic policies and institutions. With a view to the unfolding of the integration process over time, historical institutionalism maintains that actors may well seek to maximize their interests, but carry out institutional or policy reforms that transform their own positions in ways that are often unanticipated or undesired (Pierson 1996*b*: 126). In other words, member states act within constraints created by themselves and the micro-level reactions to those preceding decisions. These insights seem noteworthy, yet how exactly institutions influence policy and how they change are still not entirely clear.

Gehring's (1994, 1996) model of institutionalized international governance combines aspects of both governance and institutionalism and is compatible with an intergovernmentalist approach to grand bargains. It accounts for the impact of institutions in everyday politics and for feedback effects. Moreover, it contemplates not only the formation of new norms in EU daily decision-making, but also their application.

Institutionalized International Governance

Institutionalized international governance distinguishes between horizontal cooperation and hierarchical governance in the European Union or, respectively, between intergovernmental conferences and everyday politics. The main concerns are, however, not IGCs or preference-formation processes, but policy-shaping and policy-setting decisions, everyday EU decision-making. Gehring (1996: 241) agrees with Moravcsik's multi-step conceptualization of international cooperation and adds the stage of norm application:

In the upward (norm-molding) process unit-level interests influence the aggregate national interests which governments pursue during an international negotiation. The national interests of the participating states influence, in turn, the collective decision process about norms that defines the common interests of the participating state-actors. In the downward (norm-applying) process collectively agreed norms orient decision-making by states. State-action, in turn, commands sub-unit actors to adapt their behavior accordingly.

In treaty-amending negotiations, the member states are the major actors, and the credible threat of exit (e.g. due to attractive alternatives, significance of a certain member for the success of cooperation) is a primary source of bargaining power. Upper-level agreement by member states creates a lower level of cooperation amongst a range of governmental and non-governmental actors on which the exit option is closed. The treaty links material interests with procedural rules which orient the secondary decisions. Due to the high degree of policy differentiation in the

EU, a package deal never concerns all the issue areas of integration. Member states must comply with the agreed procedures if they do not want to put their membership into question. A selective exit is not possible. In addition, exit in implementation is excluded by mechanisms of surveillance and dispute settlement as well as by the direct applicability of EC regulations (Gehring 1994: 231–5). The member states may still bargain to pursue their interests, but they do so on the basis of allocated power resources, in particular voting rules.

Other actors such as supranational and substate entities may also be assigned institutional power (Gehring 1994: 225–8). The Commission initiates new legislation, the European Parliament influences it, and the Court of Justice delivers binding judgments. The EU institutions also provide new inlets for the intervention of subnational actors. The more integrated a particular policy sector and the more decisions are governed by majority rule, the more likely policy-making is to be characterized by transnational coalitions among subnational, national, and supranational actors (Risse-Kappen 1996: 66; Jönsson *et al.* 1998: 333–5). Pollack (1997*a*: 129–30) argues that supranational autonomy depends on the distribution of preferences among member-state principals and supranational agents, institutional decision rules, the degree of information and uncertainty, and the support of transnational constituencies.

The analytical distinction between a norm-molding process and a norm-applying process on the lower level makes it possible to conceptualize institutional feedbacks on the actors' interests (Gehring 1994: 212–13). It makes everyday EU politics resemble domestic policy processes rather than international negotiations. Institutions influence the actors' decisions and these decisions, in turn, modify the institutions. According to IIG, regimes may affect their own future development by several reflexive mechanisms. First, an international governing institution may foster future cooperation due to its very existence (e.g. expanding integration within the EU framework). Second, feedback may occur between the level of the member states and the EU level (e.g. redefinition of positions during negotiations, influence of institutions in collective decision-making). Third, cooperation causes adaptations in the behavior of substate actors which later influence national preferences. That is, as noted earlier, policy feedbacks of a major EU decision may work through everyday EC politics (in terms of issue-specific norm-molding and norm-applying processes) to influence future grand bargains. There are also several devices by which an institution may influence the calculation of actors' preferences under conditions of bounded rationality. First, the existing agreement is likely to serve as baseline criteria for the negotiations. Second, a regulatory solution in a parallel field may constitute an acceptable standard. Third, procedural norms constitute a form of linkage of decisions over time. Thus, IIG helps to capture institutional development over time and path dependence.

In spite of the apparent differences between institutionalized international governance and liberal intergovernmentalism, the two approaches stand on common ground and can be used together to provide a thicker description of the integration process. They are both grounded in regime theory, view governments as the key actors, distinguish between 'grand bargains' and 'everyday politics', and underline the importance of threats of exclusion or exit in interstate bargaining. Marrying IIG to LI provides a more powerful approach, as the following section will show.

The 'LI plus' Framework

Drawing on Peterson's (1995a: 71–6) three categories of decisions in the analysis of EU policy-making, I suggest a twofold distinction between 'grand bargains' (or history-making decisions) and 'everyday politics' comprising policy-setting as well as policy-shaping decisions. I argue that a framework based on liberal intergovernmentalism and institutionalized international governance offers the more powerful explanation. Both approaches conceive of the European Union as an international regime: its principles explain why the states cooperate; its norms and rules, what the cooperation is about; and its procedures, how cooperation takes place. In a treaty-making process, state executives are the signatories whose unanimity is required. Yet, in everyday politics, their ability to control the supranational agents or the mobilization of sub- and transnational actors is constrained.

While LI explains national preferences and intergovernmental bargains, IIG is aware of the role of sub-, trans-, and supranational actors in daily EU business, introduces the norm-applying process, and points to the closure of the exit option on the lower level of the Union's decision-making. It adds an institutional dimension and the possibility of studying feedback effects over time. Moreover, 'LI plus' proposes the use of a single theoretical framework instead of a portfolio of four different approaches (Peterson 1995a: 83–5; Peterson and Bomberg 1999: 9) which confines the actors to different levels, tries to separate 'technical' from political issues, and raises questions about the appropriate 'transmission belts'. Moreover, the impact of a 'micro-level' of domestic politics, and thus of national preference formation, is simply assumed (Peterson 1995a: 85). In spite of the heuristic division between the Union's legislative procedures (the policy-making processes) and the polity-building process that changes these very procedures, 'LI plus' presents a coherent approach. It avoids the 'level-of-analysis problem' by incorporating a multi-step approach to EU decision-making.

The new framework is called 'LI plus' since it is closer to liberal intergovernmentalism and actually develops a stronger version of LI. It distinguishes between 'constitutional' (treaty-making) and issue-specific ('everyday') norm-molding and norm-applying processes, as well as between the analytical stages of preference formation and negotiations in the norm-molding processes. The resulting five analytical steps (see Figure 3.1) are now discussed in more detail.

'Grand' EU Bargains
'Constitutional' Norm-Molding Process
   Step 1: Formation of National Preferences (Modified LI)
   Step 2: Intergovernmental Negotiations (LI)

'Everyday' EU Politics
'Constitutional' Norm-Applying Process (or Issue-Specific Norm-Molding Process)
   Step 3: National Preferences (Modified LI)
   Step 4: Treaty-Based Negotiations (IIG)
Issue-Specific Norm-applying Process
   Step 5: Application of Norms (IIG)

FIGURE 3.1. The Five Steps of the LI-Plus Framework

We start with the constitutional norm-molding process of a 'grand' EU bargain, which consists of the formation of national preferences (step 1) and intergovernmental negotiations (step 2). Step 1 proposes a modified LI approach to the shaping of domestic preferences in the framework of EU membership, by way of aggregating economic and political incentives and impediments to integration (e.g. with regard to differentiated integration). The impact of domestic institutions and of a 'socialization effect' of EU membership on national preferences needs further investigation, but in this stage and in case of a request for an exception due to 'national interests', such an effect is likely to be rather weak. Step 2 suggests an (unmodified) LI approach to intergovernmental bargaining among the member states (e.g. about the principle of flexibility). Supranational and sub- or transnational actors lack direct access to the IGC negotiations. They may only have an indirect impact via the member states. An important source of bargaining power is the option of exit or exclusion, that is, the existence of attractive alternatives and the relative intensity of preferences. Package deals are facilitated by potential issue linkages, compromises, and side-payments.

We now turn to 'everyday' EU politics, the constitutional norm-applying process (which also constitutes an issue-specific norm-molding process). It consists of the formation of national preferences (step 3) and treaty-based negotiations (step 4). Step 3 applies a modified LI approach of preference formation to the application of the treaty provisions (e.g. on closer cooperation), including possible feedbacks from the 'grand' bargain. As suggested by institutionalized international governance, the norms previously agreed in the Amsterdam Treaty orient the states' decision-making and affect the behavior and interests of substate actors. In daily EU decision-making, national preferences might well be constrained by the EU's institutional architecture. Step 4 puts forward the IIG approach for the 'negotiations' on concrete norms and rules (e.g. in a certain policy field of closer cooperation). Both the member states and the EU institutions bargain according to the envisaged procedure, and the empowered supranational actors provide new lobbying opportunities for sub- and transnational actors. Institutionally derived rights provide new power resources and are supplemented by potential issue linkages, compromises, and side-payments. The threat to establish closer cooperation outside the Union's framework remains.

Finally, we look at the issue-specific norm-applying process (step 5). Institutionalized international governance provides some guidance for the application of specific provisions (e.g. those of closer cooperation in a given issue area). The decision-making process follows the treaty rules. Sub- and transnational interest groups as well as national and European institutions play their role in implementation and may induce new policy feedbacks for future decisions.

In sum, the role of the different actors varies in each step of decision-making. The relevance of domestic institutions and substate actors is greatest in the phases of preference formation (steps 1 and 3) and norm application in a specific issue area (step 5). The member states dominate the intergovernmental negotiations (step 2), while the EU institutions join them as players in the treaty-based negotiations on issue-specific norms (step 4). Further hypotheses need to be generated about the conditions under which sub-, trans-, and supranational actors exert influence, and some of the links between the steps need further research as well.

As a preliminary 'plausibility test', the proposed framework is now applied to the Amsterdam Treaty's provisions on closer cooperation. The following section examines why flexibility has been codified and what its institutionalization implies for the Union's future.

'Closer Cooperation' in the Amsterdam Treaty and Beyond

According to the dominant legal view, the EU Treaties have become 'constitutionalized' by their subsequent amendments and by the interpretations of the European Court of Justice (Sauter 1998: 30; Mancini 1989; Weiler 1999). Among the most important principles of the Union's constitution are non-discrimination, the primacy of Community law over national law, subsidiarity, solidarity between member states, and the Community method. Closer cooperation is codified in Articles 40, 43–5 TEU and 11 TEC, which 'transform flexibility into one of the constitutional principles of the EU' (Ehlermann 1997: 60).

In the run-up to the IGC, all member states more or less realized that some kind of differentiated integration might be necessary due to British resistance in some fields and the uncertain implications of Eastern enlargement. The Community method was reaching its limits as the scale and diversity of integration increased. The motives for supporting flexibility were diverse. Some governments hoped to move ahead with deepening integration without being held back by those unwilling or unable to join. Other governments counted on a right not to participate or to opt in later. We first examine the member states' positions (step 1), then the role of the other actors, the negotiation dynamics, and the outcome of the 'grand' flexibility bargain (step 2). Statements about the future application of the new provisions on closer cooperation remain speculative. Nevertheless, some observations about steps 3 to 5 will be made.

The Member States' Positions

After diverse ideas of flexibility had been floated in the public, especially in Germany, Britain and France (cf. Lamers and Schäuble 1994; Major 1994; Balladur 1994), the issue was definitely put on the agenda in December 1995 by a joint letter of German Chancellor Kohl and French President Chirac to the Spanish Presidency (Chirac and Kohl, 1996). They suggested that flexibility be embraced as a means to enable those member states, willing and able to do so, to develop closer cooperation within the Union. In March 1996, the Turin European Council (1996: para. I.5) asked the IGC

to examine whether and how to introduce rules either of a general nature or in specific areas in order to enable a certain number of Member States to develop a strengthened cooperation, open to all, compatible with the Union's objectives, while preserving the *acquis communautaire*, avoiding discrimination and distortions of competition and respecting the single institutional framework.

While a detailed analysis of the national preference formation of the member states cannot be supplied here, an approximation based on the modified LI approach of three categories of member states can be discerned. First there are the traditional (able and willing) integrationists Germany, France, the Benelux countries, and usually also Italy. The second category is the 'reluctant' (able but unwilling) group of the United Kingdom, Denmark, and partly Sweden, as well as Austria and Finland. Finally, there are the (willing but often unable) 'cohesion' countries Spain, Portugal, Greece, and to some extent Ireland and Italy. The integrationist countries should perceive closer cooperation as a way to get rid of the laggards, while the reluctant members should welcome the possibility to opt out, and the potentially unable states should be anxious about exclusion.

Flexibility is an institutional issue, where the substantive consequences are difficult to calculate and the potential costs of exiting or being excluded depend on the policy area in question. The future application is uncertain, in particular in the first pillar, since introducing flexibility meant 'establishing rules for future rules'. In some areas, the economic interests are probably weak (e.g. Schengen, CFSP, education, culture, tourism, development co-operation), whereas in other areas (e.g. taxation, environment, social policy, capital movement, research, energy, trans-European networks) the potential economic implications for the outsiders could be more important, in particular if solidarity measures were missing. Weak, uncertain, or diffuse economic implications leave even more room for political incentives or impediments in the formation of preferences (Moravcsik 1993: 494–6).

The 1996 IGC retrospective database of the European Union (EU 1996), in particular the summaries of positions established by the IGC Task Forces of the Commission (1996*e*) and of the European Parliament (1996), as well as the material provided by Weidenfeld (1998), lead to the following brief synopsis of the member states' positions. France and Germany advocated their concept of open closer cooperation with a general clause and three pillar-specific clauses, where the Council enjoys a strong position and no member state has a right to veto. The Benelux countries firmly rejected a 'Europe à la carte' and favored flexible integration as a last resort, in terms of different speeds to be monitored by the Commission. From their point of view, the non-participating states should share the objectives and be able to join later, the Commission should play a central role, and the Council should decide by majority. By contrast, Britain insisted on unanimity and opposed any flexibility clause in the second pillar. The Nordic countries and Austria accepted the idea of a multi-speed Europe, if it did not give rise to different classes of member states. The 'Eurosceptic' countries were aware that the possibility of differentiated integration would allow their domestic and geohistorical constraints to be taken account of in further efforts of deepening, but at the same time they were afraid of the consequences of being excluded.

The countries benefiting from cohesion funds were afraid that closer cooperation would diminish their influence and rejected any exclusive 'hard core'. Spain, Portugal, Ireland, and Italy emphasized the need for solidarity and generally preferred integration at different speed to variable geometry. In addition, Portugal and Greece suggested stringent conditions such as participation by two-thirds of the member states, measures to support the states unable to take part from the outset, and a major role for the Commission. Greece even rejected the notion of a multi-speed Europe and insisted on purely transitional arrangements. After the EMU experience, the Greek government obviously tried to diminish the risk of being left behind in further fields.

As expected, the integrationist countries wanted to facilitate further deepening, while the 'reluctant' and the 'cohesion' countries tried to avoid the negative externalities of exclusion. It thus appears that a modified LI approach to the Amsterdam 'grand bargain' does provide important insights into the interplay of perceptions of risk, strategies of resistance, and reform negotiations. But this is not the whole of the story.

Non-State Actors in 'Grand' Bargains

From a liberal intergovernmentalist point of view, the role of sub-, trans-, and supranational actors in history-making decisions is marginal. Dinan (1997: 209) is probably right to observe that the issues on the IGC's agenda have not lent themselves to the kind of lobbying and Commission–private-sector cooperation that preceded the Single European Act. The main focus of the economic interest groups was competitiveness and deregulation, while flexibility received less attention. The message of the Union of Industrial and Employers' Confederations of Europe (UNICE 1997) to the Amsterdam summit simply stated that closer cooperation should not be allowed to create new obstacles to trade or to the four freedoms of the internal market.

The Treaties envisage no formal role for the Commission during inter-governmental conferences. Hence, it needed a mandate from the European Council before it could produce its report to the Reflection Group. The Commission (1996c: 21–2) firmly opposed the idea of 'a "pick-and-choose Europe" (e.g. the Social Protocol) which flies in the face of the common European project'. In its 'non-paper' of January 1997, which was more a summary of the debate than a position paper, the Commission (1997g) finally conceded that closer cooperation was on the member states' wish list and suggested that it should respect the Union's objectives, the single institutional framework, the *acquis*, the internal market, the competitive conditions as well as the institutional balance, and that it should only be used as a last resort, open to all member states. The required number of participants should be high, and the Commission should decide on the proposals to be submitted to the Council. After the Amsterdam Treaty was signed, the IGC Task Force of the Commission (1997*j*) concluded that the flexibility provisions corresponded in 'the broad lines' to its conception.

In its resolution on the IGC of March 1997, the European Parliament (1997*c*: 167–8) considered that closer cooperation as a last resort should only be possible if the institutional framework, the *acquis*, the principles of equality and of solidarity, the internal market, and the rights and interests of the non-participating states are safeguarded. The willing but not able states should obtain support, Parliament should be involved in initiation (assent), legislation, and budgetary questions (co-decision), and closer cooperation should, in principle, be transitional. No flexibility should be allowed in the first pillar if qualified majority voting (QMV) was extended. After the Amsterdam summit, the European Parliament (1997*a*: 101) deplored its weak position and the veto in cases of vital national interests and emphasized that 'more courageous and more consistent steps in the transition to the Community method would have been appropriate'.

The lack of crucial initiatives or compromise proposals by either the Commission or Parliament (Moravcsik and Nicolaïdis 1999: 70) comes as no surprise, given that it is a primary task of the Community institutions to ensure a uniform deepening and application of integration. Both the Commission and the European Parliament vividly rejected the idea of a Europe 'à la carte'. Whereas the Parliament favored a multi-speed solution, the Commission seemed to allow for some variable geometry, but under its own control and not in the first pillar. Neither of them, nor any sub- or transnational groups, played a decisive role in the institutionalization of flexibility. In these terms, the expectations of LI theory continue to be upheld, but in order further to explore the issues we should now have a closer look at the negotiation dynamics in terms of bargaining tactics, such as threats of exit or exclusion, linkages, compromises, and side-payments.

The IGC Negotiation Dynamics

Discussions on flexibility progressed only slowly. Instead of a list of areas open or closed to differentiation, the Dutch Presidency ultimately introduced broader criteria with a general clause and an enabling clause for each of the three pillars. The reasons for this gentle pace were, besides the delicacy of the issue, the inextricable links of flexibility with certain substantive issues under consideration (cf. Irish participant McDonagh 1998: 143). In addition, flexibility was tied to an extension of qualified majority voting. Eventually, a balance was struck with some progress in QMV in exchange for a 'bounded' form of flexibility (Edwards and Philippart 1997: 16–17).

With regard to a minimum threshold for closer cooperation, the main options debated were a simple majority of member states, a majority defined by population criteria, or a special two-third majority (Edwards and Philippart 1997: 14). The compromise foresees 'at least a majority of Member States' on the grounds that a lower bottom-line would have raised doubts about the Union's coherence and credibility, while a higher one might have impaired the practicability of closer cooperation. Different options were discussed also for the accession of new states. One proposal suggested that two-thirds of the member states could reject an application (Greek participant Kotzias 1998: 18). However, the governments considered that if a candidate country accepts the *acquis* and the Commission is of the opinion that all the conditions are fulfilled, it should be able to join. Otherwise, the Council's decision would not be formal but political.

Flexibility in the third-pillar areas of asylum, visas, immigration, and the control of external frontiers, where most member states had clear common interests, was less controversial (Kotzias 1998: 21, 34–5). The 'cohesion countries' Spain, Portugal, and Greece did not object to flexibility in this field, while Britain and Denmark simply wanted the possibility to opt out.

The negotiating dynamics of the Amsterdam process, at least in so far as they concerned differentiated integration, closely reflected the positions and the intensity of the interests of key groups of member states. In order to complete the picture of this 'grand bargain', we will now take a closer look at the results of the IGC.

The Outcome at Amsterdam

The European Council at Amsterdam discussed the provisions on closer cooperation in the early hours of the final morning (Duff 1997: 194–6). Flexibility in the first pillar was restricted to the powers already attributed to the Community. The British insistence on veto was accommodated by the possibility of objecting to a qualified majority vote to trigger closer cooperation for important reasons of national policy (a codification of the 'Luxembourg Compromise'). As LI would expect, some sovereignty has been pooled (QMV) to facilitate future cooperation, some sovereignty has been delegated to the Commission to protect the internal market and the *acquis*, and new procedures accommodate the divergent positions regarding the desirable degree of future commitment.

The flexibility clause in the second pillar was scrubbed in favor of a form of constructive abstention (or case-by-case flexibility). That is, a member state abstaining in a vote accepts that a decision (requiring two-thirds of valid votes) commits the Union, but is not obliged to apply it. The draft proposal had suggested that closer cooperation must respect the powers of the EC and the objectives of the CFSP and aim at promoting the identity of the Union without impairing its effectiveness in international relations. It would have been triggered by unanimity (the advocates had first proposed qualified majority, then a majority covering three-quarters of the EU population, cf. Kotzias 1998: 32–3). The watering down of this proposal was moved by Britain, Austria, Ireland, and Greece, which were not among the supporters of a common foreign policy (Duff 1997: 196).

Consistent with the assumptions of LI, the Amsterdam provisions on closer cooperation reflect to a large extent the joint French–German letter of October 1996 (Kinkel and de Charette 1997). They differ only where compromise had to be reached with the more reluctant partners such as the UK. Like the final outcome in the Amsterdam Treaty, the French–German initiative had envisaged a general clause and three specific clauses. Yet, in contrast to the final outcome, the French–German initiative had conceived of closer cooperation also in the fields of defense policy, common defense, and armament. It had envisioned no right of veto for the member states (like the final text does 'for important reasons of national policy') and only an *avis conforme* by the Commission (instead of the power to decide to submit a proposal to the Council or not). On the one hand, integrationist members sought to institutionalize their capacity to exclude other states from certain policies since they were concerned with safeguarding against future vetoes, maximizing the chances of success for EMU, and minimizing potential disruptions stemming from enlargement. On the other hand, potential outsiders sought to limit their counterparts' ability to exclude them from future cooperation by requiring a veto for the triggering stage, limiting the scope of flexibility, the control of access, and a periodic review by the Commission. In the end, France and Germany were pleased that closer cooperation was introduced, whereas Britain was satisfied that flexibility should not apply to the second pillar and that it obtained opt-outs from the third pillar and a right to veto in the first pillar (Kotzias 1998: 31).

As a result, the provisions on closer cooperation allow for multi-speed integration and variable geometry, but they exclude any à la carte integration. The member states not only put the issue of flexibility on the IGC agenda, but they dominated the discussions and the outcome. Closer cooperation may well entail some feedback effects on future grand bargains, even if the unanimity requirement still holds for intergovernmental conferences. If no consensus can be reached, member states may bypass a veto either by establishing closer cooperation on the lower level or by resorting to the exit option on the upper level in terms of integration outside the Union framework, where the choice of partners is free and no majority is needed.

Unlikely Closer Cooperation

The Amsterdam Treaty entered into force on 1 May 1999, and the provisions on closer cooperation have not been applied yet. In step 3, national preferences will be formed based on the relevant economic and political incentives and impediments to integration which the issue area in question evokes. As set out above, the process might be affected by a certain 'socialization effect' as the Amsterdam provisions are implemented within the Union's instutional architecture. In the final analysis, it can be assumed that a state will not jeopardize its EU membership if confronted with the implications of incremental deepening.

How likely is a future application of the provisions? In the first pillar, predetermined flexibility already covers a large part of the need for differentiation. Yet, closer cooperation might be applied in areas such as education and professional training, youth, culture, public health, the fight against social exclusion, tourism, energy, trans-European networks, civil defense, industry, research, environment, development cooperation, taxation, and the movement of capital (Philippart and Edwards 1999: 96; De la Serre and Wallace 1997*b*: 31; Deubner 1998: 45–7). One might add the areas of free movement of persons, which will not be submitted to QMV until May 2004 (Article 67 TEC). In fact, in those areas of the first pillar where majority decisions are possible, closer cooperation is (at least until further enlargement) less likely. In the third pillar, the fight against international crime and judicial cooperation, as well as parts of the Schengen *acquis*, are left as possible areas of closer cooperation.

The restrictive conditions make it unlikely that closer cooperation will be applied very often. The progressive states might dread the complicated procedure and the fact that they might not exclude unable members, while the reluctant states might fear the exclusion from parts of the *acquis* and the problems of late accession. Doubts may also be expressed about the justiciability of the provisions, and whether closer cooperation involving an international mixed agreement commits the Union. It is also unclear what would happen if the presidency is with a non-participating member.

Future Negotiations on Closer Cooperation

The Treaty of Amsterdam established some norms, rules, and procedures to guide the application of the flexibility principle (step 4). The general clause (Articles 43–5 TEU) stipulates that the objectives of the Union be furthered and its interests protected, the single institutional framework of the Union be respected, the *acquis communautaire* or the interests of the non-participating member states not be affected, and that it only be used as a last resort. As a rule, closer cooperation must concern at least a majority of member states and be open to all at any time.

The specific flexibility clause in the first pillar (Article 11 TEC) adds that closer cooperation may not affect Community policies, actions, or programs, discriminate between nationals, restrict trade between member states, or distort competition. Moreover, closer cooperation may not touch upon exclusive Community competences, citizenship of the Union, or go beyond the Community's powers. Regarding the procedure, member states interested in flexible integration address a request to the Commission, which may then submit a proposal to the Council. If the Commission decides not to submit a proposal to the Council, it must deliver a reasoning. Its proposal may only be side-stepped by a unanimous vote of all member states. After consulting the European Parliament, the Council then enables the states by qualified majority, unless a member state objects for important reasons of national policy. In the latter case, the Council may request by qualified majority that the issue be brought to the heads of state and government for decision by unanimity. The Commission decides over the accession of new members after delivering an opinion to the Council.

In the specific clause dealing with the third pillar (Article 40 TEU), there are only two additional norms for the initiation of closer cooperation. First, it should aim at enabling the EU to develop more rapidly into an area of freedom, security, and justice. Second, the powers of the Community and the objectives of judicial cooperation in criminal matters and police must be respected. In contrast to the procedure in the first pillar, the member states have the right of initiative, and the Council grants authorization, while the Commission and the European Parliament are only consulted. Again, the Council decides by qualified majority, unless a member state objects for important reasons of national policy. The Commission's position is weaker, since it delivers an opinion on new accessions but the participating governments decide.

The introduction of flexibility provisions in the Amsterdam Treaty conditionally reopens the exit option on the lower level, with repercussions on the threat of exclusion or exit as bargaining tactics. On the one hand, efforts to reach compromise in the Council may be discouraged as the majority might rely on closer cooperation to side-step the opposition. On the other hand, the threat of closer cooperation may encourage compromise on the part of the minority afraid of being left out. Depending on the relative intensity of preferences, the minority might also seek to bargain for substantial side-payments by threatening to launch a 'Luxembourg Compromise' veto. Its ability to do so then depends on the majority's determination to go ahead, if necessary outside the Union's institutional framework. The use of a veto brings the issue to the highest level. Their point being made with great publicity, the minority states may then be satisfied with opt-outs from closer cooperation.

Conceivable Effects of Closer Cooperation

Once closer cooperation is established in an issue area (once step 5 is reached), differentiated integration may act as a stimulus for the laggards to catch up. Still, there are no criteria for the ability to participate in closer cooperation, leaving it up to the political will and, in the first pillar, to the Commission's judgment. Those members able but unwilling are not forced to participate, but they will have to deal with the externalities of closer cooperation. It is not necessary any more to offer every member state an incentive to participate. Governments with attractive alternative coalitions are less likely to make concessions. As a consequence, the potential for issue linkages and side-payments might be reduced. Yet, since closer cooperation will be based within the Union's institutional framework, the threat might also gain some new significance (e.g. by excluding alternative paths of integration in the same issue areas).

Within closer cooperation, the relevant institutional procedures of the Treaties shall apply. All member states may take part in the deliberations of flexibility measures, but only the participating countries have a right to vote in the Council. By contrast, decision-making procedures in the European Parliament, the Commission, or the Court of Justice do not distinguish between participants and non-participants. The relative influence of the supranational entrepreneurs (and the corresponding lobbying efforts of sub- and transnational entities) depends on the issue area.

As a result, the new provisions offer scope for both future conflict and success. The analysis here, in terms of 'LI plus', enables us to think more clearly about the ways in which the future politics of 'everyday integration' may interact with the 'grand bargain' of Amsterdam, not to mention the possible consequences of the 2000 IGC.

Flexibility: Risk or Revival for Europe?

This chapter has sought to take a first step towards a theoretical grasp of flexibility. It has showed that a distinctive theoretical approach is needed for a more complete explanation of the integration process, and specifically for the analysis of the impact of flexibility provisions. The proposed multi-step approach of 'LI plus', by linking 'grand bargains' and 'everyday politics', opens up broad opportunities for future research since it can easily be generalized and applied to fields other than differentiated integration.

As argued in the early parts of this chapter, the issue of closer cooperation embodies all 'four Rs': risks, reform, resistance, and a hope for revival. The resistance of certain states against further deepening led in the past to their demand for *ad hoc* flexibility. The risk of a deadlock in integration brought about the provisions on closer cooperation, which constitute a reformative step away from the orthodox Community method and a means by which to manage increasing diversity. Flexibility may revive the deepening of integration, but it may also facilitate the 'grand enlargement bargain', which in itself focuses perceptions of risk and the need for reform (see Part III below). Variable geometry is expected to make widening easier by reassuring the integrationist member states and by acting as a safety valve. However, enlargement will increase the requirements to be met if a mathematical majority of member states is to be obtained, and may thus render closer cooperation more difficult. Facing resistance against more integration and the risk of stalemate after enlargement, flexibility can be interpreted as a reform to facilitate a future revival of the Union. Yet, it is not a substitute for institutional reform, and the IGC 2000 will have to resolve the institutional issues left open in Amsterdam. In doing so, it will have to confront the interaction theorized here, between the 'grand bargains' encapsulated in IGCs and the 'everyday integration' generated by the evolution of the Union.

4

The Paradox of the 'European Polity'

JO SHAW AND ANTJE WIENER

Introduction

This chapter focuses on features of the process of European integration which suggest that the European Union is simultaneously both 'near-state' and antithetical to stateness. The centerpiece of the chapter is the paradox of the 'European' polity with particular regard to its 'stateness'. This paradox consists of a parallel development of two dimensions: one *institutional*, the other *theoretical*. The institutional dimension can be assessed through studying the process of supra-, trans-, and infranational institutionalization, with contrasting conditions of decision-making and legitimacy attaching to the different levels observed (Weiler 1999: ch. 8). This process generates shared norms, routinized practices, and formalized rules and procedures which are part of the *acquis communautaire*, the shared political and legal properties of the EU (Gialdino 1995). As the institution that now carries a strong structuring weight within European integration over the past fifty years, the *acquis communautaire* has come to include a number of key elements of state-building processes. It entails, for example, a common market, citizenship, a common monetary policy and currency, and, with the communitarization of the Schengen *acquis*, now an increased pooling of sovereignty in relation to the emerging Area of Freedom, Security, and Justice. In sum, there is indeed little dispute among students of European integration that governance beyond the national state is a fact in Europe (Jachtenfuchs 1995). The question is how to characterize and understand this polity.

In turn, the theoretical dimension encompasses a peculiar mismatch between theories and politics of European integration that cannot escape the reference to stateness. A good example is the concept of 'integration through law' which has long dominated both legal practices and legal

Many thanks to Armin von Bogdandy and Damian Chalmers, as well as the editors, for comments on an earlier version.

studies in European integration, respectively. That is, while EC law, understood as a body of texts ('the letter of the law'), has never made explicit reference to the concept of stateness, what we might term the 'spirit of the law' which has guided the generation of the leading constitutional principles of 'direct effect' and 'supremacy of EU law' is shaped by the touch of stateness even so (Armstrong 1998; Shaw 1996; Capelletti *et al.* 1986). It follows that both dimensions, the institutional and the theoretical, underscore a recurrent, albeit often unintended and rarely rationally debated, reference to the image of the final shape of the EU as something to be kept in mind (Diez 1996). The *risk* of studying European governance then lies in the continuous *revival* of the idea of stateness, whether that takes the form of *resistance* against or *reform* towards the establishment of statelike patterns. It lies in studying a non-state polity within the frame of stateness, with all its theoretical and methodological implications.

Indeed, the perseverance of the 'touch of stateness' is quite impressive in the context of European integration studies. Two examples may suffice to demonstrate the problem. First, stateness is the implicit reference of most work on the condition of 'deficits', including deficits of democracy, legitimacy, accountability, equality, and security (Grimm 1995; Dehousse 1995; Grande 1996; Weiler 1999). This discussion of 'deficits' implies that, in the EU, many core principles of sovereign modern nation-states (Zürn 1998) are lacking. The language of 'deficit' clearly suggests a comparative dimension referring to the political form of the state, and not, for example, to international organizations. It begs the normative response to overcome the deficit (see, critically, Wiener and Della Sala 1997). Not surprisingly, normative theories provide the leading touch of stateness in this respect (Habermas 1992; Bellamy and Castiglione 1999). A second example is provided by the debate about different approaches to European integration. While this debate advanced substantially from juxtaposing neofunctionalism with intergovernmentalism in the 1980s to discussing more differentiated nuances of new institutionalisms in the 1990s (Pollack 1996), the touch of stateness has remained a constant factor none the less. While the underlying neofunctionalist assumption was that governance would eventually lead to a 'Europeanized' superstate (Haas 1964; Lindberg and Scheingold 1970), intergovernmentalists contend that the degree of institutionalization created in the process of European integration can be explained by studying member-state interests and preferences (Moravcsik 1993, 1998). While neofunctionalism thus evokes the image of the (federal) superstate, (liberal) intergovermentalism cannot account for the forming and changing institutional interests beyond states.

This chapter addresses the pitfalls of the often invisible touch of stateness and proposes a methodological perspective with a view to overcoming them. We point out that recent social and legal constructivist approaches to European integration have begun to discuss new ways of assessing the 'European' polity. Their specific validity with a view to avoiding stateness, we argue, lies in an ontological shift from a focus on the state towards analyzing the impact of norms, identities, language, and discourse on politics and practices in the 'European' polity. We specifically highlight the important insights gained through analyses of constitutionalism that have begun to set new parameters for the study and characterization of the 'European' polity. The argument develops from noting a tension between those formal elements of a 'European' constitution or the constitutional framework which have evolved so far, on the one hand, and the abstract ideas about civilized coexistence within polities which are necessarily implicated by the invocation of the term 'constitutionalism', on the other. While this tension is particularly interesting, thus far it has remained largely under-researched.

With a view to generating further empirical research, we discuss the emerging link between social and legal norms through the empirical lens of policy practices.[1] More specifically, on the basis of studying constitutional discourse and policy-making practices, we propose to trace the emergence of social norms and discuss their potential to materialize. For example, the shared reference to 'subsidiarity' or 'flexibility' as a guiding rule of constitutional bargaining at intergovernmental conferences (Shaw 1998; Wallace 2000) may, potentially, turn into a legally stipulated rule. In other words, we argue that through the routinization of practices, and/or the institutionalization of principles, social norms can, potentially, acquire the status of legal norms. We exemplify this argument by reference to the Treaty of Amsterdam. We seek to demonstrate that an example for a case that contributes to challenging the paradox of stateness is provided by the changing meaning of the principle of *flexibility*, from operating as an organizational idea to achieving constitutional status in the Treaty of Amsterdam (Curtin and Dekker 1999; Von Bogdandy 1999*a*, 1999*b*; Wallace 2000; Leslie 2000). We suggest that asymmetrical solutions such as opting-in/out possibilities emerge as the guiding norm for politics and policy-making in the EU, as well as giving rise to unusual types of legal problematics.

The chapter is organized in four further sections. The first discusses constructivist approaches in political science and law that offer an ontological focus on ideas, norms, and identities. The next section turns to the debate over constitutionalism and constitutional change in the EU as an

---

[1] See, for further detailed exposition, A. Wiener, *Governance under Changing Conditions of Democracy* (provisional title, Manchester University Press, in preparation).

approach to the paradox of stateness. Then an empirical example of a process in which social norms become gradually materialized into legal norms is discussed, focusing on the emergent principle of flexibility. Finally, we summarize our findings and reflect these back upon the promise to circumvent the cul-de-sac effect which state-centric approaches have upon the challenge theorizing the 'European' polity.

Constructivist Approaches to the 'European' Polity

A range of interdisciplinary legal-political science work offers ways of making it possible both to preserve the potential of the *sui generis* assumption about the EU and to provide guidelines for comparison. In general terms, the reformulated view of EU constitutionalism we develop in this paper on the basis of the discussion of social and legal constructivism is a case in point. Its focus is a tension between the abstract and the formal. More specifically, we argue that debates over the meaning and composition of new institutions in the 'European' polity, such as, for example, Union citizenship, or, the Schengen Convention, provide an access point for our argument, especially in so far as they instantiate the principle of flexibility and its emergence as a new norm. In the following two sections, we proceed to elaborate on the interdisciplinary approach which, as we suggest, will allow us to track norms from 'the social' to 'the legal'. The leading questions are which norms have come to guide practices and processes in the 'European' polity, and how do these norms change, that is, from social norms to legal norms?

Explaining this link between the social and the legal on the basis of an interdisciplinary perspective on norms is not entirely new, to be sure. It has been most prominently explained in Jürgen Habermas's work on the functional importance of law and its potential to generate integrity in a society that is fragmented into separate social and political spheres (Habermas 1992). The role of law in linking the validity and the facticity of norms has subsequently been applied and elaborated on in normative work on compliance mechanisms beyond the nation-state (Zürn and Wolf 1999). While this chapter endorses the link between the social and the legal, it does not share the normative thrust of the argument. That is, we do not elaborate on the problem of establishing an adequate problem-solving capacity of a political system based on law (Zürn and Wolf 1999: 282). Instead, we seek to trace the empirically observable process of norm construction and change. In the following, we elaborate on the core methodological innovations that constructivist approaches offer for this endeavor from both political science and legal perspectives.

We argue that an interdisciplinary politico-legal approach is particularly useful with a view to examining aspects of 'European' constitutionalism. Within this framework, the ontological focus on norms provides a helpful methodological starting-point for political scientists and lawyers alike. Both political scientists and lawyers are interested in questions of which norms have implications for practices and politics in the 'European' polity. Yet the respective conceptual conclusions drawn from the empirical insight of an emergence of (social) norms differ as between political scientists and lawyers. While the former are primarily interested in how norms, through their impact on identities and interests, change actors' behavior in, say, decision-making, policy-implementing, or policy-planning situations, the latter are more specifically concerned with the normative range of norms, and in understanding norms as rules, standards, or principles as well as the adjudicatory and allocative responses which they provoke. It is our contention that both perspectives taken together provide an excellent empirical starting-point with a view to comprehending the 'European' polity from a perspective that is not blurred by a touch of stateness. This position will be more specifically elaborated from the perspectives of social constructivism and legal constructivism respectively, in the remainder of this section.

Social Constructivism

It needs to be emphasized that there is no single shared constructivist approach either in international relations theory or in European integration. In the latter case, where constructivist theorizing has only recently begun to become an issue, this point needs to be made more strongly. Instead of a general theory, constructivism is understood as an umbrella approach. It is a 'middle ground' on which specific theoretical interests merge and from which various research strategies emerge (Adler 1997; Checkel 1998). It has been characterized as a methodological practice of 'establishing a middle ground' between the two poles of rationalism and reflectivism (Christiansen *et al.* 1999: 535–7). Engaging in this practice allows scholars to create an arena in which ontological shifts and meta-theoretical moves can be debated. For example, some maintain a strong interest in explaining decision-making, and generating hypotheses, albeit of a heuristic nature (Checkel 1999; Marcussen *et al.* 1999), while others are primarily interested in identifying the emergence of practices and concepts with a view to discussing their impact on political and legal processes (Koslowski 1999; Diez 1999). Crucially, the participating scholars do not necessarily share epistemological assumptions. They do, however, agree about the importance of the social for both understanding and explaining European integration (Risse and Wiener 1999: 776).

A core constructivist insight stresses the importance of communication and intersubjectivity in situations of decision-making and bargaining beyond the borders of nation-states (Kratochwil and Ruggie 1986). Actors act within an environment that is structured by the social that contributes, in turn, to shaping the structures of this very environment. The environment or the norms that emerge in this context have an impact on identities. In turn, identities influence interest formation and subsequently behavior. International relations scholars have, so far, referred to three types of norms. *Regulative norms* order and constrain behavior, in a way similar to rules. *Constitutive* norms create new actors, interests, or categories of action, and *evaluative or prescriptive* norms create the much less defined and often actually excluded category of oughtness, that is, they set the standards for socially appropriate behavior (Katzenstein 1996: 5; Jepperson *et al.* 1996). The interdisciplinary approach pursued in this chapter argues that, while for analytical reasons such distinction of types of norms may prove helpful in specific political situations, the emergence of norms in the 'European' polity actually suggests a much more closely linked interrelation between types of norms.

This link emerges very clearly in studies of the *acquis* (Wiener 1997, 1998; Jørgensen 1998). Thus, it has been shown that the structuring power and the ability to change of the *acquis* have long been grossly underestimated. The case of citizenship policy demonstrates particularly well how a methodological bracketing of the *acquis*, that is, de-linking it from its social environment, often produces misleading results. Studies that rely exclusively on a bracketed definition of the *acquis* fall short of assessing the meaning of genuinely 'European' concepts, such as, for example, the concept of citizenship of the Union. That is, studies of citizenship that refer to the contents of the *acquis* without acknowledging its embedded structure will invariably miss the social processes (and cultural ideas) that preceded the legal stipulation of citizenship. Subsequently, they find the concept to entail a 'deficit' (O'Leary 1995). In turn, studies of European citizenship that seek to understand the meaning of citizenship by studying citizenship as a practice, including the ideas and policy objectives which have been formed in the process as part of the 'embedded *acquis communautaire*' (Wiener 1998), have found the 'European' concept of citizenship to be genuine, and see it as a potentially powerful challenge indeed to nation-state citizenship (on the crucial importance of embeddedness, see also Chalmers 1999: 522). Studies of changing policy frames have similarly endorsed the importance of tracing the link between informal and formal resources of the *acquis* in the sector of environmental policy (Lenschow and Zito 1998).

In other words, by missing out on the social norms that precede the stipulation of legal norms, a gap emerges. Ignoring this gap may well imply a recurring touch of stateness, for example, by falling into the trap of 'deficit' talk. In relation to the example on citizenship, one could make the following comments: the first approach entails a normative study that is infected by the touch of stateness; the second focuses on norms and can study the interrelationship between EU and national institutions in a way that is free of that touch. To overcome this gap, it has been suggested that one could conceptualize the formal resources, that is, the shared legal and procedural aspects of the *acquis*, as embedded in a social environment. Informal resources such as ideas and social norms emerge in this environment through practices and routinization. These social norms potentially contribute to the formulation of legal stipulations, or the emergence of legal norms, if they may materialize. Analytically, the parts of the embedded *acquis* are best approached by identifying informal resources, routinized practices, and formal resources based on analyses of public discourse. It should be noted that, while this approach does have a historical institutionalist bias, that is, it acknowledges historical contingency of institutions (Pierson 1996*b*; March and Olsen 1998), it does not suggest a teleological development along a straight line from informal to formal resources. Instead, the formation of informal resources, such as social norms, and the stipulation of formal resources, such as legal stipulations, do not develop in a linear way. They are, however, interrelated through practices. Furthermore, it is important to note that, even if social norms are not included in the formal *acquis*, they still have a crucial role in the process of accepting legal norms. They have significant impact on rule-following and compliance (Zürn and Wolf 1999).

For example, studies in international relations have convincingly shown that norms have a pervasive power across national borders. Thus, the increasingly globally shared perception of human rights norms has crucially influenced agency behavior in different countries in similar ways (Jacobson 1996; Klotz 1995*a*; Soysal 1994). In this way the same norms have an impact on different actors and contexts. Equally, by examining actors' behavior in different contexts, it has been demonstrated that specific social norms have spread across borders. With a view to studying how norms matter to practices and processes in the 'European' polity, we distinguish between two basic types of norms, namely social and legal norms. More specifically, we argue that the crucial contribution which interdisciplinary politico-legal research about norms has to offer is its ability to demonstrate the link between social and legal norms and, subsequently, to discuss the constitutional potential of norms.

This approach shares the assumption that socialization matters to analyses of political decision-making (Risse and Wiener 1999: 776). Taking norms as the starting-point, it follows the observation that social meanings are discursively constructed. As such, discourse reflects institutional structures and helps to construct them in the process. Public discourse hence offers a crucial medium to assess the link between social and legal norms, or for that matter, the materialization of social norms in the legal sphere. Most generally, it has been observed that norms are profoundly 'social' once they are shared (Klotz 1995*a*). That is, communication about norms establishes their meaning and subsequently their impact. This broad definition of norms implies, for example, assumptions about behavior that are shared by the majority of individuals within a specific area, a decision-making process, a group, or, a nation. As such, norms can be crucial factors in decision-making processes. Indeed, Friedrich Kratochwil argues, for example, that 'actors *have to resort to norms*' (Kratochwil 1989: 5; emphasis in the original).

A number of political and legal scholars have stressed the impact of 'the social' on politics and policy-making in the EU. For example, it has been demonstrated that the perception and guiding force of world-views and ideas, as well as processes of socialization, are each significant for accepting or resisting norms and are hence crucial to the assessment of legitimate governance (see e.g. Jachtenfuchs 1995, 1999; also March and Olsen 1998). Equally, social ethics have been identified as shaping administrative processes (Everson 1998). In sum, it has been argued that socialization matters for political and legal processes of institution-building and decision-making. This insight crucially challenges rationalist assumptions of a 'logic of consequentialism'. Instead, constructivists refer to the 'logic of appropriateness' and/or the 'logic of argumentative rationality' instead (March and Olsen 1998; Risse 1999). Both latter rationales for political decision-making are innovative in an important way for European integration studies, in so far as they both involve a return to 'the social'. Thus, appropriateness is measured against shared norms, whereas argumentative rationality proceeds from an assumption about a belief in moral virtues, which are to be maintained from, or achieved by way of, arguing. It is precisely at this point where social constructivist perspectives on norms (and the logic of appropriateness which they generate), on the one hand, and legal-philosophical perspectives on norms (and their normative range), on the other, will merge.

Legal Constructivism

In the field of legal studies, it is in relation to the study of international law that constructivism has had probably its greatest impact, especially as regards interdisciplinary scholarship. The contribution of constructivism has been emphasized, for example, in the context of the broader agenda examining the interdisciplinary interactions of international relations and international law. More specifically, the potential of building interdisciplinary research agendas through the key insight that 'actors, identities, interests and social structures are culturally and historically contingent products of interaction on the basis of shared norms' has been noted (Slaughter *et al.* 1998: 384). It has been suggested that we should be looking to the development of research which will 'develop convincing accounts of precisely how such structures are continuously formed and transformed by discursive practice, and how they continuously set the terms by which actors interpret their own and others' identities, interests and actions' (Slaughter *et al.* 1998: 389). This suggestion follows from a focus on 'the idea that norms and other intersubjective structures are "always in process"'. The same authors emphasize also the extent to which discursive practices in relation to arguments about shared norms are situated or embedded in deeper normative structures—which in the case of international law are enumerated (non-exhaustively, one presumes) as 'states, sovereignty and anarchy' (Slaughter *et al.* 1998: 389), for which one could read in the case of the law of the European Union 'states, sovereignty and *markets*'.

For lawyers, constructivist accounts often have the particular merit of promoting a critical perspective upon the use of definitions in determining the proper scope of legal claims (Kingsbury 1998). Thus, similar to the various debates in international relations theory, critical constructivist work in legal studies is frequently posited in contrast to positivism, which would favor closed and fixed definitions of categories or claimants, on the basis of which the legal interpretative process proceeds. With a view to methodological innovation, a constructivist approach to the definitional task rejects the idea of universally applicable criteria. Instead, it posits a 'continuous process in which claims and practices in numerous specific cases are abstracted in the wider institutions of international society, then made specific again at the moment of application in the political, legal and social processes of particular cases and societies' (Kingsbury 1998: 415).

This contextualized definitional method can usefully be applied to the use of the term 'constitution' in relation to the EU. In the first instance, 'defining' the 'European' constitution is itself a contested process. Initially, the method permits us to develop an approach which is sensitive to the 'universal' abstract characteristics of constitutionalism in relation to the balancing of majoritarian power and individual rights within a structured institutional framework common to all liberal nation-states and characteristic of civilized coexistence. But this abstract universalism stands in a creative tension to a second aspect of EU constitutionalism, namely the discursive specifics of ongoing European negotiations as a *sui generis* case of polity formation outside the nation-state which results in identifiable formal outputs. In addition, it is possible to link issues of definition to the constructivist ontological focus on language and communication. Thus one could hypothesize that, in the case of 'European' polity formation, a constructivist approach is helpful precisely because the focus on communication through language proves to be a crucial factor. In this *sui generis* context, constitutionalism depends upon mediating the meanings of 'new' institutions, norms, rules (see e.g. Curtin and Dekker 1999) as well as upon adapting 'old' institutions using a comparative method.

Constitutionalism depends also upon the constructive potential of the 'community of law' which underpins the project of European integration in both symbolic and practical terms. After all, the EU is a 'pure creature of law' (Beaumont and Walker 1999: 170). It has no pre-political community out of which it has emerged as a polity. That insight does not, however, in itself guarantee a seamless and productive interdisciplinary enterprise in relation to the study of law *and* politics. For example, while political scientists have undoubtedly discovered the Court of Justice as a legal institution, some might doubt whether they have discovered 'law' (Armstrong 1998: 155). Borrowing from Jürgen Habermas (1986), Kenneth Armstrong suggests that a fruitful interdisciplinary conceptualization of the role of law in relation to the EU will see 'attempts to use law as a medium' confronting 'the role of law as an institution'. Forces external to law will necessarily be mediated through law's institutional structure. In other words, law gives a different 'reading' to social, political, and economic phenomena because of its institutional structure, which includes its normative qualities. In those terms, legal analysis can be about 'bringing the law to bear' upon phenomena hitherto studied solely in 'political' terms.

However, a legal-political constructivist analysis is a more ambitious enterprise, identifying and explicating the role of what might be termed the 'spirit of the law' as a shared norm in relation to the EU. The dominant political-science approach to the role of law and legal institutions has been used to account for the compliance of the member states (for example, the work of Karen Alter 1998*a*, 1998*b*) and to explain the phenomenon of 'legal integration' involving the acceptance of EC law by national legal orders and national courts. But it is more sensitive to the specificities of law as a normative system to argue that:

the processes of persuasion and justification on the basis of norms play a *constitutive* role in the formation of actors' identities and interests and in the structure of the international system itself. On a deeper level, this approach rejects a simple law/power dichotomy, arguing instead that legal rules and norms operate by changing interests and thus reshaping the purposes for which power is exercised. (Slaughter *et al.* 1998: 381)

However, the 'spirit of the law'—like many facets of the EU—displays a paradoxical character when observed more closely. The rhetoric of the Court of Justice may be primarily focused upon the integrative, unifying, and cohesive force of the legal order. In practice, as it develops incrementally, that same legal order both tolerates and embodies aspects of disintegration, differentiation, and disruption (Shaw 1996). This point emerges clearly from the narrative about EU constitutionalism, which has shifted from the so-called constitutionalization of the Treaties by the Court of Justice to the reconceptualization of the post-Maastricht EU as a constitutional order. Aspects of this narrative are covered later in this chapter.

While the methodological approach of this chapter focuses on social norms, and their capability to materialize and thus develop normative potential as legal norms, it should be noted nevertheless that the *theoretical* approach employed in this chapter should be contrasted with a *normative* or *ethical* approach based on moral imperatives of social organization and, especially, those which concentrate upon the European Union as an entity caught between nation-states and processes of globalization (Habermas 1999). Others have characterized this shift as the so-called 'normative turn' in studies of the European Union (Wincott 1998; Bellamy and Castiglione 1999), part of the vocation of which is to find 'the politics' in integration studies and integration theory. Nor is this chapter an attempt to add to the literature which seeks to capture the 'mixity' of the EU.[2] Moreover, while MacCormick's work (e.g. 1999), which is based on an institutional theory of law which does not privilege the nation-state but is premised on plural sources of authority for the purposes of identifying the law, is a rich framework for assessing the specific character of the EU and its legal order as escaping the conceptual constraints of both national law and international law, it does not provide a full conceptual framework for assessing the *mutual* constitution of norms between legal *and* political actors. Also outwith our consideration is the question of technocratic efficacy and functionality, which in the view of some authors might lend some degree of legitimacy to the EU, such that its pursuit can likewise be seen as a normative imperative. Still less does this project lend support to the view that the EU should become more like a liberal democratic state, because only thereby can problems of legitimacy be solved. Indeed, our questions are not directly concerned with *legitimacy* at all, whether referring to that of the Union as a whole, its institutions, or the

---

[2] See e.g. authors whose work is rooted in legal and political philosophy, although the normative stipulations about the consequences of that mixity represent important insights in EU studies: Neil MacCormick (1997*a*, 1999) or Richard Bellamy and Dario Castiglione (1997, 2000).

activities it pursues. Rather our questions represent a twofold enterprise. They involve the meta-theoretical attempt to problematize taken-for-granted conceptions often fed into the study of the Union, such as 'state', constitution, or citizenship, for the one part, and the task of disaggregating the processes and actors involved, according to the guiding norms of this process, for the other.

In sum, constructivist approaches to European integration contrast with other approaches, such as, for example, normative and conceptual approaches to the 'European' constitution, as well as 'integration-focused' approaches. While the latter struggle to escape stateness, for example, by focusing on what must be done to establish a European constitution, or by discussing the final shape of the European polity, respectively, constructivists do not focus on the whole. Instead, they propose referring to meta-theoretical approaches and new ontological perspectives, when studying European integration. Empirically, we suggest linking political and legal approaches on the basis of rules and norms that emerge from and structure the day-to-day practices of constitutional politics. We suggest that this approach has great potential for studying the processes and practices without falling into the trap of implicit recurrence to stateness in the 'European' polity, precisely because of its focus on ontology. Thus, constructivists have begun to study the impact of identity, discourse, and norms and their respective impact on explaining and understanding the 'European' polity (Christiansen *et al.* 1999). The main implications of constructivism lie in the methodological tools that prove helpful for analyzing processes of fragmentation (of concepts), as well as the process of differentiation (of legal regimes). As we will proceed to demonstrate, a focus on constitutional politics, understood as day-to-day practices in the legal and political realm as well as the high dramas of IGCs and new Treaties, provides an interesting case to prove the point. In the following section we turn to defining traditional approaches to constitutionalism and its role in nation-states and then proceed with a review of constitutionalist debates with reference to the 'European' polity.

Constitutionalism and the 'European' Polity

Constitutionalism represents a useful focus for debate as it attracts both continuing public attention in the media, where there are relatively frequent calls from commentators for a European process of constitution-building,[3]

---

[3] See J. Freedland, 'This Institution has Failed. For we, the People, have Not Spoken Yet. Europe in Crisis', *The Guardian* (17 Mar. 1999), and I. Pernice, 'Vertragsrevision oder Europäische Verfassungsgebung?', *Frankfurter Allgemeine Zeitung* (7 July 1999) 7.

and a growing degree of attention across political science and inter-national relations commentary on the EU. Continuing the cross-disciplinary theme, we investigate in this section how different disciplines address the 'touch of stateness' question in the specific context of consti-tutionalism which has significance both in relation to institution-building and at a more symbolic level. This provides a general introduction to the more specific assessment of the principle of flexibility as emergent norm in the next section.

As a concept, the 'state' evokes different—but fundamentally comple-mentary—reactions in political scientists and lawyers. For political scien-tist two aspects are crucial for defining the state. The first is the 'Westphalian state' (Caporaso 1996) that had its point of origin in the 1648 Treaty of Westphalia. The subsequently emerging international sys-tem of states was structured by mutual acceptance of territorial state bor-ders that mark the limits of foreign intervention other than by force (of war), and the rule of sovereignty became the guiding norm of inter-national politics (Krasner 1995; Lyons and Mastanduno 1995; Chayes and Chayes 1995; Biersteker and Weber 1996; Ferguson and Mansbach 1996). The second aspect equally refers to sovereignty. However, instead of relations between states within the international realm, it has been forged by the citizen–state relation which emerged in the eighteenth and nine-teenth centuries. Both definitions of the state converge around the famil-iar Weberian definition of sovereignty, as involving the monopoly of the legitimate use of force within a bounded territory (Weber 1946). States have been perceived as the key actors in world politics, whether in the process of representing interests to the outside, that is, within the inter-national state system (Morgenthau 1985; Waltz 1979), or to the inside, that is, representing the constituted power to the constituency.

The assumption of the state as the single most important actor has been challenged, in particular, by processes of globalization in a number of pol-icy areas. While an abundant amount of material has been produced to define, debate, and discuss the role and impact of a variety of actors, the role of 'the social', emphasized by Max Weber as fundamental for legit-imate state politics, has stirred little interest amongst political scientists.[4] The tension that has emerged from the process of modern state-building, on the one hand, and the increasing institutionalization of global politics, on the other, brings the Hobbesian dilemma of civilized interstate rela-tions to the fore. Can states be sovereign and still maintain profoundly civ-ilized, that is principled, relations without having to succumb to a global

---

[4] For exceptions, see early constructivists such as Kratochwil and Ruggie (1986), Young (1989), or, for that matter, Gramscian contributions to the study of international relations, such as, for example, Keyman (1997), Murphy (1994), Whitworth (1989).

Leviathan? This is the larger question which accompanies any discussion of European 'stateness'.

For the lawyer the state's systemic character is one issue which comes to the fore, in particular in relation to the constitutional settlement which underpins every modern liberal nation-state. The historical and conceptual links that hold together state, constitution, and law as a system have proved hard to break and, from time to time, it has been suggested that they should have been transferred *en masse* to the EU (Mancini 1998). The temptation towards this wholehearted embrace of stateness has occurred partly because, in spite of a general intuition that the EU is *not* a state and *never* will be a state even though it satisfies basic criteria in relation to territoriality, population, and government, legal scholars have struggled to find a convincing alternative vocabulary to express the mixity, 'betweenness', or liminality of the EU (Curtin 1996). This is unsurprising if, for example, the starting-point for an analysis is the enumeration of different types of legal order. If the starting-point for analysis accepts (what are, for these purposes, simplified) Kelsenian positivist precepts that there are essentially two forms of law, namely international law and domestic or municipal law, then the features of the law of the EU must necessarily be observed and described in relation to the (closed) conceptual systems which these types of legal order offer. Moreover, the analysis is predisposed towards a hierarchical conceptualization of the relationships between different legal orders, and diligently though the Court of Justice has pursued its vision of EC law as *sui generis* and superior in nature to national law, it has never been wholly successful in persuading national legal actors, especially constitutional courts vested with the specific task of preserving and developing the national constitution, of the appropriateness of that approach. There have been many occasions on which legal scholarship has been caught between the tension of the *sui generis* nature of the EU (in empirical if not conceptual terms) and the temptation to argue by analogy with established legal and politico-legal categories.

Yet within its own terms, there is no doubt that the European Community, specifically through the agency of the European Court of Justice, has aped stateness, at least in legal terms, because of its strong adherence to the formal properties of the rule of law and the creation of the hard legal core often contrasted with the 'soft' political domain. The juridification of intra-Community relationships between institutions and between the institutions and the member states, as well as the oft-lauded creation of rights which individual private actors can enforce in national courts against member states and (sometimes) other private actors, have all contributed to that trend. But while the instrumental character of the EU legal order is not in doubt—especially in relation to the concepts of the supremacy and direct effect of EC law—there is a great deal more uncertainty about its systematic character. The lack of systematization of the European Union after Maastricht and now after Amsterdam has often been commented upon (Curtin 1993). This commonsense presupposition about the fragmented nature of the EU as order will be problematized in the discussion of constitutionalism which follows.

Where lawyers and political scientists can most comfortably join debate is in the domain of constitutionalism, and the related notions of constitutional law and the practice of constitutional politics. These figures suggest the possibility of giving simultaneous attention to the need for order (that is, law) to give a framework to the exercise of political choice and the need for a politics to structure the exercise of formal authority. A crucial tension exists between the formal principles or framework of EU constitutionalism, which make the system work in practice, and the abstract qualities associated with a regard for constitutional ideas and practices as the framework for civilized coexistence within polities. At the points of intersection between these formal and abstract aspects, a legal-political approach to constitutionalism borrowing from constructivist methodologies can elucidate both the troubling aspect of applying notions to the EU which are traditionally associated with the state and also its constructive potential in a post-national setting (Shaw 1999) and it is upon that distinction that we must focus.

Applying, for instance, the method of contextualized definition identified in the previous section we can problematize the meanings and languages of constitutionalism in the EU. We can see that both 'a constitution' (and, to a more limited extent, the idea of a 'need' for such a constitution) and the individual elements which make up this constitution in the formal sense have become crucial shared norms involving the coalescence of law and politics. On the other hand, when constitution-making is under discussion, the language of the 'normativity' of such norms is never far away. Thus EU constitutionalism is often seen in normative terms as being about the challenge of designing good institutions for the future Euro-polity. This is normativity in the sense of filling the legitimacy deficit. In that sense, the understandable demand for constitutional formality slips into a rhetoric of seeking the supply of constitutional ideas in order to bring stability and legitimacy to the people which draws instrumentally upon the abstract attractions of constitutionalism as a set of ideas. Seen in this register, constitutionalism for the EU has more than a hint of the 'touch of stateness'. It is about identifying a single end-product, and then about naming that end-product according to the conventional toolbox of constitutionalism (liberal, republican, democratic, etc.). In formal legal terms, it is about transgressing but not ultimately transcending the established divide between domestic law, in which constitutionalism is a comfortable discourse, and international law which swings between the formal legitimacy offered by the principle of *pacta sunt servanda* operating between formally equal and sovereign states, which holds together the EU from an external perspective, and a more base power politics involving realistically unequal relations of political and economic power.

From a constructivist perspective, a more fruitful conceptualization of the emerging EU constitution in this formal sense would concentrate on disaggregating its key elements (Shaw 2000), with a view to tracking emerging norms and to ascertaining both the embeddedness of norms and their 'normativity' in the sense of their claim to authority from political authorities, including the member states. Aside from the functional provisions on the single market, Economic and Monetary Union, the flanking policies on social affairs, the environment, regional redistribution, and on internal and external security, there are four main groups of provisions within the EU Treaties—buttressed in many cases by case law of the Court of Justice—which sustain a plausible claim to be 'constitutional'. First there are provisions which address the nature of the polity, by proclaiming the existence of the Union, including the constituent Communities and forms of cooperation which comprise the Second and Third Pillars. They are buttressed by basic value statements such as Article 6(1) TEU, which commits the EU to the principles of 'liberty, democracy, respect for human rights and fundamental freedoms, and the rule of law'. So far as these provisions include also those relating to the possibilities of flexibility and closer cooperation, they often beg as many questions as they answer about the precise nature of the polity. Second are provisions which establish the rule of law and its systemic properties, and which address the authority of the Court of Justice. As a third group, we can bring together provisions regarding the key values, principles, and norms within the system, including fundamental rights, non-discrimination, and the institutionalization of Union citizenship. Finally, there is an important group of provisions governing the exercise of power within the EU, covering the whole question of competence and the limits upon it. However, these provisions have not come all at once through a single formative constitutional experience for the EU, but have been the result of gradual accretion through the original treaties, amending treaties, and their associated intergovernmental conferences, constitutional-type interpretations and rulings by the Court of Justice, and the practices of the institutions and the member states which have set up many of the constitutional cornerstones which are now being increasingly recognized.[5]

[5] A good example would be the wording of Article 6(2) TEU which is intended, *inter alia*, to set the basic conditions for admission to the EU, as well as to be a constitutional

Constitutionalism can be seen as both a risk and a source of revival for the EU. As a practice of polity-formation, for example, constitutionalism is a natural progression for a polity which continues to transgress both the boundaries of the 'traditional' international organization and the functional borders of the project of economic integration. The significance of economic integration in the original treaties establishing the European Economic Community was mixed: *functionally* it was to the fore in the sense that only limited instruments for policy development were given to the new supranational institutions and it represented the focal point of the legally binding and enforceable treaty dispositions (what were, previously, Articles 9, 12, 30, 34, and 36 EEC on the free movement of goods, for example; Poiares Maduro 1998). Yet in terms of *rhetoric*, economic integration took its place from the very beginning alongside a more ambitious if vague project for the 'ever closer union of the peoples of Europe' (as in the Preamble to the EEC Treaty, for example). In practice, it was the project of market-making which decisively relaunched what we now know as the European Union from the mid-1980s onwards, with the Single Market Program, the planning and gradual achievement of Economic and Monetary Union, and the politico-economic project of enlargement after 1989.

Explanations of these outcomes have commonly focused upon the balance of causes: autonomous institutional driving force deriving support from the logic of policy spillover, or (rational) choice of the member states. Michelle Everson has argued that market-making has in fact unleashed a set of *private* as well as *public* national and Community interests which compete for prominence at the EU level. These interests were propelled in the first instance by a fundamentally neoliberal program, but this subsequently was gradually 'socialized' over the years (Everson 1998). Constitutionalism—or, a set of choices about the formal underpinnings of the polity and the societal bargains upon which those choices are based— is, on that reading, part of a sequence of market-oriented polity-formation, capable of explanation using either of the standard toolkits of European integration studies (neofunctionalism and intergovernmentalism), but one which, we would argue, reveals its paradoxical nature most clearly when subject to constructivist analysis. For that analysis allows us to make a specifically legal-political analysis. For when the emphasis is upon the significance of constitutionalism as a question of *legal order* a different perspective emerges.

cornerstone for the present membership. Although inserted in the TEU by the Treaty of Amsterdam, it is derived directly from the so-called Copenhagen Principles, articulated when the European Council first formally acknowledged the prospect of enlargement to include the newly democratized countries of Central and Eastern Europe (European Council 1993; also *Bulletin of the EC*, 6 (1993), para. I.13).

Constitutionalism gives meaning to the idea of the EU as a 'community of law', as its most visible sign is the role of the European Court of Justice in 'constitutionalizing' the legal order. As Kenneth Armstrong has argued, the idea of the 'constitutionalized treaty' is one of the most powerful instrumental images within EC law (Armstrong 1998: 161). This is the most important facet of the formal elements of EU constitutionalism sketched above. But what, in fact, the Court has done is first and foremost to establish the federal character of the EU legal order by creating an explicit hierarchy between EC law and national law, with EC law becoming *part* of and taking precedence over national law. Remedies in national courts are guaranteed for aggrieved individuals on the basis of this dogmatic system. It has then buttressed the near-state nature of the EU by finding that the European Community—at least—holds 'sovereign powers' (not sovereignty as such), powers which are limited in nature but are increasing by incremental steps both as a result of further transfers by means of Treaty *fiat* and as a result of teleological interpretations of those powers by the Court itself and its application of the principle of implied powers.[6] Constitutionalism in this sense comes tantalizingly close to an ideal closely related to a formalized notion of the rule of law which offers a commonsense goal which many observers and commentators find it easy to accept that the EU *should* aspire to in so far as it represents a common endeavor of a collectivity of liberal states. That is, constitutionalism as a frame of reference for analysis beckons suggestively towards a normative discourse for the future of the EU in an evolving world of liberal states and even liberal post-state and post-national polities. This is a discourse which underpins implicitly much legal commentary on the EU and its legal order. It is a discourse which reveals, once again, the touch of stateness.

However, the contribution of a constructivist analysis is not limited to uncovering these touches of stateness in constitutionalism. It can also contribute to a legal-political understanding of EU constitutionalism based on shifting definitions and emerging norms. For example, an interesting question is whether the discourses of the constitutionalized treaty, and indeed the socialized market, are confined to describing and evoking a constitutionalism of the *European Community*, paying insufficient attention to the *additional* challenges of considering the *European Union* as a proto constitutional order. This is another example of seeking to define the EU's constitutional framework. Since the Treaty of Maastricht (and continuing after the Treaty of Amsterdam), an important and sophisticated debate has been enjoined amongst lawyers about how to characterize the EU in legal terms, in particular its relationship with the established

---

[6] Opinion 1/91, *Re the Draft Agreement on a European Economic Area* [1991] ECR I–6079.

legal entity of the European Community (Von Bogdandy and Nettesheim 1996; Dörr 1995; Pernice 1998, 1999; Curtin and Dekker 1999; Von Bogdandy 1999*a*, 1999*b*; De Witte 1998; Koenig and Pechstein 1998). The question has been asked whether the European Community, gathering together the three Communities (EC, ECSC, Euratom), and the EU, gathering together the 'three pillar structure' of Maastricht along with the common provisions of the Treaty on European Union, are fundamentally separate entities with separate legal orders. A specific problem is the fact that formal international legal personality is ascribed to each of the three Communities, but not to the European Union itself, although the latter acts in certain ways in the international domain as if it were a recognized legal person, and is given the objective of asserting the identity of the Union on the international scene (Article 2 TEU). On the other hand, the principle of coherence offers an important institutional counterweight to such differentiations between Community and Union (Article 3 TEU).

A number of questions are raised about the transformative process and its outcomes. Does one (EC) belong to the domain of supranationalism and the other (EU) to the domain of intergovernmentalism? Or is the picture clouded by gray areas, as Meyring suggests, especially if one has regard to the activities of the institutions in the context of justice and home affairs (Meyring 1997)? Is it permissible to focus on the EC as representing the best efforts of the integration dynamic based on the functionalities of the single market and economic and monetary union, treating the EU as the poor political relation, ignoring the cross-cutting influence of structures such as the institutional framework? Or is it correct to revert back to the categorization of EC law as a species of international law (the 'new legal order of international law' characterized by the Court of Justice in the foundational case of *Van Gend en Loos*),[7] and to assert that now international law and EC law are (re)converging (Denza 1999). To characterize this essentially *legal* debate as being fundamental to the constitutionalism of the European Union in broader politico-legal terms seems, at first sight, to be falling victim to excessive law-centrism. Is this type of formalized conceptualization of EU constitutionalism not merely replicating the pitfalls of the earlier generation for whom the constitutionalized Treaty was the central image, albeit on this occasion without the Court of Justice in the vanguard, given its relatively decentered position in the overall EU framework (Peers 1999)?

On closer inspection, it is perhaps less the narrow question of the putative fusion, interlinkage, or separation of the EC and EU legal orders, but

---

[7] Case 26/62, *Van Gend en Loos* v. *Nederlandse Administratie der Belastingen* [1963] ECR 1.

rather the related endeavor to characterize the EU in terms self-consciously based on meta-theoretical understandings and social scientific ontologies which is of significance in this context. Curtin and Dekker (1999), for example, draw on the institutional theory of law developed by Neil MacCormick (1997*b*) in order to argue that the regime established by the Treaty on European Union represents the institutional concept of the 'international organization' rather than that of the (mere) 'Treaty'. Central amongst their arguments is the way a single institutional framework operates across the entire EU system, with a resultant mixing of principles in relation to decisions and decision-making, judicial practices, constitutional practices, and practices in relation to the protection of human rights. Practices are 'borrowed' and applied, for example, in relation to the whole system when a strict interpretation seems to indicate that they 'belong' only to a part of the system. A good example has been the interpretation of transparency provisions by the Court of Justice and, most notably, by the Court of First Instance. The characterization of this system as 'layered', however, recognizes that within the basic shell there are 'various autonomous and interlinked entities with their own specific roles and legal systems' (Curtin and Dekker 1999: 132).

A related analysis comes from Armin von Bogdandy who characterizes the EU as a supranational federation (1999*a*, 1999*b*). Although the analysis builds upon an earlier argument about the unity of the EU legal system (Von Bogdandy and Nettesheim 1996), the strength of the argument comes from a juxtaposition of unifying elements (such as the assertion in the Treaty of Amsterdam of a more clearly demarcated external borders and a starker distinction between insiders and outsiders in relation to the Union: Article 11 TEU; Articles 62 and 63 EC) and elements of polycentrism and fragmentation evident in the plurality of institutional methods and configurations. While not hesitating to deploy the emotive term 'federalism', Von Bogdandy is still careful to stress its capacity to express the diffusion of the holding of power in *non-state* contexts, and to urge the integration of federalism and supranationalism as (for him) a potent blend—in a normative as well as a descriptive sense—for the Union. Although he deliberately distances his argument from 'postmodernist' arguments in relation to law, in practice Von Bogdandy relies heavily upon concepts of networks and heterarchy commonly used by such analyses.

The analyses by Curtin and Dekker and Von Bogdandy represent, in our view, an application of the notion of the 'embedded *acquis communautaire*', or 'the continuously changing institutional terms which result from the constructive process of "integration through law"' (Wiener 1998: 299). In the case of Curtin and Dekker, the emphasis is upon the contribution of certain routinized institutional practices to the constitution of the *acquis* and the transformed understanding of the EU in legal-political terms. Von Bogdandy, meanwhile, draws out the paradox of flexibility and fragmentation within a framework of unity, which is an important condition of the *acquis* since it is dependent upon its 'constitutive practices' (Wiener 1998: 300–1). It is to the concept of flexibility which we now turn, in order to develop a further empirical specification of our methodological premises, by examining the emergence and transformation of this concept as 'norm' within EU constitution-building and polity-formation.

Flexibility and the Treaty of Amsterdam

Observers have developed a number of interesting parallels between flexibility and the concept of subsidiarity which was included in the EU Treaties by the Treaty of Maastricht in 1993 (Shaw 1998; Wallace 2000). Like flexibility, subsidiarity finds a number of different forms in the Treaties, juxtaposing the 'legal' and the 'political' (De Búrca 1999). The political statement is that now contained in Article 1 TEU, about decisions being taken as closely as possible to the citizen. Its specific legal form is to be found in Article 5 EC, where it sets out conditions to the exercise of *shared* competences between the Community and the member states, including a reference to levels of appropriateness for decision-making. Flexibility meanwhile is part of the deep political penumbra of the Treaties, which comprise increasingly common differentiated solutions to the challenges of integration. In legal terms, it also has two different faces (Walker 2000). On the one hand there is the 'unplanned architectural sprawl' (Walker 2000) of *ad hoc* arrangements principally for social policy (1993–7), for EMU (1993 to the present), and for matters relating to free movement, asylum, and immigration (since the 1980s in respect of the Schengen Convention, but since 1999 only in respect of this newly 'communitarized' policy). On the other hand, there are basic principles which are supposed to govern any future and potential flexibility *within* the Treaty frameworks, setting conditions on what is constitutionally tolerable (Articles 40, 43–5 TEU and Article 11 EC).

The two concepts also arguably offer languages on the basis of which ostensibly antagonistic interests can keep a conversation going, that is, by providing a shared terminology into which very different meanings can be invested. Thus subsidiarity can be seen as a form of advanced federalism with its prescriptions on the decentralization of power, or it can be the reassertion of the statal grab for power and a symbol of a revitalized proud nationalism. Equally, flexibility in the run-up to the Amsterdam IGC was asserted as a vital principle as much by those seeking 'more Europe' through enhanced cooperation within a hard core, if need be leaving behind the laggards, as it was by those such as the then UK government which wished to place a brake on the whole principle of intensified integration by introducing increased 'pick and choose' or à la carte options (De la Serre and Wallace 1997*a*).

However, to encompass these varied meanings, as well as the specific legal terms and usages highlighted here, it is necessary to deploy a wide definition of flexibility. Thus in using the term 'flexibility', we are combining a number of different levels and dimensions of differentiation and fragmentation within the EU polity. For example, at a macro-level we include the development of complex overlapping systems of authority, exemplified by the extra-EU evolution of Schengen, the development and transformation of the cooperation in justice and home affairs before and after the Treaty of Maastricht, and the subsequent Amsterdam-inspired communitarization of Schengen and construction of the new Title IV of the EC Treaty on Visas, Asylum, etc. States—notably the UK, Ireland, and Denmark—have moved laterally across these systems of authority as they have developed greater depth. Other examples at that level include social policy from 1993 to 1997 and EMU as it continues today, in relation to the non-participants in Euro-land and their various conditions of non-participation. Flexibility also operates within the EU, as the example of open-textured concepts such as Citizenship of the Union illustrates, where the flexibility operates in a temporal sense of ensuring 'fit' and complementarity between an allegedly common Union concept and diverse national notions of citizenship.

At a more technical level in relation to the internal market flexibility has, since the date of the Single European Act, offered an outlet for national sensibilities, by allowing member states to deviate under certain conditions from harmonized arrangements on, for example, product safety (Article 95 EC). Here there appears to be a more formal convergence of the concerns of flexibility and subsidiarity, given the need for much internal market legislation—falling within areas of shared competence—to respect the principle of subsidiarity. Indeed, it is in relation to internal market legislation (broadly defined) that the Court of Justice has so far made its limited pronouncements on the effects of the subsidiarity principle. Notably in the UK's challenge to the legal basis of the working time directive, which was based on a competence to regulate health and safety matters,[8] and a German challenge to the adoption of a directive harmonizing national laws on deposit guarantee schemes,[9] the discussion

---

[8] Case C–84/94, *UK* v. *Council* [1996] ECR I–5755.
[9] Case C–233/94, *Germany* v. *Parliament and Council* [1997] ECR I–2405.

by the Court does not betray any particular sensitivity to any new inter-institutional balance which the insertion of the subsidiarity requirement into the Community legislative process might have brought about (De Búrca 1998).

If there is an emerging common agenda in the Court of Justice about the concepts of subsidiarity and flexibility, it appears to be in a general reluctance to allow these principles to fetter the judicial role. Thus, in addition to the subsidiarity case law highlighted already, in relation to flexibility the Court of Justice has shown a disinclination to allow the presence of differentiated or partial arrangements to undermine the coherence and uniformity of the legal order it has created. So it decided to classify the 'law' arising when measures were adopted under the Social Policy Agreement from which the UK opted out between 1993 and 1997 as 'Community law',[10] and it declined an invitation from the Council *not to intervene* when it concluded that it has jurisdiction to consider whether a Third Pillar measure, which it could not in normal circumstances review, was unlawful because it should have been adopted under EC Treaty provisions.[11] A more positive contribution to the embedding of these norms in the legal and political systems, by their invocation as underlying structural principles of that legal order is not, therefore, presently in view.

An important research agenda suggests itself as a result of these insights. For example, is it possible not only to track the discourse of flexibility through phases of decision-making, but also to pinpoint moments at which it transforms into 'norm', and then at some point shifts from 'the social' to 'the legal'? Such work would, for example combine studies of norms as informal resources that are influential in various policy sectors (Lenschow and Zito 1998; Marcussen *et al.* 1999) as well as research on compliance with norms (Zürn and Wolf 1999). What sort of future do we envisage for flexibility in the Court of Justice? Is it limited to the fixing of the boundaries of differentiated decisions, or will it be elevated to the status of a more general interpretative principle along the lines of the notion of 'institutional balance'? A major new research field which will prove crucial to the formation and role of the flexibility principle will be policy areas that are covered or touched by the Schengen Implementation Agreement (Hailbronner and Thiery 1997), such as, for example, research on asylum policy, visa policy, and policing.

---

[10] Case T–135/96, *UEAPME* v. *Council* [1998] ECR II–2335.
[11] Case C–170/96, *Commission* v. *Council (Air Transport Visas)* [1998] ECR I–2763.

Conclusions

In this chapter, we began by outlining the paradox of the 'European' polity, so far as it struggles—in the context of both the studies and practices of governance in relation to European integration—to escape the touch of stateness. We outlined a methodological stance which builds upon the constructivist middle ground where scholars can debate ontological shifts and meta-theoretical moves. We chose to focus on the embeddedness and embedding of norms, using the concept of the embedded *acquis communautaire* as an example of the strong structuring properties of norms, and their impacts upon actors as guiding social norms, as well as legal rules. At the same time, this paper has emphasized the fluid nature of norms: on the one hand, norms may achieve strong structuring power, on the other hand, norms are created through interaction. The processes of norm construction and rule-following are mutually constitutive. In this conclusion, it is important to highlight the relevance and interest of this analysis, which elaborates upon the general field of constitutionalism as an object of study and the specific case of flexibility.

We identified a tension between the formal and the abstract in EU constitutionalism, and subsequently sought to highlight the continuing paradoxical relationship between a non-state polity and a touch of stateness presented often implicitly in analyses of this polity. With a view to overcoming the touch of stateness, we turned to constructivist approaches, arguing that the focus on the social and an ontological shift away from state actors offers a fresh perspective on the 'European' polity as *sui generis*, yet comparable. We argue that constitutionalism might be about fundamental ordering principles which have a validity outwith the formal setting of the nation-state. Yet, in practice the ways in which these principles find expression in the EU's legal order are either frequently dependent upon premises about the 'good society' which draw directly upon the normative properties of states, or are drawn into the Court of Justice's design of a federalized 'Community of law', in which the spirit of that community draws strength from the extent to which the EU as legal order apes a statal order.

It follows that reconceived on the basis of a constructivist ontology which allows a focus on norms—and their emergence and transformation from the social to the legal—constitutionalism presents a research area that is key to understanding and explaining the specific non-state conditions of the 'European' polity. Thus, we propose identifying the emergence and impact of norms in various policy sectors. In this chapter we particularly stressed the IGC processes as an arena in which social norms emerge

(Wallace 2000). With reference to the principle of flexibility and its increasing social acceptance as well as legal insertion in the Treaties, we suggest that norms are a factor structuring, for example, the redefining of the constitutional scope of the Euro-polity as it has shifted from Community to Union, and as it transforms once again in the wake of the Treaty of Amsterdam and the vital structural and political changes which that has introduced.

III

Monetary Union:
Ideas, Interests, and Impact

5

Monetary Integration in Europe: Ideas and Evolution

AMY VERDUN

Introduction

The launching of Europe's single currency, the Euro, on 1 January 1999 was a well-prepared and long-awaited moment in the history of European integration. Earlier attempts in the 1970s had failed. The launch of the Euro in financial markets on 1 January 1999 and the planned circulation of banknotes and coins in 2002 illustrates how far the European Union has proceeded in some areas of policy-making, in this particular case, the area of monetary policy-making.

When Economic and Monetary Union (EMU) had been agreed to in the early 1990s, few political analysts expected that it would start off initially with such a large group of EU member states. Meeting the criteria for entry—the so-called convergence criteria[1]—required that national

An earlier version of this paper was presented at a workshop at York University in March 1999, at the fifth biennial conference of the European Community Studies Association USA (ECSA-USA) in June 1999 and at a luncheon seminar at the Robert Schuman Centre of the European University Institute on 15 June 1999. The author would like to thank the participants of those conferences and the seminar for useful feedback on an earlier version. Special thanks go to Tanja Boerzel, Yves Meny, Thomas Risse, Martin Rhodes, Alberta Sbragia, and the editors of this volume for useful comments and suggestions. The Robert Schuman Centre is thanked for providing facilities and funding that assisted some of the research conducted for this paper.

[1] The convergence criteria are placed in a protocol to Article 121 (ex Article 109*j*) of the Treaty of European Union. (i) Inflation rates have to be within 1.5 percentage points of the rates of the EU's three best performers in terms of price stability. (ii) No excessive deficit is to exist (public debt may not exceed 60% of Gross Domestic Product (GDP), and budgetary deficit may not exceed 3% of GDP). (iii) During the two years before entering the third stage of EMU, the national currency has to respect the 'normal' fluctuation margins in the narrow band of the ERM, 'without severe tensions' during the last two years and no devaluations shall have been undertaken on the member state's own initiative in the same period. (iv) The average long-term interest rate in the member state should not exceed those of the three best performing member states by more than two percentage points. Apart from these four criteria the national central bank would have to be independent from its national government. Also there should be no monetary financing of the budget.

member states governments make difficult adjustments. In particular it required a serious restructuring of public finance and government spending. It also meant restrictive policies in the area of monetary policy in order to guarantee low inflation and stable exchange rates, as well as making the national central bank independent from elected politicians. Yet, to everyone's surprise, countries like Ireland, Italy, Portugal, and Spain performed amazingly well on these criteria in the course of the 1990s. By contrast, France and Germany, despite their initial showing, were having more difficulty meeting the debt and deficit criteria in the second half of the 1990s. When in May 1998 the European Council formally named the *eleven* member states that were to join the single currency, many realized that, due to the sheer size of the group of participating countries, a much more far-reaching project had come to completion than had been anticipated.[2]

The focus on the role of the convergence criteria distracts our attention from the underlying reasons why EMU happened. As will be discussed in the next section, there are a large number of explanations of that process. Many analyses focus on the role of spillover from the single market and EMS, national government preferences, domestic politics, globalization, and so on. But what will be argued here is that, for a full understanding of why EMU happened, one is well advised to pay close attention to the development of ideas about monetary policy and economic and monetary integration more generally. It will also become clear that not all actors in all member states at all times hold the same ideas about the role of monetary policy. In fact, when EMU was under attack in the mid-1990s, it was because some groups (such as newly elected left of center governments) felt that EMU did not allow for a regime of policy-making that they desired. However, the underlying support for EMU was strong enough to allow 'Euroland' to be created.

Economic and Monetary Union has clearly been at the core of the development of European integration over the past decades. It has also witnessed every possible characteristic of European integration. Referring back to the four themes of this book, it has seen risks, reform, resistance, and revival. EMU was not originally incorporated in the Treaty of Rome, as it was the type of integration that the leaders at the time considered to be too *risky*. They did not dare to pursue that goal. Yet by the late 1960s, the plan to create an EMU received support as the customs union in the

---

[2] The eleven countries that have entered the third stage of EMU—more popularly known as 'Euroland'—are Austria, Belgium, Finland, France, Germany, Ireland, Italy, Luxembourg, The Netherlands, Portugal, and Spain. Greece had wanted to join, but it was rejected as it was judged as not having met the 'convergence criteria'. By contrast, Denmark, Sweden, and the UK chose not to join the third stage of EMU from the outset.

European Community had been completed. It was hoped that EMU could serve as an engine to keep the integration motor running. By the 1970s it had become clear, however, that the EMU goal had been too ambitious, given that member states held divergent views as to how to achieve EMU. EMU witnessed *revival* in the 1980s as the plan was relaunched after the Single European Market program seemed to take off, and the Exchange Rate Mechanism (ERM) of the European Monetary System (EMS) had been operating quite successfully. At this point member state governments held more similar ideas about the role and aim of monetary policy and thus monetary integration. Thus the original EMU plan was *reformed* in order to reflect these changes in ideas. The incorporation of EMU into the Treaty on European Union (TEU) at Maastricht in 1992 was a major achievement, although not achieved without considerable *resistance* from the UK government. However, by the mid-1990s doubt occurred. *Resistance* came from various member state governments and from a variety of domestic groups and European citizens. Amazingly by the late 1990s a *revival* could be seen when as many as eleven member states joined EMU. Moreover, those who were initially more skeptical were aiming at joining EMU in the near future. In addition, countries applying for membership of the EU were also keen to become part of Euroland.

This chapter examines why the plan to create EMU occurred in the European Community/European Union[3] during the 1980s and 1990s. It reviews the literature on EMU and argues the importance of taking an ideational perspective. Furthermore, the chapter discusses what challenges were posed to the plan to create EMU in the 1990s and how EMU survived. The following section reviews the various theoretical explanations of why EMU happened. It briefly discusses why the EMU plan failed in the 1970s, then moves on to discuss three approaches to explaining why EMU happened, pointing to their strengths and weaknesses. The next section discusses the 'ideational approach' and clarifies how it contributes to our broader understanding of why EMU happened. This is followed by a historical overview of the process creating EMU and illustrates the importance of the role of ideas. It elaborates how this road to EMU has advanced a particular design of EMU and discusses the development to EMU in the 1990s. The concluding section speculates about the conditions under which EMU may pose serious challenges to the integration process and offers suggestions as to how such risks can be avoided. It also indicates how a 'successful' EMU may contribute to the broader integration process.

---

[3] Before the entering into force of the Treaty on European Union, on 1 Nov. 1993, the term European Community was used to refer to the three European Communities.

Why EMU?

Let us now turn to the question of why EMU happened, by starting at why the creation of EMU failed in the 1970s. There are two authoritative analyses of the EMU process in the 1970s. Douglas Kruse (1980) and Loukas Tsoukalis (1977) have each identified reasons why EMU floundered. Though each of them focused on the domestic situation and international bargaining at the EC level, both these authors independently come to the conclusion that ultimately the EMU process failed due to divergence in ideas about the process of economic and monetary integration against a background of changed international circumstances. Two changes in particular stand out. First, the Bretton Woods Agreement collapsed. It had secured a regime of more or less stable exchange rates in Europe and *vis-à-vis* the United States since the end of the Second World War. Second, economic conditions deteriorated. As a result of the oil crisis and the economic recession that followed, European countries were confronted with lack of economic growth, unemployment, and inflation. This posed a serious challenge to West European countries that had enjoyed almost three decades of more or less continuous growth. The various national governments reacted differently to these challenges. Ultimately the governments held different views on the appropriate responses.

The eventual collapse of EMU showed that there was still too much divergence in the underlying ideas of creating a monetary union. In particular there were two distinct visions of how economic and monetary integration could be obtained: that of the 'monetarists' and that of the 'economists'. The former, consisting of the governments of Belgium, France, and Luxembourg, believed the fixing of exchange rates would lead to further economic coordination. The governments of Germany, the Netherlands, and to a lesser extent Italy held the opposite view. Economic cooperation would have to be secured before moving to further monetary cooperation (fixing of exchange rates and ultimately the creation of a single currency).

Glenda Rosenthal emphasizes the importance of policy learning and socialization among monetary experts in the process of creating the EMU blueprint in the early 1970s (Rosenthal 1975). In her view, the experts' close cooperation was at the basis of making EMU possible during the negotiations in the late 1960s and early 1970s. She also stresses the irreconcilable differences between the two schools of thought as having ultimately caused the EMU process to come to a halt.

With the renewed momentum for the EMU process in the 1990s, the analyses of EMU have resurfaced (for a more comprehensive review of this literature, see Verdun 1998*b*, 2000*a*). There have been almost as many analyses of EMU as there have been approaches explaining European integration more generally. Though not all authors have necessarily self-identified themselves as fitting one or more of the various groups of approaches explaining European integration, one could categorize the analyses in the various approaches without doing too much injustice to their rich scholarly analyses. In fact, sometimes authors have adopted approaches that fit more than one 'category'. Let us look in turn at the following approaches: a neo-functionalist/neo-institutionalist or path-dependent approach; a domestic politics approach; realist and intergovernmentalist approaches; and the globalization and interdependency approaches. Then I will point to some weakness in these approaches and how an ideational approach might offer some insights.

A neo-functionalist, neo-institutionalist, or path-dependent analysis of EMU has been offered among others by Wayne Sandholtz (1993*a*; see also Campanella 1995). The argument is that a variety of factors contributed to the relaunch of EMU. The learning that had occurred due to participation in the ERM increased the domestic support for a monetary policy aimed at price stability. In addition, the Internal Market program gave rise to a widespread sense of Euro-optimism surrounding the 1992 project. It was felt that to fully benefit from the single market, a single currency would be beneficial. Furthermore, the increasing integration of capital markets generated the need for a regime of monetary stability. EC member states considered EMU a useful vehicle to institutionalize their commitment to low inflation and to secure fixed exchange rates.

A domestic politics approach has also been made in order to explain EMU (see e.g. Martin 1993). Some scholars have examined the specific domestic situation of a given country in order to explain why EMU was supported in that country. The Italian and German cases serve as primary examples. The Italian national government had been totally incapable of governing the country effectively. European integration more generally and EMU in particular were gratefully taken on board by the political élite and the citizens as a way to deal with problems in the domestic arena (Dyson and Featherstone 1996; Croci and Picci 1999; Quaglia 1999). It is remarkable that the Italian citizens and their national governments have consistently been very pro European integration. Some authors have examined this phenomenon by adopting Putnam's two-level game metaphor (Putnam 1988; Wolf and Zangl 1996; see also Dyson 1994).

A somewhat different conclusion is reached when a domestic politics approach is used to clarify the case of Germany. Many observers have asked why the German government was willing to agree to EMU. Given that the German monetary authorities were *de facto* the hegemon, why were they willing to give up that position? Under the EMS the German monetary authorities determined monetary policy for Germany based on their own indicators of the German domestic economy. Other EMS countries, in turn, closely followed these monetary policies. Not certain that the time or conditions were right, the German central bank, the Bundesbank, was skeptical about EMU. A domestic politics approach shows that the Kohl government was willing to accept EMU because it saw EMU as being firmly based on German principles of stability and central bank independence (see e.g. Henning 1994: 228–37). The Kohl government was willing to put aside the Bundesbank's scepticism because of its own pro-European stance. Moreover, other domestic actors in Germany were in favor of EMU.

Erik Jones, Jeffrey Frieden, and Francisco Torres (1998) analyze the process of accepting EMU in various smaller member states. The interesting phenomenon here is that they find that there is no 'small country explanation' of why EMU happened. Their analyses seem to suggest that EMU occurred because it served domestic actors in different ways. It should be noted, however, that the analyses of these smaller member states—such as Austria, the Benelux, Iberian, and Scandinavian countries—point to international factors, globalization, and financial market integration as having been important for the realization by national monetary authorities of the limited room for maneuver in macro-economic and monetary policy-making. Jones *et al.* do not claim, however, that monetary integration is in any way inevitable.

The international dimension of the domestic politics approach and two-level games analyses have much in common with a realist analysis of EMU. The realist view examines the role of national governments in international politics. It would generally not expect international cooperation to occur because national governments will resist surrendering national sovereignty to a supranational organization. In this view, one can expect cooperation only when national governments would enjoy net gains from it. Let us look at two examples.

As has been briefly alluded to, the case of monetary cooperation in the 1980s shows that some governments had *de facto* given up a large degree of sovereignty over monetary policy-making. In making sure their currencies stayed in the ERM without having to be devalued too frequently, national governments—such as those of the Benelux countries, France, and Italy—had shadowed German monetary policies. This situation, in which German monetary authorities *de facto* were setting monetary policies for the EMS countries, was not very attractive for the EMS countries in the longer run. Their governments desired a greater voice in EC monetary policy. As such a realist account can understand why EMU could have emerged (Grieco 1995).

Germany had other reasons for joining EMU. German reunification implied that Germany needed to show the rest of Europe that it would remain committed to the European integration objective. Some authors argue that the EMU arrangement, as set out in the TEU, shows that Germany managed to dominate the international bargaining arena. Others reject this interpretation because the TEU wording kept the door open to member states who would not have had the German-type commitment to price stability (Garrett 1993). This kind of analysis sees the reason for German acceptance of this 'suboptimal outcome' as having to be found in the international circumstances at the time of the Maastricht negotiations. That is, German reunification and the demise of the Soviet empire led to the German government wanting to signal a broader political commitment to deepening European integration.

Closely connected to the realist approach is the liberal intergovernmentalist approach (Moravcsik 1998). Like the realist approach, this approach focuses strongly on the role of national governments, in particular those of the larger member states. This approach is referred to as 'liberal' in that it derives its understanding of 'state preferences' from the underlying economic interests in society. In this analysis, national governments are seen as 'unitary actors', not because they are, but because they can be seen to act 'as if' they are unitary. Moreover, the national governments are seen as acting rationally and aim at safeguarding the 'national interest'. The conclusion is that the EMU package in the TEU is in no way a result of unintended consequences, or path dependence. Rather, it is the result of careful negotiation and bargaining of national governments, reflecting in particular the interests of the most powerful member states. In this view the process can be best analyzed by assuming that national governments formulate preferences, then engage in interstate bargaining and finally decide whether or not to delegate or pool sovereignty (Moravcsik 1998: 473). This analysis offers us an interesting insight into the EMU process as based on bargaining between national governments, but does not credit significant explanatory power to a number of other factors identified by others as having been important to the EMU process, such as changed international circumstances, globalization, or changes in the ideas over monetary policy-making and the role of experts.

The interdependency or globalization argument to explain EMU has been made by authors such as David Andrews, Kenneth Dyson, Louis Pauly, and others. This view stresses that the EMU process cannot be understood merely by looking at path dependence, spillover mechanisms, domestic politics, or international bargaining. In this view, external developments provided the major impetus for the Maastricht Treaty. Especially structural changes in economics and politics have led national governments to redefine interests. The global integration of financial markets and the interdependence of the European economies have made national monetary authorities governments less capable of pursuing independent monetary policies (Andrews 1993; Pauly 1992). Kenneth Dyson's analysis emphasizes how bargaining happened in a framework of structures over which the actors involved had limited influence (Dyson 1994).

We can now place the various approaches into three groups: (1) the neofunctionalist, neoinstitutionalist, path-dependence approaches (NNP); (2) domestic politics, realism, and intergovernmentalism (DRI); (3) globalization, interdependence, internationalization approaches (GII).

The approaches in the NNP group emphasize the importance of institutions, spillover, and path dependence. In this view domestic and European institutions play an important role because they set the rules of the game. Spillover happens because integration in one policy area will eventually lead to further integration in that and other policy areas. Societal actors and technocrats are here also considered to be important actors. National governments are given relatively little attention in the analysis. What the approaches in this group do less well, however, is to specify *when* and *how* integration happens. It is clear from these approaches *that* integration at some point *will* happen. But these approaches fail to clarify the conditions under which integration may or may not occur. It also is not clear what determines what integration will look like. Finally, NNP sees a role for many different actors, but it is not spelled out exactly how these actors make a difference.

The approaches in the DRI group focus in particular on the role of governments in determining the outcome of the integration process. Other actors are considered merely as shaping the preferences of the national governments. National governments are perceived to aim at safeguarding their interests based on rational expectations of the outcomes, given their preferences. The latter, in turn, are derived from either the economic interests of societal actors, from the government's judgement about its role in the rest of the world, or from the specific domestic circumstances. The DRI group does a good job in explaining the behavior of national governments and also the variance between them. What is lacking in these approaches, however, is a significant role for the kinds of actors and factors that the NNP group identifies. Most importantly, we require an insight into who and what shape preferences in the first place. Ideas only play a minor role in the DRI group's analysis of integration. As will be seen below, an ideational perspective makes clear why preferences converge easily. For this to happen we need to allow space in our analysis for several non-governmental actors, as well as a learning process that led to certain ideas becoming acceptable.

The approaches in the GII group are the most eclectic of the three. They have emerged in response to the failure of the classical integration theories to pay heed to international circumstances. The GII approaches stress the way in which national governments, national and European institutions, and other actors are confronted with changes in the global economy. As a result of the increasing interdependence caused by 'globalization' and 'Europeanization', individual actors cannot act in isolation from others. The whole context in which integration is happening is determined by this change. In the European case, the fact that integration has already progressed quite significantly in various areas, means Europeanization poses a certain constraint or opportunity for further decisions. The approaches in the GII group share some of the assumptions about the integration process with the NNP group. The crucial difference is the weight placed on external constraints. As with NNP, these approaches do not spell out when the international circumstances are significant enough to lead to further European integration or standstill. To use the terms set out in Chapter 1 above, it is not clear when international factors lead to revival or resistance. The ideational approach can be used to shed some light on this issue.

Thus, the benefits of taking an ideational approach are threefold. First, it offers further understanding as to why new steps are taken in the integration process. It explains how this process occurs and who are the important actors. It thereby complements the approaches in the NNP group. Second, it adds to our understanding of the choices made by governments, keeping in mind that governments are not the only important actors. National governments in many ways reflect the consensus about policy-making as held by a wider community of experts. An ideational approach also extends our understanding about how national government preferences are formed. It places the focus beyond mere economic and strategic interests into the realm of ideas. In doing so it enriches the DRI approaches. Third, an ideational approach builds on the understanding generated by the GII group. It proposes to look at ideas in order to determine when international circumstances will or will not lead to further European integration.

Ideational Approach and EMU

The above-mentioned theoretical approaches all have the capacity to explain an element of the puzzle of why EMU happened. It is argued here that underlying all these approaches are various ideas about monetary policy. Convergence in ideas about economic and monetary integration was a crucial factor in making the EMU project possible.

First of all there are ideas about the nature of and path to economic and monetary unification. In the 1970s, as we have seen above, there was a strong disagreement between the 'economists' and the 'monetarists' on this matter. Subsequently the focus on EMU disappeared and exchange rate cooperation came to the forefront. In the course of the 1980s consensus emerged about what monetary policy still could and should do. During this decade, there was a convergence of ideas among monetary experts who believed that monetary policies should be geared towards price stability. They also agreed that there was no trade-off between inflation and unemployment. Thus there was no need to view monetary policy as being capable of redistributive tasks. Another changed view was that to be successful in guaranteeing stable exchange rates, monetary policies had to be credible (see Artis and Winkler 1997). The strategy that was subsequently adopted was to follow the German monetary policies. Finally it was thought that the room for maneuver over monetary policy in individual member states had become seriously reduced due to financial integration in Europe and the rest of the world. It had become clear that monetary authorities were confronted with what has been dubbed by Tomasso Padoa-Schioppa the 'inconsistent quartet'. This means that one cannot have free trade, free movement of capital, fixed exchange rates, and monetary policy autonomy (Padoa-Schioppa 1994: 4; see also McNamara 1998).

Related to the role of monetary policy, there is the role of economic policy. The acronym EMU stands for *Economic* and Monetary Union (*not*, as is often mistakenly thought, *European* Monetary Union). From the outset it was believed that monetary union could not occur without some further integration in other areas of macro-economic policy-making (such as fiscal policy). Early European economic integration scholars spoke about the various stages of economic integration: free trade agreement, customs union, single market, economic and monetary union, and full economic union (Balassa 1961, 1975; Tinbergen 1965). In these early writings, economic and monetary union implied some halfway house between a single market and a fully fledged economic union with integration of a broad range of areas of policy-making (thereby resembling a federal state). Thus, the question had been since the outset: how much economic integration is needed to flank monetary union? At the time of the Werner Report (1970), which set out the blueprint for EMU in the 1970s, it was still thought that considerable coordination of fiscal policy was necessary. Also it was believed that EMU would imply a larger European budget and larger transfer payments to the various member states. However, by the 1980s, ideas about what was needed to create EMU had changed considerably. True, the Single European Act (SEA) and its plan to complete the Single

Market had meant that significant progress had been achieved in this area. Perhaps more importantly, the fact that the ideas about economic and monetary integration had changed such that there was now no need to place so much emphasis on economic integration implied that there was a window of opportunity to create EMU.

In other words, a change in ideas over monetary policies emerged that made the monetary options from which to choose fairly limited. This development in ideas is crucial in order to understand why EMU happened. In addition to the change in ideas over monetary policy, the ideas also changed about the overall role of governments. As we shall see in the next section the ideas about the overall role of governments in the context of a changed international environment provided another shared belief about the options to choose from.

This ideational approach focuses on how ideas have become accepted in a wider policy community, given some of the changes in the global economy. The wider policy community referred to here involves national and international experts in the widest sense, for example, academics, bureaucrats, or 'technocrats'. In the latter category one would also count the central banking community, the research staff working at the international organizations. In the case of economic, monetary and financial issues these would include the International Monetary Fund (IMF), the World Bank, the Organization of Economic Cooperation and Development (OECD), and the European Commission (in particular Directorate General II—Economic and Financial Affairs). One would also include in this wider policy community the leading financial and economic press (e.g. *The Financial Times, The Economist*). In a way this approach builds on the research carried out by Glenda Rosenthal in the 1970s.

An ideational approach has been applied to the case of EMU by various scholars (*inter alia* Dyson 1994; Marcussen 1997, 1998a, 1998b; McNamara 1998; Risse *et al.* 1999; Verdun 1999, 2000b). These analyses show how the ideas of sound monetary policies have become embedded in the policy choices. Dyson (1994) has found that the central actors also held certain economic beliefs concerning EMS and EMU that structured their views of what were viable choices. Martin Marcussen (1998*a*) offers various ideational analyses in which he shows how ideas about monetary policy were changed and formed the basis of consensus in the 1980s. He focuses in particular on the role of central bankers. Kathleen McNamara (1998) has also showed the importance of convergence in ideas in order to understand the success of the EMS in the 1980s.

A study on the role of experts in the creation of EMU has emphasized how the final outcome of the EMU process has been predominantly constructed by monetary experts, in particular those from the central banking community (Verdun 1999). This is not to say that politics does not matter (see also Radaelli 1999). The study argues that the Delors Committee, which drafted the blueprint for EMU, operated as an epistemic community. It thereby created the kind of EMU that was logical from the perspective of the central banking community and of economists favorable to the European integration project. However, to fully appreciate the process one needs to examine why national governments decided to ask a group of mainly central bankers to draft a blueprint, and eventually to incorporate this proposal in the TEU with only minor changes. The reason is that it was the only way forward at that point in time. The consensus in ideas was held by the central bankers. Policy learning had occurred about the role of monetary policy in an interdependent world. Moreover, the status quo was not really desirable. Many believed that the German-dominated system could be replaced by a European system. Thus, a step 'forward' required that the institutional design remained close to the status quo and implied institutionalizing a German-type monetary regime. The importance and role of experts is not restricted only to the process of drafting a blueprint for EMU. Other EU committees such as the monetary committee and the committee of central bank governors (subsequently the European Monetary Institute and now the European Central Bank) also have played an important role in creating common ideas, a common language, and long-term commitment to policy objectives (Verdun 2000*b*).

Summarizing, the advantage of using an ideational approach over the other approaches discussed above is that the ideational approach provides the context in which the integration process takes place. For example, to understand how preferences are formed, it is necessary to understand the broader framework of possible acceptable positions that governments can take, given the development of common ideas. The point here is not to state that the ideational approach is superior to all others. Rather the reader is invited to consider the importance of commonly held ideas as providing a context within which the integration process moves forward or halts, as well as a vehicle which drives the integration process forward.

The Road to a Monetary and Neoliberal Mode of Governance

Based on a discussion of theoretical approaches that explain EMU, we have emphasized the importance of having common ideas about the core aim of economic and monetary policy-making. It was suggested that common ideas might underlie all of the approaches mentioned. Even though it is not the aim of this chapter to test that hypothesis, let us elaborate on this view a little further and illustrate it by looking at the evolution of

EMU and how these common ideas came about and shaped the EMU process.

The history of European economic and monetary integration is well known. The end of the Bretton Woods Agreement in the 1970s led to the so-called snake, an exchange rate agreement of European currencies. It was not very successful and was succeeded in 1979 by the EMS and its exchange rate mechanism (ERM). The ERM was unstable at the outset. Many de- and revaluations were necessary in the period 1979–83. An important turnaround came in 1983 when the French President François Mitterrand realized that he could not pursue 'socialist policies' in one country. His policies diverged so much from those in other Western countries that financial markets reacted and led to a downward pressure on the French franc. The idea was abandoned that a national government could pursue monetary policies that were significantly different from those of other West European countries. The French experience had a profound effect on other countries, in particular the Southern European states (though in the Italian case the actual change in policy took a few years longer to materialize: Walsh 1999). It became regular practice of ERM countries to closely focus on German monetary policies. This led to what some observers have called 'ten minute sovereignty';[4] once the German Bundesbank had announced to change its interest rates, the monetary authorities in surrounding countries would soon follow.

A few other factors led to further cooperation in the area of monetary policy-making. First of all, the wider global phenomenon of financial market integration and internationalization made policies more interdependent. In addition, EC member states decided in the mid-1980s to liberalize capital markets by 1 July 1990. This implied that the real capacity of national monetary authorities to pursue monetary policies divergent from others had become virtually impossible. The reason that member state governments agreed to further liberalization and integration was because they had decided that market principles should prevail. Moreover, as regards monetary policy, the focus was on low inflation and stable exchange rates. These were the objectives that were strongly supported. Once these objectives *de facto* were accepted and continued to be accepted for a number of years, they became the obvious basis of EMU.

Some observers have criticized this focus on a neoliberal model for Europe (see e.g. Gill 1997; Leander and Guzzini 1997; Moss and Michie 1998). They argue that this neoliberal Europe is doing away with good governance, and that big business and the 'tyranny' of the market

---

[4] Philippe de Schouteete paraphrased the behavior of the Belgian monetary authorities in this way.

will threaten the welfare states of Europe. The interesting observation, however, as we have seen above, is that when EMU was being negotiated, many domestic actors accepted that particular context and held similar ideas about monetary policies (Verdun 2000a). Trade unions, employers' organizations, and monetary authorities also accepted the broader globalization process. In addition, the representatives of the various domestic groups represented in the Economic and Social Committee took this particular angle on the economic and monetary integration process (Economic and Social Committee 1990, 1991).

It should be noted that those who were most concerned, that is, trade unions and the representatives of the weaker segments in society, as well as the French government in the late 1980s and late 1990s, felt that a European System of Central Banks (ESCB) needed to be flanked by some kind of 'economic government' at the EU level. But none felt that the general underlying ideas about the role or purpose of monetary policy-making or the wider deregulated, global, market-oriented focus would change (Verdun 2000a). In fact, trade unions were cautiously supportive of EMU. They wanted to participate in the discussions and create this particular type of EMU in order to put items on the agenda that they were most concerned about. Without EMU they felt they would lose even more terrain. As corporatist consultation models were giving way, trade unions felt they needed to institutionalize themselves in the European arena. By agreeing to EMU and adding their agenda points (social and employment issues), they wanted to influence the process not by fundamentally changing it but by putting it in perspective and creating other policies at the EU level (Verdun 2000a).

Perceptions of EMU held by other domestic actors in Britain, France, and Germany showed a strong support for this particular type of EMU. Employers' organizations, central banks, and Ministries of Finance were willing to embark on this new project (except that the British Treasury was unwilling to join EMU from the outset). These actors accepted EMU as a way to pursue neoliberal policies. At the same time, EMU offered a policy instrument that could be used to influence monetary policy that many had accepted as not any longer under the control of any given government or other actor. They considered EMU as a means to institutionalize the monetary policy regime but also saw it as a vehicle for regaining some power over policy-making. EMU was also taken on board as a disciplinary tool to restructure the domestic economy (public finance and the welfare state). In addition, each of the actors also had specific reasons that led them to support EMU. Even the actors that held a more reserved position *vis-à-vis* EMU were not in total opposition to it, and perceived EMU as possibly being more desirable at a future date.

As the 1990s proceeded and recession struck the EU member states, more concerns arose about EMU and its possible effect on unemployment. Also the question was posed whether a single monetary policy for the EMU-zone would at all times be good for all parts of Euroland. The discussion re-emerged about the fact that EMU was not flanked by either an 'economic government' or a serious increase in the EU budget and subsequently there were no planned increased transfer payments. The latter, referred to as fiscal federalism, is the case in mature federations.

EMU encountered difficulties in more than one way. The ERM crises in the early 1990s caused many an observer to wonder whether EMU could be rescued. The Treaty on European Union provisions had stipulated that currencies needed to stay within the narrow band of the ERM. Until 1992 currencies had nicely stayed within this narrow band. Between 1992 and 1993 currencies fluctuated heavily, which eventually led to the abandoning of the narrow bands. Although the exchange rate bands were stretched from ± 2.25 per cent to ± 15 per cent, it was obvious that the wording in the Treaty referred to maintaining the exchange rates within the original bands. It was remarkable that monetary authorities of the ERM countries nevertheless tried to aim at the 2.25 per cent bands. Most of the time they managed to meet that target. It was clear that the monetary authorities of ERM countries were convinced that keeping exchange rates within the original narrow bands was worth pursuing. The reason the bands were stretched was to avoid a currency becoming the subject of currency speculators.

Another difficulty was the meeting of the convergence criteria. Already in the Delors Report (1989) the idea was mentioned of having member states subject to limits on budgetary deficits and public debts. However the actual reference figures chosen—that budgetary deficit should not exceed 3 per cent of Gross Domestic Product (GDP) and public debt should not exceed 60 per cent of GDP—was decided by the Monetary Committee (Verdun 2000*b*). These criteria were chosen as an upper limit for debts and deficits based on some kind of average of the EC member states. The language in the Treaty was to ensure that member states whose original debt or deficit had been very high, but who had made considerable effort, would be able to join EMU. By 1993 it had become clear that most member states were unable to meet the criteria. However, by the mid-1990s the governments of Portugal, Spain, Italy, Ireland, and the Netherlands had made considerable progress towards securing a lower public debt and budgetary deficit. In Portugal and Spain, restructuring of the public sector took place. In Italy, a 'European tax' was levied which was used to reduce the budgetary deficit. Ireland and the Netherlands managed to move both their public debt and budgetary deficit in the downward direction so considerably that it soon was labeled 'ready' for EMU. By contrast, France and Germany, the two countries without whom EMU was unthinkable, were not performing as well. Speculation even arose as to whether or not both countries were guilty of 'creative accounting' in order to meet the convergence criteria. By the spring of 1998, however, with the exception of Greece, all member states who wanted to join EMU, were considered to have met the criteria (Commission 1998*d*).

Another controversial point was the Stability Pact. By the end of 1995 the German government had made clear that guarantees would have to be made that would secure that debts and deficits would remain low even after EMU had entered its final stage ('Stabilitätspakt für Europa' 1995; Artis and Winkler 1997). This pact was subsequently heavily criticized by the trade unions and others who were worried that the convergence criteria could lead to deflationary spirals and cause unemployment to rise. The compromise was a 'Stability and Growth Pact', the wording of which satisfied the advocates of both camps.

Towards the end of the 1990s another challenge to EMU occurred: social-democratic parties came to power in many of the EU member states (see Chapter 14 below). By 1998 there were left of center governments in office in France, Germany, Italy, the Netherlands, the UK, and various other member states. Social-democratic parties had traditionally been more resistant to the free operation of market principles. EMU as it was designed was very much based on a limited role for national and European governments. The convergence criteria required that governments reduced their public debt and budgetary deficits. Moreover, EMU assumed that monetary policy remained outside the influence of national politicians.

However, interestingly enough, these left of center governments did not put EMU in danger, even though some governments—such as the Jospin government of France—again voiced the need to create an economic government (Howarth 1999; see also Chapter 6 below). Rather, these left of center governments accepted EMU as a context within which they needed to develop policies that could lead to further economic growth and national redistribution. They even accepted the 'convergence criteria' and later the 'Stability and Growth Pact'. These restricted the increase of budgetary deficits and public debts to pay for increasing expenses. It is quite remarkable that even the left of center governments have accepted the overall regime that EMU requires. They have accepted neoliberal ideas of governance and institution-building in the EU.

Having said that, current governments would, of course, have a hard time departing from the ideas and rules embedded strongly in the TEU. During the IGCs in 1990 and 1991, the German government had emphasized the need to embed the rules of EMU and the mandate of the

European Central Bank (ECB) firmly in the TEU, so that future generations of politicians could not easily change the rules. This was ironic because the German government was the first government to really criticize the EMU model and the insistence on price stability as the primary mandate of the ECB. In the autumn of 1998 an SPD–Green government came to power in Germany. Its Finance Minister Oskar Lafontaine made a variety of public speeches in which he strongly disagreed with the policies of the ECB. He recommended that the ECB reduce interest rates in order to stimulate the economy. It was the prospect of exactly this kind of policy recommendation by politicians that had led those who designed EMU to embed the European Central Bank's mandate of price stability firmly in the TEU. The Prime Minister Gerhard Schröder did not share the views of Lafontaine. and this clash of views, among other reasons, eventually brought about Lafontaine's resignation in March 1999.

Until very recently, there was strong support for the 'monetarist' and 'neoliberal' mode of governance over economic and monetary policy-making as well as EMU's institutional design. This implied support for the 'asymmetrical' relationship between economic and monetary policy, and subsequently its institutional design (see Verdun 1996, 1998*a*). Thus there has been support for the transfer of sovereignty over monetary policy to the 'supranational' level and for a completely politically independent ECB to conduct this policy. At the same time budgetary and fiscal policy (macroeconomic policy-making, that is, government spending and fiscal policy) remains at the national level. The current EMU design envisages an ECB that has as its mandate to maintain price stability (which the ECB has defined as no more than 2 per cent inflation). The ECB's mandate implies that it may not endanger that objective in order to promote other macroeconomic objectives, such as economic growth or employment. The ECB's political independence is firmly anchored in the TEU: no one may seek to give instructions to the ECB.

Since the signing of the Maastricht Treaty in 1992, EMU's institutional design and policy objective have been attracting opposition from the public and domestic/European actors as well as from certain governments. In recent years these dissenting views have become more vocal. Especially after the Schröder government took office in Germany in the autumn of 1998, those that favor change to EMU's design or policy objectives have felt their position strengthened and have voiced forceful criticism. With the departure of Oskar Lafontaine some of these voices weakened. But the criticism on EMU was not merely restricted to the question of what EMU can do to improve the economic output of the EU: its institutional design was condemned as insufficiently democratic, legitimate, and accountable (Verdun 1998a).

Conclusions: Future Challenges

Economic and Monetary Union happened because there was a strong convergence in ideas about the aim of monetary policy and the design of EMU. It meant institutionalizing an exchange rate regime and monetary policies based on price stability. The contents of 'economic union' had been watered down. In contrast to the idea in the 1970s, EMU did not imply major transfer payments or the development of an economic government. These ideas were more or less abandoned in the course of the 1980s and 1990s, even though at times they would briefly reemerge. Without this strong consensus about the aim of monetary policy and the design of EMU, it is unlikely that EMU would have happened. An ideational approach nicely complements the other theoretical approaches in explaining why EMU happened.

For EMU to succeed and be a positive development in the European integration process, it is imperative that its particular design and mandate continue to receive sustained widespread support throughout the EU. If amendments are deemed necessary, proposals for change will need to receive widespread support. By contrast, if it turns out that there are stark divisions in the EU about EMU's design and objectives, EMU may end up posing a serious risk to the integration process. This is particularly the case because a change in the ECB mandate requires a change in the Treaty, and thus a unanimous decision by the European Council and subsequent parliamentary ratification in all member states.

EMU has been the result of the revival of the European integration project in the mid-1980s, which also led to a serious reform of the EU in the form of a major Treaty amendment. As we have also seen, just creating the new institutions and objectives does not mean that resistance does not occur. In fact, the 1990s witnessed quite a bit of resistance against the rigid rules imposed by the convergence criteria and the Stability and Growth Pact. Ultimately the risks of a deadlock were overcome and as many as eleven member states participated in EMU. As such EMU has ultimately contributed to the revival of the European integration process.

EMU will lead to further revival of the EU if there remains a clear consensus and widespread support for common ideas on the objectives of economic and monetary policy. By contrast, EMU may end up posing a serious risk to the integration process if governments, the ECB, societal actors, and public opinion *disagree* about the aims of monetary policy and EMU's design. EMU could also pose a serious risk to the integration process if the costs and benefits of EMU were to be unevenly spread across the EU member states, the sectors, regions, and citizens. This situation would become particularly challenging if it was perceived that no European or national government wanted to take responsibility for an uneven distribution of the costs and benefits of EMU. (On the political economy of adjustment, see Chapter 7 below.) If this was the case, and if the EU recognized the need to change its institutional design, EMU may actually lead to reform. The EU would need to change its institutions or policies to correct the imbalance. EMU has taken the EU on a road into an uncertain future, with many chances for resistance, reform, or revival. Whatever the outcome, it is a risk worth taking.

6

The Battle between ECOFIN-11 and the European Central Bank: A Strategic Interaction Perspective

MIRIAM L. CAMPANELLA

Introduction

Since its creation, the European Central Bank (ECB) has experienced strained relations with its political counterparts, the Council of Ministers and the Economic and Finance Ministers of the eleven countries taking part in the common currency (ECOFIN-11).[1] In May 1988, discussions over the appointment of the ECB president in May 1998 erupted into an ugly dispute over the name and the term length of the bank's president. The dispute intensified following the victory of the red–green coalition in Germany in September 1998. Led by the French and German Finance Ministers of the time, the battle shifted attention to less symbolic and more substantial issues: namely, the bank's monetary and exchange rate policy, and the creation of a 'gouvernment économique' (economic government). The political authorities, taken singularly as national representatives or in their clothing as European intergovernmental bodies, continued to pay lip-service to the ECB's granted independence. At the same time, they made no mystery of the claim that a coordinated policy and even an informal institution—this 'gouvernment économique'—should provide a sort of counterweight to the independence of the newly appointed monetary authorities. Thus, the ECB, greeted as the major achievement of the EMU project, was called to flex its muscles even before

The author would like to thank Sylvester Eijffinger, Ivo Maes, and David Mayes for useful comments on an earlier version of this chapter. To Maria Green Cowles, Michael Smith, and to an anonymous reviewer she is specially grateful for the final revision. The usual disclaimer applies.

[1] ECOFIN-11 and Euro-11 Group are the names given to informal meetings of the Ministers of Finance and Economic Affairs of countries participating in the Euro area. The first ECOFIN-11 meeting was held in June 1998.

it was due to begin operations. Independence from political authorities—pivotal to the new central bank—was under attack.

One of the factors urging Euro-11 political officials to take action in these delicate issues was certainly the gloomy prospect of a major economic slowdown in the eleven Euro-countries in the year to come. According to the forecasts of the International Monetary Fund in October 1998, the global 'output gap' for 1999 (the difference between actual and potential production) was predicted to be at its widest since the 1930s. The Euro economies were expected to grow at only 2 per cent, compared to the previous forecast of 3 per cent, while the threat of output and prices falling together suggested a 1930s-like crisis (IMF 1998). The government representatives were concerned that central banks in Europe as well in the USA and Japan could turn a 'deaf ear to calls for monetary expansion'. This would occur at a time when the inflation rate was a mere 1 per cent (the lowest rate for a half a century), while a deflationary trend—a 'new and possibly more dangerous' enemy—threatened.[2] For many Euro-11 countries, a persistent 12 per cent record level of unemployment exacerbated this gloomy forecast.

The ensuing institutional battle between the ECB and ECOFIN-11 was an important one. Indeed, in keeping with the themes of this volume, it posed serious risks to the independence of the European Central Bank and to the viability of the EMU project in general. The battle highlighted the government representatives' resistance to handing over the reins of monetary and exchange rate policy. In turn, the inter-institutional conflict demonstrated the ECB officials' resistance to the governments' political demands for greater macro-economic coordination. As discussed in this chapter, the outcome of the events in 1998–9 was important in that this inter-institutional confrontation may reemerge in the future. The ability of the ECB to preserve its independence will be an important determinant of the success of EMU—and the renewal of the EU project in general.

This chapter employs a strategic interaction approach (Fratianni and Hagen 1990; Muscatelli 1997) to explain the conflict between the ECB and ECOFIN-11, and incorporates the theoretical game of chicken (Morrow 1994: 93) to highlight the preferences of the two parties and ensuing dynamics. The strategic interaction approach would predict the emergence of a battle for political dominance, where the fiscal authorities are likely to want the bank to subscribe to their own preferences, while the bank resists these pressures and sticks to its own prerogatives. The resulting inter-institutional dynamic develops within a standard agent/principal relationship that links the ECB (the agent) and the Council of Ministers (the

---

[2] See 'The New Danger', *The Economist* (20 Feb. 1999), 15–16.

principal). However, as the latter has transferred monetary policy to the former in order to solve a time inconsistency dilemma with a third actor, the market constituency, the central bank can turn its attention to this third actor, the market participants, and consider them as its own constituency to which it is must be accountable.[3] The bank has the power to offset the pressures exerted by political (elected) actors, as its activity and performance are now subject to market assessment. This triangular relationship sets up what I call an 'iterated strategic interaction', which describes a two-stage strategic positioning of the principal–agent pair, and offers an interesting forward-looking view of the likely path of inter-institutional dynamics within the EMU environment.

This chapter does not adopt a standard gametheoretic approach that involves a single, one-time game of chicken in which the two groups engage in a confrontation whereby each party seeks to dominate the other. This simple strategic game situation foresees a winner and a loser, but such an outcome cannot wholly apply to the case-study in this chapter. The two contestants, in fact, are in an iterated game (Axelrod 1984). They belong to the same EMU environment, and are expected to play this game over and over again. This signals that they are bound sooner or later to learn to calculate, before any move is made, the likely consequences of the other group's move on its own payoff. As this chapter suggests, ECOFIN must recognize the ECB's motives in resisting political pressures. The ECB's resistance can be seen as an important shaping force in the inter-institutional dynamic not only in the 1998–9 dispute, but also in the years to come.[4]

This iterated game also explains why the ECB does not always engage in bitter confrontation with ECOFIN-11. Indeed, when direct governmental pressures are removed, the bank will eventually review its resistance, settling for an accommodation with political authorities. Thus, the ECB can resolve to stand by the EMU Treaties that safeguard its institutional independence, but be willing to review its own posture when political pressure does not represent a major threat to its independent status.

The chapter is developed in three sections. The first section sets out the background facts relating the strategic positioning of the parties. The sec-

---

[3] Padoa-Schioppa (1997: 86). The European economic constitution compels not only the executive and legislative branches of member government to comply with the Treaties of the EC, but also firms and private markets at large.

[4] There are, of course, other pressures on the ECB not explored in this chapter. For example, some academics have questioned the bank's self-ruling policy in terms of accountability and transparency (Eijffinger 1998; Mayes 1999). They have proposed that the European Parliament, the major democratically elected institution in the EU, as the appropriate political authority to which the ECB should have to account for its monetary policy (Tabellini 1998).

ond section further analyzes the ECB and ECOFIN-11conflict over three major issues—'economic government', target zones, and interest rate policy—and offers some preliminary conclusions regarding the future path of the EMU inter-institutional dynamics. The conclusion reviews the monetary institutional debate and discusses its implications for the future of EU monetary policy.

Background of the Battle

> The idea of a political body that interacts with the ECB is shocking: Europe and the world have moved a healthy distance from short-term political control of monetary policy.
>
> (Dornbusch *et al.* 1998: 28).

The events, which occurred between autumn 1998 and April 1999, offer some evidence of the difficulties and challenges the ECB had to face in establishing a normal inter-institutional relationship with the political and fiscal authorities. Political pressures on the ECB were evident as early May 1998 with the designation of its president. From October 1998 to March 1999, the ECB coped with many challenges, which, if they had been successful, would have definitely eroded its major institutional asset—its reputation as the central bank that was the most independent (of political pressures) in the world. The crux of this battle occurred with the arrival of German Finance and Economy Minister Oskar Lafontaine, and ended with his departure on March 11, 1999. The ECB was able eventually to resist these pressures, and the German Finance Minister resigned both as Finance Minister and as leader of the SPD. The ECB then proceeded to trim the interest rate by a 'large' half point (50 basis points) on April 8, 1999, while the Euro was depreciating against the US dollar by 10 per cent and a money supply growth (M3) was rising faster (5.1) than the bank's reference value (4.5 per cent). Why did the ECB paradoxically refuse to lower interest rates when Lafontaine and others were demanding that rates be lowered—and then proceed to trim the rates following his departure despite the monetary situation at the time? Some analysts have regarded this sequence of events as a sign that the bank is not yet a grown-up institution or, worse, as evidence of internal ECB confusion. As discussed below, this development can better be explained as part of the bank's institutional posturing *vis-à-vis* the political authorities.

The centerpiece of the row between the ECB and the political authorities was the issue of macroeconomic coordination. Though international macroeconomic coordination is a somewhat unsettled issue in the academic literature (Vaubel 1985; Gosh and Masson 1994; Muscatelli 1997), it has a certain credence in EU political circles, having been mentioned in the 1974 Werner Report. There the idea is raised of creating an institutionalized coordination body, defined as a 'center of decision for economic policy', to take the lead in community-wide economic policy. Though vague in details, the Werner Plan sketches out the creation of an economic center dedicated to putting forward the Community's interest:

> The center . . . will exercise in an independent way . . . a decisive influence over the general policy of the Community. Given that the role of the Community budget as a conjunctural instrument will be insufficient, the Community's center of decision making has to take the appropriate measures suitable to influence national budget policy. In particular, the level and the content of expenditure as well as the methods of deficit financing and the use of surpluses should be monitored and assessed. Further, *any change in the parities of the new currency or of the basket of the national currencies should be handled by this Center.* Eventually, in order to ensure the necessary link with general economic policy, its responsibility should be extended to other domains of economic and social policy which are being transferred to the Community level.[5]

Whether the Werner Plan's 'center of decision' reflected the French 'dirigiste' preference or the more generalized Keynesian mood of the 1970s is not known. However, the architects of the Maastricht Treaty and of its predecessor, the 'Delors Report', were careful not to reawaken interest in any such 'center of decision'. In the mid-1980s, with increasing capital mobility and neoliberal policy at its peak, a 'center of decision' was perceived as an old-fashioned tool. Conservatism in monetary policy, as well as the acceptance of central bank independence and of market-oriented surveillance, gained favor. At the end of the 1980s, the Delors Report mentions private markets as a means of fiscal discipline, and references to an 'economic center of decision' are dropped. With regards to monetary policy, governments were barely recognized as having the right to set exchange rate parities, and only a few vague words were said about coordination policy. In the Maastricht Treaty, governments' monetary policy is limited to coordinating and monitoring budget discipline, and not to its earlier meaning of coordination on the objectives of monetary policy. In the Stability Pact signed in Amsterdam in 1997, coordination is limited to surveillance aimed at insulating the ECB from inflationary pressure, or from the need to bail out high debt and deficit countries (Campanella 1998, 2000). The Treaty, faithful to its objective of a market economy, points out that only informal coordination should be achieved through cooperation between governments.[6]

---

[5] The author provides the rough translation from the French. The italics are the author's.

[6] The Maastricht Treaty, however, sets up a somewhat informal 'communication' line

Despite the efforts of the Maastricht Treaty architects, socialist representatives of the French and Dutch governments had on several occasions tried to pave the way to introduce coordination policy as an issue. French politicians have long held strong beliefs that central banks should be under political supervision (Howarth 1999: 10–15). Indeed, the idea of the EU 'government économique' has been spelled out since 1991 in the French draft of the Economic and Monetary Treaty.[7] The French argue that in Europe, a lack of coordination due to the incomplete political unification[8] and a bias to run lax budget policy, meant that the ECB would stick to a rigid monetary policy with higher interest rates. As a consequence, one could expect an overvalued exchange rate against the US dollar. The solution, according to the French, would be the establishment of an 'economic government' forum, made up of the representatives of the finance and economic departments of the countries participating in the single currency (ECOFIN-11), with the aim of establishing a permanent forum for macroeconomic coordination (Howarth 1999).

The arrival of the new-left governments in Europe between 1996 and 1998 (discussed by Pollack in Chapter 14 below) brought governments to power that were keen to push growth up and unemployment down. From autumn 1998, the demand for an 'economic government' began to appear in the headlines of many European newspapers. The French socialist Prime Minister Lionel Jospin was a main proponent of an 'economic government' to counter the presumed bias of the ECB towards austerity, that is, restrictive monetary policy. Italy took a lower profile on the issue. That same autumn, with the Social Democratic and Green coalition in power in Germany, German political representatives openly embraced the creation of an 'economic government' forum to offset the European Central Bank and put forward this idea on the ECOFIN-11 agenda.[9]

between the Council of Ministers, in the offices of ECOFIN and ECOFIN-11 and the ECB's Governing Council. Indeed, there are now formal 'invitations' and informal meetings with ECOFIN-11. See Duisenberg (1999*a*).

[7] As the French draft notes, 'Every where in the world, central banks in charge of monetary policy are in dialogue with the governments in charge of economic policy. Ignore the parallelism between economic and monetary matters (. . .) and this could lead to failure' (Howarth 1999: 10).

[8] References to the USA and Germany are made in support of this argument. As Louis argues, 'It is impossible to conceive of the USA Federal Reserve without the President and the Treasury Secretary, or the Bundesbank without the Finance Minister and the French Bank without the Economic and Finance Minister' (Louis 1998: 3–4).

[9] The German government took a strong stance by endorsing the creation of the 'Euro-11' group, a new informal body, which has no 'obligation to reconcile its discussions and conclusions with the run of EU business in which all fifteen governments take part, seeking consensus. The ECOFIN-11 also set itself up as a 'political check on the ECB'. On Nov. 22, 1998, this group met in Brussels to endorse a manifesto calling for the ECB to keep interest rates low in order to promote growth and jobs. Concerns emerged that ECOFIN-11, as

Though his political and economic views were known long before his appointment,[10] German Finance and Economy Minister Oskar Lafontaine shocked the economic community as he and his advisers began to express their preference for the post-stage three EMU political economy. In several speeches, the newly appointed Finance and Economy Minister set out to confront the European Central Bank on at least three points: an 'economic government', lower interest rates, and target zones. A strong advocate of Keynesian macroeconomic demand management policy who was keenly aware of the sluggish German economy, Lafontaine endorsed the French idea of a 'gouvernment économique', as a 'balancing' institution composed of the finance and economy ministers of the eleven Euro-governments. He viewed the new ECB's monetary power as reminiscent of the 'monetary superpower' embodied in the Bundesbank (BUBA). It was no coincidence, therefore, that representatives of the BUBA headed the counter-offensive. Jürgen Stark, the Bundesbank Vice-President argued that that the European Central Bank needed 'no counter-government' and no 'gouvernement économique' at all, and made it quite clear that the EBC was ready for a battle to resist political pressures. Wim Duisenberg, the newly designated President of the ECB, was also reported to have rejected the demand by the European socialist leaders to set up an 'ambitious system of target zones to stabilize the Euro, dollar and yen'.[11]

By mid-November 1998, however, there was growing support for some kind of 'gouvernement économique'. This was largely prompted by the increasing currency crisis in Latin America, gloomy forecasts of likely recessionary trends in the USA and the UK, a slowdown in continental Europe with growth forecasts being downgraded from 3.2 to 1.5 per cent, and some evidence that a deflationary trend was taking place.[12] Most socialist-led governments in the Euro zone called for the adoption of a demand-side policy that emphasized three points:

- the introduction of an 'economic government' forum under the offices of ECOFIN-11 to offset the newly created supranational monetary institution;

a qualified majority, could steer ECOFIN-15 to pass most EU economic directives or to refuse to apply fines to offending countries of public deficit limit. These actions could e.g. override the fiscal discipline of the Stability Pact. See 'The Power of Eleven', *The Economist* (5 Dec. 1998), 109–10.

[10] Lafontaine had laid out his views in a book co-authored with his wife. See Lafontaine and Mueller (1998). Other sources that detail his political views include Flassbeck (1999) and Wolfgang Munchau, 'Power Struggles over the Euro', *The Financial Times* (7 Nov. 1998), 19.

[11] See W. Munchau, 'Duisenberg Hails "Sensational" Decision', *The Financial Times* (4 Dec. 1998), 1.

[12] 'The New Danger', *The Economist* (20 Feb. 1999), 15–16.

- exchange rate management (specifically a target zones policy) to stabilize the Euro exchange rate against the US dollar and the yen;
- a sensible interest rate policy to take account of growth performance.

Thus, by late autumn 1998, the priorities of the 'new' political economy in the EU were set, and the battle between the ECOFIN-11 and ECB intensified. Figure 6.1 indicates the strategic positioning of the two parties. If political authorities gathered in ECOFIN-11 were clearly set to regain political dominance over monetary policy (German and French political representatives converged strongly on this point), the ECB was even keener to star as the BUBA's successor.

According to ECOFIN-11, the goals of the new political economy are to obtain:

> - A strategy aimed at regaining decisional power over monetary issues.
> - A lasting outcome—i.e. reversing the trend of monetary dominance achieved by a combination of globalization of capital markets and the subsequent capital mobility, so as to regain room for governments to establish fiscal dominance.
> - Sizeable political payoffs expected to stabilize the new socialist political cycle.
> The means to obtain these measures would be through ECOFIN-11, an informal institution, led by Euro member countries and functioning as an 'economic government' forum.

According to the ECB, the aims are to pursue

> - A strategy aimed at increasing and retaining a reputation of 'absolute' independence from political bodies.
> - A lasting outcome: gaining credibility for the policy of price stability.
> - Sizeable political payoffs: building up sizeable amount of credibility *vis-à-vis* market participants.
> The means to obtain these goals would be by resisting pressures for an 'economic government' by sticking to EMU blueprints.

FIGURE 6.1. Strategic Positions of ECOFIN-11 and the ECB in Autumn 1998

Another way to examine this growing battle between the ECB and political authorities is to view it in terms of a strategic game of chicken (Morrow 1994: 93). Artis and Winkler (1997: 92–4), for example, have described a game depicting the struggle for dominance between EMU finance and central bank's representatives which is similar to the one observed in this chapter. The parties are attributed with two sets of preferences: tight and lax policies. Monetary authorities score the best payoff when they impose a tight policy, and fiscal authorities score the best with a lax one. Figure 6.2 delineates these payoffs in a game of chicken, based on the preferences articulated in Figure 6.1.

		Fiscal Authorities	
		Tight policy	Lax policy
ECB	Tight policy	4, 2	−1, −1
	Lax policy	0, 2	1, 3

FIGURE 6.2. A Game of Chicken between ECOFIN-11 and the ECB

Payoffs are clearly negative (−1, −1) when the two groupings engage in confrontation, that is, when the two authorities engage in a game where no one wants to change its policy. Faced with lax fiscal policy, the monetary authorities will in the end be forced to accommodate (1, 3) and, likewise, facing a tough ECB, fiscal authorities will 'chicken out' and accept discipline (4, 2). If monetary authorities chicken out, this means that they are likely to relax monetary policy with an interest rate cut or by loosening their grip over inflation. If the political authorities, faced with a tough monetary policy, chicken out, they will be constrained by higher interest rates to accept monetary dominance and as a consequence to place discipline over public budget policy. The preferences of the two contestants are clearly set: the ECB prefers the 'tight' equilibrium (top-left) with tight monetary and fiscal policies (4, 2), whereas the fiscal authorities prefer the 'lax' outcome (bottom-right) with relaxed policies (1, 3).

Figure 6.2 portrays pretty well the dynamics of the game between the ECB and the Euro governments during Lafontaine's tenure in office. In the first three months (January 4–April 8, 1998), the ECB stuck to a tight monetary policy, maintaining interest rates at 3 per cent against an inflation rate of below 2 per cent. The ECB's monetary stance, however, changed quickly after Lafontaine's resignation. It cut interest rates by a half point and set the reference interest rate at 2.50 per cent. The cut, however, occurred at the same time as the Euro was weakening against the US dollar and M3 (money supply) hit 5.1 per cent against 4.5 per cent of the bank reference value. This circumstance can lead to payoff 1, 3. It seems that the ECB, partly but not wholly thanks to the exit of Lafontaine, and the dropping of calls for economic governance, was set to fall in line and to accommodate the preferences of Euro governments. This suggests that ECB tight monetary policy is linked to political pressures. Once these pressures are removed, the ECB can relax monetary policy.

Strategic Interaction at Work

Using a game-theoretic perspective, one can see that the two parties participate in a strategic interaction that comes with a political price: namely, the resignation of the German Finance Minister and the abandoning of any further demands for 'gouvernement économique' by the surviving French Finance Minister Dominique Straus-Kahn.[13] Euro-governments did eventually get a good payoff: a more sensible policy of lower interest rates at the time of a sharp depreciation of the Euro against the dollar. As noted, a few weeks after Lafontaine's resignation, the ECB cut interest rates.[14] As would have been predicted by a game-theoretic approach, both the Council of Ministers (under the guise of ECOFIN-11) and the ECB got their own way by looking after their own self-interest, which eventually resulted in a mutual accommodation, i.e. passive collusion. This is represented in Figure 6.3.

In essence, this represents an evolution from Figure 6.1, and signals that an iterated strategic interaction has occurred. First, the Euro-11 governments appreciate the benefits of a stubborn and independent ECB that demonstrates it is capable of: (*a*) gaining credibility, and in doing so (*b*) accommodating governments' failures in economic policy-making. Second, the ECB gains a reputation as a 'hard-nosed' independent institution, which provides smoke screens for possible governance failure in monetary policy.

Figure 6.3 also suggests that a dynamic evolution of governments' preferences has occurred. Political authorities chicken out as they realize that the ECB is prepared to stick to its prerogatives, to resist the introduction of an economic governance institution, and to reject calls for a 'target zones' policy. The scapegoat in this situation is certainly Lafontaine, the German Finance Minister. After his departure, the way was clear for the two groupings to reinstate the proper functioning of their inter-institutional relations. Governments learned the lesson that an aggressive stance against the ECB, either under the guise of a 'gouvernement économique' or under the ambitious 'target zones' policy prescription could result only in the ECB sticking to higher interest rates. Thus, the political authorities were ready to start a different inter-institutional

[13] Strauss-Kahn resigned as Finance Minister on Nov. 2, 1999, following a corruption charge.

[14] The April 8 cut has been severely criticized by academics and market agencies, not for the cut in itself but due to the Euro's depreciation. In relation to the latter, Duisenberg said in April that he was not bothered by the Euro's weakness, only to add later that he would be concerned if it fell further. *The Economist* (26 June 1999), 95.

According to the Euro-11 governments, the aims are:

- A strategy aimed at establishing normal inter-institutional relations with monetary authorities.
- A lasting outcome, namely the softening the ECB's monetary stance.
- Sizeable political payoffs to be used in the event of the emergence of difficult 'structural' economic adjustments.

The means to obtain these goals is to abandon the demand for an 'economic government'.

According to the ECB, the aims are:

- A strategy aimed at increasing and retaining a reputation for 'absolute' independence from political bodies and public opinion at large.
- A lasting outcome: gaining credibility *vis-à-vis* the monetary policy of the bank.
- Sizeable political payoffs: building up a sizeable amount of credibility so as to be able to accommodate political priorities.

The means are by: (*a*) resisting pressures for 'more' accountability and sticking to the EMU Treaties; (*b*) selling price stability against inflation targeting; and (*c*) taking decisions on interest rates only when political pressures have been removed.

FIGURE 6.3. Strategic Positions of ECOFIN-11 and the ECB after Lafontaine's Resignation

game, which is likely to produce mutual gains, even in the form of payoffs from collusion.

For the Euro governments, there are at least three payoffs. The first is in the form of cheaper debt servicing and a weaker exchange rate, which can avert the need for politically painful structural adjustments,[15] and get them, at least partly, out of a difficult situation. The second payoff is an interest rate cut[16] that can give some relief to Euro economies in terms of cheaper borrowing. A third and far more important gain has been generated from the ECB's benign neglect attitude *vis-à-vis* exchange rate targeting. The ECB anti-interventionist approach seems to have relieved the Euro economies, with a relevant weakening of the Euro against its princi-

---

[15] The IMF has urged the introduction of structural adjustments in the Euro countries (IMF 1998).

[16] On July 29, 1999, the Governing Council of the ECB decided that the interest rates on the main refinancing operations, the marginal lending facility and the deposit facility would remain unchanged at 2.5, 3.5, and 1.5% respectively (ECB Press Release, 29 July 1999).

pal competitor, the US dollar. This outcome, however, should be ascribed more to the ECB's sagacious policy than to the Lafontaine and Strauss-Kahn 'target zones'. Thus, with the changed institutional dynamics, the ECB's independence is enhanced while the Euro-11 countries benefit from greater price stability and, to a certain degree, a Euro dividend.

While European governments may enjoy these benefits now, it is not clear that they will never challenge the ECB's authority again. An economic government, exchange rate targeting, and interest rate policy are important tools in any coordinated macro-economic approach. What is evident from this episode, however, is that the ECB is determined to resist their governmental pressures. The ECB is resolved to defend its independence and, as a consequence, its credibility *vis-à-vis* its own market constituency. It is worthwhile, therefore, to review the ECB's response to the demands for economic government, exchange rate targeting, and interest rate policy during the 1998–9 period in order to ascertain the grounds on which it will oppose government pressures in the future.

Economic Governance

The rejection of an 'economic government' by the ECB seems to be a clear pre-emptive move against 'macroeconomic coordination' between fiscal and monetary policies. Christian Noyer, the ECB's Vice-President, has made several unambiguous statements about the relationship between the monetary and budgetary authorities in which he clearly plays down the call for a coordination policy. ECB independence does not 'rule out communication with politicians' and, indeed, the bank should 'have a regular exchange of information and views with the budgetary authorities' (Noyer 1999*b*). At the same time, the ECB is not and will not be prepared to enter into any form of ex-ante co-ordination of monetary and budgetary policies. For example, the ECB 'cannot promise ex-ante that interest rates will be reduced if budgetary authorities promise to reduce fiscal deficits' (Noyer 1999*b*).

An area where the ECB and ECOFIN-11 might meet to discuss macro-economic issues in the future is in the 'macroeconomic dialogue' as part of the European Employment Pact. Here, the Council of Ministers, the Commission, the ECB, and the social partners will meet to create such a 'macroeconomic dialogue'. However, as Noyer points out, the dialogue would be 'limited to an exchange of information' and would 'not interfere with the responsibility of individual policy areas' (Noyer 1999*a*). Other ECB officials are less open to this forum. Duisenberg, for example, has publicly rejected any participation in or invitation to a 'macroeconomic dialogue'.

Target Zones

The target zones argument was the major cause of disagreement between the ECOFIN-11 and the ECB. In EMU treaties, responsibility for exchange rate policy is divided between the Council of Ministers (ECOFIN) and the ECB. In particular the Council has the right to enter into formal exchange rate arrangements with non-EU countries or to formulate general orientations for the exchange rate. In the absence of such arrangements or orientations, the management of exchange rate policy is the sole responsibility of the ECB. A European Council Resolution on economic policy coordination in December 1997 indicated that ECOFIN may provide general orientations for exchange rate policy in exceptional circumstances, for example in the case of a clear misalignment. Moreover, these orientations should always respect the independence of the ECB, with the primary objective of maintaining price stability.

The ECB's firm stance against an active exchange rate policy scored an important victory *vis-à-vis* the ECOFIN-11 (Duisenberg 1999*a*). Though the ECB defense line vacillated when the Euro came under strong depreciation (June–July 1998), ECB officials were adamant in their non-activist stance for several reasons. First, most Euro area countries are exceptionally open economies, with the sum of their exports plus imports as a share of their combined GDP reaching about 53 per cent. Considering the whole Euro area in the world economy, trade in goods measured as exports and imports combined is around 26 per cent of GDP and thus only a little higher than that of the USA and Japan. Second, as a consequence of SEA and EMU, the Euro area has grown as a 'bloc' economy with a common currency and a lower exposure to world markets. Against this background, a certain instability in the Euro exchange rate because of domestic economic contingencies turns out to be less important compared with the same instability in the exchange rate of a national currency in the past. The ECB, in the words of its President, must not ignore the likely effects that instability in the exchange rate of the Euro can trigger in economic activity and prices. The ECB, Duisenberg insists, takes the exchange rate as a significant variable in the 'outlook for price stability', and it 'still undoubtedly plays an important role in the monetary policy of the Eurosystem' (Duisenberg 1999*c*).

Given these arguments, a rejection of exchange rate targeting (or target zones) is logical.[17] The Bundesbank and the US Federal Reserve also

---

[17] Exchange rate target is one of the most controversial topics in monetary literature. The consequences on a country's economy of an active stance or inactive *laissez-faire* policy are still being debated. See Krugman's seminal contribution to this debate (1993), and various reviews and assessments (Dominguez and Frankel 1993; Henning 1997; Bergsten 1997).

share this view. The issue, however, presents some intriguing political nuances in the ECOFIN-11 and ECB political debate. Leaving aside other aspects, the power to adjust the Euro exchange rate parities in exchange rate arrangements would rest on the ECOFIN-11, which can prevent the ECB from following an independent and restrictive at a time of monetary policy. This explains the ECB's strong opposition to the reintroduction by means of the 'Trojan horse' of exchange rate arrangements, and of limits and burdens to its monetary policy independence.

The insistence of ECB officials on exchange rate movements as a natural dynamic of open economies alarmed market participants to some extent. It happened when the ECB, after Lafontaine's resignation, cut interest rates by a half point at the same time as the Euro exchange rate against the US dollar was deteriorating. ECB watchers started to collect evidence that the ECB's stance on exchange rates was a covert 'mild benign neglect' policy.[18] The ECB's self-defense centered on two points. First, the Euro had depreciated because of the weak fundamentals of the Euro-economies. This contrasted with the US dollar which appreciated thanks to the continuing rapid growth of the US economy, a favorable employment situation, a fiscal situation under control, and a healthy surplus in the government budget. Second, the volatility of the Euro had been small compared to what was expected for a new currency. Noyer (1999*b*) refers to a different, more robust explanation of the ECB's anti-activist policy. Globalization was a major factor of governments and central bank's discipline, but domestic price flexibility necessitated flexibility in the long run. This flexibility includes exchange rate flexibility. Noyer (1999*b*: 2) has referred to Mundell's famous quartet theory (1961) which states that 'if three of the four conditions are fulfilled—free trade, international capital mobility and an independent domestic monetary policy focusing on the maintenance of price stability—it is not possible to maintain fixed exchange rates'. Noyer has also publicly rejected a major argument often raised by target zone sustainers (Henning 1997; Bergsten 1997). This argument takes the emergence of the Euro as an international currency, with the concomitant reduction in the number of key players in international monetary relations, as a persuasive reason for intensified exchange of information and co-ordination on international monetary issues. Noyer, however, stresses the untenability of any international monetary policy co-ordination, such as exchange rate targeting or the co-ordination of the 'global policy-mix', as it could jeopardize 'the goal of price stability and endanger the credibility of monetary policy'. With a similar argument,

---

[18] T. Barber, 'ECB Attempts to Soothe Fears over Euro's Weakness', *The Financial Times* (26 Apr. 1999), 16.

Otmar Issing, member of the Executive Board and chief economist of the ECB, argued that exchange rate targets are unsuitable to maintain economic stability.

For a large economic area like the Euro area, which has a relatively low degree of openness, stability must be mainly created and maintained at home. The Euro area cannot, unlike a small open economy, efficiently run a stability-oriented monetary policy if it has an exchange rate target. For this reason, the Eurosystem—similar to the Federal Reserve—has never considered the employment of an exchange rate target in its monetary policy strategy. (Issing 1999*b*: 2)

The ECB's resistance to 'exchange rate targeting' has involved a substantial shift of the bank's explanatory argument from a rather defensive line, in which the bank's main concern was to fend off control over its independence, to openly supporting a mild 'benign neglect' stance. Here, the 'natural' decline of the Euro exchange rate against the dollar, with a more than 10 per cent loss, has been considered to be a major positive factor in Euro economies' prospective growth (Duisenberg 1999*b*).

Interest Rate Policy

The ECB's most important tool, interest rate policy, has firmly rested in its hand. In the period covered in this chapter, the ECB has not only offered evidence that it will not abstain from activism over interest rate movements, but it has moved interest rates first down and then up three times since its investiture, acting independently of any outside pressures. The first two moves were at the end of December 1998 at the time of irrevocable fixing of bilateral parities, when the reference interest rate was set at 3 per cent from its previous 3.5 per cent and on April 8, 1999, when again interest rates were lowered by a full half point (2.5 per cent). Its third move occurred on November 4, 1999, when interest rates were raised by 50 basis points, bringing the Euro interest rate back up to 3 per cent. This last move clearly exacerbated European authorities who favored lower interest rates.

Conclusion: Resistance—A Continuing Story?

This chapter focuses attention mainly on the first eight months following the EMU third stage and makes some conjectures on the future pattern of the inter-institutional dynamic that has evolved from the relationship between the ECB and ECOFIN-11. Granted, the conflict did create some serious problems for the functioning of the new authorities. However, the chapter reveals this is a relatively common situation in which central bankers (monetary authorities) and finance ministers (political authorities) confront each other in crucial issues of monetary policy: interest rates, exchange rate, and an unclear macroeconomic coordination. Central bankers, who in many countries have gained independence from the political authorities, are prepared to resist pressures from the political authorities so as to deliver a monetary policy that essentially is anti-inflationary. Central bank resistance to political pressures is, indeed, neither episodic nor accidental. It is a stance that the bank's constituencies, markets, and general holders of money would expect as proof that their interests are being defended. This means that, if political authorities, eager to improve their political standing, are likely to challenge central bankers, the latter are no less resolved to stick to their anti-inflationary commitment in order to win market confidence.

Thus, the ECB's resistance to political pressures turns out to be a key word in understanding the relationship between the ECB and ECOFIN. The central bank's rigid commitment to its institutional objective is a counter to political authorities who are trying to gain fiscal dominance over monetary policy. This can explain the strategic interaction between the ECB and ECOFIN-11, as each party refers to different commitments and constituencies. If political authorities have clear commitments to their own domestic electorates, central bankers, too, are provided with them as they refer to market participants to increase their own assets, a successful anti-inflationary stance. Further, the ECB, as Padoa-Schioppa (1997: 87) argues, clearly aims at creating the second tier of the EU economy—the 'economic constitution of the market economy'. Its conservative nature and its own monetary commitment to price stability are indispensable ingredients for building a stable, friendly environment that favors the creation of a more robust market economy in the European Union. From this perspective, the ECB's resistance to ECOFIN pressures is extremely significant as it symbolizes the strategic positioning of the EMU supranational institution in respect of its statutory objectives (to deliver price stability), with its aim of resisting political pressures, which are often based on short-term objectives.

If this chapter were to consider the ECB–ECOFIN-11 confrontation in terms of a standard 'one-time game', there could have been two different scenarios. On one hand, the ECB as the winner would present monetary policy as one sticking to rigid price stability. On the other, the ECOFIN as the winner would place fiscal dominance over the ECB (thus threatening its independence), with wider public deficit margins being observed in the Euro area (Dornbusch *et al.* 1998). In the iterated strategic game, however, we see another scenario in which the ECB resists the pressures of political authorities, but when these pressures subside, adopts a monetary policy of 'benign neglect'. Thus the events, from January to November 1999, ended the major ECOFIN-11 and ECB confrontation, to use T. .S. Elliot's words, 'not with a bang but with a whimper'. Perhaps this mild 'benign neglect policy', diligently defended by ECB officials, can be a lasting option for the Euro area, which still retains its structural weaknesses rooted in member states' incomplete fiscal adjustments. On average, Euro member countries' budgets are far from balanced, and governments have not yet meaningfully reduced their role in the economy. Social spending programs continue to expand, financed by a still-rising tax burden measured at 45.4 per cent of GDP in the EU compared to 32.0 per cent in the USA (Kasman 1998: 20). Given this situation, the ECB might 'be seen as the building block of a Stability Culture in Europe' (Kasman 1998: 19), while allowing for some 'passive collusion' with the member states as a means to mitigate political pressures in the future.

Of course, the ECB will continue to resist strong political pressures, and to counter the macro-economic cooperation envisioned by some ECOFIN-11 representatives. This, one can argue, ultimately leads to healthy 'inter-institutional dynamics' between the ECB and ECOFIN-11 in which the diverse and even conflicting interests are openly debated and scrutinized in the public arena. Indeed, if such is the case, one can expect a continually renewed and vibrant EMU policy in the future.

7

European Monetary Union and the New Political Economy of Adjustment

ERIK JONES

Europe's economic and monetary union (EMU) did not get off to an auspicious start. Although launched with much fanfare in January 1999, the single European currency (the Euro) soon collapsed in value relative to the US dollar. Worse, concern arose that the monetary union might fall apart even before Europe's national currencies are replaced in 2002. A prominent German banker complained about the Euro's 'weakness'. The newly appointed president of the European Commission, Romano Prodi, suggested that Italy might be unable to meet the obligations of membership. And a group of economists working in the research division of the International Monetary Fund (IMF) argued that Europe's currencies were still vulnerable to speculative attack (Berthold *et al.* 1999).[1] Meanwhile, European unemployment remained above 10 per cent of the workforce and Europe's center-left policy-makers appeared unable to agree on how best to respond (Dyson 1999). Given the potential for lasting disagreement over how to manage the monetary union, the prospects for EMU's immediate future look grim. At the extreme, as Martin Feldstein (1997*a*) has argued, Europe's member states may even go to war!

Still, looks can be deceiving and the future is usually less exciting than we imagine. The problem is that, despite the debate that has surrounded Europe's EMU project, we still know very little about how the introduction of a single currency will affect how Europeans respond to economic change. The bulk of existing analysis focuses on the costs and benefits of the project—including the implications of differing institutional regimes—as well as the political motivation behind it. What it does not cover is the extent to which EMU will affect how different groups monitor developments in the economy, how they protect themselves from

[1] See, respectively, 'Euro Embarrassing, Says Deutsche Chief', *The Independent* (17 July 1999); 'Prodi's Remarks Leave the Euro Bruised and Battered: Soon may be Worth a U.S. Dollar', *Financial Post* (22 June 1999); and 'Euro Warning on IMF Website Sparks Debate', *The Independent* (2 Aug. 1999).

economic misfortune, and how they react to the necessity of changing either what they produce, or where and how they produce it. Rather, most of the existing work on EMU *assumes*, and does not analyze, the political economy of adjustment.

This distinction between assumption and analysis is important. On close examination, the assumptions made about the political economy of adjustment in Europe are open to question. For example, although Rolf Breuer, chairman of Deutschebank, claimed that the rapid drop of the Euro against the dollar undermined the currency's credibility, he went on to point out that the change in relative values would actually be good for European exports during a period of otherwise slow growth. His assumption, then, is that Europeans care about the external value of the currency even when that value is unrelated (or inversely related) to European economic performance. Such a claim may be plausible in empirical terms, no matter how illogical it appears. The history of the member states provides numerous examples of unpopular but necessary devaluations. Nevertheless, such an illogical assumption is a strange basis for asserting that the Euro's depreciation during its first six months is an 'embarrassment'. Moreover, Breuer's belief that Europeans attach symbolic importance to the external value of the Euro contradicts one of the foundations of the theoretical literature on monetary integration—which is that popular concern about exchange rates should decrease as the size of the monetary union increases (Mundell 1961: 662–3).

The economists at the IMF also rely on questionable assumptions. In their analysis, they doubt whether 'further rises in unemployment in EMU member countries are politically sustainable' and therefore suggest that national politicians may choose to leave EMU 'as the costs of staying inside . . . become too large to bear' (Berthold *et al.* 1999: 23). The assumption here is not that EMU causes unemployment—a claim that they make great efforts to justify in their analysis—but rather that any political mobilization resulting from a rise in unemployment will focus on participation in EMU rather than on any one of the numerous other factors that contribute to the problem. Even if we accept the claim that EMU contributes to Europe's unemployment problem, that is no reason to believe that membership is the only or even the most important factor behind any rise in the number of people affected. Of course it is conceivable that opposition parties or other groups representing the interests of the unemployed will attempt to use EMU membership as a rallying point. However, recent Eurobarometer public opinion polling reveals substantial commitment to EMU in all of the participating countries and such commitment usually crosses traditional party divides.[2] Moreover, even if EMU does cause

---

[2] Commission, Eurobarometer, *Public Opinion in the European Union*, 50 (March 1999).

unemployment that does not mean exiting from EMU will create jobs. Therefore, the belief that political mobilization in response to unemployment will center on EMU membership can only be regarded a weak basis upon which to conclude that 'large asymmetric shocks during the transition phase might constitute a serious challenge to the viability of EMU' (Berthold *et al.* 1999: 24).

Martin Feldstein's assumptions are almost purely speculative. Where the IMF economists suggested that political mobilization in reaction to a rise in unemployment would organize around membership in EMU, Feldstein (1997*a*: 60–2) assumes a cumulative four-step chain of causality. First, EMU would encourage deeper integration among participating countries. Second, 'there would be important disagreements among the EMU member countries about the goals and methods of monetary policy'. Third, such disagreements could underscore 'incompatible expectations about the sharing of power'. Fourth, disagreement over methods and expectations could escalate into armed conflict within the monetary union, between EMU members and non-members, and between Europe and the outside world. Drawing upon the experience of the American Civil War, Feldstein cautions that 'a formal union is no guarantee against an intra-European war'. Therefore, he concludes that the prospect of war 'is too real a possibility to ignore'.

Feldstein's reality exists by assumption. Indeed, the same criticism could be applied (though perhaps with weaker force) to the claims made by the IMF economists and by the German banker. Under different assumptions, EMU's launch could be a success as easily as a failure. Following the editors of this volume, we could conclude that the Euro's performance so far demonstrates 'that [the Euro] is behaving as a "normal" internationally traded currency'—all of which depreciate relative to other currencies from time to time, and few of which have ever sparked either a limited secession or a full-scale war.[3] However, such contrasting assessments of Europe's performance become a test of wills between EMU supporters and detractors—much like the debates underway between the pro- and anti-Europe wings of the UK Conservative Party and arguably just as unenlightening.

---

[3] Barry Eichengreen (1998: 34) recently supported Feldstein's argument with the assertion that 'there is no shortage of monetary unions which have disintegrated . . . where the decision to file for a political divorce led to the decision to go for a monetary divorce'. This may be so. However, his suggestion that the political motivation for such schisms can be equated with a desire for policy autonomy is reductionist. Even had the leaders of multinational countries he cites as examples—Austro-Hungary, the Soviet Union, and Czechoslovakia—been enlightened enough to allow the introduction of subnational currencies it is highly doubtful (to say the least) that these multinational conglomerations would have continued to exist. See e.g. Goodhart (1995: 448–9).

The problem is that argument by competing assumption can provide only limited insight on how EMU is likely to develop in the near or distant future. A more robust framework for analysis is required, one that explains both how Europeans are adjusting to EMU and how EMU is changing the pattern of European adjustment. The purpose of this chapter is to examine how the creation of EMU has resulted in a new political economy of adjustment in Europe. The central claim is that European adaptation to EMU is changing how Europeans adjust to other economic developments as well. In turn, these changes in the pattern of European adjustment will affect the stability of EMU. Some of these changes were anticipated by the economists and policy-makers who designed Europe's monetary union, and others were not. Therefore, some reconsideration of the project may be warranted, but such reconsideration can only take place on the basis of analysis and not assumption.

The chapter is divided into five sections. The first argues that, while existing analysis of EMU has paid considerable attention to the problem of economic adjustment, it has assumed (or ignored) the political and economic mechanisms that make adjustment relevant to the sustainability of EMU. The second examines how processes of adjustment differ across institutional environments. The third analyzes how the introduction of the single currency is affecting national patterns of adjustment. The fourth expands the analysis to encompass transnational processes of adaptation. The fifth concludes with an assessment of the risks this new political economy of adjustment poses for Europe and provides a preliminary assessment of scenarios for the other three 'Rs' (reform, resistance, revival) at the heart of this volume.

EMU and Adjustment

Existing analysis of Europe's economic and monetary union incorporates strong assumptions about the political economy of adjustment because it centers on the member states. For example, economists view EMU as a problem of macroeconomics—whether and how the member states should sacrifice control over their national currencies and therefore also over domestic monetary policy. Such an approach has the advantage of providing a single framework for member states to use in making the choice about participation, referred to as the theory of optimum currency areas. The idea is that politicians and their economic advisers can rely on a theoretical notion of the 'optimum' currency area as a benchmark in determining whether their national currency is too small or, presumably, too large. Using this theory and its accompanying criteria, economists can also make broad estimates of the relative costs and benefits of a given country or group of countries adopting fixed or flexible exchange rates (Kawai 1992; Tavlas 1993). From the member-state perspective, economists support EMU when the cost of sacrificing policy autonomy is less than the benefits of irrevocably fixing exchange rates.

Political scientists view EMU as a problem of international relations—whether and how the member states can make a binding or 'irrevocable' commitment to fix the value of their currencies relative to one another (and therefore also perhaps commit to other modes of behavior). Here the advantage lies not in evaluating the participation of a single member state, but rather in making assessments about the sustainability of the system as a whole. Political scientists support EMU when the institutions or agents responsible for maintaining the commitment to irrevocably fixed exchange rates are stronger than the incentive for member states to defect from the monetary union (Cohen 1993).

In both cases, the member states provide the basic (and irreducible) unit for analysis. Thus, while economists and political scientists refer to actors or processes within the member states—such as subnational regions or economic sectors—they do so for one of three reasons:

- a vertical comparison across levels of aggregation (EMU is like a member state);
- a horizontal comparison across the member states (some member states are more suitable for participation than others); or,
- a *reductio ad absurdum* (Mundell's famous dictum (1961: 660) that 'the optimum currency area is the region').[4]

Meanwhile, the member states are assumed to be subject to a common rationality: the relative cost of irrevocably fixing exchange rates *is* the incentive for countries to defect from the monetary union. The assumption is that when the relative cost of participation in EMU is high enough, Europe's member states will stay out of the monetary union in order to maintain, or will leave the monetary union in order to regain, their policy autonomy.[5] When this assumption does not hold, both economists and

---

[4] A principal exception to this trichotomy is the literature on the agglomeration effects of industrial activity under a single currency. This is dealt with below.

[5] Consider the following citation from the *New Palgrave Dictionary of Money and Finance* under the heading 'monetary unions': 'Although the international community tries to observe the rule "*pacta sunt servanda*", history is full of examples of "irrevocable commitments" to exchange rates that have broken down. The reason is simple: assuming that national governments behave rationally, they will evaluate the costs and benefits of the fixed exchange rate union [according to economic criteria]. If the costs become overwhelming with respect to the benefits, the government concerned may be tempted to change the parity, even if this means breaking an international agreement. The evaluation of the costs and benefits, in fact, may vary over time, for example in relation to economic conditions and/or to preference functions of governments' (Gandolfo 1992: 768).

political scientists are wont to decry the influence of a 'politics' beyond rationality and to regard the situation as either whimsically temporary or practically unsustainable. No matter how fervent the desire to create EMU at a particular point in time, the inexorable logic of costs and benefits must eventually take hold.[6]

This synthesis of economic and political science perspectives on EMU begs two questions. First, what are the 'costs' of sacrificing policy autonomy by irrevocably fixing exchange rates? Second, how and to what extent are states motivated by such costs? The answer to the first of these questions is relatively straightforward. According to the theory of optimum currency areas, the cost of sacrificing policy autonomy derives from the difficulty of economic adjustment. Because prices and wages do not move downward easily in the marketplace, firms cannot respond efficiently to changes in demand for their output. As a result, when the demand for exports falls in foreign markets, the government of the exporting country is faced with a trade-off: either it can try to stimulate demand at home to compensate for the shortfall (and run the risk of accelerating inflation) or it can accept an increase in unemployment. Alternatively, the government can allow its currency to depreciate relative to its foreign markets and so avoid (much of) the inflation–unemployment trade-off. The cost of EMU, therefore, is the lack of exchange rate depreciation as a policy alternative, as well as whatever inflation or unemployment results from the country's adjustment to the shortfall in foreign demand. This cost is higher the more often a country suffers from shocks (or sudden changes) to its exports and the more important the shocks.[7]

The usefulness of exchange rates in obviating or facilitating economic adjustment is disputed. In theoretical terms, the cost of giving up the exchange rate as a policy instrument rests on the assumption that changes in the exchange rate can influence developments in the real economy— which is to say output and jobs. In empirical terms, it rests on the belief that policy-makers can manage exchange rates and that they will do so to facilitate adjustment problems (Wyplosz 1997). Even accepting the theoretical condition, the empirical questions remain in contention. Few if any currency areas can be explained on the basis of an economic rationality (Goodhart 1995: 449). Moreover, while there is some evidence that countries (and currency markets) engage in exchange rate intervention in response to economic shocks (Bayoumi and Eichengreen 1998), there is

---

[6] Indeed, this is the essence of Martin Feldstein's (1997*b*) critique of EMU.

[7] This telling of the nominal exchange rate-adjustment story omits a range of complicating factors such as the possibility of price distortions resulting from asymmetric supply shocks and the nature of the demand stimulus. For a more comprehensive and yet still summary treatment, see Kawai (1992).

little evidence that movements in the exchange rate are useful in stabilizing employment—or, surprisingly, that countries suffer from a significant shock-adjustment problem in terms of unemployment (Belke and Gros 1999). Thus, even if governments can use exchange rates to facilitate adjustment problems, they may not want to do so and it may not be necessary.

The synthesis of economic and political science perspectives on EMU, then, rests on the question of state motivations. To reiterate, how and to what extent are states actually motivated by the costs of foregoing the exchange rate as an adjustment mechanism? It is in answer to this question that the strong assumption about the political economy of adjustment implicit in the member-state-centered approach is most apparent. Simply, the process through which any shock-adjustment problem is translated into a demand for state autonomy over exchange rates is a black box, with economic shocks on one side and political action on the other. When firms experience a shock to their exports they will pressure national politicians to exit from the monetary union.

Opening the box is difficult. Any attempt to establish the micro-mechanisms behind member-state preferences for or against participation in EMU threatens both the generalizability and the parsimony that are the principal advantages of existing economic and political science approaches to monetary union.[8] Moreover, without such micro-foundations, large statistical comparisons of member-state attitudes toward EMU based on structural factors such as trade integration or left-right coalition ideology are incapable of replacing the black box with an endogenous model of 'rational maximizing behavior'.[9] Not only do such studies derive their testable hypotheses from a macro- rather than a micro-economic analysis of self-interest (and so reiterate strong assumptions about individual or group rationality), but they also rely on assumptions about the effectiveness of lobbying in influencing policy outcomes. Therefore, while broad statistical comparisons can facilitate the understanding of monetary integration as a process—which, in fairness, is usually their objective—they shed little additional light on the political economy of adjustment. Indeed, the results of such studies are sometimes counterintuitive. For example, recent (and still preliminary) analysis by Jeffry Frieden (1998) suggests that, while particular interests may be able to influence exchange rate policy, that influence does not reflect (or

[8] The obvious contrast is with endogenous models of trade protection, where the micro-foundations of firm behavior and political lobbying are more easily established.

[9] The short quotation and the 'black box' metaphor are taken from Magee *et al.* (1989: 30–1). Two of the best attempts to 'endogenize' national preferences for monetary regime types in Europe are Frieden (1996) and Oatley (1997).

correlate with) a country's suitability for participation in EMU. Taken to its logical extreme, this finding suggests that the sustainability of Europe's monetary union may be unrelated to the political economy of adjustment altogether.

The Role of Institutions

Nevertheless, it stands to reason that adjustment is an important issue and therefore also a potential political problem. A sudden and unexpected drop in income, whether to a firm or to an individual, is sure to provoke some sort of reaction—in the marketplace, in the political arena, or on both fronts at the same time. Empirical evidence that trade shocks do not correlate with changes in the level of unemployment only serves to rule out or mitigate one type of response (Belke and Gros 1999). Such evidence cannot be interpreted to suggest that shocks are somehow irrelevant. Therefore, in order to question the standard assumption about the political economy of adjustment—which is that firms will respond to economic shocks by forcing governments to reconsider participation in EMU—it is necessary to provide some alternative explanation for how reactions to economic shocks play out.

Where the standard assumption is that the political response to an economic shock will be to call for a change in the exchange rate regime, the alternative is simply for firms and individuals to work through those institutions—patterns of behavior structured by rules, norms, conventions—that already exist. Thus firms could respond to a sudden shortfall in foreign demand through a reduction in dividends, delayed investment, access to credit facilities, or an internal reallocation of productive resources. Firms could also call upon pre-existing government support mechanisms or they could lobby for exceptional subsidies to be made available. If the shocks are frequent enough, firms could engage in some type of insurance activity beforehand, whether directly through contracting arrangements and futures markets, or indirectly through negotiations over flexible working-time and profit-sharing with their employees. For their own part, the employees could protect their income by negotiating multi-period contracts, severance bonuses, or even private redundancy insurance. In short, the range of responses to shocks—and therefore also to uncertainty—is as varied as the activities of states and markets.

Two examples are sufficient to illustrate the point: Finland and Ireland. Both are member states located at the periphery of Europe's monetary union and both are widely regarded as likely to suffer a substantial shock-adjustment problem within EMU. Yet neither country seems ready to abandon membership. On the contrary, concern about the danger of economic shocks has been directed at domestic institutions and not at participation in EMU. The Irish chapter of the European Anti-Poverty Network (EAPN Ireland 1999) has called for 'effective labor market and industrial support policies' to redistribute the costs of adjustment at the national level. Meanwhile, Finnish representatives of industry and labor have agreed to make additional social insurance contributions in order to create a financial buffer for use in the event of an adverse shock (EIRO 1997).

Of course both economists and political scientists are aware of the variety of responses to shocks that are available to firms and individuals. Such variety is cumbersome to analyze and difficult to rely upon in predicting outcomes. For example, it is easier to identify a correlation between the size of the trading sector and the size of the government than to anticipate what form government intervention will take (Rodrick 1998). Worse, many of the mechanisms used by firms and individuals to respond to shocks work at cross purposes, being helpful under one set of circumstances or to a particular group, and harmful under different circumstances or to another group. The institutions used in anticipating or responding to sudden shocks to income are potentially inefficient and they have important redistributive properties. Thus, as Blanchard and Wolfers (1999) argue, economic shocks by themselves cannot explain Europe's unemployment but the interaction between economic shocks and domestic institutions can.

A good example of the good and bad sides of institutionalized adjustment is multi-period wage contracting. Multi-period contracts protect employees from sudden shocks to their income. As a result, such contracts also explain to a large extent the downward price and wage stickiness in the marketplace. Firms may need to lower wages in response to an economic shock but—because of multi-period contracting—cannot. In turn, this stickiness lies at the heart of the unemployment–inflation trade-off that governments would manipulate the exchange rate to avoid in the first place. If it were not for wage rigidity (that is, if employees would accept a change in their wages from one day to the next), then countries would not need to maintain control over the exchange rate.

The bulk of empirical evidence suggests that firms and individuals respond to shocks through institutional mechanisms rather than relying on exchange rate autonomy. Such evidence includes not only Belke and Gros's (1999: 21–3) finding that changes in the exchange rate do not correlate with changes in unemployment, but also Frieden's (1998) observation that economic 'suitability' for monetary union is unrelated with the choice of exchange rate regime. Firms are generally more interested in how much their products cost in foreign markets than in the institution through which domestic prices are translated into foreign currency. Indeed, case-studies of how the member states prepared for EMU demonstrate that national approaches depended more heavily on the structure of domestic markets and state institutions than on any of the criteria economists use to define an optimal currency area (Frieden and Jones 1998).[10] More fundamentally, the central importance of institutionalized responses to shocks is evident in the fact that virtually no existing currency area is optimal—and many are clearly suboptimal—from an economic perspective.

This point can be overstated. The argument is not that adjustment is irrelevant to EMU but rather that Europe's monetary union encompasses a variety of national institutional environments where many mechanisms for adjusting to or avoiding shocks are already provided. Within this context, EMU can be interpreted as a mechanism for adjustment—or for obviating adjustment—in its own right. Such an interpretation is evident in the broad claims made by the European Commission that EMU is necessary for the completion of the internal market (Emerson *et al.* 1992). It is also apparent in the attitudes of European business leaders. From the perspective of the firm, exchange rate volatility is a shock with effects that are often more important than other shocks to foreign trade (Gros 1998). The irrevocable fixing of exchange rates between European countries represents an institutional response to the threat of exchange rate volatility.[11] Exchange rate stability will not necessarily increase trade, but it will decrease the uncertainty that surrounds it (Bacchetta and van Wincoop 1998; Sekkat 1998). As a result, monetary union is popular among large enterprises even in countries where general opposition is strong.[12]

The advantage of viewing EMU as one institution among many is that it shifts the focus from optimality *per se*. The irrevocable fixing of exchange rates and the constitution of a single monetary policy are no

[10] The case-studies are published in Pisani-Ferry *et al.* (1997) and Jones *et al.* (1998).

[11] Indeed, while 62% of respondents in the fifteen EU member states believe EMU will reduce business costs and 48% believe it will decrease exchange rate volatility, only 37% believe it will result in faster growth and 29% expect it to create more jobs. See Commission, Eurobarometer, *Public Opinion in the European Union*, 50 (March 1999): 66.

[12] Polling of business support for EMU in the UK has been the subject of considerable controversy. See 'Pole Axed: The CBI's Survey Undermines its Position on the Euro', *The Times* (21 July 1999); 'The Proof of the Poll is in the Interpretation', *The Financial Times* (26 July 1999). An interesting result, however, is that 30% of respondents could not or did not name what they thought to be 'an appropriate competitive exchange rate' for the pound to enter EMU and 57% thought the pound should enter at 2.60 Deutschmarks or higher. By comparison, the average daily spot rate for the pound–Deutschmark exchange is 2.63 for the period from 31 Dec. 1994 to 5 Aug. 1999. The CBI poll can be found both on the CBI's own website (www.cbi.org.uk) and on the MORI website (www.mori.com).

more 'optimal' than any other set of institutions in the economy (or in the polity). Like other institutions for responding to the problem of economic uncertainty, EMU should be expected to work better under some conditions and to offer advantages to some groups, but to work less well under different conditions and to present disadvantages to other groups. EMU should be expected to be inefficient and to have important redistributive properties. From this standpoint, the link between the theory of optimum currency areas and the debate between fixed and flexible exchange rates is clear: should governments intervene or should they let the markets decide? If all institutions are suboptimal, then perhaps the absence of institutions is better. Moreover, the assumption that sudden shocks to exports would result in pressure to recapture exchange-rate autonomy is wishful thinking from the proponents of flexible exchange rates *qua* market forces: better a change in the exchange rate regime than an inefficient institutional arrangement.

The institutional approach to EMU also directs attention to the question of institutional interaction and away from the structural characteristics (size of the trading sector, diversity of exports, and so forth) embedded in the theory of optimum currency areas. The economics literature has long recognized the intermediary role of institutions in support of suboptimal currency areas or inefficient monetary unions. Robert Mundell (1961) introduced the notion of the optimum currency area as that space within which adjustment already took place through efficient factor markets, meaning markets for capital and labor. Later, Peter Kenen (1969: 47) suggested that national (read monetary union-wide) fiscal institutions might play a vital role in facilitating the adjustment process. Union-wide fiscal systems redistribute financial resources across regions as well as between individuals and so could absorb any shocks to income and thus facilitate adjustment.

In the optimum currency area literature, the focus is on maximizing the efficiency of adjustment and therefore on general welfare effects. For the present argument, however, the role of domestic institutions is not to render the process of adjustment more efficient. Two or more inefficient institutional arrangements do not add up to an efficient system, nor should they be expected to do so. Rather the effect of compounding institutional arrangements is to redistribute the cost of anticipating or responding to economic shocks in a manner that is or can be—at least in broad terms—politically predetermined. The shock-adjustment problem is a problem of redistribution and not efficiency. Therefore the institutional solution should be expected to have distributive outcomes as well.

The link between domestic adjustment mechanisms and distributive outcomes is well established in the literature on comparative political economy (see e.g. Gourevitch 1986). In broad terms, groups in power design institutions that will redistribute the costs of the shock-adjustment problem onto others who have less political influence. In this context, the implications of EMU for exchange rate policy autonomy are only of secondary or derivative concern. The principal political focus of economic actors centers on the design of domestic fiscal and market institutions far more than on responding to a particular shock or shocks. This proposition explains the central dilemma concerning the attitudes of Europe's heads of state and government toward EMU. Although economists have consistently argued that the shock-adjustment problem should be addressed at the European level either through the adoption of a Union-wide tax and transfer system or through the facilitation of Union-wide labor mobility, the heads of state and government have consistently refused even to open the discussion. The member states would be hard-pressed to design a Union-wide system for facilitating adjustment without generating undesired distributional effects and do not perceive the political support for any institutionalized and Union-wide redistribution (Von Hagen and Hammond 1998; Jones 1998).

Domestic Adjustment

The problem of member-state adjustment within EMU is not whether economic shocks will occur but how the costs will be redistributed. To what extent does participation in EMU affect the ability of groups in power to predetermine the distribution of costs arising from adjustment to economic shocks? This is the question that has moved to the center of concerns about EMU in the participating countries and the answer is as yet unclear.

Recall from the start of this chapter that the political economy of adjustment encompasses how different groups monitor developments in the economy, how they protect themselves from economic misfortune, and how they react to the necessity of changing either what they produce, or where and how they produce it. Participation in EMU has an impact on all three aspects of this process: by changing the information content of prices, by altering the hierarchy of risks, and by facilitating the movement of capital, goods, and services. In turn, these changes have obscured the distribution of adjustment costs under existing national institutions. Thus while public opinion within the EMU member states is generally supportive of monetary union, respondents to public opinion polls are concerned about how much monetary integration will cost them in particular. Moreover, their attention is directed not at the possibility of an unforeseen shock necessitating adjustment under EMU but rather at the imminent adjustment to the single currency itself.

To illustrate this point it is useful to look at the rank-ordering of concerns expressed about the Euro in 1998 public opinion polls (Commission 1999*d*). Across the fifteen EU member states, 58 per cent of respondents feared losing money when exchanging their national currencies into Euros, 55 per cent worried about bank charges for converting their accounts, and 52 per cent expressed concerns about how retailers would change prices. Meanwhile, only 43 per cent of respondents foresaw difficulties in 'getting used' to the Euro, 42 per cent worried about mixing up national and European currencies, and 38 per cent feared they would not be able to understand Euro prices. Although clearly there are some psychological hurdles to overcome, the adjustment to the single currency is not so much the problem as who pays for it. Moreover, perceptions of inequity resulting from Europe's new single currency can persist even under ideal circumstances, and can have real impact through the cancellation of contracts or other disruptions to economic activity (Servet *et al.* 1998: 14–15).[13] Small wonder, then, that Europeans are overwhelmingly in favor of extending the introduction of the single currency over as long a period of time as possible.[14]

The process of converting denominations is only the most obvious impact of introducing the single currency. Less obvious, though still important, is the elimination of currency risk as a factor in making investment decisions. With the irrevocable fixing of exchange rates and the consequent reduction in transaction costs, Europe's marketplace is no longer subdivided into geographic regions with more and less stable domestic currencies. In other words, EMU eliminates two of the most important sources of geographic division in Europe with the effect being to create a more homogenous and competitive environment for business. Inadvertently, however, EMU also increases the relative investment risks associated with differing national institutional environments. Any institutional difference across countries, resulting in relatively higher production costs—or any fiscal policy change resulting in a rise in relative wages—can now exercise greater influence over the pattern of investment both within and across national boundaries (Barrell and Pain 1998). By implication, geographic risk remains a factor under EMU, but the assignment of good and bad places for investment has changed.[15]

---

[13] For a comprehensive analysis of this subject see Commission (1997*h*).

[14] See Eurobarometer 1999: 69.

[15] See e.g. 'Turning European—The Euro has Brought about a Sector Allocation Approach to the Management of European Equities, but Investors Cannot Afford to Forget Geographical Considerations', *Investors Chronicle* (23 July 1999).

A final challenge for domestic adjustment strategies arises from the operation of Europe's single monetary policy. Over the long run, the European Central Bank should provide for low inflation and low interest rates, thereby lowering the cost of capital for European firms. The introduction of the single currency should deepen European financial markets and thereby lower the cost of capital even further. These two factors together—stable financial conditions and greater liquidity—represent strong advantages that will accrue to all participants in Europe's monetary union. That is not to say that all member states will benefit equally. Countries with long histories of financial instability or with relatively limited capital markets will benefit more than those (such as Germany) with long histories of stability and already substantially liquid markets. Nevertheless, all participants will benefit. In terms of lowering the cost of capital, EMU is a win–win proposition.

The cost of maintaining Europe's stable and liquid financial markets is not so easily distributed. Changes in Europe's monetary policy will likely have different effects in different parts of the monetary union—and specifically across systematic differences in the borrowing practices of consumers or firms (Ramaswamy and Sløk 1998). Whether households rely on fixed or flexible mortgages, and firms rely on bank, bond, or equity financing can all influence the real effects of monetary policy changes within a particular member state. Moreover, econometric evidence from the USA reveals that monetary policy changes can impact more strongly across some types of industry than others (Carlino and DeFina 1998*a*). Member states which concentrate their economic activity in interest rate-sensitive areas such as manufacturing or construction will experience stronger real effects from changes in monetary policy than other member states. On both counts, therefore, it is possible to identify member states that will consistently suffer more than others from changes in the European monetary policy stance and for structural reasons (Carlino and DeFina 1998*b*; Ramaswamy and Sløk 1998).[16] These countries will face an additional set of adjustments under EMU and it would be wishful thinking to conclude that they will abandon their institutional differences altogether.

In addition to these structural differences, the monetary stance taken by the ECB will not always be appropriate to macro-economic conditions in each and every member state. This is the concern most often raised in Britain about joining EMU, and it has received considerable attention in the economics literature. Nevertheless, the universal appropriateness of

---

[16] In reviewing much the same evidence, Dornbusch *et al.* (1998) add that the impact of any change in monetary policy on the external value of the Euro could compound the regional diversification of effects.

European monetary policy is likely to be less important to EMU's future than the differential impact of monetary policy changes. To begin with, the possibility that Europe's monetary stance will not suit domestic macroeconomic conditions is one that faces each of the member states— rather than those with peculiar credit markets or industrial structures. Second any such discrepancy between European monetary policy and domestic macroeconomic conditions can be mediated through changes in national fiscal policy—even while adhering to the terms of the broad agreement between the member states to limit fluctuations in their fiscal positions (Gros and Jones 1997). A union-wide fiscal system may be more efficient, but it is unnecessary (Bayoumi and Masson 1998). Finally, the emergence and strengthening of a 'European business cycle' should mitigate the macroeconomic differences between countries.[17] As the member states of EMU move into a common pattern of slower and faster growth, the monetary stance of the ECB will become more generally appropriate even if member-state reactions to monetary policy changes continue to differ.

Whatever the case, the adaptation of national adjustment processes remains national in scope. Thus while it is unclear how the costs of adjusting to EMU will be distributed, it is clear that the formula for distributing these costs will differ (characteristically) from one participating country to another. The flurry of activity within the member states indicates an important process of institutional adaptation but few signs of institutional convergence. This is particularly the case in the area of labor markets, where the member states are developing action plans for employment under European supervision but along explicitly national lines (Pierson *et al.* 1999). However, the claim also applies to national financial markets and product markets. Although there is considerable industrial restructuring under way (see e.g. European Central Bank 1999), the emergence of a European business cycle and the completion of the internal market have not resulted in a homogenization of national institutions.[18]

---

[17] Artis and Zhang (1999) provide evidence that a European business cycle is emerging, but are cautious in asserting that this emergence is the result of European monetary integration. For the purpose of this argument, the trend is more important than the causality behind it.

[18] In anticipation of this lack of institutional convergence, writers such as Richez-Battesti (1996) have called for the creation of a European welfare state. If anything, that prospect is even more remote than the establishment of a minimal Union-wide fiscal stabilization mechanism.

European Adjustment

The institutional differences from one member state to the next make it difficult to identify stable coalitions of interests across countries. This problem was particularly evident at the European Commission, where officials in the information directorate (DG X) often complained about the difficulty of consolidating the campaign in support of EMU. The process of winning the public over to monetary union was largely a piece-meal affair, with each member state taking a slightly different approach (Frieden and Jones 1998). Nevertheless, the creation of a monetary union is a European as well as a national event. Therefore, it is necessary to ask the extent to which EMU will affect how groups monitor developments in the economy, protect themselves from uncertainty, and respond to the need for change at the European level. Has EMU affected some funda-mental shift in how Europe adjusts? The preliminary analysis is mixed both in terms of what is happening and whether it is good or bad.

To begin with, there is little indication that groups are organizing across national boundaries either for EMU or against. Moreover, and as men-tioned earlier, there is little support for the construction of Europe-wide institutions for facilitating adjustment in support of EMU. The heads of state and government have not agreed to the construction of a Union-wide tax and transfer system and they are unlikely to encourage any large-scale labor mobility across national boundaries. Finally, the European Central Bank (ECB) lacks the formal authority to conduct exchange rate policy. Thus while there was considerable speculation that the ECB would inter-vene in currency markets to support the Euro against the dollar, such intervention never materialized.[19] EMU is in many ways more an eco-nomic and monetary union of European member states than a European monetary union.

That said, EMU has generated some important Europe-wide effects. The most troubling of these is in the area of wage bargaining. And, the trouble is that, while the mechanisms at work are ambiguous, the poten-tial consequences are important—particularly in distributive terms (Calmfors 1998). According to some analysis, Europe's labor markets will become more competitive and its workforce necessarily more flexible, with

[19] See 'Euro Rises vs. Dollar Amid Speculation European Central Bank May Intervene', Bloomberg Top Financial News at Bloomberg.com (31 May 1999). Although the ECB does not have formal authority over exchange rate policy, it can intervene in foreign cur-rency markets through the European System of Central Banks. For example, during the summer of 1999 the ECB coordinated an intervention with the Bank of Japan to support the value of the yen against the dollar.

the consequence that conditions for workers will deteriorate. Other analyses suggest that real wages could increase in Europe's German core, benefiting employed workers at the expense of increasing numbers of the unemployed. Alternatively, real wages could increase in particular groups of countries—such as those that presently rely on centrally coordinated wage bargaining or those which are presently poorer and less productive and therefore have lower nominal wages. Each of these prospects raises the possibility of a significant redistribution of income at the European level and beyond the control of national institutions.

Mechanisms are the crucial components of such analyses. Depending upon the assumptions at work, the impact of EMU on wage bargaining could operate through any one of a number of channels:

- competition in product markets;
- transparency of relative wage rates; and,
- signaling between monetary authorities and wage bargainers.

Increased competition in product markets could encourage trade unions to moderate their wage claims and to accept more flexible contracts and work practices (Danthine and Hunt 1994). Greater transparency in relative wage rates could encourage a convergence in pay scales across countries (Jones 1998). And a change in the pattern of signaling between monetary authorities and wage negotiators could lead to real wage increases in Germany, in countries with centralized wage bargaining institutions, or even across Europe (Hall and Franzese 1998; Iversen 1998; Soskice and Iversen 1998). Such possibilities are contested, and under different assumptions the impact of EMU on wage bargaining can result in a general reduction in unemployment (Grüner and Hefeker 1999). Nevertheless, the prospect of substantial Europe-wide changes in wage bargaining is unsettling.

The evidence from the wage negotiators themselves is equally ambiguous—although, in keeping with the general tenor of this chapter, it is not as exciting as it could be. A July 1999 survey of wage-bargaining practices entitled 'The "Europeanization" of Collective Bargaining' produced characteristically ambivalent results (EIRO 1999). Wage negotiators in some countries, such as Ireland, have emphasized national wage bargaining as a means of maintaining competitiveness. Meanwhile, those in other countries have looked at the possibility of coordinating wage bargains across national boundaries: in September 1998, trade-union representatives in Belgium, Germany, and the Netherlands agreed to coordinate their activities 'in order to prevent possible competition on wages and working conditions, with the prospect it raises of a downward spiral'. Moreover, similar diversity can be found at the sectoral level, with some sectors retaining a purely national focus, and others—such as the metalworkers—exploring new possibilities for coordination across countries.

The impact of these different strategies of isolation and integration remains to be seen. Although wage negotiators are taking advantage of the single currency as a basis for making comparisons across countries, the role such comparisons play in setting wage claims is indeterminate. Even within multinational enterprises—where the existence of enterprise works councils greatly facilitates wage and benefit comparisons—the attitudes of wage negotiators tend to vary by sector, firm, and region. Even among the representatives of labor, the appropriate balance between the objective of coordination and the constraint of national and regional conditions is undecided. Finally, it is simply too soon to characterize the interaction between national wage negotiators and the European Central Bank. Thus, while there is considerable evidence of adaptation in the political economy of adjustment, the final distribution of costs is unclear. The potential for disruption remains unsettling and the evidence is mixed.

Conclusion: The New Political Economy of Adjustment

The ambiguous reaction of wage negotiators to EMU reveals a stable hierarchy of institutions for adjustment, with domestic institutions at the top and European institutions much further down. In this sense, at least, the new political economy of adjustment in Europe is much like the old: what goes on inside the member states is more important than how the black boxes are put together. Of course there are exceptions to the rule. Should EMU result in a sudden strengthening of one domestic group over another—for example, increasing the power of trade unions across Europe, and therefore within the member states—the resulting distributional conflict would be powerfully disruptive. This is the real concern about the impact of EMU on wage bargaining and, given the danger of rising unemployment or falling living standards, such concern is warranted. Nevertheless, despite the validity of the concern, the evidence of such a sudden shift in domestic coalitions has yet to materialize. Indeed, what is clear at the moment is that the impact of EMU has not been as dramatic as we might have feared.

If anything, the impact of EMU is likely to get even less dramatic. Given time to prepare, domestic groups are unlikely to allow themselves to be out manœuvred as a result of the single currency. On this point, the verdict of European public opinion is clear. What matters is not that Europe has a single currency, but who pays for it, and how much opportunity there is to avoid paying more than a fair share of the cost. Moreover, the focus for reform lies in the structure of national institutions and not European monetary bargains. If for some reason such efforts are to prove inadequate, and some future constituencies complain about having received an inequitable share of the cost of adjustment, then national reform efforts are more likely to be redoubled than to be rolled back.

For EMU as for any big policy innovation, reform and resistance are closely interconnected. As national adaptations to EMU progress, national resistance to leaving Europe's monetary union will increase as well. This argument can be developed as a simple extension to Paul Pierson's (1996a) 'new politics of the welfare state'. Once domestic institutional arrangements have been adapted to operate within EMU, generating the motivation to change them again will be difficult. Auspicious or no, EMU became part of the status quo on 1 January 1999. Resistance now works in its favor.[20] Following the logic of this claim, EMU has less need for revival than for consolidation. Moreover, such consolidation will be undramatic (although welcome). From inauspicious beginnings, EMU will gradually recede into the background of European politics and economics—arguably where it belongs.

---

[20] The logic of the argument can be spelled out more explicitly as follows. Once established, the direct benefits of EMU participation are high and (to a large extent) narrowly concentrated among e.g. large enterprises and tourist associations. The costs of leaving EMU are high and concentrated as well—such as for banks and retailers. Meanwhile, the costs of staying in and the benefits of leaving are diffuse. Apart from the differential effects of European monetary policy changes, the shock-adjustment problems under EMU are difficult for groups to anticipate beforehand and the adjustment to EMU itself has already been incorporated in public attitudes. Indeed, even if we accept that such costs of staying and benefits of leaving are high, because they are diffuse—and because they can be redistributed through existing institutional arrangements—the motivation to avoid or attain them through collective action will be limited.

IV

Enlargement: Understanding Past, Present, and Future

8

EU Enlargement: A Neglected Subject

HELEN WALLACE

Introduction

It is hard to find a better topic than the enlargement of the European Union to illustrate the themes of this volume: risk, that changes to the membership will prejudice what has been achieved by existing member states; reform, in order to equip the EU to withstand the disturbance of enlargement; resistance, to enlargement by the supporters of the status quo; and revival, perhaps, if somehow enlargement can be used as a ratchet for new commitments to intensify integration. All of these themes were in the debate in late 1999, as the Helsinki European Council of 10–11 December agreed to extend the negotiations for accession to include Bulgaria, Latvia, Lithuania, Malta, Romania, and Slovakia, as well as to give Turkey official 'candidate status'. Thus seven additional countries would join the 'first wave' group of the Czech Republic, Cyprus, Estonia, Hungary, Poland, and Slovenia. Add thirteen to the existing fifteen member states, and envisage over the next decade almost a doubling of membership to twenty-eight. And remember that other European countries lie beyond in south-eastern Europe and the western fringes of the former Soviet Union; here too there are aspirants to EU membership.

One might expect that the now voluminous literature on European political integration would be able to offer some analytical insights into the dynamics of change provoked by extensions to the membership of the EU. Not so: indeed, it is an oddity of the literature on the EU, and more generally on (west) European integration, that so little effort has been made to theorize about the enlargement of the EU. In reality the EU has long had an unstable membership—from six to nine to ten to twelve to fifteen members between the 1950s and 1995. Since the early 1990s it has been evident that some form of eastern enlargement was in prospect, as successive European Councils have acknowledged. From 1961 further enlargement has been a recurrent issue in the EU, and indeed part of its regular experience. There have been only brief periods unmarked by either knocking at the door by governments from other European countries, or adaptations to the arrival of new members. Yet the literature on the EU has in the main treated enlargement as an episode, or succession of episodes, rather than as a phenomenon somehow intrinsic to the integration process itself.

This neglect is in retrospect an astonishing omission, given that there are strong grounds for supposing that successive enlargements have made a good deal of difference to the character of the EU, its institutions, processes, and policies. A new generation of young scholars is addressing this 'intellectual deficit'. Until recently, however, most accounts of enlargement were historical and descriptive, generally concerned with particular periods and groups of countries, or with individual applicants. Few studies attempted to compare across enlargements, although Preston (1997), Michalski and Wallace (1992), and Redmond and Rosenthal (1998) endeavored to make some overall assessments.

Interestingly, within the practitioner community, enlargement has been treated predominantly as a series of episodes as well. Here too, one might suggest, there has been a failure to reflect on the nature of enlargement. Memories seem to be short, and lessons poorly learned, about the substantive impacts of enlargement, with each prospective enlargement appearing as the stimulus to anxieties, rather than as an event to be incorporated into a more nuanced understanding of the dynamics of integration as a result of changes to the membership of the EU.

If we were to confine our understanding of the EU to its role in economic integration, we might (perhaps) be able to stand on firmer ground. There is an established frame of analysis in economics from which to make judgements about economic complementarities or divergences that facilitate or hinder the possibilities of creating a single economic space. There is a familiar literature on trade creation and trade diversion that provides some analytical insights (Baldwin 1994; Faini and Portes 1995). There is also a literature on optimal currency areas (although somewhat contested and contestable) that offers some suggestions as to how to understand the costs and benefits of grouping particular countries within a single monetary regime (Krugman 1990; Mundell 1961). But in neither political science nor international relations is there a set of yardsticks for attempting comparable analyses. We have no convincing concept to offer of what would constitute an 'optimal political area' for integration.

At last, and not before time, a new generation of young scholars in political science and international relations has started to ask theoretical questions about the dynamics of enlargement of the European Union. Welcome recent studies, notably Friis (1997), Friis and Murphy (1999), Schimmelpfennig (1999), Sedelmeier (1998a), E. Smith (1999), and

Torreblanca (2000), represent efforts to analyze systematically the nature of enlargement as a feature of European integration. More studies are underway, or in process of publication, and seem likely to greatly extend our understanding of the impacts of changes in the membership of the EU, both in terms of the EU system as a whole and in terms of the relationship between the European and the national arenas of politics. The moment is timely, since the lengthy process of eastern and south-eastern enlargement is a prospect which is prompting a good deal of nervousness among practitioners.

Inherited Assumptions

Given the absence of 'macro' theorizing about enlargement, we have to tease out the inherited assumptions from a miscellany of empirical studies. These include accounts of the handling of enlargement as an example of EU policy-making, generally cast as 'external' policy-making; commentaries on some late-joiners as more or less awkward new partners (generally Denmark, Greece, or the UK); and analyses of the debates in applicant countries, occasionally comparative, but more often about individual countries and in the indigenous language of each country. The more horizontal literature deals to some extent with the notion of the *acquis communautaire* as the shorthand for the constituent elements and obligations of membership. Some studies address the alleged tension between 'widening' (enlargement), versus 'deepening (intensified integration). Other studies have examined institutional issues, such as the several assessments of possible changes to voting behavior in the Council of Ministers, or the accounts of possible procedural devices to manage a 'multi-speed' Union.

Several core assumptions run through these accounts, including the following:

(i) enlargement is an asymmetrical process in which the incumbent members, in the driving seat, engage with the candidates, which are supplicants and dependants;

(ii) EU membership is a powerful magnet shaping the aspirations of the candidates, which otherwise need mainly contingent, rather than systemic, explanation;

(iii) the issue for the incumbents is whether or not the candidates are desired or desirable partners in terms of their fit with the existing and established patterns of integration;

(iv) there is a big distinction between membership and non-membership in terms of what is implied for an individual country; and

(v) accession for the candidate means jumping across over this distinction, and engaging in a process of convergence with the established
template of what membership connotes; but

(vi) the governance of the EU, which rests on an incomplete polity or constrained form of collective regime (depending on one's theoretical
standpoint), may need to be protected against erosion.

These assumptions are, of course, derived from a West European experience of EU extension to include other established market economies and
democratic or democratized states. Nervousness about their applicability
to post-communist countries permeates much of the EU practitioners'
current discourse. Preservation of the established template of membership
obligations has become a central priority for many practitioners, often
flanked by an insistence on protecting the political voice of the incumbents
in the institutional arrangements of the EU. This has become the guiding
mantra for the 2000 Intergovernmental Conference (IGC), as the EU
moves from the Treaty of Amsterdam reforms to the projected Treaty of
Nice. This concern about the systemic shock of an eastern enlargement
has been in the practitioner debate since Jacques Delors's prescient speech
in January 1989, ahead of the explicit decomposition of East European
communism. Delors's preference for a European Economic Area, even for
the countries of the European Free Trade Association (EFTA), signaled a
concern lest indiscriminate enlargement undermine the inherited integration model of core Western Europe.

It is worth noting that much of the subsequent academic commentary
by EU specialists, especially those based in EU member states, has echoed
the practitioners' debate and its assumptions. In contrast, specialists on
Central and Eastern Europe have often looked through the other end of
the telescope and assumed, or advocated, that the EU has (or should have)
the political capacity to absorb new members. Similarly many economists
have shared this viewpoint, taking as their point of departure that EU
politicians mean (or should do) what they say when they assert that the
single market is the core of the EU. Part of my subtext here is that many
European academics are so influenced by their observations of practice
that they sometimes cannot see the wood for the trees, a big obstacle to
macro-theorizing or systemic insights.

Elusive Definitions of Political Integration

A striking feature of much of the scholarship on the EU in political science and international relations is thus the extent to which its parameters
have been set by EU praxis. Analyses of the politics of EU integration take

the territorial and functional boundaries of the EU as definers of the para-meters of the intellectual terrain. Commentaries on the external relations of the EU make few forays into the adjacent domain of defense, where a separate literature can be found, although Nordic scholars have often roamed more freely between these different domains (e.g. Saeter 1991; Sjursen 1998; Waever 1996). By and large the EU literature, whatever its theoretical standpoint, neglects the continental setting in which the EU is nested.

Surely there is a need to broaden our understanding of European polit-ical integration, so as to configure the enlargement dimension into a more rounded model? Three particular dimensions of European integration need to be more thoroughly articulated. First, we need to look at the range of the relationships between the interconnected countries of Western Europe, as well as those of Eastern Europe; only some of these relation-ships are articulated through the EU. Secondly, we need to reexamine the relationships between the European and domestic arenas of politics, for EU member states, but also for neighboring European countries. Thirdly, we need to relate the process of Europeanization to the process of global-ization, in order to establish in what ways EU membership provides (if it does) a distinct response or reaction to globalization.

Interconnected Europe

European countries are connected to each other through relationships that serve a variety of different purposes. These are set out at greater length elsewhere (Wallace 1999*b*) and summarized here. Essentially these purposes can be grouped under three headings: functional, territorial, and affiliational. These different dimensions of interconnectedness are all rel-evant to the way in which the EU has developed.

Functional connections are those that promote cross-border regimes to manage specific public policy functions of a socio-economic character. These are increasingly focused through EU policy regimes, but also engage a variety of other, mostly 'technical', European institutions. The point here is that the EU does not monopolize socio-economic connections. On some policy issues, European governments, and indeed actors other than governments, have preferred alternative fora. Many such fora have histor-ically involved countries other than those that happened to be EU mem-ber states. To take one current example, there is talk from the European Commission of developing an EU regime for managing civil airspace in Europe, even though there has long existed an alternative body, Eurocontrol, which has always had a wide West European membership, and latterly has included countries from Central and Eastern Europe.

The territorial dimension includes both the management of relationships between contiguous neighbors and those that relate to security and defense. The EU has certainly served a purpose (insufficiently covered in the literature) of regularizing relationships between neighbors. Sometimes the EU has adopted the relationships of EU member states with neighboring non-members, although not always. One of the problems for the EU in developing its policy *vis-à-vis* Turkey has been that the policy of the EU as a whole has had a different preference from that of governments from Greece, the closest EU member state. In short, wherever the boundary of the EU has been set, it has raised issues about the relationships of the insiders with the next set of outsiders, and vice versa.

The other aspect of territorial interconnectedness in Europe touches the more conventional issues of security. One core purpose of multilateral regime-building in Europe has been to enhance the security of the participating countries. The explicit security regimes have been mainly orchestrated through the North Atlantic Treaty Organization (NATO), and the Western European Union (WEU), as well as, in the cold-war era, the Warsaw Pact. The EU has historically played a part in this at least as an ancillary component, although views differ on how far the EU has in the past been a vehicle for enhancing collective security. But, we should note, some European countries have in the past remained outside the military alliances. In these cases, governments have chosen to pursue their security through different forms of non-alignment. Yet at the same time, it can be argued, they have also contributed to collective European security by softening the confrontation between opposing alliances. Here too there has been a kind of interdependence between different multilateral regimes with their not quite coinciding memberships.

The affiliational dimension of European interconnectedness relates to values, norms, and societal relationships. Here it is increasingly being argued that the EU is a domain in which shared values are an important part of the story. This has been partly articulated through explicit value-reinforcing codes and policies, but also in part in a more implicit reliance on shared understandings of shared values. Yet here again the appeal to shared values has never been the exclusive property of the EU. Other European organizations, again with different memberships, have been engaged, for example, the Council of Europe and the Conference on, later Organization for, Security and Cooperation in Europe (CSCE, later OSCE).

In short, interconnectedness on these three dimensions has provided different components of the European political integration process. Most, but not all, EU member countries have been involved in multilateral regimes dealing with all three dimensions, although the security arena had special features during the cold-war era. But regime membership has involved other non-EU countries, variously according to each dimension, thus with regime memberships not in practice being coterminous. In pre-cold-war Europe, all West European countries were part of this set of interconnected relationships and engaged in some of the West European regimes. In addition, and very importantly, formal relationships were buttressed by extensive informal relationships—the 'real' economy, extensive societal and cultural connections, complementary security arrangements, and élite political connections (through, for example, political party federations or political movements or interest groups). Western Europe was thus characterized by extensive shallow integration, while that part of Europe embraced by full membership of the EU was characterized by deep integration.

None the less the EU did not provide all of the channels for that deep integration process, since the security component was in large part provided by NATO and the WEU, and the helpful umbrella that this provided, even for non-aligned countries. In addition some of the affiliational dimension was channeled through other organizations. Before 1989 only a few elements of interconnectedness spread eastwards, partly through the CSCE, its three baskets (economic, security, and cultural) touching the three dimensions of interconnectedness outlined above.

In post-cold-war Europe this variety of European regimes has provided channels for extending interconnectedness eastwards. Thus a proliferation of association and partnership arrangements has opened up the scope for developing economic and functional co-operation. Most of this has been pursued by bilateral agreements between the EU and the individual countries of Central and Eastern Europe, although the technical organizations have also made some contribution to this process. In the security domain, efforts have been made to extend interconnections, partly through NATO, initially the Partnership for Peace, and for some countries full NATO membership, flanked by associate membership of the WEU for ten of the Central and East European countries and Turkey (long a full member of NATO). Alongside these military alliances the CSCE was reformed into the OSCE to provide a kind of pan-European security framework. As for the affiliational dimension, the Council of Europe was revived as a convenient first entry point into the liberal democratic European family for newly democratizing countries. Informal interconnectedness has also grown, although patchily as between both domains and countries. In other words, over the past decade most of Central and Eastern Europe has become part of this area of shallow integration, an area with, for some purposes, borders further to the east and south-east than the boundaries of the ten countries accepted in the mid-1990s as full candidates for EU membership.

What then are the implications of this account of interconnectedness and integration? First, engagement in the process of European integration involves participation in an array of European regimes. The extent of involvement for any given country varies in scope and intensity, depending on whether their membership of these different regimes spans the three dimensions of integration. Involvement across all three dimensions takes a country closer to a deep form of integration. Secondly, regime memberships need to be backed by substantive and informal interconnections if they are to provide a durable basis for deep integration. Thirdly, an enlargement of EU membership seems to become an option—for both incumbents and supplicants—at the point where all three dimensions of interconnectedness are in play. At this point the incumbents not only recognize the candidates as capable of deep integration, but also are themselves influenced by their own interconnections with the candidates. For the supplicants there is the additional requirement of accepting the tough conditionality of EU membership.

However, eastern enlargement poses some questions that were much less present in earlier rounds of enlargement in two particular respects. First, the extent of interconnectedness has been much thinner and much more recent for Central and East Europeans than for it had been for West Europeans. Secondly, the EU has edged towards embracing explicitly more of the regime-building across all three dimensions of integration. The EU is becoming more of an actor in the security domain, which is a move away from the coexistent parallelism of NATO and the EU of the past. Thirdly, the EU has aspirations to a more explicit role as regards the affiliational dimension of integration. Thus whereas in the past, memberships of different regimes, and accumulations of interconnectedness, could proceed irrespective of EU membership (as for example in the cases of the Nordic countries), nowadays it has become harder for non-EU members to build up their interconnections through other channels.

The Domestication of Europe

European integration alters the process of domestic politics within individual countries. Conventionally it has been assumed that the nature of this alteration is especially pronounced for countries that are member states of the EU. Indeed much of the literature presumes that there is a kind of template of Europeanization on which the politics of member states converge, the main features of that template having been set by the earlier members of the EU. Late-joiners are left to carry the burdens, and reap the rewards, of adjustment to match that template. This summary is misleading in two respects: it neglects the differences between EU member states in the ways in which the European dimension is 'domesticated', and it exaggerates the impact of Europeanization as focused on EU membership while neglecting the influences of Europeanization on non-members, irrespective of their accession to the EU.

First, then, comparative politics has more to offer us than it yet has by way of commentary on differences between countries in the way that Europeanization is filtered into domestic politics. Cross-border regime-building has been a crucially important feature of politics in Western Europe over the past fifty years. Yet the impacts vary greatly depending partly on the 'fit' with domestic politics and preferences, and partly on the character of the receiving political environment in terms of country-specific institutions and political cultures (Wallace 1973, 1999*a*). Thus the actual experiences of Europeanization are varied country by country, and the ways in which 'Europe' is instrumentalized in pursuit of domestic goals varies country by country. Although the European dimension is important, there are also wide-ranging areas of domestic politics which are relatively unmarked or unpenetrated by European regimes, and where country-driven characteristics remain important in explaining what happens. Thus while the Europeanization of domestic politics is important, it is not all-embracing and it is not homogenous in its impacts.

This observation seems to be increasingly borne out by such detailed comparative studies as are available, although the coverage of the literature remains patchy. Hence, it can be argued that we need to question the notion that there is a predominant single template of how Europe is domesticated in EU countries. Indeed, it might be further argued that positive impacts from Europeanization depend on both the way that European governance is construed and the differing characters of national governance and politics in individual EU member states. It is a two-way process, which has enabled significantly different countries to adapt to Europeanization in significantly and persistently different ways. In the context of enlargement the question that follows is how the two-way process is likely to operate in the case of any potential new member state. Ireland and Greece, for example, represent potently different experiences of Europeanization and its domestication; so, it might be argued, do Finland and Sweden.

Secondly, there are more similarities than are generally admitted between EU members and non-members in terms of the impact of Europeanization. The forces (political and economic) that account for the development of the EU are not restricted in their impact to EU countries. Penetrated sovereignty is a continent-wide experience, to which the EU is a specific, but not the only, response. Other European regimes, as was suggested earlier, impact on the domestic politics of non-EU members, albeit perhaps less sharply than the EU. We can begin to see from studies of countries like Norway and Switzerland evidence about extensive Europeanization that illustrates this phenomenon.

In addition, EU rules and legislation have an extra-territorial impact on neighboring and associated countries. Thus prior to their bids for accession the countries of the EFTA were, for example, to varying extents imitating EU rules in their domestic legislation in order to facilitate access for their products to the EU market, as Norway and Switzerland still do. Economic actors from such countries have found that their behavior is shaped by these extra-territorial impacts, and in this sense it is not surprising that so many of the business, trade union, and other interest associations have for many years included members from non-EU countries. Neighbors of the EU, for which the EU is by far the predominant economic partner, are sucked into unilateral regime-alignment.

Thus we should perhaps see Europeanization as comprising a spectrum of domestic responses, taking varying intensities and configurations across member and non-member countries. In this respect EU membership is about acquiring a louder voice in decision-making and negotiation about these impacts, as much as it is about the impacts themselves. Thus the line between membership and non-membership is to do with the choice between contractual obligations and imitative alignment. In this respect the cumulative enlargement of the EU over the years, combined with the expansion of its policy scope, has increasingly constrained the options of non-member neighbors. It has become harder and harder for non-members to maintain differentiated rules and practice on those policy issues where EU members have strong collective regimes.

Here a paradoxical commentary can be made. Opponents within the EU of further enlargement have often been tempted to devise alternatives to full membership for those neighbors thought likely to be disruptive. No systematic and stable formula for partial membership has yet been devised. Perhaps this is because circumstances have produced a form of partial membership in so far as neighbors increasingly imitate EU practice and rules—virtual, but voiceless, membership. This suggests that it might also be difficult to devise a formulaic version of virtual membership for currently non-candidate countries in south-eastern Europe. EU practitioners are currently seeking a mechanism of association or partnership that would encourage economic and political transformation towards EU 'norms' and practice, but would not connote a commitment to 'normal' membership.

Globalization and Europeanization

So far the discussion has been about forms of integration within a bounded Europe. But, of course, Europe is not hermetically sealed off from the rest of the world. Hence some thought needs to be given to the questions as to whether Europeanization is, in effect, the local variant of globalization, or a specific European response to globalization, or rather to be understood as a distinctive response to the circumstances and context in Europe, irrespective of the broader phenomenon of globalization. These are big issues, which have only relatively recently begun to be explored in the academic literature. This is not the place to enter into the debate in detail. Instead a few comments follow on how this debate might be pertinent to the topic of EU enlargement.

First, then, as regards the conflation of globalization and Europeanization, if this interpretation is adopted, it would seem to follow that non-EU countries in Europe are likely to be subject over time to much the same erosion of national autonomy as EU countries. Self-conscious articulation by those in the EU of their efforts to control the impact of globalization may be interesting at the discursive level, but may not be substantively important. Those in non-EU countries may have some choices about how to express their responses to the predicament, but little influence on the process. We should, however, note that Edward Smith (1999) argues that the path to EU membership was a conscious choice by some actors in the Nordic countries keen to facilitate their adaptation to the global economy.

Secondly, however, if the EU formula is instead a substantively specific response to globalization, further EU enlargement becomes a concrete policy issue for both incumbents and candidates. Incumbents have to address the question of whether a larger EU would be better or worse placed to provide a concerted response to globalization. Candidates have to consider whether or not this distinctive EU mode suits their needs or not. Here there are indeed some grounds for debate, since the EU mode is so much shaped by West European interests and inheritances. A formula which makes sense for West European countries does not necessarily suit the interests and inheritances of Central and East European countries. An argument can be made that some differences of priority and substance might more sensibly be developed to mediate the impacts of globalization. Here we might note that EU practitioners sometimes want to have their cake and eat it. There is a reluctance to accept new members until and unless candidates have pre-adapted to EU rules and practice, even to the point of criticizing candidate countries for sometimes being more obedient to global regimes, such as those required by the World Trade Organization (WTO), than to those of 'pre-accession' to the EU. Yet the

EU does not, as it were, indemnify the candidates against the costs of collision between WTO and EU requirements.

Thirdly, the debates on both globalization and Europeanization are partly about the extent to which the state remains robust faced with the incoming influences from Europe and/or the globe. In Western Europe we have a tradition of relatively strong states, developed out of a long historical process of state-building. Indeed so strong is that tradition that a good many commentators argue that the state remains the core unit of political organization. Some go further and argue that Europeanization has in practice been a vehicle for shoring up the West European state. Indeed one might argue from the experience of a country like Ireland that even relatively new, small, and vulnerable West European states have become more robust under the umbrella of Europeanization.

What is much harder to judge is how far this West European experience might set a model for the countries of Central and Eastern Europe. Their experience of state-building and state-sustainability has been so much more checkered. Even without the corrosive impact of communism many of the countries of the region had contested borders, histories of penetrated sovereignty, and a weak match between citizenship and statehood. The mix of fragmented political identities and invasive empires has provided an uncertain starting point for adapting to either Europeanization or globalization. In this respect at least there are grounds for speculating that any such adaptation might be expected to take different forms in this part of the continent.

Shallow Integration Versus Deep Integration

It has been argued above that integration in Europe flows from a great many conditions and connections in and between countries, of which only one part revolves around the formal organization of the EU. West European countries have been arrayed along a spectrum from shallow to deep integration with each other, and the lines between the more shallow and the more deep forms of integration have not entirely coincided with the boundary between EU members and non-members. To take one concrete illustration, Finland and Sweden were in the late 1990s already ahead of several long-term EU members in the extent to which they had transposed and implemented the EU legislation to regulate the single European market.

Yet to deny that there is an important difference between EU membership and non-membership would be absurd. Institutionally, politically, and juridically there is a rather high boundary between the insiders and the outsiders. Insiders have to accept and make operational, and recurrently so, the disciplines and the commitments of strict club rules and understandings. Hence two issues have permeated the practitioners' debate on enlargement. One is whether or not candidate members would be able to deliver comparable levels of discipline and commitment (for either systemic or contingent reasons). The other is whether or not the incumbents are willing to extend, and perhaps dilute the privileges of club membership by admitting new and uncertain members.

It is from this kind of debate that the asymmetrical character of enlargement is derived. The incumbents call most of the shots, it is widely assumed, in that they determine the 'whether or not' judgement on both issues. Yet perhaps this assumption needs to be questioned, or at least modified. The reality of EU experience is that enlargement has not been easily resistible. On the contrary in practice, within Western Europe, candidates have been accepted by incumbents, albeit often with a delay and on tough entry conditions. Those West European countries that have remained outside the club have kept themselves outside by exercising a preference for a kind of penetrated and modified autarchy, as the experiences of Norway and Switzerland appear to demonstrate.

Thus, at least as far as Western Europe is concerned, the notion of asymmetry needs to be re-examined, and is perhaps explained by the extent of embedded interconnectedness in this part of the continent. We may need to press the question further as regards Eastern and Southeastern Europe. Both events and analysis suggest that the EU incumbents cannot easily walk away from their non-member neighbors. Recently we have seen three events that suggest that EU members are also pulled towards engagement with these various non-members: the intervention in Kosovo; the offer of a form of 'virtual membership' (Romano Prodi's term) to troubled Balkan countries; and the extension of active candidate status not only to the other five East European associates, but also, more surprisingly, to Turkey. Sedelmeier (1998*a*, and in Chapter 9 below) offers us the basis for an explanation in his emphasis on the self-definition of the EU by its political leaders as implicated in the recovery of Central and Eastern Europe. Here values and norms seem to have played a particularly important role in shaping an EU identity that played in favor of proceeding towards eastern enlargement, however uncertainly.

Governance and Governability

Much of the recent literature on the EU focuses on the questions of governance and governability. Much of the practitioner debate on enlargement focuses on how an EU already suffering from contested governance might remain governable with an enlarged membership consisting of so many countries that seem so different from the current membership. In other words numbers and heterogeneity are presented as the two critical variables by the practitioners, and hence both are set to be addressed in the 2000 IGC. Thus the IGC agenda was declared in December 1999 as needing to address issues to do with preventing a larger number of members, and especially many small countries, from paralyzing decision-making. Some wanted to go further and reinforce the opportunities for the existing membership (or the more integration-minded among them) to press ahead in developing common policies.

It is an odd debate in so far as the cataloguing of problems is somewhat divorced from solid evidence. An evidence-based survey would surely reveal that numbers of participants in an EU negotiation make much less difference to the outcomes than is supposed. There are also well-established techniques for adapting EU legislation to accommodate different circumstances in individual member states, whether by variation of substantive provisions or by delayed implementation. Moreover the drift of policy-making in the EU towards more regime development by regulation, benchmarking techniques, or new forms of transgovernmentalism (Wallace and Wallace 2000) means that numbers as such are much less of a problem than for the older versions of common policies as exemplified in sectors such as agriculture. This drift of policy-making has, it should be emphasized, little to do with enlargement as such, and seems to be driven by different factors.

Thus evidence rather than assertion is what is needed to appraise these issues of governability. Part of the evidence that is required is a systematic assessment of the impacts of previous enlargements on the EU process of governance. Two main observations deserve more attention than they have received in much of the literature on EU integration. One is that enlargement has in the past generally been accompanied by a reinforcement of deep integration. The other is that for many late-joiners EU membership has run in parallel with an extension of positive interconnectedness and domestic adaptation.

If we look back at each round of enlargement, we can observe that in each case a stronger agenda of deep integration has been agreed. In the 1970s this failed to materialize for external as much as internal reasons (the oil-shocks, international recession, and so forth). But Iberian enlargement directly coincided with agreement on the 1992 Single Market Program and the development of more extensive redistribution mechanisms. The EFTA enlargement coincided with the move towards economic and monetary union, and, more surprisingly, with a rapid extension of EU involvement in developing a common defense policy.

Similarly many, even most, newcomers to the EU have rather rapidly adapted to EU regimes and commitments. Thus, to take the clearest cases, Ireland, Portugal, Spain, and Finland have exhibited strong trends towards accommodating the disciplines of membership, and indeed by and large have also generated support for extensions of integration. Even the more troubled cases of the UK, Denmark, Greece, Austria, and Sweden show uneven records of partial strong adjustment alongside the areas of contention internally and at the EU level.

Conclusion

To return to the themes of this volume, enlargement has indeed repeatedly and recurrently provoked debates about the risks of changes to the status quo membership. Academic commentary has sometimes echoed the practitioners' fears, and been drawn on in support of resistance to enlargement. This reflects a phenomenon among some European scholars of integration of sometimes being too close to their object of study. More sober assessment and more careful distillation of the record and the evidence suggest that there is no reason in principle to suppose that enlargement prevents reform or revival. Accession to the EU by new members has generally been only part of a broader process of Europeanization, and nested in a wider global context. Hence the adaptation by individual countries to EU membership has both preceded and followed accession. Specific domestic factors have had much to do with the process of adaptation, in some cases helping to make a 'good fit' between Europeanization and domestic adjustment, in other cases a more contested relationship.

Whether this West European experience would hold good for the countries of Central and Eastern Europe remains to be seen. But why not? In other words, comparative and historical analysis seem to suggest both that enlargement has something to do with the broader configuration of the continent (Amato and Batt 1999) and that more often than not European and domestic governance accommodate. None of this is intended to imply that enlargement is a straightforward and linear progression, but rather that it is a dynamic process. Both the context and the conditions of interconnectedness play a part. Much depends on how those involved in managing the process respond. On both of these points there is a welcome burgeoning of insights emerging from new scholarship.

9

Eastern Enlargement: Risk, Rationality, and Role-Compliance

ULRICH SEDELMEIER

Introduction

The policy of the European Union towards the Central and Eastern European countries (CEECs) displays the complexity of the relationship between the four themes of risks, reform, resistance, and revival. The 1989 revolutions presented for the EU and its member states not only new opportunities, but also the *risk* of political instability if the transformation processes should fail. The academic literature broadly agrees that the best way to avert this potential risk is to integrate the CEECs with the EU and ultimately to allow for eastern enlargement. In turn, eastern enlargement requires the EU to undertake far-reaching internal *reforms* (see e.g. Mayhew 1998; Grabbe and Hughes 1998; Avery and Cameron 1998).

In an optimistic scenario, eastern enlargement may thus lead to *revival* and a new dynamism, as it presents a window of opportunity to address accumulated contradictions of the integration model and carry out long-overdue reforms. In a pessimistic scenario, although enlargement might serve the EU's collective long-term interest, it might fail because the *resistance* from negatively affected actors might lead to a 'joint decision trap' (Scharpf 1988). Since enlargement as well as the necessary reforms need to be endorsed by all member governments, individual governments that consider themselves better off under the status quo (for example, in terms of receipts from the EU budget through agricultural and structural policies, national influence, efficiency of collective decision-making, future prospects for 'deep integration') can prevent decisions that would allow the EU to avert a common risk.

In this sense, the EU's policy towards the CEECs could be interpreted as a (test) case of collective foreign policy making (see e.g. Niblett 1995; Torreblanca 1997; K. E. Smith 1998; Zielonka 1998). From this perspect-

The argument and empirical research for this chapter are based on Sedelmeier (1998a).

ive, the decision of the Luxembourg European Council (December 1997) to open accession negotiations with a first group of CEECs in March 1998 is striking. It seems to provide an unexpected but welcome proof of the EU's ability to overcome lowest-common-denominator bargaining and of collective problem-solving. Agreement on an eastern enlargement thus seems an expression of the EU's capacity as a strategic actor in international politics.

However, the strategic coherence of the decision for eastern enlargement is far more ambiguous than this interpretation suggests: the decision to start accession negotiations was taken without any prior agreement on internal reforms. It was taken more than a year prior to the debate about policy reform undertaken by the Berlin European Council in March 1999, and despite the still fresh impression of the manifest failure to agree on institutional reform at the 1996/7 IGC.[1] More broadly, agreement was reached in the absence of any thorough debate on the shape of an enlarged EU.

Of course the EU has a track record of delivering eleventh-hour agreements and a strong aversion to difficult compromises as long as there is still scope for postponement. None the less, indications are that reforms that relate to enlargement will be piecemeal and will involve incremental tinkering, rather than thorough anticipatory adaptation. The adequacy of the policy reforms and financial perspective crafted at Berlin have been doubted (see e.g. Begg 1999), and the Cologne European Council's agreement on a limited tidying-up IGC in 2000 suggest little ambition for institutional reform. Thus, rather than a strategic collective response to a common risk, the EU's decision to enlarge seems to create its own risks for the integration project in the future.

The EU's decision to enlarge presents a number of puzzles. Why did the member governments agree on enlargement without prior agreement on reform, despite the risks and future costs that makeshift compromises create for all of them collectively? Why did they give the go-ahead, despite the uncertainty about the final shape of a deal on internal reforms? More generally, why do those member governments for which it is clear that the negative consequences of enlargement will outweigh possible benefits agree at all? For example, while their geographical position means that Ireland, Portugal, or Spain are not very vulnerable to political instability in the CEECs and are not best placed to exploit the economic opportunities of

---

[1] On the Luxembourg European Council, see e.g. Friis (1998*b*); on the eventual outcome of the debate about policy reform at the Berlin European Council, see Laffan and Shackleton (2000); Leibfried (2000); Allen (2000); on institutional reform at the 1996/7 IGC, see e.g. Sedelmeier (2000); and for a broader overview of the issue, see Sedelmeier and Wallace (2000).

enlargement, internal policy reforms entail for them the risk of losing substantial receipts from the EU budget. At the empirical level, the fundamental puzzle is why the EU committed itself to enlargement, despite the costs that arise for individual member governments which all have veto power.

At the theoretical level, this puzzle pertains to the contemporary debate in international relations between rationalist and more sociological approaches. It challenges the explanatory power of materialist rationalist approaches that exogenize interests and assume that actors maximize material self-interest in strategic bargaining. This chapter sketches how an approach that takes account of non-material factors—namely the role of collective identity that the EU has created for itself in its relations with the CEECs and the regulative norms that this identity entails—can improve our understanding of the evolution of the EU's policy towards the CEECs.

I argue that the EU's collective identity includes the notion of a 'special responsibility' towards the CEECs. It proscribes purely self-interested behavior by policy-makers acting on behalf of the EU, and prescribes a degree of accommodation of the CEECs' preferences in EU policy. This component of the EU's collective identity does not determine policy outcomes. Yet it limits the range of available policy options, by precluding certain options as inappropriate, and by reinforcing the legitimacy of others. In this way, it created scope for a group of policy advocates, primarily located inside the Commission, to obtain approval for a number of policy initiatives that incrementally, but firmly, set the EU on the path towards enlargement. However, while compliance with the EU's professed role made it difficult for policy-makers to oppose such initiatives, it did not extend to forging consensus on a strategic approach to reform and on a collective sharing of the adjustment burdens.

The chapter proceeds in three main parts. The first section traces the origins, and identifies the content, of the EU's collective identity towards the CEECs. The second section presents the analytical concepts that help to understand how this EU identity has an impact on policy outcomes. The third section contains the empirical analysis. It focuses in particular on how agreement was reached on the formal endorsement of the CEECs' eventual accession and on the agreement's significance for subsequent policy developments.

The Origin and Content of the EU's Collective Identity Towards the CEECs

This section seeks to trace the EU's collective identity towards the CEECs—in the sense of the role that EU policy-makers collectively define for themselves in their relations with the CEECs—and to identify the norms that characterize it. This section therefore analyses the discourse of EU policy-makers on the EU's role towards the CEECs. I argue that throughout the cold war and in response to the dramatic changes in the late 1980s, EU policy-makers have discursively constructed a specific role which implies a 'responsibility' of the EU towards the CEECs, in particular to support the political and economic reforms and their integration with the EU.

Broader Aspects of EU identity

There are certain norms that define the EU's identity more broadly and that could be expected to resonate particularly in its policy towards the CEECs. These include the norms embedded in the domestic structures of the member states. Liberal theories stress the importance of the identity of states defined by liberal (social) democratic norms for their international policies (see e.g. Lumsdaine 1993), especially if they interact in an international institution that is committed to these norms (see e.g. Risse-Kappen 1995). Along those lines, Schimmelfennig (1998, 1999) argues that the EU, as an international community of (European) states characterized by shared values and norms of liberal democracy, enlarges to include states that share these values.

Other norms that characterize the EU's identity more broadly were generated at the EU level. These include the notion of the EU's broader European vocation which is expressed in the commitment to enlarge in the EEC Treaty. In the preamble, the signatories state their determination 'to lay the foundations of an ever closer union among the peoples of Europe', rather than just the founding states, and explicitly call for 'the other peoples of Europe who share their ideal to join their efforts'. Article 237 EEC Treaty/Article O TEU stipulates that any (democratic) European state may apply to become a member of the EU. Fierke and Wiener (1999), for example, emphasize the importance of this commitment for the EU's enlargement policy.

Finally, it could be argued that the notion of a broader European vocation as part of the EU's self-image is not confined to an obligation to remain open. Previous enlargements have set a precedent for a special EU role in supporting democratic consolidation and market economic reforms. In part, this was implied in the original integration project (Wallace 1996: 19), and it was particularly obvious in the enlargements to Greece, Spain, and Portugal. Such a role should resonate particularly in policy towards the CEECs. Friis (1998*b*) argues, for example, that an important factor in the differentiation between the accession candidates was the ability of certain policy-makers to frame this decision as one concerning the stabilization of Central Europe.

However, while these broader norms are important, the empirical evidence of earlier membership applications, as well as from the EU's policy towards the CEECs, shows clearly that they are in themselves insufficient to prompt a decision by the EU to enlarge. In the cases of the British, Spanish, or Maltese applications, the member states were not reluctant openly to veto or block enlargement. The empirical part of this chapter shows that, in the case of the CEECs, the EU's explicit acceptance of the principle to enlarge, and its decision to start accession negotiations, has been very reluctant and incremental. These norms that relate to the EU's identity more broadly might thus be important contributing factors to a more specific role of the EU towards the CEECs. But they alone seem insufficient to trigger enlargement.

In order to understand the particular case of EU policy towards the CEECs, we need to focus on the construction of the specific identity, role, or self-image that EU policy-makers have collectively created for the EU in its relation to the CEECs, and on the behavioral norms that such an identity contains.

Discursive Creation of a Specific EU Identity Towards the CEECs

The formation of the EU's identity towards the CEECs began with the origins of the EEC and continued throughout the cold war. Statements by policy-makers from EU institutions and member governments deplored the involuntary exclusion of the CEEC societies from the integration project, and asserted that, without them, this project remained incomplete. For example, Walter Hallstein claimed that the EU did 'share one wish above all others which is to overcome the division of Europe' (Reinicke 1992: 5), and Mitterrand stated in 1980 that '[w]hat we term Europe is a second-best option which alone cannot represent all European history, geography and culture' (Haywood 1993: 275). In 1985, the Dooge Committee's report claimed that the EU had 'not lost sight of the fact that it represents only a part of Europe' and that 'any progress in building the Community is in keeping with the interests of Europe as a whole' (European Council 1985).

This discourse might have been genuine, or it might have been cold-war rhetoric, but when overcoming the division of Europe suddenly became a real possibility, it provided the script for EU policy-makers to assert a specific role for the EU in post-cold-war Europe and towards the CEECs in particular. Rather than backtracking in the face of dramatically changed conditions, there is a continuity in the discourse about the EU's role towards the CEECs which reaffirmed the EU's commitment.

EU policy-makers, individually and collectively at successive European Council meetings, couched pledges of support for the CEECs in strong normative language. At Rhodes in December 1988, the European Council reaffirmed the EU's 'determination to act with renewed hope to overcome the division of the continent' (European Council 1988) and declared a year later, in Strasbourg, that '[t]he Community and its Member States are fully conscious of the common responsibility which devolves on them in this decisive phase in the history of Europe. . . . The availability and willingness to cooperate are essential elements of the Community's policy' (European Council 1989). At the beginning of 1990, Prime Minister Haughey affirmed on behalf of the Irish Council presidency that '[t]he EC can and must do more than anyone else . . . [It] has an enormous load of responsibility towards East Europe' (Torreblanca 1997: 114); the Rome European Council in December pronounced itself 'conscious of its special responsibility towards the Central and Eastern European Countries' (European Council 1990).

The EU's own discourse was endorsed and perpetuated by outside sources. The new CEEC governments declared as their ambition to 'return to Europe' by joining the EU, and the US administration stated that the CEECs were largely 'Europe's responsibility' (Baker 1989). The continuity in the collective discourse of EU policy-makers, and the validation from outside sources reinforced the EU's self-proclaimed role and endowed it with more concrete substance: it had a 'special responsibility' towards the CEECs to use this 'historical opportunity' to overcome the division of the continent. The EU had to actively support the transformations in the CEECs and their integration with the EU. The discourse implied an EU commitment which, for those policy-makers in charge of EU policy towards the CEECs, had become closely associated to the EU's self-image. The discourse of a collective EU identity, characterized by a 'responsibility' towards the CEECs, became a central aspect of EU policy.

Policy Impact and the Uneven Effect of the EU's Collective Identity Towards the CEECs

Through the centrality of the notion of 'responsibility' in the policy discourse, EU policy-makers have thus discursively constructed a specific role for the EU, or the EU's collective identity, towards the CEECs. However, merely to establish the existence of such a collective identity is not sufficient to infer a causal effect on policy. This section therefore seeks to clarify the mechanisms through which EU identity has a policy impact.

This is not only in itself a central concern of the social constructivist research agenda (see e.g. Risse-Kappen 1994; Checkel 1998); it seems particularly necessary to understand the effect of identity on policy towards the CEECs. There was strong opposition inside EU to acknowledging even the principle of enlargement in the Europe Agreements (EAs), and incrementalism characterized the subsequent evolution of the EU's commitment to eastern enlargement. This contrasts with the virtually automatic effect on appropriate behavior that is usually associated with constructivist approaches.[2] The discursive existence of a collective EU identity that centers on the notion of 'responsibility' is thus not, as such, sufficient to generate policy outcomes that accommodate the CEECs' preferences.

This chapter argues that a crucial aspect of the effect of the EU's identity on its policy towards the CEECs is that it is *uneven* across the policy-makers involved: both the way in which and the extent to which it affects their behavior varies. In order to understand its policy impact, we thus need to consider four related concepts, namely (i) the difference between shared and collective identities; (ii) the distinction between constitutive and regulative effects of norms and identity; (iii) the difference between internalization of norms and norm-conforming behavior resulting from rationalist calculations of reputational and social costs of deviation; and, as a consequence of these, (iv) the importance of the agency by policy advocates.

Certain norms or a specific identity may be *shared* by all members of a group. But even if they are *not* commonly held, they might none the less characterize the group *collectively*, if they have become either a prominent feature of the public discourse of the group, or formally institutionalized as common property (Jepperson *et al.* 1996: 54).

The latter seems the case for the EU's identity towards the CEECs. Some member governments that fear the consequences of eastern enlargement might not share a desire to integrate the CEECs in the near future. But they have been implicated in the creation of a discourse that implies a responsibility to support their integration. The key question is then to what extent and why those that do not individually share the goals implied in the collective discourse might feel bound by it. To the extent that they do, it might be due to a regulative effect of norms and identity. It is precisely this regulative effect that pushes the boundary between 'thinner' social constructivist approaches that emphasize the role of strategic action, and more sophisticated rationalist approaches that also include non-material factors. Rather than assuming an either/or approach to

---

[2] For a similar observation, see Schimmelfennig (1999).

social construction and rational choice, this focuses on the link between rationality and norm-compliance (see e.g. Finnemore and Sikkink 1998; March and Olsen 1998).

Identity and the norms that define it can have *constitutive* or *regulative* effects on actors, or both. The effects of identity and norms are most far-reaching if they have a constitutive effect. This is the case if actors internalize certain norms or identities: if a given identity forms a large part of their multiple social identities, and if they have an effect on their preference formation and interest definition (see e.g. Jepperson *et al.* 1996). This does not mean that regulative norms do not play a role in this case. They specify standards for appropriate behavior through which a given identity is enacted in varying circumstances.

Yet norms and identity might also have a purely regulative effect. In this case, the effect is merely on behavior, not on underlying interests. They regulate behavior by prescribing or proscribing appropriate ways of acting for a given role. This is different from the quasi-material constraints on strategies that many neoliberal institutionalist accounts emphasize. However, more sophisticated rationalist approaches take account of the fact that actors might include reputational concerns and social costs of non-conforming behavior in their cost/benefit calculations (see e.g. Johnston 1999).[3]

Thus in order to understand how the uneven effect of identity affects EU policy towards the CEECs, we need to identify the relevant constitutive effects and regulative norms implied by the EU's collective identity. To the extent that policy is evaluated with regard to its compatibility with the role professed in official statements, the somewhat diffuse notion of an 'EU responsibility towards the CEECs' is a rather vague guide. None the less, as opposed to questions of specific policy detail, the prescriptions that it entails on the general principle of eastern enlargement are fairly clear.[4] The EU needs to contribute actively towards making enlargement a reality. At a minimum, eventual enlargement cannot be refused simply because it might compromise certain vested interests of the incumbents, as it presents a legitimate aim of the CEECs.

---

[3] In a similar vein, Schimmelfenning (1999) emphasizes that arguments relating to institutional norms strengthened the bargaining power of actors pressing for eastern enlargement. He argues, however, that such actors only use these arguments instrumentally, i.e. they have not internalized these norms.

[4] By contrast, it is not immediately obvious which evaluative standards it implies for an assessment of the norm-conformity or 'appropriateness' of specific EU practices on issues of policy substance, such as to liberalize trade or to establish concrete conditions for accession. These are outside this chapter's focus, but any account that analyzes the effects of identity on policy towards the CEECs cannot be complete unless it captures the effects on these issues as well (see Sedelmeier 1998*a*).

In this case, the regulative effect of identity thus operates primarily through a prohibitive norm. Since its evaluative standard is clearer for the behavior that it proscribes, rather than what it prescribes, the role of policy advocates is crucial. To have a positive effect on policy outcomes, it requires certain actors to advocate policy options with which others then conform, because they feel they cannot refuse to do so, although they might not otherwise have chosen to do so had they not been forced to justify non-compliant behavior. In turn, in order for a credible group of policy advocates to emerge, identity has to have a constitutive effect on certain policy-makers. This chapter argues that a group of policy advocates emerged around the Commission's DG I and successive commissioners for external relations and their *cabinets*. These policy-makers identify most strongly with the EU's role towards the CEECs and thus largely internalized the EU's identity in this respect.

In sum, the argument that this chapter sketches does not suggest that EU identity towards the CEECs determines policy outcomes. Nor does it suggest that identity only has an effect if actors internalize it. To be sure, material self-interests and strategic bargaining are an important part of the process. Identity affects policy by structuring the 'realm of possibilities' for available policy options, which precludes certain options as inappropriate, and reinforces the legitimacy of others (see e.g. Price and Tannenwald 1996: 148–9; Klotz 1995*b*: 461–2). It thus created the necessary scope for policy advocates to obtain agreement on incremental steps that advanced policy.

Nor does it contradict the argument if actors whose preference formation is shaped by the internalization of identity behave strategically to maximize these preferences. They might even use normative arguments strategically to induce compliance in others, or they might appeal to actors' self-interest to gain agreement. Indeed, the policy advocates frequently asserted that an accommodating policy towards the CEECs served the EU's collective self-interest. Conversely, some actors might promote similar goals for purely self-interested reasons. They might even try to legitimize their goals with reference to norms. What matters in this case is why actors—for whom norm-compliance is not clearly complementary with material interest-maximization—are susceptible to their arguments. Interesting from a theoretical point of view is the effect on policy of the interaction between the referenced regulative norms and interests definition, and between norm-compliance and rational choice, not an either/or causation. The regulative norm provided the necessary condition, which, in combination with strategic behavior by the policy advocates and the support of some actors motivated by material self-interests, led EU policy towards eastern enlargement.

Advocacy, Incrementalism, and Norm-Compliance in the EU's Policy Towards the CEECs

The EU's decision to start accession negotiations was not simply the result of a 'history-making' decision at the Luxembourg European Council in December 1997. Rather, the formal decision was the result of a number of apparently discrete decisions at different European Council meetings that made the enlargement process increasingly hard to reverse. I argue that the crucial step which started this expansive and cumulative logic of policy evolution was the formal endorsement of the CEECs' membership perspective at the Copenhagen Council in June 1993. Table 9.1 highlights the key junctures in the evolution of the EU's policy.

This section sketches how this agreement was reached and its significance for subsequent policy developments. It emphasizes the continued advocacy and the strategies of the policy advocates, the incremental nature of policy evolution, and the importance of the regulative effect of the EU's identity in reducing the scope for a veto.

The Formal Endorsement of the Principle of Eventual CEEC Membership at the Copenhagen European Council

During the negotiations of the Europe Agreements with the first three CEECs in 1991, the CEECs wanted the EAs to acknowledge a link between the agreements and their eventual membership. They were supported by the unit in the Commission's DG I (external relations) that was responsible for policy towards the CEECs (DG I-E), and external relations commissioner Frans Andriessen and his *cabinet*. These policy-makers had continued close contacts with their counterparts in the CEECs and soon acted as advocates of the CEECs' interests inside the EU and of their integration with the EU, which they regarded as the EU's responsibility and in line with the EU's role.[5]

However, the EU's overall position on the CEECs' membership perspective was highly restrictive. The member governments, except for the German and British, and parts of the Commission were strongly opposed to creating a link to eastern enlargement, or even to engage at this stage in a debate about enlargement as a longer term prospect. As a result, the negotiation directives for the Commission negotiators specified that, if the

---

[5] Interviews in a Commissioner's *cabinet*, 2 Feb. 1995; in the Commission, DG I, 23 Oct. 1995, Brussels; in the Commission, DG I, 24 Oct.1995, Brussels; in the Commission, DG I, 24 Oct. 1995, Brussels; and in the Commission, DG I, 27 Oct. 1995, Brussels.

TABLE 9.1. *Key Dates in the CEEC Enlargement Decision*

December 1990	Start of negotiations for Europe Agreements (EAs) with the first CEECs (Hungary, Poland, Czechoslovakia)
December 1991	Signing of the first EAs
June 1993	Copenhagen European Council (Endorsement of the CEECs' membership perspective)
December 1994	Essen European Council (Agreement on a 'pre-accession strategy' to prepare the CEECs for accession)
December 1995	Madrid European Council (Agreement to start accession negotiations six months after the IGC to be convened in 1996)
July 1996	Start of the 1996/7 IGC (Dealing also with institutional reform)
June 1997	Amsterdam European Council (end of the IGC; signing of the Treaty of Amsterdam) Commission's Agenda 2000 document published (Containing proposals for internal policy reform)
December 1997	Luxembourg European Council (Decision to start accession negotiations in March 1998)
March 1998	Start of accession negotiations with the first CEECs (Hungary, Poland, Czech Republic, Estonia, Slovenia—plus Cyprus)
March 1999	Berlin European Council (Agreement on the financial perspective for 2000–6—implications for reform of the CAP and Structural Funds)
June 1999	Cologne European Council (Decision to hold a short IGC in 2000 to finalize institutional reform)

CEECs should raise the issue during the negotiations, they should simply refer to the general possibility, according to Article 237 EEC, for any European state to apply for membership.[6]

The conduct of the negotiations and their final outcome on this issue was fairly close to what rationalist approaches would expect. In the intra-EU debate, the member governments' positions seemed to reflect the cost/benefit calculations of the longer-term implications that such an acknowledgment of the CEECs' eventual membership would entail. In the negotiations, the asymmetries in bargaining power between the member states and the CEECs constrained the accommodation of the CEECs'

---

[6] Interviews in the Commission, DG I, 23 Oct. 1995, Brussels; and in the Commission, DG I, 24 Oct. 1995, Brussels.

preferences.[7] Although the Council agreed to make the negotiation direct-ives more flexible in order to resolve the negotiation deadlock resulting from the dissatisfaction of the CEECs, this mainly concerned the EU's trade concessions. The Council did agree to a formulation in the preamble which acknowledged eventual membership as the 'ultimate objective' of the CEECs. This formulation fell, however, well short of acknowledging this as a mutual objective shared by the EU, and made clear that mem-bership would be far from an automatic consequence of association.

Still, the Commission negotiators inserted in the paragraph of the preamble that 'in the view of the parties these agreements will help this objective'. Although this went beyond the negotiation directives, none of the delegations in the Council wanted to object formally to it.[8] In this sense, the EA negotiations also showed that the EU's professed role towards the CEECs created a certain room for manœuver for the policy advocates inside the Commission.

Although this concession seemed to stretch to its absolute limits what the main actors on the EU side could accept, a year and a half later the EU agreed on the step that the great majority of member governments and parts of the Commission had opposed rigorously.[9] The Copenhagen European Council in June 1993 declared that 'the associated countries in Central and Eastern Europe that so desire shall become members of the European Union. Accession will take place as soon as an associated coun-try is able to assume the obligations of membership by satisfying the eco-nomic and political conditions required' (European Council 1993: 5). The continued advocacy by DG I-E and the Andriessen *cabinet* generated the essential dynamism behind this development of policy. Almost immedi-ately after the signing of the EAs, these policy advocates started to work on moving EU policy beyond the association formula. In addition to more substantive proposals, the central element of their advocacy was the for-mal endorsement of the CEECs' eventual accession as an objective shared by the EU.[10]

The extent of opposition to reopening the debate and the constraints that it imposed on a more accommodating policy were reflected in the fact that the Copenhagen declaration itself was the result of an incremental evolution. This process was marked by agreement on key documents that

---

[7] For further detail on the negotiations, see e.g. Sedelmeier and Wallace (1996); Niblett (1995); Friis (1997); Torreblanca (1997); Sedelmeier (1998*a*).

[8] Interview in the Commission, DG I, 23 Oct. 1995, Brussels.

[9] In addition to this declaration, the European Council also endorsed a unilateral accel-eration of trade liberalization and closer institutional links between the EU and the CEECs. These are not, however, subject of this chapter.

[10] Interviews in the Commission, DG I, 24 Oct. 1995, Brussels; and in the Commission, DG I, 24 Oct. 1995, Brussels.

went increasingly towards acknowledging the CEECs' membership perspective. While the individual documents did not themselves explicitly acknowledge eastern enlargement as a shared objective, they made it increasingly hard to refuse it ultimately.

The Commission's report on enlargement for the Lisbon European Council in June 1992 acknowledged that while the CEECs were 'not yet in a position to accept the obligations of membership [they have] political needs which go *beyond* the possibilities of existing agreements' (Commission 1992*a*: 8, my emphasis; see also Michalski and Wallace 1992: 63). In the report for the Edinburgh European Council in December 1992, the Commission proposed that the European Council 'should now confirm that it accepts the goal of eventual membership in the European Union for the [CEECs] when they are able to satisfy the conditions required' (Commission 1992*c*: 3). The Edinburgh European Council was too distracted with other business to discuss the Commission report in detail, but stated that at its next meeting it would 'reach decisions on the various components of the Commission's report in order to prepare the associate countries for accession to the Union' (European Council 1992*b*: 37). In the run-up to the Copenhagen European Council, the discussion in the Council focused mainly on trade concessions and the institutional framework and no longer seriously challenged the principle of membership.

Strategic Behavior and Instrumental Rationality

An important aspect of the success of the policy advocates was that they moved strategically to achieve their goals. They forged strategic alliances and informal cooperation with actors that arguably promoted an evolution of policy towards eastern enlargement for more self-interested reasons. This included support from German policy-makers, but crucially also active coordination with the UK and Danish Council presidencies in the second half of 1992 and the first half of 1993. Cooperation concerned both strategy and substance, including the insertion of policy papers drafted in the Commission as presidency papers into the Council's discussion.[11]

Tactical behavior secured the approval in the Commission of the crucial report for the Edinburgh European Council. Endorsement was obtained not simply through a process of persuasion, but by calling a vote in the College of Commissioners. Many commissioners, including President Delors, were concerned that putting enlargement on the agenda was divisive for the member states and thus detrimental for progress on the internal

---

[11] Interviews in the UK Permanent Representation, 9 July 1993, Brussels; and in the Commission, DG I, 24 Oct. 1995, Brussels.

agenda. The necessary majority was secured with the inclusion of requirements in the qualitative criteria for CEEC membership that called for the stability of democratic institutions in the CEECs and the EU's capacity to absorb new members without endangering its own momentum.[12]

Finally, an element in the policy advocates' strategy was to persuade the member governments that the prospect of eastern enlargement would increase their material self-interest, or at least not affect it negatively. For example, on the one hand they emphasized that the perspective of membership could counter the risks that the changing political situation in Central and Eastern Europe entailed, such as the threats to stability from ethnic conflicts and the risks to the reforms stemming from the increasing popular dissatisfaction (Commission 1992c, 1993a). On the other hand, the Commission supported research into the effects of further integration of the CEECs on specific EU regions and sectors, in order to demonstrate that the expected negative consequences were greatly overstated (Baldwin 1994; Faini and Portes 1995).

Regulative Norms and Identity-Related Arguments about Appropriate Behavior

The building of strategic alliances and instrumental strategies that focused on the material cost/benefit calculations of the more reluctant policy-makers thus played an important part in the agreement on the Copenhagen declaration. But this is not the whole story and not sufficient to explain this outcome. A key element of the policy process was that even EU policy-makers concerned about the material consequences of enlargement were sensitive to non-material factors associated with the regulative effects of the EU's identity towards the CEECs.

The policy advocates' strategy included presenting the member states' endorsement of the CEECs' membership perspective as a case of appropriate behavior by relating it to the EU's identity. In the internal debate they repeatedly used such normative arguments and pursued an explicit link in official documents between identity and enlargement as an important objective in its own right. For example, the policy advocates inserted into the Commission's Lisbon report a language that explicitly expressed the EU's responsibility towards the CEECs and the need to act accordingly.

The integration of [the] new democracies into the European family presents a historic opportunity. . . . The Community has never been a closed club, and cannot now refuse the historic challenge to assume its continental responsibilities and

---

[12] Interview in a Commissioner's *cabinet*, 15 Dec. 1995.

contribute to the development of a political and economic order for the whole of Europe. . . . Enlargement is a challenge which the Community cannot refuse. (Commission 1992*a*: 1–2, 9)

Another example is contained in a draft of the Commission report for Edinburgh, which emphasizes the legitimacy of the CEECs' objectives and the resulting need for the EU to endorse it: 'The merits of . . . a [clear declaration by the Community, in which it endorses the object of fully-fledged membership of these countries at a later stage] would be very substantial as it would give: satisfaction to the *justified* aspirations of these countries' (Commission 1992*b*: 5; my emphasis).

Likewise, the apparent vulnerability of EU policy-makers to the broadly based criticism of the EAs by academics, journalists, as well as CEEC policy-makers, is striking, as it was not linked to any material threats. Academic and media criticism was unanimous in denouncing the absence of a clear membership perspective, the failure to engage in a debate about constructive adaptation of the EU integration model in order to accommodate the CEECs in the long run;[13] and the limitations of the trade concessions.[14] CEEC policy-makers criticized the EAs both in an individual capacity[15] and collectively in two so-called Visegrád memoranda of September 1992 and June 1993 (Visegrád 1992, 1993), issued just before the respective European Councils with the active encouragement from the policy advocates in the Commission.

This criticism focused not only on the failure of the EU to act decisively in its own security and economic interest. It had a strong normative dimension which emphasized the failure of the EU to match its rhetoric with appropriate behavior, and to live up to the role it had declared for itself and to the expectations it had raised. Crucially, although it was not linked to material sanctions and was not made by actors with the material capabilities to sanction non-fulfilment of their demands, such criticism and the strong normative language of the policy advocates had a clear effect on member governments and the more reluctant parts of the Commission.

For example, the French government strongly perceived the need to take a much more positive approach in order to rectify the impression that France was a main obstructer of a more accommodating policy.[16] The

---

[13] See e.g. Bonvicini *et al.* (1991); Wallace (1991); Reinicke (1992); Kramer (1993); Smith and Wallace (1994).

[14] See e.g. Baldwin *et al.* (1992); Winters (1992); Hindley (1993); Messerlin (1993); Rollo and Smith (1993).

[15] See e.g Hanna Suchocka, 'Le Passage d'un système à l'autre doit être moins brutal', *Le Monde* (17 Sept. 1992); Inotai (1994); Saryusz-Wolski (1994).

[16] Interviews in the French Foreign Ministry, 3 and 10 July 1996, Paris.

Spanish government felt that its tough stance on trade issues was misinterpreted as general hostility to the eventual accession of the CEECs.[17] After a visit by the Polish Prime Minister Hanna Suchocka to Madrid, Prime Minister Felipe Gonzáles instructed the Foreign Ministry to support the Commission's proposals.[18]

Crucially, after the Commission formally put the proposal to endorse the membership perspective on the table, none of the delegations in the Council disputed it openly.[19] In the end, reservations existed mainly among the Belgian and Luxembourg governments, which had strong concerns about the possible dilution of future integration, but did not voice them formally.[20] The agreement on the financial perspective and the solution to the Maastricht ratification crisis at the Edinburgh European Council had greatly reduced the arguments that could be presented as legitimate against turning to the question of enlargement.

In sum, the way in which the Copenhagen European Council's formal endorsement of the CEECs' membership perspective as a mutual policy goal was achieved suggests that EU policy did not merely evolve within the parameters of material cost/benefit calculations of the main actors. The endorsement of the Copenhagen declaration might have been facilitated by the consideration that this statement did not entail any formally binding obligations on the EU and thus allowed for later backtracking. But although it could lead to the debate that the majority of member governments and parts of the Commission had wanted to avoid, EU policymakers responded to the criticism of their apparent failure to act in accordance to their professed role, rather than taking the stance that the EAs were a take-it-or-leave-it offer.

The regulative effect of identity created the necessary room for manœuver for the policy advocates to press for the formal endorsement of the CEECs' eventual accession as a mutual goal. EU identity limited the policy options that were acceptable as appropriate behavior. It limited the grounds for legitimate opposition by excluding argument about material self-interests. Even policy-makers in the member governments and the Commission that feared the material consequences of eastern enlargement felt inhibited to veto this step with reference to their particular self-interest.

The regulative effect of EU identity toward the CEECs is underlined in the importance of two non-material factors for the success of the policy advocates, namely the use of identity-related arguments in official

---

[17] Interviews in the Spanish Foreign Ministry, 18 and 21 June 1996.
[18] Interview in the Spanish Permanent Representation, 3 Feb. 1995, Brussels.
[19] Interview in the UK Permanent Representation, 9 July 1993, Brussels.
[20] Interview in the Commission DG I, 24 Oct. 1995, Brussels.

statements and internal discussions and the normative criticism of the EAs from both the academic community and the CEECs. However, endorsement of the policy advocates' proposal was far from automatic and relied heavily on their strategic behavior.

Even in these instances in which behavior seemed to follow more clearly a logic of appropriate behavior, it included instrumental rationality on the part of the policy advocates who used normative arguments strategically to induce compliance. Furthermore, although compliance was not induced by material sanctions and constraints, it did in part result from a strategic calculation of consequences. Crucially however, the utility function of these actors included the reputational and social costs entailed by failing to conform with the regulative norms implied in the EU's role towards the CEECs.

The Expansive Logic of the Formal Acknowledgment of the CEECs' Eventual Membership

The Significance of the Copenhagen Declaration

The acknowledgment of eventual CEEC accession as a shared objective presents a significant achievement, considering the strong initial opposition to such a move. However, at the time the assessments of the substance of the Copenhagen declaration were rather ambiguous. The declaration did not involve any legally enforceable commitment. The absence of a timetable, the qualitative formulation of the conditions for membership,[21] and in particular the provision that 'the Union's capacity to absorb new members, while maintaining the momentum of European integration, is also an important consideration' (European Council 1993: 5)—something entirely beyond the CEECs' control—provided ample scope for backtracking. The Copenhagen declaration might thus be interpreted as a limited, merely rhetorical response to the CEECs' criticism of the EAs.

The limitations of the Copenhagen declaration are on the one hand an expression of the constraints that strategic bargaining between material interest-maximizing actors placed upon a more accommodating policy. On the other hand, both how Copenhagen was achieved and its subsequent significance suggest that EU policy did not merely evolve within the parameters of material cost/benefit calculations of the main actors.

---

[21] The declaration mentions the following conditions: stability of institutions guaranteeing democracy, the rule of law, human rights, and respect for and protection of minorities; existence of a functioning market economy; capacity to cope with competitive pressure and market forces within the Union; ability to take on the obligations of membership including adherence to the aims of political, economic, and monetary union.

The benefit of hindsight allows one to establish that Copenhagen was indeed highly significant. All subsequent EU documents on policy towards the CEECs start by quoting Copenhagen as the key expression of the EU's commitment to eastern enlargement. Crucially, the Copenhagen declaration had a profound substantive impact on the subsequent evolution of policy. It provided a starting-point for an expansive logic that made it increasingly difficult to block initiatives aimed to develop policy further. Despite the strong reluctance among EU policy-makers to face up to the consequences of eastern enlargement, it paved the way to open accession negotiations with the CEECs, which is '[p]robably the most significant of the different stages of the accession process . . . because opening them implies a willingness to conclude them' (Avery and Cameron 1998: 27).

Incrementalism, Regulative Norms, Commitment and Credibility

Central to this evolution were successive agreements on limited, incremental developments of policy. The Essen European Council in December 1994 endorsed the Commission's proposal of a so-called pre-accession strategy to prepare the CEECs for accession. Its economic core was a Commission White Paper to prepare the CEECs for their participation in the internal market. Finally, the Madrid European Council in December 1995 approved an indicative date for the start of accession negotiations: six months after the conclusion of the IGC starting in 1996.[22]

This incrementalism was in part a result of the constraints on policy; in part it was a deliberate strategy of the policy advocates.[23] Similarly to the Copenhagen declaration, these incremental steps focused on apparently limited measures and questions of principle, to refuse which would have been in contradiction with the EU's identity. For example, having accepted the general principle of the CEECs' eventual accession, it was difficult to refuse the argument that the EU should present the CEECs with a workable road map that indicated the path from the general principle to actual accession.[24] In turn, having agreed to a work program for the CEECs' accession preparations, it was hard to argue against an indicative date for the start of accession negotiations, if the CEECs had by then made significant progress.

A crucial factor that reinforced this dynamic was that the Copenhagen declaration presented a certain formalization of the EU's commitment to eventual membership. Agreement to these initiatives could now be clearly presented as a test for the credibility of the EU. In this sense, when the Essen

---

[22] For further detail on this evolution see e.g. Sedelmeier and Wallace (1996); Mayhew (1998); Grabbe and Hughes (1998), Sedelmeier (1998*a*).

[23] Interview in the Commission DG I, 24 Oct. 1995, Brussels.

[24] Interviews in the Commission DG I, 24 Oct. 1995, Brussels; and in a commissioner's *cabinet*, 2 Feb. 1995, Brussels.

European Council endorsed the pre-accession strategy, it affirmed that '[the EU], in deciding this strategy, reemphasizes the commitment of the Union to the accession of the associated countries' (European Council 1994: 25).

Apparent Safeguards and Decreasing Grounds for Legitimate Opposition to Enlargement

In addition, these measures still contained safety valves that seemed to keep them limited and to provide scope to stop developments at a later stage. The Copenhagen declaration was only a declaration of principle and set conditions for membership, including the ominous provision of the EU's own dynamism. The choice of regulatory alignment as the economic core of the pre-accession strategy[25] could be seen as a safeguard against politically motivated early accessions. By making the regulatory accession requirements more explicit, it seemed to make the conditionality harder.[26] Finally, the start of accession negotiations was made conditional on successful institutional reform at the 1996/7 IGC (European Council 1995: 23). However, despite these safeguards, each of those measures had the increasingly effect of reducing the grounds of legitimate opposition to enlargement. As the EU's collective identity proscribed selfish opposition to enlargement, it restricted legitimate arguments to those that focused on the common interest of an enlarged EU.

One such common interest of all participants is the proper functioning of the internal market. Doubts about the CEECs' ability to implement the EU's regulatory regimes were thus a legitimate argument against enlargement. However, since the pre-accession strategy focused precisely on the preparation of the CEECs for the internal market, such doubts could no longer serve as a general pretext.

Another common interest of current and future members is the sustainability of the EU's dynamism after enlargement. Initially, member governments could legitimately decline to address the general question of enlargement before the ratification of the Maastricht Treaty, which was supposed to provide the necessary deepening. But the solution to the Danish ratification problem at the Edinburgh European Council made it hard to refuse to take a general position on enlargement.

A further aspect of the EU's dynamism is the effectiveness of decision-making in an enlarged Union. However, since the Madrid European

---

[25] For a discussion of a pre-accession strategy based on regulatory alignment, see Smith *et al.* 1996; for the process leading to the adoption of the pre-accession strategy and the White Paper, see Sedelmeier (1998*b*); for the follow-up in the Accession Partnerships, see Grabbe (1999).

[26] Interview in the French Prime Minister's Office, 10 July 1996, Paris; and in the French Foreign Ministry, 3 July 1996, Paris.

Council made the start of accession negotiations conditional on institutional reform at the 1996/7 IGC, it was difficult to refuse the principle. Furthermore, despite the insufficient results of the IGC, the logic of having agreed to an indicative starting date was such that the member governments decided none the less to open accession negotiations in March 1998, while agreeing on another IGC to deal with these issues. To be sure, some member governments entered into the minutes of the Amsterdam European Council their intent not to endorse any accession if the reforms should not be agreed.[27] However, it seems very hard to conceive that they would eventually veto enlargement with the argument that the results of the 2000 IGC did not go far enough.

Conclusions

This chapter's argument has both empirical implications for the EU's ability to respond strategically to a common risk and theoretical implications for the broader debate in IR theory about the relationship between rationality and norm-conforming behavior.

Enlargement, Risk, and Rationality

The central argument of this chapter is that the EU's decision to open accession negotiations was not the result of a strategic choice in response to the potential risks of instability in the CEECs. The ability to agree on enlargement despite the veto power of negatively affected member governments is thus not a reflection of the EU's capacity as a collective strategic actor in international politics. Rather, the EU's decision to pursue accession negotiations can largely be attributed to the collective identity that the EU created for itself and the regulative norms such an identity entailed.

First, although the EU was able to agree on enlargement, it could not agree to more than minimal reforms to prepare itself for enlargement. Thus, while the EU was able to avoid the risks associated with passivity *vis-à-vis* the changes in the CEECs, its activism generates its own long-term risks for the sustainability of the integration project. Second, the process through which enlargement was endorsed was very different from strategic decision-making driven by a common security rationale. The policy process has been far too incremental; every step towards further developments was strongly contested; and at virtually no point was there a thorough debate about the EU's interests and appropriate strategies for an enlarged EU.

[27] *The Financial Times* (16 Sept. 1997).

It is thus difficult to see in the enlargement decision a rational collective decision by enlightened member governments that prioritize long-term interest, or engage in collective problem-solving and burden-sharing out of solidarity with those member states that are most directly affected by potential instability in the CEECs. Nor was it the case that member states with particular interests in enlargement coerced the others into a decision that might be detrimental to the system as a whole. This chapter's analysis suggests that while member governments with more obvious material interests in enlargement provided significant support for the policy advocates, they were not the source of the crucial policy initiatives analyzed in this chapter.

Moreover, the chapter suggests that looking at EU policy primarily as case of foreign policy is seriously misleading. By overstating the importance of the security rationale, it distracts from the distinctiveness of the relationship with the CEECs. It ignores the fact that EU policy towards the CEECs is as much about the definition and enactment of the EU's identity as about a stabilization of its 'new abroad'.

To understand the decision to enlarge requires one to depart from materialist assumptions of rationality. Identification with, or the constitutive effects of, the discursively constructed role of the EU towards the CEECs led a group of policy advocates inside the Commission to continuously promote moves towards enlargement. This does not mean that calculations of the material costs and benefits of enlargement were not an important part of the story. For example, the perception of risks from possible instability in the CEECs was an important factor in generating support for enlargement, particularly from the German government. Conversely, the perception of the risks that enlargement itself could entail for future integration in the EU were important considerations that caused reluctance in the Belgian and Luxembourg governments, for example. The maximization of material interests imposed constraints on policy, which meant that it could only evolve incrementally, but these could not stop the process altogether. Albeit incrementally, policy did evolve. These successive steps made the enlargement process increasingly irreversible. The necessary scope for such an evolution was created by regulative constraints on behavior. The decisions at each stage were presented as questions of principle. Opposition with open reference to narrow self-interests would have entailed conflicts with regulative norms associated with the EU's collective identity towards the CEECs.

To be sure, agreement at each of these stages included apparent safeguards which seemed to maintain the possibility to block further evolution of policy at a later stage. To the extent that policy-makers subsequently felt inhibited to insist on a strict interpretation of these safe-

[28] Interview in the German Foreign Ministry, 13 Dec. 1995, Bonn.

guards, there might have been an element of unintended consequences facilitating a certain path dependence. The cumulative logic of policy evolution, and the increasing formalization of an EU commitment to enlargement, further limited the grounds for legitimate opposition to enlargement and raised the reputational costs of a veto.

However, as the regulative norm was primarily prohibitive, the consensus it created was primarily a negative consensus, namely 'not to block enlargement'.[28] The EU's identity was not widely enough internalized to forge a positive consensus on enlargement and on the necessary reforms. The prospect of continued muddling-through suggests a pessimistic scenario in which enlargement might lead the EU towards the 'risk'-end of the continuum identified in the introduction to this volume.

A more optimistic interpretation is that the inevitability of enlargement now condemns policy-makers to agree to the necessary reforms. EU policy-makers might thus have pushed themselves towards the reform/revival scenario (see Chapter 10 below, by Friis and Murphy). Still, in this case, the impetus for reform and revival did not come primarily from a collective strategic decision, but to a large extent precisely from the obstacles that the EU's role towards the CEECs imposes on a 'rational' defense of individual member states' narrower material self-interests.

The Link between Rationality and Norm-Compliance

These apparent shortcomings of rationalist approaches to eastern enlargement highlight the important contribution that more sociological approaches in international relations can make. However, EU policy towards the CEECs also presents a key case to support the more recent move in the theoretical debate away from either/or arguments between rationalism and constructivism. Instead, it underlines the need to focus on, and to understand better, the link between rationality and norm-conforming behavior.

The debate has already clarified that to accept interests as endogenous does not exclude strategic behavior to achieve these interests. But eastern enlargement entails cases that are not easily captured by the elegant solution of such a 'division of labor' between rationalists and constructivists (Katzenstein *et al.* 1998). It thus identifies two related key areas where further conceptual and methodological research is necessary. One is the strategic use of normative arguments and what it tells us about whether the actors that profess these norms use them instrumentally or genuinely. The other is how the strategic use of normative arguments works. The regulative effect of norms generates behavioral constraints and induces norm-compliance, although there is neither a link to material sanctions, nor a constitutive effect of actors' interest definition.

10

Enlargement: A Complex Juggling Act

LYKKE FRIIS AND ANNA MURPHY

Since the inception of the EU, in 1957, enlargement has been a recurrent phenomenon. Despite this, the current enlargement round is generally looked upon as being unique (see for instance, Eatwell *et al.* 1997; Preston 1997). The core reason for this is that the EU cannot simply dig into the toolkit of the past and apply its classical method of dealing with enlargement: that is, to concentrate on the actual accession negotiations and postpone institutional and policy reform until after accession (Preston 1997). In the present round, the EU has to tackle four challenges at the same time or, to phrase the point metaphorically, the EU has to perform a difficult juggling act.

First of all, it has to address the difficulties of integration which emerge in the actual accession negotiations (on terms and criteria for entry into the EU) with a set of applicants whose political, economic, and administrative cultures are very divergent from those of existing member states. Second, enlargement by possibly twelve countries will have major repercussions for the policies and functioning of the EU and force it to the table of internal reform. Third, the EU will have to address the challenge of 'queue-management', that is, managing the order of accession to the EU. Since it is confronted by a historically long queue it will, for the first time, have to differentiate between applicants and possibly face accusations of discrimination and of attempting to draw new dividing lines in Europe.

Fourth and finally, enlargement demands that the EU addresses its implications for the wider Europe. It must develop a stronger policy towards those neighbors which will not accede to the Union in the medium to long term. Without, for instance, a strengthened policy towards Russia and Ukraine, the accession of the countries of Central and Eastern Europe could easily draw new borderlines in Europe and, instead of achieving the desired goal of security, it could do the opposite. The same goes for its southern neighbors of the Mediterranean. In 1999, the war in Kosovo was a potent reminder of the continuing risks and threats to security and stability in South-eastern Europe. These considerations place an additional burden on the EU's enlargement process.

The very fact that the EU has to perform this juggling act not only makes this enlargement round unique but also engages the EU in a new balance between what this book describes as the four Rs: risks, reform, resistance, and revival. The risks are linked to the fact that the EU could easily end up dropping one item (or even all) in its complex juggling act. For instance, the difficulties of just managing the first challenge, negotiating accession with the most advanced countries, could lead to a situation where the EU neglects queue-management and hence creates new divisions in Europe. The institutional and policy reforms necessitated by enlargement could be forestalled due to the resistance of member states to surrendering some of their present benefits. On the other hand, the act of juggling the four challenges could itself be a catalyst for revival in the sense that the enlargement process reveals an underlying trend towards a greater preoccupation with peace and stability in the wider Europe. This may be evidenced by a shift of collective focus to expanding the foundational goals of the EU to the wider Europe. The enlargement process, which is largely driven by a security rationale, remains the primary vehicle for pursuing this objective.

Despite the fact that it is this juggling act which makes this fifth round of enlargement unique, the literature on the topic tends to focus on one challenge only, with the result that the interlinkages between them are understated. Second, the literature is largely atheoretical (for a similar criticism see Helen Wallace in Chapter 8 above). Indeed, as pointed out by Philippe Schmitter, after four previous rounds of enlargement 'all the discussion about "widening vs. deepening" is [still] taking place in a theoretical vacuum' (Schmitter 1996: 14).[1]

This chapter presents a conceptual framework which combines governance theory with the concept of boundaries to enable us to understand the juggling act. To date, governance theory, which is otherwise prominent in the EU literature, has not been directly applied to enlargement (with the exception of Friis and Murphy, 1999 and 2000*a*). Nevertheless, we argue that it provides us with the necessary conceptual bridge between the internal and external which is intrinsic to the juggling act.

The central argument of this chapter is that one can only comprehend the EU's enlargement policy if one analyses the interlinkages between the four challenges and the dynamics operating between the boundaries. We

---

[1] Most of the literature on this fifth round of enlargement is atheoretical (Maresceau 1997; Grabbe and Hughes 1998; Redmond and Rosenthal 1998; Avery and Cameron 1998; Henderson 1999; Curzon Price *et al.* 1999). For exceptions, see H. Wallace 1997 and Ch. 8 above; Miles *et al.* 1995; Preston 1997; Friis and Murphy 1999.

show this by looking at the empirical evidence from December 1997, when the EU formalized its enlargement strategy at the Luxembourg European Council, to mid-1999 when it concluded the related *Agenda 2000* negotiations. Up to mid-1999, the EU managed its juggling act by postponing key internal reforms and by launching policies short of membership towards the candidates. We argue that this juggling act can only be sustained in the short term. Given that its enlargement policy remains tied to the prospect of eventual membership and that key internal reforms have simply been postponed, the EU's ability to juggle is bound to come under immense pressure in the medium term. As will be seen, the underlying dynamic of boundary change continues to draw the EU into deeper levels of engagement with an ever-widening circle of countries in Europe and on its shores. This presents not only new risks for the juggling act but also opportunities for further revival and a rethinking of the EU project.

The chapter is broken down into three parts. The first part sets out the conceptual framework. It also highlights five boundaries which are crucial to the EU system and its enlargement policy. The second part plunges into the empirical world and analyses the EU's complex juggling act. In doing so, it focuses explicitly on the four Rs. The final, concluding section returns to the ties and tensions of the enlargement process and the dynamics of boundary change.

Governance and Boundaries: A Conceptual Framework for EU Enlargement

A variety of perspectives drawing upon governance and regulation have risen to prominence in studies of European integration (for an overview of the literature, cf. Hix 1998). Although this is diverse, scholars converge around the starting-point that the process of governing is no longer exclusively conducted by states, but also by the EU in response to the need for 'collective problem-solving' beyond the state (Armstrong and Bulmer 1998; Caporaso 1996; Marks *et al.* 1996c). Following Armstrong and Bulmer, governance can be defined as 'more complex, differentiated and diffuse systems of control than the more limited institutions and functions associated with the minimal liberal state' (Armstrong and Bulmer 1998: 255).

As was pointed out in the introduction to this chapter, the governance lens has rarely been applied to enlargement. We intend to show that it provides the necessary perspective to comprehend the present enlargement round. First, it provides us with the conceptual bridge between the internal and external by allowing us to focus on how the EU's governance system affects its capacity to act towards the outside. This bridge also connects the four challenges posed by enlargement.

Second, the very concept of governance (which is not tied to a specific geographical territory) directs our attention to boundaries. Relative to the state, the European Union is not equipped with stable, rigid boundaries. For instance it is anything but clear as to where the EU's cultural boundary lies. The malleable nature of the boundaries allows the EU to strengthen, change, or move boundaries as a means to extend governance to non-members. The ultimate form of governance is to move the institutional boundary by granting non-members full rights of participation and representation in the EU through accession. The lack of coincidence or overlap between the EU's boundaries and the porous, non-rigid nature of certain boundaries also allow the EU to extend governance beyond the Union without offering membership.

Drawing especially upon Jachtenfuchs (1995) and Scharpf (1988), two distinct kinds of governance are produced by the EU. The first is 'soft governance' and reflects the fact that EU governance extends beyond formal interaction to the development of norms, values, and institutional settings. These condition the action of its members and influence non-members. The second kind of governance produced is 'hard' and refers to the process of governing through negotiations. The EU governance system is characterized by ongoing sets of negotiations. These are by their nature protracted, favor conservative solutions (path dependency), and are often characterized by a policy of postponement. Every set of EU negotiations is bound to touch upon historical package deals (the shadow of the past), parallel, ongoing negotiations (the shadow of the present), and the prospect of future negotiations (the shadow of the future).

This tendency towards protractedness and conservatism is also displayed in the development of the EU's external policies. They emerge from agreements reached amongst the member states, followed in many cases by negotiations with an external actor. The tendency towards protractedness and conservatism is very pronounced in the case of enlargement since this not only engages the EU in accession negotiations but has far-reaching implications for the EU as a system of governance, the degree of influence of individual states in the system, and the internal distribution of costs and benefits. Indeed, enlargement involves a systemic transformation of the EU (Friis 1998*a*).

The EU's ability to govern beyond its territory and to develop policies towards non-members is also heavily affected by the nature of its boundaries. The malleable character of these boundaries means that it cannot insulate itself from the wider Europe. Changes in the boundaries affecting security are particularly sensitive for the Union. This malleability provides it with the motivation to extend governance and ultimately membership to other European states. Based upon Michael Smith's work (1996: 13–18), we identify the most salient boundaries as being institutional, legal, transactional, geopolitical, and political cultural.[2]

The institutional boundary draws a dividing line between those who participate fully in the EU's decision-making and those who do not. So far, this boundary has been very rigid, as only members have a full voice and vote in EU negotiations. Movement of this boundary is at the core of accession to the EU.

The legal boundary concerns the legal order of the European Union and, unlike the institutional one, does not correspond with the territory of the EU. Although largely concerning the EU territory, the legal boundary reaches beyond the EU through, for example, the external dimensions of its policies and voluntary imitation or assumption of EU legislation by non-members. The EU can alter this boundary through negotiations with outsiders on mutual undertakings concerning the reach of EU legal acts in the absence of accession and full access to EU legal remedies.

The EU is also equipped with a transactional boundary, set by the regulation of access to its market for goods, services, capital and persons. This boundary is not rigid, in the sense that regimes governing access differ across policy sectors and between non-members. In addition, market regulation at the global level may pry open EU markets. The EU can extend governance to non-members by manipulating this boundary through, for example, agreeing preferential trade regimes or opening access to EU funds and research programs.

Geopolitics also produces a boundary between EU insiders and outsiders, even though the EU has a limited capacity to manipulate it. For example, the cold war drew a rigid geopolitical boundary around the EC. It prevented close co-operation between the EC and its East European neighbors and precluded membership of some 'Western' European states, such as Austria, in the EU. The removal of that boundary opened up opportunities for the EU to extend governance and even membership to these states in the 1990s.

The final boundary—the political cultural boundary—refers to the fact that democratic values and principles attach to membership of the Union. States that do not respect these cannot accede. The EU itself may affect the geographical reach of this boundary by stimulating the spread of political values through policy conditionality, for example, where adherence to

---

[2] We modify Smith's institutional/legal boundary by clearly separating it into two. The institutional boundary is set by the full participation of actors in EU negotiations and institutions, whereas the legal boundary is determined by whether actors play by the EU rules.

democratic values is a condition of EU trade agreements with non-members. As European states increasingly adhere to these values, they can legitimately claim a right to EU membership. Being 'European', itself a contested concept, also constitutes an important element of the political cultural boundary. Here again, the EU has some discretion in determining for itself what is European.

EU decisions to adjust the boundaries can, because of the nature of the governance system, become intertwined with EU negotiations on 'internal' matters such as financing or institutional reform. This is most evident in the case of enlargement, which triggers policy and institutional reforms. EU negotiations, however, are not only determined by member-state preferences and power but are also conditioned by two intervening variables: the institutional setting and the unintended effects of boundary changes. The latter shape the conditions for enlargement in that, for example, the opening of the transactional boundary can create pressures for movement with respect to the institutional one.

The EU's Enlargement Juggle: Risks, Reform, Resistance, and Revival

The erosion of the geopolitical boundary of the cold war provided the initial catalyst for the EU's current enlargement round. Over time, the EU accepted the membership applications of a number of Central European states. The contours of its enlargement policy towards them and other states were shaped by the workings of the EU system, as the governance approach shows us, and by boundary changes. Unlike previous enlargement rounds, this produced a complex juggling act as the EU had to manage four interrelated challenges at the same time. These were: (*a*) accession negotiations; (*b*) internal reform; (*c*) the enlargement-queue, and (*d*) new neighbors. The following section analyzes how the EU managed this juggling act over the period 1997–9 and assesses the four Rs involved. As we will show, policy initiatives designed to meet each of the challenges had a tendency (both intentional and unintentional) to influence EU action in other areas of the enlargement process. In addition, changes at the level of the boundaries dragged the EU deeper and deeper into enlargement. Hence, one needs to analyze the interlinkages between the four challenges and the dynamics operating between the boundaries to comprehend the EU's enlargement policy.

Challenge Number 1: Managing Accession Negotiations with the Most Advanced Candidates

The Luxembourg European Council in December 1997 marked a new phase in the EU's enlargement policy.[3] After years of preparation, it moved into the negotiation phase with a first wave of candidates, namely, Poland, Hungary, the Czech Republic, Slovenia, Estonia, and Cyprus. These countries had, in July 1997, been singled out for accession negotiations by the European Commission in its report, *Agenda 2000* (Commission 1997a).

Although the decision to launch accession negotiations with just this small number of countries was linked to clear differences in development amongst the candidates, it was also influenced by recognition of the second challenge, that of agreeing to institutional reform prior to further accessions. In a clear confirmation of the EU's predilection for postponement, EU leaders did not grasp the nettle of institutional reform at the 1996 intergovernmental conference (IGC) but postponed it to future IGCs. As it was unclear how the EU would eventually streamline its institutions, the majority of member states and the Commission agreed to restrict accession negotiations to a small number of countries (Friis 1998b: 5). This decision also enabled the EU to manage these negotiations technically. The alternative at the time, the so-called regatta-option, whereby the EU would negotiate accession with all eleven candidates in parallel, was deemed to be too cumbersome.

Once this first step towards shifting the institutional boundary to six countries was taken, the remaining candidates (Latvia, Lithuania, Bulgaria, Slovakia, and Romania) perceived it as a move to redraw cultural and geopolitical boundaries. None accepted the EU's argument that it had simply differentiated between the candidates on the basis of objective criteria (Friis 1998b: 7). Denmark and Sweden, proponents of the ostensibly more inclusive regatta-option, warned of these negative effects. The Luxembourg Council, December 1997, addressed them by carving out a special place for those candidates not included in the first wave of accession negotiations. Not only were they offered an analytical examination of their ability to fulfill the *acquis*, which echoed the screening exercise underway with the first wave of EU candidates, but all were also included in the EU's enlargement process 'as part of the implementation of article O' (the enlargement article in the EU Treaty). Furthermore,

---

[3] For the enlargement policy before European Council, Luxembourg, 1999, see Sedelmeier and Wallace 1996; Friis and Murphy 1999.

these so-called second wavers were offered Accession Partnerships (see below) and inclusion in the Europe Conference.

Although the decision to negotiate accession with the most advanced candidates must obviously be seen as a clear-cut example of governance being linked to membership, these negotiations were none the less structured in a way which allowed the EU to extend governance short of membership or 'below the membership line'. In practice, the EU's strategy was to demand that candidates fulfill and enforce the *acquis* in almost all areas before they actually joined the Union (cf. Grabbe 1999; Krenzler and Everson 1998). To use our boundary terminology, the EU's strategy was to shift its legal and transactional boundaries before its institutional one.

First, candidates were obliged to follow almost all the EU's rules before they could be let in as members and obtain a voice in the system. The new accession instrument of Accession Partnerships equipped all candidates (including those in the second wave) with a detailed training plan for how and in what sequence they must fulfill the *acquis*. Should a candidate decide to prepare itself for enlargement in a different way it ran the risk of losing pre-accession aid and of falling behind the other countries in the enlargement queue (Krenzler and Everson 1998: 8). In fact, Grabbe argues that the Partnerships were so far-reaching as to represent an extension of EU influence over policy-making which was greater than that of the EU with respect to the member states (Grabbe 1999). Not only did the EU require that the applicants fulfill the *acquis*, but went beyond that by demanding, for example, reform of prisons, civil service, and social security systems.[4]

In practice, the EU's management of accession can only be understood by putting it into perspective and by analyzing it as part of a complex juggling act. Although it was guided by the objective of making the candidates fit for membership, it was also driven by the difficulties of agreeing to internal reforms and the overall resistance of member states to early membership. The conditionality of the enlargement policy bought the EU time to reform its own institutions and policies. It also shifted the burden of adjustment to the applicants (cf. also Grabbe 1999). In theory, if the newcomers applied and enforced most of the *acquis* before accession they would not require long transition phases or be as dependent upon EU

[4] To be sure, governance beyond the territory of the EU is not a novel phenomenon. Norway and Switzerland are largely within the EU's legal boundary. By comparison, EU governance in Central and Eastern Europe is much more intrusive. Although these countries accept EU governance because of their interest in membership, the intrusive nature of policy has generated accusations of 'paternalism' (Lippert and Becker 1998: 354) and a 'colonial attitude' on the part of the EU (interview with Kirsty Hughes in Ben Partridge, 'East/Central Europe: EU Shows "Faltering" Commitment to Expansion', Radio Free Europe, 1 Dec. 1998, http://www.rferl.org.

structural funds. Finally, the principle of strict conditionality was also a way for those states who were most supportive of enlargement to secure the support of those who were less enthusiastic (Friis and Murphy 1999: 221).[5]

As indicated above, the chosen strategy had many advantages in terms of enabling the EU to juggle in the short term. However, in the medium term, the strategy was anything but risk-free. First of all, negotiations on accession initially focused on the easiest dossiers and the more contentious ones such as the Common Agricultural Policy (CAP), environmental protection, and free movement of workers were put on the back burner. Many of the difficult issues of adjustment had yet to be faced. Second, high risks attended the accession of Cyprus, which was also included in the first wave of candidates. Although accession negotiations were opened there was no certainty that the EU's strategy of moving to enlargement in tandem with a solution to the division of the island would work. In principle, there was still a danger that Greece could block further progress in EU enlargement should Cyprus not be included in a first wave of entrants. As Turkey's agreement remained essential to a solution to the division of the island, it could also hinder the accession of Cyprus.[6]

Third, the insistence that applicants take on the *acquis* before they joined would exert strong pressure on the EU to shift its institutional boundary, that is, to grant membership to candidates which played by EU rules. Otherwise, it would face a serious risk of losing credibility and bitter accusations of betrayal from the candidates.

Challenge Number Two: Internal Institutional and Policy Reform

The second challenge in the enlargement process is that of internal reform. Without institutional reform, the accession of new candidates threatened to deadlock the EU. Enlargement without reform of the CAP would lead to a politically unacceptable increase in the EU's budget.

Up to June 1999, the EU postponed decisions on key reforms. This reflected the inherent tension between, on the one hand, maintaining the present system of governance and, in particular, the benefits it yielded to every member state and, on the other hand, the goal of stabilizing Central

[5] See TEPSA 1999. Moral and security concerns and expectations of economic gain drive the support for enlargement. Resistance is linked to fears about weakening the Union's decision-making capacity, the diversion of funds to the east, and loss of influence in the system. There is some concern that the applicant states do not have the necessary mechanisms to implement in full the Union's *acquis*.

[6] At the Luxembourg European Council, Turkey was only offered a place in the so-called Europe Conference—an offer it rejected. The EU revisited the relationship in autumn 1999.

and Eastern Europe through enlargement. The Berlin European Council, in March 1999, struck a compromise deal on Agenda 2000 which foresaw the expansion of the structural funds to take account of new entrants and carved out pre-accession aid, but postponed thorough reform of the CAP. As a result, the EU must revisit CAP reform before it can finalize enlargement talks with the first wavers. As Germany's State Secretary for European Integration, now Commissioner in charge of enlargement, Günther Verheugen put it, 'the agricultural part of what we resolved at the summit in Berlin will not hold until 2006—one can say that without sticking one's neck out'.[7]

As already indicated, the IGC which was concluded at Amsterdam in June 1997 postponed the necessary decisions on institutional change. In practice, this postponement was influenced by the fact that the accession of even the most advanced applicants was not imminent. So, there was, at that time, no urgent need to open up divisive debates on questions such as the relationship between small and large member states and efficiency and representation in a larger EU, particularly when faced with a skeptical public opinion (Friis and Murphy 2000*b*). The European Council of Cologne (June 1999) returned to the question of institutional reform. There, the member states agreed to convene a new IGC to deal with the leftovers of Amsterdam—the size of the Commission, weighting of votes in the Council, and possible extension of qualified majority voting (European Council 1999*b*: 8). This narrow agenda seemed to indicate that the two-phased approach to institutional reform elaborated in a protocol to the Amsterdam Treaty would be followed. The first phase would concentrate on the leftovers. In the second phase, the EU would embark on a more comprehensive reassessment of the institutional problematic before EU membership exceeded twenty. However, in principle, it cannot be excluded that this two-phased approach will be changed. Already in July 1999, Commission President Romano Prodi criticized it:

The Intergovernmental Conference is seen by some as a simple tidying up exercise after the Amsterdam Summit, with the objective of sorting out the detailed issues that could not be agreed then. I have to say that I disagree with this analysis. For me, the IGC is a crucial rendezvous for the European institutions. It is our opportunity—perhaps our last opportunity—to prepare for the potential doubling of the number of members of the Union. An IGC with only limited objectives would not, in my view, respond to this challenge. (Prodi 1999*b*)

Undoubtedly, the postponement of key internal reforms enabled the EU to maintain the juggling act in the short term. In the medium term, several question marks are raised. First of all, postponement does not

[7] 'EU Farm Deal Will Need Fixing—German Minister', Reuters, 30 Mar. 1999.

necessarily make it easier to strike a deal on internal reforms. In fact, it could undermine the juggling act. Institutional reform is a good example of this. By embarking upon two successive IGCs, a first wave of candidates may well have joined the EU when the second IGC is convened. The EU risks putting itself in a position where twenty member states will have to agree upon what fifteen members were not able to in Amsterdam! Failure to agree to reforms could jeopardize the accession of the second wave of candidates. It is therefore not surprising to see the European Policy Centre argue that 'it does seem perverse to accept the need for a big enlargement of the European Union, but a small institutional reform. The IGC should not be restricted to finishing the unfinished business of the Amsterdam Treaty if we are really planning for an EU of 25 or more members' (EPC 1999; see also Helen Wallace in House of Commons 1999: 22).

The same risk to the juggling act surrounds CAP reform. By postponing reform, the EU placed itself between Scylla and Charybdis: either it will have to reform the CAP before it enlarges (i.e. in parallel with the accession negotiations) or it will be forced to offer the newcomers long transition periods. A parallel process of negotiations, given the traditionally tortuous and lengthy debates on CAP reform and the possibility of linkage to negotiations in the World Trade Organization, could lead to overload of the EU system. The outcome could be a postponement of accession. The alternative option of negotiating accession without CAP reform offers the prospect of lengthy transitional periods for entrants as a means to facilitate accession. The size and potential of agriculture in Poland and Hungary makes this option politically unattractive to them. As it would also undermine the unity of the single market, it would meet with resistance within the EU. This approach could also complicate the accession of a second wave of candidates as, for example, Poland and Hungary could demand a shortening of their transitional periods as a precondition for further accession (Nello and Smith 1998).

Challenge Number 3: Managing the Enlargement Queue

The third challenge, that of managing the unprecedented enlargement queue, poses further complex questions for the EU. For example, how is it possible to sustain the momentum of reform among those candidates not selected for immediate accession negotiations? This is even more difficult if they perceive the EU's strategy to be one of creating new political, cultural, or religious boundaries.[8]

---

[8] Turkey's reaction to the decisions of the Luxembourg summit clearly illustrates the problem. President Demirel asked 'Is it necessary for Turkey to become a Christian country before it is let into the EU? Don't you think the times for the crusades are over?' ('Demirel wants EU to Treat Turkey as an Equal Candidate', Reuters 20 Feb. 1998,).

The EU responded to such problems, initially triggered by its decision to limit enlargement to five Central and Eastern European countries and Cyprus, by committing itself to a more comprehensive, inclusive, enlargement process. For the first time ever, it engaged in an analytical examination of the *acquis* (the so-called screening exercise) with candidates which had not yet been selected for accession negotiations and all of the second wavers were offered Accession Partnerships. This meant that they too would take over large chunks of the *acquis* prior to EU entry. The EU Commission was mandated to regularly evaluate candidates' progress and their fitness to join the first wavers in accession negotiations.

The progress of the second wavers to the stage of negotiations on accession is highly dependent on what happens with respect to internal reform and the outcome of accession negotiations with the first wavers. The conclusions of the Vienna European Council, December 1998, evidenced this linkage. Although the Commission (1998*c*) had indicated that Latvia would soon be ready to graduate to the first wave, the European Council failed to take such a decision. Such a decision would have created even greater pressure for institutional and policy reforms before the *Agenda 2000* negotiations were completed. In addition, such a decision would have reopened the entire question of graduation or queue management.[9]

The graduation question came back onto the agenda in 1998–9. Commission progress reports found that internal developments in Malta, Latvia, Slovakia, and possibly in Lithuania, meant that they could soon meet the criteria for opening EU accession negotiations (Commission 1998*c*, 1999*i*). Such a situation would leave only two countries in the second wave—Bulgaria and Romania—with possible negative repercussions for their sense of security (see also Mayhew in House of Commons 1999: 31). These fears were exacerbated by the EU's parallel ambition in 1999 to stabilize Kosovo and the surrounding region through offering the countries of South-eastern Europe a membership perspective. Bulgarian actors, in particular, voiced their fear of being effectively relegated to a third division: instead of being part of the accession process, they would suddenly find themselves in the same league as Macedonia and Albania.[10] These fears and their broader security implications were acknowledged in a statement of the Cologne summit, June 1999, which 'highlighted the importance also attaching to the prospect of accession for applicant countries with which negotiations are not yet under way' (Commission 1999*i*: 9). For this reason, it invited the Commission, in preparing its progress

[9] Denmark and Sweden would undoubtedly have made the case that Lithuania should also be upgraded, whereas countries not selected for negotiations would once again criticize the EU for drawing new boundaries.

[10] Authors' interview in the Bulgarian Ministry of Foreign Affairs, 6 Apr. 1999.

report to the Helsinki European Council in December 1999, to 'consider measures which can help crystallize that prospect for all applicant countries' (Commission 1999*i*: 9).

The eventual shift of the institutional boundary to include the first wave of applicants may also produce unintended effects for others in the enlargement queue through its impact on the transactional boundary. EU membership threatens to undermine existing levels of transaction in trade and the free movement of people between the first wave and the second wave of candidates. In the case of Hungary, the implementation of the *acquis* would require it to introduce visa and Schengen controls with respect to Romania. This is a highly sensitive issue, given the presence of a large Hungarian minority in Romania. Such restrictions would of necessity create new dividing lines (see Lavanex 1999). Romanian officials, for instance have indicated that 'Schengen could create a more effective dividing line than anything since the Cold War'.[11] Similarly, as EU members, Hungary, Slovenia, Estonia, and the Czech Republic may not be able to maintain their custom unions and free trade agreements with other candidates but may, on the contrary, have to introduce new trade restrictions with them.[12]

These unintended effects of boundary change are likely to push the EU towards making more commitments to the second wavers. However, this move will put immense pressure on the EU's juggling ability—especially in terms of keeping the ball of internal reform up in the air. Since there is no alternative to enlargement (given that the EU has coupled its policy towards the second wave applicants to the prospect of enlargement) this could lead to a make-or-break situation which could very well force the EU to rethink its integration project. A likely scenario is that the institutional boundary may be softened to allow for different kinds of membership. Such a move would not only open the door to more entrants, but it could reduce the degree of institutional and policy reform otherwise required by enlargement. It could also allow the EU to develop a strengthened policy towards its neighbors which are not candidates for membership.

Challenge Number 4: Managing Relations with the EU's (New) Neighbors

Until mid-1999, the EU was not heavily engaged with the fourth and final challenge, that of managing the effects of enlargement on countries

---

[11] Anatol Lieven, 'EU Accession Raises Visa Worry in East', *The Financial Times* (23 Feb. 1998), 2.
[12] Breffni O'Rourke, 'EU: Negotiations with Easterners Reaching Tough Point', Radio Free Europe, 22 Mar. 1999, http://www.rferl.org.

beyond the second wave. CEPS, a leading think-tank in Brussels, characterized the EU's policy towards the former Yugoslavia and Albania as being a 'poor and distant cousin to the enlargement process' (1999: 32). In practice, the limitations of this approach could be seen as a logical consequence of the fact that accession had simply not taken place.

With the invitation to begin accession negotiations with the first group of candidates, the EU's policy towards its neighbors became more distilled. Here, one can again argue that this was a response to the unintended effects of boundary changes: the initial preparations for shifting the institutional boundary to the first wavers triggered concerns (in Russia and Ukraine) that the EU was about to draw new transactional, cultural, and geopolitical boundaries with them. That the EU was conscious of these effects and their implications for its wider role in Europe was clear from the statement by Commission President, Romano Prodi: 'Apart from turning over the unhappy page in European history of the Iron Curtain, enlargement raises immediate political questions by shifting the Union's center of gravity to the East, thereby underlining the importance of relations with Russia, which will provide a yardstick for the success of any further common foreign and security policy' (Prodi 1999*a*).

Although both Russia and Ukraine were supportive of enlargement, they also questioned the EU's approach. To quote Russia's Ambassador to the EU, would this enlargement 'be the last one or would it be followed by one more which will cover the Commonwealth of Independent States?'[13] What would happen to the EU's transactional boundary: would Russia be able to maintain its trade regime with Poland and Estonia? Ukraine, for its part, was negatively affected by Poland's decision, resulting from EU pressure, to introduce visa requirements for Ukrainian citizens. Indeed, it criticized this decision as an 'unfriendly act'.[14] In order to avoid such negative effects, Russia, requested consultations on the enlargement process.[15] In early 1999, Ukrainian Foreign Minister Borys Tarasyuk appealed to the Union to improve its policy towards Ukraine in order to allow it to return to Europe and finally end 'the artificial division caused by the Cold War'.[16] More concretely, he called for a Europe Agreement (with a membership perspective) and a White Paper that would specify the main political legal, social, and economic parameters of the Ukraine's integration into the EU.

[13] *Agence Europe*, no. 7306. 'Russia calls for consultations with the European Union on the impact of EU extension towards Central and Eastern Europe' (23 Sept. 1998), 5.

[14] Hermann Schmidtendorf, 'Polens Marsch in die EU verärgert die Nachbarn', *Die Welt* (17 Feb. 1997), 2.

[15] *Agence Europe* (23 Sept. 1998): see n. 13.

[16] Ben Partridge, 'Ukraine: Minister Wants Positive Signal from EU on Membership', Radio Free Europe, 3 Feb. 1999, http://www.rferl.org

The EU responded to these concerns by launching discussions on common strategies for Russia and Ukraine at the European Council, Vienna (December 1998).[17] The common strategy for Russia was adopted at the European Council in Cologne (European Council 1999*a*).[18] Although these strategies were quite vague and did not contain major new ideas, they represented an attempt by the EU to govern below the membership line. This time, governance was not linked to accession but to EU support in a range of areas from energy policy to civic society. However, the common strategies suggested an erosion of the political cultural boundary between them and the EU, a key consideration with respect to possible membership in so far as they were explicitly based on 'shared political values' (Commission 1999*k*: 9).

The common strategy towards Russia was to be complemented by yet another initiative—the 'Northern Dimension'—proposed by Finland. A follow-up conference of Foreign Ministers representing the EU, Latvia, Lithuania, Estonia, Poland, Russia, Iceland, and Norway was scheduled to draw up an action plan for the region (see Commission 1998*a*). This was an attempt to avoid new dividing lines in northern Europe by developing regional approaches to the management of issues of common interests such as infrastructure and energy. This was also part of the EU's juggling act: Finland, in particular, took the view that the EU's concentration on enlargement to the East and the French–Spanish emphasis on developing a Southern dimension required a Northern counterpart.

The conflict in Kosovo in 1999 forced the EU to turn its attention to the security of South-eastern Europe. Before the NATO bombing campaign had come to an end, the EU launched the idea of a Stability Pact for the region. The aim of the Pact was to strengthen the countries of South-eastern Europe 'in their efforts to foster peace, democracy, respect for human rights and economic prosperity, in order to achieve stability in the whole region' (Stability Pact 1999: 2). Although the EU was in the lead in setting up the Stability Pact, it was very much constructed as a joint enterprise involving a number of institutions, such as the EU, NATO, the World Bank, and the OSCE. The initiative involved countries already included in the enlargement process (Hungary, Slovenia, Bulgaria, Romania, and Turkey) in addition to five South-eastern European countries (Bosnia and

---

[17] The concept of common strategy was introduced by the Amsterdam Treaty. It allows the Union to formulate broad policy guidelines on the basis of unanimity. Actual implementation is carried out on the basis of qualified majority. The economic crisis in mid-1998 provided an additional impetus for EU action towards Russia (for the EU's policy towards Russia before 1998, see Herrberg 1998).

[18] The common strategy for the Ukraine was scheduled to be adopted under the Finnish EU Presidency (July–Dec. 1999).

Herzegovina, Croatia, the Federal Republic of Yugoslavia, the Former Yugoslav Republic of Macedonia, and Albania).

In terms of enlargement, the most significant element of the EU's contribution to the Pact was its offer of a membership perspective to all the South-eastern European countries involved. The Pact states that

the EU will draw the region closer to the perspective of full integration of these countries into its structures. In case of countries which have not yet concluded association agreements with the EU, this will be done through a new kind of contractual relationship taking fully into account the individual situations of each country with the perspective of EU membership on the basis of the Amsterdam Treaty and once the Copenhagen criteria have been met. (Stability Pact 1999: 4)

In practice, this prospect (however distant) of EU membership acknowledged the fact that only a shift of the EU's institutional boundary could stabilize the region. It also indicated that the EU leaders' perception of the limits of the political cultural boundary had changed: the region was now unambiguously seen to be part of Europe. To quote Germany's Foreign Minister, Joschka Fischer:

There are no political, economic, cultural, religious or any other reasons why we should refrain from giving the people in Dubrovnik, Sarajevo or Belgrade what the people in Dublin, Frankfurt or Warsaw already have, namely a firm place in Europe . . . If the awful conflict in Kosovo has brought something good with it, it is that we understand our belonging together far better. (Fischer 1999; authors' translation)

Just like the case of the second wavers, this membership perspective represented an attempt to govern below the membership line. The prospect of membership was used as an incentive or carrot to encourage cooperation and reconciliation across the region. The policy was highly conditional and EU leaders took care to underline that the proposed new contractual relations, to be based on new Stabilization and Association Agreements (Commission 1999*k*), were not a 'short cut' to membership. For many years these countries, which may soon find themselves labeled as 'third wavers', will therefore have to meet strict conditionality requirements which, in practice, encourage them to import much of the EU's political and economic *acquis*. The success of this strategy will depend on the actual interest of the countries in EU accession and whether they look upon the membership prospect as being credible. Croatia and Serbia may be early test cases—in 1999, neither state fulfilled the necessary conditions for opening negotiations on Stabilization and Association Agreements (Commission 1999*k*).

As already indicated in the previous section, the opening of an EU membership prospect to the countries of South-eastern Europe raised

concerns among the second wavers.[19] Clearly confirming the close interlinkage with the enlargement process, Ukraine perceived the Stability Pact
to be yet another shift of the boundaries—its Foreign Minister stated that
'we consider it unfair and even dangerous to keep Ukraine out of the
European perspective. It is not so much the issue of reconstruction but of
the ultimate involvement in Europe and the invitation to integration into
Europe.'[20]

Finally, turning to the deep South of Europe, the EU also tried to
develop a strengthened policy towards the countries of the Maghreb and
the Middle East. These countries are in a separate category to those considered so far in this chapter, since, for the purposes of EU policy, they are
clearly not perceived to be within the political cultural boundary of
Europe. None the less security concerns, ranging from immigration to ter-
rorism, coupled with the need to balance the EU's relationships with the
East and with the South drive EU policy towards the region. The main
plank of this policy, the so-called Barcelona process, did not include the
perspective of membership but focused primarily on the transactional
boundary (Barbé 1998; Gomez 1998). The inability to use the membership
carrot and the fact that the Barcelona process is entangled with the difficult Middle East peace process were important constraints on EU action.
Hence, since its inception in 1995 the Barcelona process seems to have lost
some of its momentum. In order to counteract this (and to respond posi-
tively to the encouraging signs of regional cooperation), the EU, in spring
1999, launched a number of new initiatives including a common strategy
for the Mediterranean and a 'Euro-Mediterranean Charter for Peace and
Stability' (Euro-Mediterranean Conference 1999). To strengthen the policy even further, Portugal, echoing the Finnish Northern Dimension initiative, planned to use its Presidency in the first half of 2000 to regenerate
relations with the South by hosting an African summit.[21]

Not surprisingly, the EU's handling of this fourth challenge allowed it
to juggle in the short term, but raises difficulties in the medium term. The
unintended consequences of boundary changes push the EU into making
new commitments. In the medium term, when the EU shifts its institutional boundary to the first wave of candidates, it is likely that Russia and

---

[19] Indeed, also first wavers have voiced concerns. For a short period Slovenia and
Hungary refused to participate in the Stability Pact, since they were afraid of being lumped
together with the unstable region (cf. BBC Monitoring Europe, 17 May 1999).

[20] Reuters, 22 June 1999. The Caucasian states (Armenia, Azerbaijan, and Georgia) also
felt negatively affected by the Stability Pact and reconstruction efforts. The Commission
planned to divert funds allocated to the TACIS program, of which they were beneficiaries,
to those countries affected by the Kosovo crisis: Simon Taylor, 'Aid Cuts Threaten
Caucasus Strategy', *European Voice* (1–7 July 1999), 7.

[21] Ibid.

the Ukraine will demand more than the common strategies offer. The countries of South-eastern Europe can be expected to demand that they move into the enlargement process. An EU response to these pressures, even one short of enlargement, could still require internal reform of policies and institutions. These combined pressures on the EU system may create a scenario where the EU is no longer able to maintain the juggling act—it could drop the final 'ball' with Russia, South-eastern Europe, and the Mediterranean.

However, the juggling act and the security imperative which drives it have already forced the EU to reflect on a possible softening of its institutional boundary. The Stabilization and Association Agreements can be seen as a new attempt to find a third way between membership and association or something akin to 'virtual membership' of the EU.[22] This return to the foundational objectives of the Union (peace, security, and stability in Europe) could lead to a revival and rethinking of the integration project.

Conclusions

The core conclusion of this chapter is that the prism of governance and boundaries enables one to understand the dynamics of EU enlargement and the risks, reform, resistance, and possibilities for revival it entails. The nature of the governance system largely determines the EU's approach to enlargement. First of all, its complex structure of negotiations explains the fact that enlargement negotiations are intertwined with other sets of negotiations and touch upon the investments of member states in the system. Hence, it enables us to understand the tensions between the various parts of the juggling act and accounts for the existence of strong pressures of conservatism and resistance to both accession and the necessary reforms in advance of accession.

Second, the combination of governance and boundaries allows us to uncover a crucial independent dynamic which largely explains why the EU, despite strong resistance, has offered the prospect of membership to an ever-increasing group of countries. Or, to use the terminology of this volume, this approach allows us to uncover a dynamic that pushes the EU closer to the revival–reform end of the continuum rather than towards risk–resistance. Boundary changes produce unintended effects on other

---

[22] CEPS argued that the EU should go further than the Stabilization and Association Agreement by, for instance, allowing the South-eastern European countries some participation in CFSP and observer status in the institutions. Similar attempts to soften the institutional boundary, such as that of Commissioner Frans Andriessen (Apr. 1991) also failed (Friis and Murphy 1999: 219).

boundaries and hence act as intervening variables between state preferences and outcomes. One vivid example of this was the decision to open
accession negotiations with only six countries (which involves a shift of the
EU's institutional boundary). This differentiation between candidates had
unintended effects on other boundaries. Without further action with
respect to the so-called second wavers, it could have automatically shifted
the geopolitical, transactional, and political cultural boundaries. As a
consequence, the EU was forced to step up its policy towards the second
wavers. A similar dynamic was at play in the EU's response to the Kosovo
crisis. Once the EU enhanced its policies towards South-eastern Europe, it
had to take into consideration its effects on the enlargement candidates
and even on Russia and Ukraine. In practice, the EU's enlargement policy
is therefore not only driven by the governance system itself, but also by the
intended and unintended effects of boundary changes.

Third, the governance approach shows that there is more to enlargement than just accession. Since governance is not necessarily linked to the
territory of the EU, the EU can offer governance below the membership
line, in terms of Accession Partnerships and the Stability Pact. In practice,
there is a strong belief that accession is the key to European stability, as is
seen from the decision to offer the prospect of membership to South-
eastern Europe. However, this policy is far more credible with respect to
the first and the second wavers, who have a realistic prospect of meeting
the entry criteria. In the case of South-eastern Europe, the prospect of
membership is much dimmer, and it is almost non-existent in the case of
Russia, Ukraine, and the Mediterranean. The EU has had tremendous
difficulty in developing alternative forms of membership which are necessary to manage the Union's changing concerns with respect to these divergent countries. In practice, so far, the EU has offered all or nothing in
terms of actual membership.

In the medium term, the EU could be forced to develop alternatives to
full membership as a stabilizing tool. On the one hand, membership of the
Union in the 1990s is much more demanding than that of the EC in the
1950s. On the other hand, there is a huge divergence of capacities amongst
the candidates and between them and the existing member states. As highlighted in the chapter, the juggling dynamic has returned the EU to its
foundational goals of achieving peace and security in Europe. Should this
revival continue it will force the EU to rethink membership. Otherwise its
enlargement policy and its underlying objective to stabilize Europe may
actually fail.

V

Institutions and Identity: Capabilities, Legitimacy, and Perception

11

The European Commission: Diminishing Returns to Entrepreneurship

MITCHELL P. SMITH

The past decade of scholarship on the institutions of the European Union has produced extensive evidence of the European Commission's policy entrepreneurship. The efforts of the Commission and the institutional attributes accentuated since the Single European Act have endogenized the process of preference formation by member-state governments and helped mobilize critical constituencies for deeper integration. Despite its ability to set agendas, induce shifts in preferences of critical political actors, build policy networks, and create opportunities to advance both its institutional role and the cause of deeper integration, the Commission in March 1999 found itself severely damaged by the precedent-setting experience of mass resignation of the College of Commissioners. How can we reconcile the entrepreneurial skill developed by this institution since the 1980s with the organizational crisis experienced in March 1999? The Commission itself recognizes that its institutional integrity is at risk, for it has placed institutional reform atop its agenda in advance of the series of enlargements expected in the first decade of the new century.

Described as a 'purposeful opportunist'[1] and as occupying a strategic position at the hub of the EU system (Nugent 1995), the entrepreneurial behavior of the Commission has been widely documented (Cram 1994; Nugent 1995; Sandholtz 1993*b*, 1996; Pollack 1997*a*; Mitchell Smith 1998). Entrepreneurship has permitted the Commission to set the agenda for deeper integration, expand its responsibilities, and enhance its capacities to administer policy regimes with greater autonomy and authority. This chapter argues that, as it has engaged in these activities, the Commission has experienced diminishing returns to entrepreneurship. While entrepreneurship unquestionably has brought the Commission

---

[1] Cram suggests that the Commission often has enlarged the scope of its activities even where the legal basis for doing so is fragile. By 'purposeful opportunist,' Cram refers to an organization with well-defined, autonomous preferences that is 'flexible as to the means of achieving them' (1994: 214).

organizational benefits, the net extent of those benefits has dwindled as entrepreneurship has increased demands on the Commission in multiple ways.

Three consequences of entrepreneurship induce diminishing returns. First, and most obvious, as the Commission pursues task expansion and develops policy regimes, its workload increases. Since the resources available to perform its duties remain fixed, the Commission is likely to feel strain under its administrative burden. In fact, task expansion itself has increased wariness of an overreaching Commission among member-state governments, ultimately exacerbating resource constraints. In addition to simple resource scarcity, as the range of programs and policy objectives it pursues grows, the Commission encounters the difficulties of coordinating an array of policies that increasingly intersect and overlap.

Second, when the Commission succeeds in creating new programs or securing greater authority through, for example, ECJ decisions, it advances to a new phase in the policy process involving an oversight function. When this occurs, the Commission moves from areas of comparative advantage—policy initiation, agenda-setting, and preference formation—to areas of comparative disadvantage, including compliance monitoring and program management. The latter set of activities are awkward endeavors for a European Commission originally designed to serve as the engine of European integration, not to audit the activities of a vast number of national and subnational economic actors and manage an extensive web of programs involving a wide range of private-sector subcontractors.

Finally, interest associations frequently mobilize at the European level in response to the Commission's activities. Indeed, such mobilization has been a source of power and independence for a European Commission strategically situated at the crossroads of European Community policy-making. Mobilized interests represent the core of policy networks that have enhanced the Commission's leverage in the policy process and have often facilitated policy implementation. However, as the European polity has developed, these interests have placed intensifying demands on scarce Commission administrative resources, and have come to encroach on the Commission's autonomy and institutional capacities.

This chapter explores each of these mechanisms of diminishing returns, drawing on illustrative examples from the fields of state aid and public procurement policy, and from the Commission-administered Leonardo da Vinci job training program. The evidence suggests that, while individual instances of policy entrepreneurship and the entrepreneurial activities of individual Directorates-General may promote discrete policy objectives, the aggregate consequences for the Commission of many individual acts of entrepreneurship may be troublesome. Accordingly, the concluding section addresses the critical challenge confronting the Commission in the new century: whether the Commission can reduce the incidence of diminishing returns in the future. In order to accomplish this, the Commission must either undertake reforms to its institutional culture that restrict its activities to areas of comparative advantage or develop greater skills in additional areas, such as program management. Since the latter course would likely detract from the Commission's abilities in its existing areas of comparative advantage, the post-resignation Commission faces a trade-off between its ability to set the agenda for deeper European integration and the breadth of its policy initiatives.

Diminishing Returns to Entrepreneurship

Political entrepreneurship implies more than taking advantage of opportunities to realize central organizational interests; it involves the use of institutional resources to create such opportunities. Entrepreneurship may involve developing and selling ideas, 'coupling' new policy ideas with existing problems (Kingdon 1984), mobilizing interests in order to create a winning coalition, or configuring decision-making procedures so that they favor certain outcomes over others. In the case of the European Commission, this may include cultivating strategic ties with interest groups that can affect the preferences of member-state governments, using ideas to shape the policy agenda, or finding new means—such as an innovative legal basis—to advance critical objectives on the Community agenda when more obvious paths become blocked.

An organization may be a 'victim' of its own entrepreneurial success in several senses. First, it may begin to encounter resource constraints as its activities intensify. As the Commission succeeds in promoting a policy regime, its workload increases, stretching its limited resources even tighter. As the Commission during the 1990s sought to extend its authority to regulate the payment of subsidies by member-state governments to both private- and public-sector industries, the number of cases it had to process rose dramatically.[2] At the same time, the climate of limited tolerance among member-state governments for Commission assertiveness prohibited increases in Commission staffing.[3] For example, after the expansion

[2] The number of aid proposals outside agriculture, fisheries and transport notified to the Commission by member-state governments averaged 157 from 1981 through 1984; for 1994 and 1995 the figure was 595. See Commission 1985: 132; and 1996*f*: 76, graph 1.

[3] It appears that senior Commission officials either failed entirely to plan effective resource allocation or internalized this constraint. In the examination of allegations of fraud and corruption that precipitated the Commission's Mar. 1999 downfall, the Committee of Independent Experts found 'no evidence of any attempt by the Commission

of EU membership from twelve to fifteen states, the number of new state aid cases notified to the Commission rose from 510 in 1994 to 680 in 1995. The relevant unit of Directorate General IV had to deal with this permanently larger volume of cases while staffing remained constant.

In addition, the completion of the first phases of a policy initiative and the transition to another stage of the process may create difficulties. Because the EC system is based on the rule of law and the Commission's authority derives substantially from its sole right of legislative initiative, Commission activism often takes the form of proposing, mobilizing support for, and drafting legislation. Once legislation is successful, the responsible administrative unit must shift its efforts to monitoring compliance, a task yielding less visibility and fewer political rewards for officials than crafting legislation and organizing political support. Moreover, implementation brings EU officials into direct contact with the societal actors affected by Community legislation, and the implementation process can galvanize opposition, particularly where the affected constituency has not been involved in earlier phases of the policy-making process (Peterson 1995*a*). Essentially, as the integration process proceeds, some of the institutional gains resulting from policy entrepreneurship are slowed and, in some instances, reversed. Central elements of the single market project offer evidence of diminishing returns to entrepreneurship.

Shift to Activities of Comparative Disadvantage

Policy Implementation

The European Commission has achieved a significant degree of independence as an informal agenda-setter, and often has been able to realize its legislative preferences to a remarkable extent. None the less, legislation is only an initial step in the integration process; regulations must be transposed into national legislation, implemented, and enforced. The Commission has a critical comparative advantage as an agenda-setter and regulator, given its long time horizon, technical expertise, and political neutrality (Pollack 1997*a*). However, the Commission is at a serious disadvantage relative to national and local units of administration because its staffing is extremely limited and it is distant from the locus of policy implementation. The Commission does not have the resources to thoroughly monitor observance of Community law; it frequently depends upon individual economic actors to lodge complaints that generate much of the

to assess in advance the volume of resources required when a new policy was discussed among the Community Institutions.' See European Parliament 1999: para. 9.4.7.

Commission's leverage in the realm of enforcement. Ultimately, success in legislating integration does not necessarily mean achieving integration in practice.

The case of public procurement policy illustrates diminishing returns in the transition from agenda setting and policy initiation to implementation and enforcement. When the Commission launched the single market initiative in 1985, it gave procurement of goods and services by public authorities a central place in the program. This was so for three reasons: widespread awareness that national public procurement markets were highly protected; the tremendous size of the market for public-sector contracting; and the potential multiplicative effects of public procurement liberalization. Although public procurement received little attention during the decade and a half preceding the Single European Act, the 1985 White Paper on the single market referred to the protection of national public procurement markets as 'one of the most evident barriers to the achievement of a real internal market' (Commission 1985: 23).

In the ensuing decade, the Commission oversaw completion of the first two phases of the liberalized public procurement regime: legislating the regulatory framework and ensuring proper transposition into national law. The Commission productively deployed two strategies of policy entrepreneurship to help market the concept of a single market in public procurement to critical constituencies, including public authorities at all levels, developing compelling ideas and linking them to existing economic problems, and using the rule of law to exploit the authority granted to the Commission by member-state governments in the EEC Treaty.

First, as it did for numerous components of the single market project, the Commission invoked the 'Costs of Non-Europe' study as its core selling-point for public procurement liberalization (Commission 1988). In so doing, the Commission emphasized several potential benefits of more transparent and open public procurement: improved government efficiency and accountability, global competitiveness of European suppliers, and technological innovation. Open procurement, the Commission argued, would save governments and taxpayers money and reduce the incidence of fraud and corruption. The costs of non-Europe study estimated that competition across borders and in sectors with little prior competition, as well as economies of scale resulting from restructuring of previously protected sectors, would generate 8 to 19 billion ecus of savings annually in public expenditure (Commission 1988: 6–7). In addition, the Commission's internal market unit argued that more competitive procurement would enable Europe's suppliers to compete more successfully with non-EU countries in increasingly open procurement markets. Increased cross-border procurement would be a natural accompaniment to the liberalization and intensification of cross-border restructuring in the telecommunications and heavy electrical equipment industries (Woolcock *et al.* 1991: 29–30). Implementation of EU procurement directives, by enhancing competition, would induce price reductions and efficiency gains. Finally, because procurement markets tend to be concentrated, the relevant sectors typically are controlled by oligopolies that stifle product innovation. Intensified competition would therefore further enhance the competitiveness of European suppliers by boosting innovation in products and processes.[4]

The Commission also has exercised entrepreneurship by invoking the EEC Treaty as a basis for expansion of the public procurement regime. The Commission's favored instrument has been Treaty Article 30, which prohibits quantitative restrictions on the import of goods within the Community. While Article 30 was intended to address barriers to the sale of goods, the Commission none the less chose to invoke Article 30 before the Court as a basis for infringement proceedings against member-state governments in cases of contracting for public works. A groundbreaking instance was the 1987 Dundalk pipeline case,[5] in which the Commission brought an action against the Irish government when the Dundalk Urban District Council, in a public tender for construction of a water main, specified that asbestos cement pipes supplied by the contract awardee would have to meet a standard certified only by the Irish Standard Mark Licensing Scheme—effectively ruling out products from other countries.

The Commission's decision to pursue the Dundalk case followed both a mid-1980s review of public procurement directives that highlighted their inadequacy and the high priority given to public procurement legislation in the 1986 Single European Act.[6] A 1971 Council Directive on procedures for the award of public works contracts excluded water and energy services, making the Commission's reliance on Article 30 pivotal. The Commission argued before the Court that the terms of the public tender violated Article 30 because they excluded pipes manufactured in other member states that were the equivalent of the Irish standard mark pipes in terms of safety, performance, and reliability. The Court's decision in favor of the Commission gave the Commission a powerful instrument with which to pursue public procurement liberalization.[7]

---

[4] Public procurement represents a large proportion of total sales in such concentrated sectors as power generation equipment, computers and office machinery, aerospace equipment, railway rolling stock, and telecommunications equipment (Commission 1988).

[5] Case 45/87 [1988], *Commission* v. *Ireland* ECR 4929.

[6] The Commission's review indicated that little interpenetration of national procurement markets had resulted from the public works and supplies directives of the 1970s. See Arrowsmith and Fernández Martin 1993: 324.

[7] Subsequent instances in which Art. 30 was central include the 1989 Storebælt case, in which the Danish government was held to have violated EC law by including a Danish

In 1993 the Commission's internal market unit completed the legislative basis for the public procurement regime. While Treaty articles prohibiting restrictions on the free movement of goods, the rights of establishment, and the right to perform services within the single market (Articles 30, 52, and 59) represented the foundation for public procurement liberalization, 'positive' legislative measures supplementing these prohibitions were required to abolish restrictions that existed in practice. The set of directives endorsed by the Council between 1987 and 1993 encompassed procedures for purchasing of supplies, commissioning of works, and contracting for services by public authorities.[8] The Commission next sought to secure proper transposition of the legislation into national law. In this phase of the policy-making process, the Commission's internal market directorate for public procurement operated on the premise that the legislative framework, however imperfect, would open up the public procurement sector once it was fully in place at the national level. Moreover, the Commission had the legal authority, however cumbersome, to overcome problems of transposition of EU legislation into national law. This is illustrated by the 1995 judgment in the *Commission* v. *Federal Republic of Germany*, in which the Commission took the German government to the Court for failing to properly comply with directives governing the award of supplies and public works contracts.[9] The German government had followed its traditional administrative procedure of altering public contracting rules informally, through the use of an internal administrative circular drafted by committees consisting of representatives of local authorities, business, and labor union representatives. The Commission argued that this did not amount to proper transposition of the directives because it did not create a right for citizens and suppliers to bring alleged violations before national courts. Germany was not alone in this method of transposing the directives—Denmark, Luxembourg, and the

content clause in the terms of a public contract for construction of bridge spanning the Western Channel of the Great Belt. The clause stated that 'The contractor is obliged to use to the greatest possible extent Danish materials, consumer goods, labour and equipment.' See Case C–243/89 [1993], *Commission* v. *Denmark*, judgment of 22 June 1993, ECR I–3386.

[8] The relevant directives include Directive 89/440/EEC on public works; 88/295/EEC on supplies; 92/50/EEC on services; and, updating and consolidating the earlier legislation on public works and public supplies, Directives 93/36/EEC and 93/37/EEC, respectively. Directives governing procedures for the award of public works and supplies contracts were legislated in the 1970s, but were largely ineffectual because public authorities typically circumvented them either by splitting contracts into smaller amounts so that they would fall below the thresholds at which the directives took effect or by liberally interpreting the conditions allowing for closed public tenders in order to negotiate with favored local, regional or national suppliers. See Commission 1986.

[9] Case C–433/93 [1995], *Commission* v. *Federal Republic of Germany*; judgment of 11 Aug. 1995, ECJ (1995–8): I–2303–20.

UK all transposed the 1988 directive governing supplies contracts by administrative circular, as did Denmark for the 1989 directive on public works. In its ruling, the Court agreed with the Commission that transposing a directive by administrative practice is not sufficient to provide citizens with an awareness of the full extent of their rights and does not protect tenderers against actions by contract-awarding authorities that violate Community directives.[10] The Federal Republic introduced more formal regulations governing public contracting in 1994.

Having largely completed the national transposition phase,[11] the Commission formally had achieved a single market in public procurement; yet in practice the legislated liberalization of public procurement had little effect.[12] While the Commission had developed a rationale for the single market in public purchases and convincingly linked this policy to problems of competitiveness, fiscal profligacy, and corruption, the effort to approximate a single market in public procurement faltered in the implementation phase.

Effective implementation of public procurement legislation would require the compliance of tens of thousands of local and regional government authorities. In addition, the thousands of firms that compete for government contracts would have to perceive sufficient incentives to bear the costs of pursuing complaints in the court system. Yet suppliers who have privileged relationships with public authorities have an interest in non-implementation. Meanwhile, those who do not have such relationships and who would gain most from more competitive public tenders may perceive that the costs of filing complaints exceed the expected benefit. Since

[10] Case C–433/93 [1995], *Commission* v. *Federal Republic of Germany*; judgment of 11 Aug. 1995, ECJ (1995–8): I–2317–18.

[11] Several cases of non-transposition remained into the late 1990s. These include non-transposition of the 1993 services directive in Belgium, Germany, Greece, France, and Austria, and non-transposition of the 1993 directive governing public supplies contracts in Belgium, Germany, France, Italy, and Austria. In addition, Spain, Greece, and Portugal negotiated extensions for transposing the most recent piece of legislation, a directive consolidating rules for contracts in the utilities sector. See Commission 1996d: 51)

[12] Public procurement remains quite closed if we measure openness by the share of public contracts won by firms based outside the member state in which the tender takes place. According to the Commission, the share of public contracts awarded to direct cross-border business rose from 1.4% in 1987 to just 3% in 1995; for purchases made through importers or local subsidiaries of firms located outside the national borders of the relevant public authority, the increase has been from 4% in 1987 to 7% in 1995 (Commission 1996e: 5, para. 2.11). Moreover, in its 1996 study of the public procurement regime, DG XV asserts that, despite the completion of the legislative framework, 'many contracting entities appear to lack detailed knowledge of their legal obligations; suppliers . . . frequently seem unaware of the market opportunities that exist' (Commission 1996d: ii, para. 7). However, the Commission claims some success for its public procurement regime: the number of public tender notices actually published in the *Official Journal of the European Communities* rose from 12,000 in 1987 to 95,000 in 1995. See Commission 1996: 21.

public contracting is essentially an iterative game, suppliers may fear that they will be excluded from future tender competitions if they take an authority to their national court for violating public procurement regulations. Pursuing a perceived infringement becomes a public good with high costs to the individual firm providing the good.

Overall, even member-state governments supportive of the single market process have demanded time to digest, politically and administratively, the vast legislative program involved. Indeed, Jacques Delors's bold leadership of the European Commission from 1985 to 1995 generated a resistance to Commission entrepreneurship, leading to the lower profile, 'less but better' approach of Delors's successor, Jacques Santer (Drake 1995: 157). In effect, the tables were turned on the Commission's informal agenda-setting capacities. In some policy areas the member-state governments came to exercise this 'second dimension' of power, stifling Commission ambitions in the planning stage because of the Commission's perception that the political climate for policy initiatives was unfavorable. This was reflected in public procurement policy, for which the Commission in the mid-1990s, despite its disappointment with the results of its public procurement initiatives, all but ruled out a legislative route to improving the functioning of the single market.

Ultimately the initial successes of policy entrepreneurship in placing public procurement liberalization high on the single market agenda faded. The Commission soon found itself in a phase of the policy process in which it was dependent on unwilling private contractors to alert them to infringements, and in which the will to digest its initiatives was exhausted. Moreover, implementation of public procurement directives is substantially beyond the Commission's control, given current enforcement mechanisms. The principal instrument of enforcement available to the Commission is Article 169 of the EEC Treaty, which gives the Commission authority to take governments to the ECJ for infringement of Treaty obligations. Two problems render this a particularly blunt instrument. The first of these concerns the severe constraints on the Commission's resources relative to the huge volume of public tenders across all levels of government and public enterprises throughout the EU. Although the Commission has the authority to take action against infringements of the Treaty and supporting directives on its own initiative, in practice manpower constraints limit the Commission to launching only those cases set in motion by complaints from damaged parties.

A second difficulty with the Commission's enforcement capabilities is that the instrument available to the DG XV to pursue infringements (EC Treaty Article 169) is highly ineffective because of the cumbersome and lengthy nature of the procedure. Where the Commission believes a public tender process violates a Community directive, it sends a communication to the public authority involved requesting relevant information. If the Commission deems the response unsatisfactory, the Directorate-General for the internal market can deliver a 'reasoned opinion', calling upon the authority to comply with the directive in question within thirty days. Only if the authority does not meet these terms can the Commission bring the case before the Court. However, this process must allow time for the suspected offender to submit its observations, for assessing the submission and drafting a reasoned opinion, and, finally, for giving the party an opportunity to comply. By the time these processes have been exhausted and the case comes before the ECJ, the contract in question may already have been executed, or it may be executed during the two-year period typical for Court proceedings (Arrowsmith and Fernández Martin 1993: 336).

Ultimately, DG XV's November 1996 public procurement Green Paper was a response to stalled efforts to achieve a single market in public procurement. While more public authorities were complying with requirements of transparent procurement procedures, few contractors were responding to the new market opportunities opened to them. The Commission therefore sought through the Green Paper to broaden the constituency for public procurement liberalization by drawing trade associations and contracting entities into a dialogue about public procurement policy.[13] Despite early successes in setting the legislative agenda, promoting the single market in public procurement as one solution to problems of competitiveness and fiscal laxity, the Commission, like an institutional Tantalus, saw its goals recede as it attempted to draw near.

Program Management

The experience of the Leonardo da Vinci vocational training program demonstrates how a program emerging from Commission initiative, and which initially appeared to serve both the overarching objective of deeper integration and the Commission's institutional interests, ultimately involved the institution in activities for which it is organizationally ill-suited. In the case of Leonardo, launched in 1995 by an initiative of DG XXII, the Directorate-General for education, training and youth, the program seemed to sustain the Commission's efforts to place itself at the center of employment policy coordination among EU member-state gov-

---

[13] DG XV concluded each chapter of the Green Paper with a series of questions to which it invited responses from public authorities and contractors.

ernments. The Leonardo initiative, designed to promote innovative and transnational job training partnerships, was an outgrowth of the Commission's 1994 White Paper on Growth, Competitiveness and Employment. The 1994 White Paper represented a classic case of Commission entrepreneurship, in which Jacques Delors requested at the June 1993 Copenhagen European Council that EU heads of state and government ask the Commission to undertake a study of competitiveness and employment in Europe. For Delors, the White Paper represented an opportunity to revive institutional momentum following implementation of the European single market, and to place the Commission at the center of the debate on how to address Europe's critical unemployment problem.

As with the opening of public procurement markets, the Commission employed two forms of entrepreneurship, matching ideas to promote integration with critical policy problems and taking advantage of the Community's grounding in the rule of law. Both the 1994 White Paper and Articles 126 and 127 of the Maastricht Treaty provided a springboard for the Leonardo program. The 1994 White Paper attributed Europe's employment problems to low job-intensity growth, especially relative to Japan and the USA, where economic growth translated much more directly into jobs.[14] The White Paper cited as critical problems confronting European labor markets a skills shortage, the need to increase the 'employability' of the long-term unemployed through retraining, and the absence of a 'European area' for continued learning. The document called for the Community to facilitate exchanges of best practice and joint projects (Commission 1994: 134–5, 138). These objectives are echoed in DG XXII's 1995 White Paper on Education and Training, which specifically cites the Leonardo program as one means of achieving these goals (Commission 1995*d*). Furthermore, the Maastricht Treaty articles charge the Community with implementing a vocational training policy to support the employment programs of the member states.[15]

By presenting Leonardo as a concrete means of implementing the aims of the 1994 White Paper, the Commission gained Council approval of the Leonardo program. Despite this success for DG XXII in establishing a Commission presence in European vocational training, it did not have the staff to implement the program itself. DG XXII therefore had to contract

---

[14] The White Paper contrasted a difference of 0.4 percentage points between economic growth and job growth in the USA between 1973 and 1990 with a difference of more than 2.0 percentage points for the EC during the same period. See Commission 1994: 59, chart 5.

[15] Art. 126 of the Treaty on European Union charges the Commission with 'supporting and supplementing' the action of member states in the area of education, while Article 127 directs the Community to implement a vocational training policy, again to 'support and supplement' the policies of the member states.

out technical support for the program from its inception in 1995. While the Commission would ultimately select projects to be funded by the program, the subcontracted 'Technical Assistance Office' would oversee the complex processing procedures for the large volume of proposals submitted for consideration.

Between June 1996 and May 1997, DG XXII carried out an internal audit of its contractor following the first year of operation of the Leonardo program. The audit produced substantial evidence of a range of abuses by the French firm awarded the technical assistance contract, including fraudulent billing, overpayment of subcontractors, and nepotism.[16] A subsequent audit revealed additional instances of these practices. However, DG XXII was reluctant to act on this evidence for fear of losing the program.[17] There were indications of growing skepticism within some member-state governments about the objectives set out in DG XXII's 1995 White Paper on Education and Training (European Parliament 1999: section 5.7.1). Additionally, since there were no plans to transfer the contract for technical assistance with the Leonardo program to another company, DG XXII's Director-General feared that any disruption of the existing contract would jeopardize the continuity of the program (European Parliament 1999: para. 5.5.4). Finally, concerned that the program would be discontinued, the Commission did not pass on the evidence garnered from its internal audits to the European Parliament as its Committee on Social Affairs and Employment prepared its recommendation on the proposed Leonardo II program in October 1998.[18]

According to the Report of the Committee of Independent Experts, problems of this type were not confined to the Leonardo program. For example, similar problems occurred in the management of the MED programs designed to strengthen political and economic cooperation with the southern Mediterranean countries. In both cases, pathologies resulted from the implementation of public policies by private contractors, a practice emerging from the expansion of Commission tasks without commensurate increases in administrative resources (European Parliament 1999: section 5.8.2). The Committee of Independent Experts traces these diffi-

[16] See European Parliament 1999. The Committee, sanctioned by a Jan. 1999 resolution of the European Parliament and consisting of five members appointed by the Parliament, was approved by a European Commission facing the prospect of censure by the Parliament. The Committee first convened in Feb. 1999.

[17] For example, in Nov. 1998, the Director-General of DG XXII reported on the internal audits to Commissioner Cresson and, according to the Report of the Committee of Independent Experts (European Parliament 1999: para. 5.4.10), urged that the various problems uncovered not be permitted to disturb the overall functioning of the program.

[18] European Parliament 1999: para. 5.6. Leonardo II was adopted by the Council in Apr. 1999, with a budget of 1.15 billion Euros for the 2000–6 period, a substantial increase over the 620 million ecu 1995–9 budget for Leonardo I.

culties to the disjuncture between the transformation of the Commission 'from an institution which devises and proposes policy into one which implements policy', and the underdevelopment of the Commission's financial management capabilities (European Parliament 1999: para. 9.4.1).

Mobilization of Interests

The shift in Commission activities demanded by successful program innovation is one source of diminishing returns to policy entrepreneurship. A second source stems from political mobilization in response to the development of policy-making authority at the European level. The growing literature on interest representation in the European Union suggests that interest articulation through national channels is increasingly supplemented through interest mobilization and articulation directly at the European level (Andersen and Eliassen 1993; Greenwood and Ronit 1994). National and European political arenas are interconnected rather than autonomous political spheres (Marks *et al.* 1996a: 346). As a consequence, a growing array of interests, including not only business associations and firms, but also cities, regional development councils, social services, and environmental groups, are now represented at the European level through both formal and informal mechanisms (Andersen and Eliassen 1993: 40–1; Hooghe 1995). Policy networks and interest associations have developed at the European level even in areas such as social policy in which EU institutions wield little formal authority (Cram 1997: 21).

Institutionalist analyses of political mobilization have recognized that the actions of governments may mobilize interests by providing resources and formal or informal channels of representation or by articulating new policies or ideas that legitimate the claims of certain groups (March and Olsen 1984: 739; Pierson 1993: 601; Immergut 1998: 20). In contrast to behavioralist approaches, which depict political mobilization as a spontaneous reflection of aggregated individual preferences, institutionalist perspectives view political mobilization as a response to government policies (Cameron 1974; J. L. Walker 1991: 49–50; Immergut 1998: 6–7). Political agendas and alliances are the products not simply of preferences and circumstances, but also of past policies; from the institutionalist vantage point, policies are themselves 'politically consequential structures' (Pierson 1993: 624).[19]

---

[19] In his discussion of mobilization theory, J. L. Walker (1991: 54) asserts that 'the steady expansion of the power and responsibility of the federal government figures as one of the major causes of the recent growth of new organizational devices for linking citizens

In the EU context, Lindberg recognized as early as the 1960s the potential of the European Community system to activate additional constituencies among broader segments of society (Lindberg 1966, 1967). Several authors have since demonstrated the link between the activities of EU institutions and the mobilization of particular regional interests, as in the response to an increase in regional development funds (Marks 1992), or the proliferating representation of subnational groups in response to enhanced opportunities to pursue interests at the EU level (Hooghe 1995). Similarly, regions beset by problems of industrial decline were mobilized by the purposive efforts of the European Commission to forge a cohesive lobby to defend funding through interaction with the Council Presidency, member-state governments, and the European Parliament (McAleavey and Mitchell 1994). These studies share Lindberg's premise that the actions of EU institutions and the process of integration can stimulate the articulation of interests at the European level. This takes place through informal consultation between private interests and EU institutions; lobbying of the Commission and the European Parliament by individual businesses, business associations, and consumer and environmental groups; and legal action in the European Court of Justice. By virtue of its independent preferences and ideas about how to achieve these, the Commission represents an additional 'optio(n) for societal actors in their choice of allies and arenas' (Sandholtz 1996: 405).

Functioning as correctives to state-centric views of European integration, most historical institutionalist analyses have focused on unanticipated ways in which the institutional dynamics of the European Community have constrained member-state governments. Yet scholars have begun to recognize that policy entrepreneurship may ultimately generate constraints for the supranational actors themselves. Constituencies of the European Commission, ECJ, and Parliament comprised respectively of subnational actors (including consumer and environmental groups and transnational business), national courts, and national electorates, not only strengthen the autonomy of supranational institutions, but also 'act . . . as a constraint on the freedom of action of the supranational institutions' (Pollack 1997a: 130).[20] As Hooghe argues, while the Commission has fostered and supported the mobilization of represent-

and their government.' There may be a parallel process taking place in response to the enhanced policy autonomy and authority of the European Union's supranational institutions.

[20] As Pollack (1997a: 130) compellingly describes the duality of this situation, 'all three supranational institutions navigate constantly between two sets of institutions: the member government principals that created them and may still alter their mandates and the transnational constituencies that act both as constraint and resource in the institutions' efforts to establish their autonomy'.

ative subnational organizations, the institutionalization of this representation threatens Commission autonomy. Thus when the issue of formalizing representation of regional and local authorities became part of the Maastricht Treaty process, the Commission faced a tension between empowering subnational actors to serve as a counterweight to member-state governments and creating an additional political control on its activities (Hooghe 1995: 193–4).

The very constituencies mobilized by policy entrepreneurship make demands on Commission resources. By this mechanism, actors whose interest articulation at the European level provided leverage for the Commission to gain autonomy from member-state governments eventually generate new constraints on Commission activities. This phenomenon is well illustrated in the area of state aid policy, where private business has been a powerful advocate of the Commission's increasingly rigorous enforcement of Treaty rules restricting the granting of subsidies or other favorable treatment to public enterprises by governments. Despite its unique powers in this area, the Commission's institutional role in the process of state aid control, Court decisions, and the responses of transnational actors to the activities of the Commission have all created constraints that the Commission could not have foreseen as it developed its state aid policy in the aftermath of the Single European Act.

The EC Treaty grants the European Commission exclusive competence to require that member-state governments 'abolish or alter' aid the Commission deems incompatible with the internal market.[21] None the less, in practice the Commission's authority has developed only gradually. The process has been highly sensitive politically since member-state governments have used subsidies as an instrument of industrial policy for decades. Following the Single European Act, the Commission developed its capacities in the state aid area through decisions of the Court of Justice, articulation of an extensive framework of rules, and by fostering the mobilization of a constituency in the business community favoring rigorous control of government aid to industry (Mitchell Smith 1998). As in the development of the doctrine of mutual recognition of product standards, the Commission exploited Court rulings to increase institutional capacities. The Commission also came to rely on complaints by third parties—typically firms competing with an aid beneficiary—to help justify the aggressive application and development of its state aid regime. Using these resources as well as its Treaty authority, the Commission was able to develop its capacities to investigate state aid cases, establish precedents, make decisions, and extract compliance from member state governments.

---

[21] This authority is codified in Art. 88 of the EC Treaty, formerly (i.e. prior to the Amsterdam Treaty), Art. 93.

The Commissioner for competition policy had substantial latitude to set the state aid agenda in order to accumulate credibility and a record of rigorous, neutral and consistent application of the rules. When confronted by ministers of member-state governments lobbying on behalf of national industry, Commission officials frequently were able to counterbalance such political pressure by invoking countervailing private complaints.

The Commission's success in constructing the state aid regime and its visibility in combating subsidies especially to state-owned industries has proven a catalyst for broader attention to state aid from private-sector competitors who rely on the Commission to sustain fair competition. However, as complaints to the Commission about suspected illegal subsidies have grown in scope and number, they also have diminished the Commission's ability to independently determine the state aid agenda. The state aid unit of DG IV would prefer private actors to bring more state aid complaints before national courts, since EC Treaty provisions prohibiting the granting of aid that distorts competition in the internal market are directly enforceable at the national level. Yet the number of cases that have appeared before national courts remains miniscule, and only a fraction of these have been successful.[22] The sharp contrast between the low success rate of complaints filed at the national level and the tentativeness of national courts on state aid matters, on the one hand, with the Commission's activism in investigating suspected breaches of the state aid rules and confronting member-state governments that violate the rules, on the other, generates strong incentives for private actors to bring their complaints directly to the Commission.

Ultimately the response of private firms to Commission activism have altered the nature of state aid cases before the Court of Justice. In the past, state aid cases typically were Commission actions brought against member states for violating Treaty articles or failing to implement Commission decisions. An increasing number of cases before the Court of First Instance now consist of actions against the Commission for failing to fully investigate complaints. Prior to these cases, the rights of interested parties to do anything more than submit evidence to the Commission were nowhere codified; the Commission has been able to dismiss third-party complaints that it is not prepared to pursue, whether for political or administrative reasons. However, recent Court decisions resulting from dissatisfaction by third parties with the Commission's treatment of their complaints have imposed

---

[22] A total of 116 cases have come before national courts. Of these, only four have involved complaints by a firm against a competitor that has received aid, and twenty-four have been lodged by firms against governments that allegedly granted aid to a competitor. In only three cases—one each in Belgium, Germany, and the UK—have the firms initiating the action been successful. See Commission 1999*h*: table II.

additional burdens on the Commission to provide grounds for dismissing a complaint. These decisions have raised the prospect of third parties challenging the Commission's exclusive competence to decide whether or not to open formal procedures of investigation of a state aid.

The landmark case is the 1995 Sytravel judgment. In this case, several French security firms filed a case against the Commission for failing to rule that the French government had infringed EC Treaty Articles governing internal market competition when it set up state-owned commercial companies to provide security and other services for the French Post Office. The decision in favor of the plaintiffs suggests that mobilization of private actors and Court judgments not only empower, but also can constrain the Commission.

Beginning from the treaty language granting it legal authority to regulate aid to industry from member-state governments, the Commission used its skills as a policy entrepreneur to enlarge the realm of its authority in this policy area. In the process, the Commission increased reliance on the Community state aid regime by firms and industrial associations interested in rigorous oversight. Mobilization of these actors initially enhanced the Commission's leverage *vis-à-vis* member-state governments. More recently, the Commission's growing policy authority in the policing of state aid has created incentives for firms and national industry associations to make demands on the Commission's state aid capacities, ultimately generating constraints unanticipated by the Commission's competition DG.

Analyzing Diminishing Returns

The experience of the European Commission raises critical questions about the consequences of policy entrepreneurship generally. Do returns to policy entrepreneurship always diminish over time? To what extent does this vary by institutional setting and policy area? Are there particular strategies policy-initiating institutions can employ to reduce the costs of entrepreneurship?

The examples of public procurement liberalization and state aid control indicate that, for the European Commission, diminishing returns are an outgrowth of institutional and political factors. First, the intrusion of the institution into new areas of political life is a prerequisite for the mobilization of new constituencies and articulation of interests that generate policy feedbacks. This is more likely where the entrepreneurial institution has a broad mandate, as is the case for the European Commission. The relationship between the Commission and member-state governments is a case of incomplete contracting, in which the Commission is valued precisely because it serves as a neutral arbiter when contingencies arise that are not specifically addressed in the EC Treaties (Pollack 1997*a*). A second institutional factor that exacerbates the problem of diminishing returns for the Commission is the essentially fixed nature of its administrative resources. Even where budgets for programs (such as cohesion funds or other structural funds) increase, the Commission itself operates in an environment that is extremely hostile to the growth of bureaucracy. Therefore while expansion of both tasks and autonomy are possible, increases in administrative resources are unlikely.

Finally, the mobilization of interests at the European level has been so substantial because of the relatively open nature of policy-making in the EU, particularly at the policy-formulation phase (Majone 1996: 67, 77; McGowan and Wallace 1996). Moreover, mobilization in response to political entrepreneurship is particularly powerful because of prior organization of affected interests. Across West European societies, labor, business, environmental, and other interests have long been highly organized, though they have aimed their activities at national and regional levels. The intensification of political activity at the European level provides an incentive for these interests to redistribute their resources between levels of governance. Pre-existing groups may divide their activities in new ways between the local, regional, national, and European levels; new groups organize at European level.

Given that diminishing returns are a product of the political dynamic of the European Community and the political environment in which the Commission operates, is it possible for the Commission to prevent sharply diminishing returns in the wake of future policy entrepreneurship? Diminishing returns normally are an inevitable outcome as the production of policy, like the production of goods, increases. Therefore, the prospect of reducing the pathologies that brought about the March 1999 downfall of the Commission depends upon the extent to which the Commission is able to control task expansion. In short, the Commission faces a trade-off between the breadth of its initiatives and returns to entrepreneurship. If the new Commission follows the dictum that entrepreneurship and the quest for deeper integration should not draw the institution into activities outside its comparative advantage, the Commission will be more likely to retain its dynamism as the engine of integration without further harm to institutional integrity. In addition, while the Commission certainly cannot control the process of political mobilization emanating from the progression of economic integration, it ultimately can narrow the risks of diminishing returns by encouraging economic actors to pursue their European-level interests in national arenas, especially national courts.

In public procurement policy, a willingness to turn monitoring author-ity over to member-state institutions offers evidence of the Commission's recognition of the need to focus its activities in areas of operational strength. The Commission simply lacks the resources unilaterally to ensure effective enforcement of the directives. Neither a substantial staffing increase for the public procurement enforcement unit nor a sharp increase in the investigatory powers of the Commission are even remotely likely, given sensitivity on the part of the Council, Parliament, and the Commission itself to criticisms of EU bureaucracy. An alternative that is both politically more viable and more productive for the Commission from an institutional perspective is the development of independent regu-latory bodies at national level that would monitor the compliance of pub-lic authorities with EU law, deter violations, and help the Commission achieve a much more effective public procurement regime. Sweden already has such an authority. Recognizing the institutional benefits of shedding some enforcement tasks, DG XV in its November 1996 Green Paper on public procurement argues that national authorities should build up the credibility of the public contracting regime sufficiently to deter violations and thereby reduce the volume of complaints.[23] However, revealing one of the shortcomings of regulatory governance, member-state governments so far refuse to bear the costs of implementing such a proposal. Still, the possibility remains that existing authorities, such as Courts of Auditors, eventually will take on the task of monitoring application of public pro-curement regulations.

The Commission has made a similar proposal for turning over enforce-ment of competition regulations governing price-fixing and abuses of dominant market position to national authorities.[24] In state aid policy, another portion of the Commission's competition policy, the Commission has since the mid-1990s pursued two means of restoring its autonomy. First, DG IV has intensified efforts to encourage the pursuit of state aid complaints at the national level. The Commission directed a 1995 notice in the *Official Journal* towards both lower level national courts and private firms (Commission 1995*a*). The Commission emphasized the powers and responsibilities of national courts in enforcing state aid rules, and elabor-ated on mechanisms through which the Commission could provide infor-mation and consultation to national courts on state aid cases. The notice also emphasized that national courts, but not the Commission, can award

---

[23] Referring to the Swedish example, the Commission in its 1996 Green Paper asserts that 'With a view to monitoring application of the rules more effectively at national level, it could be worthwhile for other Member States to set up a similar body.' See Commission 1996*d*: 17.

[24] See *The Financial Times* (13 Dec. 1999), 1.

damages to competitor firms in cases of violation of Community state aid rules.

Additionally, in 1998 the Commission gained Council approval of the first of a series of regulations that will reduce its state aid caseload by exempting broad categories of state assistance to enterprises from state aid notification requirements. This includes aid to promote small and medium enterprises, environmental protection, research and development, and employment and training, all objectives consistent with the Community's competitiveness aims and all areas of activity unlikely to seriously distort competition within the single market.[25] These emergent Commission responses to the problems of overextension suggest that the Commission has learned that, rather than being a risk to its institutional interests, new forms of subsidiarity may contribute to institutional revival.

Conclusion: Policy Entrepreneurship in a Maturing European Polity

Observers of EU institutional dynamics have suggested that the vast scope of decision-making renders it difficult for member-state governments to control the development of policy (Pierson 1996*b*: 137). Yet the same may be said for the Commission, which has relatively little experience with coordination across policy areas. As the internal market has developed, policy regimes increasingly have come to overlap and even conflict with one another. For example, the attempt to liberalize the purchase of goods and services by local government authorities may disadvantage small suppliers that cannot compete across national borders, yet it is precisely small and medium enterprises that are at the core of EU-coordinated efforts to boost employment in Europe.[26] Even though it may have a comparative advantage in information resources and long-term planning, as this chapter has demonstrated, the Commission cannot perfectly anticipate the results of legislative initiatives, Court decisions flowing from cases it initiates or in response to its enforcement efforts, or the demands of constituencies newly mobilized in response to policy outputs.

Accordingly, as Europe's single market and economic integration have progressed, the nature of the encounter between the institutions of the European Union and European society has changed. In the early years of

[25] The first of these enabling regulations, Council Regulation EC 994/98, was passed on May 7, 1998.

[26] In the late 1980s the European Parliament expressed concern to the Commission about the impact of public procurement liberalization on social objectives—including the welfare of small and medium enterprises—and regional policy goals. The Commission's response to the Parliament and Council on these issues is found in European Commission (1989).

integration, the encounter was a circumscribed affair, limited largely to circles of political and economic élites. The take-off of integration following the launch of the single European market intensified the interpenetration of European and national levels, and thereby implicated more organized interests in the interaction with EU institutions.[27] The European Commission has used this process to its institutional advantage, organizing policy networks in numerous issue areas to augment its autonomy relative to member-state governments. However, as the density of such networks has increased, societal interest mobilization in response to the incentives created by Commission entrepreneurship has intensified demands on the Commission and constrained its autonomy. In this respect, the emergence of the European polity more closely resembles the development of governing capacities in some national settings, like the USA, where the expansion of government after the Great Depression was followed by the capture of state regulatory agents by private interests (McConnell 1970).

The entrepreneurship of the European Commission has been a potent institutional response to the breadth of its mandate to foster deeper integration. The very fact that it has succeeded in building governance capacities has mobilized powerful organized interests at a European level; the maturation of the European polity is reflected in the fact that constraints on the autonomy of supranational regulators have emerged not from policy failures, but from successful entrepreneurship and the progress of integration. During the 1990s, the increasing penetration of Community policies into the lives of Europeans mobilized societal interests and brought them into direct contact with EU institutions. The resulting demands on the Commission's resources, along with increasing responsibilities of monitoring compliance with Community regulations, management of an expanded array of programs, and coordination of a more diverse range of policies have put at risk the integrity of an institution originally designed to protect the EEC Treaties and promote the quest for ever closer union. At the same time, the Commission's mistakes and failures appear to have sown the seeds of reform and revival by imbuing the institution with an awareness of the dangers of overextension. As a result, in the coming decade we can expect to see a Commission that continues to skillfully use its resources to push for deeper integration and institutional aggrandizement, but with a much greater consciousness of its limitations, and a greater sense of restraint.

---

[27] As Hooghe (1995: 179) observes about the EU polity, 'The politics of multi-level governance are pluralist but with an elitist bias.'

12

Democracy, Legitimacy, and the European Parliament

ROGER SCULLY

The 1999 institutional crisis in the European Union, which saw the mass resignation of the Commission, became to many critical observers in the media and the political world not simply a specific instance of institutional failure, but symbolic of a wider malaise in the Union. Many of the debates concerning the EU in the 1990s have focused on issues of democracy and legitimacy, with even more sober critics diagnosing a 'democratic deficit' and/or a wider 'legitimacy crisis'. These concepts have been deployed to help explain much of the resistance to European integration in recent years, and as the reasons prompting many proposals for reform. In this context, it is unsurprising that the European Parliament (EP) has assumed an increasingly significant place within the EU—not least because parliamentary chambers have long been regarded as key institutions of representative democracy and as making an indispensable contribution to the wider legitimation of public authority which democracy is generally understood to convey in modern, Western political systems.

The growing significance of the Parliament constitutes one of the most important institutional reforms to have occurred in the EU in recent times. It remains, however, a change whose wider implications have been insufficiently explored. We undoubtedly know more about the EP than was the case a decade ago. Its enhanced powers have been extensively catalogued and analyzed, and greater consideration has also been paid to the internal politics of the chamber—its election, organization, and the attitudes and behavior of EP members (MEPs).[1] In developing this knowledge, concepts and methods borrowed from other contexts have often proven invaluable.[2] However, recent research remains markedly devoid of a broader compar-

[1] See Corbett et al. 1995; Raunio 1997; Bowler and Farrell 1995; Scully 1997c, 1998; Kreppel and Tsebelis 1999; for but a few examples.

[2] For instance, Hix and Lord (1996) and Raunio (1997) examine roll-call voting data, and Crombez (1997), Moser (1997), Tsebelis (1994), Garrett and Tsebelis (1996), and Scully (1997c) all deploy dimensional models of bargaining processes.

ative perspective: where does the contemporary European Parliament stand in comparison to other such institutions, others in the genus 'legislatures' or 'parliaments'?[3] This would matter little were the EP's circumstances sufficiently atypical for lessons drawn from elsewhere to be irrelevant. But in many salient respects they are not. The Parliament certainly has some unique features, including a membership from fifteen countries, and over eighty separate national parties, operating within a broader structure of multinational institutions. Yet the fundamental challenges that the EP faces—of influencing policy-making and building effective and legitimate structures of political representation—are far from unique. On the contrary, these challenges are common to parliaments across the democratic world.

This chapter examines the European Parliament using an analytical framework adapted from comparative parliamentary research. The framework points to two key dimensions: the policy impact of a chamber and the level of support it enjoys. After reviewing recent institutional reforms in the EU, I will argue that, while the EP has now attained a substantial policy role, it has been considerably less successful in securing deep-rooted support among the European public and significant sectors of the political élite. Thus, I suggest that the Parliament increasingly resembles a 'vulnerable' legislature, its lack of a solid constituency of support rendering its hard-won policy prerogatives subject to future challenges. This vulnerability is argued to lie not least in the chamber's inability to generate a sense of democratic legitimacy for the Union as a whole. Invoking the themes of this book, the broader implications of these arguments for both the Parliament and Union are assessed in the conclusion.

The European Parliament and EU Policy-Making

> The simplest and most common comparative statements about legislatures relate to the strength or weakness of particular legislative institutions . . . such statements usually refer to the importance of the legislature in the policy-making process relative to the importance of non-legislative institutions.
>
> (Mezey 1979: 23)

Assessments of the European Parliament's influence as an actor in the policy processes of the EU have traditionally been harsh. The chamber has generally been seen as a 'multi-lingual talking shop', lacking 'true

---

[3] For a partial early effort, see Hermann and Lodge (1978); a more recent work echoing the concerns of this chapter is Judge and Earnshaw (1999). Examples of a more *sui generis* approach to the EP are Corbett *et al.* (1995), Westlake (1994*a*), and J. Smith (1995).

legislative capabilities' (Thomas 1992: 4; see also Dinan 1993: 109–10). The reforms of recent times, however, mean that such a verdict is increasingly misplaced. Without conducting a detailed examination of how the EP has won a greater role in EU politics, it can easily be demonstrated that the significance of the Parliament within the Union has been transformed.

Often seen as an afterthought in the original integrationist schemes of Jean Monnet, Robert Schuman, and others,[4] the Common Assembly (as the EP was first entitled) was at first composed of national legislators delegated to serve part-time in a body with few powers. The assembly could dismiss *en masse* the High Authority (forerunner of today's Commission), but did not appoint this executive body, or have any substantial budgetary or legislative powers.[5] Early empirical work also suggested that the Parliament (as retitled from 1962) did not even help create a body of like-minded, pro-European politicians as, rather than being socialized into attitudes favorable to integration, a 'self-selection' effect led people who already held such views to serve within the chamber (Haas 1968; Kerr 1973).

Until the 1970s, then, the EP was of minimal importance. But subsequent developments have altered the picture considerably. Treaty amendments and institutional agreements have given the chamber considerably greater powers; powers buttressed by MEPs' consistent willingness to exploit their potential in a 'maximalist' fashion (Scully 1998). Let us briefly review the major elements of this process.

The Budget

In the 1970s, two treaties granted the Parliament a greater say in the Community's budgetary process.[6] The EP was given the right to propose modifications to planned 'compulsory' spending (mainly on agriculture) and to insist on amendments to 'non-compulsory' spending. Finally, a super-majority of MEPs (an absolute majority of all MEPs, and two-thirds of those voting) could reject the budget outright.[7] The Parliament and the Council of Ministers (rather than the Council alone) were desig-

---

[4] As Judge and Earnshaw observe, 'The Assembly was designed to operate at the peripheries of the grand European design' (1999: 5–6).

[5] Even if EP members are extremely dissatisfied with one or more members of the executive body, their only power is to dismiss those members and all their colleagues.

[6] These were the 1970 Treaty Amending Certain Budgetary Provisions of the Treaties, and the 1975 Treaty Amending Certain Financial Provisions of the Treaties.

[7] This power has been exercised twice, in 1979 and 1984. In the event of a rejection of the budget, the treaties allow the Community, however, to continue to exist for the following year on the basis of 'twelfths': i.e. spending carries on at a level equivalent to one-twelfth of the appropriations for the previous financial year.

nated as the budgetary authority of the Community; final declaration of the adoption of the annual budget now lies with the President of Parliament (Westlake 1994*b*: 30).

What practical impact did these reforms have? As later occurred with its growing legislative role, many MEPs sought 'to see how far [the formal powers] could be taken. Major confrontations with the Council, far from being avoided, seemed at times almost to be sought as the EP attempted to assert itself' (Nugent 1994: 180). This meant deploying rejection and amendment powers; trying to insert new budgetary lines in areas the EP wanted policy to develop (such as aid to Latin America and Asia); and pressing increases in 'non-compulsory' spending, which now constitutes almost 50 per cent of expenditure (Laffan and Shackleton 1996: 78). The Parliament's budgetary role was further enhanced by the 1988 'Inter-Institutional Agreement on Budgetary Discipline and Improvement of the Budgetary Procedure' between the Council of Ministers, Commission and Parliament, which agreed that parliamentary approval would henceforth be needed for increases in compulsory spending (Westlake 1994*b*; Nugent 1994: 180–2, 347–60).[8] The agreement, and a 1993 successor, ran parallel to multi-year budgetary agreements which allowed greater parliamentary attention to implementation issues, and to relatively small changes between spending priorities.

Beneath the immense complexity of budgetary politics in the EU,[9] Parliament is now a significant player. While few observers judge it quite the equal of the Council of Ministers, it does not simply have to agree to all or even most of the Council's agenda. Recent years have seen a shift in the prevailing agenda 'from the "high politics" of budgetary reform to management issues, particularly fraud and "value for money" issues' (Laffan and Shackleton 1996: 95), and attempts to move from confrontation between the institutions to cooperation based on Inter-Institutional Agreements.[10] But, where it occurs, this is cooperation between potentially strong competitors, not meek acquiescence by a weak Parliament to an all-powerful Council.

---

[8] This agreement was instituted to run alongside the 'Delors I' settlement, which established the main parameters for Community spending for 1988–92. A further Inter-Institutional Agreement on Budgetary Discipline and improvement of the Budgetary Procedure was finalized in 1993, to run parallel to the 'Delors II' financial deal.

[9] Laffan and Shackleton quote the senior French MEP, Jean Cot: 'Community budgetary procedure poses a challenge of logic to any cartesian mind, one which it is more sensible to bypass' (1996: 87).

[10] Inter-Institutional budgetary conflict remains present, however, as the refusal by the EP to grant discharge (approval) of the 1996 budget demonstrates. Moreover, the budget, and decisions regarding its future direction, remain the subject of fierce disputes between different EU member states.

Executive Oversight

The Parliament has made only limited progress here: partly because the EU lacks a clear 'executive branch' to oversee. An increasing number of executive functions—particularly in the developing area of foreign policy—are wielded by national governments or their representatives, who are reluctant to yield to EP scrutiny. The Parliament can still dismiss the Commission for (the equivalent of) 'high crimes and misdemeanors', and in March 1999, evidence of mismanagement in the Commission had become so obvious that MEPs seemed on the verge of using their ultimate weapon; they were only pre-empted by the mass resignation of the twenty Commissioners. The position of the EP was boosted by The Maastricht Treaty, that amended Article 158 to give the Parliament approval power over a new Commission nominated by national governments. This provision was interpreted in 1994/5 as allowing Parliament both to vote on the Commission President-designate and on the Commission as a whole; the Amsterdam Treaty formally approved Parliament's veto over the President-designate. However, practical use of Parliament's powers over the Commission is restricted: sacking the entire Commission is such an extreme act that the EP has never actually done it,[11] while MEPs voting on a new Commission may be strongly encouraged to endorse the choice of their national party leaders, as apparently occurred in 1994/5 (Gabel and Hix, n.d.). None the less, day-to-day scrutiny of the Commission is increasingly pursued by parliamentary committees, both regularly established committees with a particular policy focus and special Committees of Enquiry. The EP may also be the only institution exercising significant oversight of the new European Central Bank, now the leading economic policy-maker in Europe. Thus, even in respect of oversight, some progress has been made by the Parliament.

Community Legislation

The Parliament has made the greatest and most recent advances here. Prior to the Single European Act (SEA, ratified in 1987), parliamentary impact on European legislation was very limited. EU laws (other than Commission legislation[12]) were processed via 'consultation'. Parliament could proffer and suggest amendments to draft laws, but could compel

---

[11] See n. 5.

[12] While virtually all major EU laws require endorsement by the Council of Ministers, the Commission also has the ability to issue laws by itself. While the vast majority of these are very narrow and technical items, in terms of sheer quantity they none the less form the bulk of EU legislation (Nugent 1994: 103–4).

neither the Commission nor Council to respond to its opinion once delivered. Aside from the possibility of using delaying tactics (by failing to present its opinion[13]), the EP had no formal means to alter legislation. To exert further influence required skilled persuasion of the Commission or national governments. These institutional constraints rendered the Parliament a fairly marginal actor in EU law-making (Earnshaw and Judge 1996).

Refusal by many MEPs to accept this subordinate role generated a fierce lobby for greater powers, particularly after the Parliament became directly elected in 1979. This pressure bore some fruit in the SEA: among the Treaty's innovations was greater complexity in the legislative arena, with consultation retained for the majority of bills but two new procedures introduced for others. The 'cooperation' procedure, used for most Single Market matters, gave the EP an ability to propose amendments (which, if approved by the Commission, could be overturned only by a unanimous Council but accepted by a qualified majority of states) or issue a veto that could only be overturned by a unanimous Council of Ministers. Though far from all the chamber had wanted,[14] and while the EP's influence remained conditional on other actors, particularly the Commission, cooperation enabled the Parliament to exert more influence over law-making than many had originally expected and was undoubtedly a significant advance (Corbett 1989; Earnshaw and Judge 1996, 1997; Tsebelis 1994).

The SEA also introduced the 'assent' procedure, under which the EP got a simple approval/disapproval power over some legislation. The scope of assent was widened at Maastricht to encompass eight areas of law, mostly relating to association agreements with third countries and the accession of new members to the Union. While the 'take-it-or-leave-it'

[13] The requirement that Parliament's opinion be received *before* legislation passed was made explicit in the 1980 *Isoglucose* ruling of the Court of Justice, which stated that 'consultation of the Parliament in the cases provided for by the Treaty therefore constitutes an *essential* formality, disregard of which means that the measure concerned is void' (cited in Corbett *et al.* 1995: 191, my emphasis). This gave the EP the option of failing to offer its opinion until the Commission agreed to modify proposals in line with the EP's wishes. Nugent indicates that this power has, in fact, been employed on several occasions (1994: 176), while Corbett *et al.* document the Commission changing a proposal (on the issue of economic and monetary union) in the face of a threatened parliamentary delay (1995: 193). However, as J. Smith notes, 'MEPs are generally in favor of further integration and do not want to be seen as putting a brake on Community legislation' (1995: 83). Furthermore, a recent judgment of the Court of Justice has stated that indefinite delay is not a legitimate parliamentary tactic on legislation designated as 'urgent' by the Council (Corbett 1996: 39–40).

[14] In 1984, the EP overwhelmingly endorsed a Draft Treaty on European Union. Developed and advocated by the veteran Italian Euro-federalist Altiero Spinelli, this document demanded equal status for the EP with the Council of Ministers as the two chambers of the Community legislature. By this measure, the cooperation procedure could be counted a disappointment.

nature of assent deprives the EP of what Tsebelis (1994) terms 'agenda setting' power, this is at least somewhat balanced by the ability to irrevocably
veto things to which MEPs object. At least some in the Parliament apparently consider this power of greater value than the possibility to engage in
agenda-setting activities (Dankert 1997: 213).[15]

   After Maastricht, however, much legislation (around one-quarter) was
processed under a fourth procedure, 'co-decision'. Co-decision laws were
designated as joint Acts of the Parliament and Council (rather than the
Council alone). Co-decision allowed the EP to push forward amendments
and delay laws, and added an irrevocable parliamentary veto. While many
MEPs were disappointed by the limited scope of co-decision, most
observers have none the less seen it as a considerable step forward. Duff,
for example, suggests that, 'Maastricht marks the point in the
Community's development at which the Parliament became the first
chamber of a real legislature . . . The co-decision procedure means that it
has now come of age as a law-making body' (Duff 1994: 31; see also
Corbett *et al.* 1995; Nugent 1994). A contrary, 'revisionist' argument,
claiming that the veto at the end of the procedure was given only at the
greater cost of Parliament losing its status as legislative agenda-setter
(Tsebelis 1995; Garrett 1995; Garrett and Tsebelis 1996; Tsebelis and
Garrett 1997), has been subjected to severe theoretical criticism (Scully
1997*a*, 1997*b*; Moser 1997; Steunenberg 1997), while the empirical evidence also points in the opposite direction. The EP's success in advancing
legislative amendments has increased significantly under co-decision compared to the already high level achieved under cooperation (Jacobs 1997;
Scully 1997*a*; Earnshaw and Judge 1996; Shackleton 1999).[16] Earnshaw
and Judge (1996: 124) nicely summarize the impact of co-decision, when
added to the earlier changes:

under consultation, Parliament's role was essentially confined to communicating
its opinion from behind the metaphorical hedgerows to the Commission and the
Council . . . under cooperation, Parliament was given the formal opportunity to

---

[15] Scully (1997*c*) finds that greater numbers of MEPs turn out for votes on assent matters than do so even for other legislative procedures, even when other factors such as sched-
uling are accounted for. In a parliament that has traditionally had problems with low
attendance, this suggests that the ability to issue an irrevocable 'yes–no' decision appeals to
MEPs.

[16] Moreover, as Peterson states, 'Crucially . . . there is evidence to suggest that both the
Commission and the Council now take far more careful informal soundings amongst
MEPs and EP officials at relatively *early* stages of the policy process' (1997: 16, emphasis
in original). This implies that other institutions' knowledge of Parliament's greater power
under co-decision leads them to pre-empt EP preferences in their own proposals, and, thus,
that the greater success of the EP in passing amendments under co-decision almost certainly *underestimates* the degree to which the procedure has boosted the chamber's influence.

step onto the path in limited policy fields and for limited periods . . . Under co-decision, however, Parliament is now an equal partner in the legislative process, and has a rightful place *alongside* Council in several important policy areas.[17]

The 1997 Amsterdam Treaty revised co-decision in a manner somewhat beneficial to the Parliament, and also extended it to twenty-three further areas of EU law, mostly at the expense of the cooperation procedure. With the ratification of Amsterdam, co-decision has become the modal proced-ure, 'a major step towards a system based on bicameral parliamentary democracy at the EC level' (Nentwich and Falkner 1997: 1). Some observers see a negative aspect to the EP's growing legislative role, arguing that the chamber is now more concerned with reacting to the legislative initiatives of others than developing its own agenda.[18] But most take a positive view: that the Parliament is now a serious player in EU law-making. When this role is considered alongside its budgetary and over-sight roles, the EP must be regarded as an important player in the European policy process.

The EP in Comparative Perspective

The above discussion confirms that the European Parliament has sub-stantially increased in importance over recent years. Comparing the EP *chronologically*—that is, with itself at previous points in time—the cham-ber has clearly become a more significant policy actor. But the more inter-esting comparisons that can be made are *cross-sectional*: how does the new, more powerful EP compare to other parliaments?

Scholars have long realized that it is difficult to make such comparisons with great precision, for at least three reasons. The first is a problem of def-inition: the meaning of the key concepts, 'power' and 'influence', remains highly contested (Sparkes 1994). A second factor is one of measurement: even if definitions can be agreed, they may be hard to apply accurately and consistently across political contexts. The third reason is also a measure-ment problem, though of a very different kind: the power and/or influence of actors generally varies across time and issue areas, even within unchanging constitutional frameworks. The result is that typologies of legislatures which include the chamber's policy impact as a classifying

[17] Indeed, other authors go further than Earnshaw and Judge in indicating that co-decision has increased the power of the EP relative to the Commission, as well as to the national governments in the Council. Peterson quotes a member of the Parliament's secre-tariat as stating that 'co-decision, in effect, blows away the Commission's monopoly right of initiative. At least it makes it less tyrannical' (1997: 15; see also Jacobs 1997).

[18] Commission official, Secretariat-General, private communication.

characteristic tend to use fairly low levels of measurement rather than trying to make finer (and possibly incorrect or illusory) distinctions.

The major effort to develop and apply a typology of parliaments
remains that of Michael Mezey (1979), later refined by Philip Norton
(1984). This work remains relevant to current legislative research (e.g.
Norton 1997*b*, 1998), while offering a well-established basis for general
comparisons of parliaments. Mezey's definition of parliamentary power
and influence built upon that of Blondel (1970), who argued for it to be
understood as 'viscosity'—the degree to which the legislature could
impede the 'flow' of proposals advanced by the executive. Thus, Mezey
observed, '[l]egislatures will be salient in the policy-making process to the
extent that their presence and prerogatives act as a constraint on the executive' (1979: 25). The strength of a chamber, he contended, was grounded
primarily in an ability to exercise a veto over policy proposals, and second-
arily in being able to modify them short of veto. Mezey also recognized
that legislatures might themselves develop a policy agenda independent of
the executive. A rough but workable threefold categorization was presented: between chambers with a strong influence in the policy arena,
those with moderate influence, and those with little or no impact on policy. This framework was refined by Norton, who argued that a crucial distinction exists between policy-*making*—which implied, he suggested, the
ability of the legislature not only to 'modify or reject government measures', but also to 'formulate and substitute a policy for that proposed by
the government' (1984: 178)—and policy-*influencing*—which may involve
the rejection or amendment of government measures, but not the promotion by the legislature of its own agenda.

TABLE 12.1. *Classification of Parliaments in Terms of Policy Influence and
Degree of Support*

Policy Power/Influence	Less-Supported	More-Supported
Strong/Policy-Maker	Vulnerable	Active
Modest/Policy-Influencer	Marginal	Reactive
Little or none	Inconsequential (?)	Minimal

A further important point is that a parliament's policy role follows not
only from powers *formally* possessed, but also from an ability and/or willingness to use them. As Norton has observed, 'what is remarkable about
. . . legislatures is not their *power* to say no to government but rather their
reluctance to *use* that power' (1998: 192, emphasis added). The British
Parliament, for instance, has considerable prestige (though sullied by
assorted 'sleaze'-scandals in recent times) as the 'Mother of Parliaments',

a prestige underpinned by the central British constitutional doctrine, 'parliamentary sovereignty', which gives Parliament apparently immense powers. Unencumbered by a formal constitutional text, this doctrine dictates that Parliament can 'make or unmake any law'; indeed, it may do anything except bind the similar freedom of a successor parliament. Is Parliament therefore an all-powerful policy actor? In practice, the answer is no, because its authority is restricted in several respects: by European conventions and treaties; by informal but powerful constraints on what Parliament may legitimately do (a law could be passed, say, to suspend future general elections, but outside wartime this would be inconceivable); by some laws (such as the Parliament Acts which restrict the role of the Upper Chamber, the House of Lords); and, perhaps most importantly of all, particularly in the House of Commons, by the force of party discipline. As King (1975) argued, the notion of executive–legislative relations is often misleading, but particularly so within a parliamentary system of government where the executive emerges from the legislature, and where much behavior is governed by partisan ties. The result in Britain is a parliament with a policy role considerably more limited than its formal prerogatives would suggest.

Among legislatures across the world, the US Congress is frequently regarded as being the most powerful. In addition to a considerable oversight role with regard to the federal executive, Congress exercises substantial influence over the passage of budgetary measures and legislation. Even when possessing solid majorities of his own party in both the House and the Senate, a president is rarely able simply to push policies unhindered through the legislature. Substantial cajoling and negotiation will usually be needed, and proposals may frequently be amended substantially. At other times, the chief executive's agenda may be blocked completely, or a counter-agenda pushed through even against a presidential veto. Thus, the US Congress attained the highest ranking in Mezey's schema, a 'strong' policy role.

Congress is often regarded—not only by Americans—as unique. Yet Mezey also identified several other chambers as having 'strong' influence over the policy process. These included the parliament of Weimar Germany, the Congress of the Philippines (until 1972), and the National Assembly in Third and Fourth Republic France. Whatever the wider failings of these political systems, all possessed parliamentary chambers which took a major role in policy-making: executive policy proposals were generally subject to a high degree of viscosity.

Among those seen by Mezey as having moderate power and influence were most of the contemporary Western European parliaments, including those in the UK, Germany, and Italy, as well the Fifth Republic in France. Later work by Norton (1997*b*) has refined this, placing the parliaments of

Western Europe within his category of policy-influencers in the order depicted in Figure 12.1. Some of these chambers (e.g. the UK) possess substantial formal powers, but remain restricted in their usage of them; others (e.g. France) also have significant constitutional limits on their role. Finally, after chambers with strong or moderate policy influence, are those with little or none. These include, for example, the Supreme Soviet during the time of the USSR, and many other chambers in non-democratic systems. Such legislatures have little substantive impact: in policy terms, they are insignificant.

More important

> Italy
> Netherlands
> Sweden
> Germany
> Britain
> France
> Ireland

Less important

FIGURE 12.1. Ranking of West European Parliaments in Terms of Policy Influence (from Norton 1997*a*)

It is into this latter category that the EP would have fitted until well into the 1970s. With the growth in its budgetary authority in that decade, it moved at least partially into the role of policy influencer. In other policy areas, as has been discussed, the Parliament had informal influence prior to the 1980s, but was generally fairly marginal. If the EP was, *in toto*, within the moderate/influencing category, it was towards the lower end. But this assessment must now be radically altered: reforms have developed the Parliament's formal prerogatives and, while the EP does not yet possess all the powers held by other chambers (including many of Norton's 'policy influencers') the Parliament does *use* many of the powers it has. Taken together, these factors mean that the policy influence wielded by the EP is surely greater than that of most national chambers in the EU. As Earnshaw and Judge astutely observe, 'the irony seems to be lost on many commentators that, whilst the raw figures showing the relatively limited impact of national Parliaments on domestic legislation are dismissed as "misleading" for *underplaying* parliamentary influence . . . at the European level, raw figures are dismissed for *overstating* parliamentary influence' (1996: 102, emphasis in original).

The EP embodies three factors—separation from the executive branch, the absence of a coherent majority party or permanent coalition inside the chamber, and a strong internal committee system—which facilitate parliaments exploiting their formal powers. Thus, although its writ does not yet (and may never) run across the entire gamut of EU policy, the EP now deserves to be ranked at least towards the upper end of the category of 'policy influencer'. If future treaties expand the chamber's prerogatives much further, and if the EP retains its capacity and willingness to deploy its powers, it will certainly require ranking with those rare instances of legislative chambers with a strong policy-making role.

Support for the European Parliament

Classifying Parliamentary Support

Examining the EP's policy role places the chamber in an increasingly positive light. However, the framework outlined above includes a second dimension—that of 'support', defined by Mezey as 'a set of attitudes that look to the legislature as a valued and popular political institution' (1979: 27). Why should this be important? Mezey suggested that it was because the degree of support enjoyed by a legislature 'lends a certain degree of predictability to the policy-making dimension'. More specifically,

the policy-making dimension indicates where a legislature *presently* is located relative to the other policy-making institutions in a political system, but it offers no guidance to where that legislature *may be five or ten years later*. Only a casual survey of world events will confirm that the importance and saliency of the legislature can be subject to significant change. (Mezey 1979: 27, emphasis added)

This argument was starkly illustrated in a non-European context by the fate of the Philippine Congress—a highly powerful legislature 'right up until the time in 1972 when President Marcos suspended the institution, with hardly a murmur of domestic dissent to be heard' (Mezey 1979: 27). The sudden revocation of the chamber's powers was possible, observers contended, because the institution and its membership were held in very low esteem across the country. When Marcos challenged Congress, on his way to establishing a dictatorship, the low level of support enjoyed by the chamber among socio-political élites and the public left it with few defenders. A similar phenomenon in a democratic polity can be seen in post-war France. The National Assembly, while extremely powerful in policy terms, had slid into public disrepute as the 'House without Windows' during the latter years of the Fourth Republic. Seemingly interminable political and government instability had generated a widespread belief that the chamber took itself and its internal machinations more seriously than it did the problems of the country. This left the chamber vulnerable and with few supporters when President de Gaulle proposed the Fifth Republic constitution which relegated the Assembly to a more subservient role (Frears 1997).

There is an additional, somewhat distinct, respect in which support for the legislature is crucial. Many comparative scholars have observed that parliaments play a highly significant role legitimating a political system (e.g. Packenham 1970; Copeland and Patterson 1994). That is, by building support amongst the public and élite groups for their role as representative institutions, and thereby acting as an effective link between the public and the political system, parliaments can help stabilize the system as a whole.

Both mass and élite level support is important. Mezey argued that 'if support is to be taken as an indicator of an institution's capacity to survive, then the support of elites is more important to the legislature than the support of mass publics' (1979: 35). Yet, as much work on 'political entrepreneurs' implies, an absence of mass support creates potential opportunities for those looking to sell a message antagonistic to an institution; conversely, political élites hostile to a parliament will be more constrained from acting upon those attitudes, *ceteris paribus*, if they perceive public opinion to oppose them. In short, parliaments which enjoy higher levels of support have greater long-term security, either from challenges to their status within the political system, or from broader challenges to the system as a whole.

Mezey operationalized the concept of support as combining institutional continuity, supportive attitudes of government leaders, and popular 'distrust of the legislature coupled with charges of corruption and/or incompetence' (1979: 29). As with the legislature's policy role, it is difficult to measure support comparatively with great precision, something which again implies the need for a low level of measurement to be deployed. The framework presented in Table 12.1 deploys a simple dichotomy of 'more-' and 'less-supported' parliaments.

The EP surely warrants classification in the 'less supported' category. The lack of institutional continuity in the EU has already been indicated. While the almost 'permanent revolution' in the Union has favored the EP in recent years, evidence from a number of sources points to a parliament that lacks active support and has attracted antagonism from at least some quarters.

Among the European public, surveys reveal minimal awareness of the EP or its work, and little deep-rooted support. A Eurobarometer poll conducted less than a year prior to the 1999 EP elections, found that only 43 per cent of EU citizens claimed to have heard *anything* about the EP and its work in the news media! The same survey also found that whereas 56 per cent of citizens in the (then twelve) EU member-states agreed that the

'European Parliament plays an important role in the life of the European Union' in late 1991, the proportion agreeing with that statement by late 1998 (across the same twelve countries) actually went down by 1 per cent, despite the considerable powers accrued by the EP in the intervening years. Public perception and reality, regarding the EP, would appear to be only distant relations. This suggests that, whatever else might explain it, the decline in approval for the EP 'to play a more important role than it does now' to an average below 50 per cent in recent years (45 per cent in late 1998) is *not* an informed response to recent institutional reforms.[19] The most detailed analysis of public attitudes to the EP hitherto conducted argued that

the majority of citizens in all EC states takes up the general public opinion in an undifferentiated way and transfers it onto the whole EC and its institutions . . . [A]pproval of the EP is thus most probably based on affective ties with the whole Community on the one hand. On the other hand, it is also influenced by the transfer of a national stereotype to the EP, which is considered as an equivalent to national parliaments. (Hofrichter and Klein 1993: 52–7)

Further evidence of the paucity of deep-rooted supportive attachments for the EP are turnout levels for EP elections, generally lower than in national parliamentary polls and having progressively declined from 63 per cent of citizens in 1979 to only 49 per cent in 1999. While evidence of active antagonism to the Parliament is less widespread, it is, perhaps, suggested by the growing support in European elections for what might be termed 'anti-system parties'. Parliamentary representation for such forces increased almost fivefold in 1994 and further still in 1999. Hostility to the EP, however, may follow from media coverage: while the EP has gained greater press attention in recent years, much has concentrated on issues like the chamber's expenses system, or the waste of time and money incurred in the monthly shuttle made between Strasbourg and Brussels, which has resulted in much distinctly unflattering press commentary.[20]

The attitudes of political élites to the EP also contain considerable ambiguity. A 1996 poll of 'Top Decision Makers' across the fifteen EU states found 65 per cent of respondents to support the notion of a European government responsible to the EP, and 63 per cent agreed that 'in matters of European Union legislation, taxation and expenditure, the European Parliament should have equal rights with the Council of Ministers, which represents the national governments'. However, these averages conceal huge variations across countries, with 89 per cent of Belgian élites endorsing a European government, but support on both

---

[19] Commission, Eurobarometer, *Public Opinion in the European Union*, 50 (1999).
[20] See, for instance, 'Recommissioning Europe', *The Economist* (30 Jan. 1999), 39–40.

questions at or below one-quarter in Denmark and Finland, and below half in Portugal, Sweden, and the UK. Nor is the picture substantially clearer when one narrows the definition of political élites to those in or close to governmental office. While national governments have granted the EP its greater policy role, only in a few states—Belgium, Italy, and Germany in particular—does there appear substantial support for the chamber across the political spectrum. In many other countries, attitudes seem ambivalent at best, as seen in the June 1998 Cardiff EU summit, when national leaders joined in a high profile attack on the Parliament over the issue of MEPs' expenses. Several national leaders have also expressed a disregard for the EP. While Mrs Thatcher's hostility was well known, her successor's was no less clear. In response to the suggestion that the EP Committee of Inquiry into the BSE crisis might call for evidence from the British government, John Major retorted that: 'No Minister of the Crown would ever appear when summoned by the European Parliament . . . they should go and boil their heads!'[21]

Implications

The EP's failure to develop widespread supportive attachments alongside its greater policy role might seem regrettable but essentially unimportant. What does it matter if the EU possesses a parliament which is powerful but unpopular? Renewed attention to the findings of prior comparative research indicates some less than benign possibilities—both for the EP and the EU as a whole.

In Table 12.1, legislatures are categorized according to their classifications along the two dimensions of power and support. The categories indicate how the combination of policy powers and supportive orientations shape a parliament's role within a political system. Thus, under the 'more supported' ranking on the dimension of support, the US Congress has been labeled by Mezey an 'Active' legislature, and the British House of Commons a 'Reactive' one. Both legislatures are central to their respective political systems, not least in a symbolic role as key representative institutions.[22] Thus, the respective institutions help to legitimize the political system, as well as playing their different policy roles (substantial and more proactive in the USA compared to the UK). Most other West European legislatures could probably be considered to share the same broad category as that of the British Parliament.

---

[21] Cited in the *Independent on Sunday* (13 Oct. 1996).

[22] As Norton says, regarding the UK Parliament, 'The status of parliament as a representative body underpins the stability of the political system. Parliament serves as a magnet and as an authoritative outlet for the views of citizens' (1997*a*: 350).

Perhaps more interesting, however, is the classification of the 'less supported' parliaments. When their policy role is moderate, perhaps mainly concentrated in influencing rather than making policy, they are seen as being 'marginal'. Much of politics eludes these chambers, which have a limited role but little connection to, or support from, the rest of the polity. Offering little threat or impediment to other actors, its limited role will tend to persist, but the parliament will never, even symbolically, serve as the centerpiece of the political system. If, however, the policy role of a 'less supported' parliament becomes substantial, then a more difficult and potentially unstable situation may be created. A powerful parliament cannot be ignored. But if such a chamber is deficient in support from political élites or from the public, it may well warrant the label of a 'vulnerable' institution, its policy prerogatives subject to challenge. Such, as discussed previously, was the fate of the powerful but unpopular National Assembly in Fourth Republic France.

With a minimal policy role and support, the EP might for many years have been classified as an 'inconsequential' chamber.[23] As the EP's policy role developed, the chamber more clearly established itself within the 'marginal' category: important in certain respects, but hardly central to European political debates. As the EP's policy prerogatives have made further significant advances in the present decade, but without consolidating its support base, the EP now approaches the 'vulnerable' category: a chamber that, in an increasing number of areas, is too important simply to be ignored, but which lacks the widespread and deep-rooted support that may be required to render its position invulnerable.

This discussion offers two major implications. The first is simply that, as with other vulnerable parliaments, the greater policy role which the EP has gained over recent times is potentially subject to challenge. An institution which is powerful but unloved and unsupported risks provoking a confrontation with those who, for whatever reason, question the legitimacy of its power. Thus, in recent times the EP has had to witness various suggestions for its reform, including the addition of a second chamber of national parliamentarians (an idea endorsed at times by various figures, including François Mitterrand, and more recently toyed with by the UK government), or even more radical suggestions, like that from a leading British newspaper:

The European Parliament should be regarded as an experiment in bridging the democratic deficit that has failed. The question is: how should it be replaced? . . . A more radical idea would be to acknowledge that a directly elected parliament is anathema to the current European political identity . . . Why not bite the bullet and revert to a European Assembly of national parliamentarians?[24]

---

[23] This is my label, and not that of Mezey who originally left this cell in the table blank.

[24] *Independent on Sunday* (14 June 1998).

The second implication, of both more immediate but also more fundamental import, is that while the 'democratic deficit' (the lack of powers for
directly elected institutions in the EU) has been substantially diminished
by the greater powers given the EP, the broader 'legitimacy crisis' confronting the EU for much of the 1990s is in no way resolved by this development. There is little or no sign that granting more powers to an EP
which has little deep-rooted support among the mass public or the political élites of Europe will do anything at all to reduce levels of hostility to,
and alienation from, the exercise of public authority at the European level.
A more powerful EP may indeed make the EU more democratic in a technical sense, but it has thus far done little to accord the EU as a system of
governance the legitimacy which democracy is normally seen to accord. A
far-reaching answer to the EU's legitimacy crisis will almost certainly be
needed; it is much less certain that the EP will prove to be a substantial
part of that answer.

Conclusion

The argument advanced here is simple and straightforward. It is that, first,
and contrary to the *sui generis* attitude prevalent in much of the literature,
the EP can be evaluated and understood as an example of the genus parliaments or legislatures. Secondly, evaluating the EP in such terms,
through an application of the most prominent framework in the comparative parliaments literature, indicates that the European Parliament, while
having experienced a considerable growth in its powers in recent years, is
approaching the category of a 'vulnerable' legislature due to the lack of
deep-rooted support which it continues to experience. As such, the greater
powers which the Parliament has gained remain subject to potential future
challenges, and the EP seems highly unlikely to be capable of playing a
substantial role in building an enhanced sense of legitimacy for the EU as
a new system of governance.

The argument should not, therefore, be misunderstood. It does not predict the imminent abolition of the EP. As historical institutionalists
remind us, there is generally a certain 'stickiness' in institutional arrangements which implies that, given that the EP is established, it is unlikely to
be gotten rid of very easily. And it is quite possible to paint a more optimistic picture—of an EP gradually consolidating its centrality within the
EU political system and gradually winning the respect and support of the
peoples of the continent.[25] The argument presented is more in the nature

[25] See, for instance, 'Little Respect, Less Love, But Growing Power', *The Economist* (12
June 1999), 21–3.

of a warning for the future. While the chamber remains unable to establish itself in the hearts and minds of many European citizens and politicians as an essential feature of legitimate democratic governance, the Parliament's status will likely remain vulnerable, either to those questioning the appropriate institutional model for the EU, or those who wish to challenge the necessity and/or desirability of European integration as a whole. A comparative perspective can remind us of the essential similarity between the fundamental challenges faced by the European Parliament and other legislative institutions, and the possible implications that follow from this. Democratic governance at the European level is a new and evolving phenomenon. But it is not so new that we can readily neglect lessons that the study of other political systems have taught us.

13

Do You Hear What I Hear?
Translation, Expansion, and Crisis in the
European Court of Justice

PAUL FABIAN MULLEN

A little neglect may breed mischief: for want of a nail the shoe was lost; for want of a shoe the horse was lost; and for want of a horse the rider was lost.

(Benjamin Franklin)

Introduction

This chapter explores the implications of enlargement for the Translation Service of the Court of Justice of the European Communities (Court of Justice), a small but integral part of the multi-lingual European Union. Under the principle of equality of languages set forth in Regulation 1 of the Council, the Court of Justice is required to allow citizens of member states to bring and defend legal actions in their native language. In every case before the Court, at least some documents must be translated into all of the official languages of the Union and multiple translations of most documents before the Court is the norm. The Translation Service's task is

The author would like to thank Alberta Sbragia, Bert Rockman, Guy Peters, and Chad Damro at the University of Pittsburgh, Giuliano Amato at the European University Institute, and Giuseppe Tesauro, former Advocate General of the Court and President of the Italian Antitrust Authority, and the editors for their assistance in completing this project. I would like to thank Dr Kurt Reichenberg, Dr Kari Liiri, and Dr Ingalill Lindblom of the Court of Justice for consenting to lengthy interviews and providing information and assistance to me in Luxembourg. This chapter was researched while I was the 1998–9 European Community Studies Association Marshall Fellow at the European University Institute and I would like to thank the European Community Studies Association and the Delegation of the Commission of the European Communities in Washington, DC, for funding this Fellowship, as well as the Center for West European Studies and the University Center for International Studies at the University of Pittsburgh for additional financial support.

to translate accurately and consistently the 325,000 pages of complex legal documents the Court receives each year.

The Translation Service is already in crisis, with delays in publishing opinions of the Court. Over half the time needed to reach a decision in a case is attributable to delays in translation and delays of two years or more in publishing a decision are common. However, because of the requirements under the Treaties, the Court of Justice has almost no power to further limit the number of pages of text it translates, and the number of pages submitted for translation has steadily increased over the past decade. Moreover, the resources of the translation service have remained stagnant. This crisis will only worsen and pose great risks for the entire European Union upon enlargement.

With the expansion of the EU, the number of languages may rise by as many as five, and this will result in an increase in the number of potential language combinations (i.e. translating from Polish to French, Polish to Hungarian, Polish to Finnish, etc.) from 110 to 240. Thus, the workload of the Translation Service will more than double, even though the number of languages will increase by less than 50 per cent. Some analysts argue that the workload increases caused by the next round of enlargement will result in chaos at the Court and delays of four or more years to process cases are possible. As cases pile up, businesses and governmental institutions will be forced to operate for extensive periods of time in an environment of legal uncertainty.

In the most basic sense, this chapter concerns the impact of enlargement on the Translation Service, a service already suffering from stagnating resources and an ever-increasing workload. But in a broader sense, this chapter also concerns the European Union as an organization and the neglect that key parts of such a complex, multi-lingual organization may face when asked to change and adapt to new circumstances, challenges, and goals. Yet more than organizational efficiency is at stake. Put bluntly, the Court's reputation will suffer if it appears unable to reach decisions in a timely manner and this can only lessen reliance on and respect for European Union law.

In the first section of this chapter, I will examine the Translation Service from an organizational perspective. In effect, organizational structures and pressures operate largely to deflect attention from the internal working of entities like the Translation Service and towards the needs of the incoming candidate states. By deflecting attention from internal problems, the organizational structures become resistant to internal change. In the second section, I will describe the process of translation, and set out the nature and origin of the current crisis in the Translation Service in some detail. In the third section, I will discuss the most recent impact of enlargement on the translation regime by focusing on the recent accessions of

Finland and Sweden. Eastward enlargement will not only amplify the problems experienced in this previous enlargement, it will create significant new problems for the Translation Service. The final section will address the implications organizational structure has for potential reform, and argue, that short of chaos, potential reforms will face a great deal of organizational resistance.

An Organizational View of Enlargement

The Translation Service of the Court of Justice is a part of a larger organization, the Court of Justice. The Court of Justice is embedded in a still larger organization, the European Union. To understand the nature and source of the crisis in the Translation Service, one must understand that each of these entities faces different pressures that result in different foci of attention. As Herbert Simon (1976: 294) suggests, information is not the scarce commodity in organizations, attention is. The more complex an issue, the greater the number of competing claims on decision-makers. March and Olsen (1979: 38–9) argue that the position within a hierarchy regulates access to decisions and information, and the attention patterns depend on both. In order to allocate the scarce resource of attention, one must weigh both the substantive and symbolic costs and benefits of attention (March and Olsen 1979). In a complex decision situation, inter-organization conflict is more likely than in non-complex situations (March and Simon 1964: 119). Also, organizations and the people in them learn from prior experiences. They use past experiences to draw implications for future actions (March and Olsen 1979: 60). But not all participants will have the same view of events since the flow of information within an organization is seldom perfect and often depends on perspective. Different parts of an organization see different worlds (March and Olsen 1979: 59). For a variety of reasons—number and complexity of demands, place in the hierarchy, and perspectives on past experiences—a crisis may be obvious and critical to one part of an organization, yet may not draw the attention of the rest of the organization. The pertinent organizational question is whether individuals who are aware of the need for reform have the power to affect reform.

In this case, the power to reform the Translation Service rests almost wholly outside the service and even outside the Court itself. As discussed below, action by the Council and the Commission would be necessary to change the rules regarding translation. Cooperation of the Parliament is necessary in order to increase the Translation Services budget. The Court of Justice, unlike the United States Supreme Court and most other high courts, does not even have control over its own rules of procedure. However, the problem has not caused chaos for the organization as a whole and therefore has not yet drawn the attention of these policy-makers.

From an organizational perspective, enlargement must be looked at as a stimulus for attention. But far from being monolithic, enlargement creates a bundle of different stimuli, each of which has a different impact on the EU in general, the Court of Justice, and the Translation Service. Enlargement is, to say the least, an extremely complex issue. Scarcity of attention is most conspicuous among those who are most important to or interested in decision-making (March and Olsen 1979: 45–7). Thus, the decision-making bodies of the European Union at large—the Council, the Commission, and the Parliament—have the most demands on their agenda.

In this instance, the next round of enlargement presents a very clear challenge to the EU at large. What is new about this upcoming of round of enlargement—and therefore more interesting to policy-makers—is that the first former communist-bloc nations will likely join the European Union. Since these applicant states have many hurdles to overcome in order to join the European Union, the focus of the European Union has been largely external. The main issue is the ability of these candidate states to meet the requirements of membership rather than whether the European Union has sufficient structures in place to accept the new members (Commission 1997*a*). This external focus is not incorrect, but it is incomplete.

As will be described in some detail below, the Translation Service has inherently less symbolic and substantive interest for policy-makers than far-reaching projects such as the European Monetary Union and enlargement. Also, while the signs of trouble are visible to the service itself—increasing workload, diminished job satisfaction, and loss of skilled employees—there are few overt signs of the worsening condition in the organization as a whole. Further, the internal structures have appeared largely adequate in the past rounds of enlargement, especially with the most recent round. Thus, while the *Agenda 2000* states the administrative burden of translating five additional languages should not be underestimated, it only acknowledges this burden once in the two-volume report.

Yet, the European Union, the Court of Justice, and the Translation Service are deeply interdependent. Scholars have argued that during the Eurosclerosis period, the Court was the primary engine of integration (Weiler 1994). In forming a constitutional legal regime, the Court of Justice firmly entrenched the doctrines of supremacy and direct effect. The doctrine of supremacy[1] holds that, in conflicts between national and

---

[1] *Costa* v. *ENEL* (1964) ECR 585.

Community law, Community law takes precedence. The doctrine of direct effect states that Community law gives individuals legal rights that are enforceable by national courts.[2] The Court has also untangled the issues surrounding free movement of goods by requiring mutual recognition of the standards of the producing state (Dehousse 1989: 5–18). Stone Sweet and Brunell (1998: 105) note that as a result of the constitutionalization of the Treaties, the capacity of the member-state governments has been reduced, while the policy influence of supranational institutions, national judges, and private actors has been upgraded. Because of its institutional structures, the Court's decisions have had an almost exclusively centralizing effect on the European Union as a whole, augmenting power at the supranational level at the expense of the member states (Mullen 2000). Thus, the Court has had a central role in the process of integration—a role that may be at risk if the burden on the Translation Service is not adequately addressed.

Translation and the Court of Justice

A recent report of the Court of Justice notes that a lack of resources places the Court in a crisis situation with regard to the duration of proceedings.[3] Currently, the average amount of time necessary for the Court of Justice to reach a decision is well over a year and a half and well over half of this delay is related solely to translation.[4] References for preliminary ruling average 21.4 months from filing until judgment, direct actions take 21.0 months, and appeals take 20.3 months.[5] In a reference for preliminary ruling (Article 167), a national court refers a question to the Court of Justice to decide if European Union law is applicable. In the case of preliminary ruling, a national court will have to delay its proceedings, on average, for over twenty-one months to receive a ruling from the Court of Justice on the applicability of European Union law. If a company is alleged to have engaged in anti-competitive practices, the time necessary for a decision may easily stretch over three fiscal years, affecting the ability of the company, and other similarly situated companies, to plan and engage in commerce.

---

[2] *Van Gend en Loos* v. *Nederlandse Adminstratie der Belastingen* (1963) ECR 1.

[3] See ECJ 1999: section 2. Various translations of the 'Report on Translation' are consistent in organization, but not in pagination. Therefore, throughout this chapter I have cited sections rather than page numbers. All quotes are from the English-language version.

[4] Interview with Kari Liiri, Head of Division, Finnish Translation Service, 27 Apr. 1999, Luxembourg.

[5] Annual Report of the Court of Justice.

The main problems facing the Translation Service are a constantly increasing workload, stagnating resources, and an impending overwhelming increase in workload with the next round of enlargement. The reason that no attention has been paid to this situation is twofold. First, the pressures felt by this crisis have heretofore been largely internalized. The Translation Service has, through increases in workloads and efficiency, been able to keep up to this point. While this has created a great deal of stress internally, the impact on the organization as a whole has been slight. Second, for the most part, the previous rounds of enlargement did not create any problems visible outside the Translation Service. The second and more severe stage of this crisis will likely occur with the next enlargement, because previous experiences with enlargement will be inadequate.

Organization and Procedure

The Translation Service of the Court of Justice is organized as a directorate that reports to the Registrar of the Court. Each of the official languages of the European Union has a language division consisting of a head of division, approximately twenty lawyer-linguists, and six to ten secretaries and proofreaders. The lawyer-linguists translate from the other official language into their own native languages. Therefore, each division must have lawyer linguists with expertise in all of the other official languages.[6]

In the view of the Court, its situation is quite different that those of other institutions. The European Parliament, for example, is considering adopting a hub system for interpretation. Under this method, three main languages (English, French, and German) would be used as hubs. For example, if a speech were given in Greek, there would be no necessity to have it interpreted from Greek into Finnish. Rather, the speech would be interpreted into one of the hub languages, and then into Finnish. The benefit of this system is to decrease the number of potential language combinations. In other words, the Finnish translators would not need to interpret from the Greek, but merely the hub language. The price in any translation is the loss of nuance. If a document is translated from an original into a second language and then this translation is itself translated, much more of this nuance may be lost.[7] In the case of the Court of Justice, the nuance of language and a precise translation is essential to a level legal playing field.

---

[6] Interview with Kari Liiri, Head of Division, Finnish Translation Service, 27 Apr. 1999, Luxembourg, and ECJ 1999.

[7] *The Financial Times* (24–5 July 1999).

Each case before the court results in multiple translations of original documents into other official languages. The use of a language of the case and the adoption of French as an internal working language has helped minimize the translation burden, but each case brings its own difficulties. The language of the case[8] is used in the written pleadings or observations submitted for all oral pleadings in the action. Currently, there are twelve official languages: Danish, Dutch, English, Finnish, French, German, Greek, Irish, Italian, Portuguese, Spanish, and Swedish. To date only Irish has not been used by the Court as a language of the case. The language of the case must be used in any correspondence, decisions, or reports addressed to the parties in the case. In direct actions,[9] the party bringing the action chooses the language of the case. However, where the defendant is a member state or natural or legal person holding the nationality of a member state, the language of the case is the language of the defendant. In references for preliminary rulings (Article 167), the language of the case is the language of the national court making the reference. In appeals from the Court of First Instance, the language of the case is the language of the case used before the Court of First Instance.

The major exception to the language of the case regime is that member states are permitted to use their own language in their written statements and observations, and oral pleadings. This requirement stems from the principle of equality of languages of the member states set forth in Regulation 1 of the Council (ECJ 1999: section 2). The Court views this right as more of a matter of substantive justice than administrative convenience or national dignity. As a matter of justice, to prohibit a member state from arguing before the court places a country in a disadvantage to a member state that argues in its own language. The appearance of a level playing field for all participants is essential to the legitimacy of Court of Justice. Courts that appear to give an advantage to one side in litigation risks losing its status as a neutral arbitrator.[10]

The use of the language of the case and the adoption of the internal working language greatly reduces the burden of translation. Because the judges and advocates do not request translation of their documents into their native tongues, the Translation Service can focus on translating documents related to the substance of the case. Despite this, an Article 167 reference has several stages where documents are required to be translated

---

[8] Art. 29(1) of the Rules of Procedure of the Court of Justice. See ECJ 1999: section 2.

[9] Direct actions include actions brought by member states, institutions or legal and natural persons in an action for failure to comply with treaty obligations (Arts. 169, 170, and 171), actions for annulments (Art. 173), and for damages (Art. 178).

[10] Interview with Kari Liiri, Head of Division, Finnish Translation Service, 27 Apr. 1999, Luxembourg. Report on Translation, section 2.

into all official languages, and other stages where it may be necessary to translate to or from all languages depending on the amount of interest in the case. The Court of Justice is required to translate in every case that comes before it and it has no control over the number of cases that are brought. Thus, despite greatly limiting the need for internal translation, the Court of Justice has virtually no further control of the number of documents that are submitted for translation.

For example, under Article 167, the Court of Justice receives a request from any national court to rule on whether European Union law is applicable in a case then before that national court. The ultimate ruling in a reference may, of course, have implications beyond the parties involved. While the language of the referring national court becomes the language of the case, the reference is translated into all the languages of the European Union and published in the official journal, allowing any interested party to receive notice of the reference. Each member state receives the order in the original and translated version. The parties, institutions, and member states are entitled to file written observations and the member states are permitted to file their observations in their own languages.[11] All observations are translated into the language of the case and the internal working language of the Court of Justice. These observations are sent to the member states and parties to enable them to adopt a view as to a need for a hearing. A Judge Rapporteur is assigned to the case and drafts a report for the hearing in the internal working language and this report is then translated into the language of the case. The report for hearing is then sent to the interested parties in the language of the case. The Advocate General drafts an opinion and this opinion is translated into the language of the case. The Judge Rapporteur writes a draft judgment in the internal working language and the Chamber hearing the case deliberates and decides on the judgment. Once a judgment is delivered, it is translated into all the languages of the European Union and delivered in open court and appears on the Court of Justices Internet site on the same day. Finally, the judgment and the report of the Advocate General will appear in the *Official Journal* in all languages.[12] While the Court has limited the numbers of pages to be translated, the need for extensive translation is present in all cases before the Court.

---

[11] Art. 20 of the EC Statute of the Court of Justice.
[12] Direct Actions before the Court of Justice also have a similarly complex translation regime and the requirements for notice and delivery of judgment are virtually identical. See ECJ 1999: annex B.

Current Workloads

The number of documents that require translation has increased yearly since 1993. The yearly rate of growth of the number of incoming pages was 14.2 per cent between 1993 and 1998, increasing from 167,144 to 325,115. The yearly growth rate for outgoing work was 16.6 per cent between 1992 and 1998, increasing from 122,245 to 307,108. Since the last addition of language translation staff in 1995, the growth rate in outgoing pages has been 43 per cent.

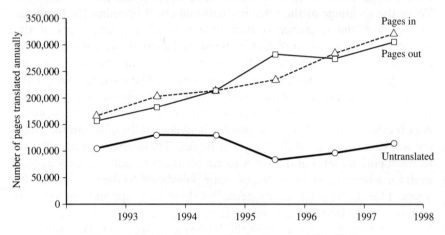

FIGURE 13.1. Translation Service Output: 1993–1998

The number of pages of untranslated work in hand has fluctuated, but is currently moving in an upward trend. The Court of Justice projects that the number of pages in hand will reach 250,000 pages by 2001 (ECJ 1999: annex C, section 6).

The numbers alone do not reflect the difficulty involved. The Court of Justice must ensure that translations are uniform across all languages. Consistency is essential. Also, since much of the law relies on statutory interpretation and precedent, the decision must be consistent with prior decisions and with the *acquis communautaire*.[13] The same terms must be translated in the same way in each case and among the languages of the various member states. Highly trained lawyer-linguists, familiar with the

---

[13] Technically, precedent does not bind the Court and previous cases do not control subsequent cases. However, in practice, the Court tends to follow its previous judgments, therefore, these judgments are important to the Court and litigants.

legislation, case law, and terms of art of the *acquis* in multiple languages are necessary for the Translation Service to properly function.

Given the adoption of an internal working language, the bulk of the translation effort is related to the translation of documents related to the conduct of cases and the publication of decisions. In 1998, 66 per cent of the pages translated were for publication in the Court Reports and 18 per cent were related to procedural documents filed by the parties. Approximately 16 per cent were related to duties such as the publication of the Annual Report of the Court of Justice and less than 1 per cent related to purely internal administrative work (ECJ 1999: annex C, section 6.1.1). The Court of Justice has taken substantial steps in limiting unnecessary translations, and the bulk of the Translation Service's time is devoted to processing case law and fulfilling other legal requirements.

Performance of the Lawyer-Linguists of the Translation Service

While the Court has eliminated virtually all extraneous translation, an additional question remains. Do the lawyer-linguists translate an adequate number of pages? As noted above, the output has been on an upward trend while the staffing has remained constant. Thus, the lawyer-linguists are doing better, but again, this begs the question, better compared to what? The translation duties between the various institutions of the European Union may not be strictly comparable, since the burdens of translation may differ. However, there are many similarities, and most importantly of all, the need to translate into multiple languages. Thus, while not a perfect measure of performance, a comparison between institutions provides at least a rough basis for comparison. In such a comparison, it appears the lawyer-linguists outperform the other institutions' linguists. As indicated in Figure 13.2, on average, the number of linguists needed to translate 100,000 pages is 124.7 for the Commission, 113.7 for the Council, 101.7 for the European Parliament, and 83.0 for the Court of Justice (ECJ 1999: annex C, section 2.1.1). For every 100,000 pages translated, the Court of Justice requires almost forty-two fewer translators than the Commission and almost nineteen less than the Council. These statistics tend to support the position of the Court of Justice, which argues that the Translation Service is at a maximum level of output under its current level of resources.

The Current Crisis

The origin and nature of the crisis are fairly simple to understand. The Court has no further ability to limit the increase in its workload, nor does it have the ability to allocate more resources to handle this workload. The

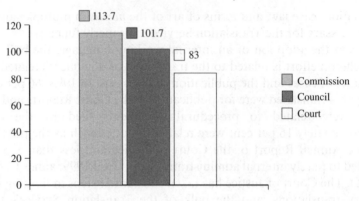

FIGURE 13.2. Linguists per 100,000 Pages

Treaties, laws, or regulations of the European Union mandate approximately 99 per cent of the Court's translation burden and the Court cannot change these requirements of its own accord (ECJ 1999: section 2). As stated earlier, the Court's ability to respond with internal conventions and increases in production are apparently exhausted. The specter of 'burnout' and loss of lawyer-linguists to other institutions is becoming an increasing worry for officials at the Translation Service.[14] Even without the previous enlargement, the workload of the Court of Justice would have increased in the past decade. Up to this point this court has, barely, been able to keep up with the demands placed upon it. Yet the delays in time necessary to publish a decision have crept upwards. In the near future, even without enlargement, both the demands and the delays may be overwhelming. With enlargement, the Court's legitimacy may come into question.

Enlargement: Learning from Past Experiences?

The most recent enlargement of the European Union saw the addition of the Finnish and Swedish language divisions. (Obviously, the third new member state, Austria, was served by the existing German language division.) According to the officials in charge of these divisions, one of the most surprising challenges was an almost complete lack of formal structure for the new divisions. Rather than any institutionalized orientation, the new services were left to their own devices, with the first translation of a decision due within ten days of commencing work. Both the Finnish and Swedish divisions experienced some early difficulties and frustration with

[14] Interview with Kari Liiri, Head of Division, Finnish Translation Service, 27 Apr. 1999, Luxembourg.

translating Court proceedings as a result of this lack of structure. Within a year or so, these services adjusted to their new tasks and experienced an increase in both efficiency and quality of work.[15]

Sweden and Finland provide some insight to the problems associated with accession. Both countries joined a well-established Union and were faced with accepting and digesting a large *aquis* prior to membership. Their languages were sufficiently different from the existing languages to create new difficulties for the Translation Service. The experiences of these two member states indicate that the eastward enlargement will be even more difficult. Both Sweden and Finland have a solid basis of administrative structures and civil law. The rule of law has not only existed, but has taken time to find a shape and a national style. The economies of these two member states have been functioning in a market-based structure. In the case of the former communist-bloc states, however, the story is different. In effect, these candidates for membership must develop a highly sophisticated economic, administrative, and legal structure where there was little or no prior structure.[16] As *Agenda 2000* states, the legal structures of the countries emerging from planned economies have neither the tradition nor administrative structures necessary to institute the rule of law. Thus the potential member states must not only establish new formal structures, but will be faced with the task of unlearning the informal norms established during approximately forty years of communist legal systems and command economies. Thus, the burden is greater for these potential members, and the burden faced by their Translation Service will be even greater than experience in accessions (Commission 1997a: ii).

The first step to accession is the acceptance of the *acquis communautaire* by the candidate states. While some adjustments or deferrals of obligations may be made during a temporary transition period, the candidate states are required to adopt the *acquis* as a condition of membership. Thus, accession negotiations are less symmetrical than typical negotiations. From the point of view of the Union, it is the applicant state that has requested to join because of the advantages membership entails (Avery and Cameron 1998: 53). Herein lies a major problem for the Translation Service. At the moment, to varying degrees, the applicant states are translating the *acquis* of the European Union, as have current members prior to their accession. The results have varied, since the individuals who translate the *acquis* may not be lawyers or well versed in

---

[15] Interview with Kari Liiri, Head of Division, Finnish Translation Service, 27 Apr. 1999, Luxembourg. Interview with Ingalill Lindblom, Head of Division, Swedish Translation Service, 30 Apr. 1999, Luxembourg.

[16] Interview with Ingalill Lindblom, Head of Division, Swedish Translation Service, 30 Apr. 1999, Luxembourg.

European Union law. This language then becomes 'official' upon accession and the member states are bound by its terminology. The results have
been mixed. In the case of Sweden, the translators have been able to work
around any discrepancies without a great deal of trouble.[17] On the other
hand, the head of the Finnish translation division has stated that the prior
translations of the *acquis* have created many problems for his lawyer-linguists by using inappropriate terminology.[18] Obviously, the burden of the
acquis will be greater for the former communist-bloc applicant states than
it was for Finland and Sweden and the difficulties in translation may well
be compounded.

Yet despite the little guidance and in some cases questionable translation of the *acquis*, the new directorates muddled through. As Figure 13.1
shows, the gap between output and pages submitted for translation actually grew as the new directorates first began their work. Obviously, it took
some time for lawsuits from the new member states of Austria, Finland,
and Sweden to become a burden on the Court. As Figure 13.1 on page 254
shows, by 1997, the increase in number of pages submitted had once again
outstripped output of the Translation Service as the impact of these new
members began to be felt. Thus, the addition of these two new languages
did not have a great immediate effect on the overall level of output. This
was due mainly to the efficiency of the Translation Service and the sacrifices made by the Court in foregoing internal translations. In the next
round of enlargement, there will be little capacity for an increase in the
internal capacity of the Translation Service, and the burden is likely to be
greater both in the new and existing language divisions.

The Next Round of Enlargement

New applicants will face the same lack of structure and likely a similarly
deficient *acquis*. Given their short history in market-based economies,
their growing pains will arguably be worse. However, it is the potential
increase in the number of existing language *combinations* that will pose the
greatest problem for these new divisions, as well as compounding the
problems of the existing divisions. With the planned eastward enlargement
of the Union, the number of official languages may well rise from eleven
(excluding Irish) to sixteen. While this rise may not seem to be substantial,
with the addition of each new language, the number of potential language
combinations multiplies. The eleven current official languages have a total

[17] Interview with Ingalill Lindblom, Head of Division, Swedish Translation Service, 30
Apr. 1999, Luxembourg.
[18] Interview with Kari Liiri, Head of Division, Finnish Translation Service, 27 Apr.
1999, Luxembourg.

of 110 language combinations. The likely addition of five more languages after the year 2000 will more than double the potential number of language combinations to 240.[19] The addition of five languages not only necessitates the addition of new directorates for each language, but a corresponding increase in the capabilities of every existing directorate. Regardless of how skilled a new Polish or Hungarian directorate may be, the existing directorates will see the number of languages they are responsible for translating increase by almost 50 per cent. In effect, approximately twenty lawyer-linguists of each existing division will be responsible for accurately and consistently translating sixteen languages. Aside from the increase in page numbers, the number of different language combinations for which each lawyer-linguist would be responsible would be beyond his or her individual capacity.[20] Simply adding a new division as in the last enlargement will be wholly insufficient. At a minimum, each existing division will have to be significantly enlarged as well. Thus, the existing crisis is likely to get much worse and 'chaos' looms. However, the organizational structures are likely to prevent any reforms in the interim.

Resistance to Reform

As discussed below, three main organizational factors act to make reform in the Translation Service unlikely, at least in the short run. First, the European Union is a complex organization and enlargement is a complex undertaking. This alone would prevent a support service such as the translation receiving organizational attention, given the fact that the Court shows few external signs of the internal crisis that is occurring. Second, however, the next round of enlargement presents both substantive and symbolic issues that have drawn the attention of policy-makers away from the internal operation of the European Union, and toward the needs of the applicant states. Finally, the Translation Service is a victim of its own success. The past experiences with enlargement will reinforce the belief of the larger organization that the current internal structures are adequate for future rounds of enlargement.

The European Union is an extremely complex organization. This inherent complexity causes a lack of attention to be given to the work of the Translation Service. The Court has been aware of the looming crisis for several years but other parts of the organization with the capacity to make the structure and fiscal decisions necessary to mitigate the crisis seem to be

---

[19] *The Financial Times* (24–5 July 1999).

[20] Interview with Kari Liiri, Head of Division, Finnish Translation Service, 27 Apr. 1999, Luxembourg.

unaware of the very nature of the crisis. Yet, this situation is to be expected in an organization as complex as the European Union. This is not a story of the 'good' Translation Service versus the 'bad' Parliament, Council, or Commission; rather, it is a story of the disparity in focus, attention, and distribution of power between large, complex parts of an organization and a small, focused, technical, yet important part. To the observer outside the service, little has changed in the past several years. While the drastic increase in the number of pages submitted for translation is the chief concern of Translation Service, the other entities are more concerned with the overt functioning of the Court of Justice. This manifests itself mainly in the amount of time necessary for the Court to reach and publish a decision. The length of this delay has increased, but not nearly as dramatically as the increase in pages submitted. In 1995, the average time for decisions was 18.7 months (average of all types of actions before the Court). In 1998, this was 20.9, an increase of 2.2 months on average. There was an increase in the time needed for a decision, but not a startling increase by any means. In short, the internal problems have heretofore not created an external trigger that would focus the Commission or Parliament's attention onto the problem.

The very nature of the next round of enlargement will draw the attention of the European Union away from the internal and towards the demands of the external. The attention of the policy-makers is focused on condition of the applicant states and their ability to comply with the *acquis,* not the ability of European Union to accept these new members. The Commission's recent White Paper on enlargement, *Agenda 2000,* is focused almost entirely on ensuring the ability of the applicant states to reform their administrative structures and to reach the fiscal standards of the European Union. Less thought is being given to whether the European Union has the structures in place to accept these candidates. In addition, a move towards budgetary discipline works against any moves toward internal budgetary increases. The main stated objective of the pre-accession strategy is to 'prepare the Central and Eastern European applicant countries for accession to the European Union' (Commission 1997*a*). Applicants must meet several political criteria and have stable institutions guaranteeing the rule of law, respect for human rights and the protection for minorities. Also, they must meet the rigorous economic criteria and establish a functioning market economy that can withstand the competitive pressures and market forces that exist in the Union. This is no small task for nations recently emerging from planned economies and having few structures capable of functioning in a market economy or under a Western conception of rule of law. The applicant nations most likely to be the next members in the European Union—Hungary, Poland, Estonia, the

Czech Republic, and Slovenia—all have made steps toward fulfilling the requirements of membership, but policy areas such as agriculture, environment, transport, and energy require further reform prior to membership (Commission 1997*a*). Thus, the focus of the *Agenda 2000* is external. For the most part, it should be. Yet, it appears to leave potential internal problem areas such as the Translation Service virtually unmentioned.

Finally, given the experience of the prior round, there is little overt reason for policy-makers to be concerned with the translation in the upcoming rounds. The fact the last round of enlargement did not cause a major increase in the delays in delivery of decision by the Court of Justice will also work against attention being paid to the Court in future enlargements. Despite the internal struggles of the service, its outward signs of performance simply did not deteriorate to the extent necessary to make its problem a problem for the European Union at large. Therefore, it is not yet a problem for the policy-makers who may undertake the necessary budgetary and structural changes that would alleviate the current looming crisis. As is often the case, the problem will have to get much worse before it gets better.

The conclusion seems inescapable, the prospect for substantial internal reforms in the short run are bleak. Yet given the focus on the applicant member states in this probable upcoming round of enlargement, one expected reform would be in the pre-accession translation of the *acquis.* This has occurred to some extent, as the European Union has provided funds to aid the applicant members in the task of undertaking a workable translation of the *acquis.* Through the PHARE program and under the auspices of the TAIEX (Technical Assistance Information Exchange Office), the European Union has provided funds and expertise to help applicant states to comply with the *acquis* (Commission 1997*a*).

Potential internal reforms fall into three broad categories: budgetary and administrative reform, language reform, and structural reform of the Court of Justice. These reforms have little prospect for implementation until Court delays caused by the looming crisis reach a level that draws the attention of the policy-makers. The officials of the Translation Service believe it will take the 'chaos' of enlargement to disrupt the Court of Justice sufficiently to draw attention to the problem. Even then, each of these areas will suffer from resistance to some extent. I will discuss these reforms below, and argue that the prospects for administrative and budgetary reforms offer the path of least organizational resistance over the long run, so are likely to be the eventual solution to the coming crisis simply because it is the easiest to implement.

Administrative and Budgetary Reform

Increases in budget are obviously one way to solve a problem of administrative overload. Yet simply adding more lawyer-linguists will not be a sufficient solution. At the moment, the translation directorate is remarkable
for the small number of administrators. As stated earlier, the organizational structure for each language division is quite flat, with one division
head overseeing all of the lawyer-linguists. The heads of division argue
that this structure is becoming unwieldy. Therefore, if the budget were to
be increased, a corresponding restructuring of the divisions would be necessary with the addition of two or more intermediate supervisors under
the division head, with each division having a three-level administrative
structure rather than the current two levels

This reform would likely be a sufficient short-run solution to the
problem. The main source of resistance would be the economizing trends
discussed above. Yet, while this might work for the next round of enlargements, the prospect of future enlargements might mean an ever-increasing
number of language combinations, and an increasingly larger bureaucracy
in Luxembourg. At some point, the sheer addition of member states will
overload the Court of Justice with cases, and cause delays regardless of the
Translation Service.

Language Reforms

Language reforms might offer some solutions to the problems of the
Translation Service. The problem, of course, is that any reforms in this
area could conflict with the principle of equality of languages of the member states set forth in Regulation 1 of the Council. Changing Regulation 1
would change relationship of the member states to the European Union
and to each other. In effect, if certain languages were adopted as 'official'
languages, some member states would be, at least in the linguistic sense,
less equal than others. Serious questions of national dignity might arise,
and any moves to limit the number of languages would likely be quite controversial.

However, reforms to the language regime do not necessarily have to
run astray of the Regulation. Using a 'hub' system where all languages
could be translated into a few of the more commonly used languages
would reduce the number of language combinations, but only at the
possible risk of reducing the reliability of the translation. In addition,
reducing the number of documents translated may help alleviate the
pressure on the Translation Service. One suggestion has been to translate
the Opinion of the Advocate General only into the language of the

case[21] and perhaps two or three of the more common languages. This Opinion tends to be a long document that is published simultaneously with the judgment of the Court, and may be quite useful to practitioners in explaining the rationale for the Court decision. However, this Opinion does not require an answer from the party, nor does it create binding precedent. Therefore, failing to translate this document would not prevent anyone from arguing to the Court in his or her own language. Yet it would make legal research more difficult for speakers of less commonly used languages. Thus, some language regime changes are possible without major structural changes or impinging upon the national dignity of the member states to any great extent. However, like budget increases, eventually the European Union may become too large for its centralized court to provide a sufficient legal system. A more decentralized system may ultimately be necessary.

Structural Changes

Structural changes in the form of decentralization may offer the best long-term solution to Court delays. Setting up 'circuit' courts modelled on the US system in the various member states is one possibility that would allow quicker resolution of cases. In fact, the current US multi-level federal court structure resulted from the pressure caused by national expansion of the US Supreme Court. Notice requirement could be relaxed since the decision would bind only the circuit in question, with Court of Justice presiding over conflicts between the circuits. The President Judge of the Court of Justice presented a similar option in recent remarks to the Council of Justice Ministers. He reiterated the view that all national courts, regardless of their status, should retain the power to refer questions to it for a preliminary ruling. However, he suggested the introduction of a filtering system that would decide the questions that need to be answered at Community level on the basis of their complexity or importance. This would involve setting up judicial bodies in each member state, having either Community or national status, with responsibility for dealing with references for preliminary rulings from courts within their territorial jurisdiction.[22] Generally, by filtering the less important cases out at an intermediate level, the Court of Justice could limit the growth in its caseload, and provide all member states access with access to a court in their own language. This would require the addition of a vast new institution whose

---

[21] Interview with Ingalill Lindblom, Head of Division, Swedish Translation Service, 30 Apr. 1999, Luxembourg.
[22] Press Release No 36/99–28 May 1998. Press and Information Division, Court of Justice of the European Communities.

reach would extend throughout the Union. It would require the agreement of the member states to undertake a financial commitment that would probably be as large or larger than the current budget of the Court of Justice. Such an investment would no doubt face considerable resistance. Yet if the bold predictions for future enlargements hold true, the burden of litigation may simply be too much for any one court. Structural reforms that offer some filtering mechanism that reduces the burden on the Court of Justice may be the best long-term solution to ensure a functioning European legal system.

Conclusion

What then will become of the Translation Service of the Court of Justice? The *Report on Translation* argues that at 'approximately 300,000 pages per year, the output capacity of the translation Directorate with its current resources has reached its ceiling' (ECJ 1999: annex C, section 6.1.2). Given the comparison of outputs with the other institutions, it is difficult to argue that the Translation Service is not operating at a very high level of efficiency. Internally, working hours are increased and job satisfaction is declining. Each year, regardless of enlargement, the caseload of the Court of Justice rises. In the short term, even without enlargement, there does not appear to be any reason to believe that Europeans will turn to the Court of Justice less frequently in the immediate future. The President of the Court of Justice predicts that the caseload will increase even without enlargement, because of the commencement of the third stage of the Economic and Monetary Union, and the entry into force of the Treaty of Amsterdam and of certain conventions drawn up under the Third Pillar of the European Union (justice and home affairs).[23] Indeed, if the *Report on Translation* is correct, the number of untranslated pages will increase to a projected 250,000 in 2001 (ECJ 1999: section 6.1.3).[24] The best-case scenario is a sharper increase in the amount of time necessary for a case to work its way through the Court of Justice. Currently, the average time it takes the Court to reach a decision has steadily increased, and what can be expected is that the pace of this trend will increase more quickly, and delays of over three years are quite plausible in the next few years.[25]

[23] Press Release No 36/99–28 May 1998. Press and Information Division, Court of Justice of the European Communities.

[24] In fact, the Court of Justice uses an 11% annual increase to predict the increase in pages in hand.

[25] *Annual Reports of the Court of Justice of the European Communities* (1995, 1998).

Yet, the real 'chaos' may occur with enlargement. The new applicant states will have greater burdens placed on them and will present greater burdens for the European Union. At this point, the delays may become so severe that they will draw the attention of policy-makers. However, as argued above, the price paid for this attention may be an inability of the Court to reach decisions in a timely manner. With potential delays of five years or more, the Court risks losing some of its relevance as a force for integration of Europe and development of the rule of law in the member states. Simply put, if the Court is seen as being unable to fulfill its mandate, member states and individuals will then become less likely to look to the Court to settle disputes and questions of law. The Court has played an important role in integrating new members into the Union by settling questions of the applicability of European law. If the crisis in the Translation Service remains unresolved, the integration of new members states into the Union will undoubtedly be much slower. This would make the next transition period more difficult and contentious as the states' rights and duties under the *acquis* would remain unresolved due to trans- lation delays. More importantly, the role the Court has played as a force for integration would inevitably lessen, and the pace of integration itself could well be delayed.

The aphorism about not fixing something 'until it is broken' is some- what misleading in the case of organizations. The breakdown needs to not only occur, but also be apparent. Otherwise, it will not garner the atten- tion necessary for it to reform. A small part of an organization such as the Translation Service may be broken for some time before it is fixed. Until delays become a problem for the organization as a whole, little is likely to be done.

Yet the focus on the applicant states is not misplaced. Their entry into the European Union has substantive importance for the economic well- being of its members and the security of the region, but is also important as symbolic evidence of the progress and stability of democratic institu- tions in Eastern Europe. The focus of *Agenda 2000* is not incorrect, but it is incomplete. Small things add up. The Translation Service is a necessary part of the Court of Justice. If it fails, the Court risks not fulfilling its core tasks in a timely manner. The need for an outward-looking policy and fis- cal constraints should not preclude a concurrent audit of internal struc- tures. If such self-examination is undertaken, then the 'chaos' of enlargement may not be a necessary prelude to reform.

14

Blairism in Brussels: The 'Third Way' in Europe since Amsterdam

MARK A. POLLACK

During the final years of the 1990s, the European political pendulum swung decisively to the left. By contrast with the early 1990s, when the prime ministers and presidents of predominantly conservative governments met to negotiate the Treaty of European Union at Maastricht, the EU in 1999 was comprised of thirteen governments with participation of left-wing parties, eleven with socialist prime ministers, including the 'Big Four' countries of Germany, France, Italy, and the UK. The triumph of these social democratic parties can be traced to the mid-1990s, most notably with the victory of Romano Prodi's Olive Tree Coalition in Italy, but it accelerated in 1997 with the landmark, landslide election of a New Labour government in Britain in May, and the surprise victory the following month of a left-wing coalition in France led by Socialist Prime Minister Lionel Jospin. Finally, in September of 1998, German voters elected a 'red–green' coalition of Social Democrats and Greens, casting out of office the Christian Democratic government of Helmut Kohl that had ruled Germany for over sixteen years.

The victory of the left, furthermore, *matters* in the context of the European Union, which has increasingly become an arena for debate between parties of the left and the right (Hix 1994). Indeed, Liesbet Hooghe and Gary Marks have recently suggested that the political debate in the European Union today can be theorized as a right–left struggle between neoliberals and proponents of what they call 'regulated capitalism'. The neoliberal project for Europe, according to Hooghe and Marks, 'attempts to insulate markets from political interference by combining European-wide market integration with the fragmentation of authority among national governments. The neoliberal project rejects democratic

The author would like to thank Corrie Potter for valuable research assistance, the editors for valuable comments and criticisms, and the Department of Political Science and the EU Center of the University of Wisconsin-Madison for research support.

institutions at the European level capable of regulating the market, but seeks instead to generate competition among national governments in providing regulatory climates that mobile factors find attractive' (Hooghe and Marks 1997*b*: 3). By contrast, the regulated capitalism project of the political left

proposes a variety of market-enhancing and market-supporting legislation to create a social democratic dimension to European governance. This project attempts to deepen the European Union and increase its capacity for regulation, by among other things, upgrading the European Parliament, promoting the mobilization of particular social groups, and reforming institutions to make legislation easier (i.e. by introducing qualified majority rule in the Council of Ministers). (Hooghe and Marks 1997*b*: 3)

If this view is correct, then we might expect the current center-left majority among EU governments to embrace the objective of regulated capitalism, and steer the Union in that direction in the coming years.

The burden of this chapter, however, is that the triumph of the left in Europe should *not* be interpreted as a Europe-wide return to traditional socialist policies, or the emergence of a more interventionist European Union, for two reasons. The first and most obvious reason is that the current hegemony of the left is unlikely to last. Indeed, the European Parliament elections of June 1999—in which the left-leaning Party of European Socialists was eclipsed by the center-right European People's Party for the first time since direct elections to the Parliament began in 1979 suggest that the European center-right remains electorally healthy, and is likely to make gains in future national elections as well.

The second reason is less obvious but more important, namely that the triumph of the European left may bring with it, not the traditional socialist policies associated with the model or regulated capitalism, but rather a 'third way' politics which attempts to move beyond both the neoliberalism of the New Right *and* the redistribution and interventionism of the Old Left. The notion of a third way is not new, of course, having originated early in the twentieth century to signify a path between the free-wheeling capitalism of the USA and the communist governments of the former Soviet bloc. In recent years, however, the term has been most closely associated with the New Labour Party of British Prime Minister Tony Blair. Since his succession to the leadership of the Labour Party in 1994, and even more since his election as Prime Minister in 1997, Blair has called, both at home and abroad, for socialist parties to 'modernize' themselves to compete in a world of economic, social, and electoral change. The primary question motivating the chapter, therefore, is whether the newly dominant European left has adopted the 'third way' philosophy of Tony Blair, or remains wedded to the interventionism implicit in Hooghe and

Marks's conception of regulated capitalism. In terms of the overarching themes of this volume, then, I examine the prospects for the Blair's proposed *reform* of the European left and its European project, as well as the *resistance* to Blair's ideas encountered in France, Germany, and throughout the European left. At stake in this debate, I suggest, is both the governing philosophy of the European left in domestic politics, and the possibility of a unified European project of the left to replace Hooghe and Marks's conception of regulated capitalism.

The chapter is organized into three parts. In the first, I examine the domestic debate within Britain regarding the *content* of the third way, as articulated by Blair and his academic muse, Anthony Giddens. Specifically, I argue that the term 'third way' can be defined in terms of three factors: a commitment to a core set of social-democratic values; a particular diagnosis of economic, social, and political change in the late 1990s; and a particular set of policy tools designed to promote social-democratic values in this changed policy context. In the second section, I examine Blair's missionary efforts during his first year in office to propagate his modernizing, third-way ideology throughout the European Union, most notably at the Amsterdam European Council of 1997, and during the British Presidency of the European Union in the first half of 1998. Third and finally, I examine the efforts by Blair and his Foreign Minister, Robin Cook, to shape the 1999 electoral manifesto of the Party of European Socialists (PES), of which Blair's New Labour is a constituent member. As we shall see, Blair was at best partly successful in his effort to proselytize the third way to the PES, but nevertheless scored a surprise victory by co-authoring a policy paper on the third way, or *Neue Mitte*, with German Chancellor Gerhard Schröder in the final week before the EP elections. The extent of Schröder's commitment to third-way policies, however, is open to question, as is the likelihood that the new Chancellor will be able to overcome considerable resistance in Germany and within his own party to any change in political strategy. Perhaps most importantly, resistance to Blair's third-way rhetoric remains considerable in Germany, France, and throughout the European left. In conclusion, I argue that the left has indeed changed throughout Europe, but that the nature of this change varies from country to country, and is unlikely to converge either on the traditional model of regulated capitalism or on Blair's 'third way' centrism. Thus, the European left will continue to face considerable challenges in identifying a single vision or project for European governance—at least in the near future.

Blairism in London: The British Debate over the Third Way

In May 1997, Tony Blair became the new Prime Minister of Great Britain, ending eighteen consecutive years of Conservative rule, and proclaiming a 'third way' between free-wheeling capitalism and traditional European socialism. Over the previous three years, since assuming leadership of the party in 1994, Blair had transformed the seemingly unelectable Labour Party into a new, 'modernized,' party of the center-left, capable of appealing to mainstream British voters. Indeed, halfway into his first term, Blair remains the most popular prime minister in the history of Great Britain. Yet an increasing number of critics from both left and right have decried the vagueness of Blair's third way. These critics charged that Blair and his fellow centrists had made clear what the third way is *not*, namely the Old Left with its antiquated attachment to state ownership of the means of production, nor the New Right with its pro-market, anti-government rhetoric. However, Blair was arguably less quick to specify what the third way *is*, at least in sufficient detail to satisfy his critics. The definition of the third way, moreover, is important not simply for British politics, but also for comparative analysis of the third way in the broader EU context. As social scientists looking for evidence of the third way in Brussels, Strasbourg, or Berlin, we must first define what we mean by the term, and operationalize it clearly so that we know it when we see it. For the purpose of such analysis, I adopt in this chapter a three-part definition of the third way, emphasizing: (1) a value framework associated with opportunity, responsibility, and community; (2) an empirical assessment of economic, social, and electoral changes in the new Europe, and the limits that such changes place on traditional social-democratic politics; and (3) a new set of policy tools designed to promote social-democratic values in this changed policy context. Taken together, these three elements—distilled primarily from Blair's political pronouncements and from the academic writings of Anthony Giddens and other British scholars—represent a baseline definition of the third way, which we can then use to examine Blair's success or failure to proselytize his approach to the rest of the EU.[1] Let us, very briefly, examine each of these three elements in turn.

---

[1] This section draws heavily on Stuart White's (1999) excellent analysis, and in particular on his discussion of the core values underlying the third way. However, I add to White's analysis a third element, namely the diagnoses by Blair, Giddens, and other third-way thinkers of the changed economic, social, and political context in which left-wing parties operate in the 1990s. This diagnosis, I argue, links together the core social-democratic values that White outlines on the one hand, with the innovative policy tools favored by advocates of the third way on the other.

A Framework of Values

Advocates of the third way typically go out of their way to emphasize that their aim is *not* to find a middle road between right and left, but rather to fashion a new politics based on the core social-democratic values of the center-left (Blair 1998: 1). The specific values, and their number, varies from author to author, with Giddens providing a daunting list of no fewer than seven core values to guide social democrats in the new politics of the center-left.[2] Most analyses, however—including the key statements of third way politics by Blair (1998) and Giddens (1998) and several studies by academics and think-tanks in the UK and abroad (White 1999; Democratic Leadership Council/Progressive Policy Institute 1999)—identify three core values underlying the third way: equality, responsibility, and community.[3]

Equality

This is of course one of the central themes of traditional social democracy, and a commitment to equality is evident in all or most of the key third-way writings. Blair, for example, make 'equal worth' the very first plank of his third-way manifesto, and Giddens similarly lists equality as the first and most important of his 'third way values'. The notion of equality can be interpreted in many ways, however, ranging from a *formal equality of opportunity*, in which every citizen enjoys a legal right to self-advancement even if she is in practical terms held back by lack of resources ('everyone is free to stay at the Ritz'), to a guaranteed *equality of outcome* for all citizens. Third-way thinkers, unsurprisingly, come down between these two polar definitions, arguing for *real* equality of opportunity for all citizens. Put simply, the core idea is that the state cannot and does not guarantee equality of outcomes in terms of income or wealth, but that it can go beyond a purely formalistic notion of equality by ensuring that each citizen enjoys sufficient skills, education, and training actually to take advantage of the opportunities offered.

Responsibility

It is one of the central themes of both American and British third-way thinking that social life entails not only rights—such as the equal right to

---

[2] Giddens's seven core values are: equality, protection of the vulnerable, freedom as autonomy, no rights without responsibilities, no authority without democracy, cosmopolitan pluralism, and philosophic conservatism (1998: 66).

[3] Blair (1998: 4–5) actually lists four core values rather than three, but the first two of these—'equal worth' and 'opportunity for all'—can without distortion be combined under the heading of equality.

real opportunity—but also responsibility on the part of individuals to their families and to society. Indeed, Giddens (1998: 65) suggests 'no rights without responsibilities' as the prime motto for his new politics. This emphasis on responsibility stands in contrast to the post-war language of the Labour Party and other social-democratic parties, which emphasized an ever-growing list of individual rights without clearly elaborating an accompanying set of individual responsibilities. However, as Giddens points out, the language of responsibilities is meant to apply not only to welfare recipients, who are often attacked by the right as irresponsible free-riders on the state, but to *all* citizens, including the wealthy who might be tempted to abandon their responsibilities to the rest of society. The principle of responsibility, and its broad applicability to all citizens in their public and private lives, most obviously informs New Labour policy on employment, which specifies the responsibility of unemployed persons to accept work or training opportunities offered to them rather than remaining on the unemployment rolls; but also manifests itself in Blair's rhetoric on the family, where his emphasis on the responsibilities of parents appears conservative, or even Victorian, by contrast with the social libertarianism of the post-1968 left.

Community

Of the three core values of the third way, community is typically less well elaborated than the previous values of equal opportunity and responsibility. At a minimum, it can be seen as a powerful rhetorical response to Margaret Thatcher's famous claim that 'there is no such thing as society. There are individual men and women, and there are families.'[4] By contrast with the extreme individualism of Thatcher's rhetoric, third-way advocates emphasize the importance of community, in two senses. First, Blair and Giddens emphasize the importance of local communities and the voluntary sector, which play a key role in providing 'social capital' or trust among individuals. These intermediate-level associations, which Blair argues have been underappreciated by both the individualist New Right and the statist Old Left, should be reinvigorated through the increased use of public–private partnerships and through devolution of government to the local and regional level. Secondly, Blair and other third-way thinkers respond to the small-state rhetoric of the New Right with an unapologetic advocacy of strong government, which has a role—albeit a new and more modest one—in third-way politics. The challenge, according to Blair, 'is to use the state as an enabling force, protecting effective communities and voluntary associations and encouraging their growth to tackle new needs, in partnership as appropriate' (quoted in Blair 1998: 4).

[4] Quoted in 'Goldilocks Politics,' *The Economist* (19 Dec. 1998), 74.

These three values—equality, responsibility, and community—can be taken as the basic normative framework of third-way politics, as formulated by Anglo-American thinkers like Blair and Giddens. As Blair argued before the French National Assembly in March 1998, 'we have to be absolute in our adherence to our basic values, otherwise we have no compass to guide us through change. But we should be infinitely adaptable and imaginative in the means of applying those values. There are no ideological preconditions, no pre-determined veto on means. What counts is what works' (quoted in Featherstone 1999: 11). Blair's emphasis on flexibility in the means available to social-democratic governments reflects in turn a second common theme in third-way thinking: the emphasis on change, and its implications for social democratic policy and politics.

Welcoming and Adapting to Change

Third-way thinkers are nearly unanimous in their view that advanced industrialized countries find themselves in the midst of extraordinary economic, social, and political changes, which challenge the traditional policies and the electoral bases of social-democratic parties all over the world. Rather than resist them, moreover, third-way thinkers generally welcome the changes they perceive in the advanced industrialized world, and argue for a rethinking of social-democratic policies to realize traditional left-wing values in a new world. Distilling a wide range of arguments to a few bullet points, we can say that third-way thinkers identify three sets of changes as particularly important.

Economic Globalization, and the Need for Social Investment

Perhaps the most common change that is identified—and to a greater or lesser degree welcomed—by the third-way advocates is economic globalization, defined in terms of the liberalization of international trade and investment and the resulting risks and opportunities presented to individuals as well as governments. In the view of thinkers like Blair and Giddens, economic globalization is on balance a positive development, bringing new opportunities and wealth for individuals in advanced industrialized countries; yet it also increases the risks posed to individuals, and the premium placed on skills as a necessary condition for competitiveness in a globalized economy. Thus, as we shall see presently, the aim of government in third-way politics is to operate within the constraints of a globalized economy, helping individuals to compete in a new and more competitive global labor market. This approach, which Ralf Dahrendorf (1999: 14) refers to critically as 'globalization plus'—'accepting the need of global markets but adding key elements of social well-being'—also sets third-way thinkers like Blair apart from protectionist sentiments among traditional social-democratic constituencies, including organized labor, and also from the mainstream of French socialism, which is far more ambivalent about the virtues of free trade and economic globalization, as we shall see below.

Globalization also has other, related effects, according to third-way analysts. For example, since the French government of François Mitterrand was forced to retreat from his Keynesian reflation of the early 1980s, it has become commonplace to argue Keynesian demand-side policies, which attempt to increase economic growth and ensure full employment through government spending and deficits, are no longer feasible in a world of extensive capital mobility. As we shall see below, Blair's third-way policies place a premium on fiscal prudence and on supply-side labor-market policies, rather than on Keynesian demand-stimulus, as the key to securing high employment in a global economy.

Social Change, and the Decline of the Left–Right Cleavage

Globalization is not the only change cited by third-way thinkers in making the case for a new approach. In addition to globalization, Giddens, Blair, and others also emphasize the extensive social changes that have taken place in the advanced industrial democracies since 1960s, and which pose new challenges to the social-democratic left, and indeed to the left–right distinction more generally. Giddens, for example, discusses the purported rise of 'post-materialist' values among Western publics, who increasingly cite lifestyle issues such as the environment, the changing nature of the family, and personal and cultural identity as core concerns, alongside the bread-and-butter economic issues that were the basis of the traditional left–right cleavage (1998: 19–21, 36). In addition, Blair and other third-way thinkers devote particular attention to the transformation of the role of women, which has in turn transformed the nature of the family and the workplace, posing new challenges for government policy. 'Reconciling such changes and opportunities to the strengthening of the family and local communities,' according to Blair (1998: 6) 'is among the greatest challenges of contemporary public policy.' Rather than turning the clock back to the traditional family with a male breadwinner and a stay-at-home wife, however, third-way politics places a premium on public policies designed to reconcile work and family life, through the provision of child care, flexible hours, and similar measures.

Electoral Change, and the Search for a New Base

New Labour is, of course, a political party, and as such it, like the other social-democratic parties of Western Europe, must be concerned with economic and social change not only in so far as they affect policy, but also and especially as they affect the electoral base of the party. New Labour modernizers and other third-way thinkers make clear that the electorate has fundamentally changed in recent years, in line with the economic and social changes emphasized above, and that social-democratic parties must adapt to a new electoral context in order to compete. Giddens, for example, argues that the rise of post-materialist issues, the decline of class voting, and the increasing salience of issues which defy a left–right classification all point to a single electoral conclusion: 'Social democratic parties no longer have a consistent "class bloc" on which to rely. Since they can't depend upon their previous identities, they have to create new ones in a socially and culturally more diverse environment' (Giddens 1998: 23). Thus for Giddens—and for Blair, who has sought to create such a cross-class constituency for New Labour in Britain—the new electoral realities call for a new governing philosophy of the center-left, which addresses concerns such as gender and ecology which were previously treated as peripheral by parties of the left.

A New Role, and New Policy Tools, for Government

When we turn from the values or *ends* of politics on the one hand, to the policies or *means* that governments use to achieve their ends, we find no single, authoritative statement of third-way policies, but rather a proliferation of both general manifestos and specific policy proposals. Nevertheless, despite the differences in specific policy prescriptions across authors, third-way thinkers generally call for a new role for government—distinct from both the interventionism of the Old Left and the non-interventionism of the New Right—and a new set of policy tools for carrying out this new role. Giddens, for example, argues for a 'social investment state' in which government will play a key role in promoting real opportunity, or what Giddens calls 'positive welfare' to all citizens. Such a shift, from the negative welfare of safety-net benefits to the positive welfare of investing in individuals to create real opportunity, calls for a fundamental realignment of policies, particularly regarding education, training, and the welfare state. Across all these areas, Giddens argues, 'The guideline is investment in *human capital* wherever possible, rather than the direct provision of economic maintenance. In place of the welfare state we should put the *social investment state*' (1998: 117). For example, Giddens suggests that government employment policy should be geared towards investment in human resources, including lifelong education and training, public–private partnerships, and family-friendly workplace policies, all of which create human capital and contribute to wealth creation and real opportunities for individuals in the labor market.

Moving from Giddens the sociologist to Blair the politician, we find perhaps the clearest statement of Blair's third-way policy orientations in a February 1998 speech in Washington, DC, in which Blair spelled out 'five clear principles of the center-left', all of which arguably follow logically from the preceding analysis:

- First, Blair argues for 'stable economic management and economic prudence because of the global economy'. In practice, this has meant fiscal restraint by the New Labour government, which has kept both taxes and spending under tight controls, while granting independence to the Bank of England.

- Second, Blair advocates 'changing the emphasis of government intervention so that it deals with education, training and infrastructure and not things like industrial intervention or tax and spend'. Put differently, Blair's third way shifts the emphasis of government intervention from demand-side stimulus and industrial policy to a supply-side emphasis on the 'employability' of individuals in flexible labor markets.

- Third, 'we must be reformers of the welfare state, otherwise the right will dismantle it'. Specifically, Blair has introduced in Britain the so-called 'New Deal' welfare-reform package, which seeks to move people from benefits into work through vocational training, child care, and other social services, and a working families tax credit designed to 'make work pay'.

- Fourth, Blair proposes 'reinventing government, decentralization, opening up government so that what counts is what works'. The most visible manifestation of this principle, consistent with Giddens's emphasis on democracy and community, is Blair's extensive program of decentralization in Britain, with the creation of new regional assemblies in Scotland and Wales, and a new elected mayor for London.

- Fifth and finally, 'we must be internationalist and oppose the right's isolationism'. In practice, Blair has arguably presented a consistent internationalist position, on issues ranging from free trade policy in the World Trade Organization, to humanitarian intervention in Kosovo, to a more positive attitude towards the European Union than either his Labour or Conservative predecessors.[5]

These principles are, of course, open to debate, and Blair's New Labour government has been closely scrutinized by critics who question whether the government's emphasis on fiscal restraint and his welfare-reform efforts have ended up hurting the poor in Britain (see the essays in Powell

[5] All quotations above taken from Martin Kettle, 'The Next Step: A Blueprint for New Labour's World Role', *Guardian* (7 Feb. 1998), 3. For a more complex but broad-ranging and insightful review of the policy tools associated with third-way thinking in Britain, see White 1999: 3–6.

1999). Nevertheless, despite the numerous criticisms of the vagueness of third-way ideology, I would argue that Blair's elaboration of the concept over the past several years, as informed and amplified by academics and policy analysts, now forms a reasonably coherent program, with a core set of values, a particular diagnosis and acceptance of social and economic change, and a new role for social-democratic governments. Whatever its merits or demerits, Blairism is (no longer) simply an electoral sound-bite. Having said this, however, we must ask how the third way might apply in the larger context of the European Union, and how well Blair's governing philosophy has traveled to the social-democratic parties of continental Europe. It is to those questions that we now turn.

Blairism in Brussels: From Amsterdam to the British Presidency

The proper definition of the third way might at first glance seem like a topic of interest only to students of British politics. The third way has, however, entered the international realm, in part because of the efforts of other social-democratic leaders to imitate Blair's success, but primarily because of Blair's prominent efforts since taking office to spread his third-way doctrine to continental Europe and beyond. In Kevin Featherstone's apt formulation, 'Blair is nothing if not a missionary with a cause and he has the drive to seek new converts' (Featherstone 1999: 10). Blair's missionary advocacy of the third way emerged clearly in his first meeting as Prime Minister with the Party of European Socialists in Malmo, Sweden, and at the Amsterdam meeting of the European Council, which agreed the basic blueprint of the Amsterdam Treaty.

The Party of European Socialists (PES) is the umbrella organization for the socialist parties of the various EU member countries, including the British Labour Party. Among other things, the PES coordinates the policies of the various socialist parties, draws up a common manifesto for election of the European Parliament, and meets regularly to coordinate the position of socialist governments in advance of the meetings of the European Council (Hix and Lord 1996). As it happens, the Party of European Socialists held such a meeting in Malmo in early June 1997, just a month after Blair's election and two weeks before the European Council was scheduled to conclude negotiations on the Treaty of Amsterdam. Fresh from the glow of Labour's historic landslide victory, Blair enjoyed star billing at the conference, which he used as an opportunity to spread his modernizing philosophy to the social-democratic parties of the continent. Blair lectured the other socialist leaders on the need for reform, telling them that, like the British Labour Party, European socialists must 'modernise or die'. In place of the statist policies of the old left, Blair argued, the left and center-left in Europe should adopt new policies emphasizing flexible labor markets, worker retraining, and a reformed welfare state, in line with Blair's own plans for Britain. 'Our task', he argued, 'is not to go on fighting old battles but to show that there is a third way, a way of marrying together an open competitive and successful economy with a just, decent and humane society.'[6]

Referring more specifically to the draft Amsterdam Treaty, Blair indicated that he would accept a proposed Employment Chapter in the new treaty, as well as the incorporation of the so-called Social Chapter—both of which had been blocked by his Conservative predecessor, John Major—but only if these emphasized labor market flexibility and avoided over-regulation of the European labor market. Blair also rejected the notion, favored by many socialists, of additional EU expenditure to increase demand and boost employment. In short, the New Labour Prime Minister and rising star of the European left was decisively *rejecting* the model of regulated capitalism, with its social and labor-market regulation, and arguing instead for a third way that would promote employment by promoting labor-market flexibility, deregulation, education, and vocational training.

As it happened, however, Blair was forced to share the stage at Malmo with Lionel Jospin of France, whose Socialist-led coalition had scored a surprise victory over the right in snap elections just days before the conference. By contrast with Blair, Jospin adopted a tone more consistent with traditional socialist views, and with Hooghe's and Marks's conception of regulated capitalism. The meeting was the first foreign appearance for Jospin since his election, and in his speech the Prime Minister attacked the neoliberal, monetarist thrust of European integration in recent years. 'Market forces,' he argued, 'if there is no attempt to control them, will threaten our very idea of civilization.'[7] By contrast with Blair's resistance to extensive European regulation, Jospin demanded an 'economic government' to coordinate economic, taxation and wage policies and provide a counterbalance to the European Central Bank. He also demanded an explicit EU commitment to growth and employment, including the commitment of new EU funds to stimulate job creation.[8] If Blair seemed to embody the third way at Malmo, Jospin emerged as the voice of the old, interventionist, Keynesian left.

---

[6] Quoted in Robert Shrimsley, ' "Am I Satisfied with Europe? Frankly No" Blair Tells EU Leaders to Follow His Example', *Daily Telegraph* (7 June 1997).

[7] Quoted in 'Europe Can't Be Built on Citizens' Backs,' *Reuters World Service*, 6 June 1997.

[8] Henri de Bresson, 'Un petit mot en anglais, quelques souvenirs d'italien . . .', *Le Monde* (9 June 1997). See also Lara Marlowe, 'Jospin Government Lays Down Conditions Likely to Delay EMU', *Irish Times* (7 June 1997).

Two weeks later, at the Amsterdam European Council, the member governments of the EU negotiated the final deal leading to the Treaty of Amsterdam, and their choices largely reflected Blair's third-way agenda. The Maastricht Social Protocol was incorporated into the Treaty, as Blair proposed, but without any changes to the voting procedures which would have made it easier to adopt new social regulations. Similarly, the member states agreed to a new Employment Chapter which formally made 'a high level of employment' an EU objective, but they rejected any harmonization of national employment laws and any additional expenditure of EU funds to increase aggregate employment. Instead, the new Employment Chapter called for the annual adoption of 'Employment Guidelines,' which would then be used by member states as the basis for their own 'National Action Plans' to reduce unemployment. As we shall see presently, this new procedure, which was voluntaristic and non-binding on the member states, would later be used by Blair as a bully pulpit or platform for his ideas about labor-market flexibility, education and training, and 'employability'. By contrast, Jospin's demands for an economic government were met only with a symbolic 'Pact on Stability and Growth', and the decision to hold a special European Council meeting during the Luxembourg Presidency in November 1997 devoted specifically to the problem of unemployment.

After his success at Amsterdam, Blair set out on an ambitious course to internationalize his third-way doctrine, most notably during the British Presidency of the European Union in the first half of 1998. Generally speaking, the Presidency of the Union is a difficult platform from which to proselytize specific national agendas. Typically, the country holding the Presidency must preside over dozens of meetings of the EU's Council of Ministers, and hundreds of lower level working-group meetings—a daunting bureaucratic challenge even for the largest EU member states. The UK Presidency, moreover, faced the additional challenges of overseeing the opening of accession negotiations with the countries of Central and Eastern Europe, and of brokering the contentious final decisions regarding the membership of the new single currency and the president of the new European Central Bank. Nevertheless, despite this overcharged schedule, Blair characteristically decided to pursue a populist, third-way agenda for the UK Presidency, which would bring Europe 'closer to the people'. 'This is the overriding priority of our Presidency,' Blair told a meeting of Dutch leaders in January, 'to help create a Europe working for the people, to make them feel more prosperous, safe and free because of what the European Union is doing.'[9] In the same speech, Blair again

---

[9] Quoted in Jenifer Chao, 'Blair Envisions a "New Third Way" for Europe', *Associated Press*, 20 Jan. 1999.

raised his third-way agenda, arguing that 'Europe has to find its own way—a new third way of combining economic dynamism with social justice in the modern world.'[10]

These third-way aspects of the UK Presidency were most evident from the beginning in the area of employment policy, where Blair and his Employment Minister David Blunkett would be called upon to lead the implementation of the Amsterdam Employment Chapter, and in particular the adoption of National Action Plans in line with the 'Employment Guidelines' adopted by the special employment summit of November 1997. Blair and Blunkett hoped to use the Presidency to press the Blairite notion of 'employability' at the European level. The basic idea behind the term, for which Blair could find support in the wide-ranging Employment Guidelines, was that the universal political goal of high employment could best be met through the use of education, training, and employment policies that encouraged and empowered individuals to find jobs, rather than through government-sponsored job-creation. This notion of employability was to be a central theme throughout the British Presidency, and indeed in Blair's broader quest to internationalize the third way beyond Britain.

Blair's international campaign continued in February with a high-profile four-day visit to Washington, DC, complete with an elaborate Anglo-American seminar (or 'wonkathon', as it was dubbed by the American press) on the third way. Intended as a follow-up to a previous seminar held at Chequers with Hillary Clinton in November of the previous year, the Washington event was larger and more far-reaching, and Blair's ambitions for the meeting were more grandiose. 'The purpose', said Blair in a widely quoted interview with the *Guardian* newspaper, 'is to craft and define centre-left philosophy for the world of today. I want to start with the ideology that links Labour and the Democrats. Then I want to bring together the Anglo-Saxon definitions of these ideas and these policies with the European ones.' He also went on to suggest the creation of a 'new standing conference of the centre-left, involving the Labour Party, the Democrats, the European socialist and social democratic parties and beyond', which would presumably act as an alternative to the long-standing, and more traditionalist, Socialist International. Finally, Blair indicated his commitment 'to engage with all sections of the European centre-left and not just the ones who appear to be most obviously close to where we are at the moment'.[11] In practice, this would mean that Blair

---

[10] Quoted ibid.

[11] Quoted in Kettle, 'The Next Step'. For useful analyses of the Washington meeting, see also 'Mr Blair Goes to Washington', *The Economist* (7 Feb. 1998); and 'Blair and Clinton Seek Holy Grail in Wonkathon', *Sunday Times* (London, 8 Feb. 1998).

would have to establish links with German and particularly French Socialists, who had proven much more skeptical of his third way than reformist social democrats in countries like the Netherlands (which had long experimented with flexible labor markets as a means of increasing employment) and Italy (where the Olive Tree Coalition of Romano Prodi was engaging in an effort to reform national finances to qualify for membership in the new single currency).

Not surprisingly, therefore, Blair's next stop on his international campaign was Paris, where in March he addressed the French National Assembly in a speech that was later called Blair's most important of the year by his aide (and now Northern Ireland Secretary) Peter Mandelson.[12] In the press, the substance of Blair's *troisième voie* speech was nearly overwhelmed by the media's emphasis on Blair's delivery of the speech in a fluent, unaccented French which contrasted with the stilted or non-existent linguistic abilities of his Conservative predecessors. Nevertheless, Blair used the occasion as an opportunity to lay out his vision of the third way 'without excessive concern for the sensibilities of the plural left', that is, the coalition of Socialists, Communists, and Greens in Jospin's government.[13] Although he resisted direct criticism of the French tradition of *dirigisme* (state management of the economy) or Jospin's proposals for a legally mandated thirty-five-hour week, Blair did attack rigid labor markets in the speech as 'another form of injustice', and went on to tell his audience that 'addiction to ideology can be fatal'. In a global economy, Blair continued, 'The role of Government becomes less about regulation than about equipping people for economic change by focusing on education, skills and technology and a welfare state the promotes work and makes it pay.' Most famously, Blair told the French legislators that 'What counts is what works. If we don't take this attitude, change traps us, paralyses us, and defeats us.'[14]

Blair's speech was applauded on both sides of the Assembly, with the center-right Gaullists applauding Blair's statement that 'There is no ideological taboo', and the center-left Socialists claiming Blair as a dynamic leader who shared their views. Nevertheless, some deputies on the left distanced themselves from Blair's advocacy of flexible labor markets, and

[12] Peter Mandelson, 'Blair's First Birthday: Best Times, Worst Times; Memoirs of a Spin Doctor', *Observer* (26 Apr. 1998), 25.
[13] Quoted in Daniel Vernet, 'Tony Blair expose sa vision du socialisme à l'Assemblée', *Le Monde* (26 Mar. 1998), author's translation: 'Il a exposé sa conception d'une troisième voie sans trop d'égards pour les susceptibilités de la gauche plurielle.'
[14] Quoted in Michael White, 'EU Must Change, Blair Tells French; Paris Speech: "Third Way" Plea Divides Assembly', *Guardian* (25 Mar. 1998), 10. See also Denis Hiault, 'Blair Will Set Out His Political "Third Way" to the French, in French', *Agence France Presse*, 24 Mar. 1998.

Jospin restricted himself to the diplomatic observation that, although they used different language to describe their policies, New Labour and French Socialists faced similar challenges.[15] Indeed, Blair's speech before the National Assembly was arguably the high-water mark of the third way in France, where it has since come under more sustained criticism among the left.

The balance sheet of Blair's efforts during the British Presidency are mixed. Most analysts agreed that the Presidency was effective and competent in the management of EU business, so that 'the trains ran on time' during the first half of 1998.[16] In addition, many critics gave Blair credit for the drastically improved tone of the UK's relationship with the European Union, which had become embittered during the final years of John Major's government by the BSE crisis of 1996, and by the Euroscepticism of a growing wing of Major's Conservative Party. Nevertheless, the UK Presidency failed to produce any tangible results, or 'deliverables', for Blair's third-way project, beyond the vaguely Blairite language about the importance of economic and political reform in the Presidency Conclusions of the June European Council meeting in Cardiff, Wales.[17] In a post-mortem examination of the UK Presidency, Peter Ludlow praises it for its efficiency and for 'normalizing' the UK's relationship with the EU only two years after the depths of the BSE crisis; yet Ludlow also presents a withering critique of Blair's political ambitions for the Presidency, suggesting that Blair's authority among the center-left in Europe is based primarily upon his electoral success, rather than his third-way ideology (1998: 581–3). Blair's missionary campaign to internationalize the third way was not over, however, and would find a new outlet in 1999 with the election of a new European Parliament—and the first left-wing government in Germany in sixteen years.

Blairism in Strasbourg, Berlin, and Paris

Every five years since 1979, the Social Democratic, Christian Democratic, Liberal, and other parties of Europe have put forward candidates in each of the various member states of the Union for direct election to the European Parliament (EP). These elections have long been referred to as 'second-order elections', since voters generally cast their votes on national

[15] Raphaelle Bacque and Clarisse Fabre, 'En Anglais, New Labour Veut Dire RPR', *Le Monde* (26 Mar. 1998).
[16] Lionel Barber, 'Solid Leadership Marks Sea Change in British Approach,' *The Financial Times* (22 June 1998), 10. See also Ludlow 1998.
[17] Lionel Barber, 'A Punctured Image', *The Financial Times* (15 June 1999), 23. For the text of the Presidency Conclusions, see United Kingdom Presidency 1999.

issues rather than on the European issues likely to be influenced by the increasingly powerful Parliament. Nevertheless, the various party families in Europe have developed close links over the past two decades, forming 'party groups' of like-minded members within the Parliament, and 'party federations' linking together the national parties and their leaders outside the EP. On the center-left of the European political spectrum, the Party of European Socialists was until recently the largest party group within the Parliament, and the federation of party group leaders has met with increasing frequency in recent years, as for example at the 1997 Malmo Congress described above. In addition, the PES has also developed the practice of adopting a common electoral manifesto for EP elections, as a supplement to the specific platforms adopted by each national party (Hix and Lord 1996).

In the run-up to the 1999 EP elections, the PES selected one of its eight vice-presidents, British Foreign Minister Robin Cook, as the primary author of its 1999 manifesto, together with Henri Nallet, the spokesman on European Union issues within the French Socialist Party. Cook's appointment represented a significant improvement in the historically poor relations between the Labour Party and its PES counterparts. In 1994, for example, then Labour Party leader John Smith had decided not to accede to the PES manifesto, because of its commitment to the adoption of a mandatory thirty-five-hour working week. By contrast, Cook and Blair imagined that New Labour would play a major role in shaping the 1999 manifesto, to be formally adopted by a Congress of party leaders in Milan in March, as a third-way document emphasizing such key Blairite themes as economic growth and employability. True to form, Blair attended the Milan meeting to press for the modernization of the European social model, and the adoption of supply-side reforms of taxation systems and labor markets. Perhaps most controversially, Blair held up the USA as a potential model for Europe, telling delegates: 'We can't argue with the fact that US unemployment is lower, growth higher—and it's not all low-skill service jobs. The prices of their goods are often more competitive. This is not an argument to undermine the European social model. It is an argument to modernise it.'[18] Despite Blair's bold rhetoric, the rest of the PES was unwilling to adopt such Blairite language for their common manifesto, which emerged as a compromise between the third-way positions of Cook and Blair on the one hand, and the more traditional socialist platform advocated by Jospin and Nallet. For example, the manifesto placed employment at the top of its list of priorities, but failed

---

[18] Quoted in 'Lafontaine Rejects "Free Enterprise" Call: "Red Oskar" and Blair Clash Over State Spending and Interest Rates', *Daily Telegraph* (3 Mar. 1999), 13.

to specify any specific strategy to that end: 'There are many positive ways to promote employment, including tax reform, the modernization of welfare systems, the promotion of new enterprises and support for the non-market sector. This may include agreed reductions in working time negotiated between the social partners.' Note the careful language in this paragraph, which includes key Blairite ideas such as tax and welfare reform alongside the working-time reductions advocated by Jospin's government in France, without committing the members to any of them. Other sections feature similarly nuanced compromises, such as the discussion of taxation, which calls for 'policy coordination to prevent harmful tax competition', a key demand of France and Germany, while stopping short of advocating full harmonization of taxation systems, which was staunchly opposed by the UK and the Netherlands (Party of European Socialists 1999). In the final analysis, therefore, the PES manifesto was not the third-way document that some of its advocates had hoped, but rather an artful compromise, which papered over the real differences among the various socialist parties, and allowed the British Labour Party to participate fully in the collective campaign for the European Parliament.

As it happened, however, the PES manifesto was not Blair's final opportunity to export the third way to continental Europe, for the German elections of 1998 had brought to power a center-left government of Social Democrats and Greens, led by centrist Chancellor Gerhard Schröder. For some months, it had remained unclear whether Schröder's government would lean towards the third-way policies of the Blair government, or the more traditional left-wing views of Jospin and the French Socialists. From the point of view of the Blairite center, the early months of the Schröder government were not promising. Unlike Blair after his triumphant 1997 electoral victory, Schröder in autumn 1998 was forced into a coalition with a Green Party that demanded dramatic reforms in areas such as nuclear power and Germany's ethnicity-based citizenship laws in return for its support for the new government. More importantly, Schröder had never managed to impose his stamp on the Social Democratic Party as Blair had on his New Labour Party. Although Schröder had won the right to campaign as the candidate for Chancellor, with his youthful and centrist image among the electorate, much of the party rank and file remained loyal to its traditionalist leader, Oskar Lafontaine, who set much of the tone for the new government in his capacity as Finance Minister.

Unlike Schröder, who stood for a vaguely defined 'New Centre' (*Neue Mitte*), Lafontaine represented the left wing of the Social Democrats, and attracted attention both at home and abroad for his unabashedly Keynesian views of the German and European economies. Lafontaine believed that the cure for Germany's record unemployment was not the

Blairite path of fiscal rectitude and labor-market deregulation, but rather a Keynesian reflation of the economy through government spending designed to increase aggregate demand. Once in office as Finance Minister, Lafontaine put these views into practice, courting controversy with his criticism of the German Bundesbank (and later of the new European Central Bank), which he argued should lower interest rates in order to speed up the recovery of the European economy. Within the so-called ECOFIN Council of Economic and Finance Ministers, Lafontaine also aroused the ire of Gordon Brown, the British Chancellor of the Exchequer, by calling for extensive EU tax harmonization, which Brown believed would be a hindrance to competition and growth in Britain.[19] Indeed, the British reaction to 'red Oskar' was aptly if hyperbolically summarized by the *Sun*, which called Lafontaine 'the most dangerous man in Europe'.

By March 1999, Lafontaine was under fire from much of the German and European business community, and from many of his counterparts, who charged that his injudicious comments about the new European Central Bank had weakened the Euro only months after its successful launch. Lafontaine responded to these pressures, and to the lack of support from the German Chancellery, by resigning without explanation from his government and party posts on March 11. The effects were dramatic, both within the European financial markets, which rose sharply on the news of Lafontaine's resignation, and within the Social Democratic Party, where Schröder seized the occasion to move his government and party decisively to the *Neue Mitte,* most notably by appointing as his new Finance Minister the centrist Hans Eichel, who immediately made known his intention to introduce significant cuts in the next German budget.

Most interestingly for our purposes, Schröder ratified his turn to the center in early June with the joint adoption of a policy paper, entitled 'Europe: The Third Way/*Die Neue Mitte*', with Tony Blair. The paper, adopted just a week before the European Parliament elections, was as Blairite as the PES manifesto was bland. Drafted largely by Peter Mandelson, the document bore none of the signs of compromise and watering down that befell the manifesto. The paper begins, as Blair so often does, with a reaffirmation of social-democratic values, followed by an extraordinarily blunt statement of the social and economic changes to which the social democratic parties of Europe are called upon to adapt.

---

[19] For good discussions of Lafontaine's views, see Peter Norman, 'Challenge to the Old Order', *The Financial Times* (23 Feb. 1998), 10; Wolfgang Munchau, 'Return to Keynes', *The Financial Times* (26 Oct. 1998), 22; and Josef Joffe, 'Let's Not Be Beastly to Germany's Most Ambitious Minister: Oskar Lafontaine's Plans for Europe's Economy Could be Disastrous, But They Won't Happen', *Sunday Telegraph* (29 Nov. 1998), 30.

'Ideas of what is "left-wing,"' it says in an echo of Blair's Paris speech, 'should never become an ideological straightjacket.' The paper accordingly goes on lay out 'a new supply-side agenda for the left', which de-emphasizes Keynesian demand management in favor of a raft of supply-side measures, including fiscal rectitude ('sound public finance should be a badge of pride for social democrats'); deregulation ('companies . . . must not be gagged by rules and regulations'); tax reform to encourage investment and employment ('corporate tax cuts raise profitability, and strengthen the incentives to invest'); and above all deregulation of labor markets married to an active program of worker education and training ('the top priority must be investment in human and social capital'). Finally, the paper ends with an open invitation to the other socialist parties of Europe to join in the renewal and redefinition of center-left politics. 'Let the politics of the Third Way and the *Neue Mitte*,' it concludes, 'be Europe's new hope' (Blair and Schröder 1999).

For Blair and New Labour, the 'Third *Way/Neue Mitte*' represented essentially a restatement of Blair's well-known views. For Schröder and the Social Democrats, by contrast, the document represented a potential revolution in a Germany that had not been scoured clean of high taxation, generous welfare benefits, and rigid labor markets by seventeen years of Thatcherism as had Britain.[20] Unfortunately for Schröder, the following week's EP elections provided an inauspicious beginning for the SPD, which suffered significant losses to the resurgent Christian Democratic Party. Nevertheless, despite this electoral set-back, Schröder pressed ahead in summer 1999 with his new-center policies, the core of which was an austerity budget that would combine tax reform with spending cuts of DM30 million in an effort to bring Germany's enormous fiscal deficit under control by 2007. On the tax side, Schröder and Eichel, the architect of the reforms, proposed a reduction in corporate taxation to promote domestic investment, coupled with an increase in so-called 'green taxes' on gasoline and electricity. Perhaps most controversially, however, the new budget included across-the-board spending cuts for almost all ministries, including reductions in spending for pensions, which would rise only at the rate of inflation for the following two years.[21] Although the proposed budget stopped short of proposing structural reforms to the German pension system, and despite Schröder's argument that there was 'no alternative' to the proposed spending cuts, the plans met with sustained opposition both

---

[20] For an excellent analysis of the very different starting points distinguishing Blair's Britain from Schröder's Germany, see Martin Wolf, 'Not the Right Way', *The Financial Times* (16 June 1999), 14.

[21] For details of the proposed budget, see Haig Simonian and Ralph Atkins, 'Hallmark of German Tax Plans is that a Deal was Made At All', *The Financial Times* (24 June 1999).

within and outside the party. Within the SPD, the Chancellor's new, business-friendly policies were attacked most publicly by the Minister-President of the Saarland, Reinhardt Klimmt, who criticized the proposed spending cuts and called for the restoration of a wealth tax on the rich, which had been abandoned by the Christian Democrats in 1997.[22]

Outside the party, opposition to Schröder's policies was voiced most loudly by the trade unions, which attacked the freeze in pension rates as unacceptable, and in a series of electoral losses for the SPD, which suffered further set-backs in state elections in Brandenburg, Thuringia, and the Saarland, and as a result lost control of Germany's second legislative chamber, the Bundesrat. In October, the political climate worsened even further with the publication of Lafontaine's impassioned biography, *The Heart Beats on the Left*, which was predictably critical of the Chancellor and his new-center policies, and called for a return to traditional left-wing politics.

Finally, during the final months of 1999, Schröder began a public retreat from his *Neue Mitte* governing philosophy. Although the government did manage to press its budget through the Bundestag by year's end, Schröder also made a series of concessions to the traditionalist left, welcoming Klimmt into his government, indicating that he might be willing to accept the wealth tax that he had earlier rejected out of hand, and even considering a proposal to lower the official German retirement age from 65 to 60. In a televised appearance on a late-night talk show, Schröder admitted to a lapse of judgment in signing the *Neue Mitte* paper without consulting more broadly within his own party; and the secretary-general of the party, Franz Münterfering, argued that the paper had 'no direct consequences' for the Berlin government.[23] In November 1999, Schröder took a controversial stance against the proposed hostile takeover of Mannesmann AG, a German telecommunications firm, by Vodaphone AirTouch of Britain, arguing that hostile takeovers could 'destroy a company's culture', and warning predators that they 'should not underestimate the power of German co-determination'. That same week, Schröder pressured a consortium of private banks to bail out Philipp Holzmann AC, a construction firm on the verge of bankruptcy, by putting up 250 million Deutschmarks ($131 million) of public funds.[24] The defense of Mannesmann, and the bailout of Holzmann, proved popular among the

---

[22] Haig Simonian, 'Chancellor's Challenge', *The Financial Times* (6 August 1999).

[23] Quoted in Ralph Atkins and Andrew Parker, 'Schröder Admits Policy Stumble', *The Financial Times* (5 Oct. 1999), 2.

[24] Edmund L. Andrews, 'Germany's Consensus Economy at Risk of Unraveling', *New York Times* (26 Nov. 1999); and Wolfgang Munchau, 'No Hostile Takeovers Please, We're German', *The Financial Times* (29 Nov. 1999).

left-wing of the SPD, and strengthened Schröder's position within the party at its year-end conference; yet these same actions suggest that Schröder will be unable or unwilling to pursue a consistent third-way governing philosophy in the face of resistance from his own party and from Germany's consensus system of decision-making.

Meanwhile, the Blair–Schröder paper was met with ambivalence or hostility in other countries, and most notably in France, where Socialist leader and Prime Minister Lionel Jospin reaffirmed the 'originality of French Socialism', which he depicted as less Atlanticist and less market-oriented than the Anglo-German approach. One must 'first be oneself rather than following the path of others', Jospin told a Socialist rally in Toulouse in June, adding that, 'We favor economic regulation worldwide and I believe this is part of a long tradition shared by leftwing political forces as well as non-leftwing political forces.'[25]

In fact, Jospin's policies during his first two years in office had proven far more pragmatic and centrist than his initial rhetoric at Malmo and Amsterdam suggested. Although Jospin and his Employment Minister, Martine Aubry, have delivered on their electoral pledge to legislate a maximum thirty-five-hour week and create thousands of state jobs for unemployed youth, Jospin's government has also broken with core Socialist policies of the past. After initially criticizing the previous government's policy of privatizing nationalized industries, for example, Jospin has quietly continued and even accelerated that process in government, selling off shares of such national landmarks as Air France. In the realm of fiscal policy, Jospin has also struck a Blairite note, emphasizing fiscal prudence so as to enable France to qualify for Economic and Monetary Union, and instituting modest tax cuts to stimulate consumption. And, in a break with the French tradition of *dirigisme*, Jospin has kept the state at arm's length as French banks, supermarkets, and other industries have negotiated both friendly and unfriendly mergers and acquisitions.

Despite this pragmatism, Jospin has been—and will continue to be— constrained in his move toward the Blairite center by the dual difficulties of maintaining a fractious pink–red–green political coalition with the Communists and Greens, while at the same time responding to a French public opinion that is deeply ambivalent about the economic and cultural implications of globalization. The nature of these constraints can be illustrated in two controversies which coincided with the French *rentrée politique* (the return to political life after the long summer vacation) of September 1999.

---

[25] Quoted in 'France's Jospin Won't Join Britain, Germany in Putting Left Behind', *Agence France Presse,* 9 June 1999.

The first of these controversies, *l'affaire Bové*, began in late August, when a group of French farmers attacked and destroyed the building site of a new McDonald's restaurant in the rural town of Millau, in protest against American tariffs on French products such as *foie gras*, Rocquefort cheese, and Dijon mustard. The American tariffs had been adopted, and approved by the World Trade Organization, in response to the European decision to ban the import of American beef treated with bovine growth hormones; yet they set off a much broader and more visceral reaction among French farmers and public opinion, which interpreted the tariffs as part of a broader American agenda of economic globalization that would eventually end in the destruction of French cuisine and the rural French way of life. In response to these tariffs, farmers from the Conféréderation Paysanne, a farmers' organization led by goat farmer José Bové, carried out the attack on the McDonald's, selected as the symbol of both American cuisine and globalization, and the perceived threat they represented to French traditions. ('McDonald's encapsulates it all', in the words of Gaillaume Parmentier of the French Center on the United States: 'It's economic horror and gastronomic horror in the same bun'.)[26] Bové was jailed for the attack, and remained in prison for nearly three weeks before being released on bail of 105,000 French francs ($17,000), raised by supporters throughout France.

Perhaps the most remarkable aspect of the Bové affair is the extraordinary support for Bové's illegal action in French public opinion, and among French political élites on the left and the right, who depicted Bové as a national hero, a martyr, and a Robin Hood of the French farmers. President Jacques Chirac said in an interview that, although Bove's methods were unacceptable, he sympathized with the farmer's grievances against the USA; at the other end of the political spectrum, Green Party spokesman Denis Baupin bluntly asserted that 'José Bové has fulfilled every ecologist's dream: dismantling a McDonald's.'[27] The Socialist Minister of Agriculture, Jacques Glavany, similarly boasted that he had never stepped foot inside a McDonald's. Finally, in a television interview in mid-September, Jospin referred to Bové as a 'strong, vigorous personality, who stems a bit from our people, with the radicalism that has always existed', adding for good measure that, 'I am not very pro-McDo', using the typical French pronunciation.[28] The following week, Jospin put the

[26] Quoted in Jon Henley, 'McDonald's Campaign Spawns French Hero: Political Activist Turned French Peasant Has Fast Food on the Run', *The Guardian* (11 Sept. 1999), 14.

[27] Quoted in Charles Bremner, 'French Farmers Fight US "Imperialism"', *The Times* (1 Sept. 1999).

[28] Quoted in Craig R. Whitney, 'Protesters Just Say No to "McDo"; Jospin Glad', *The New York Times* (15 Sept. 1999), A17.

affair in broader perspective, telling *Washington Post* reporter Jim Hoagland that the French people had a legitimate concern for the quality and safety of their food in an era of globalization. 'We do not resist globalization,' he said. 'We want to civilize globalization where we can, to harmonize it with our way of life. We don't want to be passive. We are open, but we are not masochistic.'[29]

The second controversy in France, the so-called *affaire Michelin*, erupted in September, when the Michelin tire company announced plans to cut some 7,500 jobs over three years, while at the same time reporting a 17 per cent rise in profits during the previous half-year. The news of the lay-offs provoked outrage among Michelin workers, trade unionists, and public opinion generally. In a live television interview, Jospin declared himself 'shocked' that the company would announce such lay-offs in a period of profitability and prosperity, and called on workers and unions to 'mobilize' against the decision. Yet Jospin went on to argue that, 'We can no longer govern the economy', and discounted the notion that the government could or should interfere in Michelin's decision. He added bluntly: 'The economy cannot be run by legislation and official texts . . . People must stop expecting the government and the state to be in charge of everything.'[30]

Jospin's statement was unremarkable by the standards of Blair's Britain; indeed, many British observers called it a rather innocuous statement of the obvious. Nevertheless, the remarks caused almost as much turmoil among the governing coalition as Michelin's initial decision to lay off its workers. Not surprisingly, the loudest response came from the Communist Party, whose leader Robert Hue publicly warned Jospin that he risked losing his governing majority over such pro-business views. Jospin responded the following week with a statement that his government would fight against what he called 'abusive' lay-offs by profitable companies, and penalize companies that relied too heavily on short-term contracts.[31] At the time of writing, it is unclear whether Jospin's U-turn in the Michelin affair signified a genuine change of policy, or was simply rhetoric designed to mollify the traditional left-wingers in the Communist and Socialist Parties. Nevertheless, the controversy over Jospin's remarks, together with the story of the Bové affair, illustrate clearly the difficulty that Jospin has encountered in moving his government and his party more openly to the

---

[29] Quoted in Jim Hoagland, 'France Coping with Globalization', *International Herald Tribune* (23 Sept. 1999), 10.

[30] Quoted in Claire Rosemberg, 'France's Socialist Government Steers Center', *Agence France Presse*, 14 Sept. 1999.

[31] Quoted in Barry James, 'Jospin to Fight "Abusive" Layoffs', *International Herald Tribune* (28 Sept. 1999), 1.

Blairite center in defiance of French public opinion and his coalition partners.

Conclusion

What future, then, for the renewal of the European left in general, for the
third-way reform of the EU agenda proposed by Tony Blair? Will the
Europe of the left adopt the interventionist and redistributive approach of
Hooghe's and Marks's model of regulated capitalism, or Blair's third-way
model, with its acceptance of globalization and market forces, its resistance to state intervention, and its emphasis on economic reform? If we
accept the tripartite definition of the third way offered in the first section
of this chapter as the benchmark of third-way thinking, it is hard to disagree with Featherstone's conclusion that 'the prospect of Blair selling his
domestic wares to the rest of Europe unmodified is not great in the short-
term. The values and interests of many of his peers are resistant to his
Clintonesque or neo-Thatcherite references' (1999: 12). To be sure, leaders
such as Jospin, Schröder, Italian Prime Minister Massimo D'Alema, and
Dutch Prime Minister Wim Kok are all attracted to Blair's model of electoral success, and to varying extents to his New Labour pragmatism as
well. However, the socialist leaders of continental Europe are generally
constrained by political and policy inheritances less favorable to the 'radical center' than Blair's Britain. In contrast to Blair, who controls a unified
Labour Party with an overwhelming majority in the House of Commons,
the leaders of France, Germany, and Italy must cope with internal party
battles, fractious red and green coalition partners, and thin governing
majorities that limit their scope for bold action. Furthermore, Blair has
enjoyed the luxury of implementing his third-way policies in a country
subjected to almost two decades of deregulation, privatization, and structural adjustment, so that, by the time Blair took office in 1997, most of the
politically difficult reforms had already been adopted by previous
Conservative governments. By contrast, France, Germany, and the other
countries of Western Europe have inherited very different policy legacies,
and face a much more difficult task in implementing the basic reforms of
fiscal, labor-market, and welfare-state policies demanded by Blair's modernizing agenda. In sum, I would argue that, contrary to the views of his
critics, Blair's third way *is* a reasonably coherent governing philosophy for
Britain, but that it is *not* ideally tailored for transfer to the very different
political and policy environments of continental Europe.

Should we then conclude that Blair's third-way philosophy is destined
to remain isolated in Britain, a third-way island in a continent-sized sea of

unreconstructed old socialists? Certainly not. As useful as it may be to define Blair's third way with precision and engage in a comparative analysis of third-way thinking throughout Europe, as we have done here, I would also agree with White's (1999) claim that the adoption of the third way as a benchmark can also obscure real changes taking place in socialist parties throughout Europe. Indeed, if we step away from Blair's definition of the third way and examine the evolution of French, German, and other European social democracies against their own political and policy traditions, a different picture emerges. If, for example, we compare contemporary socialist governments in France, Germany, and elsewhere in the EU with the traditional image of those countries from Shonfield's classic *Modern Capitalism* (1965), we see that even the 'traditionalist' socialist parties in France and Germany have evolved significantly, moving away from Keynesian demand-management and *dirigiste* industrial policies in favor of an almost universal (*pace* Lafontaine) acceptance of monetarism and fiscal rectitude, and a more grudging acceptance of deregulation, privatization, and labor-market flexibility. Similarly, if we compare the European policy preferences of the French, German, and other socialist governments to Marks's and Hooghe's ideal type of regulated capitalism, we find a general acceptance of the liberalized internal market and of the monetarist terms of Economic and Monetary Union, and only the dying echoes of Jospin's and Lafontaine's initial demands for an 'economic government' at the European level (see Chapter 6 above, by Campanella).

Perhaps the real lesson of Blair's crusade is that, in the words of Stuart White (1999), there is not one third way, but many. The socialist parties of continental Europe are unlikely to adopt in its entirety Blair's third way, which is poorly suited to their own domestic contexts; but nor will those parties remain frozen in a statist, Keynesian, and redistributive past. Rather, each of Europe's socialist parties will adopt—and indeed is already adopting—its own third way, combining elements of the 'traditional' and 'modern' socialism in ways that reflect the political and policy constraints specific to their own domestic contexts. Aggregating those various third ways, and articulating a coherent vision of the European social model at the EU level, will be one of the central challenges for center-left parties at the dawn of the twenty-first century.

15

On Being European: The Character and Consequences of European Identity

DAVID MICHAEL GREEN

Since the launching of the European integration project fifty years ago, scholars have debated its meaning, motives, and its proper interpretation in the context of wider debates among international relations theorists. If such debates today seem stale, it is in part because of a growing appreciation of the necessary contribution made by *both* major explanatory approaches, neofunctionalism and intergovernmentalism. It is also because facts on the ground have overtaken scholarly debate, and as such require that Europeanists reinventory their questions, concepts, and conclusions. Chief among these facts is the existence today of a viable and, in certain domains, quite consequential polity where none existed fifty years ago.

It is fitting, therefore, that Europeanists now turn their attention to the sorts of questions appropriate to the study of existing polities. What are the salient institutions of this polity, and how do they relate to each other? How deeply does the polity penetrate its respective civil society? How does it relate to the political units which comprise it and to external sovereigns? What sorts of actors and politics characterize its decision-making processes? And, what is the relationship of the polity to its body politic? The study of one particular aspect of this latter dimension has grown increasingly prominent across the social sciences, and is of special concern to political scientists. This is the question of identity, and it is crucial to the welfare and longevity of any democratic polity.

David Easton and Jack Dennis recognized this years ago, when they wrote of the diffuse support necessary to sustain polities. Such support, of which political identity is one manifestation, 'forms a reservoir upon which a system typically draws in times of crises, such as depressions, wars, and internecine conflicts, when perceived benefits may recede to their lowest ebb' (Easton and Dennis 1969: 63). In this regard, it is useful to recall that the brief history of European integration has transpired during a period of remarkable and unprecedented peace and prosperity. And yet, there are no shortage of politicians and pundits demonstrating not the least hesitation to beat up on Europe when it suits them to do so, and many among the public who follow their lead. If this is the condition of Europe during the most munificent of times, what will it be should the ill winds of war or economic hardship blow across the continent?

Thus, it is *risks*—among the four themes of this volume—which are most implicated by the question of identity. The project of European integration has shown remarkable progress in a short half-century, yet not only its future but its present as well are at risk to the extent that a European identity does not develop. Europe may be *sui generis* in many respects, but it is like any other polity in its need for a robust affective relationship with its citizenry. Slater puts the point well, in both its generic and specific applications:

Almost by definition, the building of a political community means the creation of a sense of community or solidarity among the people of a given region. It is this sense of solidarity which gives legitimacy to the Community's institutions. A viable political community needs the allegiance of its mass public as well as that of elites. In the case of the European Community, a lack of public commitment to Europe tends to be seen as a major threat to the existence of the Community. (1982: 155)

Nor are such concerns purely theoretical. Flush with the success of the SEA in the late 1980s, Europe was held in reasonably high esteem by its public. But in the 1990s, such sentiments have been replaced by anger and alienation for many Europeans, as the EU was seen at Maastricht to outrun its own legitimacy, and as the subsequent run-up to monetary union required sacrifices in several member countries. Such sentiments point to the significance of a second theme of this volume, and the consequent *resistance* to integrative initiatives which may be predicted of an alienated body politic. Moïsi illustrates the effects of these developments in France, generally one of the countries most sympathetic to the European project:

Instead of being perceived as a goal or even—less ambitiously—as a solution, the European Union is seen as either the problem or an irrelevant answer to the daily preoccupations of the French: unemployment and insecurity. In a contradictory manner, the EU is seen as being both too intrusive in a bureaucratic sense and too impotent on the international stage. From the diktats of Brussels to the failure of Europe in Bosnia, the European project is losing its allure and purpose for France. The growing discontent is shrewdly exploited by Jean-Marie Le Pen's extreme right.[1]

---

[1] See Dominique Moïsi, 'Gloom of the Sick Man: The Deep Sense of Malaise in France is Endangering Monetary Union', *The Financial Times* (13 Dec. 1996), 20.

If, as was argued above, Europe is now a grown-up polity, then it must face the challenges incumbent upon all grown-ups. In particular, if it expects the integrative achievements of the last fifty years to weather diffi-cult storms, let alone any further such developments—if, that is, Europe is to transcend the risks and resistance associated with public sentiment—then the foundations of the European project must be built on firmer ground than the shifting sands of indifference and occasional hostility which presently (fail to) buttress the Union. The best bulwark for ensur-ing the success of European institutional integration is thus an equally developed positive affect among Europeans. In short, as does any other non-autocratic polity, a successful Europe requires a mature European identity.

This chapter explorers the theme of European identification, with spe-cific reference to six questions of particular interest. (1) How widespread is the phenomenon? (2) How does Europe compare to other continents? (3) Is European identity growing over time? (4) What factors influence lev-els of identification with Europe? (5) What is the meaning of a European political identity for those who possess it? (6) How deep do such identities run?

Context, Method and Sources

The idea of European identity is not a new one, yet it is not a phenome-non which has been extensively studied. The dream of a united Europe is at least a thousand years old, having occupied the minds of poets, philosophers, and would-be emperors perhaps since the fall of Rome (Lewis 1993: 12). Most of the academic literature addressing the question of European identity is of a purely theoretical bent, typically grappling first with the question of whether a European identity is even conceivable, followed by the corollary concerning which attributes and characteristics could form the stuff of such an identity. Responses to the former question generally divide scholars into two camps—skeptics and optimists—or, in terms of more conventional paradigmatic labels for scholars of political identity, primordialists and constructivists. Those in the first group (Anthony Smith 1992, is an example) argue that Europe possesses little of the shared cultural and historical artifacts from which identities typically have been crafted, and will therefore never be able to craft one of its own, because such commonalities are difficult or impossible to fabricate. Constructivists (e.g. Wintle 1996), on the other hand, as their name implies, believe that identities can and have been shaped into existence, and thus Europe has the same prospects for forming a common identity as, say, a Britain or a France of several centuries past.[2]

European identity has also been examined empirically, though there are few such published studies. Perhaps the earliest treatment is provided by Inglehart's discussion of the topic in *The Silent Revolution*, where he finds that the three most powerful predictors of supranational identity in Europe are (in descending order): length of Community membership (higher levels are found among the Six than in later joining member states), post-materialist values, and cognitive mobilization (a constructed index combining political involvement, level of education, and informational cognizance) (1977: 340–1). Miles Hewstone's study of college students from Germany, Italy, France, and Britain provides some additional empirical data on the question of European identity, though Hewstone's interpretation of his findings sometimes seems unduly pessimistic. For example, a prompt posed in his study—'I am more loyal to the interests of the EEC than to the interests of [R's country]'—returned a mean response of 3.23 (where 1 = 'strongly disagree' and 7 = 'strongly agree') (1986: 140, 199–201). Hewstone sees this as evidence for the failure of a European identity to materialize, but given the starkness of the prompt, just the opposite conclusion seems at least as appropriate. A final study of note is that by Sophie Duchesne and André-Paul Frognier, who find, among other things, that European identity is more prevalent among the better educated and those with a higher income, but that such effects are more pronounced in less developed European countries than in those which are wealthy (1995: 209–17).

The present chapter offers an empirical analysis of European identity which seeks to expand upon previous work along several dimensions. First, it addresses a broader array of topics, as identified in the six questions listed above. Second, in looking at the key question of determinants of European identity, it examines a wider series of explanatory hypotheses than does previous work. Third, not only quantitative but also qualitative sources are employed, as the use of both is crucial to a more complete understanding of such a nuanced and subtle phenomenon as political identity. Finally, among the quantitative sources, a wide series of Eurobarometer and related surveys are utilized, ranging across multiple-question formats and nearly three decades of time.

Altogether, twenty-six existing data sets are employed, including those generated by Eurobarometer (1976–94), European Communities Studies (1971, 1973), World Values Surveys (1981–4 and 1990–3), and the

---

[2] Excellent treatments of the construction of British and French identities where they did not exist previously can be found in Colley (1992) and Weber (1976), respectively.

International Social Survey Program (ISSP) (1995).[3] In addition, another data set, the Survey of European Identifiers (SEI)—was produced specifically for this project and contains responses to a thirty-eight-question survey returned by 227 (mostly) strong European identifiers from nearly every EU member state. The respondents attended either the May 1998 Fiftieth Anniversary Congress of Europe in the Hague, or the June 1998 People's Europe Conference in London. A few were members of the British Young European Movement who responded to electronic circulation of the survey. Finally, interviews were conducted with seventy-seven Europeans—mostly identifiers—including at least one from every EU member state. Interviewed informants were drawn from delegates to the Congress of Europe and the People's Europe conferences, as well as graduate students at the College of Europe in Bruges. All interviews were conducted during the summer of 1998.

Are there any 'Europeans' in Europe?

As noted above, skeptics wonder whether a European identity is even conceivable, and thus it is fair to ask whether there are in fact any European identifiers in Europe. Table 15.1 provides a very robust answer, beyond that supplied by the above-referenced interviews of in-the-flesh European identifiers. An extensive search of extant survey data sets located fifteen containing unambiguous measures of European identity.[4] While the wording changes slightly in a few cases, these fifteen measures fall into four standard formats, as shown in Table 15.1. In format one, respondents were asked to select the geopolity to which they 'belong first of all', with choices including their town, region, country, Europe, and the world. They were then asked for their second choice from the same list. These questions were

[3] See Commission, Eurobarometer (1976–94), various authors, Inter-university Consortium for Political and Social Research (distributors); European Communities Studies (1971, 1973), Jacques-Rene Rabier and Ronald Inglehart, principal investigators, Inter-university Consortium for Political and Social Research (distributors); International Social Survey Program (1998), International Social Survey Program: National Identity (1995: computer file). ICPSR release, Cologne: Zentralarchiv für Empirische Sozialforschung (producer); World Values Study Group (1994), World Values Survey, 1981–1984 and 1990–1993 (computer file), ICPSR version, Ann Arbor: Institute for Social Research (producer): Inter-university Consortium for Political and Social Research (distributor) (1994).

[4] Scholars are not always as rigorous in their operationalization of European identity as they should be. Among other indicators, citizenship, support for integration, and the preferred polity location of various competencies have all been used to operationalize identity. While related, these are four altogether very different concepts, and should be measured and treated accordingly.

TABLE 15.1. *Identification with Europe (% of respondents)*

Dependent variable	ECS 1971	ECS 1973	EB06 1976	EC10A 1978	EB12 1979	WVS 1980–4	EB27 1987	EB30 1988	EB31 1989	EB33 1990	WVS 1990–3	EB36-0 1991	EB37-0 1992	EB41-1 1994	ISSP 1995	SEI 1998
Format one																
Eur. 1st choice	8.1	5.9	6.2	4.1	5.1	4.3					4.9					27.1
Eur. 2nd choice	12.2	13.0	11.8	11.8	13.5	9.0					12.8					46.9
Eur. not chosen	79.6	81.1	82.0	84.1	81.4	86.7					82.2					26.1
Format two																
Often							14.2	16.2	14.8	15.8		15.9	14.4			68.1
Sometimes							35.3	38.3	35.6	31.4		33.6	33.0			27.9
Never							50.4	45.4	49.6	52.7		50.5	52.6			4.0
Format three																
9–10 (most Eur.)														14.5		
7–8														22.6		
5–6														26.7		
3–4														17.5		
1–2 (least Eur.)														18.8		
Format four																
Very att'd/close												13.1			14.6	39.7
Fairly att'd/close												37.7			38.1	39.2
Not very att'd/close												30.2			32.2	15.8
Not at all att'd/close												18.9			15.1	5.3

Note: Percentages are of valid cases only ('no answer' and 'don't know' excluded). Data sets weighted by country population, and include respondents from EC/EU member states only.
The survey of European Identifiers (SEI) is not based on a random sample, and cannot be compared to the other survey data presented here.

asked in both administrations of the World Values Surveys (1980 and 1990), though they were otherwise confined to the 1970s.

The second identity question format asked respondents 'Does the thought ever occur to you that you are not only [nationality] but also a European? Does this happen often, sometimes, or never?' This format was employed during the late 1980s and early 1990s. For format three, Eurobarometer 41/1 (1994) posed to respondents the same question described in format two, but asked them to locate their response on a ten-point scale—with 1 representing 'Not at all also European' and 10 being 'Very much also European'—rather than choosing among three categorical responses. Finally, in the fourth format, a series of separate questions asked about the respondents' feelings towards the various polities/geographic levels listed under format one. For purposes of this study, the key question posed was the fourth in this series, asking 'How attached [or close] do you feel to Europe?' Respondents could choose between answering 'Not at all attached/close', 'Not very attached/close', 'Fairly attached/close', and 'Very attached/close'. This format appears in Eurobarometer 36/0 (1991), and in the ISSP survey on national identity (1995).

A look at the figures presented in Table 15.1 makes apparent two immediate conclusions. First, no matter how one slices it—including use of the rigorous, zero-sum format one question battery—there are clearly European identifiers to be found in Europe. Second, the quantity of such identifiers appears to be dependent on both the format of the question,[5] and which of the responses one considers indicative of European identification.[6] In any case, even by the most stringent test, minimally some 5 per cent of respondents should be counted as core European identifiers, with roughly another 12 per cent in a secondary group. While 5 per cent in relative terms is rather small, if extrapolated to the entire population of Europe, the figure represents nearly 20 million people, or the entire populations of Belgium and Portugal combined.

Format one represents the most stringent—and arguably unrealistic—test of European identity from among the four formats, in that it puts the identity question in competitive and zero-sum terms. If respondents are asked about their feelings toward Europe without having to rank those feelings against other identity sentiments, then a more expansive pattern of European identification emerges. Data from all three of the remaining

[5] The reason this cannot be stated more definitively is that question formats tend to aggregate in time, as Table 15.1 indicates. Thus it remains possible, however unlikely, that the differences are period effects rather than artifacts of the variation in question.

[6] In format two data, for example, should those who responded 'sometimes' be counted as European identifiers or non-identifiers?

formats suggest that something like 15 per cent of Europeans can be labeled core or strong identifiers, with roughly another 35 per cent as secondary-level, or less intense, identifiers. This leaves the remaining 50 per cent of the population for whom there is little affective sentiment toward Europe (or, possibly, active hostility—this cannot be determined by the question formats). Given the robustness of these findings, and the greater appropriateness of these question formats, it seems fair to conclude that this 15/35/50 ratio roughly but reliably captures the extent of identification with Europe.

European Identity in Time and Space

Another conclusion which becomes immediately apparent from a glance at Table 15.1 is that longitudinal analyses of European identity are nearly impossible given the structure of the data. In almost every case, unfortunately, question formats have been clustered in time, thus precluding an assessment of the fluctuations in levels of identification over time. The single exception is provided by format one questions, which are indeed clustered in 1970s ECS and Eurobarometer surveys, but also show up in the two World Values Surveys of 1980 and 1990. These appearances at least permit an examination of the trajectory of European identity over a twenty-year period.

Rather surprisingly, perhaps, given the institutional changes witnessed on the continent during the 1970s and 1980s, these data reveal a completely static pattern of identification with Europe. There are several caveats which suggest a need for a degree of caution in acceptance of this non-effect, however. For instance, it is possible that change might have appeared had another question format been employed over the period examined. Or perhaps a later data point would have captured the increasing effects of the ERASMUS educational exchange program and other developments which some have argued have produced a new generation of European identifiers. Still, while recognizing the paucity of data from which to draw conclusions, it nevertheless appears that the story of European identification is marked by stasis, not change.

Data from the World Values Surveys also permit comparison of European identification patterns across another dimension, and here the results are perhaps even more surprising. As their name implies, the surveys were administered in many countries around the globe, and the same format one question was asked in each. Remarkably, after thirty years of integration unmatched anywhere else in the world, European identity levels in 1980 were identical to the average continental identity level (first and second choice combined) for the entire sample (12.4 per cent).[7] By 1990, European identity (15.9 per cent) grew to slightly higher than the global continental identity average (13.0 per cent), but is still lower than that found in Africa (19.5 per cent). These figures should probably be read with a large degree of caution, not least for their volatility across the two survey administrations, but also because for several continents the number of countries included is small and not necessarily representative. Nevertheless, the reasonable expectation that European identity would be considerably advanced over its analogues elsewhere is certainly not supported by these data.

To the degree that the measures are accurate—and there are considerable reasons for concern in this regard—neither the longitudinal nor the geographical comparative assessments of European identity bode well for the EU. Here is a polity where extensive 'state'-building and even some quiet 'nation'-building efforts appear to have yielded little benefit in terms of an expanded sense of shared identity. Within the continent, economic and institutional integration over several decades has produced little effect on identity. Perhaps more embarrassingly, European identity may well be dwarfed by that found on other continents which possess nothing remotely approaching its institutional integrative achievements.

And yet, a historically sensitive perspective reminds us that any expectations for the development of a flourishing European identity must be tempered by a sober apprehension of the magnitude of Europe's challenge. To start with, the EU was not born *in vacuo*, but rather followed (and, indeed, was precipitated by) the most flagitious of fratricidal conflicts which, in fact, were only the most recent manifestations of at least half a millennium of the same. The bitterness and division engendered by centuries of war against 'the Other' cannot be expected to yield to a common identity overnight. Indeed, it is arguably nearly miraculous that Europeans are today as united as they are. Old hands at the College of Europe remember how in its early years French and German students shared dorm facilities, but could not bring themselves to talk to one another. In no small sense, European identity has come a long way in a short time.

This becomes even more evident when one considers its other developmental impediments, especially relative to the task faced by nation-builders of the past. Unlike them, Europe cannot rely upon coercive techniques to forge a national identity, since such practices are illegitimate

---

[7] Europe does represent two-thirds of the sample in 1980, so this finding is not entirely a surprise. However, a continent-by-continent comparison shows that European identity is dwarfed by the continental identity in certain other locations, specifically Latin America and Africa.

by contemporary standards. Moreover, unable to wield the stick, nor can it offer the carrot to the same extent states have. The CAP notwithstanding (which only seems to breed resentment even among its beneficiaries), Europe has nothing like the welfare state with which to inspire (purchase?) the allegiance of its citizenry. Nor can it employ the good, old-fashioned unifying technique of antagonism directed against an external 'Other', since such prejudice and saber-rattling, so reliable for past nation-builders, are no longer legitimate practices today—and such an 'Other' would be difficult even to define, since Europe itself is difficult to define. The continual enlargement of the EU (with even Turkey now in the membership queue) may be positive in many respects, but it certainly does not make the job of solidifying a sense of common identity easier.

What, then, is to be made of these empirical findings and their historical and comparative contexts? This question is considered in greater depth in the conclusion to this chapter, where several possible interpretations are assessed. What can be said here, however, is that under almost any scenario they probably do not speak well for Europe's strength as a polity, especially in the short term and under any adverse conditions which might manifest themselves. If, as has been argued, identity (and other forms of diffuse support) are essential to the welfare of any polity, then the fact that a half-century of progress in integration does not seem to have moved levels of European identity—either relative to previous measures or against those of continents where nothing approaching such integration has developed—suggests a Europe at risk.

Who are 'The Europeans'?

The data summarized in Table 15.1 clearly demonstrate that varying levels of attachment to Europe are to be found among Europeans, but leave unanswered whether any patterns exist which might explain and predict such differences. Elsewhere, this question has been addressed at length, and the fifteen data sets in Table 15.1 are each employed to model a broad variety of hypothesized explanations, with an even broader array of variables used to operationalize these concepts (Green 1999). The results of these ordered probit and OLS analyses comprised tables too extensive to fit within the space limitations of this chapter. Table 15.2, however, presents a summary of the findings from these analyses and from the other quantitative and qualitative sources also described above.

Such explanatory hypotheses are grouped into four broad categories. The first of these is comprised of attributional hypotheses, which turn out to be generally powerful predictors of European identity levels. The

TABLE 15.2. *Explaining Variance in Levels of European Identification:*
Summary of Hypotheses and Findings

Hypothesis	Finding
Attributional Hypotheses	
Socio-economic status: Élites will tend to identify with Europe more than non-élites.	Strongly supported
Cosmopolitanism: Cosmopolitans will tend to identify with Europe more than non-cosmopolitans.	Largely supported
Generational: Younger cohorts will tend to identify with Europe more than older	Supported by quanitative data Not supported by qualitative data.
Gender: Men will tend to identify with Europe more than women.	Supported
Attitudinal Hypotheses	
Post-materialism: Post-materialists will tend to identify with Europe more than materialists.	Supported
Ideology: Those in the centre will tend to identify with Europe more than those on the right or left.	Not supported as hypothesized Those on the left identify more closely with Europe Those on the right are less likely to identify with Europe
Non-traditionalism: European identification is associated with a wider set of non-traditional attitudes.	Not supported
Integration support: European identification is driven by support for the integration project.	Most powerfully supported, but direction of causality?
Normative: European identification is driven by universalist, pacifist, and other normative values.	Strongly supported
Social Psychological Hypotheses	
Political Efficacy: The more efficacious will tend to identify with Europe more than the less efficacious.	Mostly supported
Instrumentalism: Identification with Europe is driven by perceptions of personal or national benefits to be gained from integration.	Strongly supported for country benefit. Mixed support for personal benefit.
Minority refuge: A European identity provides a refuge for excluded national minorities.	Not supported
Socialization: European identity is the product of parental or peer socialization.	Not supported
Leadership: Europeans take identity cues from leaders they admire.	Some support, but direction of causality?

Hypothesis	Finding
Political Cultural Hypothesis	
Nationality: European identity levels vary according to nationality	Supported. Countries with high levels of European identity: France, Italy, Spain, Portugal (and Austria—appearing in one survey only) Middle/ambiguous cases: Luxembourg (probably high), Belgium, Germany, and Greece Countries with low levels: Netherlands, Denmark, Ireland, Britain (and Sweden—appearing in one survey only)
'Primordialism': European identity increases with the country's years of membership in the EC/EU	Not supported. Opposite is true.
Size of country: People in smaller countries will be more likely to identify with Europe	Not supported
Wealth of country: People in wealthier countries will be more likely to identify with Europe	Supported
Catholic culture: People in Catholic countries will be more likely to identify as Europeans	Generally supported, but depends on dependent-variable question format.
Second-World-War effect: People in former Axis countries will be more likely to identify as Europeans	Not supported.
Regional culture: European identity levels vary according to region	Supported. Those in southern countries identify more closely with Europe.

models reveal that cosmopolitans, men, and especially élites are over-represented among European identifiers. The major surprise in this category is that the generational hypothesis is not borne out by statistical data. Not only do few differences among age groups emerge when controlling for other factors but, when differences do appear, it is often those in the younger generations whom the models show to be relatively less attached to Europe. This finding is particularly anomalous because it runs directly contrary to oft-repeated assertions by interviewed informants that the younger generations are closer to Europe than their parents and grandparents. A plausible explanation for this contradiction is suggested by a reconceptualization of identity attachments in terms of stages rather than as a monolithic phenomenon which either fully exists or does not. In other words, it may be that younger Europeans are much more *comfortable* with Europe as a social space,[8] without necessarily strongly *identifying* with it in political terms.

Attitudinal factors, the second explanatory category, also provide good predictors of individuals' levels of European identification. Not surprisingly, the most powerful predictor of all of those examined is the respondent's attitude toward the integration project. Yet this finding leaves unanswered the causal direction of the relationship. That is, do supporters of European integration therefore identify as Europeans, as the hypothesis suggests, or is it that those who identify with Europe therefore support integration? Whichever is correct, the relationship is strong. But other attitudinal factors are also associated with higher levels of European identity, including Inglehart's post-materialism, leftist ideological commitments, and a normative sense of European universalism and pacifism. The only hypothesis in the attitudinal category which was not supported is the suggestion that European identities are part of a broader constellation of non-traditional attitudes.

The third category of potential explanations groups together a series of hypotheses under the banner of social psychological accounts of variance in European identity levels among individuals. By and large, these hypotheses receive less support from the collected data than those of the attributional or attitudinal categories. The major exception is the instrumentalism hypothesis, for which a strong relationship exists between perceptions that R's country has benefited from European integration on the one hand, and R's level of European identity on the other (though this relationship is less clear with regard to personal benefits from integration). There is also some support for the notion that those individuals with higher levels of political efficacy are more likely to identify as Europeans, as there is for the idea that individuals take their cues on identity from political leaders they admire. The difficulty with the latter relationship, however, is again the question of causal directionality: that is, do individuals get their identities from admired leaders, as the hypothesis suggests, or do they pick leaders to admire on the basis of prior identities? Finally, very little support could be found for the hypothesis that a European identity provides a refuge for ethnic or religious minorities among the various

---

[8] This much of the explanation seems clearly true. Younger Europeans travel, study, and associate across borders to a degree unheard of by older generations (and the EU is in no small part responsible for this, having sponsored educational exchange programs like ERASMUS and SOCRATES, in which increasing numbers of young Europeans now participate). Moreover, today's younger generations have little of the emotional baggage from the Second World War which so embittered their parents and grandparents.

member states, or for a socialization process of identity development. The data available for addressing the latter question are quite limited, but suggest that European identification is a 'vanguard phenomenon' (Duchesne and Frognier 1995: 223), and that such identifiers are, if anything, *socializers*, not *socializees*.

A final approach to explaining variance in European identity levels is the political cultural. This analysis was performed in two stages. First, a series of country dummy variables were introduced into the model, the results of which provide substantial levels of explanatory purchase, in rather consistent patterns. Thus, one nearly always finds higher levels of European identifiers among the French and Italians, for example, moderate levels among Germans and Belgians, and low levels in the Netherlands, Denmark, Ireland, and Britain (see Table 15.2 for a complete list). For the second stage of this analysis, an attempt was made to substitute conceptual measures for the proper nouns of the country dummies. Here, the results were mixed. A hypothesized 'primordialist' relationship, for example, in which those respondents in member states who were part of the Communities/Union longer would be more likely to identify as Europeans, is not supported—indeed, just the opposite seems to be more generally the case. Neither does the size of the country matter, nor which side it took in the Second World War. Wealthier EU countries do have higher levels of European identifiers, as do those which are more Catholic, though the latter relationship only shows up in some of the data. There is, finally, a geographical gradient which follows the oft-noted divisions within the continent, such that European identifiers are less likely to be found within northern countries than central countries, and are most likely of all to be found in southern member states. Of course, 'southern Europe' is every bit the proper noun as 'Italy', but the pattern may at least suggest avenues for further investigation.

Who, then, are 'the Europeans'? Three generalizations emerge from the foregoing analyses as perhaps the most significant. First, the identity belongs principally to élites, and particularly those whose interests, occupations, and social communities extend beyond provincial and national frontiers. Second, identification with Europe is, not surprisingly, also associated with a constellation of other Europe-related attitudes, such as support for integration and a belief in its personal and especially national benefits. Finally, levels of identity are partially predicted by deep cultural attributes that vary across member states. These cannot yet be much better specified, though religion and geography seem significant, while the length of EC/EU membership and recent historical factors appear to be less so (hence the reference to 'deep culture').

The implications of these findings for the risks facing the EU are mixed. Someday, in historical retrospect, Europe's élite cosmopolitans may be seen to have been the vanguard which led the remainder of the public toward a more widespread European identity. Or they may simply continue their solitary march to a different drummer than that which is heard by other Europeans. It is enormously difficult to predict the future trajectory of public affect, though in the concluding remarks to this study it is argued that the former scenario may be more likely than the latter. The fact that many informants spoke of the effect of their experience as exchange students or working abroad on their sense of European identity certainly bodes well for the potential of winning hearts and minds, and thus of diminishing risks and resistance to the polity. On the other hand, the power of deep cultural factors over such identities suggests that they are less mutable. If there is a programmatic lesson here for Europhiles, it may be, first, that the extent to which identities can be shaped is partially limited, at least in the short term, by relatively inelastic structures of political culture. But, secondly, and paradoxically, there is simultaneously a space within which to act towards producing such identity shifts within individuals, and that the way to do so is by making the case for integration and, especially, by encouraging the expansion of direct transnational experiences.

The Meaning of 'Being European'

Earlier appearing political identities—chiefly nationalisms—have tended towards being monolithic, ethnos-based, and highly emotive in character. To determine whether European identifiers conceive of their identity in similar terms, or whether the identity represents something different entirely, data from several sources have been collected and are examined in this section. Table 15.3 presents a first look at the content of European identity, for those surveyed in Eurobarometer 27 (1987). Respondents were presented with the following prompt: ' "There are different ways of feeling European. Among the following [show list], which ones come close, as far as you are concerned, to the fact of being European?" (Several responses possible.) "And still looking at this list which one appears to you the most important?" (Only one response.)' The fourth column in Table 15.3 (labeled 'EU') presents the percentage responses for the entire sample of respondents. It is preceded by three columns which break down these totals by response to a (format two) question measuring the frequency with which the respondent thinks of himself or herself as European. The final column in the table measures the degree to which identity content responses vary by identification frequency. For each content item, the first row indicates the percentage of respondents making that choice at all (out

TABLE 15.3. *Content of European Identity, by European Identity Level*
(% with % choosing as most important in italic)

	Thinks of Self as European				
	Never	Sometimes	Often	EU	Cramer's V
End rivalries/	43.7	60.6	60.8	52.1	.17***
peace	*39.0*	*44.4*	*41.1*	*41.3*	.20***a
Shared	15.4	30.8	34.6	23/6	.20***
cultural	*7.5*	*12.5*	*13.8*	*10.3*	
traditions					
Religious	7.1	13.4	15.5	10.5	.11***
philosophic	*3.1*	*3.6*	*3.8*	*3.4*	
values					
Adventure	12.1	28.3	39.4	21.7	.25***
of European	*7.2*	*14.7*	*18.9*	*11.7*	
integration					
Freedom	37.4	50.9	42.7	42.9	.12***
of travel	*23.3*	*18.5*	*14.9*	*20.3*	
Geographical	25.3	14.9	14.3	20.1	.13***
fact only	*10.2*	*4.9*	*5.5*	*7.6*	
Other	0.4	1.4	2.1	1.0	.06***
than these	*0.2*	*0.4*	*0.9*	*0.4*	
None	6.7	0.5	0.6	3.7	.16***
of these	*9.5*	*1.0*	*1.2*	*5.1*	
N				10,241	

Source: Eurobarometer 27 (1987).
Notes: aThis Cramer's V value applies to all second-row ('most important') entries in this
table. * = p ≤ .05; ** = p ≤ .01; *** = p ≤ .001.

of three possible selections), with the second row showing the percentage
picking the item as the most important of the possibilities presented.

One interpretation of the data in this table is that they are suggestive of
a rather instrumental approach to the meaning of being European. The
identity would appear to be mostly about 'freedom of travel' and especially 'peace' for those responding to this question. More than half picked
'peace' as one of their choices, and more than 40 per cent called it the most
important aspect of being European. On the other hand, the qualitative,
non-instrumental aspects of European identity which might be supposed
to be prominent are not. For example, little support is given for the notion
of 'shared religious and philosophical values' being at the core of
Europeanness. 'Shared culture and way of life' does attract more agreement, but only at approximately the same levels as what might be

described as the minimalist and maximalist definitions of being European, respectively: that it is 'only a geographical fact', or that it is 'a great adventure in forming the United States of Europe'.

The instrumental effect is displayed more clearly and in a predictable pattern when the meaning variable is arrayed against the respondent's level of European identification. The 'peace' characteristic is rather impervious to levels of European identification (at least in the second-row, 'most important' entries), with roughly 40 per cent of those who never identify with Europe and about the same proportion of those who sometimes or often do so all saying that this is the most important aspect of being European. The same is true for the few respondents who see 'shared religious or philosophical values' as most important. For those choosing the remaining categories, however, the relationship between the two variables is far more articulated. The proportion of those picking 'shared cultural traditions' or the 'adventure of European integration' rises with the level of European identification. At the same time, the proportion of those selecting 'freedom of travel', 'geographical fact only', or 'none' of the offered choices is inversely related to levels of European identity.

The latter two relationships are probably indicative of a general lack of European identity among respondents selecting those responses. But the remaining relationships suggest an interesting pattern. Overall, it appears that 'peace' is the universally most popular meaning attributed to being European, and 'shared religious and philosophical values' is universally the least, but that choice of meanings beyond that is affected by the degree of identification, such that (per the instrumentalism effect discussed above) non- and sometime-identifiers mention 'freedom of travel' more often than do frequent identifiers. Among identifiers, on the other hand, the less material concerns of culture and politics become more prominent. With some exceptions, the first-row percentages follow the same pattern,[9] as do data from other Eurobarometer surveys.

Similar findings emerged from the 1998 Survey of European Identifiers (SEI), in which 'democracy' was selected as a very important aspect of being European by 88.2 per cent of that (very Europhile biased) sample, 'peace' by 82.8 per cent, and 'culture' by 71.7 per cent. Only 38.3 per cent rated 'standard of living' as highly, with 39.3 per cent finding 'way of life' very important, and 57.1 per cent so rating 'quality of life' (for all responses, $N = 209$–12). These figures once again suggest a values-oriented (as opposed to an instrumental) bias among European identifiers. Further evidence of this inclination is given by the written-in open

---

[9] Since these latter are reflective of up to three choices from the small handful of options, they are less readily interpretable. Nevertheless, they point in the same general direction as the second-row ('most important') figures.

responses to this question, in which 9.1 per cent (of 227 respondents) mentioned political ideas or ideals, 8.4 per cent referred to social security/solidarity, and 7.4 per cent listed diversity or tolerance.

This latter theme appears even more prominently in responses summarized in Table 15.4. Here, SEI respondents were asked in open-ended questions to define the meaning of their European, national, and regional identities. The first question, for example, asked 'What does being European mean to you? What words, ideas or feelings come to mind when you think of being European?'. Similarly phrased questions were posed with regard to national and regional identities. At the European level, by far the most popular response invoked themes of diversity, tolerance, and multiculturalism. The predominance of this theme becomes even more pronounced if the related ideas of 'multilingual culture' and 'openness' (listed separately on the table) are also combined with it. What is perhaps most remarkable about this finding is the irony of an identity built around a conceptual core of diversity and tolerance—characteristics precisely in opposition to those which historically have been the stuff of political identities.

In any case, a quick glance at Table 15.4 shows that for European identifiers, the European identity evokes values-related themes above others. For this same cohort, however, national and regional identities appear to be chiefly cultural phenomena (or, especially for the regional, non-existent), with a good deal of emotional content attached. This distinction was also clearly manifest in interview after interview of European identifiers, many of whom made overt reference to the cerebral nature of their European identities, as compared to the more emotion-laden sentiments associated with national and regional identity. A Portuguese informant described the character of her European identity in terms which are probably a bit too stark to be generally representative of those interviewed, but which nevertheless provide a good sense of the flavor of Europeanness even among those generally strongly committed to the identity. For her, she noted, 'Europe is something that rings a bell in your mind, but not in your heart; it doesn't have a spirit.'

These findings offer further evidence of the scope of the task facing would-be European 'nation'-builders. Whether the future will bring changes to the character of the identity is impossible to know, but for the present, Europe does not appear to enjoy the emotional enthusiasm—and the unquestioning loyalty such fervor often produces—with historically associated national identities. Instead, this is an identity which is rationally determined, the product of cognitive rather emotive processes, and therefore one which is heavily tied to its (perceived) achievements. Once again, this suggests that the path to a wider, and perhaps also deeper, sense

TABLE 15.4. *Meaning of European, National, and Regional Identities:*
Open Response Question

Response	% of Respondents Mentioning		
	European	National	Regional
Minimal			
Nothing/None (Active answer, not blank response	3.6	9.0	30.4
Shares space/Living in Europe/ Geographical proximity	2.0		
Values-Related			
Solidarity/Collectivism/Socialism	7.1	3.2	
Humanitarian values	5.6		
Diversity/Multiculturalism/Difference/ Tolerance/Exchange	27.4	4.8	8.3
Multilingual Culture	4.6		0.6
Openness/Open-mindedness	7.6		
Liberty/Freedom	7.1		
Democracy	8.1	4.2	
Togetherness/Unity/Community	14.2		
Part of a great idea/Project/Organization/ Necessary for future	7.6	4.8	
Political system/Political culture		7.4	
Instrumental			
Security/Peace/Co-operation	21.8		
Friends/Contacts/Family	6.6		5.4
Economic progress/Benefits/Development/ Euro	5.6		4.2
Standard of living	3.0		
Cultural			
Similar lifestyles/Culture	21.3	26.5	9.5
Similar/Common Morals/Ethics/Values	4.6		
Heritage/Tradition/Destiny	13.2	7.9	3.6
History/Common experiences	8.6	13.2	6.0
Language		12.7	
Pride/Shame/Emotion/Patriotism		20.1	7.7
Home		8.5	10.7
Natural/Urban beauty/Energy/ Opportunities		3.2	9.6
Warmth/Acceptance/Comfort			5.4
Identity			5.4
N	197	189	168

Source: Survey of European Identifiers, 1998: up to three responses coded.

of shared identity for Europe—and thus to greater insurance against risks and resistance—runs through the perception on the part of its body politic that it delivers something worthwhile. Whether or not this is good news for Europhiles probably depends on the balance of achievements and failures which the future brings to the European polity. Will monetary integration succeed and be seen to enhance the prosperity of Europeans? Will Europe do a better job of responding to the next Bosnia? These are, of course, questions which cannot answered be prospectively, though they do point to the nature and the magnitude of the task at hand.

But even under the most favorable of outcomes, the idea of an emotive European identity modeled on nationalisms of the past seems a very dubious proposition. Indeed, perhaps the more interesting question concerns the degree to which Europe may not be so uniquely challenged in this regard, in the contemporary political culture of developed countries. In Europe today, neither nationalism (Dogan 1994) nor religion inspire the emotional punch, the loyalties, nor the behavioral imperatives of earlier times. Perhaps it is the case that the challenge of European identity is unique only to the extent that historical inertia gives older identities the small advantage of residual emotional content that any newer identity would not, by definition, possess. But such an advantage may be rapidly diminishing in a postmodern world where all the verities of the past have instead become variables—the 'melting of all solids'—a possibility explored further in this essay's conclusion (see also Green forthcoming).

The Depth of European Identification

'Who will die for Europe?', asks Anthony Smith (1995: 139), and it is well that he should. Though the question puts the matter in its most extreme construction, it nevertheless directs attention to a critical aspect of European identity. We know, that is, that some Europeans identify as such, but what is the depth of that identity? Answering this question ultimately requires reference to measures of sacrifice, even if 'the ultimate sacrifice' is not necessarily its best measure. Again, there is both quantitative and qualitative data upon which to draw in measuring the depth of European identification. The analysis proceeds in the direction of increasing specificity, beginning with discussion of the overall importance of the European integration project, and then moving to willingness to make national and then personal sacrifices of various types for Europe and for fellow Europeans.

Eurobarometer 30 (1988) asked respondents to select those political and cultural institutions and movements of our day worthy of the greatest concern. The text of the question read: ' "In your opinion, in this list (show list) which are the great causes which nowadays are worth the trouble of taking risks and making sacrifices for?" (Several answers possible.)' Included in the list were such items as human rights, world peace, freedom of the individual, the struggle against racism, and others. Table 15.5 presents frequency distributions from the survey, again arrayed against the identity frequency variable, for three of the prompted responses: 'defense of my country', 'my religious faith', and 'the unification of Europe'. The data in the table indicate that, of the three causes, Europeans still hold national defense as most worthy of taking risks and making sacrifices (though, interestingly, less than 30 per cent of respondents are of this opinion, even for this most popular cause). Approximately 15 per cent of respondents believe European unification to be worthy of risks and sacrifices, a figure which, incidentally, is equivalent in size to the cohort labeled 'core identifiers' above. While 15 per cent is not a lot relative to the whole of the sample, it may be considered a rather remarkable amount for a movement which is simultaneously young, controversial, sometimes threatening to the established political order, and generally rather vaguely specified.

TABLE 15.5. *Causes Worth Risks and Sacrifices, by European Identity Level (%)*

	Thinks of Self as European				
	Never	Sometimes	Often	EU	Cramer's V
Defense of my country	29.8	30.8	25.8	29.5	.04***
My religious faith	17.8	19.5	19.7	18.8	.02*
The unification of Europe	10.0	21.2	33.2	18.1	.22***
N					11,379

Source: Eurobarometer 30 (1988).
Notes: * = p ≤ .05; ** = p ≤ .01; *** = p ≤ .001

Relative to the popularity of the other causes, moreover, the figure becomes even more impressive. Roughly the same number of those sampled believed Europe as worthy of risk and sacrifice as their religion, and only about 11 per cent more respondents held that opinion with respect to their country than with regard to Europe. Considering the centuries and even millennia of tradition (and traditions of sacrifice, at that) associated with faith and country, these are remarkable comparisons indeed. Given the rather diminished figures for all three measures, however, the headline emerging from Table 15.5 may have less to do with the relative depth of European identity than the degree to which contemporary Europeans resist all such calls on their health and wealth. In any case, turning to the figures broken down by identity level, it is not surprising to find that the degree of identification with Europe has little effect on the extent to which respondents think risks or sacrifices are worthwhile for their country (V = .04) or their religious faith (V = .02), but has enormous implications for their opinion with respect to European unification (V = .22). Indeed, more than three times the proportion of those who frequently think of themselves as European support risk or sacrifice for European unification (33.2 per cent) than do those who never think of themselves as European (10.0 per cent), as might be expected. And, just as might also be expected, 55.3 per cent of the generally Europhile sample of SEI respondents also described European unification as worthy of risk and sacrifice.

The identity depth measure discussed so far is silent with respect to who or what would be taking or making the posited risks and sacrifices for each cause—it simply asks whether the cause is worthy of risk and sacrifice as a general proposition. A more specific scenario places the respondent's country in the role of active agent, and also specifies a particular need to be addressed. The following question was posed in Eurobarometers 8 (1977), 10 (1978), 15 (1981), and 24 (1985): 'If one of the countries of the European Community other than our own finds itself in major economic difficulties, do you feel that the other countries including [R's country], should help it or not?' Responses to these questions display a remarkable willingness to sacrifice on behalf of other Europeans—that is, a depth of European identity—to the extent that more than 80 per cent in every survey answered this question affirmatively, and, astonishingly, nearly 90 per cent did so in two of the four surveys (the proportion answering affirmatively in the four surveys was 88.2, 87.7, 83.2, and 85.3 per cent, respectively). There are national variations on these levels, of course, but these do not obscure the more remarkable finding that support for the notion of assisting other countries is quite robust, in no member state ever falling below two-thirds of the sample, and on average approaching 90 per cent. This consistent mean at so high a level is rare among surveyed opinion questions in general, but is perhaps even more astonishing for a question involving sacrifices.

A third level of specificity regarding the depth of identity brings the issue directly to the respondent, testing his or her willingness to personally sacrifice for Europe or Europeans. Three question prompts were employed across Eurobarometers 5 (1976), 10 (1978), 13 (1980), 15 (1981), 18 (1982), and 24 (1985) to generate the data in Table 15.6, all concerning willingness

TABLE 15.6. *Various Questions Regarding Personal Sacrifice, by Nationality (% agreeing)*

	France	Belgium	Neth	Germany	Italy	Lux	Denmark	Ireland	UK	Greece	Spain	Portugal	EU	Cramer's V	N
EB 5 (1976) Accept a European tax voted by the EP?	84.8	87.4	84.6	76.5	88.9	92.3	55.7	80.3	57.5	—	—	—	77.0	.28***	7,001
Sacrifice (e.g. taxes for another EU country?															
EB 10 (1978)	41.8	34.8	68.3	36.1	72.4	41.9	51.2	45.4	39.0	—	—	—	48.3	.30***	7,305
EB 15 (1981)	32.4	24.5	57.0	36.9	73.6	56.6	47.8	46.3	38.8	60.4	—	—	46.5	.33***	18,040
EB 18 (1982)	34.6	24.4	46.9	38.7	56.2	39.0	32.5	26.7	24.1	45.2	—	—	38.1	.23***	8,374
EB 24 (1985)	44.5	26.3	57.1	40.3	69.6	54.4	34.9	34.7	41.5	52.6	48.4	47.5	48.1	.23***	10,290
EB 13 (1980): Okay for use of taxes to aid neediest regions of															
own country	89.2	84.0	89.1	85.0	90.3	95.2	90.0	93.5	86.4				87.8	.07***	179,478
EU	30.6	30.6	54.3	60.2	44.8	44.1	24.6	27.5	19.0				38.5	.31***	173,041

* = p ≤ .05; ** = p ≤ .01; *** = p ≤ .001; EB = Eurobarometer.

to pay a European tax. Clearly, the structure of the sacrifice and perhaps even the phrasing of the prompt affect the depth of sacrifice supported. The general European burden posited in Eurobarometer 5 generates much higher agreement than the specific and personal tax burden of the question asked in Eurobarometers 10, 15, 18, and 24. Moreover, these latter measures—which call for *personal* sacrifice in the form of additional *taxes*—are supported by about half the nearly 90 per cent reported above who favored the same sort of transnational aid by their *countries* for other EU countries struggling economically.

Close to 80 per cent agree with the first question in Table 15.6, though there is very wide variation across national frontiers (V = .28), ranging from 55.7 per cent in Denmark to 92.3 in Luxembourg (or 88.9 in the larger country of Italy). When the second prompt is employed, on the other hand, the agreement rate falls to a fairly consistent 46 to 48 per cent (Eurobarometer 18 is the one exception). Remarkably, this rate of agreement for the entire sample is mostly consistent despite enormous variance across countries (V ranges from .23 to .33), as well as within countries across the four surveys. Finally, the pairing of aid questions from Eurobarometer 13 provides an interesting comparative measure of the depth of European identity relative to national identities. Close to 90 per cent of respondents would be willing to pay taxes to aid needy regions of their own countries, and that figure is quite consistent across the countries sampled (V = .07). When asked to make the same sacrifice for needy regions of the EC, though, less than half as many (38.5 per cent) would agree to do so, though the variance between countries is extensive (V = .31), ranging from 19.0 per cent agreement in Britain to 60.2 per cent in Germany, more than three times the British commitment. In any case, according to these figures, the depth of European identification is clearly less than the national, by a vast degree.

The intersection of a European identity measure and an identity depth measure in the same survey is relatively rare, but the European Communities Studies of 1971 and 1973 support the intuitive supposition that the two phenomena are related. Of those who selected Europe as their first identity (Format One) in the 1971 survey, 27.4 per cent were definitely willing to make sacrifices for European unification, while 16.6 per cent of those choosing Europe as a second identity were so willing, and only 8.2 per cent of those who did not choose Europe first or second were willing to sacrifice (N = 7,016). In the 1973 survey, the analogous figures were 16.3, 13.6, and 6.2 per cent, respectively (N = 11,163).

A final and quite interesting collection of survey data is summarized in Table 15.7. This table presents the results of various tests of willingness to make sacrifices on behalf of various polities. The data thus provide an

excellent opportunity to examine identity depth in a context that is comparative in two dimensions: across types of sacrifice, and across beneficiaries of such sacrifice. The downside of the data is that it is derived from
the SEI instrument, and thus reflects the sentiments of mostly strong
Europhiles. While responses to these questions from a representative sample of Europeans would certainly be preferable, these data may at least
provide a sense of willingness to sacrifice for Europe at its current plausible limits. The data in Table 15.7 were gathered by asking SEI respondents
a set of four questions, repeated three times—once each with respect to the
respondent's country and region, and for Europe. For each of the twelve
resulting questions, respondents could check one of three boxes marked
'Not very willing', 'Possibly willing', or 'Very willing'. The questions
posed were:

What sort of sacrifices would you be willing to make for the sake of . . .
    . . . your country;
    . . . your region or province (e.g., Scotland, Bavaria);
    . . . Europe or the EU?
(1) . . . Accept a modestly lower standard of living to help raise the standard of
    living in poorer parts of . . .
        . . . your country?;
        . . . your province?;
        . . . Europe?
(2) . . . Pay additional taxes to ease a crisis in another . . .
        . . . province?;
        . . . community/town?;
        . . . European country?
(3) . . . Serve in a volunteer corps for a year?
(4) . . . Fight in a war in a time of crisis, or approve of a family member doing so?'

   Comparing first the four tests of willingness to sacrifice to one another,
it is largely the case that they descend in order of popularity, regardless of
which polity is in question, just as might be expected a priori based on the
ascending level of sacrifice these tests would be expected to entail for most
individuals. Of course, a more interesting question concerns what respondents would be willing to sacrifice on behalf of one polity relative to what
they would give for another. Based on the figures in Table 15.7, the answer
to this question can be interpreted in at least three ways, all providing valid
and interesting commentary on the relative depth of competing identities.
   In the first instance, it might be noted that the depth of national identity still trumps its regional and continental rivals. But, this is true in only
three of the four tests when looking at the 'very willing' category, and in
only two of the four tests when looking at combined 'possibly' and 'very
willing' categories. Thus, secondly, one might just as well note the relative

TABLE 15.7. *Willingness to Sacrifice for Regional, National, and European Polities, by Type of Sacrifice* (%)

Polity	Lower Standard of Living			Pay Additional Taxes			Serve in a Volunteer Corps			Fight in a War during Crisis		
	Not very willing	Possibly willing	Very willing	Not very willing	Possibly willing	Very willing	Not very willing	Possibly willing	Very willing	Not very willing	Possibly willing	Very willing
Region	26.7	47.6	25.7	28.2	47.2	24.6	41.6	38.9	19.4	65.6	25.4	8.5
Country	15.2	51.0	33.8	14.4	53.6	32.1	34.8	38.8	26.4	54.4	30.1	15.5
Europe	19.6	50.3	30.2	18.6	50.5	30.4	31.3	39.5	29.2	52.3	33.2	14.6

Source: Survey of European Identifiers, 1998. $N = 189–209$.

depth of European identity evident in these figures, especially considering again that the European polity is weak, young and controversial. That nearly 15 per cent of respondents would be very willing to fight a war on behalf of Europe in a crisis is quite noteworthy, though it must be remembered again that this is a highly biased sample. Finally, perhaps the most interesting conclusion to be drawn from the table is the relative equality of the three polities when it comes to respondents' willingness to make sacrifices. In particular, members of the SEI sample are equally inclined to sacrifice on behalf of Europe as for their countries, while the depth of identity with respect to their regions is lower, but not vastly so.

As a final data source, interviewed informants (again, largely but not exclusively Europhiles) were also queried on the depth of their identification with Europe. The verbal prompt put to them read:

People are often asked to make certain sacrifices for the benefit of their country, such as paying taxes to aid a less developed region, serving in a volunteer corps, or even fighting in a war during a time of crisis. How would you feel about being called upon to make similar sacrifices at the European level?

The initial response of many informants to this question ran along the lines of 'We are already doing so', either in the form of VAT or other taxes, or perhaps preparation sacrifices in the run-up for monetary union. Whether or not informants made that comment, however, they almost always agreed in principle with the idea of making sacrifices on behalf of Europe. There were certainly some who did not wish to do so, including the Dane who said 'I would probably prefer to make sacrifices in Denmark. I'm still not European enough', or the ardent British Euroskeptic (and nationalist) who said 'I would rather go to jail', and seemed to mean it. On the other hand, there were those who were equally enthusiastic about the prospect of paying dues to Europe. A Portuguese informant said 'I would do it without any problem. I hope to have the chance to do this.' A British businessman pronounced his preference for making sacrifices at the European level over the national, including fighting in a European army, or paying taxes to Brussels (while noting that he felt sure his sentiments were unusual among the European public generally, let alone the British).

These represent the two extremes of responses to this question. Yet there was little real variation—most expressed a general willingness to make sacrifices on behalf of the European polity, as did the Spanish informant who said he had no problem with European taxes and the like, noting, 'I could make the same sacrifices for Brussels as for Madrid.' The typical responses did not give the impression that informants were necessarily motivated by affection for Europe, however (though that sentiment may have been preventing a knee-jerk rejection of the prospect of sacrifices for Europe). Rather, informants projected a sense of fair play which caused them to recognize that benefits must be paid for, regardless of the polity providing them. For example, one Italian informant said, 'I am a citizen and am receiving benefits, so I would have no problem contributing.' The only caveats to this general willingness to sacrifice in return for benefits provided were concerns expressed about the implementation of programs associated with those sacrifices. Informants wanted a Europe which made demands of them to be efficient, democratic, and fair. A Swede, for example, said 'I would have no problem if all others made the same sacrifices, because I believe in the European idea', while an Irish informant noted that 'It would depend on what Europe is doing in return.' If Europe were providing quality services, that is, she would have no problem making the necessary sacrifices to support them.

Some rejected military service in principle, regardless of the polity in question, while others had pragmatic concerns about the notion of a European military (e.g. language incompatibility, non-democratic political institutions making deployment decisions, relations with national service). There were, again, the extremes of those who rejected the idea completely, such as the British informant who simply found the idea too foreign from his notion of military service, and those who actively embraced it, such as the Belgian who said 'I would be glad to serve Europe', or the French student who was already trying to fulfill his national military/civil commitment in European institutions. Generally, however, the idea of European military service was approached with the same pragmatic detachment that characterized most responses to questions of sacrifice for Europe. It seemed fair and necessary in principle, and therefore informants understood the need to contribute, just as they did within their national communities. Their only stipulation was that such sacrifices met their definitions of good governance (also applied universally to all polities): efficiency, fairness, and democracy.

As with so many of the other dimensions discussed in this chapter, assessing the depth of European identification requires making interpretive judgements of the data, particularly of the 'Is the glass half-full or half-empty?' variety. Perhaps more so than elsewhere, however, these findings provide rather positive indications with respect to the welfare of the European polity. That is, there appears to be more depth to the sense of shared European community than might otherwise be expected, even when personal financial sacrifices are at stake—though of course still less than for the nation. Yet even among the Europhiles the sense of non-emotive rationality surrounding such attitudes is palpable. Many Europeans seem to see these sacrifices in terms of mutual responsibilities which are required to maintain the political systems of which they are a part, and perhaps little more. Still, the above-mentioned comparison made in Eurobarometer 13 of willingness to sacrifice for another part of the country against willingness to sacrifice for another part of Europe seems particularly telling. Arguably, these questions measure respondents' sense of the boundaries of shared community. Presumably, more would sacrifice for another part of their region or city than the nearly 90 per cent who would sacrifice for another part of their country. Likewise, it would be reasonable to expect that fewer would sacrifice for another part of the world than the nearly 40 per cent who would sacrifice for another part of Europe. And, thus, while not nearly as many as for their respective nations, a considerable proportion of Europeans nevertheless see themselves as 'in it together' enough to make a personal sacrifice to aid others in what is perceived to be a shared community.

European Identity in Perspective

This volume attends to the state of the evolving European state. In the present chapter, it has been argued that no polity may expect to survive and prosper long on a foundation weakened by the absence of strong affective ties to its citizenry. Europe has been blessed to be born, grow, and prosper during the best of times, but such peace and prosperity are no more a given than is the EU itself, and arguably the latter's fortunes are dependent on the former. It is relatively easy to support (or tolerate) a political community in flush times, but what happens when circumstances are more challenging, 'in times of crises, such as depressions, wars, and internecine conflicts, when perceived benefits may recede to their lowest ebb' (Easton and Dennis 1969: 63)? In this regard, it is instructive to ask both why the idea of France survived occupation, and why the Soviet Union did not survive the will to coerce its maintenance. A meaningful answer in both cases must resort to notions of diffuse popular support generally, and of identity particularly. What, then, will be Europe's fate should it encounter such a crisis, especially given the already well-demonstrated capacity of national politicians and press to use the EU as a whipping boy for all manner of domestic maladies? In the end, it is the bulwark of popular identity and other forms of diffuse support which must provide Europe its insurance policy against such risks.

   Is such a policy in effect? Or has it lapsed, its premiums long unpaid? The foregoing empirical discussions have demonstrated that there *are* 'Europeans' in Europe, though such identification is limited in several dimensions. It has been shown that this circumscribed identity appeals to rather a small (and probably static in size) segment of the population, at least with substantial potency, and that the membership of this segment is disproportionately élite and cosmopolitan. Moreover, even when European identity does exert an appeal to individuals, it is to their minds and not their hearts, with all the behavioral consequences attendant on an entreaty limited to the cognitive, and contingent upon reciprocal performance. Finally, there appears to be some depth to European identification, but not at the same level as the national, and—again—not necessarily based on emotional content.

In short, a European identity exists, but within limitations which make it nearly unrecognizable by lights of the political identities which have populated the landscape over (at least) the past two centuries. This much is clear. Precisely how these characteristics should best be interpreted, however, is far less evident. One possibility is that Europe presents political analysts with a *sui generis* case, a beast unlike any other in the polity jungle. According to this interpretation, European identity does not appear to be growing, for example, because the EU itself is *not* growing. It will continue to be what it is, and comparisons to nation-states or other political communities are not illuminating.

Another possibility—perhaps no more or less probable based on the evidence at hand—posits just the opposite conclusion. Here, the often fruitful likening of Europe's progression to the nation-state analogue is extended, and today's EU is simply a snapshot of a polity on a developmental trajectory, at perhaps the same location as France or Britain several centuries back. Such a perspective reasonably asks that we give Europe adequate time to develop, while simultaneously noting the fantastic strides it has made in fifty years, a very short period by historical standards.

There is a third possibility, as well, and one which is arguably the most likely of the three. James Caporaso (1996) has looked at the European Union and asked whether it ought to be viewed as a postmodern 'state', with all the shifting structural complexity such an appellation implies. It is a very good question, and one which might also be asked of the European 'nation'. By such lights, then, Europe would become neither the aberration nor the laggard among political communities, but rather the harbinger of a world in which identities are multiple and contextual, shallow and shifting, rationally contingent, values-driven, and drained of emotional content. Europe's present—this 'marketization' of political identity—may thus preview the fate of other postmodern polities, especially after one or two iterations of generational replacement have depleted their populations of those raised under the tutelage of powerful nationalisms. Of course, such a scenario does not address the diffuse support dilemma any more than does the first, or (in the short run) the second. It only evens the field, leaving all political communities (and probably other, non-political associations as well) in the same unhappy boat, on the same unpredictable seas, seeking one and all to capture popular affect as conditions permit.

In the end, any of these projections may prove accurate. Europe may be wholly unlike traditional political communities, or it may be slowly moving in the same direction they have traveled. Or perhaps the opposite is true, and these others will move toward Europe's model. In terms of the welfare of the European polity, it hardly matters, except for the long-term prognosis of the second model. Otherwise, though, Europe remains in any of these scenarios a polity at risk.

VI

Policy-Making: Challenges in a Changing European Union

16

EU Trade Policy: The Exclusive versus Shared' Competence Debate

SOPHIE MEUNIER AND KALYPSO NICOLAÏDIS

Introduction

As the European Union enters the new millennium, it will face institutional and policy challenges that might destabilize its fragile institutional status quo. The Amsterdam Treaty can be interpreted mostly as a stop-gap compromise, which postponed major institutional reforms that will, at some point, become unavoidable. This is particularly true in the case of trade policy—the oldest, and one of the most successfully integrated policy sectors in the EU.

From its very creation, the European Community had spoken in international trade negotiations with a single external voice.[1] The principles of supranational competence over trade matters and unity of external representation in trade negotiations sharply distinguished the Common Market from other preferential trading arrangements, such as the European Free Trade Association. Recently, however, member states have started to question this transfer of sovereignty to the supranational level, especially with respect to the new trade issues of services and intellectual property. In 1994, the European Court of Justice introduced the caveat that the Community and the member states actually shared competence in these areas. The 1997 Amsterdam Treaty further reinforced these restrictions to transfers of sovereignty in the realm of trade by allowing member states to decide what competence to delegate on a case-by-case basis at the outset of a negotiation. This move could create the European version of the American fast-track procedure of delegation of trade authority, with all

---

[1] For an overview of the issue, see Meunier and Nicolaïdis (1999) and Johnson (1998). This chapter directly builds on the arguments and historical narrative first presented in Meunier and Nicolaïdis (1999).

the havoc and uncertainty, as well as political benefits, associated with it. It is worth asking whether this development is likely to serve the interests of the EU.

More generally, trade policy is a critical case of the risks, resistance, and reforms faced today by the European Union. It is in the area of trade that member states have accepted, for the longest time, to pool their sovereignty and delegate representation. The same reasoning should continue to apply today as the EU needs to deal with an ever-expanding trade agenda. If no reform of the institutions and decision-making procedures can be implemented in the realm of trade, then reform cannot be implemented anywhere. Yet institutional reform is crucial for the credibility and survival of the European Union as a world actor, especially in light of new EU commitments to a substantive Common Foreign and Security Policy. How can the EU be expected to start speaking with one voice in the controversial realm of foreign policy if it has stopped doing so in the traditionally easier realm of trade?

This chapter starts from the premise that the policy equilibrium established during the Amsterdam revision of the Treaty is unlikely to be sustainable in the face of several upcoming challenges. These include the relaunching of multilateral trade negotiations under the aegis of the World Trade Organization (WTO), including the unsuccessful start of the 'Millennium Round' in Seattle in November 1999; the expected enlargement of the EU to some of its Eastern neighbors; and the proliferation of bilateral and plurilateral agreements between the EU and its trading partners. In light of this new trade agenda, the EU's internal coordination and legitimation process is bound to become even more complex and demanding as new actors become concerned by trade negotiations. What risks will these challenges pose to EU trade policy? How should the trade policy-making process be reformed in order to address these challenges? What might be the consequences of failure to implement any institutional change?

Clearly, the institutional machinery associated with trade policy has always been geared towards striking a balance between member-state control and unity of representation. We argue that this balance should not only be maintained, but control by member states and participation by non-state actors should be strengthened, for normative reasons—democratic accountability remains at the national level for the foreseeable future—and for strategic reasons—the bargaining power of the EU decreases if outsiders believe the Commission, an unaccountable body, is free to agree to what it wants. At the same time, unity of representation *vis-à-vis* the outside world is more necessary than ever before. In order to square this circle, internal debates prior and during negotiations need to be more transparent and binding for the Commission. As a quid pro quo, the Commission's authority should be increased at the ratification stage through systematic use of majority voting for *all* issues on the trade agenda.

The first section of this chapter presents the different modes of competence delegation in trade and examines the traditional rationales for sharing sovereignty over trade matters. Next, we explore the evolution of the delegation of trade competence in the EU from the Rome to the Amsterdam Treaties. The third section analyzes the upcoming challenges to EU trade policy institutions, with a special focus on the new multilateral negotiations and the Eastern enlargement, and hypothesizes on the potential consequences of failure to reform the institutions. In conclusion, we make some policy recommendations, while addressing the relationship between trade policy reform and democratic accountability.

Modes of Control and Allocation of Competence in Trade Policy

Who should speak for Europe? Our argument in brief is that the answer to the question depends on the stage of the negotiation and the kind of relationship established between the spokesperson and its principals. The debate over exclusive competence acts as a proxy for the real debate over such relationships. In examining the specific field of trade policy-making in the EU, we apply principal–agent theory to highlight and understand the stages of negotiation and respective modes of control, and the distinction between exclusive and shared competence in the EU.

Principal–Agent Theory and International Negotiations

The delegation of competence can be analyzed through the lenses of principal–agent theory (Pollack 1997*a*; Coglianese and Nicolaïdis 1998). This theory is relevant both to the why and how of delegation in any context where tasks are not conducted directly by their ultimate beneficiaries and shapers. Only recently has principal–agent theory been applied to the context of negotiations (Meunier and Nicolaïdis 1999; Mnookin *et al.* 1999). In short, delegation occurs when tasks are too complex or time consuming to be conducted by the principal, or when the presence of agents helps to make agreements stick. In the case of external EU negotiations, the 'why' question does not need much discussion. We are interested here in 'how' delegation occurs.

The theory starts from the premise that in any agency relationship, *agency costs* can be due to: (1) differences in interests between agents and principals; or (2) information asymmetries which come from the fact that agents usually know more about their task than their principals do, while principals usually know more about what they want accomplished. In the context of negotiations, agency costs occur because the negotiator knows more about the constraints of external negotiations while the principals know more about their bottom line (Nicolaïdis 1999). Agency costs also occur because the agent's interests might not be aligned with that of his or her principals, if for instance the fact of a deal matters more to the agent than its content. The prescriptive challenge is to create institutional arrangements to minimize such agency costs. This can be done through 'mechanisms of control'—for example, the different constraints under which agents must operate. It is important to note that such mechanisms are not neutral in the 'external game', as they can serve to signal to outside parties which concessions can be made. How these mechanisms operate is the key determinant for whether, or to what extent, the EU actually 'speaks with one voice'.

The Stages of Negotiation: Mandate, Representation, and Ratification

Any formalized negotiation involving agents negotiating on behalf of principals can be divided into four stages: (1) the design of a negotiation mandate; (2) the representation of the parties during the negotiations; (3) the ratification of the agreement once negotiated; and (4) the implementation and enforcement of the agreement once it is brought into force. Whether the Community is perceived to speak with 'one voice' is most relevant during the negotiations but is also affected by signals sent at the mandate stage and expectations created about the ratification stage. The agreement can of course still unravel at the enforcement stage, demonstrating that any apparent unity before that point was actually flawed, since one or several parties were not able to act on their commitment.[2]

What does this mean in the context of external EU negotiations? The conduct of trade policy in the EU can be seen as a two-tiered delegation, spelled out in Article 113, which was renumbered Article 133 by the Treaty of Amsterdam:

(1) in terms of substantive authority: delegation from the individual member states and their parliaments to the assembly of European states, acting collectively through the Council of Ministers;
(2) in terms of procedural authority: delegation from the Council of Ministers (principals) to the European Commission (agent).

---

[2] This situation has never occurred in the history of the EU, so we leave the enforcement stage aside.

Two fundamental questions emerge from this two-tier delegation of authority. How much control does each individual state retain over trade policy? How much control do the member states as a collective retain over its conduct by the Commission? At each of the stages of international negotiations mentioned above, the principals (in this case, the states, individually or collectively) use different procedures and mechanisms to bind or control their agent (the Commission) and limit its margin of manœuver throughout the negotiations:

Initial Mandate

The Commission has sole competence to elaborate proposals for the initiation and content of international trade negotiations. The key policy discussions take place in the 'Committee 113/133',[3] which examines and amends Commission proposals on a consensual basis, before transmitting them to the Committee of Permanent Representatives (COREPER) and subsequently the General Affairs Council, which then hands out a negotiating mandate to the Commission. In theory the mandate is agreed upon by qualified majority. We will say that control is exercised at this stage by adopting a more or less *flexible* mandate. This depends in turn on the complexity and sensitivity of the issue, as well as the degree to which national positions have been already shaped prior to the negotiations.

Ongoing Representation

Commission officials represent the Union under the authority of the Commissioner in charge of external economic affairs and conduct international trade negotiations, within the limits set by the Council's mandate. Member states are allowed to observe but not speak in WTO plenary sessions, although they are of course involved in much of the 'informal diplomacy'. We will say that control is exercised at this stage by granting more or less *autonomy* to the Commission through formal and informal channels.

Ratification

At the conclusion of the negotiations, the Council approves or rejects the trade agreement, in principle by qualified majority. The European Parliament has little say in this process; it is informed on an informal basis and consulted before ratification upon initiative of the Commission. We will say that control is exercised at this stage by reducing the Commission's *authority* and thus uncertainty of the member states' vote.

---

[3] 'Committee 113', named after Article 113(3), is composed of senior civil servants and trade experts from the member states as well as Commission representatives. It was renamed Committee 133 after the Amsterdam Treaty came into force.

TABLE 16.1. The Four Stages of Delegation

	Authorization (flexibility of the machine)	Representation (autonomy)	Ratification (authority)	Enforcement
Exclusive competence (Art. 113/133 and 235, EC Association Agreement)	113/133 Committee → Council (qualified majority)	Commission e.g. 'unity of representation' (ongoing informal consultation)	Council (formal: qualified majority); informal: veto at least by big states)	Commission (exclusive)
Mixed competence (Art. 113/133 EC in the WTO Arts. 113 and 235)	113 Committee → Council (unanimity) and member states	Commission (ongoing informal consultation) Some member-state involvement	Council (unanimity) and parliamentary ratification in each member state	Commission with delegated authority (in consultation)

Source: modified from Meunier and Nicolaïdis (1999).

In sum, flexibility (at the mandate stage), autonomy (during the negotiations) and authority (over ultimate ratification) can be seen as the three fundamental characteristics of the Commission's role as an agent of the member states in the international arena (Nicolaïdis 1999).

Exclusive versus Mixed Competence

The Commission negotiates on behalf of the member states under two types of legal framework: exclusive and mixed competence. In theory, the core difference between exclusive and mixed competence comes at the ratification stage. Mixed competence in trade simply means that delegation of authority is granted on an *ad hoc* basis for negotiation purposes rather than systematically. Individual member states retain a veto both through unanimity voting in the Council and through ratification by their own national parliament. Under exclusive competence, on the other hand, a qualified majority vote in the Council stands as ratification. So it would appear that exclusive competence implies that the EU speaks with one voice, that of the Commission, while mixed competence leads to a concert—or a cacophony!

In practice, the difference is more blurred. On one hand, exclusive competence does not guarantee a single voice. Powerful member states still exercise an informal veto both at the mandate and the ratification stages, to the extent that the Luxembourg compromise extends to the trade area. Conversely, member states have managed to speak with one voice in areas of mixed competence or common foreign policy (as exemplified by 95 per cent of the decisions taken in common in the United Nations or the negotiations over association agreements with Eastern and Central European countries). The principle of unity of representation by the Commission is valid under both configurations, even while in both cases individual member states usually seek to reduce Commission autonomy to the extent tolerated by their partners. Nevertheless, the expression of dissent is dampened, the incentives for seeking compromise increased, and the role of the Commission enhanced in areas of exclusive competence.

Thus, when we ask 'who should speak for Europe' we need not assume that the answer is unequivocally linked to the technical issue of competence. The question arises whatever the configuration. But, as we will now see, this is how the debate has come to be framed in the last decade.

As we go through our historical narrative, we must differentiate between tiers of delegation. For the first tier of delegation from member states to the Union, formal competence does matter, as it determines national veto power at a minimum in the Council and at a maximum through national parliamentary ratification. For the second tier of delegation from the Council to the Commission, the core trade-off is between unity of representation during the negotiations and constraints imposed at the mandate and ratification stages. Conceptually, we need to think of flexibility, autonomy, and authority as variables that can be traded off irrespective of the formal competence arrangement. For instance, mandates handed down by the Council have traditionally been very flexible, not least because the resort to consensus has forced states to agree on the smallest common denominator. Some insiders argue that this is in part the root of the problem: it is because the Commission is so 'free' at the outset that it must 'pay' in terms of authority later. Similarly, if member states feel that they have lost control of the Commission during the negotiations, there will be a higher likelihood of difficulties at the ratification stage. It is with an eye to these trade-offs that we now turn to a historical overview of the issues.

The Evolution of Trade Competence in the EU

Trade policy came under supranational competence from the very beginning of the European Community, which was originally founded as a common market. Internally, it meant that barriers to trade between the member states had to be abolished. Externally, it meant that trade policy had to be integrated—mostly through a common external tariff and a unified external representation.

Supranational Competence in Trade: From Theory to Practice

When the founders asked themselves 'Who should speak for Europe?' their answer was in theory straightforward, but in practice quite ambiguous. In theory the fact that external trade fell under the category of 'exclusive competence' seemed to mean that the Community would indeed speak with one voice. In practice, however, this is one area of exclusive competence where member states retained a great amount of control over the Commission. The member states initially 'won' that battle on two counts. For one, Committee 113 had a competitor at the outset, namely the trade incarnation of the COREPER, which would have meant that member-state input into trade negotiations would primarily be controlled by national delegates living in Brussels. Committee 113, on the other hand, was staffed by representatives from the capitals, less prone to 'capture' by Brussels 'ideology'. By the 1970, Committee 113 had established itself as the sole forum for trade decision-making, enshrining direct input from the capitals (Johnson 1998). Second, it was unclear at the outset who should chair and coordinate the meetings of the Committee, the member states (through the Council) or the Commission. In the end the former solution prevailed, again ensuring greater control of the agenda by the member states (Johnson 1998).

As with other areas of EU policy-making, the gap between theory and practice has been the greatest with regards to voting procedures. Although qualified majority is the official voting rule governing trade policy decisions, the *modus operandi* has proven more complex. First, unanimity was used during the initial trade negotiations in which the EC participated, the Dillon Round and Kennedy Round of GATT. According to the original Treaty, the Council of Ministers was to take trade policy decisions unanimously until January 1966, the end of the transitory period. Qualified majority voting would have been automatically instituted after this date, had De Gaulle's 'empty chair' crisis of 1965 not triggered the 'Luxembourg compromise,' according to which a state can veto a decision otherwise taken according to qualified majority if vital national interests are at stake. The 1985 Single European Act restored the primacy of majority voting. In practice, however, member states have always managed to reach consensus on a common text and at the ratification stage, as with most other areas of policy-making in the EU. But as we will see, it does matter that discussions are held in the Council 'under the shadow of the vote'. It is worth noting that not only trade negotiations but also EU decisions on trade sanctions fall under qualified majority voting. The Maastricht Treaty explicitly formalized this in its revisions to Article 228.

Challenges to the EU's Exclusive Competence in Trade

During the two decades following the Treaty of Rome, the Commission successfully negotiated on behalf of its members two major trade rounds under GATT, as well as a host of bilateral trade agreements. The emergence of new issues onto the international trade agenda in the mid-1980s, however, prompted the member states to question the clear foundations of the Community's trade competence. The 1986 Uruguay Round was designed, in part, to negotiate over three categories of 'new issues': intellectual property rights, trade-related investment measures, and services.[4] The question of trade delegation in the EU came to be framed as follows: who, of the Commission or the member states, was responsible for negotiating these issues? Several member states, reluctant to give up forever entire new sectors of their trade policy, insisted on being granted their own competences with respect to the 'new issues', arguing that these were not covered under the definition of trade given in the Treaty of Rome.

Were new issues actually covered by Article 113? If not, would this not mean they fell under mixed competence? And if they did, should member states not have a greater say in their negotiation? On one hand, the term 'commercial policy' was not defined in the Treaty of Rome, thereby suggesting a broad coverage. On the other hand, Article 113 provides illustrations of the 'uniform principles' on which the policy is to be based and many would follow Michael Johnson, former UK President of Committee 113, in arguing that 'these examples were understood early on as restricting the coverage of Article 113 to trade in goods and related issues such as the operation of industrial standards' (Johnson 1998).[5] Examples include 'changes in tariff rates, the conclusion of tariff and trade agreements, the achievement of uniformity in . . . measures to protect trade such as those to be taken in the event of dumping or subsidies' (Article 113(1)). Indeed these all fit the trade-in-goods paradigm. But the list also includes 'the achievement of uniformity in measures of liberalization'—a term that would seem to encompass liberalization of imports of banking services as

---

[4] Services in particular, ranging from telecommunications to professional accreditation, included areas that had traditionally fallen under domestic jurisdiction and where concerns about externalities and consumer protection were generally more acute than for trade in goods.

[5] Johnson adds '(other) commercial matters such as finance and services were clearly understood to remain within the competence of the individual member states' (1998: 8).

well as typewriters! In short, anything could be read into the texts them-selves.

The issue of competence was not resolved at the outset of the negoti-ations, which led to a prolonged debate as to how negotiations should proceed. In the end, a compromise was found between negotiating and legal imperatives: it was agreed that the Commission should conduct the negotiations on all aspects of the round. Some have argued that the Commission had actually more margin of manœuver in the new issues because it was not bound by the traditional procedures laid out in Article 113. We believe that the Commission, indeed, managed to have a great deal of autonomy in these realms during the round, but only because the new issues were so 'new' and complicated.

Instead, the dispute over internal competence crystallized during the Uruguay Round over the EC-US 'Blair House Agreement' on agriculture. This was paradoxical since this agreement had nothing to do with the 'new issues'. The Blair House deal was negotiated in November 1992 by an autonomous Commission after six years of deadlock in the agricultural talks (Woolcock and Hodges 1996; Meunier 1998). When US negotiators leaked details of the agreement, France denounced the Commission's abuse of power and declared its absolute opposition to the deal. After sev-eral months of intense lobbying, France eventually rallied several member states (including Germany) around its position. After difficult exchanges with the USA, the agreement was eventually renegotiated partially, with symbolic concessions to France's position. Nevertheless, the Blair House crisis represented a turning-point in the delegation of negotiating author-ity to the supranational representatives, seriously putting into question the informal flirtation with majority rule and increased autonomy of the negotiators that had started to prevail (Meunier 2000).

The issue of competence arose more formally during the Uruguay Round on two fronts. First, who would ratify the final agreement? After heated debates, both the Council President and the External Trade Commissioner signed the Final Act of the Round on 15 April 1994 on behalf of the Community, while representatives of each member state signed in the name of their respective governments. In a half-way house between mixed and exclusive competence, individual member states asserted their competence symbolically, but without requiring parliament-ary ratification[6] (Arnull 1996). A second controversy erupted over the question of membership in the WTO, itself an outcome of the Uruguay Round.[7] Again in a spirit of compromise, the Commission suggested that

---

[6] Although some states chose to undergo such ratification.

[7] This question constituted an unavoidable legal challenge for the EC, even though the rest of the world left it up to the Europeans to decide how this would be settled. The EC

the member states become contracting parties in the WTO, provided that they accepted the principle of unitary EC representation and thus reaffirmed exclusive competence. The member states all but agreed that they should be the members, but they were now wary of giving the Commission free rein during the negotiations.

In order to solve the competence dispute, the Commission decided to bring the issue to a head. If member states were not going to compromise politically, perhaps their objection could be overruled legally. This decision was not without controversy inside the Commission, where Legal Services and the Directorate General for External Affairs (DG 1) had differing assessments about their chance of success in the legal sphere.[8] The 'optimists' prevailed, however, and in April 1994, the Commission asked the European Court of Justice for an 'advisory opinion' on the issue of competence. The optimists believed that the judges would back the Commission's stance and confirm that the scope of exclusive competence extended to new issues.

The Council and eight member states opposed the Commission's reasoning.[9] As we have argued elsewhere, member states picked their sides in the competence debate as a function of their preferences along two dimensions, economic interest and ideological bias (Meunier and Nicolaïdis 1999). France was at the helm of the 'sovereignty' camp mostly for ideological reasons, with new concerns over national sovereignty in the wake of the almost disastrous referendum on the ratification of Maastricht in 1992 and a growing mistrust *vis-à-vis* the Commission as a result of the Blair House episode. The United Kingdom, traditionally one of the most pro-liberalization states in the EU, opposed the formal expansion of Community competence to the 'new issues' in trade out of a traditional ideological bias against any expansion of supranational authority. Germany resisted transfers of sovereignty on ideological grounds, mostly because German regulators were highly protective of their powers. It can also be argued that Germany was less secure about its competitive position regarding services than France and the UK and therefore less supportive of the liberal stance taken by the Commission. Finally, countries

had never formally substituted the member states in GATT, whose creation preceded that of the Community. Since the GATT was only an 'agreement' with signatories but no members, the question of Community membership never formally arose (Denza 1996). For all practical purposes, therefore, the EC—represented by the Commission—had been accepted by the other GATT partners as one of them. Moreover, formally replacing the member states by the EC could have a cost, since the individual voting rights of member states in GATT would give way to a single vote. Since GATT operated by consensus, however, this had more symbolic than practical significance.

[8] Private interview with EU Commission official, Apr. 1999.

[9] These countries were: Denmark, France, Germany, Greece, Netherlands, Portugal, Spain, UK.

motivated by sectoral concerns, such as Greece (shipping) and Portugal (textiles), preferred to keep their sovereignty over the new trade issues. On the other side of the spectrum, irrespectively of their economic competitiveness in services, countries with traditionally pro-integrationist stances—for example, Italy, Belgium, and Ireland—strongly backed the Commission. These countries, especially the smaller ones, recognized that without the negotiating umbrella of the whole Community, they were always at the mercy of the EU's big trade partners.

The Court knew that this dispute over trade competence was going to be a test-case of its approach to European external relations, and more generally European integration, in the post-Maastricht era. In their November 1994 opinion, the European judges confirmed that the Community had sole competence to conclude international agreements on trade in goods.[10] In a controversial move, however, they also held that the member states and the Community shared competence in dealing with trade in the 'new issues'.[11] More specifically, among these, only 'crossborder' trade in services, that is one of the 'modes of services delivery' according to the official jargon—counted as traditional trade.

Several legal scholars suggested that the judges could plausibly have gone the other way, ruling instead in favor of exclusive Community competence (Bourgeois 1995; Hilf 1995). We have identified elsewhere at least four arguments in favor of a more expansive reading of the Treaty of Rome (Meunier and Nicolaïdis 1999). First, the Court could have applied a requirement of consistency: external powers ought to be implied by internal powers. This had been the basis of its former jurisprudence.[12] With the application of the Single Market Program to the broadly uncharted field of services, the Single Act seemed to call for a similar scope expansion on the external front. Second, the Court could have argued in favor of adaptability, as it had in the past. Given the rapidity of changes in the world economy, not foreseen at the time of the Treaty of Rome, trade policy should retain a dynamic and evolutionary character. Third, on the substantive front, denying their character as trade issues stems from an

---

[10] Including agricultural products and products covered by the European Coal and Steel Community and Euratom treaties.

[11] Court of Justice of the European Communities, *Opinion 1/94*, 15 Nov. 1994, I–123. (1) The Community has sole competence, pursuant to Article 113 of the EC Treaty, to conclude the multilateral agreements on trade in goods. (2) The Community and its Member States are jointly competent to conclude GATS. (3) The Community and its Member States are jointly competent to conclude TRIPs.

[12] In case No. 22/70. *Commission* v. *Council*, the Court concluded that 'whenever Community law has created for the institutions of the Community powers within its internal system for the purpose of attaining a specific objective, the Community has authority to enter into the international commitments necessary for the attainment of that objective even in the absence of an express provision in that connection'.

outdated analytical understanding of the actual nature of services and intellectual property issues. In the post-Uruguay Round era it seems more than a little odd to deny the label of 'trade' to three of the four forms of services delivery across borders defined internationally in the General Agreement on Trade in Services (GATS) as constituting 'trade in services'. Finally, the fourth argument against the Court's judgment is a political one, appealing to the very nature of the European Union. By 1994, it could be argued, the Community had matured and acquired a real external personality. On the internal front, the Maastricht Treaty had created general expectations about the establishment of an international identity for the Union and a deeper coherence between external economic policies and foreign policy. On the external front, exclusive competence was consistent with the expectations of Europe's trading partners regarding its role and standing in multilateral negotiations. In short, the Court's opinion denied the EU a competence that the rest of the world already took for granted.

We see in this judgment one more piece of evidence that the ECJ's rulings reflect calculations over political acceptability (Rasmussen 1986; Weiler 1991; Burley and Mattli 1993; Alter 1998*b*). The European Court of Justice refrained from (re)establishing exclusive competence for new trade issues because of a change in its assessment of the weight given to sovereignty concerns by some member states in this area. The recapture of formal power by the member states was also part of a more general trend in the EU. In the aftermath of the Maastricht ratification debates, it had become clear that the member states were increasingly wary of further devolution of sovereignty to the supranational level. By making a ruling which respected the national governments' sovereign powers instead of promoting further European integration, the Court acted to preserve its own role in the EU's institutional edifice.

The extremely cautious wording of the decision leads us to believe that the Court was trying to suggest how trade policy could still be conducted efficiently under the status quo until politicians sorted out the issue themselves at a later time. In order to allow for the evolutionary nature of trade, the language of the Court was quite imprecise, leaving room for interpretation when future conflicts on 'new issues' arose. In effect, the Court sent the ball back to the politicians. To avoid future competence disputes, they would have to amend the treaty either by following the Court's opinion to enshrine this new sharing of sovereignty in the texts or by explicitly 'expanding' Community trade competence to include new issues.

The Court's ruling can be read as advocating the kind of trade-offs that we highlighted at the outset of this chapter. In effect, the Court reduced the *authority* of the Commission by creating uncertainty at the ratification stage. At the same time, however, the Court insisted that this conclusion should not jeopardize the principle of unity of representation during the negotiations. To achieve this result, it encouraged the adoption of a code of conduct designed to govern relationships between the member states and the Commission. This would, on one hand, reassure the member states as to their input during the negotiation, but at the same time enshrine Commission *autonomy* as the sole legitimate voice for the Community as a whole. Such a code of conduct was discussed and elaborated in the subsequent presidencies.

The Amsterdam Compromise and the Current Policy Equilibrium

The Commission was determined to use the opportunity of the 1996 Inter-Governmental Conference (IGC) to revisit the ruling of the Court on 'mixed competences'. It expected some help in this endeavor from the significant evolution in national positions regarding trade competence in the two years following the Court's judgment. The 'sovereignty' camp had shrunk from a majority to a minority, consisting of France, the UK, Denmark, Portugal, and Spain. By contrast, the 'expansionist' camp had gained considerable support with the reversal of the German trade authorities, to whom it seemed to have become clear that Germany had more to lose than to gain in keeping future agreements captive to the protectionist demands of Portugal or Spain. Greece and the Netherlands had also changed sides, the former as it switched strategies simply to obtain an exception for shipping, and the latter as it came closer to the Commission while taking over the presidency. In addition, the three new member states (Austria, Sweden, and Finland) were all firmly with the expansionists. Despite their growing numbers, however, the expansionists failed to create any sort of operational alliance as they sought to retain power over other institutional issues during the Amsterdam conference. The revision of Article 113 was not their top priority. Moreover, it appeared unrealistic to waste political capital on an issue where France and the UK were decidedly on the other side.

As the IGC negotiations were coming to a close, the sovereignty camp became willing to contemplate a compromise over the scope of competence in exchange for extensive exceptions and guarantees. In a late draft, the Dutch presidency proposed to extend the Commission's exclusive competence *post hoc* to the areas of which it had been in charge during the Uruguay Round: further negotiations in the services sectors covered under the General Agreement on Trade in Services (GATS) and the Trade-Related Aspects of Intellectual Property Rights (TRIPs) code would also continue to be under exclusive community competence. In essence, the Community would have exactly the same powers in trade over existing services that it had over trade in goods, with both the mandate and the adoption of the agreement being agreed to under qualified majority voting. At the same time, there would be no open-ended granting of authority for potentially new services sectors or new national measures that may become the object of external negotiations at a later stage. In addition, some member states insisted on the explicit inclusion of a series of exceptions to the new scope extension. The protocol thus proceeded to exclude maritime and air transport services and to reproduce extensively the broad exceptions stated in the WTO charter.[13]

At the end of the day, the proposed compromise had become fraught with so many exceptions, caveats, and the introduction of cumbersome control procedures that the Commission itself persuaded the Presidency to withdraw it. Even though the proposal represented a limited success on scope expansion, the Commission preferred the status quo—better to keep options open and gamble on a better future political climate in the Court as in the Council. The member states eventually agreed to a simple and short amendment to Article 113 (renumbered 133), allowing for future expansion of exclusive competence to the excluded sectors through a unanimous vote of the Council. The newly adopted paragraph 5 states that: 'the Council, acting unanimously on a proposal from the Commission and after consulting the European Parliament, may extend the application of paragraph 1 to 4 to international negotiations and agreements on services and intellectual property insofar as they are not covered by these paragraphs'.

Interpreting the Amsterdam Compromise

If anything, the Amsterdam compromise is simply a stop-gap measure—a recognition that in practice and in the long run, the Community will have to find a consistent basis for its negotiations in all areas of international trade. The result of future battles over competence is in no way predetermined, since, through the new Article 133(5), the scope of the Article can be extended permanently and generally, in relation to a named international institution or on a case-by-case basis. Organizations that deal with services and intellectual property issues are thus also covered. The Court could also review its opinion under better political auspices.

As it stands, everyone seems to agree that the Amsterdam compromise was a face-saver for the Commission. Members of the Commission tend

---

[13] Exceptions ranged from activities connected with the exercise of official authority or the participation of member states in the International Monetary Fund to measures adopted to protect the stability of the financial system or regarding citizenship, residence or employment on a permanent basis of third country nationals.

to downplay the magnitude of their defeat by pointing out that in practice they will continue to be the EU's single voice on all issues and that, whatever the legal basis, ratification always requires consensus. In the end, we believe that the Amsterdam compromise ought to be interpreted as a victory for the sovereignty camp. At a minimum, it is a statement that extension of Community competence should be the result of case-by-case political decisions rather than some uncontrollable spillover. It represents one among several examples of 'hybrid' decision-making procedures introduced at Amsterdam, falling between classical Community delegation and pure intergovernmental approaches (Moravcsik and Nicolaïdis 1998). These procedures need not be threatening if handled adequately.

Other interpretations view such 'ad-hocism' as a dangerous move towards multi-tier procedures and fragmentation in the external economic field. Legal scholars tend to view this result as anathema to the spirit of the Treaty since it allows for a broad-based expansion of competence without constitutional revision. Indeed, Community competence can now be extended to new issues (beyond those envisaged by the aborted compromise) without having to go through a formal revision of the Treaty. But is this such a bad result? It could be seen as a significant gain for the parties concerned with efficiency, such as the Commission, at least when compared with the situation prevailing under the Uruguay Round. In the most optimistic interpretation, this outcome could become an EU version of the American fast-track whereby member states decide at the beginning of a negotiation that the end result will be ratified on a qualified majority basis. This in turn gives added importance to the initial phase where the mandate is shaped. Discussions are likely to be more transparent, democratic, and broad-based since there is more at stake. The *flexibility of the mandate* may be reduced in such a context; but under our analytical framework, this may allow for greater autonomy and authority for the Commission down the road. Reasserting member-state control is quasi-impossible under permanent exclusive competence. This new provision may give greater flexibility to the Council, allowing it to revisit past decisions if necessary. Arguably, the very possibility of such flexibility—or the 'reversibility of delegation'—may make it more acceptable to delegate powers to the Commission in the first place (Coglianese and Nicolaïdis 1998).

In the end, the Commission can choose not to invoke the new provision under Article 133(5) and go into the negotiations without an explicit extension of exclusive competence, as it did during the Uruguay Round. In doing so, it would test the member states in their commitment to unity of representation. It would also signal its disapproval of the Amsterdam compromise. This approach might be playing with fire, but might be the only way for the Commission to keep the debate open.

Upcoming Challenges to Trade Policy Institutions

Does the institutional outcome reached in Amsterdam represent a stable policy equilibrium? The answer to this question depends in part on one's interpretation of the meaning of the reformed Article 133. Most importantly, however, it seems that a series of challenges might put the EU procedures for making trade policy, and more generally EU institutions, at risk if no serious reform is undertaken. We believe that upcoming challenges such as, in particular, the relaunching of multilateral negotiations under WTO and the future enlargement of the EU to its Eastern neighbors will put heavy pressure on the existing institutional mechanisms for trade policy-making in the EU. If these are not reformed, the EU faces the potential erosion of the international effectiveness that it has painstakingly acquired over four decades of existence.

Central Challenges to Trade Policy Institutions

The Relaunching of WTO Negotiations

The new Millennium Round negotiated under WTO auspices was supposed to be launched in Seattle in November 1999 at the initiative of Sir Leon Brittan, the former trade commissioner. The EU insisted on framing the trade negotiations in very broad terms, encompassing issues such as competition policy, labor standards, and food safety, in order to offer the world a 'managed' globalization. As an echo to the Rio Summit on Environment held in 1992, the EU also insisted that the round be based on the premise that negotiated rules over free trade ought to be compatible with sustainable development.

These negotiations pose a number of new challenges. First of all, the former 'new issues' have now taken a life of their own and a number of conflictual points need to be addressed. As one example among many, the rise of electronic commerce through the Internet forces a reappraisal of the scope and content of the GATS. Member states are likely to disagree strongly over the right solution. How, for instance, should 'virtual goods' such as CDs and videos downloaded across borders through the Net be classified? As goods or services? If they are considered goods, US demands for liberalization will be harder to resist unless the so-called audiovisual exception is extended to the realm of goods. There is likely to be some degree of disagreement between member states over such issues. But the fact is that an analytical question such as classification may be resolved on grounds that put one issue under shared competence and not the other. This does not seem very conducive to effective negotiations.

The 'new issues' that were tackled in Seattle and will be addressed in the next multilateral negotiations make the competence controversy more acute. These so-called 'trade and . . .' issues include trade and environment, trade and labor, as well as trade and competition law—although each of these topics may be taken up under different premises depending on how far along the discussions have progressed. These 'trade and . . .' issues have one characteristic in common: they engage policy and advocacy communities well beyond the trade arena, from environmental activists to trade unions and competition regulators. Given such a broad base of input, the need for one EU voice is all the more acute.

Overall, the EU offered a fairly united front during the Seattle conference. The European Parliament was more involved than in the past (still informally), with a delegation of Euro MEPs forming part of the EU delegation. A conflict over competence arose, however, between the member states and the Commission on the issue of biotech. Several states, as well as some members of the European Parliament, accused the EU negotiator, Pascal Lamy, of having exceeded his negotiating mandate by accepting the setting up of a biotechnology working group. This episode suggests that, as the topics discussed become more symbolic and domestically sensitive, any attempt by the Commission to overstep its mandate will be increasingly visible and publicly denounced.

The emergence of these new issues also creates a particular problem for the external representation of the EU. The question is no longer only 'who speaks for Europe', but also 'who speaks for the Commission'? The preeminence of the new Directorate General for Trade (formerly Directorate General for External Relations) is being undermined by the proliferation of the 'trade and . . .' issues. One exception to this preeminence was in the case of agriculture, whose DG has traditionally been the principal actor making the EU's external trade policy on agricultural matters. With the expansion of trade into so many new domains traditionally the '*chasse gardée*' of domestic polities, however, directorates in various parts of the Commission (such as on social and environmental affairs) can now legitimately claim involvement in the trade policy-making process. If intra-Commission disagreements exist (and they are bound to happen) and internal cohesion proves difficult to achieve, the trade policy process will be delayed. One consequence might be a reduced practical effectiveness of the Commission in international trade negotiations (Johnson 1998).

The Enlargement of the European Union

The institutional procedures for making trade policy were originally designed for a Community composed of six members. The more countries joined the EU, the more cumbersome and inadequate these institutional procedures became. Several practitioners have argued that the sheer size of the reformed Committee 133 now impedes its work (Johnson 1998). The traditional practice of hammering out a consensual compromise over lunch, for instance, does not work smoothly when there are fifteen national representatives and their assistants around the lunch table. Moreover, one could expect the policy process to be delayed and rendered less efficient by the existence of potential vetoes in the hands of fifteen, and potentially more, member states.

Each enlargement brought along an expanding array of specific trade interests—'free market' pressures with the accession of Great Britain, new interest in the shipping industry with the enlargement to Greece, protectionism in agriculture with the joining of Spain and Portugal, etc. Along with an increased diversity in trade interests came an increased number of internal contradictions within the Community. The next enlargement will be no exception to the rule. This fragmentation of EU interests could lessen the external efficiency of the EU as an international trade negotiator.

Why is Institutional Reform Necessary?

Failure to reform the EU's institutional structures and implement change in decision-making procedures will have several consequences. First, it will affect the attitude and behavior of Europe's trade partners and negotiating opponents. Procedures for granting trade authority shape the expectations of Europe's partners, and thus its role in the global trading system. The uncertainties created by the system of mixed competence in the new issues tend to spill over into all other areas of trade negotiations, since issues are increasingly negotiated as package deals. Above all, contested authority tends to render third countries more reticent to conduct negotiations with, and make concessions to, Community representatives. The Blair House renegotiation debate was followed by other deals negotiated with a single voice by the Commission on behalf of the whole Community, only to be reneged on later by the member states.[14] Because negotiations are an iterated game, the growing uncertainty that the concluded deal will hold through may weaken the long-term credibility of the Commission. Moreover, the EU might be hampered in its more frequent offensive endeavors by the constant threat of having one of its increasingly numerous member states break ranks (Meunier 2000). Foreign negotiators will attempt the 'divide and rule' strategy of seeking bilateral deals with 'friendly' member states when the supranational negotiating authority is

---

[14] In 1997 the Council attacked trade deals with Mexico and Jordan. 'Trade deal debacles bring criticism of Union mandate', *European Voice* (10–16 July 1997).

contested. Indeed, US negotiators have already started to exploit these institutional uncertainties as bargaining leverage, for instance by contesting the legality of the negotiators' competence when the proposals are not in the USA's favor.[15]

Moreover, failure to implement institutional change in EU trade policy could have a significant impact on the nature of the international political economy as a whole. How the EU negotiates affects the world system, directly as the largest trader, and indirectly as a potential model for other regional systems. Fragmented actors facing each other in complex multilateral negotiations are less likely to be able to come up with packages of linked deals and more likely to heed internal protectionist forces. If the EU is presenting a less than unified front with competing competences when negotiating international trade deals, it could result in an increasingly protectionist pressure on the world economy: the collective position of the EU will be more easily captured by the most conservative member state and Commission negotiators, who have traditionally held a free-trade bias, will enjoy less negotiating autonomy (Meunier 2000). Since the EU has become the most consistent promoter of liberalization package deals in the wake of the Uruguay Round, such a shift would be bound to have profound repercussions on the dynamics of multilateral trade negotiations.

Conclusion: A Prescriptive Analysis of Trade Competence

The common commercial policy, cornerstone of the original Common Market, was initially conceived for six member states trading goods with a limited number of countries. Considering that membership is now fifteen countries, that trade now involves services, intellectual property, and a host of other new issues, and that more than 130 countries are now members of WTO, the EU's common commercial policy has been extremely resilient and adaptable. Nevertheless, as we have argued, the current institutional procedures need to be reformed in order to resist the challenges to be expected from the relaunching of multilateral trade negotiations and the next enlargement of the EU. The member states have included in the Amsterdam Treaty a timid revision of Article 113 which might open up the way for a more *ad hoc* approach to competence-sharing in the future. The Amsterdam policy equilibrium might not be very stable, however, and member states may want to revisit their decision-making procedures before the next institutional crisis explodes.

Which institutional arrangement should replace the existing policy mechanisms? The first arrangement that we can recommend is a pragmatic

---

[15] Private interview with DG I official, Apr. 1997.

approach that would preserve member states' sovereignty while enabling the EU to reap the benefits of centralized negotiating power. Indeed, the member states have attempted for many years to draft a Code of Conduct designed to delineate practically the respective roles of each actor in the trade policy-making edifice. No Code of Conduct has ever been formally adopted by the Council, however, as the member states have never wanted to put down on paper an acknowledgment that the system of mixed competences is not a practical one.

Another avenue through which some reform of the EU trade policy-making process could be undertaken is a legal one. With its Opinion 1/94 the European Court of Justice paved the way for the current confusion of responsibilities with its recognition of a coexistence of competences in some non-goods cases. Perhaps the Commission can find a case to give the European judges another opportunity to set a precedent—a case in which goods and services are so inextricably linked that it becomes impossible practically to disentangle the respective competences.

The Amsterdam dynamics illustrated the tension between two options: carving out exceptions to exclusive competence or adapting the initial 'pure' system with the caveat of a code of conduct that would give more say to member states during the actual negotiations. If disgruntled states can neither easily question the autonomy of the Commission, nor easily assert the Luxembourg compromise at the ratification stage in areas of exclusive competence, their only recourse is to take back competence altogether. In the last four years, the shared competence battle served as a proxy for a redefinition of the mechanisms of delegation to the Commission in all of the common commercial policy. If the Commission did not seem willing to give up much of its autonomy during international negotiations, member states would seek to reduce the scope of its authority where they still could (for example, over new issues). This may imply that, if the Commission is willing to negotiate under a higher degree of scrutiny on the part of the member states, it may not have to leave ratification to the uncertainties of national parliamentary procedures. Conversely, the Commission could promote a US-like 'fast-track' approach where the battle would be fought mostly ahead of, rather than during, the negotiations. The Commission would negotiate as it wishes, under the important caveat that anything negotiated would be submitted to the Council for ratification. However, this kind of approach is unlikely to be appropriate for the EU. One of the challenges of EU trade policy-making is to make trade-offs between national as well as sectoral interests. Member states have traditionally been unwilling to let the Commission control such trade-offs (Woolcock 2000). The dispute will thus likely continue as negotiations are conducted. The Commission vehemently opposed suggestions during the Amsterdam conference that the presidency of the Council be present during trade negotiations alongside the Commission. There is little doubt that Europe could no more effectively 'speak with one voice' under such a scenario. Instead, the Commission and the member states need to strengthen the Code's authority. As we have seen, there are pros and cons to each of these approaches. Both seem more effective, however, than the current situation, where not only trade authority but the procedures whereby it is granted constantly need to be renegotiated.

This chapter has highlighted some of the consequences that could derive from a failure to implement any institutional change in the common commercial policy. Change may be more difficult to implement today than at the time of the Amsterdam conference, however, while it also seems more necessary. The public demonstrations in Seattle showed that trade policy is now a 'hot topic', with many citizens openly concerned about the effects of trade liberalization. In some sense, the discourse against the WTO echoes the discourse against the EU. The Seattle failure represents a serious *risk*, not only for the multilateral trading system, but also for the EU. If the EU trade policy-making process does not answer public expectations about democracy and accountability, this might pose risks for the credibility and legitimacy of the EU as a whole. Also, Europe is increasingly endorsing, willingly or not, a leadership role in the multilateral trading system. It stands to lose more from multilateral failures than the USA, and therefore cannot let its own institutional defects and hesitations prevent it from playing this leading role in liberalizing world trade. In the face of these risks and challenges, how can a *reform* of EU trade policy be undertaken? While reform 'from above', such as a formal redistribution of competences, is ultimately necessary, we believe that in the short term increasing trust and communication are needed. There is little doubt that an attempt to expand exclusive competence to areas of domestic regulation, such as the environment, would provoke tremendous resistance from public opinion. *Resistance* to further transfers of sovereignty has clearly been demonstrated in recent cases, such as the French outcry against Brussels rulings in the British beef case and the growing awareness and opposition of NGOs to trade liberalization. Trade policy is both the oldest cement binding the EU member states together and one of the most pressing issues facing the EU today. How the EU manages to achieve a balance between negotiating efficiency, on one hand, and democratic legitimacy, on the other, will determine, to a great extent, how it can *revive* itself in all the other domains.

17

Flexibility or Renationalization: Effects of Enlargement on EC Environmental Policy

INGMAR VON HOMEYER, ALEXANDER CARIUS,
AND STEFANI BÄR

Introduction

Eastern enlargement of the European Union poses a challenge to European Community environmental policy. In particular, Central and Eastern European candidate countries have great difficulties in adopting the environmental chapter of the *acquis communautaire*, the common body of Community legislation. The European Commission concluded in its *Agenda 2000* that 'none of the candidate countries can be expected to comply fully with the [environmental] *acquis* in the near future, given their present environmental problems and the need for massive investments' (Commission 1997*a*: 67). The Commission has made pessimistic statements of this kind on several occasions. So far it has only given such a bleak prognosis for the environmental sector.

Why is the Commission so pessimistic about the adoption of the environmental *acquis*? The second part of this chapter looks at the progress made so far by candidate countries in adopting EC environmental legislation. Against the background of the results of the Commission's 'screening' of the compatibility of the environmental legislation of five candidate countries with EC law in 1999 we discuss some of the difficulties which these countries face in the process of 'approximation'—the formal transposition of Community law into national law, its implementation and enforcement (Commission 1997*b*: 8). We particularly stress problems of implementation linked to financial and administrative constraints.

In chapter 1 above, Cowles and Smith point out that European integration 'is increasingly difficult to develop any 'grand theory' unifying the whole field of analysis' because 'there are a number of coexisting and often competing forces operating on the EU'. The history of integration is not one of absolutes but of balances and nuances. The forces driving the 'four

Rs' of risk, reform, resistance, and revival are simultaneously present in the integration process—albeit to a different extent at different times and in different issue areas.

Taking these observations as a departure, we discuss the consequences of Eastern enlargement for EC environmental policy through the lenses of two alternative theoretical frameworks, liberal intergovernmentalism and historical institutionalism. Rather than theory-testing, the purpose of this exercise is to illuminate how coexisting and competing forces mediate the impact of Eastern enlargement on EC environmental policy.

Drawing on a liberal intergovernmentalist approach, we argue in the third part of this chapter that the widespread use of transition periods for the adoption of the environmental *acquis* poses a serious risk for EC environmental policy because it may lead to a partial renationalization of environmental policy-making. This may happen if the budget for the EU's pre-accession strategy, which supports candidate countries in meeting the conditions of accession, remains relatively low. But the risk of renational-ization would also increase if EC decision-making becomes more cumber-some. This is likely to happen if member states do not agree on far-reaching reforms of decision-making procedures, in particular of the system of voting in the Council of Ministers.

Although liberal intergovernmentalism suggests that the budget of the pre-accession strategy will remain too low and member states will fail to agree on major reforms, a process of institutional adaptation of EC envir-onmental policy may limit the risk of renationalization. Using a historical institutionalist framework, we look in part four at the priorities and imple-mentation of the pre-accession strategy and the Commission's regulatory strategy. The way in which the Commission influences the pre-accession strategy may to some extent compensate for an insufficient budget. In addition, the Commission's Directorate General (DG) Environment's pursuit of an increasingly flexible regulatory approach may limit rena-tionalization in the long run. Flexible regulation provides for transition periods, limited exceptions, delegation of decision-making to expert or regional bodies. Therefore it may accommodate a further increase of diversity among member states more easily than the traditional, more rigid approach to environmental regulation.

Challenges of Enlargement

The difficulties associated with the adoption of the environmental *acquis* by candidate countries are manifold. Problems include negotiation of transition periods for the adoption of parts of the *acquis*, post-accession implementation of the respective agreements, a high probability that most candidate countries will be environmental 'laggards', and issues linked to certain common characteristics of the environmental situation in candidate countries.

Adoption of the Acquis Communautaire

According to official Commission statements, the five 'ins' with which detailed accession negotiations have already started—the Czech Republic, Estonia, Hungary, Poland, and Slovenia—will be able to legally transpose the environmental *acquis* in the medium term (cf. Commission 1998*h–j*). However, the Commission is increasingly skeptical regarding the ability of these countries to complete transposition by the time of their envisaged accession—Hungary plans to accede in 2002, the remaining four 'ins' in 2003. The recent 'screening' exercise revealed that progress has been slow in most countries. As a DG Environment official put it: 'It was clear [. . .] that very little has already been transposed [. . .] it is highly doubtful whether legal transposition will be accomplished by the candidates own official target-dates for accession' (J. Jørgensen 1999: 1–2).

Indeed, the candidate countries' law-making capacities are severely overburdened by the adoption process. Frequently, this is the result of political conflicts delaying the passage of legislation through parliaments, lack of administrative resources, and the fact that contextual conditions influencing the way in which European legislation may be transposed—for example, property rights or administrative structures—are still in the process of being established.

Although there are problems regarding formal transposition, effective implementation poses an even bigger challenge. Table 17.1 presents those environmental directives for which the 'ins' indicated either during the screening (Commission 1999*b, c, f, g, j*) or in their position papers for the accession negotiations (Conference on Accession 1999*a–e*) that they may need transition periods, mainly because of implementation problems. Of the three larger countries Poland and Hungary announced that transition periods may be necessary for full implementation of about twenty Directives. This would be slightly less than a quarter of the eighty-nine legal acts contained in the *Acquis Guide* (Commission 1997*b*)—a Commission document listing EC environmental legislation to be adopted by candidate countries. Allowing this number of transition periods would be a far cry from the EU's official position that candidate countries should adopt the whole *acquis* at the time of accession.

In its comments on the screening results, the Commission indicates that there may even be a need for more and longer transition periods, in particular for Poland and the Czech Republic (cf. Von Homeyer *et al.* forthcoming). Poland was the only country which had not answered the Commission's implementation questionnaire, leaving the Commission with only 'scattered' knowledge of the state of implementation of the environmental *acquis* (Commission 1999g: 20–1). The Czech Republic indicated a need for relatively few transition periods, but the Commission expects that more than twice as many transition periods will be necessary. Even this estimation may be too low if approximation is not speeded up (cf. Commission 1999b). It should also be noted that all 'ins' have indicated the need for transition periods for the implementation of major pieces of legislation, for example the Urban Waste Water Treatment, the Integrated Pollution Prevention and Control (IPPC) (with the exception of Estonia), and the Packaging Waste Directives. However, several other transition periods only concern relatively minor adjustments.

Costs are a big problem in implementing the environmental *acquis*. For the areas of air pollution control, waste management, water pollution control and waste water disposal—the sectors requiring by far the most investment—the Commission estimates financing requirements of about EUR 120 billion for all ten candidate countries, of which about EUR 65

TABLE 17.1. *Screening results for the environmental acquis: Transition periods as indicated by the accession countries*

	Cz	Est	H	Pl	Slo
Horizontal Legislation					
Information on Ambient Air Pollution (97/101/EC)			T		
Nature Conservation					
Trade in Endangered Species (338/97/EC)					T
Birds Directive (79/409/EEC)	2005*	2010*	T	T	2004–6
Habitats Directive (92/43/EEC)	2005*	2010*	T	T	2004–6
Water Quality					
Urban Waste Water Treatment Directive (91/271/EEC)	2008–10*	2010*	2015*	2015*	2017
Groundwater Directive (80/68/EEC)		2006*	2007*		
Nitrate Pollution from Agricultural Sources (91/676/EEC)	2006*	2008*		2010*	
Discharge of Dangerous Substances (76/464/EEC)	T	2006*	2009*	T	T
Abstraction of Drinking Water (75/440/EEC)		T		2010*	
Drinking Water Directive (80/778/EEC)	2006	2013	T	T	

	Cz	Est	H	Pl	Slo
Bathing Water Directive (76/160/EEC)			T		
Fish and Shellfish Water (78/659/EEC & 79/869/EEC)		T		T	
Industrial Pollution and Risk Management					
Integrated Pollution Prevention and Control (96/61/EC)	2012*		T	2010*	2011*
Air Pollution from Industrial Plants (84/360/EEC)			T		
Large Combustion Plants (88/609/EEC)			T		
Chemicals and Genetically Modified Organisms (GMOs)					
Control of Major Accident Hazards (Seveso II) (96/82/EC)			T		T
Air Quality					
Air Quality Framework (96/62/EC)			T		
Ozone Depleting Substances (EC/3093/94)				2005*	
VOC Emissions from Petrol (94/63/EEC)		2007		2009*	
Quality of Petrol and Diesel Fuels (98/70/EEC)				2009*	2004*
Emission from Non-road Mobile Machinery (97/768/EEC)				T	
Sulphur Content of Liquid Fuels (93/12/EEC)	2005				
Waste Management					
Waste Framework (75/442/EEC)				2012*	
Hazardous Waste (91/689/EEC)			T	2012*	
Hazardous Waste Incineration (94/67/EC)			T		
Emission of Dioxins and Furans (97/283/EEC)			T		
Packaging and Packaging Waste (94/62/EC)	2005*		T	2007*	2007*
Shipment of Waste (EEC/93/259)				2012*	
Disposal of Waste Oils (75/439/EEC)			T	2005*	
PCB/ PCT Disposal (96/59/EC)			T		
Batteries and Accumulators (91/157/EEC)			T		

Sources: Screening reports (Commission 1999*b, c, f, g, j*) and those listed under *.
Notes: T = transition period without specification of length; number = indicated end of transition period; * = source is a position paper (Conference on Accession 1999*a–e*).

billion is earmarked for the five 'ins' (cf. Environment Policy Europe 1997: 18, 97). While the necessary investment in countries which are particularly weak economically, such as Romania and Bulgaria, may pose the biggest challenge, the 'ins' also face problems. Poland, for example, had environmental investments of EUR 1.8 billion in 1997 (cf. Commission 1999g: 21). However, given that the Polish investment requirement for the implementation of the environmental *acquis* alone is estimated at EUR 35 billion—according to the World Bank costs could even exceed EUR 50 billion (1998: 1)—this is only a fraction of the money needed.

The administrative requirements for implementation of the environmental *acquis* pose additional problems. The environmental *acquis* is substantially more comprehensive today than at the time of the EC's southern enlargement, as a result of the creation of the Internal Market. EC environmental legislation has also grown more complex in recent years, placing higher demands on member-state institutions responsible for implementation. Public participation requirements, flexible implementation based on sophisticated concepts such as Best Available Technique (BAT), an integrated approach to different environmental problems, and integration of environmental concerns into other policies have contributed to this development. Implementation requires technical expertise and effective structures for management, co-ordination, consultation, monitoring, and enforcement. These preconditions are frequently lacking in candidate countries. Administrative structures often still tend to be centralized, either because regional administration does not exist or because regional and local agencies lack competencies, autonomy, and/or resources. This causes problems in areas such as the issuing of permits and public participation (OECD 1999: 67–9).

Other implementation problems are a general lack of legal awareness and empirical legitimacy of public law and state intervention (Carius *et al.* 1999a), and weak civil societies—for example the number and effectiveness of NGOs or business associations is low (Jancar-Webster 1998). The environmental industry also remains underdeveloped and there is a long and enduring tradition of implementation failure (OECD 1998, 1999: 69)

Transition Periods

The screening results show that a relatively large number of transition periods will have to be agreed upon, at least if accession takes place within significantly less than ten years. This raises challenges—and risks—for European environmental policy in several respects. First, there is a danger that parts of the environmental *acquis* may be used as bargaining chips in the accession negotiations. Complete adoption of other chapters of the *acquis* may be traded for additional transition periods in the environmental sector, because full adoption of EC environmental legislation will in any case not be possible by the date of accession (cf. EP 1997: 5). This practice would reduce the importance of environmental legislation *vis-à-vis* other parts of the *acquis* (cf. K. E. Jørgensen 1999: 15).

There is also a danger that transition periods may lead to more delays in the implementation of the environmental *acquis*. Despite the wave of environmental reforms in the early 1990s in most candidate countries, today environmental protection ranks low on the political agenda. The economic and social problems of transition dominate politics (Baker and Jehlicka 1998: 9–11). The need to adopt the *acquis* is therefore an important motivator for candidate countries to remain active in environmental policy-making. However, extensive use of transition periods would significantly reduce this 'external' pressure and might lead some candidate countries to postpone implementation of EC legislation until close to the end of transition periods, rather than proceeding step by step over their complete duration. Failure to implement in time may require further extension of transition periods.

Finally, long transition periods may push candidate countries to join the group of environmental 'laggard' countries after accession. This group tends to oppose a high level of environmental protection. Core members are the countries which joined the EU during its southern enlargement—Spain, Greece, and Portugal (cf. Andersen 1998: 208). Like these countries, candidate countries will belong to the group of economically weaker member states which are more reluctant to bear the costs of environmental protection. As well as having insufficient financial resources, candidate countries lack strong environmental policy traditions which could generate the political will to play a more proactive role. Although most candidate countries developed comprehensive environmental legislation—which may occasionally be stricter than EC standards (cf. Davies 1999: 7)—severe implementation deficits persist. If candidate countries were still a long way even from the implementation of existing Community legislation by the time of accession, the chances that they would then try to block legislative initiatives in the Council which aim at high environmental standards would rise sharply.

Different Environmental Situations

A final challenge results from the particular characteristics of the environmental situation in candidate countries. There are systematic differences between the state of the environment in Central and Eastern Europe and the EU. These can partly be attributed to different paths of economic development since the Second World War, which are now in the process of being revised. Therefore, the picture of candidate countries as 'societies in transition' is to some extent also valid for the environmental situation in candidate countries.

The most notable difference between the state of the environment in the EU and in many candidate countries is the marked contrast in the latter between heavily polluted 'hot spot' regions, such as the so-called 'Black Triangle' between Poland, the Czech Republic and Germany, and expansive, relatively unspoiled areas, which are often marked by exceptionally high levels of biodiversity (cf. European Environment Agency 1998: 149; Regional Environment Center 1994: 10). This contrast can often be attributed to the long predominance of centralized planning in candidate countries. For decades planners concentrated on building up heavy industries which tended to be particularly damaging to the environment. Inefficient use of resources further compounded environmental problems. However, many other areas remained unspoiled because these industries were concentrated in a few regions.

Since the late 1980s the situation in many 'hot spots' has improved as a result of economic recession, restructuring, stricter and better enforced laws, and significant investment into environmental protection. Nevertheless, substantial problems remain to be solved in the 'hot spot' areas (cf. Stehlík 1998: 272–3).

In addition, increasing convergence with the environmental situation in Western Europe is not limited to the reduction of pollution levels in the 'hot spots'. It is also visible in the rise of new environmental threats to urban areas and, in particular, to the hitherto relatively unspoiled natural regions. This trend is increasingly evident, for example, in the dramatically expanding volume of road traffic in both urban and rural areas, rising levels of consumption accompanied by a growing production of waste, intensifying land use, etc. These 'new' environmental problems are still less severe in candidate countries than in most member states. However, it will only be possible to preserve the specific positive features of the environmental situation in candidate countries if these countries manage to follow a more sustainable path of development than the one pursued so far by member states. This would require, among other things, that candidate countries give special priority to implementing EC legislation capable of addressing the new problems. Examples include measures to integrate environmental concerns into other policy areas (cf. Commission 1998*g*) and to promote public information and participation; the planned directive on 'strategic' environmental impact assessment (Commission 1996*d*); Directive 96/61/EEC on IPPC. However, these directives are often particularly difficult to implement in candidate countries (see below).

How will the EU cope with these challenges? Different theoretical perspectives on policy-making lead to different expectations. As illustrated in the following two sections, liberal intergovernmentalism tends to emphasize risks. It suggests that the increasing number and diversity of member states, lack of radical reform of decision-making, and a growing gap between environmental policy 'leaders' and 'laggards' (cf. Héritier 1994) will fuel partial renationalization of EC environmental policy. By contrast, historical institutionalism focuses more on how the challenges may trigger both defensive and innovative processes of institutional adaptation which could lead to a new stage in the evolution of EC environmental policy rather than to its partial demise.

Risks of Renationalization

Liberal intergovernmentalism assumes that executive actors at the top of member-state governments make major decisions concerning European policy-making. Domestic economic interests with a particularly high stake in policy outcomes exert the strongest influence on the interests which executive actors pursue. Given this, the relative power and the intensities of the interests of member-state governments determine policy outcomes. Supranational institutions, in particular the Commission, are less influential. Although they may gain some short-term autonomy from their 'principals', the member states, supranational 'agents', by and large, function as efficient instruments, executing the will of the most powerful member states (cf. Moravcsik 1993).

According to liberal intergovernmentalist assumptions, member states would only be willing to bear the costs of extending EC environmental policy to candidate countries if this yielded net benefits for them.[1] Generally, the extension of the environmental *acquis* would have three main benefits for member states. Perhaps most importantly, it would eliminate the competitive advantage for industries in candidate countries caused by environmental standards which frequently continue to be significantly lower than Community standards. Rapid adoption of EC environmental legislation would also create export markets for member states' environmental industries. Finally, member states could benefit from a reduction in transboundary pollution. However, it seems safe to assume that these benefits would be significantly smaller than the estimated EUR 120 billion needed for full implementation of the most cost-intensive EC Directives in candidate countries.

[1] The interests of candidate countries are secondary because the conditions for accession are largely formulated unilaterally by the EU (cf. Caddy 1997).

Given limited economic and other substantive benefits but very high costs of implementing EC environmental standards in candidate countries, liberal intergovernmentalism predicts that member states will refuse to bear these costs. In fact, the two major EU assistance programs for candidate countries only contribute a small fraction of the total costs of implementing the environmental *acquis*. An annual sum of EUR 1.56 billion has been earmarked for the Phare program for the period 2000–6. It will be decided during the run of the program how much of this money will be spent on the environment. The history of Phare suggests that the figure will be relatively low. Between 1990 and 1996 only about 8 per cent of Phare assistance was spent on the environment. Although this proportion is likely to rise because of a recent reform of Phare which focuses assistance more strongly on accession requirements (as discussed below), spending on the environment will remain limited due to urgent investment needs in other sectors.

Starting in 2000, additional money will be forthcoming from the Community's new Instrument for Structural Policies for Pre-Accession (ISPA). For the period 2000—6 an annual budget of EUR 1.04 billion has been allocated to ISPA. Of this, about 50 per cent is to be spent on improving the environmental infrastructure in candidate countries. Although this amounts to a dramatic increase in spending, it is still far from sufficient. Even assuming that, in addition to ISPA, one quarter of the Phare budget will be spent on the environment, the total sum will only reach EUR 910 million annually.

The financing gap (cf. OECD 1999: 128–9) and the problems in adopting the environmental *acquis* imply that approximation is likely to be far from complete by the time of accession. In this case liberal intergovernmentalism predicts that member states will partly renationalize environmental policy. Renationalization may be defined as a tendency for member-state governments to pursue environmental policy at the national rather than the European level. This does not necessarily imply that existing EC environmental law is formally repealed. Rather, member states may obstruct the adoption of new environmental legislation. They may also try to undermine implementation and enforcement (cf. Jordan 1999*b*: 71).

To some extent the Treaties limit possibilities for renationalization because member states are obliged to adhere to Community law. However, from a liberal intergovernmentalist perspective the effectiveness of such limits is low because the medium- to long-term development of EC legislation reflects member-state interests. There is in fact a significant implementation deficit of EC environmental legislation (Commission 1998*e*; Jordan 1999*b*) and member states have tried to repeal or weaken various directives after they had been adopted (Sbragia 1996: 252).

Against this background, renationalization may also result from another scenario. With enlargement, the rise in the number and diversity of Council members is likely to increase the risk of protracted decision-making and indecision due to more 'cycling' between a higher number of different winning coalitions (cf. Wilming 1995: 85–120). In cases of 'cycling', majority voting will in itself not lead to a decision because there is no stable majority for a particular outcome. 'Cycling' happens if the aggregate choices of voters depend on the way in which the sequence of alternatives is presented to them. Diversity of preferences and a high number of relevant issues tend to increase the risk of 'cycling' (cf. Riker 1980).[2]

Perhaps more importantly, the future Central and Eastern European member states will, as mentioned above, probably be environmental 'laggards'. On the basis of present voting rules, they, or an alliance between them and old member-state 'laggards', could form a blocking minority in the Council (cf. Dehousse 1998: 147). Even if member states did manage to agree, the agreement would often be on a low level of environmental protection, reflecting the interests of a potential blocking minority of 'laggards' who have an advantage in bargaining because the fallback outcome of no legislation is usually closer to their interests than to those of the 'leaders' (cf. Scharpf 1988).

However, if no EC legislation is in place, then member states may adopt laws at national level.[3] Under certain conditions they may also do so under Article 95(4) and (5) and Article 176 EC if existing Community environmental legislation is not sufficiently strict. While these provisions have rarely been used (Shaw 1998: 77–8), 'leaders' may be willing to use them if faced with consistently lower EC environmental standards as a consequence of enlargement.[4]

Liberal intergovernmentalism also predicts partial renationalization in case of substantially incomplete adoption of the environmental *acquis* at the time of accession. In particular, economically weaker member states

---

[2] For a good illustration of the basic idea, see Elster (1989: 155). In addition to diversity of preferences and the number of relevant issues, the empirical incidence of the theoretical concept of 'cycling' is likely to depend on factors such as the time horizons of actors, possibilities for issue linkages or package deals.

[3] The freedom of member states to adopt national legislation is limited in that national legislation must conform to the Treaties, in particular to Arts. 28–30 EC. These provisions and the relevant jurisdiction of the European Court of Justice generally prohibit trade barriers between member states but also provide for limited exceptions for purposes of environmental protection.

[4] In addition to the legal restrictions (cf. n. 3) such a trend would also be limited by the fact that in some cases higher standards at the national level might entail loss of economic competitiveness for the industries of the respective member state. However, this has not kept several member states from notifying the Commission of their intention to adopt or retain stricter national standards (cf. Albin and Bär 1999: 186).

which compete most directly with new members will only willingly continue to bear the costs of relatively high environmental standards if new members reciprocate. If, however, new member states do not fully implement the environmental *acquis*—or do so only after long transition periods—this will create incentives for the economically weaker old members to reduce their competitive disadvantage by neglecting implementation, too. This will further aggravate the existing implementation deficit. As a consequence, the credibility of European environmental policy will decline sharply, perhaps leading all member states to prefer national measures.

For environmental 'leaders', reform of decision-making procedures offers an alternative to renationalization. They could change voting rules in the Council in an effort to reduce the opportunities of the growing group of 'laggards' to form a blocking minority. However, any general reform of EC decision-making will be determined by factors which are largely independent from considerations of environmental policy, such as member-state population and more general possibilities of groups of countries to form majorities (cf. Midgaard 1999). Moreover, given the potential size of this new 'laggard' group, 'neutralization' of this group would require quite radical reform, for example simple majority voting *and* significantly stronger proportionality between member-state populations and voting weights in the Council.

Such radical reform may form part of a larger effort to democratize EU decision-making. But it is unlikely to come about as a reaction to the interests stressed by liberal intergovernmentalism, that is, substantive, clearly identifiable gains for member states which offset the sharply rising risk for a member state of being outvoted on any single issue. According to intergovernmentalism, member states do not easily give up their individual chance (or what is left of it) to influence specific policy outcomes (cf. Moravcsik 1993: 510–11; Wilming 1995: 179–80). Moreover, even radical reform of decision-making may not prevent renationalization. If high environmental standards are adopted against the will of a minority of 'laggards', the latter may obstruct implementation and enforcement (cf. Jordan 1999*b*: 84–5).

Institutional Adaptation

Historical institutionalism provides an alternative theoretical perspective to liberal intergovernmentalism and leads to a different assessment of the likely consequences of Eastern enlargement. Rather than partial renationalization, the consequence of enlargement may be adaptation of EC environmental policy-making.

Although there is no agreed definition of historical institutionalism, most historical institutionalists stress two issues. First, institutions structure political struggles (Steinmo and Thelen 1992). This means that change tends to be path-dependent because efforts to alter political institutions are often themselves affected by the institutional structures which are the object of change. In particular, actors have limited capacities for information processing. It is not only difficult for them to monitor institutional development but, more importantly, they frequently depend on the institutions which they try to affect to develop relevant cognitive and normative orientations. Put differently, while the broader social context in which political institutions operate may alter institutions, institutions also structure the context.

Second, institutional actors, for example the European Commission, may have considerable autonomy *vis-`a-vis* the broader social context. They have their own institutionally shaped interests (cf. Hooghe 1999; Bach 1992) and can act accordingly (cf. Pollack 1997*a*). Given that societal actors often depend on these institutions to develop cognitive and normative orientations, 'ideas' (for example, political programs, causal explanations, normative judgments) are particularly important for explaining institutional influence. Within certain limits, institutional actors may influence their context by choosing one set of 'ideas' over an alternative one (Hall and Taylor 1998: 961–2).

Historical institutionalism suggests that path dependency and institutional stability may, but need not, stifle policy innovation. Whether or not institutions promote innovation often depends on contextual factors (cf. Steinmo and Thelen 1992: 16). For example, the European Commission is generally more innovative and successful in the pursuit of regulatory rather than redistributive policies. This may be explained in terms of different contexts. Member states impose high constraints on the Commission's autonomy to pursue redistributive policies. This has induced the Commission to follow a reactive, conservative approach, reflecting its interest in defending hard-won financial resources. By contrast, the Commission is less constrained with respect to regulatory policies because member states do not directly pay for these policies. Most costs are borne by societal actors who have to comply with EC regulations. Consequently, the Commission's approach tends to be more activist in this area (cf. Majone 1996).

Against this background, a historical institutionalist approach suggests that with respect to Eastern enlargement the Commission should be relatively unconstrained by its 'principals', the member states, or other interested parties in the pursuit of its institutional interests because there is a high degree of uncertainty about the long-term consequences of enlargement (cf.

Schimmelfennig 1999). The fact that member states have difficulties in evaluating enlargement gives the Commission the opportunity to develop and implement its own enlargement program. As argued in the following section, the priorities and implementation of the EU's pre-accession strategy have, in fact, been strongly influenced by one of the Commission's principal interests, which is to ensure that candidate countries adopt the complete *acquis*.

The Commission's influence and strategy can be expected to vary depending on whether it needs to adopt redistributive or regulatory policies to achieve its aims. Although the Commission has been able to influence the pre-accession strategy, the financial resources available for the adoption of the environmental *acquis* to a large extent continue to reflect the narrow constraints which member states impose on most EU redistributive policies. Therefore, the effect of the pre-accession strategy on reducing the risk of renationalization of EC environmental policy is likely to be limited, in particular in the longer term.

However, the Commission may try to reduce the risk of renationalization further by increasing the flexibility of its regulatory approach. DG Environment has previously reacted to efforts by member states to renationalize parts of EC environmental policy in a similar way. Therefore it does not need to invent an entirely new approach to cope with the risks of Eastern enlargement but can chose to follow a path which has been gradually developed since the mid-1980s. Given the greater room for maneuver which the Commission has enjoyed in regulatory matters in the past, it seems unlikely that member states would strongly resist a more flexible regulatory approach. The costs of more flexibility would again be borne primarily by societal actors.

The Pre-Accession Strategy

As pointed out above, the budget of the pre-accession strategy is too limited to meet the challenges of enlargement, particularly in the environmental field. However, in recent years the Commission has gained considerable control over the priorities of the pre-accession strategy and the way in which it is implemented. To some extent it has managed to compensate for a lack of financial resources by influencing the selection of priorities and implementation in a way which reflects its own institutional interest rather than member-state interests (cf. Everson and Krenzler 1998: 7–10). The Commission has also been able to raise additional member-state and other financial resources for the pre-accession strategy.

The pre-accession strategy evolved in two main steps. First, after the European Council summit in Copenhagen had formulated the basic conditions for accession, the 1994 Essen summit called on the Commission to prepare a White Paper and designate those parts of the *acquis* which are essential for the Internal Market as priority areas for approximation. This approach satisfied member states because it privileged aspects of enlargement from which they could gain most, namely trade liberalization and the creation of a 'level playing field' for economic competition. However, privileging Internal Market legislation was unsatisfactory from the Commission's point of view. Unsurprisingly, DG Agriculture opposed the strategy and DG Environment was not enthusiastic either (cf. Sedelmeier and Wallace 1996: 382).

It remains unclear whether the Commission ever intended to fully implement the Council decision and discriminate between parts of the *acquis*. The Commission used its informal agenda-setting power (cf. Pollack 1997*a*: 124–8; Cram 1993) to advance its interest in ensuring that candidate countries would have to adopt the complete *acquis*. In the White Paper on Internal Market legislation, which purportedly implemented the Council decision, the Commission also announced measures to ensure approximation of legislation *not* covered by the White Paper (Commission 1995*c*: 19). Subsequently, DG Environment established the Development of Implementation Strategies for Approximation in Environment (DISAE) facility and, in early 1997, published the *Acquis Guide*—a comprehensive document designed to assist candidate countries in adopting the entire environmental *acquis*.

Publication of the Commission's *Agenda 2000* in June 1997 marked the second step in the development of the pre-accession strategy. The Commission proposed an enhanced strategy, programmed by Accession Partnerships focusing on the adoption of the whole *acquis*. The Commission's strong influence on the formulation and implementation of the enhanced pre-accession strategy is evident in its central role in the reform of Phare, the establishment of ISPA and the SAPARD agricultural accession fund, and in negotiating Accession Partnerships—a bilateral exercise between the Commission and candidate countries which is dominated by the Commission (cf. Caddy 1998: 90–9).

The establishment of the ISPA and SAPARD funds underlines the Commission's interest in speeding up the adoption of the whole *acquis*, rather than privileging Internal Market legislation. The two accession funds aim at preparing candidate countries for the structural funds and the CAP—two EC policies which, due to their financial implications, are particularly problematic in the context of Eastern enlargement but are not directly linked to the Internal Market. The new guidelines for the Phare program replaced 'demand driven' by 'accession driven' programming. This means that expenditure is no longer guided by recipient countries' needs but is linked to the requirements of accession as identified in the

Accession Partnerships. This further increased the Commission' influence on the implementation of Phare (cf. Commission 1997*i*).

The Commission also managed to raise additional member-state and candidate country resources for the pre-accession strategy. For example, while ISPA, SAPARD, and Phare funds may be used for the practical implementation of projects falling under the priorities identified in the Accession Partnerships and candidate countries' National Programs for the Adoption of the *Acquis* (NPAA), a considerable amount of available resources is to be spent on project preparation. This allows the Commission to exert influence on the selection and design of a larger number of projects. The practical implementation of projects will then be co-financed by candidate countries, bilateral member state aid, and international financial institutions.

This strategy is also evident in 'twinning' projects. Twinning is a major part of Phare. It supports member-state experts in assisting candidate countries in institutional capacity building for the implementation of selected parts of the *acquis*, including environmental legislation. Twinning allows the Commission to utilize member-state experts, who are seconded to candidate countries, and candidate country staff to implement the *acquis*. Only member-state expenses are reimbursed. However, reimbursement often does not cover real costs and member states have to pay for project preparation. The Commission uses competition to induce member states to participate. States failing to win projects lose the opportunity to replace bilateral aid by partially EU-financed twinning projects. Against this background bilateral aid may be increasingly replaced by 'cheaper' Community programs which are largely controlled by the Commission.

Twinning also illustrates the Commission's relative independence from member states in the implementation of Phare. For example, the Commission decided to rely on the long-term secondment of member-state experts as the 'back-bone' of twinning projects, despite opposition by some, and skepticism by most, member states. Candidate countries tended to oppose the plan, too. The UK, Ireland, the Netherlands, Portugal, and others argued that availability of suitable member-state personnel would be a major problem (cf. Commission 1998*f*).

Bureaucratic procedures for approval of twinning projects illustrate the Commission's conservative approach to control over redistributive policies. Although the Commission had initially promised to handle twinning flexibly, the rules gradually became increasingly detailed and similar to the older Phare rules for investment projects. This bureaucratic approach considerably delayed approval of twinning projects. Several member states even threatened to raise the issue of excessive bureaucracy in the Council.

The Commission proposal to limit the level of Community aid for ISPA projects to 85 per cent provides another example of the Commission's path-dependent approach to redistributive policies. Although several important member states preferred a ceiling of 75 per cent, the Commission, supported in particular by Spain and Portugal, wanted to avoid creating a precedent for changing similar provisions for the Cohesion Fund.[5] Other features of ISPA may also illustrate conservatism and path dependence because ISPA was largely modeled on the Cohesion Fund.

Flexible Environmental Regulation

Although the pre-accession strategy may be more effective in supporting the adoption of the environmental *acquis* than its 'official' budget suggests, it is unlikely that it will be sufficient to avoid partial renationalization. Flexible regulation offers more innovative ways to adapt EC environmental policy to the long-term consequences of an enlarged and more diverse Community because it promises to accommodate a larger spectrum of different ecological conditions, economic capacities, and political aspirations (cf. Holzinger 1999).

Flexible regulation may involve possibilities to deviate from EC standards under certain conditions (flexible regulation 'proper') or giving a wide leeway to actors implementing legislation ('flexible implementation'). Flexible regulation 'proper' may be based on temporal ('multiple speeds'), geopolitical ('variable geometry'), or substantive criteria for differentiation. Temporally flexible regulation requires the application of transition periods and allows member states to progress towards fully harmonized standards at different speeds. By contrast, geopolitically flexible regulation establishes permanently different standards between groups of member states. Finally, substantively flexible regulation allows for differentiation according to objective variations, for example in ecological conditions.[6] Flexible implementation may, among other things, be based on

---

[5] Cf. 'EU/Agenda 2000: Despite Difficulty Raised by Spain, General Affairs Council Makes Progress Concerning Pre-Accession Instruments', *Bulletin Quotidien Europe*, No. 7330 (26–7 Oct. 1998), 13. After the Berlin summit reaffirmed the 85% maximum level of aid for the Cohesion Fund, the way was cleared for a compromise. As demanded by a majority of member states, the ceiling for ISPA was set at 75%. However, the Commission may increase the level to 85%. This decision can then only be overturned by a qualified majority in the Council, which has to decide within a period of three months.

[6] This classification differs from the one developed by Stubb (1996: 290) who equates substantive differentiation according to 'matter' with the concept of 'Europe à la carte' where 'a member state is allowed to pick-and-choose [. . .] from respective policy areas'. We understand substantive differentiation as relating to objective factors, the presence of which will frequently not coincide with member state borders. Substantive flexibility therefore mostly allows for regionally or locally differentiated standards.

delegation of decision-making to expert bodies, public participation, and economic incentives (cf. Carius *et al.* 1999*b*: 31–7).

A historical institutionalist approach suggests that the Commission is likely to pursue a course of institutional adaptation which increases the flexibility of environmental regulation. As argued above, the Commission has a record of pursuing relatively innovative policies in the regulatory arena. In particular, however, it has reacted to challenges of renationalization in the past which are similar to the ones posed by Eastern enlargement by increasing the flexibility of its regulatory approach. Therefore, DG Environment can draw on an existing set of ideas and practices regarding flexible regulation.

The general tendency to increase the flexibility of EC environmental legislation can be traced back to the mid-1980s, when the Single European Act (SEA) was negotiated. On the one hand, the SEA created possibilities for a limited renationalization of environmental policy. Under certain conditions the new Articles 100*a*(4) and 130*t* EEC allowed a member state to keep—perhaps also to adopt new—national environmental regulations deviating from EC standards. The SEA also introduced the subsidiarity principle (Article 130*r*(4) EEC) which limited EC environmental competencies to cases where the Community can attain Treaty objectives better than member states. The UK in particular used the principle to argue for a partial renationalization of environmental legislation (Golub 1994: 21).

On the other hand, the SEA introduced the concept of temporally flexible regulation into the Treaty. Article 8*c* EEC allowed for transition periods if certain economies were disproportionately burdened by measures to create the Internal Market (cf. Ehlermann 1995: 8; Beck 1995: 150). This provision was particularly relevant for Spain and Portugal which had only recently joined the Community and were expected to block the adoption of Internal Market legislation if they were not granted transition periods. For example, at the level of secondary legislation, Directive 88/609/EEC on Large Combustion Plants was temporally flexible in that it granted Spain a special transition period for compliance with important requirements. Directives 85/337/EEC on Environmental Impact Assessment and 90/313/EEC on Access to Information improved the general conditions for flexible implementation by establishing common procedures for public information.

In the early 1990s the trend towards more flexible environmental legislation became markedly stronger against the background of the rising awareness of the implementation deficit of EC environmental legislation and, more importantly, calls by Britain, Denmark, and Germany for partial renationalization of environmental policy (cf. Holzinger 1999: 12; Collier 1996: 11). The Maastricht Treaty introduced Article 130*s*(5) EC, which allowed for transition periods if new environmental standards caused excessive costs for member-state administrations. More importantly, the EC adopted the Fifth Environmental Action Program (Commission 1993*b*). This document called for a wider application of more flexible instruments, such as public participation, education, and economic incentives. Articulating flexible regulation/implementation as an official strategy, the program provided a set of politically legitimated 'ideas' which DG Environment used in its effort to resist renationalization (cf. Zito 1999: 28–31).

The EC subsequently adopted a number of flexible measures. Regulations EEC/1836/93 on Eco-Audits and EEC/880/92 on Eco-Labels create economic incentives to motivate environmentally friendly behavior. The EC's Auto-Oil-Program aims at close cooperation with industry and, more recently, NGOs in the development of an integrated approach to pollution caused by road traffic (cf. Commission n.d.). Directive 98/70/EC on the Quality of Petrol and Diesel Fuels, which is part of the program, contains temporally and substantively flexible provisions allowing a member state to delay full compliance if it can demonstrate that otherwise 'severe difficulties would ensue for its industries' (Article 3). The Directive also permits adoption of stricter standards in certain regions if 'atmospheric pollution [. . .] can reasonably be expected to constitute a serious and recurrent problem' (Article 6(1)).

The IPPC Directive features delegation of decision-making and participation. Definition of BAT as the basis for standard setting is delegated to a special agency. Industry and environmental NGOs participate in the deliberations of the respective expert committees. Public participation is also prescribed in the licensing procedure (cf. Scott 1998).

The adoption of framework directives allows for more flexible implementation. For example, the planned Water Framework Directive (Commission 1997*k*) combines temporal and substantive flexibility with flexible implementation. Member states are given an unprecedented transition period of sixteen years, with possibilities of further delaying full compliance for another eighteen years. The Directive delegates the formulation of comprehensive river basin management plans to specialized regional authorities and provides for participation by stake holders and the public (cf. Bär *et al.* 1999; Matthews 1999).

Despite existence of a broad range of concepts and practices of more flexible EC environmental regulation, it cannot be ruled out that member states will resist further expansion of flexible regulation. For example, the planned Water Framework Directive, which was the Commission's 'flexible answer' to member-state pressure to repeal several older Water Directives (cf. Kraemer 1998: 389–90; Jordan 1999*a*), has met with considerable member-state resistance. Nevertheless, the basic conditions for relatively innovative EC regulation have not changed because costs are still primarily borne by societal actors rather than member-state governments. If anything, the speed at which EC environmental legislation is adopted has increased over recent years (cf. Jordan *et al.* 1999).

In addition, the Amsterdam Treaty introduced two new provisions which may increase the flexibility of EC regulation. First, according to Article 11 EC a group of member states may under certain conditions agree on common measures which are more far-reaching than existing Community legislation. DG Environment considers this new possibility of differentiation according to geopolitical criteria potentially useful to prevent stagnation of EC environmental policy as a result of enlargement (cf. Commission 1999*e*: 46). Second, Protocol 21 of the Amsterdam Treaty on the application of the principles of subsidiarity and proportionality emphasizes the use of framework Directives and flexible implementation in general (cf. Scott 1998). In fact, DG Environment officials seem to regard flexible regulation as increasingly important to avoid stagnation and renationalization of EC environmental policy in the long term.[7]

However, there are other limits than member-state resistance to the effectiveness of flexible regulation as a means to avoid renationalization. Given that even member states have trouble implementing, for example, the IPPC Directive, most flexible EC environmental regulation will initially be even more difficult to implement in candidate countries due to traditionally centralized administrative structures, lack of experience, less developed civil societies. It is therefore only in the medium to long term that flexible regulation may be successful in preventing renationalization of EC environmental policy. Moreover, there is always a certain risk that flexible implementation, in particular, may lead to *de facto* renationalization if European rules leave too much leeway to national and subnational public authorities and societal actors who are charged with implementation (cf. Commission 1999*e*: 17; Knill and Lenschow 1999: 17).

Conclusion

This chapter has looked at some of the potential consequences of Eastern enlargement. Candidate countries face serious problems in adopting the environmental *acquis*. Therefore, a large number of transition periods will have to be agreed upon if accession is to take place within significantly less than ten years. This may lead to a downgrading of environmental policy

---

[7] Interview, DG XI, 10 Feb. 1999, Brussels; Interview, DG XI, 5 Jan. 1999, Brussels.

vis-à-vis other EC policies during the accession negotiations. More importantly, widespread use of transition periods may contribute to factors pushing candidate countries to join the group of environmental 'laggards' after accession. At the same time, systematic differences between the state of the environment in candidate countries and in member states are likely to further increase the diversity of challenges and opportunities for environmental protection in an enlarged Union.

With its emphasis on economic interests and the power of member-state governments to control developments at the EU level, liberal intergovernmentalism highlights the risks of Eastern enlargement. It suggests that partial renationalization is likely to result from two factors. First, the costs of providing sufficient support to avoid numerous long transition periods for the full implementation of the environmental *acquis* in candidate countries will be much higher than the benefits from doing so for member states. Second, it is unlikely that member states will agree on sufficiently radical reform of EC decision-making rules to prevent the rising number of environmental 'laggards' from blocking the adoption of strict EC environmental standards after enlargement. This situation may induce all member states to prefer partial renationalization.

Historical institutionalism focuses on the way in which institutions structure relations between actors, in particular by influencing cognitive and normative orientations. It draws attention to institutional interests and the capacity of institutional actors to act relatively autonomously. According to this perspective, processes of institutional adaptation to the risks of Eastern enlargement may lead to reform of EC environmental policy. The Commission might influence the priorities and implementation of the pre-accession strategy in a way that increases the strategy's effectiveness as an instrument to assist candidate countries in the implementation of the environmental *acquis*. In addition, a more flexible regulatory approach may mitigate long-term risks stemming from the fact that candidate countries are likely to be environmental 'laggards'. Since the mid-1980s the Commission has reacted to member-state efforts to partly renationalize EC environmental policy by introducing increasingly flexible regulation. DG Environment seems well prepared and willing to expand on the concepts and practices of flexible regulation developed so far in an effort to manage the long-term risks of Eastern enlargement for EC environmental policy.

Our discussion suggests that Eastern enlargement creates new risks for, and potential resistance to, EC environmental policy. Simultaneously, we observe efforts by the Commission to contain, and adapt to, these risks. There is significant potential for reform of EC environmental policy. Some observers recommend a more flexible regulatory approach not only to address the long-term risks of enlargement but also to cope with a host of other problems facing EU environmental policy (cf. Holzinger 1999; Scott 1998). Against this background, the incentives generated by Eastern enlargement to adopt a more flexible regulatory approach may in the long run even lead to a more general revival of EC environmental policy.

18

How Defense 'Spilled Over' into the CFSP: Western European Union (WEU) and the European Security and Defense Identity (ESDI)

J. BRYAN COLLESTER

> In Kosovo we have all come face to face with the European future, and it is frightening.
>
> George Robertson, British Defense Secretary

Introduction

Has the phoenix risen from the ashes? Like the fabled ancient bird of Egyptian lore, the European Union is regenerating itself again. This time it is the elusive common defense policy. The EU is significantly reshaping the distant objectives and tepid language on European defense in Title V of the Treaty on European Union (TEU). In the language of the TEU, the European Union committed itself to 'the eventual framing of a common defence policy, which might in time lead to a common defence'. But that 'eventual framing' has come about with unwonted and certainly unexpected rapidity. Broadening its Common Foreign and Security Policy (CFSP), the EU is now seeking to forge a viable defense policy, which includes the capacity for autonomous action, backed up by credible military forces, the means to decide to use them, and the readiness to do so.

Although the EU has long been an economic giant and a military midget, the *New York Times* headline proclaimed: 'European Union Vows to Become Military Power.'[1] It reported that leaders of the fifteen member states had decided finally to make the European Union 'a military power for the first time in its 42 year history, with command headquarters, staffs

---

[1] 'European Union Vows to Become Military Power', *New York Times* (4 June 1999), A1.

and forces of its own for peacekeeping and peacemaking missions in future crises like those in Kosovo or Bosnia'. And when Gerhard Schröder, German Chancellor and President of the European Union opened his May press conference in Cologne, he beamed: 'This is a good day for Europe.'[2]

To those who follow the European Union less closely, attaining the capacity to defend itself or others—a time-tested definition of sovereignty—might seem both natural and inevitable. Over the years, however, that elusive capability has proved neither natural, nor inevitable—until now. Decisions by the EU, however, which reached a crescendo in December 1998 to December 1999, show the Union most serious about creating a European Security and Defense Identity (ESDI) to underpin its Common Foreign and Security Policy. And it is doing so by formally adopting the capabilities and structure of the Western European Union (WEU). Moreover, to signal unmistakably its overt commitment to the development of a defense capability, the EU appointed Javier Solana, the widely respected former Secretary-General of NATO, to the new post of Secretary-General of the Council and High Representative for Common Foreign and Security Policy. Solana, now the putative foreign secretary for the Union, has been 'double-hatted' as the Secretary-General of the WEU as well.

The EU's decision to expand CFSP to include defense is dramatic and significant, and it raises the obvious questions: why this momentous change, and why now? Analysis of those questions is the focus of this chapter. Like the volume itself, this chapter will use the 'four Rs', *risk, reform, resistance,* and *revival,* to circumscribe this story, for the experience of the Union's CFSP, its security policy, and finally its defense policy has been one of fluctuation among those forces. The '*risk*' of including defense in CFSP, for example, has been judged in quite varied ways by the member states. Britain until Prime Minister Tony Blair's 'sea-change' has been among those states most adamantly opposed to making defense a common European policy.[3] France, to the contrary, has long advocated independence of European action to supplement its Gaullist stance on NATO and US military hegemony.

Reform, like risk, is a variable force. But the reform, the reshaping of Union policy on defense, has been steady and concrete to the observant. For others, the reforming of defense policy appears almost meteoric since the last Intergovernmental Conference (IGC) in which the WEU was

---

[2] 'Europeans Impressed by Their Own Unity', *New York Times* (4 June 1999), A16.

[3] In an interview, an official of the WEU was asked about 'the single greatest problem' that stymied the WEU's development as a supranational entity. He responded, with visible frustration, 'Britain . . . Britain!'

embraced by the EU, although at arms length. Part of the task of this chapter will be to assess the reforms and their effect—the 'spillover' in functionalist vocabulary—which has made possible major, region-wide corporate mergers in the defense industry. Heretofore the lack of uniform national policies and standards allowed the development of very few Union-wide defense assets and left American providers with ready markets. But with the ink scarcely dry on the new European Defense Charter, EADS (the European Aerospace, Defense and Space Company), the world's third-largest defense contractor, has been formed. EADS is an immediate beneficiary of the new common defense policy and should also be a bulwark against 'spillback' or disintegration.

Resistance, of course, is the counterforce to reform of the Union's CFSP. Beginning with the Rome Treaty, members of the European Community treated foreign policy as an intergovernmental endeavor. Resistance to what became CFSP was overwhelming, and, of course, resistance to a common defense policy was vigorous and tenacious, the projected European Defense Community (EDC) having met an ignominious fate at the hands of the French National Assembly in 1954. But resistance to a defense-capable CFSP diminished as conditions changed, globally and nationally. As the cold war ended, it fed Balkan instability and the Bosnian imbroglio. Then came the Serbian atrocities and ethnic cleansing in Kosovo, watched daily on CNN (Cable News Network) and other news services by millions of horrified viewers world-wide, including those in Western Europe who empathized with the plight of their hapless eastern neighbors. This incessant media horror show was a major catalyst, which by reducing resistance against military action made reform of defense policy possible.

Finally, reforms underway in the EU, in the WEU, and in NATO, helped mitigate the resistance to a CFSP having a defensive capability. And those reforms have led to a *revival* of a concept conceived by René Pleven in the early 1950s, a common European army. Of course that plan, encapsulated in the EDC, was not a blueprint for today's still-opaque outline of a common defense policy. As the editors of this volume aver, there are probably grand conflicts and grand bargains ahead, as well as 'balances and nuances' to accommodate, as the European project evolves into a polity of yet undetermined size, dimension, and complexity.

In order to explain the interaction of the four Rs, *risks, reforms, resistance*, and *revival*, and this long-awaited expansion of the CFSP into a potentially viable defensive capability for the EU, this chapter focuses on the convergence of a set of significant political and institutional forces. It begins by considering some of the salient developments in the WEU's half-century of existence which have led to this remarkable and quite historic linkage between the EU and WEU and the ultimate revival of a common defense policy. The next section reviews the cardinal events between December 1998 and December 1999 which reformed the EU and CFSP and led to the revival of a common defense policy (ESDI) by formally integrating the EU and WEU capabilities. The following section examines how the media phenomenon called the 'CNN-effect' gave impetus to the British government's move to forestall another tragedy like Bosnia from happening in Kosovo. It was this move by Britain, long the opponent of an independent European defense pillar, which catalyzed EU member governments to agree upon a historic change in defense policy and to deepen the CFSP. The coming together of long-term institutional changes with governmental interests and with the perception that 'something had to be done' thus constitutes the driving force behind the 'spillover' of defense policy into the CFSP.

The final section of the chapter suggests some of the conditions that may forestall integration 'spillover' from turning into intergovernmental 'spillback'. Like the original functionalist ideas of Jean Monnet in which the market provided the cement to weld together national public policies, so today's cement is the (Europe-wide) regionalization and globalization of the defense industry. With mega-mergers taking place in corporate Europe faster than in any previous decade—and because of the size, the capitalization required, the workforce employed for these mega-corporations—it seems highly unlikely a single member state could withdraw or substantially circumscribe its defense policy, which is based on a European-wide procurement policy. Thus integration seems sustainable, now that the EU has agreed upon a platform of common policies in defense. In considering the potential for retreat or 'spillback', it is also important to consider the role of the USA in the further and future integration of the European defense pillar. While the USA has given its blessing and Bill Clinton his vocal support, some members of the US Congress and others are not so sure an independent European pillar will not undermine NATO and the Atlantic Alliance. The outcome of this new relation will bear watching closely.

WEU Prepares for the European Security and Defense Identity (ESDI)

WEU will be developed as the defence component of the European Union and as the means to strengthen the European Pillar of the Atlantic alliance. To this end, it will formulate a common European defence policy and carry forward its concrete implementation through the further development of its own operational role.[4]

_____
[4] WEU Maastricht Declaration of 10 Dec. 1991.

The Western European Union has worked quite creatively for more than a decade to be prepared to provide defensive capability to the EU, or to integrate into it. And it has done so largely without publicity and with minimal favorable press. This section, however, is not intended as a history of the WEU; several good monographs are available for that purpose (cf. Cahen 1989; Archer and Butler 1992; WEU Secretariat-General 1996). None the less, WEU might be thought of as a toolbox, an instrument which the European Union now is impelled to include under its CFSP. This section highlights the nature of the WEU, including its political organization, and its military capability—which is considerably older than the EU itself.

Since its founding in 1948 as the Brussels Treaty Organization (BTO) by Belgium, the Netherlands, Luxembourg, France, and the United Kingdom, the WEU has served various purposes, beginning with security, until eclipsed by NATO in 1949. Alfred Cahen (1989: 25), the BTO's first secretary-general, noted: 'at the very beginning the [WEU] had the defence structure necessary for carrying out its mission. However, with the signing of the Washington Treaty, its implementation and the subsequent establishment of NATO, the Organization gave up these defence structures and transferred its military activities to the North Atlantic Treaty Organization.' The BTO officially became the Western European Union in October 1954, when the Paris Agreements were signed modifying the Brussels Treaty and including West Germany and Italy in the organization. It became a liaison organization in 1958, a back-channel between the six continental members of the European Community and Britain. Following Britain's admission to the EC in 1973, the WEU became moribund until called into the service of France's European designs by President François Mitterrand in 1984. Britain, NATO, and the USA looked upon this Trojan horse as suspect and illegitimate, a burden the WEU had to bear until the USA in particular decided to reverse its traditional opposition for domestic political and economic reasons following 1989.

Conceptually, what accounts for this unheralded growth of WEU? It appears to be neofunctionalism or growth and development spawned internally by the organization's Eurocracy. It was integration kept alive by those members whose success and failure were tied to the success or failure of WEU. It was *integration by the back door*. And although it sometimes seemed as if the era of grand plans and 'supranational' integration had ended, beneath the veneer of intergovernmentalism and nationalism, European defense has remained as conceptually vital as it did at the Hague in 1987, where WEU ministers adopted 'The Platform on European Security Interests', the first definition of a European security identity. It grew, however, at the 'nuts and bolts' level (the functional level) until early 1999 when the WEU's integration into the EU became more than a distinct possibility.

There are a number of ways in which the WEU's organization, its military force capability, and the actions in which it has participated might fit with the EU. The WEU's membership is, of course, an important factor. The WEU has twenty-eight members in four categories. There are ten full *members* who belong not only to WEU, but also to the EU and to NATO. There are three *associate members* who do not belong to the EU, but do belong to NATO, and there are five *observers* (cold-war 'neutrals', except Denmark) who belong to the EU but not to NATO (reverse of associate members). Finally, there are ten *associate partners*, newly democratic states from Central Europe who have signed 'Europe Agreements' with the EU. From such a *mélange* of categories, membership has long been one of the signal barriers to integrating WEU into the EU.

Major WEU policy is formulated by the Council of Ministers, which is composed, uniquely, of member's foreign *and* defense ministers. The Council is chaired for six months on a rotating basis and has been synchronized with the EU presidency. The Secretariat is located not far from the Brussels headquarters of the EU. A Permanent Council of member-state representatives meets under the Secretary-General's direction and provides day-to-day management. WEAG, the Western European Armaments Group, successor to the Independent European Program Group (IEPG), provides national cooperation on arms procurement for 13 participating members. The 115-member Parliamentary Assembly, which meets twice each year, and the Institute for Security Studies (the think tank) meet in Paris in more grandiose quarters. To the south in Torrejon, Spain, near Madrid, the WEU established in 1993 a Satellite Centre for the interpretation of satellite data and crisis monitoring. It uses commercially available imagery gathered by satellites and high-resolution imagery from the Franco-Italian-Spanish Helios defense observation satellite.

The heart of WEU's military capability lies in the Defense Planning Cell and the Situation Center, both housed in the Brussels headquarters. The Planning Cell, for example, responsible for the 'Forces Answerable-to-WEU' (in WEU-speak that is FAWEU, pronounced 'fah woo'), has expanded assets committed to WEU by 25 per cent between 1996 and 1998. In addition to the Planning Cell, the WEU now has a permanent military staff headed by a lieutenant-general (3-star) and a Military Delegates' Committee. Also, the presidencies of the EU Council and WEU were harmonized on 1 January 1999, to facilitate compatibility and interoperability. Manifestly the WEU has discovered a viable defense rationale and is building an organization to respond to that rationale.

The WEU Planning Cell was tasked with developing a listing of available defense forces in November 1994, in the *Preliminary Conclusions on the Formulation of a Common European Defence Policy*. That listing of 'forces-answerable', FAWEU, updated in 1995, and continuing since, has grown steadily upward in quantity and quality. Those forces may come from any of the twenty-eight member states, although as a practical matter the core comes from the ten full members. National forces available as 'forces-answerable' are identified or 'counted' in 'units'. A unit could be, for example, a ship, or a battalion, or a squadron. In July 1996, the Planning Cell contained over 2,000 units of forces-answerable. It should be noted, however, that forces-answerable have come not only from full members of WEU. Associate members also may make units available, and, in fact, the first armed helicopters came from associate members.[5]

And the Planning Cell does 'exercise' the forces-answerable. Phase I of Crisex 95/96 began in December 1995. Not only troops were involved, but also the WEU Council, the political and military officials, and the Planning Cell. Phase I is considered a political planning phase. In Phase II of the exercise held in June 1996, the commander and a multinational staff were selected, and an operations plan adopted. In Phase III, held in December 1996, a CJTF (combined, joint task force, see below) plus the commander and key staff were deployed. After each phase an assessment, a kind of post-audit, is carried out.

Using strategy provided by the WEU Council, the Planning Cell then develops 'contingency plans' to use the FAWEU. Those plans, however, are not designed for a specific country, an Iraq or a Bosnia. Instead planning is called 'generic', and a force-package would be designed using five parameters: (1) size of threat, (2) distance from deployable force, (3) intensity of the conflict, (4) projected time, and (5) cost of the operation. Generic plans for humanitarian and rescue-type operations, the lower end of the Petersberg tasks,[6] have been written, are available to be used in exercises. Generic plans are now being written for traditional peacekeeping operations and the use of force in crisis management situations.

The European Corps, or EUROCORPS, which grew out of the Franco-German brigade, is part of the FAWEU and active at about 50,000 troops. France, Italy, Spain, and Portugal have organized a European land force (EUROFOR) and a maritime force (EUROMARFOR), both are FAWEU. In addition, WEU has four other multinational units at its

---

[5] Interviews with WEU Planning Cell officials, 5 July 1996.

[6] In a suburb of Bonn, Germany, members signed the Petersberg Declaration of 19 June 1992, agreeing to prepare for the effective implementation of conflict prevention and crisis management measures, including humanitarian and rescue tasks, and peacekeeping, including peacemaking.

disposal to a total of seven: the Multinational Division (central) consisting of Belgian, British, Dutch, and German units, the UK–Netherlands Amphibious Force, the Headquarters of the First German–Netherlands Corps, and the Spanish–Italian Amphibious Force.

Although actual 'combat experience' has been mostly planning, WEU has carried out several security operations indicating the capability for more extensive use. Although, WEU and the EU are cooperating in the policing and administration of Mostar in the former Yugoslavia, the first WEU military operation was mounted in 1988 in which mine-sweepers were used under its command in the Persian Gulf during the Iran–Iraq War. Subsequently WEU participated, double-hatted, with NATO in a naval blockade of Iraq during the 1990–1 Persian Gulf War. WEU and NATO also began cooperating in 1992 in a joint naval arms embargo in the Adriatic (Operation SHARP GUARD). In 1993 WEU provided assistance to Bulgaria, Hungary, and Romania in their efforts to enforce UN sanctions on the Danube, and in May 1997, as tensions in Kosovo were rising, WEU sent a Multinational Advisory Police Element (MAPE) to Albania to help with training for border policing and public order.

One of the potentially most useful capabilities of WEU is actualizing an innovative concept called 'combined, joint task forces' (CJTFs), which permits WEU members, at the EU's behest, and with NATO assent—and NATO assets—to form military task forces structured for a particular operational purpose (Gordon 1997). These purposes might include humanitarian relief, peacekeeping, or peace enforcement. 'Combined' signifies two or more states (e.g. France and Germany) are participating in a task force, and 'joint' means two or more services (e.g. army and navy) are involved. So a CJTF is a 'deployable, multinational, multiservice formation generated and tailored for specific, contingency operations'. The CJTF concept allows the WEU, and thus the EU, to avail itself of NATO (and hence US) assets without subjugating itself to the USA. For the EU, such a force is extremely important. It may also be an operational nightmare.

At the EU's 1996 Intergovernmental Conference, the WEU sought to make its case for integrating into the EU's CFSP. Recognizing concerted opposition from several quarters, not least Britain, the WEU proposed three positions for the IGC to consider: (1) *integration*: after which the WEU would cease to exist independently; (2) *future integration*: in which the WEU would retain its extant legal and operational structures, but would work toward integration into the CFSP; or (3) *cooperation only*: WEU would retain its independent and intergovernmental organization and develop closer ties to NATO. The IGC rejected the first position, while accepting the broad outlines of the second. Now, of course, those plans WEU made in preparation for the 1996 IGC are available for execution.

The WEU straddles the evolution between the European Union and NATO, for without a defensive capability, the EU must remain a rump polity incapable of securing its own sovereignty without NATO. But so long as NATO is under the hegemony of the USA (perceived or actually), EU defense decisions will be made by the Americans, a politically intolerable condition.[7] The WEU had become a necessary aspiration, a linchpin of the CFSP, but it remained in expectant limbo, being permitted neither to succeed, nor to fail, for its success would come at the expense of national sovereignty, and its failure would come at the expense of European integration (Holland 1998*b*).

The conclusion to the 1996 IGC, formalized as the Amsterdam Treaty (2 October 1997), adopted new and concrete links between the EU and WEU without opting for either a maximalist or minimalist position. The Treaty stated quite simply that the EU '*shall . . .* foster closer institutional relations with the WEU with a view to the possibility of the integration of the WEU into the Union' (emphasis added). But subsequent events in Europe significantly enhanced the rationale and momentum of the WEU. Elections in the UK and in Germany brought new and moderate socialist governments to power, as well as new views on the WEU and on NATO. The continuing progress and promotion of the Euro enhanced the Europeanist and integrationist approaches to organizations and institutions, and, finally, Russia's antipathy to NATO's eastward expansion muted the efforts of the Atlantic Alliance, and its new strategic concept, to become the sole and multi-purpose defense capability.

A Year of Dramatic Change: December 1998–December 1999

Of the many elements converging to make reform of the CFSP possible,[8] perhaps the first significant event occurred on 1 May 1997, when the

---

[7] This is the problem alluded to regarding CJTFs. By way of illustrating US capacity, almost two-thirds of the air power projected against Serbia on behalf of the Kosovars were US platforms.

[8] Some of the major agreements made by states participating in the EU and/or in NATO and which preceded PM Tony Blair's election in the UK and laid the groundwork for member states to decide to enhance CFSP and defense policy were as follows. 1991 Treaty on European Union (TEU) or Maastricht Treaty established the CFSP as the 'second pillar', 'which might lead to a common defence'; 1992 Petersberg Declaration defined the 'role or tasks' WEU would carry out for the EU: humanitarian and rescue tasks, peacekeeping tasks, and combat forces in crisis management, including peacemaking (Van Eekelen 1993, 1994); 1994 NATO Brussels summit agreed to support the development of a European Security and Defense Identity and of 'separable but not-separate forces'; 1996 Berlin

British voters, after a Clintonesque campaign, turned out the Thatcher–Major Eurosceptic Conservatives and elected New Labour's Tony Blair (see Chapter 14 above), who was manifestly more disposed towards Europe than his predecessor. Britain's financial titans in 'the City' were not yet ready to join the Euro-zone, but Blair was interested when French president Jacques Chirac called to suggest a joint defense initiative, giving the EU a voice in military affairs for the first time.[9] So began the EU's auspicious year of dramatic change in defense policy. Britain was important to France for two reasons: first, Britain is the only other European nation that can field significant forces for combat anywhere; second, it was the British, with their commitment to the USA and to NATO, who had continuously blocked French aspirations for a European defense capability independent of the Americans.

When the European Council met informally at the lakeside in Pörtschach, Austria, in late October 1998, Tony Blair outlined his three steps to give the CFSP greater credibility. His third step was to provide 'Europe with its own effective military capability able to take on Petersberg tasks.'

Blair's interest in Europe and his willingness to lead Britain past his Thatcherite predecessors back into Europe is an intriguing domestic political story,[10] but the importance for Europe became clear in early December 1998, when Prime Minister Blair and French President Jacques Chirac met in the seaside resort of St Malô to coordinate and to extend their planning for defense. They agreed the EU 'must have the capacity for autonomous action, backed up by credible military forces, the means to decide to use them, and the readiness to do so . . . [which require] strengthened armed forces that can react rapidly to the new risks' (M. Walker 1999).

The St Malô plan became the new European Defense Charter and was adopted by the EU the following week at the Vienna summit. In April,

---

Ministerial: NATO agreed to consider and develop the Combined Joint Task Forced concept as well as to make the Deputy SACEUR a European in charge of any European-led CJTF; 1996 Amsterdam Treaty provisions for the Union to 'avail itself' of the Western European Union to implement Petersberg Tasks.

[9] Ulrich Beck, professor of politics at Munich University, noted: 'Kosovo could be our military euro, creating a political and defense identity for the European Union in the same way as the Euro is the expression of economic and financial integration.' *New York Times* (28 April 1999), A11.

[10] Cornish (1999) reaches a different conclusion based on his reading of events tho Mar. 1999, asserting that the British, despite all the rhetoric which sounds WEU-favorable, are still intergovernmental and committed to NATO. He notes the UK has a 'preference for NATO' and 'The EU (or any other institution) should not be allowed to challenge NATO's primacy.' Still, he acknowledges 'it is still too early' to determine where WEU will fit into the future defense spectrum.

George Robertson, British Secretary of State for Defense, speaking to Harvard's Kennedy School of Government, told his audience: 'If Europe is serious about shouldering more of the burden in the future conflicts, it must improve its defense capabilities. Whether we act as Europeans or through NATO, our aims will amount to nothing if our armed forces cannot meet our political aspirations.'[11] In May at the WEU Council meeting, Robertson told the ministers of the WEU: 'The European Union has long been an economic giant and military midget . . . With this meeting we have taken a considerable step toward a common European security and defense policy.'[12]

Chancellor Schröder added his endorsement to the plan in June 1999 at the conclusion of Germany's European Council presidency from January to June 1999. Not wanting to be overshadowed by the Franco-British initiative, Schröder also made defense one of his primary focuses at the Cologne ministerial. Although former CDU Chancellor Helmut Kohl had been broadly supportive of deepening integration, including security, Schröder was emotionally unattached to the post-Second-World-War integration, and the election of Social Democratic chancellor and his Green Foreign Minister, Joschka Fischer, cast doubts on continued German support for integrating defense. The Green party was known for its opposition to advancing German military defenses, and that posture did not augur well for advancing European defense arrangements. But Fischer surprised his 'fundi' supporters in the party and backed Schröder, including the NATO bombing of Kosovo.

At the Cologne meeting of the European Council in June, the members agreed: 'We are now determined to launch a new step in the construction of the European Union.' That step, absorbing the functions of the WEU, was stated in more ponderous language in Annex III to 'The Presidency Conclusions' of the Cologne European Council.

[W]e task the General Affairs Council to prepare the conditions and the measures necessary to achieve these objectives, including the definition of the modalities for the inclusion of those functions of the WEU which will be necessary for the EU to fulfil its new responsibilities in the area of the Petersberg tasks. In this regard, our aim is to take the necessary decisions by the end of the year 2000.[13]

The *New York Times,* (4 June 1999: 1/16) added: 'They [the European leaders] echoed language first used by President Jacques Chirac of France and Prime Minister Tony Blair of Britain six months ago after two crises

---

[11] 'The Future of European Defense', *The Christian Science Monitor* (26 Apr. 1999), 9.
[12] 'Dependent on U.S. Now, Europe Vows Defense Push', *New York Times* (5 May 1999), A12.
[13] 'European Council Declaration on Strengthening the Common European Policy on Security And Defence', Annex III, in European Council (1999*b*).

in the Balkans showed how far Europe still had to go to be taken seriously as a military power, even on its own continent.'[14]

At the Cologne summit in early June, Schröder also announced that the EU's fifteen members had agreed that 'Mr CFSP' (or in French, *Monsieur PESC*), the Union's foreign-policy czar would be in place by late 2000. The Secretary-General of NATO Javier Solana would assume that post. Solana's name inspired respect, signaled achievement, and, most of all, was an acknowledgement that NATO and the EU would get on well together. Importantly, and not unexpectedly, the new strategic doctrine of NATO, formally adopted at the Washington summit in 1999, specifically welcomed this new European role and identity, calling for a NATO head-quarters for WEU-led operations. At Cologne the EU members formally agreed to absorb the functions of WEU.

In addition, Schröder, after two days of bilateral talks in May with President Chirac in Toulouse, said France and Germany planned to remodel the EUROCORPS into a rapid-reaction force within a new European Union defense role. At length, Britain, France, and Germany, it appears, are all speaking similar 'defense' language and seem ready to commit to the next step of integration: operationalizing a European defense with its own decision-making capability and in close coordination with NATO. This step, finally, gives meaning to the language from the Berlin NATO ministerial in 1996: using 'separable but not separate forces'.

The momentum continued during the autumn. On 15 November, Solana, the newly appointed Secretary-General of the EU Council's General Secretariat and 'High Representative' for foreign and security policy, was 'double-hatted' and made Secretary-General of WEU. Officially, then, Solana, the EU's 'Mr CFSP', could attend NATO meetings. The EU had thus placed in one portfolio the oversight and direction of its own defense policy, as well as the instruments and assets of the Western European Union. The EU members had spoken clearly and acted boldly on defense. The negative sentiments of incompetence and over-reliance on the USA were replaced with the positive sentiments of a new assertiveness of Europe's role in defense, with the new-old idea of a European pillar. The catch phrase on defense in the European press was 'not too much America, but too little Europe'.

As proof of their sincerity, France and Germany offered to revamp EUROCORPS, the force of 50,000 troops headquartered in Strasbourg, and to take control of the headquarters of NATO's peacekeeping force in Kosovo in 2000. Europe was seeking to begin to redress immediately the incompetence and incapacity, which had plagued the Union and catalyzed

[14] *New York Times* (4 June 1999), 1/16.

the whole movement to make defense a viable part of the CFSP. Then in early December 1999, the French and German Defense Ministers signed a declaration indicating their intent to form a multinational European air transport command. The purpose of this integrated command is to facilitate the coordination of *all* available airlift means, both military and civilian.

Finally on 11/12 December 1999, the European Council meeting in Helsinki reiterated 'its determination to develop an autonomous capacity to take decisions and, where NATO as a whole is not engaged, to launch and conduct EU-led military operations in response to international crises'. In overt language, the Council directs its members to develop specific force capabilities. As noted in Annex IV (Annex I) of the 'Conclusions of the Presidency':

To develop European capabilities, Member States have set themselves the headline goal: by the year 2003, cooperating together voluntarily, they will be able to deploy rapidly and then sustain forces capable of the full range of Petersberg tasks as set out in the Amsterdam Treaty, including the most demanding, in operations up to corps level (up to 15 brigades or 50,000–60,000 persons). These forces should be militarily self-sustaining with the necessary command, control and intelligence capabilities, logistics, other combat support services and additionally, as appropriate, air and naval elements. Member States should be able to deploy in full at this level within 60 days, and within this to provide smaller rapid response elements available and deployable at very high readiness. They must be able to sustain such a deployment for at least one year. This will require an additional pool of deployable units (and supporting elements) at lower readiness to provide replacements for the initial forces.

As never before the political will to build a defense capability inside the EU *seemed* evident. But was the deed done? Not all were convinced. One knowledgeable analyst called the new arrangements 'a funeral disguised as a wedding'.[15] Nor could one forget the words of Jacques Poos, the former Luxembourg Foreign Minister who gained widespread notoriety in 1991 by announcing the 'hour of Europe' had arrived (Europe would save Bosnia)—an announcement followed by several years of under-achievement.

One of the biggest tests of the new commitment will be financial, the need to expend enormous sums of tax dollars to upgrade European military capabilities.

Of the Europeans, only the British and French had anything remotely approaching American capability. The French had two medium-size aircraft carriers, the obsolete Foch being actually faster than the new Charles de Gaulle. The British

---

[15] Michael Mandelbaum appearing on the Jim Lehrer *Newshour* (9 June 1999).

had two small carriers whose usefulness had been demonstrated in the Falklands War, but whose limited ability to project force depended on the short- and vertical-takeoff Harrier jets. (M. Walker 1999)

German analyst Josef Joffe adds: 'We essentially have WWII armies with no projection capability, no satellites, no ships, no aircraft carriers, and we're talking about very serious money.'[16]

US Defense Secretary William Cohen noted in 1999 that Europe's NATO members were collectively spending $44 billion annually on research and development and procurement, compared with America's $82 billion. In overall military spending, the Europeans trailed the USA by $174 billion to $270 billion. As a result, says US Ambassador to NATO Alexander Vershbow, 'the U.S. provides the lion's share of the strategic lift, logistical support and intelligence assets needed to sustain military operations beyond NATO territory. If the European Security and Defense Identity is to mean anything in practice, it must address these questions of capability.'[17]

Finally, there are other issues like operationalizing the CJTF concept, the role and participation of the USA, and many others—but they are not new challenges. The sea-change, however, is in the apparent will of the major EU member states to develop a defensive capability within CFSP, so that future Bosnias and Kosovos can be swiftly and effectively mitigated.

From a 'conceptual' point of view, the story until now has been almost exclusively an intergovernmental one, focusing on institutional design and 'deals'. As such, it has privileged the role not only of governments but of certain governments in particular (those of Britain, France, and Germany). None the less, it is also clear that the availability of certain organizational assets, especially those in the WEU, played a considerable role in facilitating the new initiatives undertaken during 1999. The next section will broaden this perspective to show governments reacting to other forces, like popular anguish over the events in the Balkans, which have been a further part of the revitalization of European defense.

The Kosovo Catalyst: Towards Integrating Defense

Kosovo [is] the historic catalyst which pushed the EU into adopting at the Cologne summit a formal European Defence Identity, aimed at

---

[16] Joseph Joffe appearing on the Jim Lehrer *Newshour* (9 June 1999).

[17] 'A New Line of Defense: Operation Allied Force is a testing ground for the idea of a coordinated, independent European defense force', *Time International* (12 April 1999), 153/i14: 42+(1).

giving the EU the military tools to ensure the peace of its own continent.

Guardian (7 June 1999)

Europe is a region of glaring, even harsh, contrasts. In the West, national integration is shaping the European Union. In the East, there is national disintegration. In the West there are questions of how to deepen and widen the integration of the EU. In the East there are questions of national separation, retribution, and ethnic cleansing. And alongside the pictures of jubilant Berliners surging over the hated Wall on that heady, almost undreamed of day in November 1989, are mass graves being unearthed in Bosnia . . . and again in Kosovo. The century began with the Balkans in war and it was to end, sadly, with the Balkans in war.

There is, however, a crucial difference between the end-of-century wars in Bosnia and in Kosovo. In Bosnia, Europeans and particularly those member states of NATO and the WEU, sought to excuse themselves from ultimate military responsibility for the atrocities. They were unprepared to go to war. The European Union had no defense policy, or capability, its apologists righteously asserted, and the USA was the preeminent leader of NATO, anyway. Thus, they asserted, the USA with its superior force, firepower, and capability should lead militarily in Bosnia. After the unfortunate intervention of an international force led by the United Nations, NATO became the surrogate international force charged with staunching the Balkan bloodshed.

With excruciatingly predictable consequences, the tragedy in Kosovo followed the inexorable logic of the tragedy in Bosnia. Following a demand for independence from a Serbia led by Slobodan Milosevic, the Serb military mercilessly retaliated with ethnic cleansing. But there was a difference. The daily roster of death and destruction had begun again, carried this time into living rooms in vivid 'living color'. The UK *Guardian* (7 June 1999) wrote that public opinion driven by the 'CNN-effect' made 'Kosovo the *historic catalyst*[18] which pushed the EU into adopting at the Cologne summit a formal European Defence Identity, aimed at giving the EU the military tools to ensure the peace of its own continent'.

While scholars disagree over the import and impact of the 'CNN-effect',[19] foreign affairs writer Michael O'Neil has described it as: 'People

[18] Italics added.

[19] Many studies have shown that US foreign policy is strongly influenced in a variety of ways by media coverage (Robinson 1999). Such a relationship is called the 'CNN-effect' and has been largely responsible for focusing government attention on pressing world problems. However, an analysis of media coverage of Somalia by Steven Livingston and Todd Eachus (1995) debunks the CNN-effect. (See also Mermin 1997.) They claim that, since the Bush administration's decision to intervene preceded extensive media coverage of the country's political and social problems, cause and effect had been reversed. Warren

expand[ing] their horizons of interest so that . . . popular opinion intrudes into the chambers of presidents and kings.'[20] And that popular opinion which intruded was angry and frustrated and demanded an end to the atrocities in Kosovo. Palliative answers about Bosnia no longer sufficed, and interestingly, and importantly, public opinion in Britain reacted dramatically. The state until then most willing to follow NATO and the USA and least willing to entertain plans of an independent European defense capability, Britain, harbored a public opinion willing to support military measures against Serbia and Milosevic. The *Independent* noted:

Through all the mood swings of the commentators on the war in Yugoslavia, two things remain unwaveringly fixed. One is British public opinion, which made up its mind from the start that the war was just, and soon after the start of it that it would have to be fought on the ground as well as from and in the air. *The Independent*'s opinion poll on May 24, 1999, found 65 per cent support for the war, and 58 per cent support for the sending of ground troops.

But even *before* the war in Kosovo reached fever pitch, *The Times* reported on March 31, 1999, that: '[the] public in the United States, Britain and, less clearly, France support military action more strongly than do politicians. Even the deployment of ground troops is backed by a majority in Britain.'

Two points emerge from this dissection of the horrors in Kosovo seen round the world: first, public opinion played a key role by demanding the British government's decision to take an activist, military posture against Serbia, a posture even more strident than the USA or most of the European Union's other members. Second, having been among the most intergovernmentally minded of all EU members on defense, and reluctant to consider integrated European approaches to defense, Britain's about-face on an integrated European defense made possible plans for integrating the WEU into the EU and the meaningful development of an ESDI.

'Spillover' to Further Integration or 'Spillback' to Intergovernmentalism?

Reviewing the long history of plans for an integrated European defense dating back to 1954, any analyst should conclude defense has been among the most jealously guarded of national capabilities. From that observation one might assume that further development would also be member-state driven and intergovernmental. Certainly, the relatively rapid agreement on

---

Strobel (1996) also asserts that the media (CNN-effect) has not pressured officials into making spontaneous changes in foreign policy, but it has changed how foreign policy is managed. 'It is like a shimmering desert mirage, disappearing as you get closer.'

[20] Steve Bell, 'Impact Of the Global Media Revolution', *USA Today* (Mar. 1999), 28(1).

creating an ESDI reflects that tendency towards intergovernmentalism. The events from the St Malô European Defense Charter to the agreement on creating a 'separable-but-not-separate' European force at the Helsinki Council of Ministers meeting lasted just over a year. But clearly it is also more than intergovernmentalism. Prime Minister Blair surely reacted to an acutely incensed and aroused public, when he gave the final and necessary assent to creating an EU instrumentality capable of making some common decisions on defense. Indeed, the first major common decision has already been made. At Helsinki in December 1999, the Union decided to create a European defense force with some 50,000 troops, the capacity to deploy in sixty days and to remain for at least twenty-four months (see above).

In addition to the interaction between governments and the broader political climate, it is important to note the role of existing European institutions. While it is true that the WEU was reactivated at the instigation of the French government in February 1984, it also had the strong support of the European Parliament and the WEU Assembly. Moreover, at a point in the WEU's history (the mid-1980s) when Eurosclerosis had set in and integration stagnated, the WEU's evolution depended on its own internal mechanisms and personnel, a period which should best be characterized as neofunctional. Indeed, as Donald Puchala's insightful review of the current theoretical debate between institutionalists and intergovernmentalists noted, the 'institutionalists evoke the neo-functionalist tradition' (Puchala 1999). Institutions, once established by governments, take on a life of their own and become the 'entrepreneurs of further integration'. This is the 'spillover' effect, produced in this case not by the inherent logic of task expansion but by the practices of institutional cooperation. Puchala continues: 'Ever since the flourishing of neo-functionalism during the 1960s . . . institutionalist interpretations have constituted the conventional theoretical wisdom of European Union studies.' Neofunctional-institutionalism remains a powerful explanatory tool, and it is clear that it helps us to explain the convergence of forces around European defense in recent years.

Sorting through which cause links to which effect is difficult at best. Michael Smith identifies an intriguing starting-point for his analysis of the relationship between the European Union and the changing European order he calls 'critical neoliberal institutionalist'. He notes: 'a neoliberal-institutionalist approach thus draws attention . . . to the complex and subtle interactions . . . between the persistent vitality of states and the increasingly dense web of international relations and private networks centering on the European Union' (Smith 1996). Clearly, the causes for integration and the current integration of defense are many, and sorting out the primal one is probably an exercise in futility.

At the same time, it is important to understand that the decisions reached at Helsinki in December 1999 and the newly created institutions are not set in stone. It is not certain that they cannot be repatriated or 'renationalized'. Of course, if the new institutions can 'spill back', they are not truly integrated. In functionalist terms, what will forestall 'spillback', or enhance 'spillover'? One major piton in the rock face of national defense is the economics of arms procurement. To put it simply, alongside the convergence of governmental strategies and public feelings, the push for European defense has both been conditioned by and has encouraged the restructuring of defense industries. For example, a European defense pillar independent of the USA (at least separable from US military assets) will require Europe to develop or acquire what the military calls 'legs', or airlift capacity. Rather than buying C17s in the USA from Boeing at $200 million to move troops and materiel, European taxpayers and their governments will demand to purchase armaments at home. Airbus Industrie's A400M now in development will be that C17 replacement, at less than half the cost ('only' about $90 million). And military procurement is both a WTO-acceptable subsidy for tightly budgeted European governments and a potential jobs program for European high unemployment.

The advantages (and necessity) of 'buying European' has also spawned a new dimension in European arms production. Germany's Daimler-Chrysler Aerospace and the French Aérospatiale Matra have formed the third largest global aerospace company in the world after Boeing and Lockheed Martin, which will be called European Aerospace, Defense and Space Company (EADS). EADS will be also primarily a private endeavor (85 per cent), which will be based neither in Munich nor in Paris, but in the Netherlands. It will be listed on the major European stock exchanges. And the plan is that the French government (owner of the 15 per cent public share) will not even be represented on the board of the EADS management, to ensure market-based decisions drive its corporate policies. In short, now that EU member governments have finally made a momentous commitment to integrating public policy, so have the private corporate 'members' of Europe made a momentous commitment to integrating economic policy. Decisions now being made by corporate Europe may well be the cement which will make permanent, or irreversible, the watershed decisions on defense integration.

There is a second variable, however, which will have an almost incalculably large influence on whether European defense policies spill over into new dimensions or spill back to the more nationally controlled policies of the past: US assent (Brenner 1998). Without question the USA is the world's '400 pound gorilla' in defense. The French, in begrudging recognition, call the USA a 'hyper-power', rather than 'just' a superpower. Of course, the USA is the hegemon in nuclear power (Russia's vast but aging capability not withstanding), but even in conventional weapons the USA is without peer. Some 80 per cent of the sorties flown in Kosovo were American, and the USA (at 3.2 per cent of GDP) outspends on defense every European country, allocating more than double Germany's 1.5 per cent.

For now, at least, the US military's global commitment and capability and its long-standing control of NATO commands will give it a commensurate voice in European military decisions. Significantly, the development of the European Defense Charter and a European military force do not really challenge any of the basic defense assumptions on which both NATO and the USA work. To the contrary, each step of the European pillar has been tailored to work within NATO, or if independent of NATO, never against it.

When President John Kennedy first put forward the notion of a 'European Pillar' in 1962, he saw the advantages of an independent military capability for Europe, which had the ability to carry out actions in situations in which the USA or NATO had decided not to act. President Bill Clinton has reaffirmed US support for an independent military force on numerous occasions, but still there is concern in the USA. Presidential aspirant and US Senator John McCain has worried out loud that Europe is drifting away from NATO, while others in the administration and Congress share the same concerns privately.[21] They worry that, at least in the short run, an independent European military policy is likely to exacerbate industrial rivalries in the traditionally US-dominated field of military aerospace and high-tech military electronics.

Michael O'Hanlon, a defense analyst at the Brookings Institution in Washington says it is 'regrettable' the USA sends mixed messages. 'On the one hand we want our allies to do more and to spend more, but at the same time we worry about how much they might distance themselves from us in doing so . . . Certainly, Mr. Cohen has been encouraging European nations to spend more on defense.'[22] The US position seems to be to proceed, but with caution. US Secretary of State Madeleine Albright has described the position of the USA as the '3-D don'ts': don't *duplicate* NATO efforts, don't *decouple* from the Atlantic Alliance (and USA), and don't *discriminate* against non-EU allies—the USA, Canada, Norway, Iceland, and Turkey. Still, 'proceed' precedes 'caution' The European Union has made a significant decision to include defense in its Common Foreign Security Policy, a decision which can be beneficial both to the EU

[21] *Washington Post* (10 Dec. 1999), 46.
[22] *The Christian Science Monitor* (9 Dec. 1999), 1.

and to the USA. In the words of French Foreign Minister Hubert Vedrine: 'The European Union as such should be able to intervene with its own means to defend its interests and its values. It should have the will and the capacity to do so.' 'Today Europe wants to play its full role.'[23]

Conclusion

So, has the phoenix risen? It may be too early to tell, but it appears that *reform* of the CFSP and *revival* of significant integration in the defense sector are occurring. Never before have the core members of the EU, NATO, and WEU agreed that an integrated defense policy and a common defense capability are necessary. They have selected in Javier Solana a uniquely qualified leader to organize and facilitate the next steps forward. In addition, they have asked for an accounting of existing forces and capabilities, and they have begun a major process to bring the WEU toolbox into the CFSP ambit, as well as committing themselves to build a European defense force of some 50,000 troops by 2002/2003. Those are major changes, which have evolved largely since the election of New Labour in Britain. And since the UK has long been the most intergovernmental and intransigent on the EU's role in defense, its acquiescence portends a sea-change. It should be pointed out, however, that the UK is also the most 'NATO-minded' of the major EU members, and that a cardinal aspect of the change in the UK position is that they now see the EU's strengthening as a key factor in the development of NATO. The USA may find the UK is much less easy to detach from EU defense positions in the future, and this may well have big implications for an enlarged NATO.[24]

It is not merely the member states' actions but a convergence of forces that have promoted the WEU and the ESDI. Clearly Kosovo was a catalyst to the process, and the evidence strongly suggests that the CNN-effect was critical in complementing and, perhaps, goading Prime Minister Blair's own instincts to align Britain and the European Union more closely. Furthermore, the long gestation period of the WEU well demonstrates the principles of neofunctionalism in which an organization and its élites nurture integration, allowing spillover to occur and preparing for that time when governments, the ultimate executives of the democratic will, see the necessity and utility of supporting further integration.

Although the member states of the EU have been able to evolve a new integrated institutional structure for defense within the CFSP, the ques-

---

[23] *The Christian Science Monitor* (9 Dec. 1999), 1.
[24] I want to thank Michael Smith for this observation.

tion arises whether this most nationally dominated of public policies will go forward (spill over) and enhance the integration process of the Union, or cause 'spillback' and inhibit the process of further European integration. One positive indicator of further spillover came with the almost immediate merger and development of European-wide conglomerates in the defense industry. Until recently, armaments largely had national markets and were also tied to national public policy. With the creation of very large conglomerates like EADS, which, when completed, will be driven by a European or even global market rather than nationally, the manœuver room for national military policy will be significantly circumscribed, much in the same way that Monnet saw national options for war foreclosed by the region-wide economic integration of coal and steel. Alternatively, although the USA has supported the principle of a European defense for more than three decades, in practice it might see its own leadership role and self-image as global leader questioned. More to the point, however, if the independent European defense policy were to challenge NATO (or even appeared to), that would cause a serious and negative US reaction, with the potential to exacerbate underlying centrifugal forces in ESDI and thus to encourage 'renationalization' or 'spillback'.

What then are the steps ahead? The members of the EU have decided they must take a final big step to reform a process, common European defense, begun fifty-five years ago. But in so doing they open another chapter, for the path and particulars of the next phase of the CFSP are neither determined, nor clear.

19

Resisting Reform or Risking Revival? Renegotiating the Lomé Convention

MARTIN HOLLAND

Our goal is clear, to revitalize ACP–EU relations; open new horizons and boost the chances of success. ACP–EU relations are still a key part of the Union's identity . . . On the threshold of the 21st century the ACP countries are looking forward, perhaps for the first time, to real prospects for development . . . This is not the time to slacken our efforts or downgrade the quality of our partnership. We should rather raise our political sights in the best sense of the term.
(Commissioner for Development, Joao de Deus Pinheiro, in Commission 1997*f*: foreword, original emphasis)

These ambitious words on the future of EU–ACP (African, Caribbean, and Pacific) relations set in motion the reform process of the Lomé Convention. First introduced in 1975, Lomé has represented the EU's principal treaty-based relationship with the developing world. Lomé was originally introduced as an Anglo-French compromise to accommodate historical links with a number of former European colonies (principally those of the UK, France, and Belgium). The early conventions were renewed every five years and their attraction has consistently grown: for example, while Lomé I had forty-six signatories, by 1985 the third Convention covered sixty-six ACP states. By the end of the fourth convention (which expired in February 2000) Lomé had increased its membership to seventy-one developing countries. In the context of 1970s, Lomé was depicted as an innovative partnership and benevolent contribution to development. In the context of the 1990s it was characterized as antiquated, unequal, and seemed increasingly out of kilter with the new direction of the global economy. Consequently, the prospects for a new Lomé V agreement were under serious threat, with radical reform seemingly the only option if the convention was to be maintained. More generally, Lomé stood as a test case for assessing the EU's future international actor capabilities and the prospects for an integrated approach to foreign policy and external relations.

It is in this context that the chapter examines this reform process that has dominated European development policy during the late 1990s. The process exemplifies each element of this collection's thematic structure: risks, reform, resistance, and revival. The continuation of EU-level development policy is arguably at risk. The nature of the reform has highlighted conflicting EU and ACP perspectives. Resistance (from the ACP and certain member states) has been evident, if somewhat diverse in effectiveness, while the motivation driving the process has been to revive and invigorate a policy sector that is commonly agreed to have failed to meet its objectives.

The chapter is divided into four sections. First, the theoretical context of the reform process is considered. Two specific integration approaches are adopted to provide this necessary location: Hill's 'capabilities-expectations' thesis (1993) and the multilevel governance approach of Marks, Hooghe, and Blank (1996). Hill's contribution provides a link between Lomé, the civilian nature of the EU as an international actor, and the Common Foreign and Security Policy (CFSP). The multilevel governance school emphasizes the complexity of the Lomé process and helps to identify a number of separate policy sectors and actors instrumental to the reforms.

Second, the anatomy of the reform process identifies three decision-making stages: the Green Paper (Commission 1997*f*), the Commission guidelines and the Council negotiating mandate. This innovative and consultative process lasted for more than three years and, perhaps paradoxically, the hallmark of this seemingly open process was an inequality in negotiation strengths. (It should be noted that this analysis does not cover the final outcome of the negotiations which were only concluded in early 2000, after this chapter was written.)

Third, the motivations driving, and resistance to, the reform agenda are examined. Empirical evidence related to past policy failure is presented. A key conceptually driven question is who are the main agenda-setting actors? Contrasts are drawn between the member states, the Commission and the European Parliament, between the member states themselves (the UK and Germany especially) as well as within the Commission. On the ACP side, internal solidarity is examined and the asymmetrical negotiating framework explored.

In the final section, the chapter considers a number of further questions (political and economic conditionality, global liberalization agendas, and WTO compliance) and critically places the Lomé reform within a global context. In particular, the question of subsidiarity is raised: simply, what type of development policy does the EU perform best? Does it merely duplicate bilateral development strategies or can we identify policy concerns that are better dealt with collectively? More generally the problems associated with policy coherence, complementarity, and cooperation both at the EU level and between the EU and member states are addressed. In this regard, the chapter implicitly recalls the theoretical debates outlined earlier. The argument is that the reform of Lomé faces the policy challenges that are familiar in other sectors, and that the scope and scale of the policy are significant and complex with respect to the EU's presence as an international actor.

Theoretical Contexts

Where should development policy in general, and Lomé in particular, be located within the integration debate? Is it best understood as an aspect of intergovernmentalism or of *communautaire* action? The Treaties suggest part of the answer. The 1993 Treaty on European Union (TEU) provides a general guide to the objectives of EU development policy. Article 130 states that Europe's policies should be 'complementary' to those of the member states. Both political and economic objectives are specified. Politically, EU policy has to contribute to 'consolidating democracy and the rule of law, and to that of respecting human rights and fundamental freedoms'. Economically, policy has to foster 'sustainable economic and social development . . . particularly (of) the most disadvantaged', to facilitate the 'gradual integration of the developing countries into the world economy', and to serve to eradicate poverty. Critics claim that these objectives have only succeeded in heightening expectations that cannot be met.

Importantly, development policy is also implicitly linked to the CFSP (Article C of the TEU Common Provisions) whereby the EU ensures 'the consistency of its external activities as a whole in the context of its external relations, security, economic and development policies'. And yet if development policy constitutes an aspect of the CFSP (in its broadest sense) how can this be reconciled with Pillar II limitations? The Lomé example amply illustrates the fallacy of compartmentalizing the EU's external relations between the first and second pillars. In any definition of national foreign policy, relations with the developing world are typically regarded as part of that policy domain. The EU's unique pillars partially obscure this logic. To adopt Allen and Smith's terminology, Lomé forms part of the EU's 'presence' in the international system (1991). Once accepted as part of the EU's personality as an international actor, it then becomes appropriate to locate the Lomé process within the general CFSP theoretical literature. Hill's 'capabilities-expectations' thesis is used here as a guide to examine this CFSP linkage and to locate development policy in a wider, but appropriate, foreign-policy-sector context.

Hill reminds us that the civilian nature of Europe's international role demands a wider definition of foreign policy than that offered by CFSP, a recognition of the context within which European foreign policy operates and a clearer demarcation between the EU's expectations and its capabilities to act (1993: 312–15). In doing so, Hill identifies those tasks that the EU should play if it is to be considered an effective actor in the international system. Four of these directly apply to EU–Lomé relations: a global intervention role, conflict mediation, joint supervision of the world economy, and as facilitator of First–Third World relations. The following analysis of the Lomé reforms provides a case-study against which to test the EU's international character and to gauge, in development policy at least, the extent to which the expectations-capabilities gap has been bridged.

The TEU also emphasizes the trinity of the three 'Cs'—cooperation, coherence, and complementarity—as the criteria around which development policy is constructed. This further helps to locate Lomé conceptually and suggests that the theoretical debate on multilevel governance could be useful for understanding the reforms. A variety of substate, state, and supranational actors and institutions influence the reform process and it is this complexity that in part shapes the policy outcome. As Marks, Hooghe, and Blank state, '[P]olicy-making in the EU is characterized by mutual dependence, complementary functions and overlapping competences' (1996: 378). For the multilevel governance approach to be valid, the authors state that:

- the Council shares decision-making authority with supranational institutions;
- individual States cannot guarantee desired outcomes through collective decisions; and,
- sub-national interests can influence State action (1996).

Indeed, the addition of actors external to the EU (the ACP states, the EU–ACP institutions) suggests that the Lomé process exhibits an even more extreme form of multilevel governance than that theorized for explanations for intra-EU policy sectors. As the following analysis illustrates, no single actor or institutional explanation captures the nuances of the reform decision-making process. The complex interaction of levels of authority, spheres of activity, and policy-making procedures, are all necessary components of a more comprehensive understanding. While conceptualization would be simpler if, for example, intergovernmental theory could be used to explain all aspects of EU activity, such simplification only serves to create an unrealistic decision-making model. Lastly, the adoption of a 'multilevel' perspective also argues that the relevance of integration theory is not limited to domestic policy spheres: as argued here, integration theories can inform us about external relations as well.

Both of these conceptual frameworks inform the following examination of the Lomé reform. Together they help to clarify the scope of Europe's international role, the expectations of external and internal actors, the multilevel agendas and motivations driving reform, and locate this policy sector within the overarching integration debate. At risk is the EU's credibility as the leading exponent of First–Third World relations. The revival of development policy is also questioned, particularly the EU's role in this sector. And competing actors illustrate varying degrees of resistance to policy reform.

The Anatomy of Reform

By the mid-1990s the old certainties pertaining to development policy were under threat and a new global agenda began to shape the EU's policy towards the Third World. In essence, the economic record indicated that, on all measures, ACP states had declined over the twenty-five years of the convention. Aid had proved to be ineffective and trade increasingly marginal (see next section). Furthermore, the demise of the cold war reduced the geostrategic importance of many ACP states, making them increasingly peripheral to Europe's interests. The status quo was confronted and challenged. The demand for reform was driven by the policy failures internal to Lomé as well as by a wider agenda that came to characterize the EU's external relations in the post-communist world of the 1990s. In general, a new intellectual rationale was driving Europe's external relations, emphasizing democracy, security, and economic liberalization. Arguably, on all of these criteria past Lomé practices had been inadequate. Indeed, economic market reforms were not an original objective of Lomé I or II, and these early conventions avoided any hint of political conditionality. If somewhat belatedly, the 1997–9 Lomé IV reform process finally located the convention within the broad democratization issues that had symbolized the EU's changed relations with Eastern and Central Europe in the 1990s. Simply, the political and economic consequences of the fall of the Berlin Wall on November 9, 1989, only finally began to have policy resonance for the ACP a decade later.

Reflecting this context, this section summarizes the evolution of the post-Lomé IV debates and identifies three phases of change: the 1996/7 Green Paper, the subsequent Commission guidelines, and the eventual 1998 negotiating mandate.

The Green Paper Options

In November 1996 the Commission issued its discussion Green Paper on the future of Lomé, the implications of which appeared far-reaching for Europe and the developing world. The traditional EU–ACP consensus in framing development policy was confronted by a divisive and perhaps paradigmatic change. The Green Paper specified four basic options, two of which involved radical reform.

- The maintenance of the status quo, based on the present contractual system of non-reciprocal preferences. Under this system ACP goods were given tariff-free access to the EU market without the Lomé countries being required to offer European exports reciprocal free access to ACP markets.
- A uniform application of the EU's Generalized Scheme of Preferences (GSP) for the ACP states, thereby removing the anomaly of differential treatment for different parts of the developing world. GSP provides reduced tariff advantages to specified countries and is one of the EU's most common and effective frameworks for trading relations.
- The introduction of uniform reciprocity in which EU exports to the ACP would enjoy the same preferential access to the ACP market as ACP products currently do in the European market. After an asymmetrical transitional period it was proposed that all ACP countries be required to extend reciprocity to the EU in line with WTO rules (creating, in effect, a single EU–ACP free trade area).
- Equally radically, differentiated reciprocity was proposed where different groups of ACP states were to receive different reciprocal arrangements with the EU (creating multiple free trade areas) (European Commission 1997*f: passim*).

Despite assertions from the Commission that the document neither constituted policy nor presumed a preferred outcome, it was clear from this new agenda that EU–ACP relations had reached a watershed. Even before the lengthy negotiations commenced in September 1998 it was apparent—despite the 'consultative' nature of the process—that the EU was insistent on reciprocity and free trade underpinning the new basis of 'partnership'. The original convention placed the notion of equal partnership as its core principle; however, as each renegotiation of the convention has suggested, the equality in the relationship appeared diminished. They were partners perhaps, but increasingly under the EU's terms and conditions. For some, it was not surprising, then, that the Commission floated the idea of root-and-branch reform, not cosmetic incrementalism, for Europe's development policy.

The Green Paper was designed to initiate a broad participatory and transparent policy debate; over the subsequent nine months there was intense commentary on these proposals from the ACP member states as well as the European Parliament. Not surprisingly, the ACP as well as Parliament vigorously opposed the most radical aspects. A special EU–ACP ministerial conference was convened in addition to the normal EU–ACP Joint Council meetings and consultation fora were held in each of the three main ACP regions. Each member state was invited to make their own submissions at the Working Group level and a variety of expert bodies and interested parties from civil society, non-governmental organizations, and the private sector were consulted from February until the final preparatory rapporteurs conference in late September 1997. This broad inclusive approach, while virtuous, appeared to many to be somewhat of a consultative charade, given the implicit agenda to modernize and streamline development cooperation.

The Commission Guidelines

Based on the results of this extensive, albeit compressed, consultation in October 1997, the Commission issued its policy guidelines for negotiating the future of the ACP–EU dialogue (which in turn formed the basis for the negotiation mandate agreed to by the Council in June 1998). The guidelines sought to reconcile 'flexibility and efficiency with a multi-pronged, integrated approach to cooperation', thereby placing the EU–ACP partnership on a new footing (Commission 1997c: 3). In essence this meant constructing a new overall agreement with the ACP that permitted differentiation and was open and flexible enough to accommodate changing circumstances. The five principle components were:

- The alleviation of poverty was reaffirmed as the cornerstone of the new partnership.
- The reform of financial management and technical cooperation procedures were advocated. The simplification and rationalization of cooperation instruments, as well as a greater involvement in and responsibility for development programs by the ACP, was proposed.
- Enhanced cooperation and economic partnership proposals modified the original Green Paper free-trade position: however, 'regional or subregional economic cooperation and partnership agreements linked to the overall EU–ACP partnership agreement' were called for.
- The introduction of geographical differentiation, while maintaining the ACP as a single group, was one of the two most contentious principles. Despite the ACP's claim of a collective identity and political will, the Commission remained insistent on differentiated procedures within the

collective ACP umbrella. As many as six subregions (four in Africa, the Pacific, and the Caribbean) were suggested.

- A stronger political dimension built on the existing conditionality that emphasized legitimacy and effective governance and a shared political vision. The incorporation of 'good governance' as a core criterion was to prove especially sensitive. While a widely debated and contentious concept, for the EU good governance can be regarded as 'managing public affairs in a transparent, accountable, participative and equitable manner showing due regard for human rights and the rule of law' and has both political and institutional dimensions (Commission 1998*b*: IIB.12).

This renewed political dialogue as a core principle with the developing world drew its authority from the EU's desire to enhance its capacity—and credibility—in external relations. Development policy formed one part of this wider agenda.

The EU sought from the ACP a commitment to pursue reforms in the political, economic, social, and environmental spheres consistent with Europe's definition of 'good governance' described above. Human rights and democratic principles constitute the heart of the dialogue: indeed, these two conditions have been part of every agreement signed between the EU and third countries since 1995. From a Lomé perspective, the application of human rights is associated with a wide range of social, educational, and gender policies. Democratic principles are similarly linked to development. Although the Commission did not specify a precise model, the EU does insist on the fundamental features of representative democracy being developed—the separation of powers, independence of the judiciary, regular free elections, and the rights to information and freedom of expression.

In the guidelines, good governance is regarded as crucial to development and constitutes a permanent feature of the political dialogue. The concept involves the open and responsible management of economic and social development as well as the prevention and eradication of corruption. A further permanent feature will be conflict prevention and settlement, enhancing the EU's credibility as an international actor as well as clearly linking development policy to CFSP. Obviously, as issues arise and the political context of relations changes, core topics will be modified or expanded. This breadth and openness of the political dialogue, as proposed by the Commission, is its most important feature and circumstances will dictate whether the dialogues will be multilateral, regional, or even bilateral.

The guidelines identify the creation of an adequate institutional capacity to support development as a key area where the EU can play a distinctive role. In particular, the capacities of the state and the public service within the context of democratization are identified as priority areas for reform and support. An efficient state with appropriate and effective delivery mechanisms is a development prerequisite. As history has shown, aid and policy direction has proved inadequate where developing countries have lacked the institutional infrastructure to effectively implement policy. Capacity building is therefore a guiding criterion for assessing the EU's involvement in cooperation agreements—and covers not just institutional capacities, but all aspects of civil society and economic sectors. For example, the state must have effective decentralization structures if democratic practices are to become secure. A free media, increased women's participation, and a willingness of the state to allow mechanisms for a pluralistic balance of authority ('civil society') are fundamental to fostering the democratic process. Similarly, a market economy is seen as the only foundation on which such a democratic process could properly flourish.

The significant changes to the economic partnership were premised on the widely held view that Lomé trade cooperation had been a failure (see next section); consequently, the Commission guidelines proposed a number of policy reforms. First, they recommended that the system of unilateral trade preferences be replaced by a more balanced and country-specific partnership. The underlying motivation was the ubiquitous desire to incorporate the ACP into the world economy. While an overall EU–ACP agreement was to be maintained, strengthening regional integration by signing individual EU agreements with Africa (subdivided in West, Central, Southern, and East), the Caribbean, and the Pacific was promoted as a long-term objective. The initial prospects for developing regional integration proposals look positive: however, the creation of any regional groupings remains at the ACP's discretion. Even in the most advanced existing regional cooperation schemes there are significant disparities between members.

This diversity persuaded the Commission that differentiated agreements were essential within the context of an overall agreement. This differentiation would recognize the need for differing levels of reciprocity and asymmetrical liberalization timetables. Changing the existing uniform Lomé provisions is a complex and lengthy process: two stages were identified. From 1998 to 2000 the overall general framework was to be negotiated with specialized regional agreements adopted from 2000–3 (either non-reciprocal cooperation agreements for least developed countries (LDCs) or reciprocal free trade areas for the economically stronger ACP states). Once in place, the regionalized economic cooperation agreements would introduce the concept of reciprocity to trading relations and form the basis for eventual free trade. While WTO exemptions may initially be required, an important longer term EU objective is to harmonize preferences progressively and make them compatible with WTO provisions without the need for waivers. As the sensitive banana, sugar, and beef regimes have shown, such waivers are always open to challenge by affected third parties.

The Council Negotiating Mandate

The Council's negotiating mandate was finally agreed in June 1998, with formal negotiations commencing three months later. The timing was important, as the UK held the presidency for the first half of 1998 and the recently elected British government had strong views on development priorities. The changes and similarities from both the Green Paper and the Commission guidelines are outlined below. Irrespective of the institutional openness of the process and the novelty of the consultative Green Paper, the negotiations between the EU and the ACP were vastly unequal. Those changes that did appear in the negotiating mandate were more likely to reflect the influence of the member states or the European Parliament than the ACP. For example, whether the current levels of access and preferences could be maintained was an area of dispute. While the Council supported the Commission's general trade liberalization thrust, a number of member states (the UK and the Scandinavian countries in particular) were critical of this being imposed on all ACP states and promoted alternative mechanisms for those ACP states unable or unwilling to move towards reciprocity and liberalization.

During the last week of the 1998 British presidency, the General Affairs Council approved the negotiating directives for a new EU–ACP agreement. At one level this decision indicated that there was consensus on the European side pertaining to the future direction and objectives of the development partnership. However, this consensus only came at the cost of compromise, bargains, and reservations. The British presidency managed to forge an agreement that permitted the least developed countries to retain their existing Lomé preferences rather than adopt the new free trade regime. This meant that, for these forty countries, non-reciprocal zero duty access to the European market was maintained. This constituted a significant policy change from the most radical of the Green Paper proposals and while there was general consensus on this principle, the timeframe remained problematic. The EU was divided between those Northern states that wanted this provision to be phased out within five years and those, such as Spain, that argued for a much longer timeframe.

Policy towards those remaining ACP countries that were not LDCs highlighted the tensions within the European 'consensus' and emphasized the key role played by the presidency. The Dutch, thinking beyond the ACP mandate, wanted the GSP approach extended to all developing countries; conversely Spain objected to any discussion of GSP, arguing that this was outside the remit of the Lomé talks. France, Italy, and Germany were concerned that the GSP option would actually undermine the free trade objective of the negotiations. It was finally accepted that any ACP country that was either unwilling or unable to join a free trade regime would retain at least the current preferences offered through the GSP system. This signaled a substantive change of position within the member states and is indicative of the persuasive power of the UK presidency. Consequently, with respect to trading relations at least, the 1998 negotiating mandate was more sympathetic to the ACP's development agenda than a radical reading of the earlier Green Paper had anticipated.

In summary, the June mandate established:

- maintenance of the present Lomé rules until at least 2005;
- negotiations to take place between 2000 and 2005 on economic partnership agreements between the EU and six regional subgroups;
- the introduction of free trade by 2015 at the earliest between the EU and countries suitable for economic liberalization;
- a review of the banana, beef, and sugar protocols in 2004 in the light of the new Lomé agreement and WTO obligations; and,
- a general review in 2004 on asymmetrical timetables for FTAs and future measures to be taken for countries unwilling or unable to join FTAs.[1]

The underlying objectives of the EU were summarized by the Secretary-General of Commission DG VIII as consolidating commercial ties and facilitating regional integration within a comprehensive framework that encompassed trade, investment, and development. These initiatives, however, would still require the consent of the WTO for any waivers involving non-reciprocity, as well as its agreement that a fifteen-year transition period was acceptable. More crucially, the ACP states remained opposed to the new trading regime and 'good governance' conditionality.

Resistance, Actors and Motivations

The economic motivation behind the reform agenda was clear-cut. A quarter-century of EU aid and development had largely failed to improve the ACP economies or see them reintegrated to any significant degree within the global economy. Despite benign intentions, the non-reciprocal

---

[1] *Agence Europe*, 7252 (1998).

preferential access for Lomé products failed to improve either the value or the balance of EU–ACP trade. Some critics argued that First–Third World dependency had become even more deeply embedded during this period (Grilli 1993). The preferences given to certain raw materials had the perverse effect of maintaining a primary-product-based neocolonial economy. As late as 1993, four-fifths of ACP exports to Europe were composed of food and raw materials (including fuel) (Commission 1995*b*). This economic record came under renewed scrutiny during the 1990s: the economic demands of Eastern and Central Europe and calls for financial constraint within the EU budget from key member states (principally Germany) combined to make policy reform a priority.

The economic case is compelling. Analyses are united in identifying the economic decline of the ACP over the last quarter-century. The current seventy-one Lomé states have a combined population in excess of 600 million (including now all of sub-Saharan Africa). However, as described in Table 19.1, after a promising rise in the value of ACP exports under Lomé I and II, from a peak of 26.8b ECU in 1985, this figure had fallen to just 18.6b ECU a decade later. By way of comparison, from a similar base in 1985 (26.0b) EU imports from Asia had more than tripled by 1994, standing at 83.9b ECU. Indeed, while the ACP could claim to be the leading developing country exporter to the EU prior to the 1980s, this position had deteriorated to such an extent that by 1994 the ACP group had fallen to bottom position. The ACP share of EU imports stood at just 3.4 per cent compared with 4.9 per cent (for Latin America), 5.7 per cent (the Mediterranean), and 15.5 per cent (Asia). A similar pattern is evident in the EU's export markets. The value of EU exports to the ACP had fallen from its 1985 peak of 17.4b ECU to 14.9b by 1994. Conversely, EU exports to Asia, Latin America, and the Mediterranean all substantially increased during this period and were worth 70.7, 28.4, and 33.1 billion ECU respectively by 1994. The only positive aspect of this trading profile is that, while in general decline, the balance of trade with the EU has consistently favored the ACP under all four Lomé Conventions. Given this context, the reform of the existing ineffective Lomé trading preferences was to prove irresistible.

Turning from economics to politics, the leitmotiv of Lomé has always been its claim of partnership. The 1999 negotiating process, however, was marked more by inequality and one-way conditionality than parity. Not that such an outcome was particularly surprising or unique. Each of the successive Lomé revisions had seen the European perspective predominate, leading Ravenhill (1985) to describe the relationship as one of 'collective clientelism'. Once the 1999 negotiations on substantive issues began, significant differences became apparent between the EU and the ACP

TABLE 19.1. *EU—Developing Country Trade (1976–1994)*

	1976	1980	1985	1990	1992	1994
EU Imports to EU (ECU bn)						
ACP	10.5	19.4	26.8	21.9	18.0	18.6
Asia	6.7	16.0	26.0	50.9	66.4	83.9
Latin America	8.3	13.7	25.8	25.7	24.8	26.7
Mediterranean	9.6	16.4	32.3	29.8	30.3	30.8
All LDCs	70.7	114.3	128.9	143.8	145.6	165.9
All non-EC	157.7	269.9	399.7	461.5	487.6	543.2
Exports from EU (ECU bn)						
ACP	9.6	15.7	17.4	16.6	17.0	14.9
Asia	7.5	13.1	29.4	41.0	47.1	70.7
Latin America	7.7	12.0	13.5	15.6	20.4	28.4
Mediterranean	12.3	19.8	29.8	28.5	28.6	33.1
All LDCs	550.9	83.4	121.7	134.2	153.1	193.3
All non EC	141.3	221.1	380.8	415.3	436.1	541.8
World	292.9	475.1	811.8	1,076.6	1,137.8	1,297.9
% share of EU imports						
ACP	6.7	7.2	6.7	4.7	3.7	3.4
Asia	4.2	5.9	6.5	11.0	13.6	15.5
Latin America	5.3	5.1	6.5	5.6	5.1	4.9
Mediterranean	6.1	6.1	8.1	6.5	6.2	5.7
All LDCs	44.8	42.4	34.7	31.2	29.9	30.5
All non-EC	100.0	100.0	100.0	100.0	100.0	100.0

Source: Commission (1997*f*).

negotiating mandates. The greatest resistance to change focused on the trade provisions and on political dialogue. The actors and motivations driving this resistance are examined below.

Creating a common ACP position was not without difficulty: a consensus had to be constructed on broad policy positions that accommodated the particular requirements of seventy-one sovereign states, drawn from three continents with often dissimilar economic needs. That a consensus was found in part reflected the fact that the ACP negotiating mandate on trade was reactive and forged in response to the EU's free trade agenda. The significant differences between the EU and ACP mandates covered three issues. First, the ACP proposed a longer FTA transition phase (ten years as opposed to five suggested by the EU). Second, the ACP sought to retain as much as possible of the existing Lomé provisions and protocols—not just for the least developed countries as suggested by the EU, but also for what the ACP denoted as 'highly vulnerable countries', those with 'small economies' or with economic levels only marginally above

LDC definitions (such as Zimbabwe and Ghana). Third, and most optimistically, the ACP called for improved access for agricultural products and for a relaxation in rules-of-origin requirements. This issue underlined the multilevel complexities of decision-making and the linkage between internal EU economic and political questions and external relations: simply, domestic lobbies make it difficult to make CAP concessions that favor Lomé producers. In addition, the ACP countries were concerned that even the status quo was not assured and that unilateral non-tariff barriers might in the future emerge (based on social or environmental criteria).

Turning to the political aspects of the mandate, there was a broad European consensus on the main elements contained within the Green Paper: democratization, human rights, and good governance. The increased importance of the political dialogue was also emphasized. However, there was no unanimity between the developing countries and the EU on the content and application of these concepts. The agenda was principally Euro-centric and met significant resistance from the ACP.

The extension of political conditionality was the most contentious issue. Just like economic conditionality which specifies economic conditions and requirements to be met before loans or aid is given, political conditionality set conditions concerning democratic practices, the rule of law, human rights, and participation which had to be observed. For the ACP the concept of partnership and new forms of conditionality were viewed as antagonistic. The ACP did not challenge the conditionality introduced in Lomé IV. What was resisted was the EU's agenda to extend the scope of good governance as a development *prerequisite*, particularly given the varied interpretations of what constituted good governance. While the ACP subscribed to the principle of good governance, they rejected the European position that it should be the principle on which aid is made conditional. They argued that good governance is in part a result of institutional development and sustained efforts to build national capabilities (especially legislative, judicial, and executive): these levels of institutional development vary widely across the ACP and can only be improved through continued and guaranteed support. Indeed, to make aid conditional could perversely undermine such institution-building.

This resistance seems unlikely to prevail. The asymmetry that has typified successive Lomé agreements seems destined to be extended to good governance. The concept, defined in European terms and by European standards, could be incompatible with individual ACP cultures and institutional capacities. Common assumptions and motivations guiding the good governance agenda cannot be presumed. Not only are the standards of good governance Euro-centric, but the EU exercises the unilateral right to suspend any form of development assistance if it concludes that good governance has been breached. The exclusion of any joint mechanism for measuring good governance or any joint procedures for suspension produced vociferous ACP opposition. Article 366 of the revised Lomé IV provides for suspension where one of the 'essential elements' of the convention is breached—and good governance has come to be regarded as such an essential feature by the EU. The suspension clause is implemented when the Council (on a Commission or member-state initiative) decides by QMV to open consultations with an offending ACP state. The state concerned then has a maximum of thirty days to address the EU's objection. Failing this, the EU can evoke either partial suspension of the Lomé provisions (acting by QMV) or their full suspension where the member states are unanimous.

A similar pattern of marginalization can also be detected in the nature of the proposed political dialogue. Despite shared concerns (conflict prevention, post-conflict reconstruction, and sustainable development), the EU's priorities (such as human rights, democracy, drugs and crime, gender equality) were given a high profile. In contrast, the ACP agenda was largely dismissed: the ACP were concerned how EU activities impacted negatively in the developing world (such as arms sales, activities of European transnationals, and even nuclear testing). Migration further underlined the two conflicting perspectives. The EU saw this exclusively in terms of poverty, human rights, conflict, and illegal immigration. The ACP, conversely, wanted to expand the agenda to cover the treatment of ACP immigrants in relation to Schengen and the free movement of individuals—something the EU was loath to do.

Institutionalizing the political dialogue was also important. While there was common agreement on a flexible approach and a reinforced dialogue, the EU faced, as it does with virtually all third countries, an expectations–capabilities gap. The ACP value and seek frequent high-level contacts. The question is whether the EU can accommodate these demands in its already overcrowded international calendar. The EU also sought to expand the scope of contacts to non-state actors, or civil society. For some ACP members this posed problems pertaining to civil–state relations. Finally, the ACP and the EU had differing positions regarding future accession to the ACP group. The ACP wished to incorporate newly independent territories as well as Cuba, thereby breaking the 'colonial' perception of membership while the EU was reluctant to commit to such an open agenda.

Clearly, the ACP states were not driving the Lomé reform process—Europe was. But which institution within the EU was dominating the agenda? Was it key member states, the Commission, the European Parliament, or even a range of subnational actors? As in other EU policy sectors, the question of 'who pays' in part suggests an explanation. The financing of Lomé once again draws attention to the consequences and contradictions of intergovernmentalism as a policy framework and underlines the value of a multilevel approach to understanding decision-making complexity. While Lomé is a common EU policy and based on a bilateral treaty, its funding does not come out of the EU budget, but from the member states by way of direct contributions to the European Development Fund (EDF). France and Germany provide virtually half of these funds (24.3 and 23.4 per cent respectively) and the UK and Italy a further quarter (12.7 and 12.5 per cent each). In total the EDF provided funding for Lomé of 12,987m ECU under the five-year EDF 8 program (plus another 1,658m through the European Investment Bank) (Commission 1996*b*: 6). However, while EDF funding is significant, the EU's collective aid is typically exceeded by the bilateral programs of France and Germany and the combined sum of the Fifteen's bilateral development programs amount to around four times the Lomé figure.

The influence of France in shaping Lomé policy towards francophone interests is well documented and partially explained by its role as the single most important financial contributor. However, an innovation in the mid-term Lomé review process was the initial intervention by Germany for radical reform, motivated by financial considerations. Changes in government in both Germany (1998) and the UK (1997) altered the earlier parameters of the negotiations. The role of the UK presidency has already been noted above and should not be minimized as a crucial factor in extending non-reciprocal preferences for the least developed countries. Similarly, the new SPD–Green German federal coalition assumed the EU presidency of the first half of 1999 and was influential in addressing the question of Third World debt, albeit through bilateral rather than EU mechanisms. This focus on key member states is reminiscent of the polity-making role in Moravcsik's liberal intergovernmentalism (1993). While important, limiting an explanation of the Lomé reform process to just these factors is unsound: the role played by the Commission was at least of equal significance.

The Commission's role *vis-à-vis* the member states underlines the implicit value of a multilevel governance approach to the Lomé policy sector. Without diminishing the ultimate political authority of the member states in determining the final decision, the Commission was the agenda-setter and defined the margins of reform through its Green Paper and 1997 guidelines. Both documents introduced the possibility of creating regional free trade areas and replaced the status quo as the basis of negotiations. The Commission's input was fundamental to radical reform. It would be misplaced to minimize the final political authority of the member states in decision-making (particularly given the influential role played by the British and German presidencies). However, it would be equally unbalanced to disregard the fact that the member states were reacting to the ambitious agenda outlined by the Commission. The context within which decision-making was undertaken was primarily shaped by the Commission.

The emergence of a free trade agenda can be seen as the outcome of an intra-departmental competition. Traditionally, Lomé and development policy had been conducted exclusively through DG VIII, with DG I having competence over external economic relations more generally. Under Sir Leon Brittan, a pervasive free trade agenda had been promoted that was to affect and redefine the parameters of development policy. A foretaste of this change was evident in the negotiations with post-apartheid South Africa. Although a developing country, the EU was insistent on defining negotiations with South Africa on the basis of free trade. The twenty-three rounds of negotiations spanning three years were concluded in May 1999 when the EU signed its first free trade agreement with an ACP state (Holland 2000). Clearly DG I had defined the context of these negotiations and a similar tendency is apparent in the Lomé reforms.

The wider involvement of other actors also supports such a multilevel approach to the Lomé reform. First, the Green Paper was consultative and as a process sought to involve a variety of actors, including interest groups, civil society, and the ACP states themselves. The ACP–EU institutions, as well as the European Parliament, played a formal role. Although their policy influence was moderated by an unequal negotiating basis (as discussed above), the multiplicity of actors below the member-state level and the complexity of their relationships demands a theoretical framework that reflects the essence of multilevel governance. To exclude the ACP states from any explanation of the reform outcome would be unjustified. Although primarily reactive in nature, their consent was a precondition to reform. Had the ACP been more cohesive and more effective, clearly their importance as an actor in the reform process would be enhanced. However, their weakness does not contradict the general theoretical point that more than one level of analysis is needed to interpret the reform process.

In summary, the necessary conditions for multilevel governance set out above have been exceeded. Shared decision-making and limitations on state authority are present, with additional actors and institutions external to the EU contributing to this diffuse decision-making network.

Risking revival?

The Lomé process raised several issues that confront existing assumptions and in doing so create risks for institutions, actors, and policy sectors. The most challenging of these relates to the question of subsidiarity. The TEU was of mixed parentage, mixing both intergovernmental and *communautaire* principles. Its problematic progeny, subsidiarity, defined the scope of integration, both past and future, and provided a mechanism whereby policy competences could be assigned to the appropriate level of governance: the Community or the member state. The onus is on the center to demonstrate that policy is more appropriately and more effectively executed collectively than it is bilaterally.

Legally, the concept of subsidiarity is confined to Pillar I competences, and even here its application to internal policies has been controversial. However, subsidiarity can also be usefully applied (if in a political rather than legal sense) to external relations. In relation to Lomé and development policy in general, the concept questions whether a specific role can be defined for the EU that is both distinct and superior to those already played by the member states individually. Again, the onus is on the EU level to demonstrate that it provides the better mechanism for conducting and delivering development policy than the member states (Holland 1998*a*: 17). By linking the issue of subsidiarity to the reform process, the continuation of European-level policy competence in this sector is put at risk. Indeed, the very rationale for reform—that twenty-five years of Lomé policy had largely failed—arguably confirms that doing things at the EU level is demonstrably not superior to bilateral action. What, then, is the evidence?

Lomé is not an exclusive policy sector. Development policy is an area of mixed competences, with parallel national and EU policy levels existing in tandem. While respecting the three 'Cs' (cooperation, coherence, and complementarity), what is the demarcation between these two levels? What can the EU do best? The emphasis on good governance and human rights conditionality is perhaps one such area where collective rather than individual action is appropriate. Such principles, at least from an Eurocentric position, are universal, not specific, and therefore appropriate to uniform application. Similarly, building institutional capacity can suggest a distinct collective European role. Paradoxically, the one characteristic that is widely accepted as being unique to Lomé, that of 'partnership', is under threat. Despite remaining a core Treaty principle, the notion of partnership has effectively lost meaningful content. Partnership denoted equality, equitable processes, and a consensual decision-making style. The anatomy of reform described above confirms the process as one of unequal negotiation, agenda-management, and implicit coercion tantamount to a *fait accompli*.

In other respects, differentiation is also problematic. While TEU Article 130 does define the EU's objectives, it fails to establish why the various policy elements it outlines are distinctly European. Is it the case that the EU can more effectively promote 'sustainable economic and social development' or be the best vehicle for the reduction of poverty? Indeed, given the ambitions of these objectives and the limited capacity of Lomé programs and available European Development Fund financing, the EU clearly does not have the capacity within its existing own resources to satisfy these demands or expectations. Conversely, perhaps poverty alleviation does constitute a potential EU-specific policy objective. The scale of the issue and the need for coordination could suggest at least a clear EU-level function.

Shared rather than exclusive competences may be the answer to this policy sector. Parallel EU and member-state programs and mechanisms (that are complementary and coordinated) may provide added value that neither level can achieve independently. The danger, however, is of duplication: it is hard to justify the EU simply offering a sixteenth program to complement the member states. As it is principally an intergovernmental agreement, the Fifteen can choose between committing their individual development resources bilaterally or through Lomé. The 1997–2000 reform of Lomé has underlined this choice and for the first time since its inception in 1975 has forced its supporters to justify the continuation of a collective approach.

More controversially, does the EU even need a development policy such as Lomé? Variable geometry or Europe à la carte would suggest that at best it is a candidate for 'flexibility' rather than a core function. The EU's involvement as an international actor, at least in part, can provide a rebuttal. There are compounding expectations that the EU will continue to play a leading role in First–Third World relations (supporting Hill's hypotheses outlined above)—from the ACP, the international system, supranational institutions, member states, and subnational lobbies. Integration is not an internal phenomenon without external implications and consequences. Whether Lomé can match these expectations to its capabilities more successfully than has been achieved in Europe's foreign policy in general remains, however, as yet unanswered.

In conclusion, while the final outcome of the Lomé reform will only be known in 2000, this analysis has outlined the policy direction and the probable implications, both for the ACP states and for the EU. In the context of a shrinking EU budget, enlargement, and Central and Eastern

European priorities, the possibility of the renationalization of development policy with the Third World cannot be ignored. Despite the pillarization of Maastricht, an essential aspect of the new relationship from the European perspective is to incorporate development policy within the ambit of the EU's foreign policy. Consequently, in line with Article J(1), development cooperation must serve the objectives of the CFSP and as such provides a further test for assessing the EU's future international actor capabilities.

Although it is too early to predict with absolute accuracy the eventual resolution of the global versus regional format debate, it is clear that the outcome will reflect the wider trading agenda being actively pursued by the EU: the progressive assimilation of the developing countries into the wider world economy, and the promotion of the longer term objective of global free trade. While the very weakest developing economies may require prolonged protection, the EU's emphasis seems clearly in favor of 'leveling up' trading relations on the basis of normal country-to-country reciprocity. This (and Europe's free-trade agenda) is clearly linked to WTO obligations that seek to dismantle trade barriers (albeit in an asymmetrical fashion). Whatever post-Lomé arrangements are devised they will have to comply with the broader WTO multilateral trade liberalization program.

Faced with this reality, radical reform has been embraced (if more enthusiastically by the EU than the ACP) as the remedy for revival. Despite the eleventh-hour concessions brokered by the 1998 British Presidency, a transition to regional free trade agreements is set to dominate the future of the Lomé relationship. While this has been an EU-driven agenda, the external motivation has been global in the form of the WTO. The banana saga added weight to those who sought a fundamental change to Lomé's non-reciprocal basis. Despite a prolonged appeal process through the WTO, Europe's banana regime which gave favorable access and tariff concessions to ACP products over those grown elsewhere, by US multinationals in Latin America for example, was ultimately found to be contrary to WTO trade rules. The presumed protection and preferences provided to ACP producers by Lomé were simply illegal. Despite the economic plight of several Caribbean Lomé producers, the ruling demonstrated that the EU's bilateral agreements were not sacrosanct, but subject to normal forms of international regulation such as the WTO. Similarly, the ill-fated Seattle WTO Millennium Round of negotiations sensitized many within the EU to addressing perceived incompatibilities with existing regulations, in order to strengthen Europe's case for widening global liberalization in areas such as services, competition, and labor standards (European Commission 1999*a*). The revitalization of Lomé called for by

Pinheiro, the then Commissioner for Development, is best understood through this wider context, once again indicating the multilevel nature of EU decision-making. The case of Lomé has illustrated inflated expectations (on the part of the EU and the ACP) as well as an inadequate capacity to deliver policy objectives. It also confirms, however, that the Lomé reform process can only be understood within the broader context of the EU's attempt to establish a more effective and coherent international European presence.

BIBLIOGRAPHY

Adler, E. (1997). 'Seizing the Middle Ground: Constructivism in World Politics', *European Journal of International Relations*, 3: 319–63.

Albin, S., and Bär, S. (1999). 'Nationale Alleingänge nach dem Vertrag von Amsterdam. Der neue Art. 95 EGV: Fortschritt oder Rückschritt für den Umweltschutz', *Natur und Recht*, 21/4: 185–92.

Allen, D. (1998). '"Who Speaks for Europe?": The Search for an Effective and Coherent External Policy', in J. Peterson and H. Sjursen (eds.), *A Common Foreign Policy for Europe? Competing Visions of the CFSP* (London: Routledge).

—— (2000). 'The Structural Funds and Cohesion', in H. Wallace and W. Wallace (eds.), *Policy Making in the European Union*, 4th edn. (Oxford: Oxford University Press).

—— and Smith, M. (1991). 'Western Europe's Presence in the Contemporary International Arena', in M. Holland, (ed.), *The Future of European Political Cooperation: Essays on Theory and Practice* (London: Macmillan).

Alter, K. (1998a). 'Explaining National Court Acceptance of European Court Jurisprudence: A Critical Evaluation of Theories of Legal Integration', in A.-M. Slaughter, A. Stone Sweet, and J. H. H. Weiler (eds.), *The European Court and National Courts: Doctrine and Jurisprudence* (Oxford: Hart Publishing), 227–52.

—— (1998b). 'Who are the "Masters of the Treaty"?: European Governments and the European Court of Justice', *International Organization*, 52/1: 121–47.

Amato, G., and Batt, J. (1999). *The Long-Term Implications of EU Enlargement: The Nature of the New Border*, Final Report of a Reflection Group (Florence: European University Institute).

Andersen, M. S. (1998). 'Environmental Policies in Europe', in J. J. Hesse and T. A. J. Toonen (eds.), *The European Yearbook of Comparative Government and Public Administration* (Baden-Baden: Nomos Verlag), 205–26.

Andersen, Svein S., and Eliassen, Kjell A. (1993). 'Complex Policy-Making: Lobbying the EC', in S. S. Andersen and K. A. Eliassen (eds.), *Making Policy in Europe* (London: Sage), 35–53.

Anderson, J. (ed.) (1999). *Regional Integration and Democracy* (Lanham, Md., and Oxford: Rowman & Littlefield).

Andrews, David (1993). 'The Global Origins of the Maastricht Treaty on EMU: Closing the Window of Opportunity', in A. W. Cafruny and G. G. Rosenthal (eds.), *State of the European Community: the Maastricht Debates and Beyond* (Harlow Essex and Boulder, Colo.: Longman and Lynne Rienner), 107–24.

Archer, Clive, and Butler, Fiona (1992). *The European Community: Structure and Process* (New York: St Martins Press).

Armstrong, K. (1998). 'Legal Integration: Theorizing the Legal Dimension of European Integration', *Journal of Common Market Studies*, 36/2: 155–74.
——and Bulmer, S. (1998). *The Governance of the Single European Market* (Manchester: Manchester University Press).
Arnull, A. (1996). 'The Scope of the Common Commercial Policy: A Coda on Opinion 1/94', in N. Emiliou and D. O'Keeffe (eds.), *The European Union and World Trade Law* (Chichester: John Wiley and Sons).
Arrowsmith, Sue, and Fernández Martin, Jose M. (1993). 'Developments in Public Procurement in 1992', *European Law Review*, 18/4 (Aug.), 323–45.
Artis, M., and Winkler, B. (1998). 'The Stability Pact: Safeguarding the Credibility of the European Central Bank', *National Institute Economic Review*, 163: 87–98.
——and Zhang, Wenda (1999). 'Further Evidence on the International Business Cycle and the ERM: Is there a European Business Cycle?', *Oxford Economic Papers*, 51: 120–32.
Aspinwall, M. (1998). 'Collective Attraction: The New Political Game in Brussels', in J. Greenwood and M. Aspinwall (eds.), *Collective Action in the European Union* (London: Routledge).
Avery, Graham, and Cameron, Fraser (1998). *The Enlargement of the European Union* (Sheffield: Sheffield Academic Press for UACES).
Axelrod, R. (1984). *The Evolution of Cooperation* (New York: Basic Books).
Bacchetta, Philippe, and van Wincoop, Eric (1998). 'Does Exchange Rate Stability Increase Trade and Capital Flows?' Manuscript (New York: Federal Reserve Bank of New York).
Bach, M. (1992). 'Eine leise Revolution durch Verwaltungsverfahren: Bürokratische Integrationsprozesse in der Europäischen Gemeinschaft', *Zeitschrift für Soziologie*, 21/1: 16–30.
Baker, J. (1989). 'A New Europe, a New Atlanticism: Architecture for a New Era', speech at the Berlin Press Club, 12 Dec., *Europe Documents*, 1588 (15 Dec.).
Baker, S., and Jehlicka, P. (eds.) (1998). *Dilemmas of Transition: The Environment, Democracy and Economic Reform in East Central Europe* (Ilford: Frank Cass).
Balassa, B. (1961). *The Theory of Economic Integration* (London: Allen and Unwin).
——(ed.) (1975). *European Economic Integration* (Amsterdam and Oxford: North-Holland and American Elsevier).
Baldwin, Richard (1994). *Towards an Integrated Europe* (London: CEPR).
——*et al.* (1992). *Monitoring European Integration, iii: Is Bigger Better? The Economics of EC Enlargement*, CEPR Annual Report 1992 (London: CEPR).
Balladur, E. (1994). 'Pour un nouveau traité de l'Elysée', *Le Monde* (30 Nov.).
Bar, F., and Murase, E. M. (1999). 'Charting Cyberspace: A US–European–Japanese Blueprint for Electronic Commerce', in R. H. Steinberg and B. Stokes (eds.), *Partners or Competitors? The Prospects for US–European Cooperation on Asian Trade* (Lanham, MD, and Oxford: Rowman & Littlefield).

Bär, S., and Kraemer, R. A. (1999). *Analyse des Entwurfs für eine Wasserrahmen-richtlinie* (Berlin: Ecologic).

Barbé, E. (1998). 'Balancing Europe's Eastern and Southern Dimension', in J. Zielonka (ed.), *Paradoxes of European Foreign Policy* (The Hague: Kluwer Law International), 117–29.

Barrell, Ray, and Pain, Nigel (1998). 'Real Exchange Rates, Agglomerations, and Irreversibilities: Macroeconomic Policy and FDI in EMU', *Oxford Review of Economic Policy*, 14/3: 152–67.

Barrett, G. (1997). 'Justice and Home Affairs Cooperation: An Overview', in B. Tonra (ed.), *Amsterdam: What the Treaty Means* (Dublin: Institute of European Affairs).

Bayoumi, Tamim, and Eichengreen, Barry (1998). 'Exchange Rate Volatility and Intervention: Implications of the Theory of Optimum Currency Areas', *Journal of International Economics*, 45: 191–209.

—— and Masson, Paul (1998). 'Liability-Creating versus Non-Liability Creating Fiscal Stablization Policies: Ricardian Equivalence, Fiscal Stabilization, and EMU', *Economic Journal*, 108: 1026–45.

Beaumont, P., and Walker, N. (1999). 'The Euro and the European Legal Order', in P. Beaumont and N. Walker (eds.), *Legal Framework of the Single European Currency* (Oxford: Hart Publishing).

Beck, H. (1995). *Abgestufte Integration im Europäischen Gemeinschaftsrecht unter besonderer Berücksichtigung des Umweltrechts*. Europäische Hochschulschriften. (Frankfurt am Main: Peter Lang).

Begg, I. (1999). 'Reshaping the EU Budget: Yet Another Missed Opportunity', *ESCR 'One Europe or Several?' Programme, Policy Paper*, 1/99.

—— and Peterson, J. (1999). 'Editorial Statement', *Journal of Common Market Studies*, 37/1 (Mar.), 1–12.

Belke, Ansgar, and Gros, Daniel (1999). 'Estimating the Costs and Benefits of EMU: The Impact of External Shocks on Labor Markets', *Weltwirtschaftliches Archiv*, 135/1: 1–47.

Bellamy, R., and Castiglione, D. (1997). 'Building the Union: The Nature of Sovereignty in the Political Architecture of Europe', *Law and Philosophy*, 16: 421–45.

—— —— (1999). 'The Normative Turn in European Union Studies: Legitimacy, Identity and Democracy', EURCIT Working Paper, www.reading.ac.uk.

—— —— (2000)., ' "A Republic, if you can Keep it": The Democratic Constitution of the European Union', in Z. Bankowsk and A. Scott (eds.), *The European Union and its Order* (Oxford: Blackwell).

Bercusson, B. (1994). 'Social Policy at the Crossroads: European Labour Law After Maastricht', in R. Dehousse (ed.), *Europe after Maastricht: An Ever Closer Union?* (Munich: Law Books in Europe).

Bergsten F. C. (1997). 'The Impact of the Euro on Exchange Rates and International Policy Cooperation', in P. R. Masson, T. H. Kruege, and B. G. Turtleboom, (eds.), *EMU and the International Monetary System* (Washington, DC: International Monetary Fund).

Berthold, Norbert, Fehn, Rainer, and Thode, Eric (1999). 'Real Wage Rigidities, Fiscal Policy, and the Stability of EMU in the Transition Phase', *IMF Working Paper WP/99/83* (Washington, DC: International Monetary Fund).

Biersteker, T. J., and Weber, C. (1996). *State Sovereignty as Social Construct* (Cambridge: Cambridge University Press).

Blair, Tony (1998). *The Third Way: New Politics for a New Century* (London: Fabian Society).

——and Schröder, Gerhard (1999). 'Europe: The Third Way/*Die Neue Mitte*', on-line at http://www.labour.org.uk/views/index.html.

Blanchard, Olivier, and Wolfers, Justin (1999). 'The Role of Shocks and Institutions in the Rise of European Unemployment: The Aggregate Evidence', *NBER Working Paper*, 7282 (Cambridge: National Bureau for Economic Research).

Blondel, Jean (1970). 'Legislative Behavior: Some Steps Towards a Comparative Measurement', *Government and Opposition*, 5: 67–85.

Bomberg, E., and Burns, C. (1999). 'The Environment Committee of the European Parliament: New Powers, Old Problems', *Environmental Politics*, 8/4: 174–9.

Bonvicini, Gianni, *et al.* (1991). *The Community and the Emerging Democracies: A Joint Policy Report* (London: RIIA).

Bourgeois, J. (1995). 'The EC in the WTO and Advisory Opinion 1/94: An Echternach Procession', *Common Market Law Review*, 32: 763–87.

Bowler, Shaun, and Farrell, David (1995). 'The Organizing of the European Parliament: Committees, Specialization and Co-ordination', *British Journal of Political Science*, 25: 219–43.

Brenner, Michael (1998). *Terms of Engagement: The United States and the European Security Identity*, The Washington Papers, 176. (Westport, Conn.: Praeger for The Center for Strategic and International Studies).

Bretherton, C., and Vogler, J. (1999). *The European Union as a Global Actor* (London: Routledge)

Buiter, W. (1999). 'Willem in Euroland', *Journal of Common Market Studies*, 37/2: 181–209.

Bulmer, S. (1998). 'New Institutionalism and the Governance of the Single European Market', *Journal of European Public Policy*, 5/3: 365–86.

Burley, A. M., and Mattli, W. (1993). 'Europe Before the Court: A Political Theory of Legal Integration', *International Organization*, 47/1.

Caddy, J. (1997). 'Harmonization and Asymmetry: Environmental Policy Co-ordination Between the European Union and Central Europe', *Journal of European Public Policy*, 4/3: 318–60.

——(1998). 'Sowing the Seeds of Deliberative Democracy? Institutions for the Environment in Central Europe: Case Studies of Public Participation in Environmental Decision-Making in Contemporary Hungary', Ph.D. dissertation (Florence: European University Institute).

Cahen, Alfred (1989). *The Western European Union and NATO: Building a European Defence Identity within the Context of Atlantic Solidarity* (London: Brassey's Atlantic Commentaries, 2).

Calmfors, Lars (1998). 'Macroeconomic Policy, Wage Setting, and Employment: What Difference Does EMU Make?', *Oxford Review of Economic Policy*, 14/3: 125–51.

Cameron, David R. (1974). 'Toward a Theory of Political Mobilization', *Journal of Politics*, 36/1 (Feb.), 138–71.

Campanella, M. (1995). 'Getting the Core: A Neo-institutionalist Approach to EMU', *Government and Opposition*, 30/3: 347–69.

——(1998). 'EU Fiscal Discipline after 1999: The Pact of Stability', *ECSA Newsletter* (Fall)

——(2000). 'The Political Economy of EMU Fiscal Discipline: A Rational Choice Perspective', in K. A. Eliassen and S. S. Andersen (eds.), *Making Policy in Europe*, 2nd edn. (Beverly Hills, Calif.: Sage).

Capelletti, M., Seccombe, M., and Weiler, J. H. H. (1986). 'Integration through Law: Europe and the American Federal Experience—A General Introduction', in M. Cappelletti, M. Seccombe, and J. H. H. Weiler (eds.), *Integration through Law: Europe and the American Federal Experience*, i (Berlin: Walter de Gruyter), 3–68.

Caporaso, James A. (1996). 'The European Union and Forms of State: Westphalian, Regulatory or Post-Modern?', *Journal of Common Market Studies*, 34/1: 29–52.

——(1998). 'Regional Integration Theory: Understanding our Past and Anticipating our Future' in W. Sandholtz and A. Stone Sweet, A. (eds.), *Supranational Governance: The Institutionalisation of the European Union* (Oxford: Oxford University Press).

——(1999). 'Toward a Normal Science of Regional Integration', *Journal of European Public Policy*, 6/1: 160–4.

Carius, A., Von Homeyer, I., and Bär, S. (1999*a*). 'The Eastern Enlargement of the European Union and Environmental Policy: Challenges, Expectations, Speeds and Flexibility', in K. Holzinge and P. Koepfel (eds.), *Environmental Policy in a European Union of Variable Geometry? The Challenge of the Next Enlargement* (Basle: Helbig & Lichtenhahn).

——(1999*b*). *Umweltpolitische Aspekte der Osterweiterung der Europäischen Union*, Study for the German Council of Environmental Advisors (Berlin: Ecologic).

Carlino, Gerald, and DeFina, Robert (1998*a*). 'The Differential Regional Effects of Monetary Policy', *Review of Economics and Statistics*, 80/4: 572–87.

——(1998*b*). 'Monetary Policy and the U.S. States and Regions: Some Implications for the European Monetary Union', *Working Paper, 98-17* (Philadelphia: Federal Reserve Bank of Philadelphia).

Cecchini, P. with Catinat, M., and Jacquemin, A. (1988). *The European Challenge 1992: The Benefits of a Single Market* (Aldershot: Wildwood House).

Centre for European Policy Studies (1999). *A System for Post-War South-East Europe*, Working Document, 131 (Brussels: CEPS).

Chalmers, D. (1999). 'Accounting for "Europe"', *Oxford Journal of Legal Studies*, 19/3: 517–36.

Chayes, A., and Chayes, A. H. (1995). *The New Sovereignty: Compliance with International Regulatory Agreements* (Cambridge: Cambridge University Press).

Checkel, J. T. (1998). 'The Constructivist Turn in International Relations Theory', *World Politics*, 50: 324–48.

——(1999). 'Social Construction and Integration', *Journal of European Public Policy*, 6/4: 545–60.

Chirac, J., and Kohl, H. (1996). 'Schreiben des deutschen Bundeskanzlers und des französischen Staatspräsidenten, Helmut Kohl und Jacques Chirac, an den amtierenden Vorsitzenden des Europäischen Rates, den spanischen Ministerpräsidenten Felipe Gonzáles, veröffentlicht am 6. Dezember 1995 in Bonn und Paris (gekürzt)', *Internationale Politik*, 51/8: 80–1.

Christiansen, T., and Jørgensen, K. E. (1998). 'Negotiating Treaty Reform in the European Union: The Role of the European Commission', *International Negotiation*, 3/3: 435–52.

——— and Wiener, A. (1999). 'The Social Construction of European Integration', *Journal of European Public Policy*, 6/4: 528–44.

Coglianese, C., and Nicolaïdis, K. (1998). 'Securing Subsidiarity: Mechanisms for Allocating Authority in Tiered Regimes', in S. Woolcock (ed.), *Subsidiarity in the Governance of the Global Economy* (Cambridge: Cambridge University Press).

Cohen, Benjamin J. (1993). 'Beyond EMU: The Problem of Sustainability', in Barry Eichengreen and Jeffry Frieden (eds.), *The Political Economy of European Monetary Unification* (Boulder, Colo.: Westview Press) 149–65.

Colley, Linda (1992). *Britons: Forging the Nation, 1707–1837* (New Haven, Conn.: Yale University Press).

Collier, U. (1996). *Deregulation, Subsidiarity and Sustainability: New Challenges for EU Environmental Policy*, EUI Working Papers, 96/60 (Florence: European University Institute).

Commission (1985). *Fourteenth Report on Competition Policy* (Luxembourg: Office for Official Publications of the European Communities).

——(1986). 'Communication by the Commission to the Council: Public Procurement in the Community', COM (86) 375 final (19 June).

——(1988). *Research on the 'Cost of Non-Europe'*, i. *Basic Findings, Executive Summary of 'The Cost of Non-Europe in Public Sector Procurement'*, WS Atkins Management Consultants (Luxembourg: Office for Official Publications of the European Communities).

——(1989). 'Communication by the Commission to the Parliament and Council: Public Procurement: Regional and Social Aspects', COM (89) 400 final.

——(1992a). 'Europe and the Challenge of Enlargement', *Bulletin of the EC*, supplement 3/92, reproduced in A. Michalski and H. Wallace, *The European Community: The Challenge of Enlargement* (London: RIIA), 157–167.

——(1992b). *Towards a Closer Association with the Countries of Central and Eastern Europe*, SEC (92) 2301 (2 Dec.).

——(1992c). *Towards a New Partnership with the Central and East European*

Countries, draft for a report by the Commission to the European Council in Edinburgh. Brussels (3 Nov.).

——(1993*a*). *Towards a Closer Association with the Countries of Central and Eastern Europe*, SEC (93) 648 (18 May).

——(1993*b*). *Towards Sustainability, Fifth Environmental Action Programme*, COM (94) 465. (Brussels: Office for Official Publications of the European Communities).

——(1994). *White Paper: Growth, Competitiveness, Employment: The Challenges and Ways Forward into the Twenty-First Century* (Luxembourg: Office for Official Publications of the European Communities).

——(1995*a*). 'Notice on Cooperation between National Courts and the Commission in the State Aid Field', *Official Journal of the European Communities*, 312 (23 Nov.).

——(1995*b*). *Trade Relations between the European Union and the Developing Countries* (Luxembourg: Office of the Official Publications of the European Communities).

——(1995*c*). *White Paper: Preparation of the Associated Countries of Central and Eastern Europe for Integration into the Internal Market of the Union*, COM (95) 163 final as of 3 May (Brussels: European Commission).

——(1995*d*). *White Paper: Teaching and Learning: Toward the Learning Society*, COM (95) 590 (Luxembourg: Office for Official Publications of the European Communities).

——(1996*a*). *The Impact and Effectiveness of the Single Market*, Communication from the Commission to the European Parliament and Council, available from http://europa.eu.int/comm/dg 15/en/update/impact/smtocen.htm.

——(1996*b*). *InfoFinance (1995): The European Development Fund*, DE 85 (Luxembourg: Office of the Official Publications of the European Communities).

——(1996*c*). *Intergovernmental Conference, Commission Opinion: Reinforcing Political Union and Preparing for Enlargement* (Brussels and Luxembourg: Office of the Official Publications of the European Communities, 28 Feb.).

——(1996*d*). *Proposal for a Council Directive on the Assessment of the Effects of Certain Plans and Programmes on the Environment*, COM (96) 511 final (Brussels: European Commission).

——(1996*d*). *Public Procurement in the European Union: Exploring the Way Forward*, COM (96) 583 final (Brussels, 27 Nov).

——(1996*e*). Task-force 'Conférence intergouvernementale', 'Positions des États membres sur les thèmes à l'ordre du jour de la Conférence intergouvernementale 1996' (Brussels, Apr. 1996), http://europa.eu.int/en/agenda/igc-home/general/fiches/cover.htm.

——(1996*f*). *XXVIth Report on Competition Policy*, COM (96) 126 final.

——(1997*a*). *Agenda 2000*, COM (97) 2000 of 15 July (Brussels: European Commission).

——(1997*b*). *Commission Staff Working Paper: Guide to the Approximation of European Union Environmental Legislation*, SEC (97) 1608 as of 25 Aug. (Brussels: European Commission).

Commission (1997c). *Communication to the Council and the European Parliament: Guidelines for the Negotiation of New Cooperation Agreements with African, Caribbean and Pacific (ACP) Countries*, COM (97) 537 final (Brussels: European Commission).

——(1997d). *External Aspects of Economic and Monetary Union*, Europapers 1, DG II: Economic and Financial Affairs (July).

——(1997e). 'For a Stronger and Wider Europe', Press Release IP-97 660, DO/97/97 (Brussels: European Commission).

——(1997f). *Green Paper on Relations between the European Union and the ACP Countries on the Eve of the Twenty-First Century: Challenges and Opportunities for a New Partnership* (Luxembourg: Office of the Official Publications of the European Communities).

——(1997g). 'Grundsatzpapier der Europäischen Kommission zur Flexibilität und verstärkten Zusammenarbeit', *Internationale Politik*, 3: 109–13 (CONF/3805/97, Brussels, 21 Jan. 1997).

——(1997h). 'Le passage à l'euro: Assurer l'acceptation et la confiance des consommateurs', 27 Nov. (Brussels: European Commission, DG XXIV)

——(1997i). *New Orientations for Phare: Non Papers on 1. Accession Partnership, 2. Phare Investment Support, 3. Phare Institution Building* (Brussels: European Commission).

——(1997j). 'Note d'analyse sur le traité d'Amsterdam' (Brussels, 7 July), http://europa.eu.int/en/agenda/igc-home/eu-doc/commissn/tfcig.htm.

——(1997k). *Proposal for a Council Directive Establishing a Framework for Community Action in the Field of Water Policy*, COM 97) 49 final (Brussels: European Commission).

——(1998a). 'Communication from the Commission: A Northern Dimension in the Union's Policies', COM (98) 589, final (Brussels: European Commission).

——(1998b). *Communication to the Council and Parliament on Democratization, the Rule of Law, Respect for Human Rights and Good Governance: The Challenges of the Partnership between the European Union and the ACP States*, 24 Feb. COM (98) 146 (Brussels: European Commission).

——(1998c). 'Composite paper. Report on progress towards accession by each of the candidate countries' (4 Nov.). http://europa.eu.int/comm/enlargement/report_11_98/composite/index.htm.

——(1998d). *Convergence Report*, DG II (Brussels: European Commission).

——(1998e). *Fifteenth Annual Report of the Commission to Parliament and the Member States on Monitoring the Application of Community Law*, COM (98) 317, as of 31 July (Brussels: European Commission).

——(1998f). *Minutes of the Meeting with National Contact Points (MS and CCs): Institution Building* (Brussels: European Commission).

——(1998g). *Partnership for Integration: A Strategy for Integration Environment into European Union Policies*, COM (98) 333 as of 27 May (Brussels: European Commission).

——(1998*h*). *Regular Report from the Commission on Progress towards Accession: The Czech Republik*, http://www.europa.eu.int/comm/dg1a/enlarge/ report_11_98/czech/index.htm.

——(1998*i*). *Regular Report from the Commission on Progress towards Accession: Estonia*, http://www.europa.eu.int/comm/dg1a/enlarge/report_11_98/estonia/ index.htm.

——(1998*j*). *Regular Report from the Commission on Progress towards Accession: Hungary*, http://www.europa.eu.int/comm/dg1a/enlarge/report_11_98/hun-gary/ index.htm.

——(1998*k*). *Regular Report from the Commission on Progress towards Accession: Poland*, http://www.europa.eu.int/comm/dg1a/enlarge/report_11 _98/poland/index.htm.

——(1998*l*). *Regular Report from the Commission on Progress towards Accession: Slovenia*, http://www.europa.eu.int/comm/dg1a/enlarge/report_11_98/slovenia/ index.htm.

——(1999*a*). *Communication to the Council and European Parliament over the EU's Stance in view of 'Millennium Round' of World Trade Organisation (WTO)* from *Agence Europe*, Europe Documents, 2151–52 (29 July).

——(1999*b*). *Czech Republic: Screening Results. Environment, Enlargement*, MD 286/99, DS286/99 (Brussels: European Commission).

——(1999*c*). *Estonia: Screening Results. Environment, Enlargement*, MD 284/99, DS 284/99 (Brussels: European Commission).

——(1999*d*). 'European Public Opinion on the Single Currency', *Monitoring Europinion*, special edn. (Brussels: European Commission, DG X).

——(1999*e*). *The Global Assessment: Environment and Sustainable Development Policy beyond 2000*, draft at 16 July 1999, DG Environment (Brussels: European Commission).

——(1999*f*). *Hungary: Screening Results. Environment, Enlargement*, MD 282/99, DS 282/99 (Brussels: European Commission).

——(1999*g*). *Poland: Screening Results. Environment, Enlargement*, MD 283/99, DS 283/99 (Brussels: European Commission).

——(1999*h*). 'Report on the Application of EC state aid law by the Member State courts' (4 June), http://www.europa.eu.int/comm/dg04/aid/en/app-by-member-states/index.htm.

——(1999*i*).'Report Updating the Commission's Opinion on Malta's Application for Membership', COM (99) 69 final (Brussels: European Commission).

——(1999*j*). *Slovenia: Screening Results. Environment, Enlargement*, MD 286/99, DS 286/99 (Brussels: European Commission).

——(1999*k*). 'The Stabilisation and Association Process for Countries of South-Eastern Europe', Commission Communication to the Council and the European Parliament, COM (99) 235, 26 May (1999).

——(n.d.). *The European Auto Oil Programme: A Report by the Directorate Generals for: Industry; Energy; and Environment, Civil Protection and Nuclear Safety.* (Brussels: European Commission).

Conference on Accession to the European Union (1999*a*). *Estonia. Position Paper*

EU Membership Negotiations: Chapter 22 Environment (Tallinn: Government of the Republic of Estonia, 2 Aug.).

Conference on Accession to the European Union (1999*b*). *Negotiating Position of the Government of the Republic of Hungary on Chapter 22 Environment* (Budapest: Government of the Republic of Hungary, 29 July).

——(1999*c*). *Negotiating Position of the Republic of Slovenia on Chapter 22 Environment* (Ljubljana: Government of the Republic of Slovenia, 27 July).

——(1999*d*). *Poland's Position Paper in the Area of 'Environment' for the Accession Negotiation with the European Union* (Warsaw: Government of the Republic of Poland, 13 Oct.).

——(1999*e*). *Position Paper of the Czech Republic on Chapter 22 Environment* (Prague: Government of the Czech Republic, 14 July).

Copeland, Gary, and Patterson, Samuel C. (1994). *Parliaments in the Modern World: Changing Institutions* (Ann Arbor, Mich.: University of Michigan Press).

Corbett, Richard (1989). 'Testing the New Procedures: The European Parliament's First Experiences with its New "Single Act" Powers', *Journal of Common Market Studies*, 27: 359–72.

——(1996). 'Governance and Institutional Developments', *Journal of Common Market Studies*, 34: 29–42.

——Jacobs, Francis, and Shackleton, Michael (1995). *The European Parliament*, 3rd edn. (London: Longman).

Cornish, Paul (1999). 'Britain, the WEU and NATO', in Carl Lankowski and Simon Serfaty (eds.), *Europeanizing Security? NATO and an Integrating Europe* (AICGS Research Report, Washington, DC: American Institute for Contemporary German Studies).

Cowles, Maria Green (1995). 'Setting the Agenda for a New Europe: The ERT and EC 1992', *Journal of Common Market Studies*, 33/4: 501–26.

——Caporaso, James, and Risse, Thomas (2000). *Transforming Europe: Europeanization and Domestic Change* (Ithaca, NY: Cornell University Press).

Cram, L. (1993). 'Calling the Tune without Paying the Piper. Social Policy Regulation: The Role of the Commission in European Community Social Policy', *Policy and Politics*, 21/2: 135–46.

——(1994). 'The European Commission as a Multi-Organization: Social Policy and IT Policy in the EU', *Journal of European Public Policy*, 1/2 (Autumn): 195–217.

——(1997). *Policy-Making in the EU* (London: Routledge).

——(1999). 'The Commission', in L. Cram, D. Dinan, and N. Nugent (eds.), *Developments in the European Union* (London and New York: Macmillan and St Martin's Press).

Croci, O., and Picci, L. (1999). 'European Monetary Integration and Integration Theory: Insights from the Italian Case', paper presented at the workshop 'Conceptualising the New Europe: European Monetary Integration and beyond', Victoria, BC (15 and 16 Oct.).

Crombez, Christophe (1997). 'The Co-Decision Procedure in the European Union', *Legislative Studies Quarterly*, 22: 97–119.

Crouch, C. (ed.) (2000). *After the Euro: Shaping Institutions for Governance in the Wake of European Monetary Union* (Oxford and New York: Oxford University Press).

Curtin, D. (1993). 'The Constitutional Structure of the Union: A Europe of Bits and Pieces', *Common Market Law Review*, 30/1: 17–69.

——(1996). 'Betwixt and Between: Democracy and Transparency in the Governance of the European Union', in J. A. A. Winter, D. M. Curtin, A. E. Kellermann, and B. de Witte (eds.), *Reforming the Treaty on European Union: The Legal Debate* (The Hague, Boston, Mass., and London: Kluwer Law International), 95–121.

——and Dekker. I. (1999). 'The EU as a "Layered" International Organization: Institutional Unity in Disguise', in P. Craig and G. de Búrca (eds.), *The Evolution of EU Law*, (Oxford: Oxford University Press) 83–136.

Curzon Price, V., Landau, A., and Whitman. R. (eds.) (1999). *The Enlargement of the EU* (London: Routledge).

Dahrendorf, Ralf (1999). 'The Third Way and Liberty: An Authoritarian Streak in Europe's New Center', *Foreign Affairs* (Sept./Oct.): 13–17.

Dankert, Piet (1997). 'Pressure from the European Parliament', in G. Edwards and A. Pijpers (eds.)., *The Politics of European Treaty Reform* (London: Pinter.)

Danthine, Jean-Pierre, and Hunt, Jennifer (1994). 'Wage Bargaining Structure, Employment, and Economic Integration', *Economic Journal*, 104 (May): 528–41.

Davies, A. (1999). 'Balancing Act: Meeting EU Environmental Standards. New Assistance Programmes Aim at Filling the Funding Gaps' *Green Phare*, 1/2: 6–7.

De Búrca, G. (1998). 'The Principle of Subsidiarity and the Court of Justice as an Institutional Actor', *Journal of Common Market Studies*, 36/2: 217–35.

——(1999). 'Reappraising Subsidiarity's Significance after Amsterdam', Harvard Jean Monnet Working Paper, 8/99, http://www.law.harvard.edu/Programs/JeanMonnet/papers/99/990701.html.

Dehaene, J.-L., von Weizsäcker, R., and Simon, D. (1999). 'The Institutional Implications of Enlargement: Report to the European Commission', available from http://www.law.harvard.edu/Programs/JeanMonnet/dehaene.html.

Dehousse, Renaud (1989). *The Institutional Dimensions of the Internal Market Programme* (Florence: European University Institute).

——(1995). 'Constitutional Reform in the European Community: Are there Alternatives to the Majoritarian Avenue?', *West European Politics*, 18/3: 118–36.

——(1998). 'Institutional Models for an Enlarged Union: Some Reflexions on a Non-Debate', in Renaud Dehousse (ed.), *An Even Larger Union? The Eastern Enlargement in Perspective* (Baden-Baden: Nomos Verlagsgesellschaft).

De la Serre, F., and Wallace, H. (1997*a*). *Flexibility and Enhanced Cooperation in the European Union: Placebo rather than Panacea?*, Research and Policy Paper, 2 (Sept.) (Paris: Notre Europe; English version of 1997*b*).

De la Serre, F., and Wallace, H. (1997*b*). 'Les Coopérations renforcées: Une fausse bonne idée?', *Études et Recherches*, 2 (Paris: Groupement d'études et recherches 'Notre Europe'; French version of 1997*a*).

Delors Report (1989). *Report on Economic and Monetary Union in the European Community*. Committee for the Study of Economic and Monetary Union (Luxembourg. Office for Official Publications of the EC).

Democratic Leadership Council/Progressive Policy Institute (1999). *The Third Way*, http://www.dlcppi.org/ppi/3way/3way.htm.

Denza, E. (1996). 'The Community as a Member of International Organizations', in N. Emiliou and D. O'Keeffe (eds.), *The European Union and World Trade Law* (Chichester: John Wiley and Sons).

——(1999). 'Two Legal Orders: Divergent or Convergent?', *International and Comparative Law Quarterly*, 48/2: 257–84.

Deubner, C. (1998). 'Die verstärkte Zusammenarbeit im System der Europäischen Union', *SWP-AP*, 3064 (Ebenhausen: Stiftung Wissenschaft und Politik).

Deutsch, K. *et al.* (1957). *Political Community and the North Atlantic Area* (Princeton: Princeton University Press).

Devuyst, Y. (1999). 'The Community Method After Amsterdam', *Journal of Common Market Studies*, 37/1: 109–20.

De Witte, B. (1998). 'The Pillar Structure and the Nature of the European Union: Greek Temple or French Gothic Cathedral, in T. Heukels *et al.* (eds.), *The European Union after Amsterdam: A Legal Analysis* (The Hague: Kluwer Law International).

Diez, T. (1996). 'Postmoderne und europäische Integration: Die Dominanz des Staatsmodells, die Verantwortung gegenüber dem Anderen und die Konstruktion eines alternativen Horizonts', *Zeitschrift für Internationale Beziehungen*, 3: 255–81.

——(1999). 'Speaking "Europe": The Politics of Integration Discourse', *Journal of European Public Policy*, 6/4: 598–613.

Dinan, Desmond (1993). *Historical Dictionary of the European Community* (Metchuen, NJ: Scarecrow Press).

——(1997). 'The Commission and the Reform Process', in G. Edwards and A. Pijpers (eds.), *The Politics of European Treaty Reform: The 1996 Intergovernmental Conference and Beyond* (London: Pinter), 188–211.

Dogan, Mattei (1994). 'The Erosion of Nationalism in the West European Community', in Max Haller and Rudolph Richter (eds.), *Toward a European Nation?: Political Trends in Europe—East and West, Center and Periphery* (Armonk, NY: M. E. Sharpe).

D'Oliveira, H. U. J. (1995). 'Union Citizenship: Pie in the Sky?', in A. Rosas and E. A. Rosas (eds.), *A Citizens' Europe: In Search of a New Order* (London: Sage).

Dominguez, K. M. and Frankel, J. A. (1993). *Does Foreign Exchange Intervention Work?* (Washington, DC: Institute for International Economics).

Dornbusch, R., Favero, A., and Giavazzi, F. (1998). 'Immediate Challenges for the European Central Bank', in D. Begg, J. V. Hagen, C. Wyplosz, and K. F.

Zimmermann (eds.), *EMU: Prospects and Challenges for the Euro* (Brussels, CEPR).

Dörr, O. (1995). 'Zur Rechtsnatur der Europäischen Union', *Europarecht*, 30/4: 334–48.

Drake, Helen (1995). 'Political Leadership and European Integration: The Case of Jacques Delors', *West European Politics* 18/1: 140–60.

Duchesne, Sophie, and Frognier, André-Paul (1995). 'Is there a European Identity?', in Oskar Niedermayer and Richard Sinnott (eds.), *Public Opinion and Internationalized Governance* (Oxford: Oxford University Press), 193–226.

Duff, Andrew (1994). 'Building a Parliamentary Europe', *Government and Opposition*, 29: 147–65.

——(1997). *The Treaty of Amsterdam: Text and Commentary* (London: Federal Trust, Sweet & Maxwell).

Duisenberg, W. (1999*a*). 'First Experiences with the Euro' (26 May), http://www.ecb.int.

——(1999*b*). 'Hearing before the Parliament's Committee on Economic and Monetary Affairs' (23 Nov.), http://www.ecb.int.

——(1999*c*). 'Press Conference' (4 Nov.), http://www.ecb.int.

Dyson, K. (1994). *Elusive Union: The Process of Economic and Monetary Union in Europe* (London and New York: Longman).

——(1999). 'Benign or Malevolent Leviathan? Social Democratic Governments in a Neo-Liberal Euro Area', *Political Quarterly*, 70/2: 195–209.

——and Featherstone, K. (1996). 'Italy and EMU as "Vincolo Esterno": Empowering the Technocrats, Transforming the State', *South European Politics and Society*, 1: 272–99.

EAPN Ireland (1999). *The Social Consequences of EMU for Marginalized and Socially Excluded Groups in Ireland* (Dublin: Irish Chapter of the European Anti-Poverty Network).

Earnshaw, David, and Judge, David (1996). 'From Co-operation to Co-decision: The European Parliament's Path to Legislative Power', in J. Richardson, (ed.), *European Union: Power and Policymaking* (London: Routledge).

————(1997). 'The Life and Times of the European Union's Co-operation Procedure', *Journal of Common Market Studies*, 35: 543–64.

Easton, David, and Dennis, Jack (1969). *Children in the Political System: Origins of Political Legitimacy* (New York: McGraw-Hill).

Eatwell, J., Ellman, M., Karlsson, N., Nuti, D. M., and Shapiro, J. (1997). *Not 'Just Another Accession': The Political Economy of EU Enlargement to the East* (London: Institute for Public Policy Research).

Economic and Social Committee (1990). *Economic and Monetary Union in the European Community* (Brussels: Economic and Social Committee, Jan.).

——(1991). *Additional Opinion on Economic and Monetary Union* (Brussels, Feb.).

Edwards, G., and Philippart, E. (1997). 'Flexibility and the Treaty of Amsterdam: Europe's New Byzantinum', *CELS Occasional Paper*, 3 (Cambridge: Centre for European Legal Studies).

Ehlermann, C. D. (1995). *Increased Differentiation or Stronger Uniformity*, EUI Working Paper Robert Schuman Centre, 95/ 21 (Florence: European University Institute).

——(1997). 'Flexibility', in *Making Sense of the Amsterdam Treaty* (Brussels: European Policy Centre), 59–60.

——(1998). *Differentiation, Flexibility, Closer Cooperation: The New Provisions of the Amsterdam Treaty* (Florence: European University Institute, Robert Schuman Centre).

Eichener, V. (1993). *Social Dumping or Innovative Regulation? Processes and Outcomes of European Decision-Making in the Sector of Health and Safety at Work Harmonization*, EUI Working Papers in Political and Social Sciences, 92/28 (Florence: European University Institute).

Eichengreen, Barry (1998). 'European Monetary Unification: A *Tour d'Horizon*', *Oxford Review of Economic Policy*, 14/3: 24–40.

Eijffinger, Sylvester (1998). 'Accountability of Central Banks: Aspects and Quantification', paper presented at ECSA Europe–World Conference, Brussels (Sept.).

EIRO (1997). 'Social Partners Reach Agreement on EMU Buffer Funds', http://www.eiro.eurofound.ie/(1997)./11/features/FI9711138F.html (Nov.).

——(1999). 'The "Europeanization" of Collective Bargaining', http://www.eiro.eurofound.ie/(1999)./07/study/TN9907201S.html (July).

Elster, J. (1989). *Nuts and Bolts for the Social Sciences* (Cambridge: Cambridge University Press).

Emerson, Michael *et al.* (1992). *One Market, One Money* (Oxford: Oxford University Press).

Environment Policy Europe (1997). *Compliance Costing for Approximation of EU Environmental Legislation in the CEEC* (Brussels: Environment Policy Europe).

EPC (1999). 'Peter Sutherland Criticises Cologne Summit "Narrow Reform"', www.TheEPC.be/normal/Challenge_Europe/Press_release/SutherlandPressht m.htm.

Euro-Mediterranean Conference of Foreign Ministers (1999). Stuttgart, 15–16.4, Chairman's formal conclusions, Press Release, (16 Apr.), 7395/99.

European Central Bank (1999). *Possible Effects of EMU on the Banking System in the Medium to Long Term* (Frankfurt: European Central Bank).

European Council (1985). 'Report by the Ad Hoc Committee for Institutional Affairs to the European Council', *Bulletin of the European Communities*, 3/1985: 102–11.

——(1988). 'European Council in Rhodes, 2–3 December 1988, Presidency Conclusions', *Bulletin of the European Communities*, 12/1988: 8–13.

——(1989). 'European Council in Strasbourg, 8–9 December 1989, Presidency Conclusions', *Bulletin of the European Communities*, 12/1989: 8–18.

——(1990). 'European Council in Rome, 27–28 October 1990, Presidency Conclusions', *Bulletin of the European Communities*, 10/1990: 7–13.

——(1992). 'European Council in Edinburgh, 11–12 December 1992, Presidency Conclusions', *Bulletin of the European Communities*, 12/1992: 1–40.

——(1993). 'European Council in Copenhagen, 21–22 June 1993, Presidency Conclusions', *Europe Documents*, 1844/45 (24 June).

——(1994). 'European Council in Essen, 9–10 December 1994, Presidency Conclusions', SN 300/94 (10 Dec.).

——(1995). 'European Council in Madrid, 15–16 December 1995, Presidency Conclusions', SN 400/95 (16 Dec.).

——(1996). 'Conclusions of the Presidency of the Turin European Council, 29 March 1996', *Bulletin of the European Union*, 3: 9–12.

——(1998). 'Presidency Conclusions', Vienna European Council, 11 and 12 Dec. 1998, http://europa.eu.int/council/off/conclu/dec98.htm.

——(1999*a*). 'Common Strategy for the European Council on Russia, Annexes to the Presidency Conclusions, Cologne European Council, 3 and 4 June 1999', http//:europa.eu.int/council/off/conclu/june1999/annex_en.htm.

——(1999*b*). 'Presidency Conclusions, Cologne European Council, 3 and 4 June (1999)', http//:europa.eu.int/council/off/conclu/june(1999)./annex_en.htm.

European Court of Justice (1999). 'Report on Translation of the Court of Justice of the European Communities', Luxembourg (23 Mar.).

European Environment Agency (1998). *Europe's Environment: The Second Assessment* (Luxembourg: Amt für amtliche Veröffentlichungen der Europäischen Gemeinschaften).

European Parliament (1996). *White Paper on the 1996 Intergovernmental Conference, Volume II: Summary of Positions of the Member States of the European Union with a View to the 1996 Intergovernmental Conference*, http://europa.eu.int/en/agenda/igc-home/eu-doc/parlment/peen2.htm.

——(1997a). 'Amsterdam Treaty: Resolution of 19 November 1997', *Official Journal of the European Communities*, C 371 (8 Dec.): 99–104.

——(1997*b*). *Opinion for the Committee on Foreign Affairs, Security and Defence Policy on the Commission Communication 'Agenda 2000': For a Stronger and Wider Union*, Committee on the Environment, Public Health and Consumer Protection, COM (97) 2000-C4-0371/97 (Brussels: European Parliament).

——(1997c). 'Resolution of 13 March 1997 on the Intergovernmental Conference', *Official Journal of the European Communities*, C115 (14 Apr.): 165–8.

——(1999). 'Committee of Independent Experts—First Report on Allegations Concerning Fraud, Mismanagement and Nepotism in the European Commission', Brussels (15 Mar.), available from http://www.europarl/eu.int/experts/en/default.htm.

European Union (1996). *The 1996 Intergovernmental Conference Retrospective Database*, http://europa.eu.int/en/agenda/igc-home.

——(1999). 'Council Gives Green Light for Reform of the EU Competition Rules Applicable to Vertical Restraints', available from htttp://europa.eu.int/rapid/start/cgi/guesten.ksh (5 May).

Everson, M. (1998). 'Beyond the *Bundesverfassungericht*: On the Necessary Cunning of Constitutional Reasoning', *European Law Journal*, 4/4: 389–410.

——and Krenzler, H. G. (1998). *Preparing for the Acquis Communautaire: Report of the Working Group on the Eastward Enlargement of the European Union*, EUI Working Paper RSC, 98/6 (Florence: European University Institute).

Faini, Riccardo and Portes, Richard (eds.) (1995). *European Union Trade with Eastern Europe: Adjustment and Opportunities* (London: CEPR).

Featherstone, Kevin (1999). 'The British Labor Party from Kinnock to Blair: Europeanism and Europeanization', paper prepared for the European Community Studies Association's Sixth Biennial International Conference, Pittsburgh (2–5 June).

Feldstein, Martin (1997*a*). 'EMU and International Conflict', *Foreign Affairs*, 76/6: 60–73.

——(1997*b*). 'The Political Economy of European Economic and Monetary Union: Political Sources of an Economic Liability', *Journal of Economic Perspectives*, 11/4: 23–42.

Ferguson, Y. H., and Mansbach, R. W. (1996). 'Political Space and Westphalian States in a World of "Polities": Beyond Inside/Outside', *Global Governance*, 2: 261–87.

Fierke, K. M., and Wiener, A. (1999). 'Constructing Institutional Interests: EU and NATO Enlargement', *RSC Working Paper*, 99/14 (Florence: European University Institute).

Finnemore, M., and Sikkink K. (1998). 'International Norm Dynamics and Political Change', *International Organization*, 52: 887–917.

Fischer, J. (1999). 'Rede bei der Vorbereitungskonferenz zum Stabilitätspakt für Südosteuropa Petersberg' (27 May), http://www.auswaertiges-amt.de/6_archiv/2/r/r990527b.htm.

Flassbeck H. (1999). 'Employment, Stability and Efficiency: Strategic Essentials of European Economic Policy', unpublished paper.

Fratianni, M. and Hagen, J. V. (1990). 'Public Choice Aspects of European Monetary Unification', *Cato Journal*, 10: 389–411.

Frears, John (1997). 'The French Parliament: Loyal Workhorse, Poor Watchdog', in P. Norton (ed.), *Parliaments in Western Europe*, 2nd edn. (London: Frank Cass).

Frieden, Jeffry A. (1996). 'The Impact of Goods and Capital Market Integration on European Monetary Politics', *Comparative Political Studies*, 29/2: 193–222.

——(1998). 'The Political Economy of European Exchange Rates: An Empirical Assessment', Manuscript (Cambridge: Harvard University, Department of Government).

——and Jones, Erik (1998). 'The Political Economy of European Monetary Union: A Conceptual Overview', in Jeffry Frieden, Daniel Gros, and Erik Jones (eds.), *The New Political Economy of EMU* (Lanham, Md.: Rowman & Littlefield), 163–86.

Friis, Lykke (1997). *When Europe Negotiates: From Europe Agreements to Eastern Enlargement* (Copenhagen: Institute of Political Science, University of Copenhagen).

——(1998*a*). '. . . And then they were 15: The EU's EFTA-Enlargement Negotiations', *Cooperation and Conflict*, 33/1: 81–107.

——(1998b). '"The End of the Beginning" of Eastern Enlargement: The Luxembourg Summit and Agenda-Setting', *European Integration online Papers* (*EIoP*) 2/7, http://eiop.or.at/eiop/texte/(1998).-007a.htm.

——and Murphy, A. (1999). 'The European Union and Central and Eastern Europe: Governance and Boundaries', *Journal of European Public Policy*, 37/2: 211–32.

————(2000*a*). *The Enlargement of Europe: Theory, Practice and the Boundaries of Governance* (London: Sage).

————(2000*b*). '"And Never the Train shall Meet?" The EU's Quest for Legitimacy and Enlargement', in M. C. Williams and M. Kelstrup (eds.), *Power, Security and Community—International Relations Theory and Politics of European Enlargement* (London: Routledge).

Gabel, Matthew, and Hix, Simon (n.d.). 'The Ties that Bind: MEP Voting Behavior and the Commission Investiture Procedure', unpublished paper.

Gandolfo, Giancarlo (1992). 'Monetary Unions', in Peter Newman, Murray Milgate and Jeahn Eatwell (eds.), *The New Palgrave Dictionary of Money and Finance* (London: Macmillan), 765–70.

Garrett, G. (1993). 'The Politics of Maastricht', *Economics and Politics*, 5/2: 105–25.

——(1995). 'From the Luxembourg Compromise to Codecision: Decision Making in the European Union', *Electoral Studies*, 14: 289–308.

——and Tsebelis, George (1996). 'An Institutionalist Critique of Intergovernmentalism', *International Organization*, 50: 269–99.

————(1997). 'More on the Co-Decision Endgame', *Journal of Legislative Studies*, 3: 139–43.

Gehring, T. (1994). 'Der Beitrag von Institutionen zur Förderung der internationalen Zusammenarbeit: Lehren aus der institutionellen Struktur der Europäischen Gemeinschaft', *Zeitschrift für Internationale Beziehungen*, 1/2: 211–42.

——(1996). 'Integrating Integration Theory: Neo-functionalism and International Regimes', *Global Society*, 10/3: 225–53.

Gialdino, C. (1995). 'Some Reflections on the *Acquis Communautaire*', *Common Market Law Review*, 32: 1089–121.

Giddens, Anthony (1998). *The Third Way: The Renewal of Social Democracy* (Oxford: Polity Press).

Gill, Stephen (1997). 'An EMU or an Ostrich? EMU and Neo-Liberal Economic Integration: Limits and Alternatives', in P. Minkkinen and H. Patomäki (eds.), *The Politics of Economic and Monetary Union* (Boston, Mass., Dordrecht, and London: Kluwer), 207–31.

Golub, J. (1994). *The Pivotal Role of British Sovereignty in EC Environmental Policy*, EUI Working Paper RSC, 94/17 (Florence: European University Institute).

Gomez, R. (1998). 'The EU's Mediterranean Policy: Common Foreign Policy by the Back Door?', in J. Peterson and H. Sjursen (eds.), *A Common Foreign Policy for Europe? Competing Visions of the CFSP* (London: Routledge).

Goodhart, Charles A. E. (1995). 'The Political Economy of Monetary Union', in Peter B. Kenen (ed.), *Understanding Interdependence: The Macroeconomics of the Open Economy* (Princeton: Princeton University Press), 448–505.

Gordon, Philip H. (1997). 'Does the WEU have a Role?', *The Washington Quarterly*, 20/1: 125–40.

Gosh, A. R., and Masson, P. R. (1994). *Economic Cooperation in an Uncertain World* (London: Blackwell).

Gourevitch, Peter (1986). *Politics in Hard Times: Comparative Responses to International Economic Crises* (Ithaca, NY: Cornell University Press).

Grabbe, H. (1999). *A Partnership for Accession? The Implications of EU Conditionality for the Central and East European Applicants*, EUI Working Paper, RSC, 12 (Florence: European University Institute).

——and Hughes, K. (1998). *Enlarging the EU Eastwards* (London: Pinter for the Royal Institute of International Affairs).

Grabitz, E. (ed.) (1984). *Abgestufte Integration: Eine Alternative zum herkömmlichen Integrationskonzept?* (Kehl am Rhein: N. P. Engel Verlag).

Grande, E. (1996). 'Demokratische Legitimation und Europäische Integration', *Leviathan*, 3: 339–59.

Grant, W. (1997). *The Common Agricultural Policy* (London: Macmillan).

Green, David Michael (1999). 'Who Are "The Europeans"?: European Political Identity in the Context of the Post-War Integration Project, doctoral dissertation (University of Wisconsin-Madison, Department of Political Science).

Green, David Michael (2000). 'The End of Identity? The Implications of Postmodernity for Political Identification', *Nationalism and Ethnic Politics*, 6/3 (Fall).

Greenwood, J., and Aspinwall, M. (eds.) (1998). *Collective Action in the European Union* (London: Routledge).

Greenwood, Justin and Ronit, Karsten (1994). 'Interest Groups in the European Community: Newly Emerging Dynamics and Forms', *West European Politics*, 17 (Jan.): 31–52.

Grieco, Joseph M. (1995). 'The Maastricht Treaty Economic and Monetary Union and Neo-Realist Research Programme', *Review of International Studies*, 21: 21–40.

Grilli, E. (1993). *The European Community and Developing Countries* (Cambridge: Cambridge University Press).

Grimm, D. (1995). 'Does Europe Need a Constitution?'. *European Law Journal*, 1/3: 282–302.

Gros, Daniel (1998). 'External Shocks and Labor Mobility: How Important are they for EMU?', in Jeffry Frieden, Daniel Gros, and Erik Jones (eds.), *The New Political Economy of EMU* (Lanham, Md.: Rowman & Littlefield), 53–81.

——and Jones, Erik (1997). 'Does EMU Need to Converge on the US Model?' Manuscript, (Brussels: Centre for European Policy Studies).

Grüner, Hans Peter, and Hefeker, Carsten (1999). 'How will EMU Affect Inflation and Unemployment in Europe?', *Scandinavian Journal of Economics*, 101/1: 33–47.

Gstöhl, S. (1998). *The Reluctant Europeans: Sweden, Norway and Switzerland in the Process of European Integration (1950–1995)* (Geneva: Ph.D. thesis, Institut Universitaire de Hautes Études Internationales).

Haas, E. (1958). *The Uniting of Europe: Political, Social and Economical Forces 1950–1957* (London: Stevens & Sons).

——(1964). *The Uniting of Europe: Political, Social, and Economic Forces 1950–57*, 2nd edn. (Stanford, Calif: Stanford University Press).

——(1975). *The Obsolescence of Regional Integration Theory* (Berkeley, Calif.: University of California, Institute of International Studies).

Habermas, J. (1986). 'Law as Medium and Law as Institution', in G. Teubner (ed.), *Dilemmas of Law in the Welfare State* (Berlin: Walter de Gruyter).

——(1992). *Faktizität und Geltung* (Frankfurt am Main: Suhrkamp).

——(1999). 'The European Nation-State and the Pressures of Globalization', *New Left Review*, 235: 46–59.

Hailbronner, K., and Thiery, C. (1997). 'Schengen II and Dublin: Responsibility for Asylum Applications in Europe', *Common Market Law Review*, 34: 957–89.

Hall, Peter A., and Franzese, Robert J., Jr. (1998). 'Mixed Signals: Central Bank Independence, Coordinated Wage Bargaining, and European Monetary Union', *International Organization*, 52/3: 505–35.

——and Taylor, R. C. R. (1998). 'The Potential of Historical Institutionalism: a Response to Hay and Wincott', *Political Studies*, 46/5: 958–62.

Haywood, Elizabeth (1993). 'The European Policy of François Mitterrand', *Journal of Common Market Studies*, 31/2: 269–82.

Henderson, K. (1999). *Back to Europe: Central and Eastern Europe and the European Union* (London: Taylor & Francis).

Henning, C. R. (1994). *Currencies and Politics in the United States, Germany, and Japan* (Washington, DC: Institute for International Economics).

——(1997). *Cooperating with Europe's Monetary Union*. (Washington, DC: Institute for International Economics).

Héritier, A. (1994). ' "Leaders" and "Laggards" in European Policy-Making: Clean Air Policy Changes in Britain and Germany', in F. van Waarden and B. Unger (eds.), *Convergence or Diversity? The Pressure of Internationalization on Economic Governance Institutions and Policy Outcomes* (Avebury: Aldershot).

Hermann, Valentine, and Lodge, Juliet (1978). *The European Parliament and the European Community* (London: Macmillan).

Herrberg, A. (1998). 'The European Union and Russia: Towards a New Ostpolitik?', in C. Rhodes (ed.), *The European Union in the World Community* (Boulder, Colo.: Lynne Rienner), 83–105

Hewstone, Miles (1986). *Understanding Attitudes to the European Community: A Social-Psychological Study in Four Member States* (Cambridge: Cambridge University Press).

Hilf, M. (1995). 'The ECJ's Opinion 1/94 on the WTO', *European Journal of International Law*, 6: 245–59.

Hill, C. (1993). 'The Capability-Expectations Gap or Conceptualising Europe's International Role', *Journal of Common Market Studies*, 33/3: 305–28.

Hindley, Brian (1993). *Helping Transition through Trade? EC and US Policy towards Exports from Eastern and Central Europe*, EBRD Working Paper, 4 (London: European Bank for Reconstruction and Development).

Hix, Simon (1994). 'The Study of the European Community: The Challenge to Comparative Politics', *West European Politics*, 17/1: 1–30.

——(1998). 'The Study of the European Union II: The "New Governance" Agenda and its Rival', *Journal of European Public Policy*, 5/1: 38–65.

——(1999). *The Political System of the European Union* (Basingstoke and New York: Macmillan and St Martin's Press).

——and Lord, Christopher (1996). *European Political Parties* (London: St Martin's Press).

Hoffmann, S. (1966). 'Obstinate or Obsolete? The Fate of the Nation-State and the Case of Western Europe', *Daedalus*, 95/3: 862–915.

Hofrichter, Jurgen, and Klein, Michael (1993). *The European Parliament in the Eyes of EU Citizens* (Mannheim: ZEUS).

Holland, M. (1998*a*). 'Do Acronyms Matter? The Future of ACP–EU Relations and the Developing World' *Baseler Schriften zur europäischen Integration*, 35 (Basle: University of Basle).

——(1998*b*). 'EU Agenda: The Common Foreign and Security Policy', *New Zealand International Review*, 23/3: 29.

——(2000). 'A Suitable Subject for Experimentation . . . ? Policy towards South Africa and the Evolution of the European Union as an International Actor (1977–2000)', *Observatoire des Relations Internationales dans l'hemisphere sud*, ORIHS Pamphlet, 4 (Grenoble and Canterbury: University of Kent at Canterbury).

Holzinger, K. (1999). *Optimal Regulatory Units: A Concept of Regional Differentiation of Environmental Standards in the European Union*, Preprint aus der Max-Planck Projektgruppe Recht der Gemeinschaftsgüter 1999/11, (Bonn: Max-Planck-Institut).

Hooghe, L. (1995). 'Subnational Mobilisation in the European Union', *West European Politics*, 18 (July), 175–98.

——(1999). 'Commission Officials and European Integration', paper presented at the ECSA Sixth Biennial International Conference, Pittsburgh, 2–5 June.

——and Marks, G. (1997*a*). 'Contending Models of Governance in the European Union', in A. W. Cafruny and C. Lankowski (eds.), *Europe's Ambiguous Unity* (Boulder, Colo.: and London: Lynne Rienner).

————(1997*b*). 'The Making of a Polity: The Struggle over European Integration', *European Integration Online Papers* (*EIoP*), 1/004, http://eiop.or.at/eiop/texte/(1997).-004a.htm.

————(1999). 'The Making of a Polity: The Struggle over European Integration', in H. Kitschelt, P. Lange, G. Marks, and J. D. Stephens (eds.), *Continuity and Change in Contemporary Capitalism* (Cambridge and New York: Cambridge University Press).

House of Commons (1999). 'European Union Enlargement, Third Report' Foreign Affairs Committee, Session 1998–1999.

Howarth, David (1999). 'French Aversion to Independent Monetary Authority and the Development of French Policy on the EMU Project', paper presented at the ECSA Sixth Biennial International Conference, Pittsburgh, 2–5 June.

Immergut, E. M. (1998). 'The Theoretical Core of the New Institutionalism', *Politics and Society*, 26/1: 5–34.

Inglehart, Ronald (1977). *The Silent Revolution: Changing Values and Political Styles Among Western Publics* (Princeton, NJ: Princeton University Press).

Inotai, András (1994). 'Die Beziehungen zwischen der EU und den assoziierten Staaten Mittel- und Osteuropas', *Europäische Rundschau*, 22/3: 19–35.

International Monetary Fund (1998). *World Economic Outlook: Financial Turbulence and the World Economy* (Washington, DC: IMF).

Issing, O. (1999*a*). 'The Eurosystem: Transparent and Accountable or "Willem in Euroland"', *Journal of Common Market Studies*, 37/3: 503–19.

——(1999*b*). 'The Monetary Policy of the ECB: Stability, Transparency, Accountability' (25 Oct.), London, http://www.ecb.int.

Iversen, Toben (1998). 'Wage Bargaining, Central Bank Independence, and the Real Effects of Money', *International Organization*, 52/3: 469–504.

Jachtenfuchs, M. (1995). 'Theoretical Perspectives on European Governance', *European Law Journal*, 1/2: 115–33.

——(1999). 'Ideen und Integration: Verfassungsideen in Deutschland, Frankreich und Großbritannien und die Entwicklung der EU', unpublished *Habilitationsschrift*, University of Mannheim, June.

Jacobs, Francis (1997). 'Legislative Co-Decision: A Real Step Forward?', paper presented to the ECSA Fifth Biennial International Conference, Seattle, 29 May–1 June.

Jacobson, D. (1996). *Rights Across Borders* (Baltimore: Johns Hopkins).

Jancar-Webster, B. (1998). 'Environmental Movement and Social Change in the Transition Countries', in S. Baker and P. Jehlicka (eds.), *Dilemmas of Transition: The Environment, Democracy and Economic Reform in East Central Europe* (Ilford: Frank Cass), 111–26.

Jepperson, R. L., Wendt, A., and Katzenstein, P. (1996). 'Norms, Identity, and Culture in National Security', in P. Katzenstein (ed.), *The Culture of National Security: Norms and Identity in World Politics* (New York: Columbia University Press), 35–7.

Johnson, M. (1998). *European Community Trade Policy and the Article 113 Committee* (London: Royal Institute of International Affairs).

Johnston, Alistair Ian (1999). 'Treating Institutions as Social Environments: The Role of Persuasion and Social Influence in Eliciting Cooperation', paper prepared for the ISA Annual Meeting, Washington, DC, 16–20 Feb.

Jones, Erik (1998). 'Economic and Monetary Union: Playing with Money', in Andrew Moravcsik (ed.), *Centralization or Fragmentation: Europe Facing the Challenges of Deepening, Diversity, and Democracy* (New York: Council of Foreign Relations), 59–93.

——Frieden, J., and Torres, F. (eds.) (1998). *Joining Europe's Monetary Club: The Challenges for Smaller Member States* (New York: St Martin's Press).

Jönsson, C., Bjurulf, B., Egström, O., Sannerstedt, A., and Strömvik, M. (1998). 'Negotiations in Networks in the European Union', *International Negotiation*, 3/3: 319–44.

Jordan, A. J. (1999*a*). 'European Community Water Standards: Locked in or Watered Down?', *Journal of Common Market Studies*, 37/1: 13–38.

——(1999*b*). 'The Implementation of EU Environmental Policy: A Policy Problem Without a Political Solution?', *Environment and Planning C: Government and Policy*, 17/1: 69–90.

——Brouwer, R., and Noble, E. (1999). 'Innovative and Responsive? A Longitudinal Analysis of the Speed of EU Environmental Policy-Making, 1996–97', *Journal of European Public Policy*, 6/3: 376–98.

Jørgensen, J. (1999). 'Speaking Point: Screening the Environmental Acquis with the "Ins"', Informal Environmental Council, Weimar, 7–9 May.

Jørgensen, K. E. (1999). 'The Social Construction of the Acquis Communautaire: A Cornerstone of the European Edifice', *European Integration Online Papers*, 3/6, http://eiop.or.at/erop/texte/1999-006.htm.

Judge, David, and Earnshaw, David (1999). 'Locating the European Parliament', paper presented to the ECSA Sixth Biennial International Conference, Pittsburgh, 2–5 June.

Kasman, B. (1998). 'Living with Low Inflation', *Economic Research* (7 Oct.).

Katzenstein, P. (ed.) (1996). *The Culture of National Security* (New York: Columbia University Press).

——Keohane, Robert O., and Krasner, Stephen D. (1998). 'International Organization and the Study of World Politics', *International Organization*, 52/4: 645–85.

Kawai, Masahiro (1992). 'Optimum Currency Areas', in Peter Newman, Murray Milgate, and Jeahn Eatwell (eds.), *The New Palgrave Dictionary of Money and Finance* (London: Macmillan), 78–81.

Kenen, Peter B. (1969). 'The Theory of Optimum Currency Areas: An Eclectic View', in Robert A. Mundell and Alexander K. Swoboda (eds.), *Monetary Problems of the International Economy* (Chicago: University of Chicago Press), 41–60.

Kerr, Henry H. (1973). 'Changing Attitudes through Institutional Participation: European Parliamentarians and Integration', *International Organization*, 27: 45–83.

Keyman, F. E. (1997). *Globalization, State, Identity/Difference: Toward a Critical Social Theory of International Relations* (Atlantic Highlands, NJ: Humanities Press).

King, Anthony (1975). 'Modes of Executive-Legislative Relations: Great Britain, France and Germany', *Legislative Studies Quarterly*, 1: 11–34.

Kingdon, John W. (1984). *Agendas, Alternatives and Public Policy* (Boston, Mass.: Little Brown & Company).

Kingsbury, B. (1998). '"Indigenous Peoples" in International Law: A Constructivist Approach to the Asian Controversy', *American Journal of International Law*, 92/3: 414.

Kinkel, K., and de Charette, H. (1997). 'Gemeinsamer Diskussionsbeitrag des deutschen und des französischen Aussenministers, Klaus Kinkel und Hervé de Charette, für die Regierungskonferenz zur verstärkten Zusammenarbeit, veröffentlicht am 18. Oktober 1996 in Bonn und Paris', *Internationale Politik*, 52/3: 72–5.

Klotz, A. (1995*a*). *Norms in International Relations: The Struggle against Apartheid* (Ithaca, NY: Cornell University Press).

——(1995*b*). 'Norms Reconstituting Interests: Global Racial Equality and U.S. Sanctions against South Africa', *International Organization*, 49/3: 451–78.

Knill, C., and Lenschow, A. (1999). *Governance im Mehrebenensystem: Die institutionellen Grenzen effektiver Implementation in der europäischen Umweltpolitik*, Preprint aus der Max-Planck-Projektgruppe Recht der Gemeinschaftsgüter 1999/1 (Bonn: Max-Planck-Institut).

Koenig, C., and Pechstein, M. (1998). *Die Europäische Union*, 2nd edn. (Frankfurt am Main: Mohr).

Kortenberg, H. (1998). 'Closer Cooperation in the Treaty of Amsterdam', *Common Market Law Review*, 35/4: 833–54.

Koslowski, R. (1999). 'A Constructivist Approach to Understanding the European Union as a Federal Polity', *Journal of European Public Policy*, 6/4: 561–78.

Kotzias, N. (1998). 'Die Regierungskonferenz und die flexible Föderung (?) der Integration', in F. Breuss and S. Griller, *Flexible Integration in Europa: Einheit oder 'Europe à la carte'?* (Vienna: Springer), 1–40.

Kraemer, R. A. (1998). 'Subsidiarity and Water Policy', in F. Nunes Correia (ed.), *Selected Issues in Water Resources Management in Europe* (Rotterdam: A. A. Balkema), 387–417.

Kramer, Heinz (1993). 'The European Community's Response to the "New Eastern Europe"', *Journal of Common Market Studies*, 31/2: 213–44.

Krasner, S. D. (1995). 'Compromising Westphalia', *International Security*, 20/3: 115–51.

Kratochwil, F. V. (1989). *Rules, Norms, and Decisions: On the Conditions of Practical and Legal Reasoning in International Relations and Domestic Affairs* (Cambridge: Cambridge University Press).

——and Ruggie, J. G. (1986). 'International Organization: A State of the Art on an Art of the State', *International Organization*, 40: 753–75.

Krenzler, H. G, and Everson, M. (1998). *Preparing for the Acquis Communautaire*, EUI RSC Policy Paper, 6/98, (Florence: European University Institute).

Kreppel, A. (1999). 'The June 1999 Elections, Amsterdam, and the Perils of Ideology', *ECSA Review*, 12/4: 8–10.

——and Tsebelis, George (1999). 'Coalition Formation in the European Parliament', *Comparative Political Studies*, 32: 933–66.

Krugman, P. (1990). 'Policy Problems of a Monetary Union', in P. De Grauwe and L. Papademos (eds.), *The European Monetary System in the 1990s* (London: Longman for CEPR and the Bank of Greece).

Krugman, P. (1993) *Exchange Rate Instability* (Cambridge, Mass.: MIT Press).

Kruse, D. C. (1980). *Monetary Integration in Western Europe: EMU, EMS and Beyond* (London and Boston, Mass.: Butterworth).

Laffan, B. (1997). 'From Policy Entrepreneur to Policy Manager: The Challenge Facing the European Commission', *Journal of European Public Policy*, 4/3: 422–38.

——O'Donnell, Rory, and Smith, Michael (2000). *Europe's Experimental Union: Rethinking Integration* (London: Routledge).

——and Shackleton, Michael (1996). 'The Budget', in H. Wallace and W. Wallace (eds.), *Policy-Making in the European Union*, 3rd edn. (Oxford: Oxford University Press).

————(2000). 'The Budget', in H. Wallace and W. Wallace (eds.), *Policy-Making in the European Union*, 4th edn. (Oxford: Oxford University Press).

Lafontaine O., and Mueller, C. (1998). *Keine Angst vor der Globalisierung* (Bonn: Dietz Verlag).

Lamers, K., and Schäuble, W. (1994). *Überlegungen zur europäischen Politik* (Bonn: CDU/CSU-Fraktion des Deutschen Bundestages, 1 Sept.).

Lavanex, S. (1999). *Safe Third Countries, Extending the EU Asylum and Immigration Policies to Central and Eastern Europe* (Budapest: Central European University).

Leander, Anna, and Guzzini, Stefano (1997). 'Economic and Monetary Union and the Crisis of European Social Contracts', in Petri Minkkinen and Heikki Patomäki (eds.), *The Politics of Economic and Monetary Union* (London: Kluwer), 133–63.

Leibfried, Stefan (2000). 'The Common Agricultural Policy', in H. Wallace and W./ Wallace (eds.), *Policy Making in the European Union*, 4th edn. (Oxford: Oxford University Press).

——and Pearson, P. (1996). 'Social Policy' in H. Wallace and W. Wallace. (eds.) *Policy Making in the European Union*, 3rd edn. (Oxford: Oxford University Press).

Lenschow, A., and Zito, A. (1998). 'Blurring or Shifting of Policy Frames? Institutionalization of the Economic–Environmental Policy Linkage in the European Community', *Governance*, 11/4: 415–41.

Leonard, Dick (1998). 'Eye on the EU', *Europe*, 4/1 (Sept.): 379.

Leslie, P. (2000). 'Abuses of Asymmetry: Privilege and Exclusion', in K. H. Neunreither and A. Wiener, *European Integration after Amsterdam* (Oxford: Oxford University Press).

Lewis, David (1993). *The Road to Europe* (New York: Peter Lang Publishing).

Lindberg, Leon (1966). 'Integration as a Source of Stress on the European Community System', *International Organization*, 20: 233–65.

——(1967). 'The European Community as a Political System: Notes toward the Construction of a Model', *Journal of Common Market Studies* (5 June): 344–87.

——and Scheingold, S. A. (1970). *Europe's Would-Be Polity: Patterns of Change in the European Community* (Englewood Cliffs, NJ: Prentice Hall).

Lippert, B., and Becker, P. (1998). 'Structured Dialogue Revisited: The EU's Politics of Inclusion and Exclusion', *European Foreign Affairs Review*, 3/3: 341–65.

Livingston, Steven, and Eachus, Todd (1995). 'Humanitarian Crises and U.S. Foreign Policy: Somalia and the CNN-effect Reconsidered', *Political Communication*, 12/4: 413–17.

Louis J.-V. (1998). 'L'EUM et la Gouvernance Économique', paper presented at ECSA Europe–World conference, Sept.

Ludlow, Peter (1998). 'The (1998) UK Presidency: A View from Brussels', *Journal of Common Market Studies*, 36/4: 573–83.

Lumsdaine, David H. (1993). *Moral Vision in International Politics: The Foreign Aid Regime 1949–1989* (Princeton: Princeton University Press).

Lyons, G. M., and Mastanduno, M. (1995). *Beyond Westphalia: State Sovereignty and International Intervention* (Baltimore: Johns Hopkins Press).

McAleavey, Paul, and Mitchell, James (1994). 'Industrial Regions and Lobbying in the Structural Funds Reform Process', *Journal of Common Market Studies*, 32/3 (June): 237–58.

McConnell, Grant (1970). *Private Power and American Democracy* (New York: McGraw-Hill).

MacCormick, N. (1997a). 'Democracy, Subsidiarity, and Citizenship in the European Commonwealth', *Law and Philosophy*, 16: 331–56.

——(1997b). 'Institutional Normative Order: A Conception of Law', *Cornell Law Review*, 82: 1051–70.

——(1999). *Questioning Sovereignty* (Oxford: Oxford University Press).

McDonagh, B. (1998). *Original Sin in a Brave New World: An Account of the Negotiation of the Treaty of Amsterdam* (Dublin: Institute of European Affairs).

McGowan, F., and Wallace, H. (1996). 'Towards a European Regulatory State', *Journal of European Public Policy*, 3/4: 560–76.

McNamara, K. R. (1998). *The Currency of Ideas: Monetary Politics in the European Union* (Ithaca, NY: Cornell University Press).

Magee, Stephen P., Brock, William A., and Young, Leslie (1989). *Black Hole Tariffs and Endogenous Policy Theory: Political Economy in General Equilibrium* (Cambridge: Cambridge University Press).

Majone, G. (1995). *The Development of Social Regulation in the European Community: Policy Externalities, Transaction Costs*, EUI Working Papers, 95/2 (Florence: European University Institute).

——(1996). *Regulating Europe* (London: Routledge).

Major, J. (1994). 'Europe: A Future that Works', William and Mary Lecture (University of Leiden, 7 Sept.).

Mancini, G. F. (1989). 'The Making of a Constitution for Europe', *Common Market Law Review*, 26/4: 595–614.

——(1998). 'Europe: The Case for Statehood', *European Law Journal*, 4/1: 29–42.

Manin, P., and Louis, J.-V. (eds.) (1996). *Vers une Europe différenciée? Possibilité et limite* (Paris: Éditions A. Pedone; Brussels: TEPSA).

March, James G., and Olsen, Johan P. (1979). *Ambiguity and Choice in Organizations* (Bergen: Universitetsforlaget).

————(1984)., 'The New Institutionalism: Organizational Factors in Political Life', *American Political Science Review*, 78/3 (Sept.): 734–49.

March, James G., and Olsen, Johan P. (1998). 'The Institutional Dynamics of International Political Orders', *International Organization*, 52: 943–59.

—— and Simon, Herbert A. (1964). *Organizations* (New York: John Wiley & Sons).

Marcussen, M. (1997). 'The Role of "Ideas" in Dutch, Danish and Swedish Economic Policy in the 1980s and the Beginning of the 1990s', in P. Minkkinen and H. Patomäki (eds.), *The Politics of Economic and Monetary Union* (Helsinki: Ulkopoliittinen Instituutti (The Finnish Institute of International Affairs)), 75–103.

—— (1998*a*). *Ideas and Elites: Danish Macro-Economic Policy-Discourse in the EMU Process*, Ph.D. dissertation, Aalborg University, Institute for Development and Planning, ISP-Series, 226 (Apr.).

—— (1998*b*). *Central Bankers, the Ideational Life-Cycle and the Social Construction of EMU*, EUI Working Papers, 98/33 (Florence: European University Institute).

—— *et al.* (1999). 'Constructing Europe? The Evolution of French, British and German Nation State Identities', *Journal of European Public Policy*, 6/4: 614–33.

Maresceau, M. (ed.) (1997). *Enlarging the European Union* (Harlow: Longman).

Marks, G. (1992). 'Structural Policy in the European Community', in Alberta M. Sbragia (ed.), *Euro-Politics* (Washington, DC: Brookings).

—— (1993). 'Structural Policy and Multilevel Governance in the EC', in A. Cafruny and G. Rosenthal (eds.), *The State of the European Community, ii. The Maastricht Debate and Beyond* (Boulder, Colo.: Lynne Rienner), 391–410.

—— Hooghe, L., and Blank, K. (1996*a*). 'European Integration from the 1980s: State-Centric v. Multi-Level Governance', *Journal of Common Market Studies*, 34/3: 341–78.

—— Nielsen, F., Ray, L., and Salk, J. (1996*b*). 'Competencies, Cracks and Conflicts: Regional Mobilization in the European Union', in G. Marks *et al.* (eds.), *Governance in the European Union* (London and Thousand Oaks, Calif.: Sage).

—— Scharpf, F. W., Schmitter, P. C., and Streeck, W. (1996*c*). *Governance in the European Union* (London and Thousand Oaks, Calif.: Sage).

Martin, L. L. (1993). 'International and Domestic Institutions in the EMU Process', *Economics and Politics*, 5/2: 125–45.

Matthews, D. (1999). 'The EBB and Flow of EC Environmental Instruments: Why the Need for a New Framework Approach to Community Water Policy?', paper presented at the ECSA Sixth Biennial International Conference, Pittsburgh, 2–5 June.

Mayes, D. G. (1999). 'Evolving Voluntary Rules for the Operation of the European Central Bank', *Current Politics and Economics of Europe*, 8: 357–86.

Mayhew, Alan (1998). *Recreating Europe: The European Union's Policy Towards Central and Eastern Europe* (Cambridge: Cambridge University Press).

Mazey, S. (1998). 'The European Union and Women's Rights: From the Europeanisation of National Agendas to the Nationalization of a European Agenda?', *Journal of European Public Policy*, 5/1: 131–52.

Mermin, Jonathan (1997). 'Television News and American Intervention in Somalia: The Myth of a Media-Driven Foreign Policy', *Political Science Quarterly*, 112/3: 385(19).

Messerlin, Patrick A. (1993). 'The EC and Central Europe: The Missed Rendez-vous of 1992?', *Economics of Transition*, 1/1: 89–109.

Meunier, S. (1998). 'Divided but United: European Trade Policy Integration and EC–US Agricultural Negotiations in the Uruguay Round', in C. Rhodes (ed.), *The European Union in the World Community* (Boulder, Colo.: Lynne Rienner).

——(2000). 'What Single Voice? European Institutions and EU–US Trade Negotiations', *International Organization* (Winter): 103–35.

——and Nicolaïdis, K. (1999). 'Who Speaks for Europe? The Delegation of Trade Authority in the EU', *Journal of Common Market Studies*, 37/3: 477–501.

Meyring, B. (1997). 'Intergovernmentalism and Supranationality: Two Stereotypes for a Complex Reality', *European Law Review*, 22/3: 221–47.

Mezey, Michael (1979). *Comparative Legislatures* (Durham, NC: Duke University Press).

Michalski, Anna and Wallace, Helen (1992). *The European Community: The Challenge of Enlargement* (London: Royal Institute of International Affairs).

Midgaard, Knut (1999). *Schemes of Voting Weight Distributions in the EU: Possible and Actual Justifications*, Arena Working Papers, WP 99/25, http://www.sv.uio.no/arena/publications/wp99_25.htm.

Miles, L., Redmond, J., and Schwok, R. (1995). 'Integration Theory and the Enlargement of the European Union', in C. Rhodes and S. Mazey (eds.), *The State of the European Union,* iii. *Building a European Polity* (Boulder, Colo.: Lynne Rienner), 177–94.

Millett, Timothy (1992). 'The Role of the European Court of Justice in Relation to Public Procurement', *Public Procurement Law Review*, 1.

Milward, A. (1992). *The European Rescue of the Nation-State* (London and New York: Routledge).

Mnookin, R., Susskind, L., and Foster, P. (eds.) (1999). *Negotiating on Behalf of Others* (London: Sage).

Moravcsik, A. (1993). 'Preferences and Power in the European Community: A Liberal Intergovernmentalist Approach', *Journal of Common Market Studies*, 31/4: 473–524.

——(1995). 'Liberal Intergovernmentalism and Integration: A Rejoinder', *Journal of Common Market Studies*, 33/4: 611–28.

——(1998). *The Choice for Europe: Social Purpose and State Power from Messina to Maastricht* (Ithaca, NY, and London: Cornell University Press and UCL Press).

——(1999). 'Is Something Rotten in the State of Denmark? Constructivism and European Integration', *Journal of European Public Policy*, 6/6: 669–81.

——and Nicolaïdis, K. (1998). 'Federal Ideals and Constitutional Realities in the Amsterdam Treaty', *Journal of Common Market Studies*, 36 (Annual Review of Activities): 13–38.

Moravcsik, A. and Nicolaïdis, K. (1999). 'Explaining the Treaty of Amsterdam: Interests, Influence, Institutions', *Journal of Common Market Studies*, 37/1: 59–85.

Morgenthau, H. J. (1985). *Politics Among Nations: The Struggle for Power and Peace*, 6th edn. (New York: Knopf).

Morrow J. D. (1994). *Game Theory for Political Scientists* (Princeton: Princeton University Press).

Moser, Peter (1997). 'The Benefits of the Conciliation Procedure to the European Parliament: Comment to George Tsebelis', *Aussenwirtschaft: The Swiss Review of International Economic Relations*, 52: 57–62.

Moss, B., and Michie, J. (eds.) (1998). *The Single European Currency in National Perspective: A Community in Crisis?* (Basingstoke: Macmillan).

Mullen, Paul Fabian (2000). 'A New Institutional Model of Courts: Courts and Intergovernmental Relations', paper presented at the Annual Meeting of the Midwest Political Science, Chicago, 27–30 Apr.

Mundell, R. (1961). 'A Theory of Optimum Currency Areas', *American Economic Review*, 51: 657–75.

Murphy, C. N. (1994). *International Organization and Industrial Change: Global Governance since 1850* (Cambridge: Polity Press).

Muscatelli, V. A. (1997). 'International Macroeconomic Co-ordination', in V. A. Muscatelli (ed.), *Economic and Political Institutions in Economic Policy* (Manchester: Manchester University Press), 98–133.

Nello, S. S., and Smith, K. E. (1998). *The European Union and Central and Eastern Europe: The Implications of Enlargement in Stages* (Aldershot: Ashgate).

Nentwich, Michael, and Falkner, Gerda (1997). 'The Treaty of Amsterdam: Towards a New Institutional Balance', *European Integration online Papers*, 1/15.

Neunreither, K. H. and Wiener, A. (2000). *European Integration after Amsterdam. Institutional Dynamics and Prospects for Democracy* (Oxford: Oxford University Press).

Niblett, Robin C. H. (1995). 'The European Community and the Central European Three, 1989–92: A Study of the Community as an International Actor', Ph.D. thesis, Oxford University.

Nicolaïdis, K. (1999). 'Minimizing Agency Costs in Two-Level Games: The Controversies over Trade Authority in the United States and the European Union', in R. Mnookin *et al.*, *Negotiating on Behalf of Others* (London: Sage).

Norton, Philip (1984). 'Parliament and Policy in Britain: The House of Commons as a Policy Influencer', *Teaching Politics*, 13: 198–202.

——(1997a). 'Introduction', *Parliamentary Affairs*, 50: 349–56.

——(1997b). 'Legislatures in Perspective', in P. Norton, P. (ed.), *Parliaments in Western Europe*, 2nd edn. (London: Frank Cass).

——(1998). 'Conclusion: Do Parliaments Make a Difference?', in P. Norton (ed.), *Parliaments and Governments in Western Europe* (London: Frank Cass).

Noyer, C. (1999a). 'The Euro as an International Currency', Tokyo (6 July), http://www.ecb.int.

——(1999*b*). 'Globally liberalized capital markets and the conduct of monetary policy', Vienna (11 Nov.), http://www.ecb.int.

Nugent, Neill (1994). *The Government and Politics of the European Union*, 3rd edn. (Durham, NC: Duke University Press).

——(1995). 'The Leadership Capacity of the European Commission', *Journal of European Public Policy*, 2/4 (Dec.): 603–23.

Oatley, Thomas (1997). *Monetary Politics: Exchange Rate Cooperation in the European Union* (Ann Arbor, Mich.: University of Michigan).

OECD, Organization for Economic Co-operation and Development (1998). *Building Capacity in the Environmental Goods and Services Industry in the Central and Eastern European Countries: Agenda for Action* (Paris: OECD).

——(1999). *Environment in the Transition to a Market Economy: Progress in Central and Eastern Europe and the New Independent States*, Centre for Co-operation with Non-Members (Paris: OECD).

O'Leary, S. (1995). 'The Relationship between Community Citizenship and the Protection of Fundamental Rights in Community Law', *Common Market Law Review*, 32: 519–54.

Packenham, Robert A. (1970). 'Legislatures and Political Development', in A. Kornberg and L. Musolf (eds.), *Legislatures in Developmental Perspective* (Durham, NC: Duke University Press).

Padoa-Schioppa, T. (1994). *The Road to Monetary Union in Europe: The Emperor, the Kings, and the Genies* (Oxford: Clarendon Press).

——(1997). 'Government and the Market', in V. A. Muscatelli (ed.), *Economic and Political Institutions in Economic Policy* (Manchester: Manchester University Press).

Party of European Socialists (1999). *PES Manifesto for the (1999) European Elections* (as adopted by the PES Congress of 1 March 1999 in Milan), online at http://www.eurosocialists.org/election/en/1.asp?LANGUAGE=E.

Pauly, L. W. (1992). 'The Politics of European Monetary Union: National Strategies, International Implications', *International Journal*, 47 (Winter): 93–111.

Peers, S. (1999). 'Who's Judging the Watchmen? The Judicial System of the Area of Freedom, Security and Justice', *Yearbook of European Law*, 8.

Pelkmans, J. (1995). 'Condemned to Conflicts, Cooperation and Consensus: The EU and US in the Uruguay Round', in F. Breuss (ed.), *The World Economy After the Uruguay Round* (Vienna: Service Fachverlag).

Pernice, I. (1998). 'Constitutional Law Implications for a State Participating in a Process of Regional Integration: German Constitution and "Multilevel Constitutionalism" ', in E. Riedel (ed.), *German Reports on Public Law, Presented to the XV. International Congress on Comparative Law* (Baden-Baden: Nomos), 40–66.

——(1999). 'Multilevel Constitutionalism and the Treaty of Amsterdam: European Constitution-Making Revisited?', *Common Market Law Review*, 36: 703–50.

Peters, B. G. (1998). 'Policy Networks: Myth, Metaphor and Reality', in

D. Marsh (ed.), *Comparing Policy Networks* (Buckingham: Open University Press).

Peterson, John (1995*a*). 'Decision-Making in the European Union: Towards a Framework for Analysis', *Journal of European Public Policy*, 2/1: 69–93.

——(1995*b*). 'EU Research Policy: The Politics of Expertise', in C. Rhodes and S. Mazey (eds.), *The State of the European Union, iii. Building a European Polity?* (Harlow and Boulder, Colo.: Longman and Lynne Rienner).

——(1997). 'States, Societies and the European Union', *West European Politics*, 20/4: 1–24.

——(1999*a*). 'Jacques Santer: The EU's Gorbachev', *ECSA Review*, 2/4 (Fall): 4–6.

——(1999*b*). 'The Santer Era: The European Commission in Normative, Historical and Theoretical Perspective', *Journal of European Public Policy*, 6 /1: 46–65.

——(2000). 'US–EU Trade Negotiations after the Uruguay Round: Get Away from Me Closer, You're Near Me Too Far', in M. Pollack and Greg Shaffer (eds.), *Transatlantic Governance in the Global Economy*.

——and Bomberg, E. (1998). 'Northern Enlargement and EU Decision-Making', in P.-H. Laurent and M. Maresceau, M. (eds.), *The State of the European Union*, iv (Boulder, Colo., and Harlow: Lynne Rienner and Longman).

————(1999). *Decision-Making in the European Union* (New York: St Martin's Press and Macmillan: New York and Basingstoke).

——and Jones, E. (2000). 'Decision Making in an Enlarging European Union', in J. Sperling (ed.), *Two Tiers or Two Speeds? NATO and EU Enlargement Compared* (Manchester and New York: Manchester University Press).

——and Sharp, M. (1998). *Technology Policy in the European Union (*London: Macmillan).

——and Sjursen, H. (eds.) (1998). *A Common Foreign Policy for Europe? Competing Visions of the CFSP* (London: Routledge).

Philippart, E., and Edwards, G. (1999). 'The Provisions on Closer Co-operation in the Treaty of Amsterdam: The Politics of Flexibility in the European Union', *Journal of Common Market Studies*, 37/1: 87–108.

Pierson, Christopher, Forster, Anthony, and Jones, Erik (1999). 'Changing the Guard in the European Union: In with the New, Out with the Old?', *Industrial Relations Journal: European Annual Review (1998)*, 30/4 (Dec.): 277–90.

Pierson, Paul (1993). 'When Effect Becomes Cause: Policy Feedback and Political Change', *World Politics*, 45: 595–628.

——(1996*a*). 'The New Politics of the Welfare State', *World Politics*, 48/2 (Jan.): 143–79.

——(1996*b*). 'The Path to European Integration: A Historical Institutionalist Analysis', *Comparative Political Studies*, 29/2: 123–63.

——(1998). 'The Path to European Integration: A Historical Institutionalist Analysis', in W. Sandholtz and A. Stone Sweet (eds.), *Supranational Governance: the Institutionalisation of the European Union* (Oxford: Oxford University Press).

Pinder, J. (1985/6). 'European Community and Nation-State: A Case for a Neo-Federalism?', *International Affairs*, 62/1: 41–54.

Pisani-Ferry, Jean, Hefeker, Carsten, and Hughes Hallett, Andrew (1997). *The Political Economy of EMU: France, Germany and the UK*, CEPS Paper, 69 (Brussels: Centre for European Policy Studies,May).

Poiares Maduro, M. (1998). *We the Court: The European Court of Justice and the European Economic Constitution* (Oxford: Hart Publishing).

Pollack, M. A. (1996). 'The New Institutionalism and EC Governance: The Promise and Limits of Institutional Analysis', *Governance: An International Journal of Policy and Administration*, 9: 429–58.

——(1997a). 'Delegation, Agency and Agenda-Setting in the European Community', *International Organization*, 51/1: 99–134.

——(1997b). 'Representing Diffuse Interests in EC Policy-Making', *Journal of European Public Policy*, 4/4: 572–90.

——(1998). 'Beyond Left and Right: Neoliberalism and Regulated Capitalism in the Treaty of Amsterdam', *University of Wisconsin Working Paper Series in European Studies*, 2/2, http://polyglot.lss.wisc.edu/eur/works/pollacktitle. html.

Powell, Martin (ed.) (1999). *New Labor, New Welfare State?* (Bristol: Policy Press).

Preston, C. (1995). 'Obstacles to EU Enlargement: The Classical Community Method and the Prospects for a Wider Europe', *Journal of Common Market Studies*, 33/3: 451–63.

——(1997). *Enlargement and Integration in the European Union* (London: Routledge).

Price, Richard, and Tannenwald, Nina (1996). 'Norms and Deterrence: The Nuclear and Chemical Weapons Taboos', in Peter J. Katzenstein (ed.), *The Culture of National Security: Norms and Identity in World Politics* (New York: Columbia University Press), 114–52.

Prodi, R. (1999a). President-designate of the European Commission, Speech to the European Parliament, Strasbourg, 4 May, http://europa.eu.int/comm/commissioners/prodi/speeches/040599_en.htm.

——(1999b), Speech by Romano Prodi, President-designate of the European Commission to the European Parliament, 21 July, http://europa.eu.int/comm/commissioners/ prodi/speeches/210799_en.htm.

Puchala, Donald (1999). 'Institutionalism, Intergovernmentalism and European Integration', *Journal of Common Market Studies*, 37/2 (June): 317.

Putnam, Robert, D. (1988). 'Diplomacy and Domestic Politics: The Logic of Two-Level Games', *International Organization*, 42/3: 427–60.

Quaglia, Lucia (1999). 'Italy in EMU: Conversion to "Fiscal Virtue" ', paper presented at the Fourth UACES Research Conference, University of Sheffield, 8–10 Sept.

Ramaswamy, Ramana, and Sløk, Torsten (1998). 'The Real Effects of Monetary Policy in the European Union: What Are the Differences?', *IMF Staff Papers*, 45/2 (June): 374–99.

Rasmussen, H. (1986). *On the Law and Policy in the European Court of Justice, A Comparative Study in Judicial Policy Making* (Dordrecht: Martinus Nijhoff Publishers).

Raunio, Tapio (1997). *The European Perspective: Transnational Party Groups in the 1989–94 European Parliament* (Aldershot: Ashgate).

Radaelli, C. M. (1999). 'The Public Policy of the European Union: Whiter Politics of Expertise?', *Journal of European Public Policy*, 6/5: 757–74.

Ravenhill, J. (1985). *Collective Clientalism: The Lomé Conventions and North-South Relations* (New York: Columbia University Press).

Redmond, J., and Rosenthal, G. G. (1998). *The Expanding European Union. Past, Present, Future* (Boulder, Colo.: Lynne Rienner).

Regional Environmental Center (1994). *Strategic Environmental Issues in Central and Eastern Europe*, Regional Report, 1 (Budapest: Regional Environmental Center).

Remmer, K. L. (1997). 'Theoretical Decay and Theoretical Development: The Resurgence of Institutional Analysis', *World Politics*, 50 (Oct.): 34–61.

Reinicke, Wolfgang (1992). *Building a New Europe: The Challenge of System Transformation and Systemic Reform* (Washington, DC: Brookings).

Rhodes, R. A. W. (1997). *Understanding Governance: Policy Networks, Governance, Reflexivity and Accountability* (Buckingham: Open University Press).

Richardson, J. (1982). *Policy Styles in Western Europe* (London: Allen & Unwin)
——(ed.) (1996). *The European Union: Power and Policy-Making* (London and New York: Routledge).

Richez-Battesti, Nadine (1996). 'Union économique et monétaire et État-provi-dence: La Subsidiarité en question', *Revue Études Internationales*, 27/1 (Mar.): 109–28.

Riker, W. H. (1980). 'Implications from Disequilibrium of Majority Rule for the Study of Institutions', *American Political Science Review*, 74: 432–46.

Risse, T. (1999). ' "Let's Argue!" Persuasion and Deliberation in International Relations', European University Institute, Florence.
——Engelmann-Martin, D., Knopf, H.-J., and Roscher, K. (1999). 'To Euro or Not to Euro. The EMU and Identity Politics in the European Union', *European Journal of International Relations*, 5/2: 147–87.
——and Wiener, A. (1999). 'Something Rotten and the Social Construction of Social Constructivism: A Comment on Comments', *Journal of European Public Policy*, 6/5: 775–82.

Risse-Kappen, Thomas (1994). 'Ideas Do Not Float Freely: Transnational Coalitions, Domestic Structures, and the End of the Cold War', *International Organization*, 48/2: 185–214.
——(1995). *Cooperation Among Democracies: The European Influence on U.S. Foreign Policy* (Princeton: Princeton University Press).
——(1996). 'Exploring the Nature of the Beast: International Relations Theory and Comparative Policy Analysis Meet the European Union', *Journal of Common Market Studies*, 34/1: 53–80.

Robinson, Piers (1999). 'The CNN Effect', *Review of International Studies*, April, 25/2: 301–9.

Rodrick, Dani (1998). 'Why do More Open Economies have Bigger Governments?', *Journal of Political Economy*, 106/5 (Oct.): 997–1032.

Rollo, Jim, and Smith, Alasdair (1993). 'The Political Economy of Eastern European Trade with the European Community: Why so Sensitive?', *Economic Policy*, 16: 139–81.

Roper, J. (1997). 'Flexibility and Legitimacy in the Area of the Common Foreign and Security Policy', paper presented to the European Institute for Public Administration Colloquium on 'Flexibility and the Amsterdam Treaty', Maastricht, 27–8 Nov.

Rosenthal, G. G. (1975). *The Men Behind the Decisions: Cases in European Policy-Making* (Lexington, Mass., Toronto, and London: Lexington Books and D. C. Heath).

Sabatier, P. (1998). 'The Advocacy Coalition Framework: Revisions and Relevance for Europe', *Journal of European Public Policy*, 5/1: 98–130.

Saeter, M. (1991). 'European Security in Transformation', in H. Wallace (ed.), *The Wider Western Europe: Reshaping the EC/EFTA Relationship* (London: Pinter for Royal Institute for International Affairs).

Sandholtz, W. (1993a), 'Choosing Union: Monetary Politics and Maastricht', *International Organization*, 47/1: 1–39.

——(1993b). 'Institutions and Collective Action: The New Telecommunications in Western Europe', *World Politics*, 45/2: 242–70.

——(1996). 'Membership Matters: Limits of the Functional Approach to European Institutions', *Journal of Common Market Studies*, 34/3: 403–29.

——and Zysman, J. (1989). '1992: Recasting the European Bargain', *World Politics*, 42/1: 95–128.

Saryusz-Wolski, Jacek (1994). 'The Reintegration of the "Old Continent": Avoiding the Costs of "Half-Europe"', in Simon Bulmer and Andrew Scott (eds.), *Economic and Political Integration in Europe: International Dynamics and Global Context* (Oxford: Blackwell), 19–28.

Sauter, W. (1998). 'The Economic Constitution of the European Union', *Columbia Journal of European Law*, 4/1: 27–68.

Sbragia, A. M. (1996). 'Environmental Policy: The "Push-Pull" of Policy-Making', in H. Wallace and W. Wallace (eds.), *Policy-Making in the European Union*, 3rd edn. (Oxford: Oxford University Press).

Scharpf, F. (1988). 'The Joint-Decision Trap: Lessons from German Federalism and European Integration', *Public Administration*, 66/3: 239–78.

——(1999). 'Selecting Cases and Testing Hypotheses', *Journal of European Public Policy*, 6/1: 164–8.

Schimmelfennig, Frank (1998). 'NATO, the EU, and Central and Eastern Europe: Theoretical Perspectives and Empirical Findings on Eastern Enlargement', paper presented at the Third Pan-European International Relations/ISA Conference, Vienna.

——(1999). *The Double Puzzle of EU Enlargement: Liberal Norms, Rhetorical*

Action, and the Decision to Expand to the East, Arena Working Paper, 15 (Oslo: Arena).

Schmitter, P. (1996). 'Examining the Present Euro-Polity with Help of Past Theories, in G. Marks *et al.* (eds.), *Governance in the European Union* (London: Sage), 1–15.

Scott, J. (1998). 'Flexibility in the Implementation of EC Environmental Law', paper presented at the conference on 'Flexible Environmental Regulation in the Internal Market' at Warwick University, July.

Scully, Roger M. (1997*a*). 'The European Parliament and Co-Decision: A Rejoinder to Tsebelis and Garrett', *Journal of Legislative Studies*, 3: 93–103.

——(1997*b*). 'The European Parliament and the Co-Decision Procedure: A Re-Assessment', *Journal of Legislative Studies*, 3: 58–73.

——(1997*c*). 'Policy Influence and Participation in the European Parliament', *Legislative Studies Quarterly*, 22: 233–52.

——(1998). 'MEPs and the Building of a "Parliamentary Europe"', *Journal of Legislative Studies*, 4: 92–108.

Sedelmeier, Ulrich (1998*a*). 'The European Union's Association Policy Towards the Countries of Central and Eastern Europe: Collective EU Identity and Policy Paradigms in a Composite Policy', Ph.D. Thesis, University of Sussex, Apr.

——(1998*b*). 'Regulatory Governance in the EU and Regulatory Alignment of the CEECs: Competing Policy Paradigms for the Internal Market?', paper presented at the British Council's Ionian Conference 'Making Enlargement Work', Athens and Corfu, 14–17 May.

——(2000). 'East of Amsterdam: The Implications of the Amsterdam Treaty for Eastern Enlargement', in Karlheinz Neunreither and Antje Wiener (eds.), *European Integration: Institutional Dynamics and Prospects for Democracy After Amsterdam* (Oxford: Oxford University Press), 218–37.

—— and Helen Wallace (1996). 'Policies towards Central and Eastern Europe', in H. Wallace and W. Wallace (eds.), *Policy Making in the European Union*, 3rd edn. (Oxford: Oxford University Press), 353–87.

————(2000). The EU and Eastern Enlargement: Squaring a Larger and More Divers Circle, in H. Wallace and W. Wallace (eds.), *Policy Making in the European Union*, 4th edn. (Oxford: Oxford University Press).

Sekkat, Khalid (1998). 'Exchange Rate Variability and EU Trade', Economic Papers, 127 (Brussels: European Commission, DG II, Feb.).

Servet, Jean-Michel, in cooperation with Carla Collicelli, Carole Bourgoyne, and Norbert Reich (1998). 'Summary of Experts Report Compiled for the Euro Working Group/European Commission-DG XXIV on Psycho-Sociological Aspects of the Changeover to the Euro', MS (Brussels: European Commission, DG XXIV).

Shackleton, Michael (1999). 'The Politics of Co-decision', paper presented to the ECSA Sixth Biennial International Conference, Pittsburgh, 2–5 June.

Shaw, J. (1996). 'European Union Legal Studies in Crisis? Towards a New Dynamic', *Oxford Journal of Legal Studies*, 16/2: 231–53.

——(1998). 'The Treaty of Amsterdam: Challenges of Flexibility and Legitimacy', *European Law Journal*, 4/1: 63–86.

——(1999). 'Postnational Constitutionalism in the European Union', *Journal of European Public Policy*, 6/4: 579–97.

——(2000). 'Process and Constitutional Discourse in the European Union', *Journal of Law and Society*, 27/1.

Shonfield, Andrew (1965). *Modern Capitalism* (New York: Oxford University Press).

Simon, Herbert A. (1976). *Administrative Behavior: A Study of Decision-Making Processes in Administrative Organization*, 3rd edn. (New York: The Free Press).

Sjursen, H. (1998). 'Missed Opportunity or Eternal Fantasy? The Idea of a European Security and Defence Policy', in J. Peterson and H. Sjursen (eds.), *A Common Foreign Policy for Europe? Competing Visions of the CFSP* (London: Routledge)

Slater, Martin (1982). 'Political Elites, Popular Indifference and Community Building', *Journal of Common Market Studies*, 21/1: 69–87.

Slaughter, A.-M., Tulumello, A., and Wood, S. (1998). 'International Law and International Relations Theory: A New Generation of Interdisciplinary Scholarship', *American Journal of International Law*, 92: 367–97.

Smith, Alasdair *et al.* (1996). 'The European Union and Central and Eastern Europe: Pre-Accession Strategies', *SEI Working Paper*, 15 (Mar.).

——and Wallace, H. (1994). 'The European Union: Towards a Policy for Europe', *International Affairs*, 70/3: 429–44.

Smith, Anthony D. (1992). 'National Identity and the Idea of European Unity', *International Affairs*, 68: 55–76.

——(1995). *Nations and Nationalism in a Global Era* (Cambridge: Polity Press).

Smith, Edward (1999). 'Re-regulation and Integration: The Nordic States and the European Economic Area', Ph.D. thesis, University of Sussex, Jan.

Smith, Julie (1995). *Voice of the People: The European Parliament in the 1990s* (London: Royal Institute of International Affairs).

Smith, Karen E. (1998). *The Making of EU Foreign Policy: The Case of Central and Eastern Europe* (London: Macmillan).

Smith, Michael (1996). 'The European Union and a Changing Europe: Establishing the Boundaries of Order', *Journal of Common Market Studies*, 43/1: 5–28.

Smith, Michael E. (1998). 'What's Wrong with the CFSP? The Politics of Institutional Reform', in P.-H. Laurent and M. Maresceau (eds.), *The State of the European Union,* iv (Boulder, Colo.: Lynne Rienner).

Smith, Mitchell P. (1998). 'Autonomy by the Rules: The European Commission and the Development of State Aid Policy', *Journal of Common Market Studies*, 36/1 (Mar.): 55–78.

Snyder, F. (1998). *EMU Revisited: Are We Making a Constitution? What Constitution are We Making?*, EUI Working Papers, Law, 98/6 (Florence: European University Institute).

Soskice, David and Iversen, Torben (1998). 'Multiple Wage-Bargaining Systems in the Single European Currency Area', *Oxford Review of Economic Policy*, 14/3 (Autumn): 110–24.

Soysal, Y. (1994). *Limits of Citizenship: Migrants and Postnational Membership in Europe* (Chicago: University of Chicago Press).

Sparkes, A. W. (1994). *Talking Politics: A Wordbook* (London: Routledge).

'Stabilitätspakt für Europa' (1995). *Auszüge aus Presseartikeln*, 75, 7 Nov.

'Stability Pact for South Eastern Europe' (1999). Cologne, 10 June, http://www.seerecon.org/KeyDocuments/KD1999062401.htm.

Stehlík, J. (1998). 'The Environment in the Czech Republic and the Association Agreement', in B. Lippert and P. Becker (eds.), *Towards EU Membership: Transformation and Integration in Poland and the Czech Republic* (Bonn: Europa Union).

Steinmo, S., and Thelen, K. (1992). 'Historical Institutionalism in Comparative Politics', in S. Steinmo, K. Thelen, and F. Longstreth (eds.), *Structuring Politics: Historical Institutionalism in Comparative Analysis* (Cambridge: Cambridge University Press), 1–31.

Steuenenberg, Bernard (1997). 'Codecision and its Reform: A Comparative Analysis of Decision Making Rules in the European Union', in B. Steuenberg and F. van Vught (eds.), *Political Institutions and Public Policy: Perspectives on European Decision Making* (Dordrecht: Kluwer).

Stone Sweet, A., and Brunell, T. (1998). 'Constructing a Supranational Constitution: Dispute Resolution and Governance in the European Community', *American Political Science Review*, 92: 63–81.

—— and Sandholtz, W. (1998). 'Integration, Supranational Governance, and the Institutionalization of the European Polity', in W. Sandholtz. and A. Stone Sweet (eds.), *European Integration and Supranational Governance* (Oxford: Oxford University Press), 1–26.

Strobel, Warren P. (1996). 'The CNN Effect', *American Journalism Review*, 18/4 (May): 32–6.

Stubb, A. C. G. (1996). 'A Categorization of Differentiated Integration', *Journal of Common Market Studies*, 34/2: 283–95.

Tabellini, G. (1998). 'Inflation Targeting and the Accountability of the European Central Bank', paper presented at the Third ECSA World Conference, Brussels 17–18 Sept.

Tavlas, George (1993). 'The "New" Theory of Optimum Currency Areas', *The World Economy*, November, 16/6 (Nov.): 663–85.

Teivainen, Teivo (1997). 'The Independence of the European Central Bank', in Petri Minkkinen and Heikki Patomäki (eds.), *The Politics of Economic and Monetary Union* (Boston, Mass., Dordrecht, and London: Kluwer), 54–74.

TEPSA (1999). 'Enlargement/Agenda 2000 Watch', 1 June, Institut für Europäische Politik in co-operation with the Trans European Policy Studies Association, http://www.tepsa.be.

Thatcher, M. (1998). 'The Development of Policy Network Analyses: From Modest Origins to Overarching Frameworks', in T. König (ed.) 'Modeling

Policy Networks', special issue of *Journal of Theoretical Politics*, 10/4: 389–416.
Thomas, S. T. (1992). 'Assessing MEPs' Influence on British EC Policy', *Government and Opposition*, 27: 3–26.
Tinbergen, J. (1965). *International Economic Integration*, 2nd revised edn., (Amsterdam and New York: Elsevier).
Torreblanca, José Ignacio (1997). 'The European Community and Central Europe (1989–1993): Foreign Policy and Decision-Making', Ph.D. Thesis, Instituto Juan March de Estudios e Investigaciones (Madrid: Ediciones Peninsular).
——(2000). *The European Community and Central Europe* (Aldershot: Ashgate).
Tsebelis, George (1994). 'The Power of the European Parliament as a Conditional Agenda Setter', *American Political Science Review*, 88: 128–42.
——(1995). 'Will Maastricht Reduce the Democratic Deficit?', *APSA Comparative Politics Section Newsletter*, 6: 4–6.
——and Garrett, Geoffrey (1997). 'Agenda Setting, Vetoes and the European Union's Co-Decision Procedure', *Journal of Legislative Studies*, 3: 74–92.
Tsoukalis, Loukas (1977). *The Politics and Economics of European Monetary Integration* (London: Allen & Unwin).
UNICE (1997). *UNICE's Message to the Amsterdam Summit (16–17 June 1997)*, Brussels, 6 June, http://europa.eu.int/en/agenda/igc-home/instdoc/social/unamsten.htm.
United Kingdom Presidency, (1998). 'Cardiff European Council, 15 and 16 June (1998), Presidency Conclusions', http://presid.fco.gov.uk/meetings/cardiff/docs/engfinal.shtml.
Van Eekelen, W. (1993). 'WEU Prepares the Way for New Missions', *Nato Review*, 41/5 (Oct.): 19–23.
——(1994). 'The Emerging Operational Role of the SWEU: Planning for a European Defense', *European Brief and Parliamentary Brief* (Brussels).
Vaubel R. (1985). 'International Collusion or Competition for Macroeconomic Policy Coordination? A Restatement', *Recherches Économiques de Louvain*, 51: 223–40.
Verdun, A. (1996). 'An "Asymmetrical" Economic and Monetary Union in the EU: Perceptions of Monetary Authorities and Social Partners', *Journal of European Integration/Revue d'integration européenne*, 20/1 (Autumn): 59–81.
——(1998a). 'The Institutional Design of EMU: A Democratic Deficit?', *Journal of Public Policy*, 18/2: 107–32.
——(1998b). 'Understanding Economic and Monetary Union in the EU', *Journal of European Public Policy*, 5/3: 527–33.
——(1999). 'The Role of the Delors Committee in the Creation of EMU: An Epistemic Community?', *Journal of European Public Policy*, 6/2 (June): 308–28.
——(2000a). *European Responses to Globalization and Financial Market Integration: Perceptions of Economic and Monetary Union in Britain, France and Germany*, International Political Economy Series (Basingstoke: Macmillan; New York: St Martin's Press).

Verdun, A. (2000*b*). 'Governing by Committee: The Case of the Monetary Committee', in T. Christiansen and E. Kirchner (eds.), *Administering the New Europe: Inter-Institutional Relations and Comitology in the European Union* (Manchester: Manchester University Press).

Visegrád (1992). Memorandum of the Governments of the Czech and Slovak Federal Republic, the Republic of Hungary and the Republic of Poland on Strengthening their Integration with the European Community and on the Perspective of Accession, Prague, Warsaw and Budapest, 11 Sept.

—— (1993). 'Aide-memoire of the Governments of the Czech and Slovak Federal Republic, the Republic of Hungary and the Republic of Poland, Prague, Warsaw and Budapest', 2 June.

Von Bogdandy, A. (1999*a*). 'Die Europäische Union als supranationale Föderation', *Integration*, 22: 95–112.

—— (1999*b*). 'The European Union as a Supranational Federation: A Conceptual Attempt in the Light of the Amsterdam Treaty', MS (June).

—— and Nettesheim, M. (1996). 'Ex Pluribus Unum: Fusion of the European Communities into the European Union', *European Law Journal*, 2/3: 267–89.

Von Hagen, Jürgen, and Hammond, George W. (1998). 'Regional Insurance Against Asymmetric Shocks: An Empirical Study for the European Community', *The Manchester School*, 66/3 (June): 331–53.

Von Homeyer, I., Kempmann, L., and Klasing, A. (1999). 'EU Enlargement: Screening Results in the Environmental Sector', *Environmental Law Network International (ELNI) Newsletter*, 2: 43–7.

Waever, O. (1996). 'European Security Identities, *Journal of Common Market Studies*, 34/1: 103–32.

Walker, Jack L. (1991). *Mobilizing Interest Groups in America* (Ann Arbor, Mich.: University of Michigan Press).

Walker, Martin (1999). 'The New European Strategic Relationship', *World Policy Journal*, 16/2 (Summer): 23–8.

Walker, N. (2000). 'Theoretical Reflections on Flexibility and Europe's Future', in G. de Búrca and J. Scott (eds.), *Constitutional Change in the EU: From Uniformity to Flexibility?* (Oxford: Hart Publishing).

Wallace, H. (1973). *National Governments and the European Communities* (London: RIIA/PEP).

—— (1991). 'The Europe that Came in from the Cold', *International Affairs*, 67/4: 647–63.

—— (1996). 'Politics and Policy in the EU: The Challenge of Governance', in H. Wallace and W. Wallace (eds.), *Policy Making in the European Union*, 3rd edn. (Oxford: Oxford University Press), 3–36.

—— (1997). 'Pan-European Integration: A Real or Imagined Community?', *Government and Opposition*, 32/2: 215–33

—— (1999*a*). 'The Domestication of Europe: Contrasting Experiences of EU Membership and Non-Membership', 6th Daalder lecture (Leiden: Leiden University, 13 Mar.).

——(1999*b*). 'Whose Europe is it Anyway?', *European Journal of Political Research*, 35/3: 287–306.

——(2000). 'Flexibility: A Tool of Integration or a Restraint on Disintegration?', in K. H. Neunreither and A. Wiener, *European Integration after Amsterdam* (Oxford: Oxford University Press), 175–91.

——and Wallace W. (eds.) (1996). *Policy Making in the European Union*, 3rd edn. (Oxford: Oxford University Press).

————(2000). *Policy-Making in the European Union*, 4th edn. (Oxford: Oxford University Press).

——and Young, A. (eds.) (1997). *Participation and Policy-Making in the European Union* (Oxford: Clarendon Press).

Walsh, J. I. (1999). 'Political Bases of Macroeconomic Adjustment: Evidence from the Italian Experience', *Journal of European Public Policy*, 6/1: 66–84.

Waltz, K. (1979). *Theory of International Politics* (New York: McGraw-Hill).

Weber, M. (1946). 'Politics as Vocation', in H. H. Gerth and C. Wright Mills (eds.), *From Max Weber: Essays in Sociology* (New York: Oxford University Press), 77–128.

Weber, Eugen (1976). *Peasants into Frenchmen: The Modernization of Rural France, 1870–1914* (Stanford, Calif.: Stanford University Press).

Weidenfeld, W. (ed.) (1998). *Amsterdam in der Analyse: Strategien für Europa* (Gütersloh: Bertelsmann Stiftung).

Weiler, J. H. H. (1991). 'The Transformation of Europe', *Yale Law Journal*, 100.

——(1994). 'A Quiet Revolution: The European Court and its Interlocutors', *Comparative Political Studies*, 26: 510–34.

——(1997). 'The Reformation of European Constitutionalism', *Journal of Common Market Studies*, 35/1: 97–131.

——(1999). *The Constitution of Europe: 'Do the New Clothes Have an Emperor?' and Other Essays on European Integration* (Cambridge and New York: Cambridge University Press).

Werner, P. *et al.* (1970). 'Report to the Council and the Commission on the Realization by Stages of Economic and Monetary Union in the Community', *Bulletin of the EC*, supplement 11, Doc 16.956/11/70 (8 Oct.).

Westlake, Martin (1994*a*). *A Modern Guide to the European Parliament* (London: Pinter).

——(1994*b*). *The Commission and the Parliament: Partners and Rivals in the European Policy-Making Process* (London: Butterworth).

WEU Secretariat-General (1996). *Press Review* (WEU Secretariat-General, Information Section/Political Section, Brussels, 28 June): 124.

White, Stuart (1999). 'Two Papers on the Rhetoric and Substance of New Labor and the "Third Way"', paper prepared for presentation at the Annual Meeting of the American Political Science Association, Atlanta, 2–5 Sept.

Whitworth, S. (1989). 'Gender in the Inter-Paradigm Debate', *Millennium*, 18/2: 265–72.

Wiener, A. (1997). 'Assessing the Constructive Potential of Union Citizenship: A

Socio-Historical Perspective', *European Integration online Papers*, 1(017), http://eiop.or.at/eiop/texte/(1997).-017a.htm.

Wiener, A. (1998). 'The Embedded Acquis Communautaire. Transmission Belt and Prism of New Governance', *European Law Journal*, 4: 294–315.

——and Della Sala, V. (1997). 'Constitution-Making and Citizenship Practice: Bridging the Democracy Gap in the EU?', *Journal of Common Market Studies*, 35/4: 595–614.

Wilming, C. (1995). *Institutionelle Konsequenzen einer Erweiterung der Europäischen Union: Eine ökonomische Analyse der Entscheidungsverfahren im Ministerrat* (Baden-Baden: Nomos Verlag).

Wincott, D. (1995). 'Institutional Interaction and European Integration: Towards an Everyday Critique of Liberal Intergovernmentalism', *Journal of Common Market Studies*, 33/4: 597–609.

——(1998). 'Does the European Union Pervert Democracy? Questions of Democracy in New Constitutionalist Thought on the Future of Europe', *European Law Journal*, 4/4: 411–28.

Winters, L. Alan (1992). 'The Europe Agreements: With a Little Help from Our Friends', in CEPR, *The Association Process: Making it Work, Central Europe and the EC*, CEPR Occasional Paper (London: Centre for Economic Policy Research), 11: 17–33.

Wintle, Michael (1996). 'Cultural Identity in Europe: Shared Experience', in M. Wintle. (ed.), *Culture and Identity in Europe: Perceptions of Divergence and Unity in Past and Present* (Aldershot: Avebury), 9–32.

Wolf, D., and Zangl, B. (1996., 'The European Economic and Monetary Union: "Two-level Games" and the Formation of International Institutions', *European Journal of International Relations*, 2/3: 355–93.

Woolcock, S. (2000). 'European External Trade Policy: A System under Strain', in H. Wallace and W. Wallace (eds.), *Policy-Making in the European Union*, 4th edn. (Oxford: Oxford University Press).

——and Hodges, Michael (1996). 'EU Policy in the Uruguay Round', in H. Wallace and W. Wallace (eds.), *Policy-Making in the European Union*, 3rd edn. (Oxford: Oxford University Press).

————and Schreiber, Kristin (1991). 'Public Procurement', in *Britain, Germany and 1992: The Limits of Deregulation* (London: Pinter).

World Bank (1998). *Poland Complying with European Environmental Legislation*, Final Report, Europe and Central Asia Environmental Unit (Washington, DC: World Bank).

Wyplosz, Charles (1997). 'EMU: Why and How It Might Happen', *Journal of Economic Perspectives*, 11/4 (Fall): 3–21.

Young, O. R. (1989). *International Cooperation: Building Regimes for Natural Resources and the Environment* (Ithaca, NY: Cornell University Press).

Zielonka, Jan (1998). *Paradoxes of European Foreign Policy* (The Hague and Boston: Kluwer Law International).

Zito, A. R. (1999). 'Task Expansion: A Theoretical Overview', *Environmental and Planning C: Government and Policy*, 17/1: 19–36.

Zürn, M. (1998). *Regieren Jenseits des Nationalstaates. Globalisierung und Denationalisierung als Chance* (Frankfurt am Main: Suhrkamp).

——and Wolf, D. (1999). 'European Law and International Regimes: The Features of Law beyond the Nation State', *European Law Journal*, 5/3: 272–92.

INDEX

Note: References to tables are indicated by the letter 't' following the page number.